Green Iguana

IGUANA RESEARCH
Special
I-391
Award
PARTICIPANT

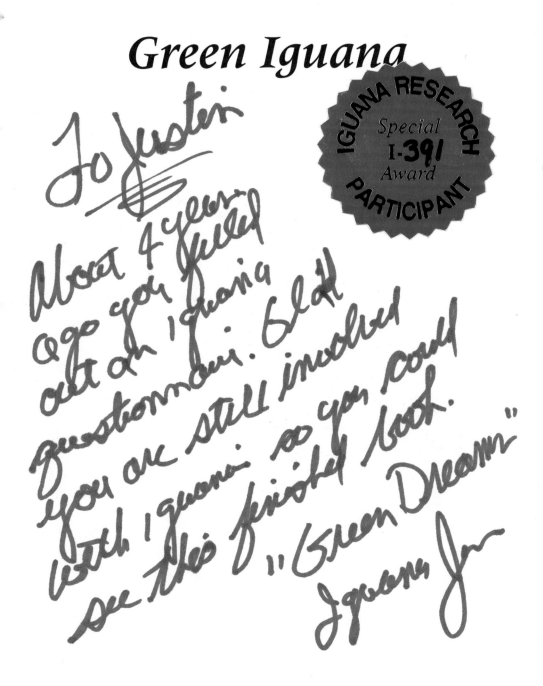

To Justin

About 4 years ago you filled out an iguana questionnaire. Glad you are still involved with iguanas so you could see this finished book.

"Green Dream"

Iguana Jim

Green Iguana—

The Ultimate Owner's Manual

James W. Hatfield III

Dunthorpe
press
Portland, Oregon

Published by
Dunthorpe Press
P.O. Box 80385
Portland, Oregon 97280

Cataloging-in-Publication Data

Hatfield, James W., 1945–
     Green iguana : the ultimate owner's manual
/ by James W. Hatfield. — Portland, OR:
Dunthorpe Press, c1993.

     p. : ill. (some col.) ; cm.

     Includes index.
     ISBN: 1-883463-48-3

     1. Iguana. 2. Lizards as pets. I. Title.

SF459.L5H   639.39'95 dc20

GREEN IGUANA — THE ULTIMATE OWNER'S MANUAL

Every effort has been made to make this book as complete and as accurate as possible.
However, there could be mistakes both typographical and in content. Therefore, this text
should be used only as a general guide and not as the single source. The purpose of this
manual is to educate and entertain. Dunthorpe Press and the author shall have neither
liability nor responsibility to person, pet, or entity with respect to any loss or damage
caused, or alleged to be caused, directly or indirectly by the information contained in this
book.

Printed in the United States of America

To Monkey Boy,

thanks for the adventure

Contents

Figures

Foreword

To get a quick overview of what this book covers, look at the table of contents. You will see that the book explains just about every aspect of keeping a healthy and happy pet iguana.

Even though the book is intended to read like a good novel—fun, interesting, exciting—it is laid out like a manual, as the book's subtitle states. As such, it's intentional that some information will appear in multiple chapters or sections, and you may be instructed to flip to another page or chapter for more details on a particular topic.

I attempted to present the information in a personal and friendly manner, and at times you may feel as if I am right in your home talking with you about your iguana. And like a good friend who wants only the best for you and your lizard, I may at times get tenacious or even forceful about the specific care requirements for your iguana. My ultimate goal is to improve the lives of green iguanas, and I take that goal very seriously.

Some Helpful Hints for Using This Book

All manuals have their own idiosyncrasies and ways of presenting material and highlighting main ideas, and this book is no exception.

In this book, most chapters include "AT A GLANCE" sections, which consolidate or clarify points coming up in that chapter. Also included are "SIDE-BARS," which explain something pertinent to the chapter but slightly out of the flow of the text. One of my favorite sidebars (located in Chapter 7, Medical Troubleshooting) contains a couple of chilling paragraphs about viruses.

An ancient Chinese proverb said, "One picture is worth more than a thousand words." Taking that proverb to heart, I have included a number of both hand-drawn illustrations and computer-generated drawings to make specific topics easier to understand. Graphs and charts probably weren't considered pictures by the ancient Chinese poet, but you'll find many in this book, and I believe they will help certain statistics come to life. And of course there is a consolidated section of color and black-and-white photos (which should appease the Chinese gods). In addition, scattered among the chapters are halftones (photographs) that put a visual face on particular topics.

Throughout the book I have included hundreds of quotations from iguana owners, veterinarians, scientific researchers, iguana wholesalers, retail store people, and iguana breeders to reinforce or clarify specific ideas. These quotations came from my several years of research on iguanas.

Deciphering the "Codes"

Quotations from iguana owners and veterinarians are in italics. The person quoted is identified by a code number that was assigned through my questionnaire research ("I" numbers are for iguana owners, "V" numbers are for veterinarians). Next comes their first name (to preserve anonymity), age (where available, to add some dimension to the person quoted), and state or country (to show the geographic scope of where iguanas and their owners and veterinarians are located). Here are examples of how these attributions appear:

—I-818, Donna, 38 yrs., Texas
—V-132, Dr. Willard, 55 yrs., Washington

Many quotations from iguana owners include brackets with additional information about individual iguanas (when this information was provided to me). For example, you might see something like the following:

[SVL: 9", TL: 2' 9", 2 yrs. 6 mo., 3 lbs.]

"SVL" refers to the iguana's Snout-Vent Length, or the distance from the tip of their nose (snout) to their vent (where they defecate), and is the scientific way to denote body length; "TL" refers to the total length, or SVL plus the tail length; age is in years and months; and weight is in pounds and ounces. The purpose of including these values is to help you better imagine the iguana being discussed.

In some quotations, especially in Chapter 8, Domestication, you will see iguana owners referring to how wild or tame their iguanas seem using a numbering system from 1 to 50. This was one of the questions I asked in my questionnaire to iguana owners. In this rating system, 1 is very tame while 50 is a "monster from hell" iguana. Details on my iguana questionnaire research are presented in Appendix A.

Quotations from scientific researchers, iguana wholesalers, or books and magazines are not italicized. These quotations are attributed to a researcher, by name or by description of the research, or to a publication title. The number in parentheses refers to the full citation of the scientific research quoted, which is located in Appendix J. Here is an example of how these attributions appear:

—John A. Phillips, iguana researcher (#46)

A Final Preliminary Note

Over the years, I've heard a number of people complain that various iguana pet-care books conflict with each other. These people express the desire for a single, non-controversial, final word on iguana care. Sorry, but you'll no doubt find information in this book that conflicts with what's in at least a few of the other books.

On the TV show *The X-Files*, they claim "The truth is out there." In the case of iguana care, the truth surely is out there, but the world of research hasn't yet unearthed all the answers on what makes these fascinating green lizards tick. This book represents what I feel to be the latest and most comprehensive guide to green iguana care, based on what we know today.

If you decide to join the ranks of iguana owners, I hope that this book might help your green friend live a long, healthy, happy life. I welcome your input.

James W. Hatfield III
Portland, Oregon

Mythical Iguana of the Mayas

O urs is not the first generation to feel that iguanas are special. The drawing on the opposite page is a rendering from an incised human bone found in the Temple of the Jaguar (Temple I) at the great Mayan city of Tikal, in what is now Guatemala. This temple was constructed in about 700 AD, and the incised bone was part of a fabulous burial offering of jade, alabaster, pearls, pots, and shells found with the remains of Au Cacau, a great Tikal king.

In the drawing, the dead king sits in the center of a canoe thought to represent his soul's passage to and from life on earth and life in the Mayan otherworld (death). The Mayas believed that kings (but not common people) did not really die, but rather traveled back and forth between the two worlds, with the aid of the canoe and chosen animal companions.

Second from the rear of the canoe is an iguana, one of the four chosen animals of the dead king (the other animals are, from left to right, a spider monkey, a parrot, and a dog; propelling the canoe are the Stingray Paddler and the Jaguar Paddler). When I was at Tikal, many of the guides and archaeologists told me that there was much speculation as to the purpose for each animal. But most believe the animals represent deities, or gods. The king chose those animal deities he wanted to accompany him.

Another theory is that each animal is associated with a color. In this theory, the iguana is very special because it represents green (the earth). Without the iguana's presence on the canoe, the dead king cannot return to the world of the living.

And you thought you were getting an ordinary pet.

Introduction

B efore 1988 I didn't know anything about iguanas. During a two-week vacation in the jungles near Puerto Vallarta, Mexico, I had my first glimpse of these lizards. One day when I returned to town, I saw a young local boy holding a dinosaur-like animal that was as colorful as a Salvador Dali painting. The creature looked so beautiful, I asked the boy if I could hold it.

Including tail, the lizard I held was easily five feet long. It looked ferocious with its huge jaws and its claws sharp enough to shred my skin. But it just settled into my arms like a big alley cat wearing a green leather coat. The lizard's eyes, which looked almost human, seemed to have a higher level of awareness than I expected from a reptile. At that moment, I fell in love with the look and feel of this animal.

It took me more than a year to purchase this lizard, called a common green iguana (*Iguana iguana*), for myself. I spent most of that year deciding whether to get a hatchling, juvenile, or adult iguana. I also had to ask myself if I was ready to accept the responsibilities of owning this or any other pet. I finally chose a healthy, feisty, 3-month-old iguana about 15 inches long.

By the time I brought him home I already had a habitat set up, as instructed by the pet store. I thought the rest of our relationship would be a piece of cake. It wasn't. Several times a week for the next few months I had to call the pet store for guidance. I had purchased the only book then available on pet iguanas, but it was 15 years old and badly outdated. I struggled to get any information on iguanas, and what little I got was either wrong, conflicting, or didn't address my particular problems.

Search for Knowledge

The lack of information on caring for my own iguana spurred me to spend more than six years trying to fill my head with answers to all my iguana questions.

Fired by fanaticism, I began by sending inquiries to more than 60 herpetological (reptile and amphibian) societies in the United States, and I joined three of them. Over the six-year period, I sent out almost 1,000 questionnaires directly to iguana owners, as well as questionnaires to veterinarians, pet stores, wholesalers, and zoos. In many cases I talked directly with manufacturers of products used for iguanas.

I attended international herpetological seminars and conferences, read scientific publications and trade journals, and did follow-up research at leading colleges and universities. I even attended a seminar for veterinarians on iguana medicine and surgery. I talked with recognized experts in a range of iguana-related fields, including state, federal, and international wildlife agencies.

I looked at hundreds of pet iguanas, plus I kept a detailed and exacting daily log book on my own pet iguana, Za.

My research also took me to Mexico and Central America several times. One summer, the Jalapa Ecology Institute near Veracruz, Mexico, invited me to work with them on an iguana egg research project in the jungles. Another invitation came from the Director of the School of Veterinary Medicine and Zoology in Oaxaca, Mexico, to study iguanas on the coast with one of the school's researchers.

This book is a compilation of all the information sources in which I've immersed myself for these years. In the end, I discovered that if you bend over backwards, jump through hoops of fire, follow all your leads, never give up, and let one desire drive you like a laser beam to your goal, eventually you get answers.

Iguanas Desperately Needed Help

I believe it would be unjust to convey the idea that an iguana is a simple pet to care for and that everyone should have one. This would be greatly unfair to iguanas. I believe only those with a genuine interest and the commitment to follow through should own iguanas, or for that matter, any pet. Having worked in and out of the pet industry, I have continually witnessed a "possession" factor that humans have. They come into a pet store and see an animal that they are attracted to and want to "possess" it. A short time down the road, the person loses interest in it and the animal begins to be neglected. When a person takes an animal into captivity they essentially become God to that animal. Likewise, they need to be ready to dedicate part of themselves to this new obligation. It takes a long learning curve for some to realize and appreciate this.

—I-508, Bryan, 27 yrs., Kentucky

Have you ever read a pet care book that argues against purchasing the animal described in the book? Well, this one does. And unlike many authors who refer to an iguana as a "specimen," I won't. If you want specimens, collect rocks.

This is the '90s and we have to take care of our environment and the animals in it. Part of this means being responsible for the pets we purchase and care for and respecting the future resources of the areas they come from. If we don't start now to take a stand for what is right, we will end up with a planet of concrete where the only wild animals are found in zoos.

When I began my research, I learned that approximately 90% of iguanas were dying once they left their homeland (Mexico, Central America, or South America) to become pets in the United States or Europe. Most died on their way to becoming pets or because their owners lacked basic information on care, feeding, and housing. I initially started putting this book together for one reason: to keep alive those pet iguanas that are already here.

At first, however, I worried that a detailed care manual might defeat my purpose by inspiring more people to purchase iguanas. Then I remembered the old adage, "Knowledge is power," and realized that one way to discourage impulse buying was to inform people of the requirements necessary to have an iguana as a pet. I felt that most impulse buyers would think twice if they knew the extent of the care required for an iguana. I figured that after the facts were presented, most of the people left would be dedicated potential iguana owners.

Iguanas' natural habitat is freedom in the tops of jungle trees. I feel strongly that people should not keep iguanas as a novelty or collector's item, as some kind of caged, exotic "thing" to show off to their friends. The iguanas I have seen over the past six years are too intelligent, too alive, for that rot-in-the-cage routine.

Some people say that an iguana is "just" a lizard, with a pea brain. But the qualities in the hundreds of iguanas I have seen as pets, and in my own pet iguana, indicate that they are much smarter than most people give them credit for. No, they can't play chess, but they are trainable and adaptable, and many are smart enough to have trained their owners to do their bidding. They are nothing like the lizards you find in your backyard. As such, they need to be treated differently.

Finally, I hope this book improves the lives of iguanas currently in captivity—as well as those in the wild—by encouraging people to purchase captive-bred, not wild-caught, iguanas.

Think Before You Buy

All animals have good and potentially bad qualities, including iguanas. Iguanas are not for everyone—due to their specific requirements, potential size and longevity, and possibly expensive veterinarian bills. They have the ability to do inadvertent damage to you, your household, and other pets. Also, adult male iguanas during their breeding season can get quite aggressive toward just about any person or thing.

You also need to consider that the cost of setting up an iguana's habitat typically far exceeds what you'll pay for the animal itself. The habitat (I prefer the word "habitat" to "cage") includes a structure, special lights, heat sources, and more (see Chapter 4, Housing). It's important to understand that if you don't have the money to purchase the total environment at one time, **don't** get the iguana. Iguanas aren't puppies or kittens, who can survive in make-shift temporary shelters.

Iguana Qualities

Even though this book was written for those iguanas who are already pets, I am sure that many readers of this book will decide to purchase an iguana. Reasons for owning a pet iguana are many, as will be explained in Chapter 2, Iguanas as Pets. With proper care, time, and patience an iguana is a great pet to have around the house, especially for those allergic to cats or dogs or whose living spaces otherwise preclude a pet.

Iguanas all have their own "special" personalities. They are very beautiful to look at, with relatively low-cost maintenance and care (once the basic habitat is set up). Iguanas feel great to hold and play with and can be house-trained easily. Once tamed, they like to "take it easy" and are not demanding pets. They also don't make any kind of irritating sound; in fact, they have no vocal sound at all. And, of course, you will have a one-of-a-kind, very different pet. But that doesn't mean you'll be alone as an iguana owner. Millions of iguanas have been brought into the U.S. as pets.

There's no hard scientific research on the life span of a captive iguana, but most people in the iguana community believe that 12 to 15 years is typical, about the same as a domestic house cat. The oldest iguana I have found lived to be 29 years old. Iguanas have the best chance of attaining this longevity with the right environment, excellent food, and sunlight. An iguana as a pet is a potentially long-term responsibility, and if you follow the information in this book and use good judgment, your iguana could be with you for many years.

Summary

Nearly everything you'll need is in this book, <u>but you have to read it before the information can help you or your iguana.</u>

One last reminder: Iguanas are exotic animals that have special, mandatory requirements for their survival. These requirements are <u>not flexible.</u> If, after all these warnings, you still believe you have the dedication and seriousness of purpose to own an iguana, I urge you to use this book to help guide you and your green iguana to a rewarding companionship.

CHAPTER 1

Iguana: The Species

The Iguana is the Birth of Mexico, a Serpent like the Pope's Anathema, of a terrible Front, but harmless; a glittering Comb on the Head, with a Bag under the Chin; a long Tail, and sharp Bones on its Back, standing up in the form of a Saw.
—an early description of iguanas in Mexico, in the book
An Essay Towards a Natural History of Serpents
by Charles Owen, published in 1742 in London

PUTTING THE GREEN IGUANA IN CONTEXT

Green iguanas may be gaining in popularity as pets, but they still qualify as exotic animals. When you own an exotic pet, it's like having a little piece of the animal's exotic homeland right in your house.

Besides choosing a common green iguana for all the special qualities only this type of lizard can offer, you're also choosing the opportunity to identify with the iguana's place of origin. And the more you know about your animal's natural home and habitat, the better prepared you'll be to make wise decisions about its care.

This chapter looks at your new pet's background as a species and in the wild, while giving you some insight into how scientists group and describe iguanas. It also introduces you to an iguana's body parts and how they function, which will help you understand what food iguanas eat and how they digest it, how they keep warm, how they defend themselves, and many other basic activities. So with those goals in mind, let me introduce you, briefly, to the heritage of the common green iguana.

Are Iguanas Really Little Dinosaurs?

Let's begin our introduction to iguanas by saying what common green iguanas (*Iguana iguana*) are not. They are not and were not dinosaurs, at least according to Dr. Robert Bakker.

Bakker is a paleontologist who graduated from Yale University with a degree in geology with departmental honors of exceptional distinction in 1968, received a Ph.D. from Harvard, taught at Johns Hopkins University, and now is the dinosaur curator at the Tate Museum in Casper, Wyoming. In his expeditions, he has named two species of Jurassic dinosaurs and 11 species of early mammals. He has detected new dinosaurs among mislabeled museum fossils. He was also a technical advisor for the book and movie *Jurassic Park*, and he was the only scientist mentioned by name in that movie.

Bakker contends that today's descendants of dinosaurs are birds, not reptiles—a viewpoint that contradicts what many other paleontologists believe. If you want more details about Bakker's controversial theories, read one of his many books.

When I talked with Bakker in Portland he told me, "I've kept iguanas. I've kept green and spiny-tailed iguanas. Iguanas are among the most advanced plant-eating lizards. They are far more advanced, in many ways, than any dinosaur. Iguanas didn't begin to evolve until the last dinosaur was already extinct. When you're looking at an iguana, you're being insulting to 'lizarddom' and 'dinodom' to confuse iguanas with dinosaurs." Now that we know what iguanas aren't, let's find out what they are.

Categorizing Living Organisms

A green iguana is a lizard, but not all lizards are iguanas. So who decides what creatures are what, and why?

Scientists categorize and arrange living things into groups to provide a systematic inventory of all of nature. This process of categorizing is called "classifying," and people who do this work are called taxonomists.

The Greek philosopher Aristotle attempted the first known classification of living organisms, some 2,300 years ago. In the 18th century, Karl von Linné (who later Latinized his name to Carolus Linnaeus) of Sweden established some very precise rules to make order out of the apparent disorder of the natural world.

The study of classification and all of its ramifications deserves a course at a university, rewarding you with three or four college credits. In this book it is covered very quickly just to let you know more about how your pet iguana fits into the grand scheme of all life.

To give you some comparison, the table on page 31 shows how three different organisms, including the green iguana, fit into the classification system. Because common names of plants and animals often vary from place to place, taxonomists use Latin for all classification titles for universal understanding and clarity. They also use the standardized format of italicizing the genus and species name (the last two categories of classification) for each organism, with the genus name capitalized and the species name not capitalized (e.g., *Iguana iguana* or *Homo sapiens*).

The orderly placement of a specific type of organism is accomplished by increasingly refined groupings based on common traits, including physical structure. It's as if the creature or plant were dropped through a multi-layered sifter. It keeps dropping through ever-finer grades of screening until it can go no further, and finally arrives alone in its own specific category—the final resting place, its species status. A species is generally defined as a potentially interbreeding population in nature; if two animals cannot physically or genetically breed, they are classified as different species.

So let's see what happens when we put a common green iguana, a human, and a Douglas fir tree into the imaginary classification sifter, and what gets eliminated along the way.

Classification	Green Iguana	Human	Douglas Fir
Kingdom	Animal	Animal	Plant
Phylum	Chordata	Chordata	(doesn't apply)
***(Division [plants])**	(doesn't apply)	(doesn't apply)	Spermatophyta
Class	Reptilia	Mammalia	Gymnospermae
Order	Squamata	Primata	Coniferales
Suborder	Sauria	———	———
Family	Iguanidae	Hominidae	Pinaceae
Genus	*Iguana*	*Homo*	*Pseudotsuga*
Species	*iguana*	*sapiens*	*taxifolia*

All creatures start at the top of the "sifter," at the **kingdom** level, which separates organisms the most broadly. When the common green iguana passes through the sifter, its inclusion in the Animal category automatically eliminates plants and all lower forms of life (e.g., algae, fungi, slime molds) from its classification.

At the **phylum** level, the screening is still relatively wide. (*For plants, this level is called division rather than phylum.) Iguanas share the Chordata designation with all other animals that have a backbone or at least a dorsally located central nervous system. Animals eliminated are creatures such as worms, mollusks, and insects.

As you can tell, an iguana's identifiable characteristics first emerge at **class**, where it fits into the category called Reptilia. Creatures of the Reptilia class are cold-blooded vertebrates with lungs and scaly skin, that hatch on land, and that share some skeletal similarities. Reptiles, as we more commonly call them, include turtles, crocodiles, and snakes as well as lizards.

As members of the Reptilia class of animals, lizards—which include iguanas—are ancient beasts. Fossil hunters in a Scottish quarry (East Krikton Limestone) recently discovered a 338 million-year-old reptile, which is 40 million years older than previously found. The specimen was nearly complete—almost 8" long and containing bones characteristic of the reptilian skull, spine, and hind ankles (*Nature*, Dec. 7, 1990, reported by *Science News*). It's not an iguana, but it is a distant relative.

The next level of refinement, **order**, further separates the reptiles. Iguanas—as well as snakes and other lizards—are members of the order Squamata, or "the scaly ones," which makes up about 95% of living reptiles. At this level turtles, tuatara, and crocodilians are no longer included. In the **suborder** Sauria, all the other reptiles drop out except lizards.

The Iguana Family

The **family** called Iguanidae includes every type of lizard commonly referred to as an "iguana," plus the chuckwallas. (Previously, Iguanidae also encompassed basilisks, anoles, horned lizards, and other lizards, but these genera now belong to other families—yet another example of taxonomists' perpetual refinement of their classifications. Taxonomists are known to intellectually fight over established classifications, as new or conflicting evidence arises.) As an interesting side note, any animal classification ending in "idae," as in Iguanidae, refers to the family level.

The Iguanidae family has eight separate genus types, each with a slightly different form, but all recognizable as "iguanas." They all have a scaly body and a medium to long tail; their arms and legs have a distinctive, well-developed structure with five digits and claws on each limb; and they have moveable eyelids.

The **genus** *Iguana* is where your pet finally stands out from the rest of the reptiles. A couple of other genera (plural of "genus") in the Iguanidae family, notably *Cyclura* and *Ctenosaura*, can also be purchased as pets. Because this book is about *Iguana iguana*, I will only touch lightly on the other Iguanidae genera.

• *Cyclura* is a large, powerful, truly prehistoric-looking lizard found in the Caribbean islands (eight species). As pets, they cost from $500 to more than $1,000 each. Only captive-raised animals are allowed to be sold, because all *Cyclura* species are on the endangered (CITES I) list. Some *Cyclura* species have red, orange, pink, blue, yellow, and other bright colors, while others (notably the rhinoceros iguana, *Cyclura cornuta*) are grey or blue-grey. A common name for *Cyclura* is rock iguanas.

• *Ctenosaura* looks most like a cross between a *Cyclura*, with its dull leathery skin, and a green iguana, with a similar body structure. They are often called spiny-tailed iguanas because of the distinctive spikes on their tails.

• *Amblyrhynchus* (consisting of only one species, *cristatus*) is the Galápagos marine iguana, which spends time in the ocean eating its favorite food, seaweed. The Galápagos Islands, made famous by the 19th century voyage of Charles Darwin, comprise 13 main islands and dozens of islets located about 600 miles off mainland Ecuador in South America.

• *Conolophus* is the Galápagos land iguana. The two species in this genus are land-dwelling vegetarians that eat many parts of the cactus that grows wild on the hot and dry islands.

• *Dipsosaurus* is a desert-dwelling iguana found in the Southwest U.S., Mexico, and islands in the Gulf of Mexico.

• *Sauromalus*, commonly referred to as a chuckwalla, is found in the deserts of the Southwest U.S., Mexico, and islands in the Gulf of California. There are six species in this genus.

• *Brachylophus* is a gorgeous, rare, and endangered iguana, often called the Fijian banded iguana, that lives on the islands of Fiji and Tonga in the South Pacific (two species). It looks somewhat like a very slender *Iguana iguana*, except with different color patterns, a smaller head, and much less prominent spines.

With the exception of all *Cyclura* and *Brachylophus* species, iguanids are not endangered. Even so, nearly every type of iguana—including *Iguana iguana*—is threatened in at least part of its range due to loss of habitat and increasing pressure (or outright predation) by human populations.

We have now arrived at the final filter where your lizard, *Iguana iguana*, stands out. This is the reason this chapter is called "Iguana: The Species."

Species for the *Iguana* genus classification has two representatives: *Iguana iguana* and *Iguana delicatissima*. *I. delicatissima* is found only in the Lesser Antilles, a group of islands in the Atlantic Ocean between Puerto Rico and the northern coast of Venezuela.

I. delicatissima looks almost identical to *I. iguana* in color and body shape, except that *I. delicatissima* lacks the large cheek scale (subtympanic shield or plate) that is found on *Iguana iguana* (see illustration on page 45).

As I mentioned earlier, taxonomists are always trying to improve classifications that seem incorrect. For example, some time ago *Iguana iguana* was further divided into subspecies: *Iguana iguana iguana* and *Iguana iguana rhinolopha*. You may have seen green iguanas with little "horns" on their nose. Some researchers felt this was a sub-species of iguana, but over time this category was dropped as more research became available. If you happen to see this *rhinolopha* subdivision in a book or magazine, you can assume the publication is using outdated information.

> *I would say her head is blunt and flat, not having much to compare her to. I was flabbergasted the first time I saw a female with horns on her nose! Mine does not have them.*   —I-795, Dawn, 24 yrs., Ohio

From here on, this book will be concerned only with *Iguana iguana*, more often called the common green iguana.

IGUANA IGUANA IN ITS NATURAL HABITAT

The ability to subsist on mature leaves of a wide variety of plants, a diet exploited in the Neotropics by only a few other arboreal herbivorous vertebrates such as sloths and howler monkeys, may be an important factor explaining the large geographic range and wide variety of habitats occupied by *Iguana iguana*.
                                    —A. Stanley Rand, iguana researcher (#25)

The green iguana is an extremely successful lizard. It is found throughout the warm environments of the Neotropics, with the only exception being the high Andes where they are excluded. They are found in swamps, savannas, deserts, rain forests, dry forests, and scrub forests. As long as it's warm and Neotropical, you'll find green iguanas.

—Gordon H. Rodda, iguana field researcher (#27)

Iguana iguana, your pet lizard, is found from the bottom half of Mexico (primarily in coastal regions), south through Central America, and in almost all the countries in South America, stopping at but including one northern part of Paraguay (see the map, facing page).

In the Lesser Antilles, along with many *Iguana delicatissima,* small numbers of common green iguanas are found. One of the many guesses as to how iguanas got from the mainland to these islands is that they were brought as live food on board ships sailing from Central and South America. Perhaps some escaped or were released once the boats arrived at the islands.

Iguanas stick to relatively low altitudes—no higher than 800 or 1,000 meters (about 2,600 to 3,300 feet) (#43)—because higher altitudes are too cold for them. Remember, iguanas are ectotherms (cold-blooded animals) and can't produce their own heat; having to live in cold weather would eventually kill them.

Iguanas are arboreal, which means they live in trees. Interestingly, the green iguana is the only reptile that both lives in trees and feeds on them. Adult iguanas live mostly in the jungle's high canopy, where they find plenty of sunshine for basking, food, and few predators. The adults come down to the ground to move from tree to tree or to mate—not much else.

Iguanas are also diurnal animals, which means they are active during daylight and sleep at night (the opposite of diurnal is nocturnal). For an iguana to maintain a normal relationship with its reality, it is important that you supply a period of light and dark each day. Twelve to 14 hours of light and the rest darkness is the standard formula to use. This is explained more in Chapter 4, Housing, "Photoperiod."

Other "Wild" Iguana Populations

Since the start of the pet trade of iguanas, these adaptable lizards have also escaped or been released by pet owners and have set up home (as invasive species) in southern Florida and on the islands of Oahu and Maui, Hawaii.

Florida

We captured a 3-foot iguana in the woods one day (no kidding!). Because we were unable to tame this individual or get it to eat, we returned it to the same place we'd found it. Three others lived there in the wild in addition to this one.

Figure 1.1: Approximate location of *Iguana iguana* in the world (#43). Dots represent location, not density.

We had no idea where they came from or how long they had been there. They ranged in size from 1 foot to 5 feet.   —I-467, Kris, 32 yrs., Florida

As Lt. Thomas Quin, wildlife inspector for the Florida Game and Fresh Water Fish Commission, said to me: "Most of the population was established either through intentional liberation of the animals or escapes. Many iguanas are in the Fort Lauderdale and Palm Beach areas."

SIDEBAR

Iguanas as Food

> Ten years ago there were iguanas everywhere; now you see very few. People eat the iguanas and their eggs.
> —Tomás, Belize river guide, 1993

Most of the iguanas in Latin America are disappearing because of loss of their habitat, not because of the pet trade. In many places I've gone, jungles were burning or smoldering to make room for cattle grazing land. No trees were left, so no place for iguanas to live.

In the wild, iguanas are caught for their skin but mostly for food. I even found a book in Central America that had a recipe for iguana stew. As one taxi driver told me, "Iguanas taste like chicken—exactly like chicken." In Costa Rica the price per pound of iguana meat is higher than for beef, if you can even get iguana meat (it's actually illegal to sell iguanas in Costa Rica).

If you saw iguanas in the market for sale, you might ask, "How can people eat these beautiful creatures we call 'our' pets?" But some of these countries are very poor, and money, clothes, and food are scarce. People there eat whatever they can to get nourishment each day. As one person told me when I was in the jungles of Guatemala, "If it moves, it's dinner."

People eat iguana meat, but they also eat the eggs of gravid females. It is thought that a male (human) who eats these eggs becomes more "macho" or virile. Killing one gravid female also kills 20 to 60 members of the future generation. Often near Christmas, hundreds and thousands of female iguanas are killed for their eggs as part of the holiday celebrations.

This is the most serious and saddest part about eating iguanas—killing future generations of the lizards. Because of ignorance and superstition, the natural proliferation of iguanas is interrupted. In many Latin American countries it is against the law to sell iguanas or their eggs, but years of tradition often supersede man-made laws.

Figure 1.2: (Opposite, top) Author in Mexican market where live iguanas are sold as food along with chickens, ducks, pigs, and goats. Photo by: A. H. Iles

Figure 1.3: (Opposite, bottom) Close-up of iguanas that are being held by the author. Notice that their claws have been tied together so they can't run away. Photo by: A. H. Iles

Quin also said that there are about 300 wildlife dealers in Broward and Dade Counties (Ft. Lauderdale to Miami) and some of these are "major, major importers. If you go around to the back door [of some of these importers] they [iguanas] are running all around. They might throw one out the back door because they though it was dead. . . . It revives itself and [there's] another iguana in Florida.

"When I worked in Florida I got a complaint about every two weeks or so about a green alligator. And of course I knew what it was . . . and you would go out there and catch an iguana," Quin said.

But the biggest changes to Florida came after Hurricane Andrew touched down in August 1992. "After the hurricane we now have baboons and 22-foot pythons roaming around in South Florida. . . . There were untold reptiles introduced, changing Florida forever. We can never come back from the biological pollutions caused by this hurricane. After Andrew there are probably thousands . . . well into the thousands [of iguanas now in Florida]."

Hawaii

Hawaii is a string of isolated islands, and because of that even the smallest introduced animal or plant has the potential to destroy a natural balance that has evolved for centuries. Trying to get a non-native animal into the state of Hawaii now is as difficult as breaking into Fort Knox. But in the old days they didn't check everyone's purse or bag, and small iguanas got into the country. In addition, many people didn't know that Hawaii follows strict import rules and may have unintentionally brought in unwanted animals.

At some point, some people with these pets might have decided they no longer wanted their lizards and released them. Unlike New York City, where people flush snakes down the toilets to get rid of them, in Hawaii people with unwanted reptiles only have to walk outside. Living in an idyllic environment like Hawaii, with plenty of warm sunshine, humidity, and lots of green plants to eat, iguanas not only survive but can easily grow into big monsters.

Sean McKeown was the supervising herpetologist at the Honolulu Zoo from 1975 to 1983. He wrote a book about the reptiles and amphibians of Hawaii and is very knowledgeable on the subject. He said that distribution records show that iguanas were established in Hawaii around the 1950s, and now there are breeding populations in several locations, including Waimanalo, Upper Manoa Valley, and Nuuanu Valley, all on the island of Oahu. Remember, Hawaii is more or less a "closed loop"; what comes in usually stays there.

"It's clear when you see these iguanas that they are from a number of accidental or purposeful releases over the years, because you see individuals that look very different from each other. Some look Mexican or South American. There's a real mix of them out there," said McKeown. (For a look at a wild iguana in Hawaii, look at the color section in this book.)

McKeown estimates that there may be a few thousand iguanas on the island, "but [the iguanas'] range and population is not increasing very much." One reason they are not rapidly increasing is lack of population density. Even though there are quite a few iguanas, they are spread out over a wide area, reducing the chances that males and females will find each other to mate and reproduce.

The number-one problem facing iguanas in Hawaii is the same as in their natural home range of Latin America—urban sprawl, which destroys natural habitat. Hawaii is truly a paradise, and more and more people want to live there. As a result, the verdant, lush jungle areas are being destroyed to make room for homes, apartments, and businesses.

Habitat destruction negatively impacts mostly adult iguanas, but in the long run it affects egg production, hatchlings, and juveniles, too. On the other hand, adult iguanas in Hawaii are less susceptible to predators.

Because adult iguanas stay mostly up in trees, their only likely predators are tree climbers or large birds. In Latin American countries, snakes, monkeys and coatimundis are some of the main iguana predators—all of which are missing in Hawaii. Hawaiian hawks are rare, so they'd be unlikely to wipe out the iguanas. And owls fly at night, when iguanas are sound asleep and hidden.

Hatchlings and small juvenile iguanas spend more time near the ground, where creatures such as mongooses, feral cats, and dogs could kill them. In addition, feral pigs can disturb and eat iguana eggs, which are laid underground.

It is illegal to keep an iguana as a pet, even if a person finds a stray one in the jungle someplace. It is also illegal to transport iguanas between islands. Despite this fact, it's not uncommon now to find escaped pets on islands besides Oahu. McKeown ended our conversation by saying: "Hawaiian laws are extremely hard-nosed about having an iguana as a pet."

I recently spent time in Hawaii (Oahu) looking for wild iguanas. Whenever I got close to talking with someone who actually had an iguana as a pet, the subject would quickly change. After talking with Domingo Cravalho, Jr., who works for the Plant Quarantine branch of the Department of Agriculture in Honolulu, I found out why. He said, "The Governor has indicated that this year [1996] we should take a strong stance [on illegal animals], especially snakes." A fine of $25,000 and one year in jail is the maximum penalty that Hawaii can hand out to people caught with illegal animals, including iguanas. That's pretty good incentive to clam up when some iguana book author comes around asking questions.

Regional Characteristics

I don't think you can follow human boundaries, political boundaries. . . . There would be no rhyme or reason the way the iguanas look relative to political boundaries. I think you are going to find very distinct differences between the ecological regimes the animals are going to live in. If it is a dry island species, you are going to have the short wide snout and if you have more jungle foliage you are going to have a longer, thin snout. That sort of thing.

I think the iguanas from South America are bigger than the

ones from Central America . . . and that is robustness [bigger body]. Some we had here [San Diego Zoo] were up in the mid-20 pound range for weight. Huge things!

—John A. Phillips, iguana researcher (#14)

The iguanas from Mexico, Central America, and South America do exhibit some different physical characteristics. The most apparent differences include the length and structure of the body; head shape; long or rounded nose; straight, curly, or extra-long dorsal spines; and of course subtle color and skin pattern distinctions.

However, for example, you can't say that all iguanas from Mexico have the little horns on their noses. When I was in the jungles of Mexico, there were iguanas that had the horns and some that didn't, and they all lived in the same general area.

Mexican

At this time iguanas are rarely imported from Mexico in large numbers, so you probably won't see these as hatchlings in pet stores. Adult iguanas from Mexico tend to have the following characteristics:

- Main body color is typically green on hatchlings, but turning brownish orange on the arms and parts of the body as the iguana gets older
- Long spines
- May have small horn-like protrusions on the snout
- Long, pointed snout
- Longer rather than wider bodies (SVL usually greater than in bulkier-looking South American iguanas)

SIDEBAR

Iguana Body Measurements

Before comparing the size of iguanas from different countries, we need a standard measurement. The most widely accepted measurement of an iguana's length is the distance from the tip of its nose (snout) to its vent (where it poops). This is the measurement that iguana scientists use, and it's called the snout-vent length (SVL).

The tail isn't included because tails can break off. Throughout this book, in quotations from iguana owners and researchers, the SVL abbreviation will be used when appropriate. I'll also use the abbreviation TL (which is total length, or the combined SVL plus tail length), as well as ages and weights of individual iguanas, whenever that information was supplied to me.

Central American

Central American iguanas don't have the blues or bright green (adults) that South Americans do. They are more grey and silverish. Their banding on the body stands out more. Very, very intelligent. Personality and size-wise my favorites. They tame down faster—they're the ones that I can actually train. I'm not able to train Suriname iguanas.   —I-11, Patty, Washington

In many parts of El Salvador and Nicaragua there are no iguanas to be found [due in part to the destructive effects of war in these countries].   **—Gordon H. Rodda, iguana researcher (#27)**

No iguanas are currently being shipped from Costa Rica, Panama, Honduras, or Nicaragua. The iguanas coming from Guatemala and El Salvador are farm-raised animals. Because Central America is a small area, there are not many dramatic physical differences between these and Mexican iguanas.

South American

My iguana from Suriname [South America] has a Roman-type nose, rounded upward slightly, which is apparent from the time they are hatched. A lot more blues and turquoises on them (adult).   —I-11, Patty, Washington

South America is a huge continent—about twice the land mass of the entire United States, and stretching from just north of the equator to the most southerly continental land outside of Antarctica—and consequently there are more opportunities for iguanas to display physical characteristics that vary with different regions.

Iguanas from South America can have some or all of the following physical characteristics:
• Roman hump-type nose (short snout)
• Tend to have shorter spines
• Less orange color, often with blue to bluish tones or other colors
• Face scales may have black outline that gives a more dramatic look
• SVL often less than Mexican or Central American counterparts, but with a sturdier, huskier body

There are only a few places in South America where iguanas are shipped to the U.S. as pets, and those countries include Colombia, Peru, Suriname, and Guyana. I talked with one importer who said that some of the other countries, such as Brazil and Venezuela, are being considered for future iguana farms.

In the photo section of this book is a great picture of a male iguana from Venezuela. These iguanas have a very distinctive rose color during breeding season, as well as huge and very beautifully shaped heads with distinctive markings.

For a while, iguanas from Suriname (formerly Dutch Guyana, located at the northeastern corner of the continent) were the prize iguanas because the hatchlings had bright green bodies, bluish heads, and distinctive patches of color on their shoulders. After that rage subsided, attention turned to the iguanas from Peru, with their overall bluish tinge. What country is next?

The choice of where your hatchling iguana comes from is usually a function of the time of year you purchase your lizard. Iguanas in different parts of the world hatch at different times of the year, and the distributors or wholesalers can sell only what they receive. An exception is those farmers who keep their iguanas a little longer to ensure stronger, healthier animals for shipping.

Variety of Color Patterns

For a year and a half my iguana had a very turquoise head and neck, which faded into a grayish-green body. In the past half year much of the turquoise has been lost and developed into brown flecking over the sides of the body. He is now 2 years old.   —I-39, Stephen, 19 yrs., Connecticut

The ontogenic changes of the iguana [i.e., the development of an individual iguana over time], in both color and spinosity [i.e., spine length and shape], are . . . correlated with changes in habits and in biotope [i.e., the environment in which it lives], resulting in good camouflage at all times.
                    —Robert W. Henderson, iguana researcher (#44)

Hatchlings and juveniles are bright green on top and almost phosphorescent green on their undersides. Because they spend much of their time near the ground, their bright green color on top allows them to blend in with the established foliage of bushes or small trees, while their phosphorescent green undersides meld with light-green new shoots.

Hatchlings are camouflaged for the habitat they live in and eat on, and they are extremely difficult to see. Even when I knew what part of a bush to observe iguanas in, I would always be surprised, even startled, when I saw them. About the only thing that allows them to stand out is when they move, which they don't do very often.

As opposed to when she was a juvenile, her overall color has faded from bright green to a more subdued green and the stripes are more pronounced.
                    —I-754, Karen, 33 yrs., New Mexico

An iguana's body color and patterns change as it grows from a hatchling to an adult. The usual progression is that a hatchling's body is a bright green and any shoulder patterns are clear and bright. Some people describe the color pattern around the shoulders as looking like a vest. But as the animal becomes older, the shoulder patch often fades and its body takes on more browns, oranges, or muted colors.

In the adult stage, iguanas no longer spend their time in the bushes, but live up high in the trees. When I canoed up the Macal River in Belize, the adult iguanas were in huge trees (125′ to 150′ tall) next to the river. The trees weren't elms but had some of the same mottling on the bark, with colors of light brown and grey. Out on the limbs the newer growth was a dull green, sometimes with orange or small blotches of gold—all the colors displayed by adult iguanas in that area.

Unless an iguana's tail has been broken off at some point, it will typically have bands of brown or black in camouflage patterns. Most iguanas' stomachs have black stripes, which people often refer to as tiger stripes.

Over the years, people have written and told me the various colors their iguanas exhibit. The following are just some of their descriptions:

- Head—Grey, bluish grey, light blue, robin's egg blue, orange
- Body—Phosphorescent/fluorescent green; bright, vibrant lime green; pea green; dark green; light green; gray-green. Also light brown, dark brown, beige, tan, rusty orange/brown, pumpkin orange, turquoise, black, white, brown with black speckles, grey with black markings, mottled, black stripes on belly
- Eyes—Brown, orange, gold, grey, green
- Dewlap—Green, orange, black dots, black and white speckles, grey

My iguana [1 yr. 4 mo.] has blue on the lips and under the eyes; blue and white on the dewlap and lower jaw; a greyish brown snout and top of the head; blue large [cheek] scale; and blue stripes on the underbelly.

—I-892, Steven, 22 yrs., Illinois

Iguana A [5½ yrs.] has more color and always has been unusually brilliant. She has shades of turquoise blue with lots of blue and blue-green on her head and neck. She has none of the gold and orange that Iguana B [7½ yrs.] has. A very distinct, bright stripe of light blue is on each shoulder.

Iguana B is not nearly as colorful as Iguana A. He has light stripes (black and green) on his belly and lower sides; a very pale green stripe on his shoulder and forearm; gold ranging to orange on his belly and dewlap; bright green underneath mixed with the gold; and pale blue highlights all over.

We had one other iguana with a much different coloration than these two. This iguana was bright kelly green all over with very little other coloring. It had very faint stripes, a lime green belly, and no shoulder stripes.

—I-467, Kris, 32 yrs., Florida

EXTERNAL BODY PARTS

You might have glanced ahead in this section and thought, "Why all the information on an iguana's body parts? I can see they have legs, a tail, two eyes, and nostrils. Why do I need to know about all this, anyway?"

Color Changes

Iguanas don't change color in relationship to what they are resting on, like a chameleon does. But they can get an overall lighter or darker color in response to changes in temperature, stress, health, or mood.

When an iguana is cold and is exposed to a heat source, it will often darken to absorb the heat faster. And just the opposite can happen: The lizard will lighten in color to help reduce an already overheated body.

Stress can also cause lightening of color, especially on the head. The first few times I took my iguana to his new veterinarian, his head would get pale from the stress of the experience.

While color changes are normal in an iguana, you must also be alert to color changes that signal ill health. Prolonged dark or very light coloring, or an overall "muddy" look, can be a sign of medical trouble. For more details read Chapter 7, Medical Troubleshooting, "Color Changes."

There are several reasons why it makes sense to learn as much as possible about your new green companion. For starters, if "pets" up until now have meant dogs, cats, or even rodents, it's likely that iguanas have body parts that are unfamiliar to you. Even the familiar-looking parts may have different functions in reptiles than in more "traditional" pets. And even if you're a long-time herp fan, or have owned iguanas in the past, you'll probably want to soak up as much information as you can about your pet.

I'll remind you frequently throughout this book that I'm not a veterinarian or a professional scientific researcher. This book is not intended to fill the role of a veterinarian's handbook or comprehensive reference book for working scientists. It is a pet-care book, and all the information in these sections is being presented in an easy and fun way with the goal of helping pet owners better understand, appreciate, and care for their iguanas.

As you read the descriptions of the external and internal body parts, be sure to look at the drawings on pages 45 and 62 for the body part locations if you are confused.

Skin and Scales

All animals have their own special outer coverings. Humans have skin and a little bit of hair, while other animals have fur, feathers, or shells. When it comes to iguanas, scales are the outer protective covering.

An iguana's skin is designed specially to retain moisture. What we call the

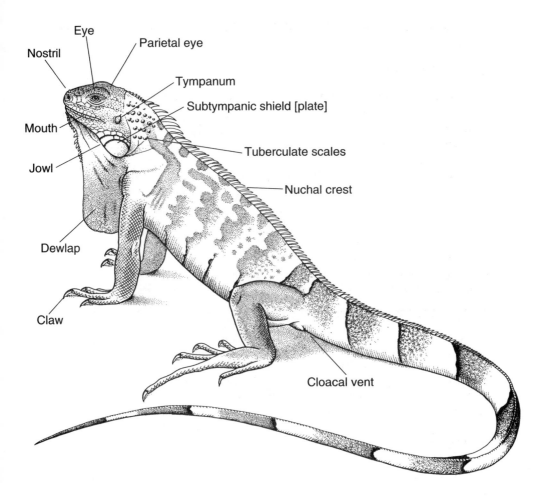

Figure 1.4: External anatomy of *Iguana iguana*. Illustration by: Kendal Morris

scales are actually individual, thickened skin cells in the outer layer of skin (epidermis) that are composed mostly of keratin, a hard, waterproof protein that's the same substance that makes our fingernails and toenails so tough.

Not every area of the iguana's skin is keratinized into hard scales, however. The folds between scales have very little keratin—a good thing, because otherwise the iguana's skin would be more like an armored suit, stiff and immobile. As it is, the iguana's skin is very flexible.

Some of these same types of keratinized skin cells modify into other structures, such as spines, claws, nose horns, or round, raised scales (e.g., on the neck).

Spines

> We decided we had to find a method of identifying each iguana without catching them and it turned out to be very easy. The iguana has this lovely feature of a characteristic array of crest scales that's visible even under poor lighting conditions, and it's visible from both sides. Looking through a telescope, we counted the first 60 dorsal crest scales of the fringe along the back and scored each for its characteristics and drew a picture of them for each animal. Some iguanas had such distinct scales that we did not need to go beyond the first 10 scales. By doing this it turned out we could keep track of all the animals in the area. There was really no practical limit to the number of animals that could be tracked.
> —Gordon H. Rodda, iguana researcher in Venezuela (#27)

Spines are merely keratinized skin cells, and can be thought of as specialized scales. Iguanas have a long crest of spines that extends from their necks (nuchal spines), all the way down their backs (dorsal spines), and down further to their tails (caudal spines). They also have a crest of spines along the lower edge of their dewlaps.

The spines are longest in the neck and shoulder area. Spines can be curved, straight, long, or short, depending on what region or country the lizard comes from.

As to the question of whether an iguana can regrow broken spines, the answer depends on the iguana and how badly damaged the area is. Long ago people would have given a flat "no" response, but I have seen young and old iguanas regenerate spines that have been broken off. Again, it depends on how deep the damage has occurred and how healthy the lizard is.

> *She [SVL: 12", TL: 4' 4", 2 yrs., 6 mo.] is missing most of her body spines. She has only 2½ spines on her upper neck. (I say "½" because one is rounded off and very slowly getting longer with each shed.) They were all missing when I got her (a side effect of malnutrition or rough handling??) and my vet did not seem too hopeful that they would grow back. Maybe it is wishful thinking, but I can see small bumps protruding from the "holes" that I swear were not that large two years ago. If they are growing in it is a very slow process, but it doesn't matter; I am happy with her the way she is.*
> —I-795, Dawn, 24 yrs., Ohio

Head

> *My large male [iguana] has a boxy, Dick Tracy head.*
> —I-289, Janice, 43 yrs., Illinois

Let's take a look at some of the most obvious and important components of an iguana's head.

Jowls

> One of the most significant characters between males and females is the width of the jaws. Males have huge, wide jaws but they don't bite with them very much. However, they do look intimidating. Both sexes have these enlarged [cheek] scales . . . [that] are very distinctively colored. The masseter muscle is hypertrophied and it lies under that large scale, which is actually conical and not flat. It is much more pronounced in large males. I would speculate that through evolutionary time sexual selection has resulted in hypertrophy of big, wide jaws and enlargement of that scale. The function is to give them the appearance of larger size.
> —Gordon H. Rodda, iguana researcher (#27)

The jowls are located at the iguana's jaw line, and as an iguana grows, so do its jowls. I often call them puff bags because of how they look and feel. If you touch an iguana's jowl, you will notice that it feels like a soft pillow.

All iguanas have jowls, but they're more prominent on adults than young iguanas, and sexually mature males have the largest jowls. At 3½ years, my iguana had the largest jowls I had ever seen; they extended dramatically from his face. He also had a large head to carry those jowls.

Jowls are another attribute to help iguanas look bigger than normal. Sometimes males will enlarge their jowls as part of their defensive or combat displays. The male iguana with the biggest head, jowls, and body gets the best food, light, heat, and access to mates.

In one test, it was proven that male iguanas with the largest heads and jowls usually won all their "mock" fights (i.e., the fights resolved by body language alone, and that didn't escalate to actual physical fighting). Because iguanas don't really want to get into fights and get injured, they often swagger, puff up, and extend body parts to intimidate their opponents.

Cheek Scale

A single, large cheek scale is located just below the exterior ear (tympanum) on each side of the iguana's head, near the corner of the jaw, directly on the jowls. Because of this location, it is called the subtympanic shield or subtympanic plate. It also goes by the common name of helmet scale because in the adult, it is large and sticks out like an ancient war helmet. It has an iridescent shine like the shell of an abalone and is often outlined in black, which makes it more distinct.

Some iguana biologists speculate that the purpose of this large scale is as a "bluff" eye, designed to ward off predators. When an iguana gets into protective mode and extends its dewlap, the cheek scale becomes more prominent. It's possible that to the predator, the cheek scale looks like a large eye of the now-expanded lizard.

Eyes

Iguanas' eye color ranges from gold or orange to brown or grey. The lower eyelid has what looks like a line of mascara on it. Iguanas in the wild are constantly in the sun, and this black line may help to reduce the sun's glare, much like the black smear that football players put under their eyes.

Iguana eyes differ somewhat from human eyes, so scientists assume that iguanas see the world slightly differently than we do. Humans have both cone cells—color detectors—and rod cells, which are extremely light-sensitive but don't detect color. This mix of cones and rods allows us to see in color as well as in dim light. But the mix also means that our daytime color vision isn't as good as if we had only cones in our retinas.

The retinas of iguanas' eyes contain large numbers of cone cells and double cone cells, both of which are used to perceive color and contrast. For this reason, scientists assume that iguanas see colors more vividly than humans do.

While iguanas have excellent full-color daytime vision, they don't see well at night or in dim light. We humans have enough rod cells in our retinas to per-

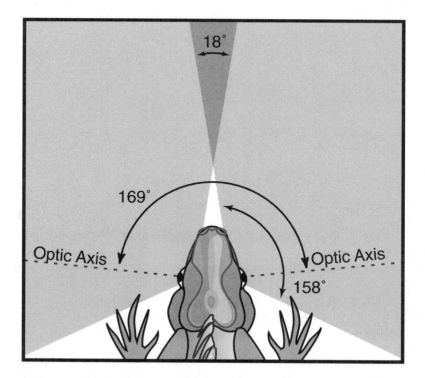

Figure 1.5: This vision diagram shows that green iguanas have good peripheral vision and that even with eyes on the sides of their head, they still have a small range of binocular (stereoscopic) vision straight ahead. Original concept courtesy of Lynn Wiegard

mit some night vision, but it's nowhere near the night vision of an animal with mostly rods in its retina, such as a cat. On the other hand, a human's vision at night is much better than an iguana's.

To test an iguana's vision in low light, take the iguana from a bright room to one with dim light and watch the lizard's reactions. Often it will paw at the air or squirm in your hand to get away. Iguanas don't like this sudden transition, probably because it renders them literally blind.

Interestingly, however, iguanas' eyes can detect ultraviolet light, which we can't. "They can see anything you can, plus ultraviolet" (#14).

Iguanas' eyes are located on the sides of their head. As a result, iguanas have only a small field of stereoscopic (binocular) vision, or area in which they can see an object with both eyes at once. Iguanas' peripheral vision is good, but they will turn their head to point one eye directly at movement or an object of interest to get a better look. Iguanas have limited depth perception (depth perception is possible only with binocular vision, like humans have), so they most often watch things with only one eye at a time. Some people speculate that iguanas are such fearless jumpers precisely because they can't accurately judge how far it is to the ground if they miss their jump target.

Iguanas' mostly monocular (one-eyed) vision gives them birdlike eye and head movements. They will cock their head to one side to get a better view. For example, if you offer an iguana something to eat, the lizard will usually bite at the food from the side, so it can see what it is eating. If you want your iguana to see something clearly, show it to your lizard from the side rather than directly in front of its nose.

Watch how an iguana moves its head to look at something in its environment, and you can tell a lot about what it is "thinking."

I can always tell when my iguana is getting ready to climb up something, whether it be my leg or a tree. He slants his head sideways, focuses one eye intently on his intended destination, and licks at the air. Then he carefully licks the object he is planning to climb. When he licks my leg—look out, he's on his way up!

He does basically the same thing when he sees something that he wants to eat, focusing one eye on the target and licking the air.
                                                —I-467, Kris, 32 yrs., Florida

Eye Movements

Pupils dilate or contract when iguanas are excited or upset—or thinking/analyzing.
                                                —I-237, Diane, 44 yrs., Texas

As the quotation indicates, iguanas also use their eyes as communication tools. Except for an occasional loud exhale, iguanas make no sounds. They rely on body language to communicate with other iguanas and with potential predators (and with humans). This reliance on body language is one reason that iguanas are so visually oriented—they're continually scanning their environment for cues. Iguanas also find the eyes of other iguanas to be very inter-esting. The eye is a stimulus to an iguana.

When an iguana closes its eyes while resting, the eyelids meet in the mid-dle. During deep sleep, the bottom eyelid comes up to the top of the eye. Igua-nas also have an extra eyelid that humans lack, but that many other animals have. This transparent eyelid is called a nictitating membrane, and you can often see it after your iguana has blinked. The nictitating membrane is hinged on the inner side of the iguana's eye, helping to keep the eye clean and moist.

If an iguana doesn't want you around, it will just close its eyes.
—I-626, Gail, 48 yrs., New York

If I hold a piece of food up to him when he is not hungry (rarely), he will quickly close the eye nearest to the food. He will keep his eye tightly shut until I take the food away. I guess that he wants it to go away and reasons that if he can't see it, it must be gone. It's funny because it's only the one eye that he closes when he does this, not both. The other is wide open!
—I-467, Kris, 32 yrs., Florida

When an unwanted or unfamiliar object comes up close to their face, igua-nas will often close the eye nearest the object. Perhaps it's a stress response. By closing the eye, the "thing" goes away and the iguana might feel safer. Often, when you pet their head, the eye closest to you will close. If your iguana is truly enjoying the experience, both eyes will shut. Take a peek over their head: Is the other eye open or closed?

On occasion, an iguana might protrude or bulge its eyes for a second or two. It often looks like the lizard's eye is going to pop out of its socket. Some-times this happens when the iguana is starting to go to sleep, other times it may happen with the eyes open. My iguana used to do this at least once a month and would scare me to death in the beginning. I had a couple of other people write and tell me that their lizard did the same thing, which made me feel much better.

One possible explanation for this protruding behavior was given to me by an iguana researcher, who said it's a way they momentarily relax their eyes. When my iguana was about 3 years old I put my finger next to his bulging eye and he turned his head and gently pushed against the finger to rub his eye.

After that, every time Za bulged his eyes I placed a finger on both sides of his head so he could rub one or both eyes if he wanted to. I did not move my fingers, as I didn't want to injure the eye; I let him apply the pressure and dura-tion he wanted. He rubbed or put pressure against my fingers for a few seconds, then blinked his eye three or four times, as if he were trying to clear something off the lens of the eye. I felt like I helped him itch, rub, or relax an area that was difficult to reach.

Parietal (Third) Eye

During World War II, small towns across the U.S. had observation towers to look for enemy planes that may have sneaked below radar and into the country. The towers were usually manned 24 hours a day by civilian volunteers. Perhaps they should have had one civilian and one iguana in those towers.

It turns out that iguanas have a third eye—more often called the parietal eye—located in the center of the top of their heads. It's called a parietal eye because it's positioned between the two parietal bones of the skull. It looks like a round or oval, colorless scale, but it actually has a working lens a few tenths of a millimeter across. The parietal lens can detect only light and darkness, not colors or images—perfect for spotting shadows cast by planes flying overhead.

As an example, one day when my iguana was in the enclosed yard, he suddenly turned his head sideways and looked up into the blank sky. He kept looking, looking, while remaining immobile, totally engrossed, and even puffed up slightly. I looked up, too, but couldn't figure out what had captured his interest. A minute or two later, I saw a jet plane, high in the sky, too high to be seen a minute ago (by me), much less heard. Za tracked the plane the whole way across the sky, until it was out of sight. Then he relaxed back to his "normal" posture and continued walking across the lawn. He did this often when he was outside, each time alerted by his third eye to planes long before I could hear or see them. (See parietal eye illustration on page 52.)

Iguanas' third eyes are very useful in the wild. As iguanas bask in the sun, they can literally keep one eye on the sky—detecting the shadows of possible bird predators, like the skill Za used so effectively to track planes in our yard.

The parietal eye is a true, functioning eye. What you're seeing when you look at the top of your lizard's head is the lens, and there's a retina beneath it. Light hitting the retina sends signals to a parietal nerve, which leads into the parietal foramens—a hole at the top of the iguana's head bones (you can see it clearly in the iguana skeleton photo on page 76). The nerve signals then travel to the pineal body on the brain, then to the brain stem.

To test some hypotheses about what the third eye does, researchers looked at what happened when the eye was either stimulated or blocked from "seeing." Believing that iguanas can detect shadows with their third eye, researchers put little blinders on the iguana's "normal" eyes, then shined a strong light to make a shadow that passed over the iguana's head. When they did this, the iguana flinched.

Another test, and one that I don't recommend trying at home, is to cover the third eye (scientists sometimes even remove it surgically—ah, the quest for knowledge . . .) and observe how the lizard reacts. And what does it do? The lizard continues to move and eat and act normally in many ways, but it doesn't seem to know when to get out of the sun.

From these tests, researchers confirmed that the third eye acts as a kind of dosimeter—a way of "counting" the amount of sunlight the iguana has absorbed, and when enough is enough. The parietal eye is crucial to let iguanas

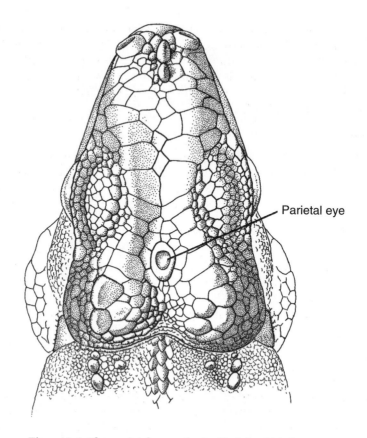

Figure 1.6: The parietal eye, often called the "third eye," is another sensory organ an iguana uses to gain information about its environment.
Illustration by: Kendal Morris

know whether to stay in the sun or move to the shade. Iguanas without a third eye (or with their third eye covered) could spend too much time in the sun and perhaps overheat and die.

The third eye is also believed to affect a number of hormonal systems, including the thyroid and the pituitary glands, which direct a wide range of activities and behaviors in iguanas. According to Richard M. Eakin, in his book *The Third Eye* (University of California Press):

The flux and interplay of hormones [produced by] the endocrine glands . . . modify . . . the behavior of the animal. The regulation of one important aspect of that behavior, to which we believe the parietal eye contributes, is the daily cycle of activity . . . called the circadian rhythm.

Every animal and plant has a circadian—or "around a day"—rhythm, during which physiological activities rise and fall. "Light is the principal external factor regulating the circadian rhythm," according to Eakin. In iguanas, it appears that the third eye is crucial for an appropriate circadian rhythm. In addition, the third eye most likely affects iguanas' breeding behavior. All in all, it's a pretty powerful little organ.

Nose

An iguana's nose, or snout, is exactly where you'd expect it to be: at the extreme front of its head. Rather than a distinctive nose that sticks out from the face, like a human's nose, an iguana's nose more closely resembles a dog's snout: two nostrils that sit above the rounded, protruding front of its face.

Nostrils

At the end of the iguana's snout are two clearly visible nostrils. Inside the nostrils is a nasal chamber with two separate functions. It stores accumulated liquid from the iguana's salt glands until the lizard snorts the liquid out, and it also is responsible for iguanas' sense of smell. Air-borne scents, breathed in by the iguana, go first to the nasal chamber. Air breathed in through the nose also goes to the lungs, just as you would expect it to do.

Ears

Humans have internal ears; the flap of curved skin we call the ear is really just to catch sound waves, which are then funneled inside the ear canal to the ear drum and the other mechanisms for hearing. Iguanas, on the other hand, have external ear drums, though the other sound detection and conversion mechanisms are inside. The ear drum, or tympanum, appears as a thin, hard, plastic-like covering just above the jowls and cheek scale (see drawing on page 45).

Iguanas have an ear on each side of their heads, located on about the same horizontal level as their mouths, but much further back on their heads, almost to where the neck begins. The ear is round or oval-shaped, with a slight depression covered by the tympanum.

Iguanas turn their heads at any sound that is unfamiliar. If you want to get an iguana's attention, make a sound he's never heard.
                                        —I-626, Gail, 48 yrs., New York

Iguanas have excellent hearing, and they will turn their attention to even faint sounds. Humans are most sensitive to the frequencies associated with human speech—in the 2,000 to 5,000 hertz (hz) range. We hear sounds beyond this range, but this is where we hear the best. Iguanas hear best between 500 and 3,000 hz, which means that humans and iguanas both hear well between 2,000 and 3,000 hz.

For the musically inclined, 500 hz is the B above middle C; 2,000 hz is two

"Snorting" or "Sneezing"

[Many people] refer to the action of nasal salt gland as "sneezing." I personally find this annoying, as sneezing, wheezing, abnormal discharges, etc. should be attended to immediately—this terminology may encourage first-time owners to be less concerned should their iguanas get chilled and exhibit symptoms of respiratory illness. I prefer to use "snorting," as it clearly defines normal behavior while acknowledging that iguanas can get colds. The snottiness and discomfort we associate with sneezing is not normal in iguanas; the vigor associated with, say, a snorting stallion, is. —I-515, Lynn, 21 yrs., Canada

All iguanas snort, and snorting performs a valuable function. As herbivorous (plant-eating) animals, iguanas have to eat large quantities of plants to receive the nutrients they need to live. But many plants also contain large amounts of potassium, which iguanas don't need. Reptile kidneys are not known for their efficiency in ridding the body of potassium and other specific wastes.

Instead, the iguana has a rhinal (nose) salt gland that acts as a back-up kidney. It is specialized to remove excess amounts of sodium, potassium, bicarbonate, and chloride—i.e., various salts—from the iguana's body. Many factors affect the precise composition of the salty fluid, including diet.

The ducts of the salt gland drain into the nasal chamber as salt-filled fluid. When a pool of this fluid has collected, the iguana simply snorts it out its nostrils.

All of that nasal discharge salt sprays on the glass every day. I probably clean the glass two times a day. —I-843, Brendon, 20 yrs., Georgia

octaves higher; 3,000 hz is the F# three octaves above middle C; and 5,000 hz is the D# four octaves above middle C. Play these notes on the piano for your iguana, and you'll probably notice that the iguana pays most attention to the notes that fall within its range of greatest sensitivity.

One interesting note is that iguanas' hearing is tied to their body temperature: They hear best when they are at their "ideal" temperature (i.e., around 85°F or so). Much above or below their optimal temperature, iguanas' hearing diminishes, especially in response to high tones.

Like humans, iguanas have Eustachian tubes that equalize the pressure between the outside air and the air in the middle ear. In an iguana, the Eustachian tubes open into the roof of the mouth and lead back to the middle ear. These tubes are vital for helping the iguana hear sounds accurately.

The ear not only acts as a device for hearing, but also is an organ of balance and motion detection. It's the same in humans: When we get infections or injuries to our inner ear, we suffer loss of balance and coordination.

Dewlap

The funniest incorrect name I have ever heard given to describe an iguana's dewlap is "wattle," which is the name given the flap of skin under a chicken's neck. The iguana's dewlap is more than a large flap of loose skin; it has multiple purposes, ranging from temperature control to communication.

Because blood circulates through the dewlap, an iguana can extend it on hot days to catch a cool breeze and cool down its body—much like water circulating through a car's radiator keeps the engine from overheating. At the other end of the temperature spectrum, the dewlap can also help the lizard warm up (e.g., first thing in the morning, so it can digest its food). The iguana extends the dewlap and aligns its body at a right angle to the sun, enabling the big skin flap to act as a great solar collector.

> *I've made an observation about dewlaps. My older iguana's was always hanging down, fully expanded, whereas the younger iguana keeps hers tucked up against her throat. I worried there was something wrong with her, and examined her dewlap carefully for unshed skin, etc. There was nothing. Interestingly enough, once the older iguana was gone, the younger one began carrying her dewlap down in the normal position.*
> —I-866, Kate, 41 yrs., California
> [AUTHOR'S NOTE: Dewlap position along with that of several other iguana body parts can demonstrate dominance. This young iguana was smart to hold up her "pride" for safety.]

The dewlap is also used for communication. The male's dewlap is usually larger and more pendulous than the female's, but both the male and female use their dewlaps in greeting and as part of mating and territorial displays. If you've ever seen an iguana react to its reflection in the mirror, or to another iguana in its territory, you've seen the extended dewlap response. Iguanas also extend their dewlaps and bob their heads as a greeting, to acknowledge the presence of another creature, such as their owners.

If you run your fingers gently along the front edge of the dewlap, near the row of spines that edge it, you will feel the long, thin hyoid bone, which supports, extends, and retracts the dewlap. The hyoid bone, actually made of cartilage, also has some branching cartilage that supports the tongue. It's a delicate and important mechanism, and that's why certain leashes and harnesses are not recommended for iguanas because they could possibly damage this supporting network (see Chapter 8, Domestication, "Iguana on a Leash").

Trunk

For the purposes of this section, we'll consider the "trunk" as everything from the neck to the vent, including appendages (arms, legs) but not including the head or tail.

Neck

An iguana's neck area is protected from attackers by a thickened, fleshy ridge; by spines that are the longest on the lizard's body; and by protective scales (tuberculate scales) that look like small rivets, or the pointed stud collars seen around Doberman Pincer guard dogs. These "rivets" also add another level of physical texture and beauty to an already spectacular creature.

Arms and Legs

Initially, if I even touched him he would push his hand out rapidly to stop me, as if gesturing, "get away from me." —I-511, Deborah, 41 yrs., Virginia

Iguanas have distinctively shaped, chubby-looking, and very sturdy legs. They walk on "all fours" and use both arms and legs to climb and to raise and lower their bodies.

As the previous quotation said, iguanas also use their arms or legs to signal the times when they don't want to be touched. In this behavior they are not trying to inflict pain, just discourage you from getting close. Still, you should try to respect your iguana's wishes when it "tells" you in this clear way that it isn't in the mood to be touched. An exception would be if the iguana starts to do it all the time, in which case you need to reassert your dominance, gently, by continuing to pet the iguana even after it starts tying to bat your hand away.

Frequently, they will use an arm or leg to scratch themselves—usually the legs are used to reach the head or neck, and the arms to reach the lower back. When resting or sleeping, iguanas commonly throw their arms back along their sides, palms facing upward, and/or kick their legs straight back along their tails. It's a sign of relaxation and happens only when they feel secure with their surroundings. Many people think this is very cute.

I love how my iguana just all of a sudden throws his front arms back along the side of his body. —I-494, Jim, 25 yrs., California

Hands and Feet

An iguana's hands and feet work more like scaly grappling hooks than flexible extensions to grasp or hold objects. The fingers don't have the flexibility of a human hand, nor do they move independently. The pads on iguanas' hands and feet are soft like a cat's, but the most striking feature of the hands and feet are the claws.

Claws

The only thing indicating that an iguana is a good climber is its claws. They are sharp and pointed like the spiked shoes that telephone linemen use to scurry up a telephone pole.

> We are talking ecologically about a very successful animal which has not diversified. It appears to have evolved fairly recently from an animal which was terrestrial in its habits, so it is not that well adapted an animal for living in trees, although it is normally thought of as an arboreal creature. The one adaptation it has becomes apparent if you have ever picked up an iguana. It has very sharp claws, and it uses these to climb.
> —Gordon H. Rodda, iguana researcher (#27)

Iguanas' claws, like their scales, are created from keratinized skin cells. The cells at the top of the claw have far more keratin than the cells in the underside, so the upper side of the claw is stronger. As the claw grows, the tougher upper portion of the claw curves over the weaker underside, giving the iguana's claw its distinctive shape.

Vent

If you hold an iguana vertically, with its belly facing you, you can see its vent, a slit covered by a fold of skin where the body meets the tail. Inside the vent of both male and female iguanas are the reproductive organs, and it's through this opening that iguanas excrete both urine and feces.

Femoral Pores

On the inside of the iguana's thighs (hind legs) is a row of about 12 to 20 large pores called femoral pores (because they run along the femur bone of the upper thigh). The femoral pores in hatchlings are quite small, like tiny pinpricks. The pores of adult iguanas are generally larger in males than in females, and sexually mature males' femoral pores often develop spinelike "spurs" that protrude distinctly during breeding season (see drawing on page 59). These protrusions are actually a soft waxy substance thought to be important in iguana communication; see "Femoral Pore Secretions" on page 84 for details.

Tail

> On the average, the tail length [of *Iguana iguana*] will be about 60 to 67 percent of the total length of the animal.
> —John A. Phillips, CRES (Center for Reproduction of Endangered Species, San Diego Zoological Society) (#14)

The tail of an iguana is a multipurpose appendage. Iguanas use their tails for balance when climbing, as an undulating propellant while swimming, and

SIDEBAR

Defecation

Unlike humans and many other animals that have two separate orifices for excreting urine and solid wastes, iguanas are more simplified: one opening, two separate but mixed waste products. Iguana feces contain a leader and trailer that is a creamy white, pasty substance, sometimes solid, sometimes more fluidy. Both are normal.

> *His poop <u>stinks</u>! Much worse than a cat or dog.*
> —I-753, Kelly, 26 yrs., Pennsylvania
> [AUTHOR'S NOTE: The smell is a function of what the iguana has eaten. Often too much protein can cause this smell.]

After defecating, an iguana lifts its tail high and to the side of the feces until clear of the mess, then rubs its vent on a solid surface to wipe it clean. Given the proper space, an iguana never drags its tail through its feces; they are very clean animals.

as a formidable whip-like weapon against attackers. Being hit by the tail of a juvenile iguana can raise a welt that lasts for several hours, while full-grown iguanas are capable of breaking the legs of a dog or cat with one swift strike.

An iguana's tail is not prehensile, meaning the iguana can't wrap its tail around a limb like a monkey or a chameleon can, but the tail does have some flexibility. Iguanas use their tails while climbing to enhance their balance and even as a brake while climbing down. I frequently saw my iguana push his tail against a limb as he was coming down, using the tail as a kind of brace or brake to slow his descent and help control his movements.

Many of the lizards you find in your backyard can snap part of their tail off if being attacked or threatened by a predator (this action is called "caudal autotomy"). If the predator grabs hold of this tail, the lizard can give a quick snap and the tail falls off, releasing the lizard. To avoid attack, the lizard can also snap the tail and run off, leaving the broken tail as a wiggling diversion (the tail continues moving from residual nerve twitches). The idea is that the predator attacks the tail as the real lizard (with luck) escapes. In these types of lizards, the tail will regrow in time.

Not surprisingly, young iguanas can also "drop" their tails. They often face more predators than adults, and have fewer defense mechanisms. The ability to sacrifice its tail and regrow a new one is important for young iguanas. But there is a short window of time in which a hatchling has the ability to regenerate a complete tail.

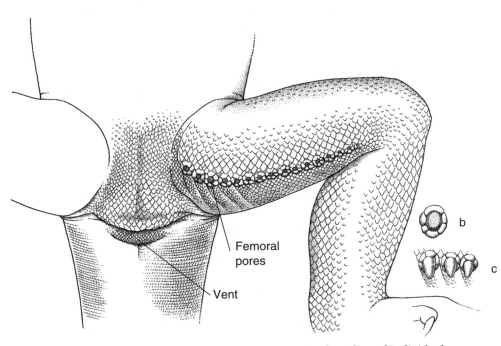

Femoral
pores

Vent

b

c

Figure 1.7: On the inside thighs of all green iguanas is a long line of individual rounded pores. These femoral pores are part of an iguana's communication system and are more apparent in sexually mature males, especially during breeding season. The insert shows them normally (b) and during breeding season (c). Illustration by: Kendal Morris

Young iguanas can regenerate their tails because several of the tail verte-brae have fracture planes, or grooves where the vertebrae can snap relatively easily. As the iguana grows, however, these fracture planes begin to fuse and the lizard loses its ability to easily sacrifice its tail.

Unlike the backyard lizards described earlier, which spend their entire lives on the ground, iguanas are arboreal, and as they get older they spend more and more time in trees and bushes. As a result, older iguanas benefit more from an intact tail—as I mentioned earlier, the tail is important for balance and climbing and is an effective weapon—so there's less advantage to being able to sacrifice it. That's probably why older iguanas take longer to recover from tail loss.

When an older iguana loses part of its tail, the wounded end heals over and repairs itself internally. Often some regrowth takes place, but the new tail is dark, often black, with none of the natural colorings and markings of the orig-inal tail. And the regrown tail never reaches its original full length. If the break was not clean, the tail may even grow back at an odd angle.

It's important to take care of your iguana's tail, to try to keep it intact. Cap-tive environments pose many more closely spaced objects, tight corners, twists, and turns than an iguana's natural environment, so it's up to you to be aware and help prevent tail-threatening situations.

INTERNAL BODY PARTS

Unless you have plans to become a reptile veterinarian, you will probably never get a chance to see the internal body parts of an iguana (see page 62). But I feel that knowing some basic facts about the inner workings of your lizard can help you detect when something may not be right, or help you understand why certain foods or habitat considerations are necessary. At the very least, it's interesting to know what's under the skin of these fascinating reptiles.

The following explanations are intended to provide only an overview of internal anatomy; I have tried to keep them short and simple. I hope from the discussion of an iguana's organs you also learn a little bit about how these organs work in your own human body, as well.

Circulatory System

Humans have a rather simple circulatory system: The heart pumps blood to the lungs; oxygenated blood goes out to the body tissues; and de-oxygenated blood returns to the heart, where the whole process begins again. Iguanas have a double circulation system, in which their blood passes through the heart twice. Blood flows from the heart to the lungs, back to the heart, then out to the body tissues before returning again to the heart. This more complex circulatory system, which is common in reptiles, is an important adaptation for iguanas, such as for temperature control and prolonged underwater swimming.

Heart

An iguana's heart has three chambers—two atria and one ventricle—instead of the four chambers (two atria and two ventricles) found in humans. The iguana heart's single ventricle keeps oxygenated blood (i.e., from the lungs) from mixing with deoxygenated blood (from the body tissues) by timing its contractions to control blood pressures and by a muscular ridge that functionally divides the ventricle. This three-chambered configuration is what makes their double circulation system possible.

Interestingly, iguanas are able to direct a proportion of their blood flow away from their lungs when they are not using them, such as when the lizard is submerged under water. This adaptation helps explain how iguanas can easily spend 20 minutes or more underwater. Why bother sending blood to the lungs if it won't get more oxygen from them? Instead, the blood stays in the tissues, where all the available oxygen goes to such crucial functions as detoxifying the liver and kidneys.

It's unlikely that you could hear an iguana's heartbeat, even with a stethoscope; it doesn't make a distinct "lub-dub" like a human's heart. And even trained veterinarians find it difficult to locate an iguana's pulse points. If you could monitor your iguana's heartbeat, however, you'd find that it got faster or slower depending on a wide range of variables, especially body temperature.

Blood

In every animal, the blood and blood vessels deliver oxygen and other nutrients to the body's organs, and remove the wastes created by the organs. The blood is a very sophisticated transportation system, carrying hormones, immune cells, nutrients, and other substances to where they should be.

This circulating transportation system is also important in reptiles to distribute heat evenly through the body. Remember, reptiles are ectothermic ("cold-blooded") animals that depend on external heat sources; humans are endothermic ("warm-blooded") mammals with a kind of internal furnace that maintains our body heat even when outdoor temperatures change, within a certain range. As an iguana basks in the sun, its body surface and the blood in vessels just below the skin become warmer than its internal organs. When blood warmed at the iguana's surface flows back through the lizard's body, it helps warm the iguana, from the outside in.

Spleen

The spleen removes old and ineffective blood cells from the bloodstream and produces new blood cells. The spleen also produces lymphocytes, cells that patrol the body through the blood, looking for harmful bacteria.

Respiratory System

Just as with humans, iguanas' breathing can be affected by all kinds of factors, including stress, exertion, and being underwater. As I've mentioned previously, iguanas can stay underwater for many minutes at a time. They can also hold their breath on land, and it can be pretty scary for a pet owner who doesn't know this can be done.

When my iguana was just over 3½ years old, he sometimes held his breath during power struggles with me, when he was frustrated that I wouldn't let him do something he really wanted to do. Za would just hold his breath for a couple of minutes, then expel it all in one big breath.

Once I realized that holding his breath wasn't hurting him, it was actually quite funny. I would talk to him and say, "Are we acting like a little twit today?" Sometimes I would hold my own breath and let it out in a big roar at the same time he did. When I tried this trick, he usually stopped "playing" hold-the-breath.

Several times Za was frightened by something he saw outside the window and his breathing sped up, as if he had just run a new record for the mile. At first when I held him, he didn't want to stay; I had to gently but firmly hold him until he settled down. Petting his head and talking calmly and quietly reduced his anxiety. He also seemed to like the side of his head pressed against the side

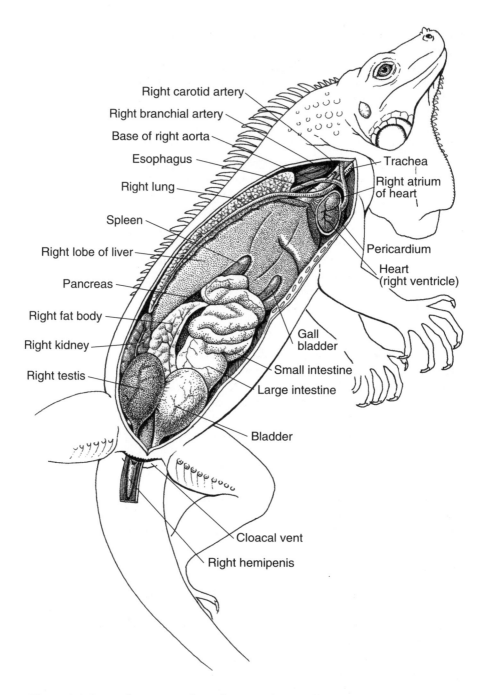

Figure 1.8: Internal anatomy of a male *Iguana iguana*. Illustration by: Kendal Morris

of my face during this time. (Actions like this made it easy to forget that it was a lizard I was holding.)

I experimented once with leaving him alone to see how long it would take for his breathing to calm down by itself. It didn't. In fact, his breathing became more labored and he became more frightened, until I picked him up and held him.

Lungs

In humans, movements of our ribcage and diaphragm—the partition of muscles and tendons below the lungs—assist our breathing. Iguanas have lungs, but they don't have a diaphragm, so they have to rely on the muscles of their ribcage to help move air in and out of their lungs.

Trachea

The trachea—commonly called the "windpipe"—is an air passageway reinforced with cartilage so that it always remains firm, clear, and open. The trachea leads from the mouth and at the other end branches into two bronchi, each of which connects to a passageway to one of the two lungs.

Glottis

The glottis is a pair of skin flaps that protects the opening of the trachea. In humans the glottis is mostly open, which is why we are able to inadvertently "breathe" in our food from time to time. In iguanas, these flaps remain closed except when the iguana is actually taking a breath or exhaling. The glottis forms a seal that keeps inhaled air in the lungs, and that prevents an iguana from breathing in its food as it munches on its favorite plants.

Digestive System

The digestive system involves all the body parts needed for eating and absorbing food and for eliminating what can't be digested. As you'll read in Chapter 5, Feeding, iguanas have a special digestive system ideally suited to their herbivorous diet.

Mouth

Before food can be digested, it has to be made into smaller parts. An iguana's mouth contains numerous small teeth; a muscular, pink tongue; and a small number of salivary glands. A very important difference between human and iguana digestion occurs in the mouth, specifically in the saliva. Human saliva contains digestive enzymes that actually begin breaking down food. But iguanas have only a small amount of clear, mucous saliva that lacks digestive enzymes. Iguana saliva is used simply to lubricate the food and help it pass through the rest of the digestive tract.

Teeth

Dozens of small, thin, sharp teeth line the inside of the iguana's jaws. Owners of hatchling or juvenile iguanas may be surprised to learn that iguanas have teeth because they are so hard to see. But in large juvenile and adult lizards the teeth are clearly visible and quite effective. An adult's teeth are like the razor-sharp teeth of a piranha fish, and it's a trip to the hospital for stitches if you're bitten by a large adult iguana. I know, because I made the trip on two separate occasions when I wasn't paying attention to my iguana's "attitude" during breeding season.

Iguanas don't chew their food like we do; their teeth are designed specifically to shear off vegetation. Each iguana bite creates perforations on a leaf, forming a sheet of what looks like irregularly shaped postage stamps. The iguana can then rip off the perforated leaf pieces as easily as we tear off a postage stamp from the sheet or roll.

Humans' teeth sit in the middle of the jawbone, whereas iguanas' teeth are seated on the inner sides of the jawbones. If our adult teeth wear or fall out they are not replaced naturally by our bodies, but iguanas are constantly replacing damaged or loose teeth throughout their lives.

An iguana might have 80 to 120 teeth at any one time. As the iguana grows and its jaw lengthens, it adds more teeth behind those it already has—as many as four per year. Iguanas also shed teeth regularly, so they always have sharp plant shears. New teeth grow up directly behind the ones currently in use, so when the old tooth is shed the new tooth is already in the same spot, ready for use.

At any moment, every second tooth in the jaw is in the process of being replaced. This pattern ensures that the iguana has at least half a set of evenly distributed, mature teeth along its jawline at all times. Iguanas might replace their teeth five times a year, which means that an iguana produces literally thousands of teeth throughout its lifetime.

Tongue

An iguana's tongue is thick and muscular, slightly forked, with many functions. It can be used as a tool to bring food into the mouth, to manipulate the food, for face cleaning, and as a sensory device. The tip is usually a darker pink than the rest of the tongue.

Because iguanas don't produce much saliva, their tongue tends to be slightly tacky. Your lizard will often use this slight tackiness to its advantage to help bring leaves into its mouth more easily.

Once an iguana has gotten something into its mouth, it slowly opens its jaws and pushes its tongue under the food. With the food pressed against the roof of the mouth, it will draw its tongue back, forcing the food further back. The iguana then closes its jaws on the food to hold it in position before easing the tongue under the food again. It repeats this cycle with its tongue to push food back until it's in position to swallow.

Because an iguana's tongue doesn't have a lot of control and flexibility, the lizard can't wipe its face clean like a cat, but iguanas do use their tongues to dislodge food or other foreign materials from around their mouths. If that doesn't work, they'll typically rub their face against a limb, rock, or the ground to clean it. (That's only one reason for including a rich assortment of items in the habitat interior.)

An iguana's tongue has another, very important, function: as a sensory device. You may notice your iguana flicking its tongue to "taste" the ground, the air, and various objects. Like some other reptiles, amphibians, and mammals, iguanas possess an extra sense organ called the vomeronasal organ, or Jacobson's organ (discussed in the next section), which is located in the roof of the mouth.

Jacobson's Organ

The Jacobson's organ, or vomeronasal organ, allows iguanas to pick up faint scents by flicking their tongues on objects or in the air. A very sensitive organ, it gives the iguana sensory information that lies somewhere between taste and smell. Iguanas don't have a great sense of smell—unlike dogs or cats, iguanas are not designed to rapidly sniff in all the air they need to pick up faint scents—and iguanas don't lick objects in the same way as many other animals do. So the Jacobson's organ provides additional sensory information to the iguana.

Here's how it works: An iguana flicks its tongue on an object, on the ground, or in the air, picking up faint traces of scent molecules. The slight fork in the tongue (though not nearly as forked as a snake's) brushes against the roof of its mouth, where there is a slight indentation. This is the location of the vomeronasal ducts, which lead to the vomeronasal organ. This sensory system enables iguanas to extract a great deal of useful information about their environment and about other iguanas, including the difference between males and females and perhaps between specific iguana individuals.

Many animals, including most reptiles, have Jacobson's organs; the ones in iguanas are not as highly developed as, for instance, a snake's. Iguanas are primarily visual animals, and they use the Jacobson's organ as a secondary rather than a primary sense organ.

Pharynx

The pharynx is a simple tube that connects the mouth to the esophagus, after which the food heads toward the stomach.

Esophagus

The iguana's esophagus serves as both a roadway to the stomach and a temporary storage site for food that has been eaten. It can distend, or stretch, to hold quite a bit of food. This capability comes in handy for iguanas, who must eat large amounts of plant material to meet their bodies' nutritional requirements. The muscular esophagus contracts to help push food toward the stomach and also secretes mucus to lubricate food for easier movement.

Stomach

Food digestion—the process of breaking down food into a form that the body can use—begins in the stomach. The stomach produces gastric juices, a mix of stomach acid and enzymes that starts breaking food down into water-soluble molecules that can be absorbed and used by the body's cells. The stomach acid also kills a lot of the bacteria and other nasty stuff that comes in with the food. In addition to this chemical breakdown, the stomach mechanically breaks down food by contracting to squish the food.

Small Intestine

From the stomach, partially digested food goes to the small intestine. Two ducts open into the first part of the small intestine (the duodenum); one duct transports pancreatic juice from the pancreas, and the other transports bile produced by the liver, via the gallbladder. These fluids contain digestive enzymes that continue the breakdown of the food. The pancreatic juice also neutralizes the stomach acid that is mixed with the food—important because although the stomach can cope with the acid, the intestines can't. The small intestine is where water and various minerals, including calcium, are absorbed by the iguana's body.

Pancreas

As mentioned above, the pancreas produces pancreatic juice, an enzyme-filled fluid that helps break down food in the small intestine. The pancreas also produces insulin and glucagon, which are important for regulating how much sugar enters the body's cells. Insulin lets more sugar into cells; glucagon lowers the amount of sugar. Without insulin, cells can't get the sugars they need, the sugars build up in the blood, and the kidney gets rid of the sugars before the body can use them. Lack of insulin, known as diabetes, is apparently rare in iguanas.

Liver

The liver has a number of important functions. It produces bile, which helps break down fats in the small intestine. The liver can also remove carbohydrates, proteins, and fats from the bloodstream and either break them down or store them. Finally, a female iguana's liver uses stored fat to produce yolk that feeds developing iguanas in her eggs.

Gallbladder

The gallbladder is a stretchy sac that stores bile (produced by the liver) until it's needed. The presence of food in the duodenum, the first segment of the small intestine, triggers the gallbladder to excrete bile.

Hindgut

Cellulose, the main component of plants, can't be broken down in the stomach. Humans cannot digest this cellulose—also called "fiber"—but we use it as "roughage" to keep everything in our digestive tracts moving along smoothly. To digest cellulose, iguanas rely on a population of microscopic organisms (microflora) that live in a special digestive appendage. This appendage, called the hindgut, is located between their small and large intestines.

Folds in the iguana's hindgut divide it into chambers that slow the movement of food, providing nooks and crannies for the microflora to inhabit so they're not flushed out with the feces. The microflora create a fermentation process (fermentation is the breakdown of the complex molecules in organic compounds, in this case the food the iguana eats).

Hindgut fermentation is responsible for 30% to 40% of the energy an iguana extracts from its food, which is more than occurs in the stomach and small intestine combined. As a result of their hindgut, iguanas can digest cellulose and use it for nutrition—and not, as in humans, simply as an intestinal roto-rooter! The hindgut is also covered in Chapter 5, Feeding, "Hindgut," but from a slightly different perspective.

Large Intestine

After food has been fermented in the hindgut, it travels to the large intestine, which includes the colon and the rectum, the last section of digestive tract where nutrient absorption takes place. Any solids remaining in the large intestine are formed into feces for easy excretion from the body.

Kidney

Iguanas, like humans, have a pair of kidneys that filter toxic substances from the blood, excrete urine, and recover water. In mammals, urine is mostly urea (a highly soluble, crystalline solid). In iguanas, urine is almost entirely uric acid (a white, colorless, crystalline substance), with only 5% urea. The uric acid accounts for the white semi-solid portion of the excrement of iguanas (and of birds). Iguanas' kidneys have ureters (tubes) that transport urine to the bladder for storage.

Urinary Bladder

A bladder provides an important convenience: This stretchy sac stores urine produced by the kidneys, so animals can rid themselves of the urine occasionally rather than having it dribble out continuously. Iguanas have a bladder, although snakes don't. While urine is being stored in an iguana's bladder, the lizard can reabsorb some of the water before expelling the urine out of its body.

Cloaca

At the end of the iguana's digestive system is the cloaca, a cavity into which both feces (from the large intestine) and urine (from the kidneys) empty. The cloaca has three chambers. The first chamber stores the feces until the iguana gets the urge to excrete them. Urine drains into the second chamber from the kidneys, where the urine is produced, and from the urinary bladder, on its way out of the body.

The third cloacal chamber has a separate function in male and female iguanas. In females, it receives sperm during copulation. In males, the hemipenes start to evert (turn outward) in this chamber before they push out through the vent for copulation.

Vent

The vent, the external opening to the cloaca, is located on the underside of the iguana's body (near where the tail meets the body), protected by folds of skin. Both feces and urine are excreted through the iguana's vent. It's also the opening through which the males' hemipenes extend; in females, it's the opening where copulation takes place.

Hormonal System

Every animal has a variety of glands that excrete hormones crucial for regulating every function in the body. Some hormones spur action, others stop action, and all of them affect each other and work in a complex, constantly shifting dance.

Pituitary Gland

The pituitary gland produces hormones that affect a variety of bodily processes: regulating an iguana's growth rate, stimulating the muscular contractions of the digestive tract, controlling the reabsorption of water by the kidney, and helping to control the function of the reproductive organs and the adrenal gland.

In addition, the pituitary gland produces a hormone that acts on melanin, a dark-colored substance in skin cells that controls their degree of pigmentation. When melanin clumps together in the center of cells, most of the cell has no melanin, so the overall effect is that the skin appears light-colored. When the melanin spreads out over the entire cell area rather than congregating in the center, the skin looks darker.

Adrenal Gland

The adrenal gland produces adrenaline, a hormone also called epinephrine, that spurs every body cell and system to work faster. You've probably heard of, and experienced, an "adrenaline rush." It can happen whenever you face a scary or startling event, such as having to give a speech in front of a large crowd or nearly avoiding an accident while driving.

Any time an animal faces a "close call" or other event perceived as threatening, the body goes into a "fight or flight" mode, ready to either put up a fight or run like hell to get out of harm's way. In either case, adrenaline is released to prime all the body's muscles and other parts required for fighting or fleeing.

Adrenaline also slows or shuts down functions not crucial to handling the immediate crisis, such as digestion or the immune response. That's why it is important that your lizard's life is not stressful, which causes adrenaline to flow unnecessarily. Such a reaction could affect proper digestion and weaken its immune system, making it more vulnerable to infection and illness.

The adrenal gland also produces hormones that help regulate the movement of sodium through the iguana's body cells. These hormones help the iguana's salt glands decide how much sodium to remove from the body through snorting. In addition, the adrenal gland produces hormones that affect reproductive organs and the body's use of carbohydrates.

Thyroid Gland

The thyroid produces a hormone that increases metabolism, or the rate at which cells do the things they do. An iguana with low levels of thyroid hormone will be lethargic or slow, and will grow more slowly than is normal for its age. At the other extreme, high levels of this hormone can cause the iguana's body to put too much effort into growing, causing the lizard to form thick bones and become hyperactive and nervous.

The hormones produced by the thyroid are also involved in the actual process of skin shedding in iguanas, including the growth of new skin layers.

The thyroid gland needs iodine to create the hormones it releases. Iguanas, like humans, need a certain amount of iodine in their diets, although no one really knows how much is enough, or too much. To complicate matters further, some plants contain compounds called goitrogens, which reduce the amount of iodine an iguana can extract from the food it eats. Cruciferous foods—broccoli, cabbages, kale, Brussels sprouts, etc.—are known to contain goitrogens (see Chapter 5, Feeding, "Go Easy on Some Veggies"), so feeding your iguana large amounts of these vegetables may rob it of iodine that its thyroid gland needs.

Humans often turn to iodized salt to make sure we get enough iodine in our diets without thinking about it. The assumption is that adding a "normal" amount of iodized salt to the foods we cook and eat will provide all the iodine we need for healthy thyroid function. It's important that you do not add table salt, iodized or otherwise, to your iguana's diet. If you feed your iguana properly, it will get enough of everything it needs.

Parathyroid Gland

The parathyroid gland regulates the levels of calcium and phosphorus in the iguana's body. As you will read in Chapter 5, Feeding, the ratio of calcium to phosphorus, known as Ca:P, is one of the most crucial balances needed for a healthy iguana. Two parathyroid hormones, calcitonin and parathormone, help maintain the appropriate levels of calcium and phosphorus in an iguana's blood.

An animal's body constantly shuffles small amounts of calcium between the blood and bones. It's a delicate balance, in constant flux, and if it's not done right an iguana can easily suffer from metabolic bone disease. Calcitonin causes calcium to be removed from the blood and deposited in the bone, while parathormone removes calcium from the bone and returns it to the blood, as well as signaling the kidney to retain calcium.

Iguanas' calcium balances are also affected by intestinal absorption of food, the amount of calcium in their food, and the amount of heat and sunlight they receive. As I said, it's a complicated balance, and I urge you to read Chapter 5, Feeding, for a more thorough discussion.

Thymus

The thymus is an important part of the immune system. It is a gland that protects the body from infection by producing antibodies against viruses and by making lymphocytes, which patrol the body for bacteria and other things that shouldn't be there. In iguanas, hormones produced by the thymus also seem to be involved in the frequency of skin shedding.

Skeletal System

The skeletal system is simply all the bones of the structural frame that give an animal its shape and support its organs, muscles, and skin. For a wonderful glimpse of an iguana's skeletal system, look at the photos on pages 72–77.

While I was researching this book, I heard that some researchers were preparing and assembling a complete iguana skeleton. I knew this was a special event, and the first time to my knowledge that anyone had done this. For nearly a year I kept in close contact with the "assembler," Stanlee Miller, Curator of Vertebrate Collections at Clemson University, until the project was completed.

David Lewis, a photographer at Clemson, took more than 30 perfect photos of the skeleton, including a special angle I requested from underneath the iguana. (To do this, he put the iguana skeleton on a piece of glass and shot it from below.) I feel lucky to have such original photos to share with you.

Male/Female Physical Characteristics

A very interesting fact about iguanas is that gender is determined by X and Y chromosomes, not by temperature or humidity like some other reptiles (e.g., alligators).
—John A. Phillips, iguana researcher (#14)

Because an iguana's genitalia are inside its body, you have to look at the secondary sex characteristics to determine gender. The problem is that these secondary characteristics are not well defined until the iguana reaches sexual maturity. As a result, it's extremely difficult to tell whether your young iguana is male or female. Recently, however, I talked with a company in California that is working to develop and market a test (a chemical DNA analysis) so pet owners can identify the gender of their iguana even at the hatchling stage. The company hopes to have the test available soon.

Here are some clues to whether an iguana is a male or female—but again, most of these are not obvious until an iguana reaches sexual maturity:

• Males tend to have bigger heads, jowls, and dewlaps than females, and the older ones have bigger bodies in general. The cheek scale (subtympanic scale) is often larger in males than in comparably sized females.

I notice males have larger dewlaps and they also have larger heads with protruding jowls when they reach maturity. In the females the jowls tend not to puff out but to lie flat, giving a less formidable appearance.
                                        —I-200, Dianna, 47 yrs., Washington

Males may invest energy into . . . morphological characteristics, such as large head, etc. Our data support this finding, as males [iguanas] begin to invest in large relative head size by 15-17 months of age, while females do not.
                                        —Nancy C. Pratt, iguana researcher

• Especially during breeding season, the base of the male's tail bulges or appears swollen (this is where the male's hemipenes are located).
• Males' femoral pores (a row of raised, circular pores on the inside thighs) are larger in diameter than females' and rise further from the surface of the skin during breeding season. The males' femoral pores often exude a waxy substance during this time.
• Head bobbing appears to occur more often in male iguanas (see "Head Bobbing" on page 83).

One way to determine if you have a male or female iguana is to have a <u>qualified reptile veterinarian</u> probe the cloaca. The probe ("depth gauge") is usually made of stainless steel, with reference markings for determining depth. **I don't recommend** <u>this procedure as a standard practice, as this area in iguanas is delicate and can be torn if the probe is not properly lubricated or inserted.</u> In addition, the person interpreting the probe depth data must have proven experience with this procedure, or the readings are meaningless. I mention it here to enlighten and scare those people contemplating having their lizard probed.

On page 78 is an illustration of the probing procedure. It's included not to show how the process done, but to highlight the internal differences between males and females. As you can see in the illustration, a male has the deeper "pockets," which makes sense as this is where they store their hemipenes.

I have met and talked with several wholesalers and distributors of iguanas who say they can identify male and female iguanas at the hatchling stage. These people see thousands of hatchlings each year and develop a very good eye for the subtle differences between the genders.

At a recent Reptile Expo, one of these distributors and I took 25 hatchlings and made our own guesses as to which lizards were males and which were females. Surprisingly, we both came up with about the same guesses—which might demonstrate that a "practiced eye" can see differences. But since we couldn't verify our results, who knows for sure.

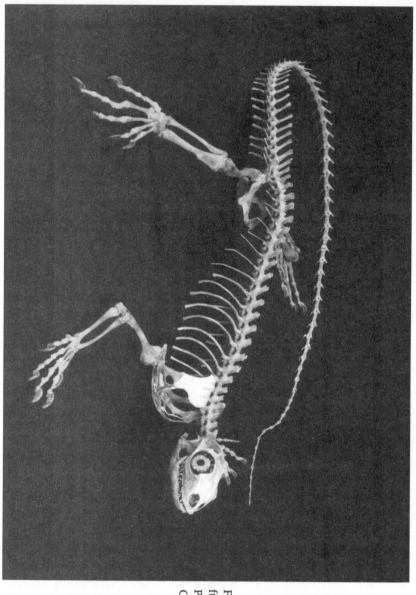

Figure 1.9: Rare photo of
full iguana skeleton.
Photo by: Dave Lewis,
Clemson University

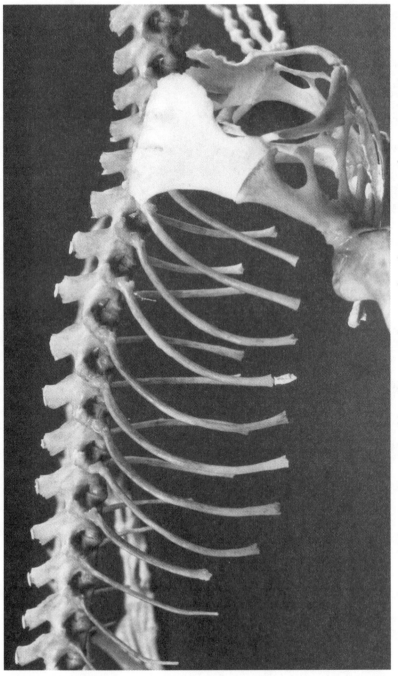

Figure 1.10: Close-up look at an iguana's shoulder, rib cage, and spine. Photo by: Dave Lewis, Clemson University

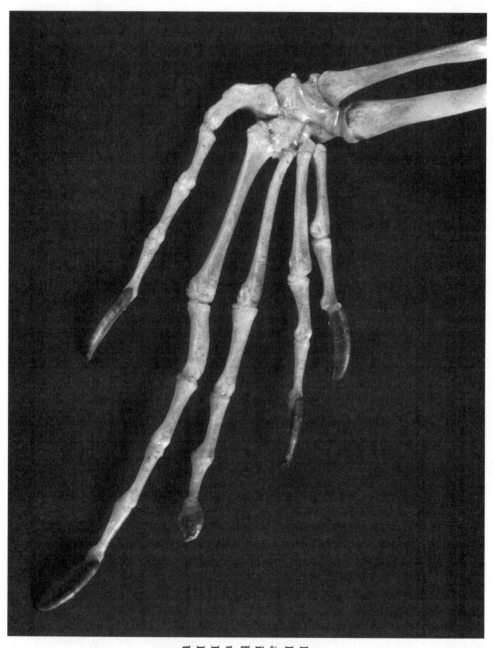

Figure 1.11:
Detail view of
all the
individual
bones making
up the foot.
Photo by: Dave
Lewis, Clemson,
University

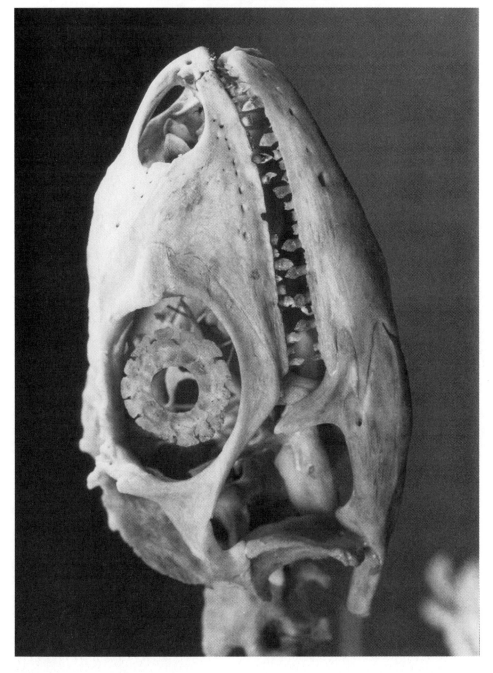

Figure 1.12: This view shows an iguana's teeth and eye socket. Photo by: Dave Lewis, Clemson University

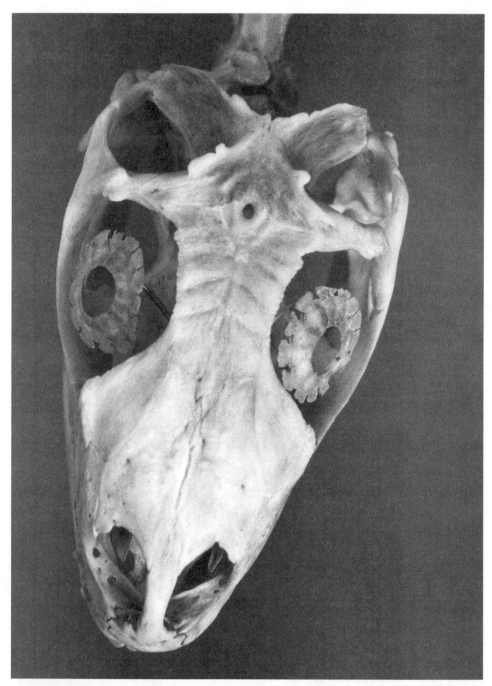

Figure 1.13: The view from the top of the iguana's head reveals where the parietal eye is located. Photo by: Dave Lewis, Clemson University

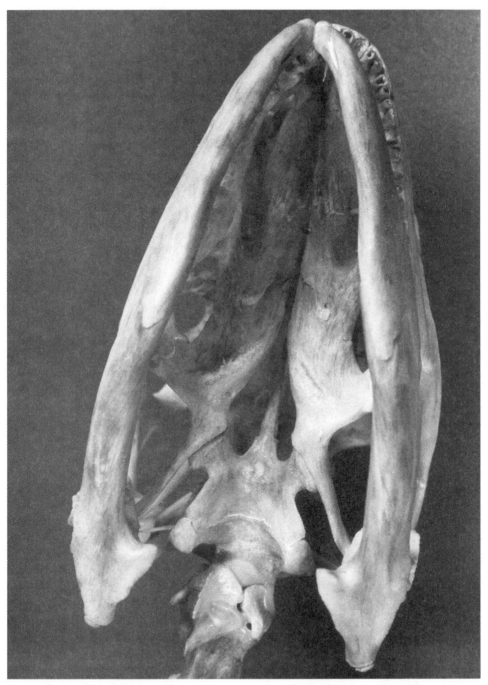

Figure 1.14: View from underneath the iguana's jaw. Photo by: Dave Lewis, Clemson University

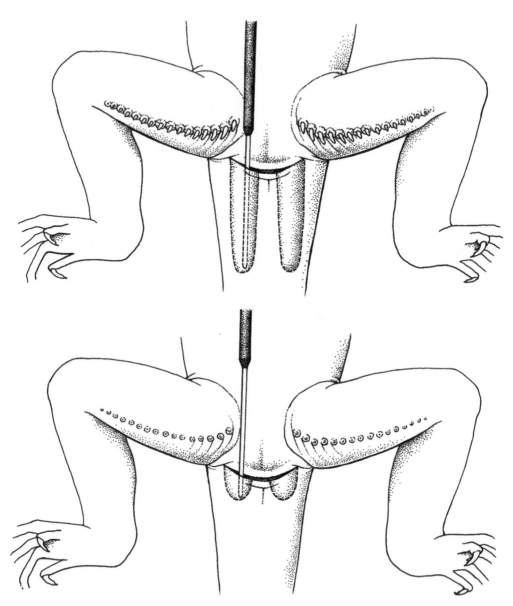

Figure 1.15: It is very difficult to identify a male or female iguana from their physical characteristics. One way is by use of a probe (not recommended!). In the illustration you can see that the male has deeper "pockets" to store his two penises. Illustration by: Kendal Morris; concept courtesy of *Iguana Times*, a newsletter of the International Iguana Society, Inc.

Male Body Parts

The way I first observed that my iguana was definitely a male was when he was about 1½ years old. When iguanas defecate, they usually finish the process by tightening up to squeeze any feces that may still remain. One day, I noticed what looked like part of my iguana's intestines come out his vent as he finished defecating. I immediately thought it was an intestinal prolapse (where part of the intestine falls out of the vent—a potentially serious medical condition). Luckily, I remembered that an iguana owner a year before had told me a story just like this about her iguana. What I saw was my iguana's hemipenes.

This experience is quite common with sexually mature male iguanas. After filling out one of my iguana questionnaires on his "female" iguana, an owner wrote back several months later with an additional comment: "Emmy revealed 'herself' while going to the bathroom today." In fact, Emmy is a male!

Hemipenes

Male iguanas don't have one penis, they have two—and they are called hemipenes. The hemipenes look like pink pieces of flesh, with no actual form resembling a mammalian penis. Whereas the human sperm passes through a central tube in the penis, iguana sperm is carried via a "seminal groove," or trough, on the surface of each hemipenis.

The hemipenes are located internally on the underside of the tail, just below the vent in a kind of pouch, or pocket. In sexually mature male iguanas, you can often see the bulge on either side of the base of the tail where the hemipenes lie.

During copulation, a combination of muscle action and increased blood pressure everts a hemipenis (i.e., turns it inside out), extending it from its storage place into the cloaca and out through the vent. The hemipenes roll out of themselves much like a sock that you roll on and off your foot. When mating, an iguana uses only one of its two hemipenes, which is inserted into the female's cloaca after flipping her into position and wrapping his tail under her.

As mentioned earlier, sexually mature male iguanas can also evert their hemipenes as they defecate, often with the final push of the feces out of their body. During breeding season, a sexually mature male iguana can also masturbate if no females are around. My iguana used to do this during each breeding season. The semen looks like melted, soft mozzarella cheese. Once left on a limb or other object, the semen dries into a "crispy" appearance, like cheese left in a hot frying pan.

Testicles

Iguanas' testicles (also called testes) produce sperm and the hormone testosterone. Unlike the external testicles of humans, which hang down in a pouch, iguanas' are located inside their bodies. In fact, they're up high in the body—occupying approximately the same location as female iguanas' ovaries.

The iguana stores sperm in his testicles and epididymis (a structure attached to the surface of the testicle and containing excretory ducts) until needed. Seminal fluid is added to the sperm to increase the total volume of semen, just like in humans. During mating, contractions of the ducts force semen out of the testicles to the cloaca. From there, the hemipenis acts like a trough to direct the semen out of the body (and, if copulating, into the female's cloaca).

Female Body Parts

The female's head is decidedly female. She [5 yrs.] has never developed pouches on her jowls like the male [5 yrs.], nor does she ever extend her dewlap. She is much more sleek around the head and shoulders than the male.

—I-626, Gail, 48 yrs., New York

While male iguanas during breeding season can get aggressive and nasty, females are more reserved. Some females do get "snappy" close to the time they release their eggs, when they are trying to find, build, or defend a nesting site. In general, females are mostly identified by being "not male"—smaller heads and jowls, slimmer bodies, no enlarged femoral pores, no bulge at the base of the tail.

Female iguanas' most defining feature, of course, is their ability to produce eggs. They can develop and lay eggs whether or not they have mated with a male—much as chickens lay eggs regardless of whether they've been fertilized by a rooster. For this reason, and because of the special needs of gravid ("pregnant") females, it's important that you know if you have a female nearing sexual maturity (see Chapter 3, Choosing Your Pet, "Size Options: Adult," for details).

Ovaries

The ovary produces eggs, also called ova (plural of ovum), along with the hormones estrogen and progesterone. When they're still in the ovaries, the eggs look very different from the way they look when they are finally laid.

Each mature ovum in the female iguana's ovary begins as a single cell with no yolk. The egg contains half the genetic material needed to create a new iguana. (The other half of the genetic material comes from the male's sperm when it fertilizes an egg.)

While still in the ovary, the egg develops a yolk supply. The yolk is what feeds the developing iguana while it's still in the egg. This is just like chicken eggs: The yellow yolks are the developing chicks' food supply. When baby iguanas hatch from their eggs, they often still have a yolk sac attached to them, which they consume as their first food after hatching.

Oviduct

At a certain point, the ovary releases eggs into the female iguana's oviduct, where fertilization can take place if sperm are present. Regardless of whether the eggs are fertilized, though, they develop a supply of albumin (the egg "white") and a membrane wrapping. In time, a specialized shell gland coats the egg in a shell that consists mostly of calcium.

A large female iguana might store 50 eggs in the lower end of her oviduct—regardless of whether they've been fertilized or not—until she finds a place to deposit them. In general, older iguanas produce more eggs than younger ones, which may be a function of body size.

When a female iguana finds an appropriate nest site, the eggs are expelled into the cloaca and out through the vent. It's important to note that female iguanas do not want to lay their eggs just anywhere. Their instincts drive them to find the conditions that will best ensure the healthy development and hatching of their eggs.

If you own a female iguana, you need to know how to recreate these ideal egg-laying conditions. Your iguana's life may depend on it. Please look at Chapter 9, Breeding, "Nesting (or Egg-Laying) Box," for important information on how to create these conditions.

Eggs

Reptile eggs differ slightly from chicken or other bird eggs. In chicken eggs, the yolk is suspended in the middle of the egg shell and the egg can be rotated in any direction without affecting the chick developing inside. In reptile eggs such as iguanas', the yolk is not suspended and simply sits on the bottom of the egg, with the baby reptile developing on top of it. As a result, an iguana egg has a definite "top" and "bottom," so it shouldn't be rotated. If you turn an iguana egg while it's developing, the yolk might settle on top of the developing baby iguana and smother it.

Reptile eggs also differ from bird eggs in that the shells are not hard, but are soft with a leathery feel. And reptile eggs increase in size even after they have been laid because they absorb water from their surroundings.

COMMON IGUANA BEHAVIORS

In this section you will find many of the common behavior patterns and characteristics that iguanas can present, both in the jungle and in your home. By knowing an iguana's natural behaviors in the wild, you can better understand why your pet reacts in a particular way around you.

As I said in the introduction, this book is an owner's manual, so much of the information presented here will also be found in slightly different forms in other chapters. That way, even if you don't read the book cover to cover at one sitting, there's more of a chance you'll pick up the crucial information along the way. Also, maybe reading a particular point presented in a different way will reinforce or make the idea clearer for you.

Thermoregulatory Behaviors

An iguana can't generate its own heat internally, yet a number of crucial functions depend upon it reaching certain body temperatures. To raise or lower its temperature the lizard has natural behaviors, known generally as thermoregulatory behaviors, designed to accomplish this crucial temperature control.

Basking

Basking is the iguana's single most important thermoregulatory behavior. It's a way for iguanas to use the environment to control their internal temperature. Iguanas in the wild start their day by angling their bodies toward the sun in such a way as to get the most direct concentration of heat. Once their bodies are warm, they are able to digest their food properly and function at optimum levels.

The rest of the day the iguana will move in and out of the sun to modify its internal temperatures. This thermoregulation process is discussed in more detail for pet iguanas in Chapter 4, Housing, "Heat."

Panting

If an iguana gets too warm, it will first try to move away from the heat source or seek shade. If this doesn't solve the problem—or if the iguana is in a place where it is unable to get out of the heat and starts to get too hot—the lizard will open its mouth wide, like an overheated dog, and pant. Unlike humans, iguanas can't cool down by sweating. During panting, an iguana's tongue will often arch or stick out to expose more surface area. Blood circulates through the tongue, and cooler air passing across the surface of the tongue will help cool the lizard's body.

If you see your lizard panting, it means the iguana is overheated and should immediately be moved to a cooler place. But <u>don't</u> stick the lizard in a bucket of cold water. This would be a tremendous shock to the lizard. You can offer water to drink or take a wet towel and rub it across the iguana's body, which will slowly bring the lizard's temperature down.

Communication Behaviors

Iguanas make no sound, so they rely on body language and other visual cues to communicate with each other, or with you. For example, if they want to communicate anger or aggression, they will first try to do it with body language. Like many animals, iguanas don't want to get into actual physical fights with each other; there are no veterinarians in the jungle to patch them up.

Fights between iguanas are usually ritualistic—they try to threaten or intimidate each other through animated body language. But if that doesn't work, they are capable of violent fighting.

Head Bobbing

You'll probably witness a variety of head movements by your iguana, particularly if you have a male, and especially after it reaches sexual maturity. Iguanas move so little in the course of their everyday life that any movement stands out. Individual iguanas vary in how often they head-bob, and for what reasons.

Head bobbing starts as early as the hatchling stage and gets more refined with age. Juvenile iguanas typically have different "styles" of head bobbing than adults, but the purpose is similar regardless of the iguana's age.

In iguanas, the juvenile display, like the adult signature display, appears to signal advertisement of position.
—John A. Phillips, iguana researcher (#9)

To those who have never seen an iguana head-bob, it's a funny sight. It looks much like those plastic dogs placed in the back windows of cars, whose heads bounce up and down when the car hits a bump or turns tightly.

In real life, an iguana head bobbing is not a joke but a physical way to let other iguanas in the area know things such as:

- "I am in control of this territory."
- "This is my food/heat/branch/female iguana. Find your own."
- "Here I am, so don't think I don't see you."
- The iguana equivalent of "Me Tarzan, you Jane."
- "I'm in a bad mood today; keep your distance."
- "I am about to rip your head off if you don't leave now!"

Both male and female iguanas will bob their heads in various circumstances, and both genders use it as part of the mating ritual. But sexually mature males tend to bob more frequently and vigorously than females, and sideways as well as up and down, especially during the breeding season. Males use head bobbing to defend their territory and to attract females, as well as to ward off other males.

For iguanas in the wild, particularly males, head bobbing gets more frequent and pronounced as the iguana gets bigger and more dominant.

Conspicuous advertisement of social status is common in natural populations, with large, dominant males displaying about 5 times more frequently than smaller, subordinate individuals. . . . Because amplitude of individual [head bobbing] displays is correlated with snout-vent length (SVL) of the lizard, amplitude of the display of each male will change as the animal matures.
—John A. Phillips, iguana researcher (#46)

The Friendly "Hello" Head Movements

Iguanas will head-bob even if other iguanas are not around, and they will even bob at you. It's their way of acknowledging your presence, their territory, your respective positions in the "hierarchy," and so on. Most times when they start doing it—especially if the bobbing consists of almost relaxed-looking up and down motions—just ignore it and continue touching and petting them as usual.

One form of head bobbing is called by scientists a "signature" display or bob. In the signature bob, the iguana dips its head downward and then abruptly throws it upward and pauses, ending with a series of vertical bobs of decreasing amplitude. This movement is often used to advertise spatial position, to say, "Here I am, and this is my territory," especially as the individual moves into a new area.

> The amplitude of the signature display and its frequency after even minor positional changes suggest that the display developed as a conspicuous form of communication.
> —John A. Phillips, iguana researcher (#46)

Head Bobbing to Signal Aggression

> An observer recorded . . . both the species-specific signature bob, which is probably used in territorial advertisement, and the rotary head nod, which signals aggression.
> —Allison C. Alberts, iguana researcher (#35)

The rotary head-nod is another type of display. In this case, the lizard rapidly twists its head back and forth along the long axis of its body, like a dog shaking water from its head. This motion is thought to be an active display of aggression toward another animal. It is common to see a subordinate animal retreat from an area after a dominant one has exhibited this display. If the iguana does not retreat, it puts itself at risk of being chased away, or worse, being attacked physically by the dominant male.

Head bobbing can also look more like head ratcheting—quick, jerky movements rather than a smooth up-and-down motion. It looks almost as if the lizard is under a strobe light. These jerky movements often signal extreme irritation or the prelude to an aggressive act. Watch out.

Femoral Pore Secretions

In addition to visual displays, iguanas also communicate with each other through olfactory means (i.e., smell). On the inside of an iguana's thighs are a row of circular femoral pores. In males during breeding season, these pores exude a soft waxy substance that carries a pheromone, or scent, produced by glands under the skin. (See page 59 of this chapter for a drawing of femoral pores.)

What we do know is that pheromones, or natural scent-giving compounds emitted by the body, play a powerful role in sexual activity
among animals. For example, a mere whiff of androsterone, a
pheromone secreted by male boars, is enough to cause a sow in
heat to turn around and assume the mating position.
—from an article on human and animal pheromones (#41)

For many years, people didn't understand the purpose of iguanas' femoral
pores or their waxy secretions. Researchers analyzed the males' secretions and
believe that iguanas use them to communicate territorial messages.

Femoral gland secretion may play a role in dominance and home
range marking in male green iguanas. Gland size in displayers [i.e.,
sexually mature males displaying aggressive behavior and orange
body coloration] exceeds that of non-displayers by 18 months of
age. In our study, femoral pore diameter was sexually dimorphic by
15-17 months of age.
—Iguana research by the Center for Reproduction of
Endangered Species (CRES), San Diego (#10)

. . . femoral pore diameter [is] also associated with social dominance in this species [*Iguana iguana*].
—research on iguana growth, hormones, and behavior (#35)

Males drag their legs over rocks, branches, and grass—or, as pets, over
couches, their habitat, and carpets—leaving traces of the pheromone to mark
their territory or advertise their position in the social structure of the group. In
fact, if you handle a male iguana in breeding who has prominent femoral pores,
you'll often find your clothing covered with what looks like chalk dust.

To other iguanas, there's a lot of information left behind by these femoral
pore secretions. They can flick the traces with their tongues and analyze them
using their Jacobson's organ (see page 65 for a description of how this works).
The iguana may be able to tell if the last iguana that walked by was a male or
female, a stranger, or a known iguana.

In the green iguana, chemical signals, especially those produced
by the femoral glands, appear to contain information sufficient to
confer individuality.   —John A. Phillips, iguana researcher (#46)

What's really startling is that the waxy substance excreted by the femoral
pores is fluorescent. All the members of the iguana family excrete a substance
with fluorescence, but the specific color varies from species to species. And
because iguanas are able to see in the ultraviolet light range, they may also be
able to see the femoral pore secretion trails, which are visible in UV wavelength
ranges.

Tongue Flicking

At the receiving end of communication, an iguana uses its eyes, ears, and nose to pick up the cues in its environment regarding everything from avoiding possible predators to finding a food source. An iguana is also fortunate to have an additional tool for gathering sensory information, called the Jacobson's organ, that it uses in conjunction with its tongue. As described on page 65, the Jacobson's organ analyzes scent molecules of objects, food, or other items that the iguana picks up by flicking its tongue.

Iguanas use this tongue-flicking action to gain important sensory information as they move around their habitat or places in your home. Almost like a dancer: one, two, three steps forward, flick, flick, two steps forward, flick, flick.

In an effort to help my iguana experience new objects without fear, I would introduce new things to him slowly. As I brought the object close to him, his eyes would dilate, his body would get a little bigger, and he would flick his tongue out when the object got within range. Sometimes it looked as if he would almost spit his tongue out as he strained to touch the object but at the same time trying to keep a safe distance. Once his tongue touched the object four or five times he relaxed, as though the information collected had been analyzed and the object deemed safe.

Judging from my own observations and those of other iguana owners, these lizards will also often flick their tongue several times when they are about to jump to a new landing spot. Perhaps this flicking provides them with an added dimensional cue.

Territorial and/or Aggressive Behaviors

Iguanas are very territorial. Consequently, whenever they are allowed into a room (or the whole house) they will investigate the area from top to bottom. They think it's their territory and they need to know its boundaries. At some times, especially when males are in breeding season, iguanas will feel the need to defend their territory from real or perceived threats, and this often leads to aggressive behavior. In captivity, a male pet iguana in breeding may become quite challenging to live with.

Head Bobbing

As already discussed, head bobbing serves many communication functions, but most have something to do with declaring, defending, or acquiring territory. Although head bobbing is often benign, it can also be a precursor to aggression. Over time, by observing your iguana carefully, you can learn what it "means" by its various head-bobbing movements.

"Launches"

I witnessed my iguana run full force from the inside of his habitat trying to get me during breeding season (presumably to bite, take me to the ground, and make me promise I will never enter his territory). The only thing that stopped him was the habitat glass. I heard a loud "thunk" and at first I thought he broke his neck or at least his nose. But after hitting full force and bouncing back, he just walked off like nothing happened.

This kind of extreme reaction usually happens only during breeding season. After this launch, I covered that section of the glass (to block his view of people as well as his own reflection) so he wouldn't be stimulated to repeat the attack.

Body Compression ("Puffing Up")

An adult iguana orients broadside to a threat, flattens the body laterally, extends the dewlap, and opens the mouth.
—"Predation and the Defensive Behavior of Green Iguanas" (#4)

There is some sort of sense that my iguana has for other males. As soon as another male comes into the house my iguana knows it immediately and starts to puff up, getting that defensive stance and posture, the whole aggressive attitude. He is a real bully.   —I-237, Diane, 44 yrs., Texas

During aggressive encounters, males will often compress their bodies laterally so they appear larger and higher off the ground to their competitors. It's like a young boy who puffs up his chest to look bigger than he is to scare off a possible bully.

When facing a dominant, puffed-up iguana, a submissive iguana will often press its body firmly against the ground. In this way, it is signaling that it recognizes the dominance of the other lizard and that there's no need to fight.

Tail Whipping

Often when an iguana is about to smack you with its tail it will twitch it ever so slightly, nervously, then BAM.   —I-531, Freda, 29 yrs., California

Tail whipping is an iguana's main defense and may begin with a wide sweeping movement of the entire tail, from one side to the other. This is usually the threatening or warning phase of tail whipping. Just before whipping, an iguana will often twitch just the tip of the tail, perhaps as a final signal. To strike, the iguana cocks its tail, aims, then snaps the tail like a whip at its target. Sometimes the iguana whips you so fast, all you are aware of is that something just hit you.

In a small iguana, a tail whip doesn't amount to much, and is mostly just startling. Large iguanas, on the other hand, can defend themselves with extremely accurate whiplashes of their muscular tails—which can quickly put stinging welts on your flesh.

Biting

Biting is pretty much an iguana's final defense. If the iguana can't run away, if puffing up and posturing hasn't worked, if tail whipping wasn't possible or effective, and the threat—whatever it is—remains, an iguana can bite.

As with tail whipping, a bite from a hatchling or young juvenile is startling but rarely painful. But adult iguanas, especially large ones, can bite fast, hard, and to the bone.

Most often, iguanas attack each other (or you) with mouths open or semi-open. The main purpose of biting is to inflict pain, so you (or the other iguana) will think twice about messing with this individual again. It can signal either aggression or defensiveness. The scariest bite is the one that comes when an iguana lunges at you.

Male iguanas also use biting during mating, but only to secure a firm hold on the female iguana's neck during the sexual act. In this case, the biting is more of a controlling strategy than a vicious action. Many times, the female iguana emerges unscathed if she goes along with the "program."

I'm also convinced that iguanas can adjust how hard they bite—the degree of crunch—to communicate a point. For example, following surgery my iguana needed a month of daily antibiotic shots, delivered in his thigh. My job was to hold Za as my girlfriend, who had experience giving shots, handled the actual injections. It was apparent that the liquid antibiotic often stung as it was injected. Za hated being injected and we hated doing it.

One day, as I was getting Za ready for his injection on the couch, he swung his head around and caught my finger in his mouth. The surprise was that he held the finger with firm but gentle pressure, without tearing my flesh or inflicting pain. He was big and strong enough to have shredded my finger, but he didn't. I know it sounds like anthropomorphizing, but I think he was just letting me know that he really hated the shots, and could I please make them stop. What other kind of logical conclusion could there be?

Hissing

I have heard of only adult iguanas performing this expression of irritability and aggression, and only a few at that. When hissing does happen, it's caused by the iguana filling its lungs with air and then forcing the air out through its mouth.

Dewlap

As explained earlier (see page 55), the iguana's dewlap is an elegant, multifunctional flap of skin. In the context of territorial or aggressive displays, the dewlap will be extended as part of the display, held stiffly away from the neck and chest. It adds to the "I'm bigger than you are" effect that an iguana is trying to communicate.

Fighting

As I've said before, most fighting among iguanas is ritualistic, where the goal is to try to intimidate the opponent without really hurting each other. Young iguanas will practice these rituals, which most often take place over food, heat, or territory.

If the ritualistic puffing up, head bobbing, tail whipping, and other behaviors don't work, iguanas can hurt each other quickly and seriously. When an iguana receives a bite from another iguana, the bite gets infected very easily and frequently develops into an abscess.

In the wild, after a fight is over, the defeated animal is usually not followed or "finished off." In fact, a dominant male in the wild may even tolerate the subordinate in the same area. In a captive situation, where space is limited, this probably isn't true. I have heard of numerous violent attacks when two iguanas were caged together. I don't recommend keeping two iguanas, especially two males, and especially two males who have already had at least one fight, in the same habitat.

Movement Behaviors

Sometimes an iguana's most obvious movement behavior is its lack of movement. Iguanas spend most of their day staying in one place, and when they do move it's usually slowly. This habit is a good defense against predators because it makes them hard to see. When not stationary, iguanas exhibit a number of forms of locomotion.

Jumping

The ability of an iguana to jump from branch to branch, or floor to chair, is due to its long hind legs. The iguana compresses its energy into these large hind legs and releases it in great leaps. As one iguana owner said, "They jump like funny-shaped frogs."

You can tell when your iguana is about to jump by the way it positions its rear legs, but also by how it holds its head and studies the place where it is likely to jump. In the wild, iguanas often jump from tree to tree or bush to bush. They also have been known to miss and fall out of the trees.

One aspect of jumping is landing on the target; another is missing the mark, which is more commonly called falling. Many people have told me how they were at some coastal Mexican resort, eating lunch or lounging in the sun, when all of a sudden an iguana would fall out of the tree next to them. Healthy iguanas have an uncanny ability to fall from high places without getting hurt.

I have climbed in 15-foot trees trying to capture iguanas only to see them jump to the ground and run away. One of my guides in Belize said he saw an iguana jump, miss the tree limb, and fall 100 feet into the river and swim away.

Following are some pet owners' observations of their iguanas about to jump. If you see your iguana making these movements, it's a good time to intervene if you don't want your lizard jumping on that particular object.

When he is about to jump, he will look up at where he wants to go, then go perfectly still and lower his belly while tensing his claws.
                                                —I-916, Lucretia, 32 yrs., California

When they are about to jump, they look around and often will rear up on their hind legs, pawing at the air in front of them, then suddenly leap.
—phone conversation with pet owner
[AUTHOR'S NOTE: Previous experiences indicate that this seems to happen when the distance to be jumped is almost too far to complete.]

When she is going to jump she cocks her head to the side, seems to judge the distance with one eye, looks straight ahead with both eyes, then she jumps.
—I-620, Suzanne, 33 yrs., New York

She [SVL: 4", TL: 14", 5 mo.] has a penchant for jumping onto anything she thinks she can; some days, in her mind, a wall and doors fall into this category.
—I-830, Elisa, 27 yrs., New York

Climbing

Because an iguana not only lives in trees but gets its food there, you would think they would be better climbers. Perhaps evolution hasn't caught up with their lifestyles. If it weren't for their sharp claws, they would probably fall out of the trees even more often than they do.

[Iguanas] are most awkward in trees, except when resting motionless, and frequently fall down. They seem to persist in climbing. . . . An iguana climbing around in a tree looks quite as much at home there as would the average dog.
—James D. Lazell, Jr., iguana researcher (#32)

She is quite humorous when she tries to climb. I can practically hear the gears grinding as she considers whether or not she can reach a certain place.
—I-795, Dawn, 24 yrs., Ohio

Running

In the wild, you very seldom see an iguana running for any long distance. As soon as an iguana is threatened, it escapes into the undergrowth of the jungle, which can be quite thick.

An iguana running on all four legs achieves extremely fast speeds for short bursts. But put an iguana in an open stretch of land with a predator in pursuit, and you will see something very surprising: The iguana will run like a human, upright, on its hind legs.

Unless a large open area is available . . . little observation of the bipedal running of iguanas can be made. It takes an iguana a few yards of quadrupedal running [i.e., on all four legs] before it can push itself up off the ground with its front legs and really run. Their forelegs are usually clapped against the chest, and the tail is curved

upward for about its first third, then trails under the control of wind and gravity. Young iguanas, especially, hold their forelegs up at right angles to the body when running. This gives them the bizarre appearance of clasping the handlebars of an invisible bicycle as they zoom along.
—from "The Lizard Genus *Iguana* in the Lesser Antilles" (#32)

Swimming

Iguanas are graceful at only two times: when running, and when swimming. . . . When swimming, iguanas flatten their limbs along the body and tail base. All speed is achieved by undulations of the tail, and this is considerable. Iguanas swim well and frequently; they commonly escape pursuit by diving into . . . bodies of water.
—James D. Lazell, Jr., iguana researcher (#32)

If an iguana is on the ground, it runs away from predators. If it is up in a tree, it usually moves to the back side of a limb or trunk to hide. But if the threat is extended or comes too close, the iguana will drop into a river or lake, if available. I've witnessed this several times during my research trips to Latin America.

As soon as they hit the water they press their arms and legs against their body for streamlining. They wiggle their long, powerful tails back and forth, which gives them great propulsion. There are all kinds of rumors about how long an iguana can stay underwater. I observed one underwater for 15 minutes, and I have heard of submersions of up to 30 minutes.

When I was on the southwest coast of Mexico, I observed a different kind of swimming technique. I had some local people take me out in a canoe to examine some iguanas. After examining each lizard, I released it into the water. But instead of diving underwater like they had every other place I'd observed them, these iguanas kept their heads on the surface while the rest of their bodies used the same swimming motion as if underwater. This gave them the advantage of seeing where they wanted to go.

INTELLIGENCE

While these animals are very likely to be non-moving most of the year, one should not suspect from that lack of physical activity that they are in any sense simple. They are not behaviorally simple, they are certainly not evolutionarily simple, and they are assuredly not simple minded.   —Gordon H. Rodda, iguana researcher (#27)

They seem to be more intelligent than certain books led me to believe.
—I-833, Donna, 36 yrs., New York

They are lower vertebrates—but you know, some of these guys are pretty in-
telligent.   —phone conversation with an iguana owner

He [SVL: 7½", TL: 2' 2", 1 yr. 7 mo.] shows signs of intelligence such as beg-
ging for food and going into the kitchen when he hears wrappers or bags being
opened.   —I-892, Steve, 22 yrs., Illinois

One of the enduring debates about nearly any kind of animal, including
humans, centers on intelligence. With non-human animals, we typically rate
intelligence in terms of memory, ability to learn, and problem-solving skills, as
opposed to instinctive behaviors or reactions. Without getting into the grander
issue of what intelligence is, and all the different kinds of intelligence, let's look
at what some pet owners, veterinarians, and iguana researchers say about the
intelligence of iguanas.

Memory

I am surprised at how much iguanas remember.
                                     —I-183, Mary, 24 yrs., Massachusetts

One of my iguanas was given to me by a friend who raised it from a hatchling.
My iguana hates my friend with a passion and whips his tail when he hears
her voice.   —identification withheld as a courtesy
    [AUTHOR'S NOTE: This experience is not a fluke. I have seen sev-
eral cases where an iguana remembers a negative experience like this.]

My iguana [SVL: 16", TL: 3' 5"] is very intelligent. The vet gave me some cal-
cium to give her orally for a short time. I put this substance in a syringe (minus
the needle) and squirted it in her mouth. The second time I approached with the
syringe she took one look and went into the "Iguana from Hell" mode. I was
surprised by her obvious ability to remember [after one experience].
                                     —I-490, Kate, 37 yrs., Oregon

One time my iguana had to be injected with a strong antibiotic, and the
veterinarian wrapped Za in a towel to control any wild flailing. This was a one-
time shot, but Za remembered the "bad" experience. Nearly every day of his
life, he got to soak in the bathtub, and when his time was up I always dried him
with a towel. For the first few days after the towel-wrapped injection experience, Za would try to run away as I dried him off.
    When he started to flip out I just let him run out of the bathroom into my
office. Each day he allowed more time to be towel dried, until he "understood"
that nothing bad was going to happen to him with towels in the bathroom.
The fact that he remembered that one unpleasant experience at the veterinarian's and generalized the association to towels seems impressive.
    When iguanas' visual learning capacity was tested experimentally, re-

searchers discovered that this species is capable of distinguishing between two complementary colors such as red-green, blue-yellow, or black-white, as well as between test pairs such as narrow versus wide stripe, green dots against brown, wavy lines, and similar patterns.

Such acquired knowledge was retained in memory for up to 5 months. In comparison to lizards with smaller brains and body size, the learning and retention capabilities of iguanas seem greater.

We live in a townhouse development where all of the houses look similar. However, my iguana [SVL: 15", TL: 3' 4", 3½ yrs., 7 lbs.] knows exactly which is his house, no matter whether we are in the back or the front of the townhouse building. He seems very insecure outside, preferring to go back into the house almost as soon as I take him outside. When he becomes insistent to go back inside, he leads me right up to our front or back door and waits for me to open the door. I think he would even ring the doorbell if he could reach it!
—I-704, Marilyn, 41 yrs., Maryland

Recognition

During visits to the Bahamas, I observed that *Cyclura* [a type of iguana that's a close relative to *Iguana iguana*] distinguished the race of the people there. For visiting white tourists, the *Cyclura* would come up and beg food, but when the black residents showed up, the iguanas would flee.
—conversation with an iguana researcher
[AUTHOR'S NOTE: The researcher felt that the reason the iguanas ran away was because only the local black people hunted and ate these iguanas.]

On the ranch there was a herd of horses in the area and the iguanas didn't pay attention to them, but if a horse with a rider came along, the iguanas would run away.
—iguana researcher in Venezuela (#48)

I once had an iguana brought into my clinic who'd been treated by another veterinarian for anorexia with multiple injections over a fairly long period of time. This relatively large (8 lbs.) iguana was easily managed for a general exam, but upon returning to the exam room with a variety of syringes [minus the needles] to show the owner how to assist feedings (by squirting pureed veggies into the pet's mouth), I received "the iguana evil eye" and from 3 feet away he whipped me with his tail so quickly that the noise of the slap and the sting were the only evidence I had that he had whipped at all!
Morals:
They're faster than they look . . .
The tail is more mobile than it looks . . .

Yes, they do recognize people and objects and will let you know which they like or dislike! —V-135, Dr. Debra, Washington

They recognize people, including the ones they don't like.

I had a friend who would tease my iguana a little when he was over visiting. Every time my iguana saw him come in the room, she would run and hide! When he came near, she would start hissing and trying to bite him.
—I-43, Taryn, 27 yrs., Alaska

They do get very familiar to a face and voice. Sometimes when strangers come and look at them they know that these people do not belong and can put on an "anti"-attitude. —I-793, Lynn, Michigan

She seems to recognize certain people and will "hide" (flatten out on the opposite side of her basking branch) when someone she doesn't know comes in our house. —I-620, Suzanne, 33 yrs., New York

My friends will try to put my iguana away into the cage and the iguana will scratch and whip, but when I come into the room my iguana settles down right away. —I-571, Sam, 13 yrs., Oregon

He knows who I am. He acts differently when he sees me than with other people. —I-769, Yolanda, 20 yrs., Michigan

Awareness

There is something about them—they are much more like a parrot than other lizards I have had. They seem more aware.
—I-180, Dave & Katherine, 50 yrs., Michigan

He likes watching and listening to everyone and everything around him and he seems to learn from his observations. —I-690, Irene, 34 yrs., Texas

If I stared too long at my iguana when he was fast asleep in his habitat late at night, he usually woke up. How did he know I was there? I would stand perfectly still and any small sound was stopped by the habitat glass and the thick walls. But again, I was not moving. I don't have a scientific answer. My guess is they have some level of awareness to pick this up—just as sometimes you can tell if someone nearby is staring at you.

He knows that he is not allowed to wander out of the kitchen or go into the living room, although he tests his parameters from time to time. The main thing that irritates me about him is a few times he has gone into my living room when I was not home and knocked over all my potted plants in an effort to be

in there. I know this because the times when I have arrived home and "caught
him in the act," he has tried to hide under the couch or behind the curtain to
keep from being seen.   —I-704, Marilyn, 41 yrs., Maryland

[AUTHOR'S NOTE: If the iguana is consciously hiding to avoid
verbal punishment, it could mean the iguana can remember past punishment and has some awareness of the consequences of its actions.]

"Trainability"

Iguanas are easily house trained and tend to defecate in the same place. I
found this absolutely amazing—remember, these are lizards, not mammals!

We were amazed that we could catbox train him [SVL: 11", TL: 3' 5", 3½ yrs.,
2½ lbs.] so easily. We had never tried because we thought he was too old to
learn. He got the hang of it immediately!   —I-690, Irene, 34 yrs., Texas

The other day I took my iguana out of his cage. Twice he tried to walk behind
the cage. Had he ended up behind the cage, it would have been impossible for
me to get him. As he was walking toward the back of the cage I said, "Come
here. Don't go back there." Both times he instantly turned and came back to me.
My son remarked, "I can't believe he just listened to you."
                        —I-872, Dave, 34 yrs., New Jersey

Chapter 8, Domestication, devotes an entire section to training your
iguana, including some specific techniques, that shows the full extent of iguanas' trainability.

Playfulness/Mischievousness

Sometimes I think iguanas are much smarter than we give them credit for.
Like crows and ravens, they can be mischievous. I have seen and heard of iguanas doing perverse things. For instance, one iguana had free run of a pet store
that sold exotic birds. The lizard had its own place to defecate, near its habitat,
but it preferred to climb on top of specific bird cages and defecate directly on
their heads. The store owner thought it was pretty funny.

I believe that iguanas do get bored, and outings or interesting items to play
with are important. Often I have seen my iguana [SVL: 15", TL: 3' 6", 5 yrs.]
climb up a chair, snake through the rungs of it, and jump down, only to climb
back up again, jump down. . . . I have also seen him chase moths (a truly
comedic, and invariably unsuccessful, endeavor). If he is bored, he will come to
see what I am doing and get in the way.   —I-515, Lynn, 21 yrs., Canada

His biggest kick is stealing from the dog food bowl, which is located in the bed-
room so our potbelly pig doesn't find it. Our iguana knows that I won't let him

have any, so he waits until I am not looking and makes a mad dash to grab a few bites before it is taken away. If he is already sunning in this room, I will check up on him to see if or when he is making his way to the bowl. He won't move while I am watching. He waits until I leave and then, bamm—there he is—smacking his lips on that dog food! He tries to be very nonchalant to say the least, and this in itself can be quite comical.   —I-690, Irene, 34 yrs., Texas

My favorite story about my iguana is the "games" she plays. The pet store people said iguanas don't play. My vet even raised his eyebrows a bit. OK . . . tell me what this sounds like to you!

Last August, I'd had my iguana for 12 months. I'd always gone to her, sought her out. One afternoon she circled the room and then jumped up on the couch. She was smaller then and jumping on the couch was a new task. I put my fingers at the edge of the couch so she could have a foothold. She climbed up onto my lap and sat, allowing me to pet her for several minutes. Then she ventured out onto my knees. She paused and then jumped off, out into the room as far as she could. I had to laugh. I patted the couch and called to her, "Come here!" To my amazement, she turned and scampered back, again jumping up on the couch, hooking her nails on my conveniently placed fingers. Once again she climbed onto my lap and enjoyed a minute or two of head petting and spine pulling (the ones on her neck she enjoys having lightly pulled). Then back out onto my knee and another leap!

Over and over she did this. I'm not sure how many times that first day. Nearly every day for 3 weeks we played this game. She would vary it at times. Sometimes she'd use my leg (one crossed over the other) as a slide! She'd slide down to my ankle and then jump down. And always she'd pause and look back. Also, she'd vary the spot where she'd jump onto the couch. Sometimes to the left side instead of always the right side. Or sometimes she'd jump directly up to my knees. Okay . . . maybe I was just the high spot in the room, or I was being her tree. But regardless, I was being sought out by her! We were really interacting and I can't tell you how special that felt.

The second week of the game, I began counting her jumps and slides. One day it was near 20. Another day it was 32 (honest!) and then it was me that had to stop playing, to get ready for work.

After about 3 weeks of this, the frequency decreased. But now and then there are new games. A couple of weeks ago we played the "curtain game" about 10 times. Up the curtain she goes and very shortly she reaches out. I rush over and reach up and she walks onto my hands. I carry her over to the couch and sit. She scampers away and goes directly to the curtain. From the top, once again she reaches out and I go "rescue." No matter where I put her in the room, it was a beeline to the curtains. I'd hardly have time to get settled sitting down and there she'd be, reaching. But I didn't mind. It was fun!

Another time: she'll play "in and out of the cage," over and over. Another time: up on the wooden ledge at the bottom of the cage, then down, then up. . . . The games seem to be repeating new movements or behaviors, over and over.

She still plays the "onto couch, onto lap, knees, and down" game some-
times, but not very often (I wish it were!) and not more than once or twice.
                                   —I-706, Melodie, 41 yrs., Tennessee

Learning and Adaptability

One morning last month, I had fallen asleep on the couch. When I awoke I
looked for my iguana, but he was nowhere in sight. I looked all over the house
and finally found him sitting in the empty tub patiently waiting for me to run
the water for his bath and daily constitutional.
                                       —I-493, Marcia, 40 yrs., Alaska

They will "study" places that they have never been and then attempt to get
there. Example: I am doing a painting job in an inside dormer of my house. My
male "watched" the aluminum ladder for a day with that "side view, one-
eyed" look. He studied the bottom and the top. The next day he had learned to
climb an aluminum ladder and I found him basking in the dormer window.
                                        —I-626, Gail, 48 yrs., New York

When confused, seeing something for the first time, or trying to figure out
what is going on, iguanas have very expressive faces. They often will cock their
head, open their mouth just the slightest, or look as if they are analyzing the situation. Skeptics will call this anthropomorphizing, but people with iguanas
will say the lizard is "thinking."

If I establish eye contact then close my eyes, he slowly closes his, too.
                                        —I-849, Amie, 22 yrs., Oregon
    [AUTHOR'S NOTE: I've heard this from several other people, too.]

We had a water dragon in the cage with our iguana. When a water dragon dis-
plays its territorial instinct it waves its arm in a circular motion. Typically, an
iguana simply bobs its head. The iguana learned to spin its arm in a circular
motion.   —I-11, Patty, Washington
    [AUTHOR'S NOTE: In other words, the iguana observed the ter-
ritorial behavior of another species and used it.]

The first few times my iguana rode in the car, he ducked his head when we
drove under an overpass. Za's parietal eye (third eye), which is light-sensitive,
responded to the shadows cast by the overpass. Ducking his head was a natural
and common reaction to possible threat from a predator. What's impressive is
that after only a few times in the car he "learned" that he didn't have to duck
his head in this situation.

I learned that a cerebral cortex is required for "learning." Since reptiles have no
cerebral cortex [you wouldn't expect them to be able to learn things]. However,

I have observed learning and conditioning (two different types of behaviors by definition) [in reptiles]. My iguana certainly seems "curious" a lot.
                                                          —V-85, Dr. Sue, New York

I've got a large morning glory vine in the living room, and he [iguana] likes to sneak in there and contemplate a route that will take him up to that hanging pot. I see him sitting in the center of the room, staring penetratingly at the lounge chair, the table behind that, the window, screen, and the vine for a few minutes . . . then he moves into action and attempts to scale up all of the aforementioned things so that he can destroy my plant. It's pretty funny—you can almost hear him thinking as he stares at each component of his plant access route.   —I-515, Lynn, 21 yrs., Canada

CONCLUSION

Now that you have a feel for iguanas' wild heritage and how all their body parts work, you'll be more prepared to create a healthy, happy environment if you decide to bring an iguana into your household.

The next chapter explains what you can expect from an iguana who shares your home with you.

CHAPTER 2

Iguanas as Pets

Pet (pet) n. 1. Any animal that is domesticated or tamed and kept as a favourite, or treated with indulgence and fondness.
—Oxford English Dictionary

As stated in the introduction, I do not use the word specimen in this book to describe an iguana. I never called my cat or dog a specimen because they were my pets. An iguana deserves the same respect.

By the same token, iguanas are not toys for children's entertainment. They are living animals that feel pain and stress and that need to be nurtured. It's unacceptable to store these creatures in a box and take them out for only a few minutes' entertainment every so often.

If you are going to purchase an iguana just to look at, go to the zoo or watch PBS shows. I'm convinced, as is my veterinarian, that reptile/human interaction plays a vital role in iguanas' upkeep and health—both mental and physical.
—I-407, Ruth, 32 yrs., Ohio

IS AN IGUANA RIGHT FOR YOU?

Before we get into the details of what it's like to have an iguana as a pet, and what they require for health and happiness, I want you to carefully consider whether an iguana is right for you at all.

An iguana is not like many other urban pets. The iguana needs much in the way of care from an owner. If you require a pet with convenient habits that will allow you "hassle-free" pet ownership then DO NOT BUY AN IGUANA! However, if you would like to witness for yourself and your family something of the beauty and complexity of nature, and if you are not afraid of making a commit-

ment to take the time and effort to care for your pet, then the iguana just may be the pet for you.
>—Dr. Patrick J. Morris, veterinarian at the San Diego Zoo
>and Wild Animal Park

Before purchasing a cute little 3-inch hatchling, look at and handle a 4- to 8-pounder and ask yourself where you'll put him when he's that big.
>—V-135, Dr. Debra, Washington

The following comments by a veterinarian are a good reality check <u>before</u> you purchase an iguana:

Give careful consideration before you purchase an iguana. Ask yourself:

a) Can I provide the proper environment, diet, care, husbandry, and medical care in order for this animal to thrive?

b) Do I have a genuine interest in these creatures or is this a "yuppie-puppy" that is more of a fad?

c) Am I willing to take the responsibility to educate myself about the species in general, and do I have a willingness to continue to learn and educate myself through the different life stages of this animal?

d) [If the iguana is for my child] will I be willing to take over as primary care-giver if my child loses interest in the pet? (!)
>—V-111, Dr. Richard, 37 yrs., Tennessee

Getting an iguana and not following through with proper care can be a disaster for the lizard. The following story illustrates the extremes of iguana care: a bad previous owner that severely neglected an iguana, and a caring, observant new owner.

I seem to have a knack for caring for "under the weather" iguanas. The latest iguana, who came to me without even a name, belonged to an 8-year-old who just had to have an iguana for Christmas. It was kept at his father's house, where the boy spent every other weekend. The iguana was housed in an old slate-bottom aquarium-type tank with plywood on top held down by bricks.

When my husband and I picked up the iguana at the father's house, I could tell there was big trouble from the smell coming from inside the cage.

The iguana was so thin that his pelvis, ribs, and base of tail stuck out sharply. Worst of all, he was covered with black crust. When we got home, I could see that the iguana was half on a hot rock and half on the slate bottom of the tank (no substrate). He opened his mouth as a threat and it was very pale pink, almost white inside.

*He had not lashed his tail at me and then I realized **that his stomach and back legs were stuck to the tank floor.** I got him loose and put him in*

a sink of warm water, Betadine, and baby shampoo. While he soaked I pre-
pared a larger cage for him and we got the mite-infested tank out of the house.
I had to assume that he also had ticks and worms.

After the bath I greased him with baby oil and triple antibiotic ointment
and put him in the new warmed tank with UV light shining. He drank a lot of
the water that I offered him, but refused to eat even when I put the food dish
right in front of him. After a day I started feeding him baby food laced with vit-
amins out of an eyedropper, and soon he would open his mouth when offered
the eyedropper. I soaked him and greased him with the antibiotic ointment
daily.

It took about a week for all the mites to come off and some green coloration
to return. He could not walk due to the black crust on his legs. It was hard, like
wearing a cast, but it eventually came off. Under the crust there was no skin or
scales. It looked like uncooked chicken.

The skin is filling in now; the front legs and toes will be fine, I think. The
stomach and tail will be very scarred. The hind legs are a bit better, skin is
coming in and he can walk and climb a little. His back feet are very bad, how-
ever; one toe came off and I think three will on the other foot. He eats solids now
and has filled out very quickly.

*I think he will be all right, very scarred, but alive. He will **not** be going*
back to his former owners, but will stay here with me.

—I-833, Donna, 36 yrs., New York

You need to know all the long-term responsibilities and demands that your new iguana will put on your lifestyle, so you won't create another situation like the previous one. Remember, having an iguana could be a 12- to 15-year responsibility, or more. Ask yourself, is an iguana really something that will work in your life?

I want to make it clear that I am <u>not</u> encouraging people to purchase iguanas as pets. Too many people want an iguana for all the wrong reasons: because the iguana is a fad, an ego trip, a way to be temporarily "cool"—in other words, a thoughtless impulse. Others simply don't think through the implications and responsibilities that go along with owning an iguana, such as that these lizards grow very big, live a long time, have very specific requirements for housing, warmth, food, and so on. I hope to thoroughly discourage all of these people from adding an iguana to their households.

Important Considerations of Iguana Ownership

As with any pet, I feel that a great deal of time should be invested in educating
yourself about care and maintenance, especially since an iguana's needs are dif-
ferent than the usual household pets (cats, dogs, hamsters, etc.) and this can
lead to a lot of problems and heartbreak if you don't do some research before
you make a purchase. I feel there should be a true commitment to all your pets

and you should be able to take on the responsibilities or seriously reconsider getting the animal.   —I-690, Irene, 34 yrs., Texas

These animals are not for everyone. . . . RESEARCH, RESEARCH, RESEARCH before purchasing a herp of any kind. If you are not willing to give the time or just don't have it, and this pertains to any animal, get a plant instead!
                                              —I-754, Karen, 33 yrs., New Mexico

Levels of Care Required

It should be stressed to iguana owners that knowledge of husbandry is critical! Ninety-five percent of illness is due to poor husbandry.
                                              —V-135, Dr. Debra, Washington

No matter what kind of pet you have, from ants to yaks, there is a minimum amount of daily care required. You'll find that caring for iguanas properly takes both time and money. The best way to find if an iguana fits into your lifestyle is to attend a local herpetological society meeting (see Appendix B) and talk with some iguana owners.

Among iguana owners, there is a vast difference of opinion on how difficult, time-consuming, or complicated iguanas are to care for. It's really not the pet that makes the difference, it's the <u>pet owner's</u> attitude. What's difficult for one person may be simple and fun for another.

Opinion A: Iguana Care is Easy

Despite their exacting requirements for heat, habitat, food, etc., iguanas are considered simple pets to care for by some owners. They feel that once the iguana's habitat is put on automatic control, the rest of the care is pretty simple.

Watching him [6-year-old iguana] as he's grown up and knowing the effort I've put into him was well worth it. I've become very attached to him.
                                              —interview at herpetological conference

It was my choice to acquire them and it's my responsibility to care for them. Once I learned how to properly care for the iguana, the rest was easy. They simply do not require the time and attention that other, more social pets do.
                                              —I-467, Kris, 32 yrs., Florida

Iguanas don't waste energy and usually stay in one place most of the day. They move only for food, warmth, or to examine something new in their habitat or environment. Theirs is a very efficient lifestyle.

Opinion B: Iguana Care is Difficult

I have definitely concluded that the care of an iguana is neither simple nor easy, and the majority of iguanas are not being cared for adequately. If you are

unwilling to follow the recommendations for proper iguana care, then you should probably choose a different type of pet. It is so unfair to these amazing lizards to be pulled out of their natural world and dropped into the hands of someone with only a fleeting interest in their care. These lizards will die a slow death in most cases and the result is shameful. You should not undertake the keeping of these lizards unless you are committed to good-quality care. But iguanas seem to adapt to captivity well (if cared for properly).
                                    —V-69, Dr. Alynn, 39 yrs., Mississippi

For the average pet owner, I don't think they make good pets. In general, I discourage people from getting an iguana as a "pet." For the person who has a genuine interest, desire, and a willingness to strive to provide a suitable pseudoenvironment, they can be a fascinating animal. But iguanas are "on the brink" as to domestication and tameness, not like a dog or cat, or even "pocket pets" such as smaller mammals, which have shared man's "environment" for centuries. And most people don't think about this and the extensive special care required to see an iguana thrive.
                                    —V-116, Dr. Richard, 37 yrs., Tennessee

The only pet more difficult to care for is a horse.
                                    —I-624, Debbie, 40 yrs., Florida

As for ease of care, they require more attention than my snakes, cat, or my deceased dog. More specifically, they require daily feeding; my snakes don't. They require a more specialized diet than any of my other pets. And, lastly, their living quarters are more specialized.
                                    —I-508, Bryan, 27 yrs., Kentucky

I would like you to say in your book that it is not that easy to raise iguanas properly. I hear all the time that they are very easy to care for and that it's a pet for everyone. We know that's not true.   —I-801, Tom, 16 yrs., California

Most of the information necessary to care for your iguana is found in this book. Before you purchase an iguana, you need to read Chapters 4, Housing; 5, Feeding; 6, Special Care; 7, Medical Troubleshooting, and pertinent sections (i.e., depending on if you have a male or a female iguana) of Chapter 9, Breeding. This way you will be able to make an informed decision and know how to care for your new pet.

Don't expect the pet store staff (or veterinarian, for that matter) to teach you "everything you need to know about caring for an iguana in one short lesson." Seek the knowledge on your own. I get really tired of people saying, "Well, they didn't tell me that!" It's your responsibility to find out.
                                    —V-116, Dr. Richard, 37 yrs., Tennessee

I agree completely with Dr. Richard. Knowledge is power, and the more knowledge you have about your iguana, the more likely you'll have a healthy, long-lived pet.

The whole concept, everything involved with iguanas, boils down to common sense. —South American commercial iguana breeder

Whether you find it easy or difficult to care for your iguana depends less on the iguana than on your outlook and expectations. In the final analysis, the relative ease or difficulty is less important than how much you enjoy the time that must be spent caring properly for these very alive animals.

Every animal, whether a dog or a cat, requires something that we don't like to do, but that's the responsibility we assume when acquiring one.
                                        —I-39, Stephen, 19 yrs., Connecticut

Growth

The major way iguanas avoid being eaten is simply by growing quickly to a large enough size that they are too big for most predators to handle.   —Gordon H. Rodda, iguana researcher (#27)

When iguanas first hatch they are all roughly the same size, but they may not grow at the same rate or end up the same size, especially in captivity.

Examination of growth in wild hatchling suggests that at an age of approximately 180 days, SVL of individual lizards can vary by as much as 70%.
—"Differential Resource Use, Growth, and the Ontogeny of Social Relationship in the Green Iguana" (#9)

Among wild iguanas, the ability to acquire a steady, high-quality food source may be the main factor either limiting or enhancing growth. But a captive iguana has more factors affecting its growth, including amount of freedom, stress encountered, and the iguana's genetic makeup, habitat size, and proper temperature.

One of the best ways to ensure proper growth is to maintain the correct habitat temperature. I believe one reason my iguana was so large was that he always had the proper temperature in his habitat. On the other hand, one of the most powerful growth inhibitors is when two (especially male) iguanas are housed together. This kind of stress should be avoided.

The present study indicates that growth and dominance are closely tied, and that this relationship may have implications for reproductive success among males.
—John A. Phillilps, iguana researcher (#9)

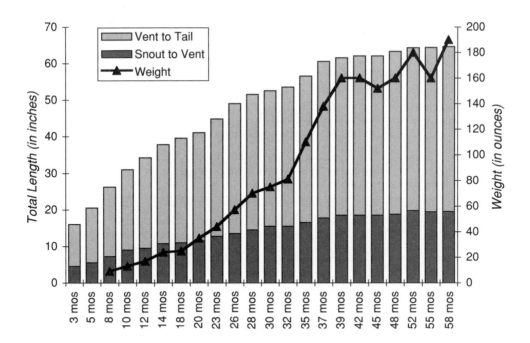

Figure 2.1: This growth-rate study for one iguana lasted about 5 years (#43). Just one interesting point is that when the SVL stabilized at around 32 months, the iguana's weight increased rapidly as he "filled out."

An iguana's growth rate is the greatest during the first three months after hatching (#9). The two charts in this section (pages 105 and 106) are to help give a general idea of how your iguana might grow over time.

When I originally got my iguana at 3 months old, he was only 15" long and so light I couldn't guess his weight. When Za was just over 5 years old he was 5' 5½" long and weighed 13 pounds. But I knew and accepted all aspects of his adult size, including his large habitat. Many people are not so prepared.

People often want and like the idea of a large lizard, but when faced with the reality of the requirements necessary to keep an animal like this, they often have regrets.

> *The pet store didn't tell us how much care an iguana needed when they get as large as ours is now [SVL: 20", TL: 4' 4", 8 yrs.]. If I had known then what I know now, I probably would not have purchased him; but now I am attached to him.* —I-654, Bill & Kathy, 28 yrs., Illinois

> *I probably won't get another green iguana. I didn't know how big they can get.* —I-832, Adam, 14 yrs., Illinois

Hatchling Number	5/24/93	7/23/93	8/20/93	11/7/93	1/16/94	5/23/94
1	26	29.5	22.6	35.3	40.6	39.7
2	21	31.2	32.6	43.7	50	64
Total · 3	26	31.5	37.3	49.1	56.5	68
Length · 4	25	27.8	29	39.4	46.5	65.9
(cm) · 5	23.5	27.7	31	38.1	55.2	59.5
6	26	29.2	36.1	42.5	49.8	70
7	24.5	33.5	40.8	55.2	56.1	69
Average Length	24.6	30.1	32.8	43.3	50.7	62.3
1	7.5	8	8.6	11	12.3	15.9
Snout- · 2	6	7.75	9.5	11.8	13.8	18
Vent · 3	7.2	9	10.6	12.9	15.7	19.1
Length · 4	7	7.5	8.4	10.5	12.9	18.3
(cm) · 5	7	8	9.1	10.6	15.6	16.8
6	7.5	8.5	10.1	12	13.7	19.5
7	7.25	9.75	12.3	15.8	16.1	20
Average Length	7.1	8.4	9.8	12.1	14.3	18.2
1	15	15	15	40	50	127
2	14	20	23	50	75	168
Weight · 3	13	23	31	76	112	195
(grams) · 4	14	15	18	41	61	189
5	14	14	18	31	99	140
6	15	16	30	45	77	244
7	14	35	48	111	108	245
Average Weight	14.1	19.7	26.1	56.3	83.1	186.9

Figure 2.2: This short growth-rate study was done by Roger Lamb of England, with his own iguanas that he bred and hatched at his home.

WHO ARE IGUANA OWNERS?

A pet industry lobby group reports that about 3 percent of U.S. families own iguanas, and that about 7.3 million iguanas are believed to be in captivity in the U.S. [1995].
—*The Vivarium*, a magazine by the American Federation of Herpetoculturists (#45)

Don't feel you are the only one on the planet that wants or has an iguana as a pet. The last seven years has seen a dramatic increase in the number of live iguanas brought in to the United States destined to be pets, as illustrated in the chart in Chapter 3, Choosing Your Pet, "Qualities to Look For." And this chart doesn't reflect the large number of iguanas sent to Europe from Latin American countries.

Appendix A has a chart that gives an idea of who some iguana owners are, how old they are, their gender, and where they live. This information comes from my research with hundreds of iguana owners in the U.S., Canada, and Europe.

My research found that iguana owners span almost every profession and are about evenly split between men and women. I was a little surprised that so many iguana owners were female. At the beginning of my research, I would have guessed a proportion more like 80% men and 20% women. I was happy with the surprising results.

Most of the people who requested my iguana questionnaire were over 18 years old. Even though my survey (which wasn't a scientific sampling) doesn't show many children as pet owners, I know through real-life experiences that they are. Despite the fact that children get iguanas, I need to emphasize that iguanas are **not** an appropriate pet for children. These lizards require a high level of exacting care, and adult iguanas can be very large and hard to handle.

Most people who call our Iguana Rescue call because the animal was bought for a child, then the first time the iguana bites or whips his tail the parents don't feel the animal is to be trusted with their children and they want to get rid of the iguana.   —I-730, Brigitte, 32 yrs., Alaska

Iguanas are not pets for children, as they need responsible care and grow to be quite large. Iguanas make better pets for people who are really willing and mature enough to move over and make room for the needs of such an exotic pet.
                    —I-200, Dianna, 47 yrs., Washington

Although I don't recommend iguanas as pets for children, there are exceptions:

I was one of those moms who absolutely refused to have a green, slimy creature in my home! Well, following two years of convincing and my son saving his money ($200—which I thought he would never do!), we became the proud owners of one beautiful green iguana. My son wrote me endless lists of "reasons iguanas make great pets." Also, I had the opportunity to visit our friend's very tame 3-year-old iguana. Now, a day doesn't go by that I don't spend "quality time" with the iguana. He is fascinating and I enjoy watching his personality unfold as time goes by.

A word of caution I would give other mothers or fathers is if you let your child have an iguana, you must take an active part in the animal's feeding and care. Also, remember to make friends with your iguana as a hatchling. Don't wait until it's 5 or 6 feet long.
                    —I-719, mom of Lucas, 14 yrs., Indiana

WHY PEOPLE OWN IGUANAS

I didn't expect my iguana to have such a definite personality. I thought only animals with high intelligence developed personalities distinctive to them. I always admired reptiles as being one of the most successful animals on earth (here much longer than mammals). My iguana is fascinating, dignified, beautiful, clean, friendly, calm, agile, and has a delightful personality with "cute" likes and dislikes.   —I-100, Char, 44 yrs., Illinois

I have never loved a pet like I do my iguana. I can't explain why, but I do.
                    —I-365, Marilyn, 53 yrs., New York

SIDEBAR

Pet Iguanas in Latin America?

Iguana ownership is big in the U.S., Canada, and Europe. But I found it to be extremely rare to find pet iguanas in most places where iguanas actually live in the wild.

I always ask people I meet in Latin American countries: "Does anyone have iguanas as pets in this village, town, or city?" I usually showed photos of my pet iguana to make sure we were talking about the same kind of animal. Almost always, people would see the photos and back up as though they had seen a ghost. Then they said, "No, no one here has one for a pet. Why would we?"

One rare exception came when I was in Guatemala doing iguana research. I went to a market one day wearing my "Green Iguana—The Ultimate Owner's Manual" T-shirt (which has a big, four-color illustration of an iguana on the back), and a local veterinarian started a conversation with me. After chatting a while, she said she had about 30 clients who have iguanas as pets. One client lived about two hours away and rode the bus with his iguana, which she said was huge. The iguana owner transported the large lizard in a mail sack on the bus to keep it and the human bus riders calm. In all the time I have spent in Mexico and Central America, this was the first I ever heard of local people having iguanas as pets.

For all of you ready to make the informed decision to own an iguana, an iguana as a pet offers some great advantages. They are relatively easy to care for once you establish a basic habitat for them and learn what is required.

An iguana is an amazing pet. When most people think of lizards they think of those little brown things that scurry around in their backyards. So when you tell friends that you have a lizard as a pet, they are likely to look at you as if you'd fallen off your bike at a young age and hit your head on something solid and pointed.

> *My pet iguana [SVL: 13", TL: 3' 5", 7+ yrs.] has exceeded all my expectations. I love him. He is like my baby. I will be devastated when he dies.*
> —I-633, Lynne, 29 yrs., Michigan

Each green iguana has a definite personality, likes, dislikes, and moods that change from day to day, week to week, and year to year. The wonderful thing is that the longer you own an iguana and allow it to interact with you, the more its personality keeps unfolding, layer upon layer.

We never thought a "lizard" would have a personality! But she showed us, shortly after she was tame, her true personality.
—I-808, Priscilla, 25 yrs., Iowa

[I like] their individuality and personality. No two are the same.
—I-714, Roger, 36 yrs., England
[AUTHOR'S NOTE: This is a pretty powerful statement, because the owner has 15 iguanas.]

I can easily say that Za, my iguana, was one of the most fascinating, exciting, and rewarding pets I have ever had, and I've owned a lot of different creatures, including cats, dogs, an African lion, a mountain lion, an ocelot, a margay, snakes, gophers, mice, rats, lizards, turtles, frogs—even a frog that ate mice—and many more. But Za was something special. So often, I swore that he must be a mammal masquerading as a lizard. He even slept at night like a house cat.

Iguanas even offer advantages over many other types of pets. You can't get fleas, Lyme disease, mange, ringworm, ticks, or rabies from an iguana. They don't need special shots, vaccines, or registration tags. They don't cause allergies, like fur animals, or require long, rigorous walks.

They are not like dogs that knock over garbage cans and spread the trash all over the neighborhood, or urinate on your car's clean tires. While a wet dog smells like a moldy burlap bag, iguanas have a pleasant, neutral smell. They don't howl ear-piercing decibels at sirens in the middle of the night or bark incessantly like your neighbor's dog. In fact, iguanas make no vocal sounds.

Unlike cats, iguanas don't require smelly "poop boxes," kick cat litter all over the floor, or cover the furniture with loose fur. Iguanas don't make you endure the sound of them puking up hair balls or screeching like a demon in a horror movie when in heat. And iguanas don't use your couch as a scratching post, shredding it to pieces.

An iguana is not messy like a bird that often throws food and seeds, or molts and leaves feathers all over the house. And unlike a pet fish's aquarium, an iguana's house, if knocked over, won't turn into an instant lake. Because of the low risk iguanas present, many apartment complexes don't require a special pet deposit, making iguanas ideal for small-apartment living.

Iguanas can be affectionate in their own way if properly tamed. Over time, they can become true "pets" with an individual personality and continually unfolding character.

When you ask "normal" people (whoever they are) what animals they keep as pets, the majority would probably say a cat or dog. If these are the average pets that people keep, then what are the qualities and characteristics of these animals that make them so desirable? And what, if anything, do iguanas have in common with these animals?

In the next few sections I have categorized some of the reasons people own pets in general, or iguanas in particular. By looking at these characteristics, you can easily see whether your desires for a pet fit what an iguana offers. I've also

---

AT A GLANCE: *Reasons People Own Iguanas*
- Companionship
- Identification with iguanas
- Care requirements
- Life span
- Allergies to fur pets
- Limited living space
- Always wanted an iguana
- Alternative to traditional pets
- Feel part of a group
- Exotic appearance of iguanas

---

included a fair number of quotes from iguana owners who, after all, are best qualified to answer the question, "Why have an iguana as a pet?"

Companionship

One of my iguanas will often come to me and put one foot on me, and just sit there. I think it's his way of seeking companionship.
—I-519, Ellen, 40 yrs., Louisiana

Companionship means you feel a bond of closeness with your animal, and you enjoy its company.

After talking with many people over the years, I have found that companionship is probably the number-one quality considered when people choose "normal" pets. The level of companionship desired covers the full spectrum, from people who want minimal companionship from their animal (e.g., an A-type, fast-paced, career-oriented person) to those seeking an animal that stays with the owner all of the time (e.g., an elderly person living alone).

The following quotations about iguana companionship are the result of long periods of interaction, with much caring lavished on the relationship. As iguanas get older, deeper levels of closeness can develop—but the average iguana will never be as devoted to you as a dog might be.

My iguana [SVL: 8", TL: 2' 4", 1½ yrs.] is very attached to me. He loves to snuggle up to me and he looks to me for protection when he feels threatened (e.g., around other people he doesn't know, at the vet, around other animals). The vet said my iguana is the wimpiest male iguana he's ever seen; he behaves like a cat. At the vet's, my iguana scooted along the exam table, crawled into my arms, and hid his head in the crook of my arm for safety. I almost cried—it was

so sweet. The vet was amazed. He'd never seen anything like it. My iguana obviously has bonded to me as much as I have to him.
                              —I-753, Kelly, 26 yrs., Pennsylvania

I love my iguana from the bottom of my heart. He is more than part of a collection. He's a friend and a pet. He is very outgoing and sometimes will just come walking down the stairs when we are watching TV and sit in the living room with the family.   —I-171, Andrew, 34 yrs., Minnesota

I am very attached to my iguana [SVL: 12½", TL: 2' 9½", 5½ yrs.]. He's outlasted at least three boyfriends so far.
                              —I-333, Phyllis, 22 yrs., California

She [SVL: 14½", TL: 3' 9½", 4 yrs.] nudges her nose into my hair and falls asleep on my shoulder.   —I-824, Joy, 56 yrs., New York

He's the most precious creature I have ever had the pleasure of living with. He's so sweet and puts up with me always making a fuss over him.
                              —comment from person at herpetological conference

Once we brought an iguana into our lives it was like having a child. In fact, I still refer to our iguanas as our "babies" and our "kids" among friends.
                              —conversation at a herp club meeting

He's a friend and he's nice, but not too nice. You know, not like a dog. He thinks on his own.   —I-360, Maxine, 12 yrs., California

My iguana [3 yrs.] is a great pet. He is a hell of a lot easier to get along with than some former boyfriends, and he smells better. He also doesn't drink, smoke, or leave the toilet seat up.   —I-493, Marcia, 40 yrs., Alaska

Because of my close companionship with my iguana, I can certainly relate to all these stories. Most of the time when my iguana was out of his habitat, he would sit in my office on his favorite chair (level with the bottom of the window) so he could watch the birds and squirrels all day. But if I got up and left the room for more than an hour or so, he would usually go back to his habitat on his own. I liked to think that he enjoyed my companionship and that when I left, part of his reason for being in the room left, too.

Identification

By identification, I mean the overall look, feel, attitude, or "aura" of your pet and how you feel being associated with it. Do you feel proud to have this animal as your pet? A pet is a natural reflection of who you are and what you are about. You have probably seen people who resemble their dog; this is the ultimate in pet identification.

When considering an iguana as a pet, ask yourself how strongly you identify with the physical and behavioral characteristics of these green lizards. Does
the idea of being an iguana owner make you feel special, or would you feel
uncomfortable or embarrassed?

Care: Requirements

I picked an iguana over other lizards because they don't require live food.
                                            —I-609, Cindy, 37 yrs., Florida

You don't need a wheelbarrow to clean out their cage!
                                            —I-725, Marie, 23 yrs., Maryland

Having a different kind of pet, no matter what kind, requires new knowledge. The basic food and housing conditions for an iguana are not complicated
but they are **specific** and **absolute.**

By picking a healthy iguana in the beginning, you can solve many possible
future problems. If you address these situations effectively, care for your iguana
in the future can be minimal.

Life Span

Life span depends on the genetics of the animal. If someone has an
iguana that lives 15 years, they should feel lucky. Keeping an
iguana healthy and happy for 15 years is a chore. Half is luck and
half is hard work.
                    —John A. Phillips, Center for Reproduction of Endangered
                                Species (CRES), San Diego Zoological Society

No one wants a pet that's going to die in a week, a month, or even a year.
We all want a pet that will live a long time so we can watch it develop and
enjoy and share time with it. But no animal lives forever, not even humans.

Some iguana-owner friends of mine once found an orphaned baby opossum and kept it as a pet. I asked how long it was supposed to live, and they said
about three years. At the time, they had owned it for nearly two-and-a-half
years. Many months later I was talking with them about their iguana and happened to ask how their opossum was doing. They said it had died. The three
years were up.

Every living thing has a "minute-timer" type of existence, and each individual animal has its own allocation of sand. Some have more, some have less,
but one day the sand will run out—we call this death. For an American human
male born today, the life expectancy is 72.8 years; for females, it's 79.7 years.
For opossums, it's three years.

How long will your iguana live? Because there is not much information on
longevity for iguanas in captivity (or even in the wild), we have to make edu-

cated guesses by talking with iguana owners. Our guess in the iguana community is that an iguana can live approximately 12 to 15 years, similar to a cat, if properly cared for.

If you purchased an iguana six or seven years ago, there is a good chance it would have died within the first few months. In those days, nearly all the iguanas shipped to the U.S. had been taken out of the jungle instead of raised on farms. A large percentage of these animals died from the stress of capture and shipment. Of the lizards that survived to become pets, many died from inadequate care caused by inaccurate, faulty, and downright stupid information.

Today, most iguanas are farm-raised and are shipped under much better conditions, and the information on proper care is much improved. I met with an iguana owner in California that I believe had the oldest iguana to date, which died at just over 29 years old (see photo on page 114). This iguana was raised during the "dark period" when there was little proper care information for iguanas, making it even more amazing that he lived so long.

With an enriched environment, excellent care, and the right food, an iguana might reach or exceed the estimated 12 to 15 years. But even with everything exactly perfect, things can take your iguana from you early.

My iguana died shortly after his fifth birthday. It was devastating. I had spent wonderful, exciting, and fun days with Za for many years. He was given the best care possible from the very first day. No expense of time, money, or care was spared. When he died, it was as if I had lost my best friend.

I had a detailed necropsy done on him (like an autopsy, but for animals). It took almost two months to check all of his organs, muscles, and bones. The pathologist said that Za was the healthiest, biggest, best-conditioned iguana he had ever seen. He also said that Za's bones were rock hard. During the necropsy, they found cancer inside Za. At the time, I didn't know that iguanas could even get cancer, but two months after Za's death a woman wrote me and said that she had her iguana put to sleep because it was being eaten up by cancer.

The sands of time eventually run out for everything and everybody, so enjoy your iguana every day.

Allergies

Sometimes we aren't allowed to have our first-choice pet. Life, with all its idiosyncrasies, often forces us into choices we had not foreseen. Sometimes this is a pain in the butt, and sometimes it's a new and exciting adventure.

People with allergies frequently can't own dogs, cats, or other fur-bearing animals. If they want a pet, they must consider new options, such as reptiles.

I got an iguana because I'm allergic to dogs, cats, birds, rabbits, hamsters, and I don't like fish that much. So reptiles were basically the only choice.
                                        —I-719, Lucas, 14 yrs., Indiana

Figure 2.3: Don Burnham of California proudly shows off his pet iguana, "Iggy," who he had for 29 years. After enjoying a very long life, Iggy died in July of 1994. Photo by: A. H. Iles

My husband is allergic to mammal fur. Dogs and cats are impossible inside the
house, and our two pet rats eventually gave him a case of asthma.
                              —I-885, Paul & Meredith, 15 & 47 yrs., Oregon

Limited Space

In the good old days, families and their pets had lots of room to live. Now
it seems as if fewer people can afford to own a house, and the actual size of
today's lots and homes is frequently smaller than in past decades. In addition,
many people live in apartments or condominiums. These reduced living spaces
often restrict the ownership of traditional pets such as dogs or cats. But if the
desire for a pet is strong enough, there are usually options; many people find an
iguana to be ideal.

I got my first iguana because I was living in an apartment that didn't allow cats
or dogs.   —I-650, Helen, 31 yrs., Ohio

I am living in an apartment complex and the owners really restrict your pet
options. An iguana fits in perfectly with their requirements and my life.
                                          —I-707, Donna, 28 yrs., New York

Always Wanted

Maybe when you were a kid, your parents didn't let you have that special
pet you really wanted. When I was a kid growing up in a small rural town in
California's Central Valley, I really wanted a monkey. My parents were completely puzzled as to why I wanted such a pet, because no other kid in town
wanted one. Instead, they allowed me to have a turtle and a cat. For many
people, that dream pet was an iguana.

What is really funny is that when I was younger, I always wanted bigger and
bigger lizards and my mother always said, "When you move out, you can get
whatever you want." It finally dawned on me one day that I am moved out,
let's get what you always wanted. —I-817, Matthew, 24 yrs., New York

I was always fascinated with reptiles, especially lizards, and my mother
wouldn't let me have one, so I couldn't resist the temptation to get one when I
got married and moved to my own house.
                                       —I-259, Kathleen, 39 yrs., New York

Many years ago (maybe 25?) in high school biology class, some student brought
in an iguana. I can't quite recall its length, or its exact color. I'm not sure if I
petted it; I must have. I went home that day and told Mother that I wanted
"one of those." As I recall we even went to a pet shop and saw one there. Mother

said, "Absolutely not; someday when you have your own house." Time passed.
I forgot about it. Now I have one.   —I-706, Melodie, 41 yrs., Tennessee

I had [an iguana] as a small boy, but was not allowed to keep it in the house.
It died because it was too cold outside. I always wanted another one. Finally 20
years later I got one. Now as an adult I give my iguana the best care.
                                              —interview at herpetological conference

Alternative to "Traditional" Pets

I wanted an iguana because I'd had traditional pets and I wanted something
unusual. My husband hates snakes and barely tolerates my iguana, so it took
me a year to talk him into letting me get one. I guess he picked the lesser of two
evils, because I had to sign in blood that I would never get a snake if he let me
have a lizard.   —I-609, Cindy, 37 yrs., Florida

While some people are forced to have non-traditional pets because of allergies or small living spaces, as I mentioned earlier, still others want an alternative to traditional pets for reasons beyond practicality.

I love reptiles and my mother said that I couldn't have any animal that might
eat our cat. So an iguana was a natural choice.
                                              —I-638, Jennifer, 23 yrs., California

I wanted a reptile that grew big enough to see me as a whole entity, as does a cat
or dog.   —I-626, Gail, 48 yrs., New York

We like our iguanas [7 yrs. & 3 yrs.]. They are much more entertaining than
dogs or cats.   —I-554, Anthony, 29 yrs., Texas

I like it because [iguanas] don't bark.
                                              —I-31, Jason & Michelle, 22 & 23 yrs., California

I think it is important to show that the iguana is not some kind of rare, weird
pet, but one that can be enjoyed by the whole family.
                                              —I-602, William, 40 yrs., Illinois

They are less expensive to feed and clean than most dogs or cats. And they don't
eat your shoes.   —conversation with person at pet store

Feel Part of a Group

Whether you planned it or not, having an iguana makes you part of a special group.

As I mentioned earlier, it is estimated that 7.3 million iguanas are believed

SIDEBAR

Cat-Like Qualities

Of all the traditional pets that people own, iguanas are most often compared to cats.

In general, iguanas seem much closer to cats than dogs, with their general indifference to people, their inability to be taught dumb tricks, the fact that they don't sniff your privates, and that they at least try to excrete in the same place.
—I-369, David, 36 yrs., Virginia

He [SVL: 15½", TL: 4' 4", 3 yrs., 7 lbs.] likes to climb up onto the handlebars of my bicycle in the kitchen and snoozes in the afternoon like a cat.
—I-493, Marcia, 40 yrs., Alaska

They are nearly feline in their behavior, and being a cat person as well, I really liked that about them. —I-556, Sharon, 40 yrs., New York

I love to sit and hold him [SVL: 13", TL: 2' 5", 3½ yrs.] while I watch TV. It's just like holding a cat on your lap. I can talk to him and pet him while we watch football together. —I-693, Kimberly, 26 yrs., Pennsylvania

I plan to maintain an iguana companion as long as I am able, as my life-long replacement for cats. —I-515, Lynn, 21 yrs., Canada

They remind me of a cat: They understand (probably not, but they make you feel that they do) but just don't care one way or the other. They display (like a cat) an air of independence that almost makes you want to gain their approval or acceptance. —I-632, Cynthia, 38 yrs., California

Remember, even though iguanas as they get older (if healthy and happy) do mellow out and have some "cat-like" characteristics, they are not cats. If you want all that a cat offers, then get a cat. Case in point: A pet store owner once told me of a woman who returned an iguana when she found out that it was not like her cat. Iguanas should be appreciated for their own definite qualities.

to be in captivity in the U.S. So right off the bat, you're in an exclusive club, and one that's growing each year. There is even a magazine aimed at people interested in the family Iguanidae (called *Iguana Times*).

Exotic

> *Having an iguana is like having a little dinosaur running around in your living room.*   —I-690, Irene, 34 yrs., Texas

The green iguana looks exotic, with its vivid color bands, patches, and patterns and the spikes on its back, neck, and throat.

But getting an iguana just because it's exotic is not a good idea. If this is the only reason for choosing an iguana, your interest will fade quickly, the iguana may not be cared for properly, and it might have to be given away. On the other hand, if exotic is one of several other stronger reasons, then it's an added bonus.

> *[My iguana has an] impressive stance, holding himself high, like he is "king of the room."*   —I-364, Lynda, 30 yrs., Maryland

> *Lizards are exotic pets—and like an expensive car, should not be purchased unless the owner is willing to spend the time, money, and energy for its upkeep.*
>   —I-493, Marcia, 40 yrs., Alabama

PET BEHAVIOR

A pet iguana's behavior is often the reflection of its food, habitat, previous owner (if any), freedoms allowed, care given, and whether it was wild-caught or farm-raised. When your iguana is at the hatchling stage, it seems like a lizard. But in time, the iguana becomes more mammal-like. Its personality starts to develop, and it likes to be touched and to interact with humans.

The next few sections address some qualities that iguana owners have asked me to bring up in my book. They are included to give you a clearer picture of what your iguana can become.

For more details about your iguana's natural behavior in the wild, look at Chapter 1, Iguana: The Species, "Common Iguana Behaviors."

Personality

> *All my iguanas are different in personality, just like not all people are the same.*
>   —I-733, Linda, 37 yrs., California

Everyone has their own definition and desires when it comes to the personality of their pet. The dictionary defines personality as "habitual patterns and

---

SIDEBAR

Serene, Calming Influence

I know from experience that there's something almost mystically peaceful—yet powerful—about holding an iguana, especially a big iguana. When I held my iguana, I felt a tranquillity and calm come over me. From the stories I've received from other iguana owners, it's clear that I'm not the only one who has experienced iguana-induced serenity.

I enjoy watching my iguanas. I find it relaxing to hold, feed, and watch them. It helps me unwind after work. —I-685, Julie, 36 yrs., California

They are great to release tension after a hard day. I go to the greenhouse where they live and watch them interact. This allows me to relax. The tranquillity that they provide me just by caring for them, this I never expected.
—I-794, Andrés, 30 yrs., California

After dinner, I sit down at TV or whatever and spend petting and cuddling time with him (I enjoy this immensely, and I think he does, too).
—I-705, Linda & Paul, 45 yrs., California

I have suffered from traumatic nightmares for several years as a result of being physically and sexually abused. Shortly after I "bonded" to my iguana, he appeared in a dream—much, much larger than he is now (about the size of a 20-pound dog). When I was being threatened in my dream, my iguana protected me by biting and whipping the person. It was probably the most empowering moment of my life. I knew the next morning that he was the best pet I could ever have picked.
—a 26-year-old female; name withheld for her privacy

---

qualities of behavior of any individual as expressed by physical and mental activities and attitudes" (*Webster's New World Dictionary*, Second College Edition).

A pet's personality is in the eye of the beholder. For example, most people would be hard pressed to recognize an individual personality in a fish. But if you ask owners of tropical fish, they might go on and on about the special quirks of each of their fish.

Some people want a pet with a powerful, impossible-to-miss personality, while others prefer a more independent pet. Pets that have subtler personalities are brought to light by the sharp and keen awareness of a loving pet owner. People who have an iguana or have spent time around them often say the same thing: Iguanas have personalities, and each is a little different. In fact, people are frequently quite startled and amazed to see that these big green lizards have such discernible, individual traits.

The best way to provide insight about iguanas' personalities is to let iguana owners do the talking. The stories here hint at the wide range of personality traits that an iguana might exhibit.

I once read in a book that iguanas don't have personalities, but I strongly disagree. Even though they don't purr like a cat or bark like a dog, and they don't do tricks or cuddle with you, [my two iguanas] both have their own way of showing you how they feel.   —I-747, Stephanie, 22 yrs., Illinois

Our iguana seems to have a "Garfieldish" attitude toward things. She [SVL: 8⅓", TL: 2' 1", 1 yr. 10 mo.] takes things in stride yet maintains a delightful curiosity in her surroundings. She can be very funny and playful, perhaps without even trying.   —I-926, Robert & Virginia, California

Independent and somewhat defiant, she doesn't do anything she doesn't want to do . . . like my girlfriend.   —phone conversation with pet owner

After owning my iguana for more than six years, I have come to the absolute conclusion that they have definite personalities. My iguana seems to respond with more character than other reptiles, more personable than the blank stare of a snake.   —conversation at pet store

He has an attitude and look to him that says, "I am the most important thing in the world and you are nothing."   —I-615, Jamie, 15 yrs., California

She [7-year-old iguana] can be very sweet and she seems to always know when I have a problem. I like that she has her own personality; some pets seem to be as dead as a doornail.   —I-806, Tiffany, 14 yrs., Texas

My iguana [SVL: 13", TL: 3' 8", 2½ yrs.] really appears to have feelings. We can tell when he is content and when he is irritated.   —I-895, Julie & Jim, 25 yrs., Texas

We've had our iguana [SVL: 15½", TL: 3' 8½", 10½ lbs.] for 28 years. He now is kind of like a grumpy old man.   —I-600, Don, 69 yrs., California

I like their aloofness. It gives them some dignity.   —conversation with pet store employee

Whenever he [SVL: 15", TL: 4' 5", 4 yrs.] is in trouble or feels he's in danger he comes running to me. And of course I am so honored.   —I-3, Peg, 38 yrs., California

His personality—tons-o-moods! There is an unusualness about an iguana. Ours [SVL: 12½", TL: 4' 5½", 3 yrs.] is such a mush (e.g., falling asleep on our laps, licking our necks when perched on our shoulders, leaning into our scratching him, etc.). —I-853, Eva & Scott, New Jersey

I love their independent attitudes—the tolerant and accepting nature (sometimes), their holier-than-thou, I-don't-need-you attitude. I suppose I believe that when they do accept me completely, I'll know that it's genuine, and not just because it's their nature. That's what makes them so unlike other pets. —I-632, Cynthia, 38 yrs., California

Affectionate?

I wouldn't say that iguanas are able to have real affection for someone, but they do develop a trust in their human care-giver and I think that says a lot. It makes me feel good to know that I have earned their trust. —I-312, Darla, 38 yrs., Ohio

Some say that an iguana can't be affectionate. Perhaps that's true in the standard human or mammalian model, but over time iguanas trust you to pull things out of their eyes, help comfort them when they're injured, and give them shots that hurt. Trusting for a non-domesticated animal is a big leap of faith and may be a close relative of what we label affection.

Iguanas are not like dogs that grovel, drool, slobber, and follow you around like you are a god, making you feel special in a grand way. Iguanas are subtle. Because their offering of "affection" is not constant like a dog's, perhaps it is more appreciated. To have a reptile seek you out is very special, and it happens <u>only</u> when you put a lot of time into developing a close relationship.

But not everyone thinks their iguanas are particularly affectionate.

I often tell people that my iguana [SVL: 17", TL: 4' 4", 5 yrs.] keeps me humble. When I come home from work the dog is all over me with "I love you, it's great to see you." The iguana expresses, "Just feed me, bitch." It gives balance to my life. —I-476, Marie, 23 yrs., Virginia

Of the qualities that I don't like, the biggest would be that he doesn't show affection like my dog or cats. He's just as happy if I handle him or not. —I-609, Cindy, 37 yrs., Florida

Even though iguanas are pretty intelligent, as far as herps go, they are not going to give you the affection of a dog or cat. —I-171, Andrew, 34 yrs., Minnesota

I don't think people should buy an iguana expecting a close personal relation-ship with them because they will be disappointed. On the other hand, they don't require a whole lot of attention.   —I-665, Molly, 17 yrs., Oregon

But do iguanas ever like us, the people who take care of them? I have a biased opinion and believe they do.

Iguanas learn to trust and depend on you. Trusting and depending is a kind of liking.   —I-11 Patty, Washington

One evening when my iguana Za was about 9 months old (SVL: 7½", TL: 2' 2½", 9 oz.), he was on his favorite human chair in my apartment and I was on the couch. He had already eaten and was content to sit on his warm heating pad at the top of this padded chair. Suddenly he got up on all four legs, looking at me nervously like he just received a message from God and had to deliver it.

Sure enough, he hopped onto the floor, walked all the way across the room, climbed up on the couch, sat on my knee, and looked into my eyes for about 30 seconds. I petted him and he went back to "his" chair and laid back down. True, he didn't deliver a verbal message, but I interpreted his actions to be that he wanted to be near me.

Several months after that, I was sorting papers on the living room floor, while Za sat in that same chair. Za repeated the nervous body movements and then left the chair, walked across the floor into the middle of the stack of papers, and sat down and looked up at me. I gave him a couple of strokes on the head and he went back to the chair on his own. He repeated this same pattern several other times over the next couple of years.

What did he have to gain in any of these situations, where he didn't need food or heat? I think he just liked me and was interested in my activities. Below are a number of quotations from iguana owners about the closeness they have achieved with their pets. Most of these are older iguanas who have had many years of bonding with their caregivers.

I didn't expect these reptiles to be playful or affectionate, just interesting and pretty. I was very pleasantly surprised as the years passed to discover one by one all the different qualities and personalities and diversity of behavior.
                                    —I-200, Dianna, 47 yrs., Washington

My iguana [SVL: 13", TL: 3' 5", 7½ yrs.] follows me around the apartment. Many times he is right "under foot" like a puppy dog would be.
                                    —I-633, Lynne, 29 yrs., Michigan

I didn't expect it [SVL: 9", TL: 2' 3", 2½ yrs.] to be cuddly like a dog or cat.
                                    —I-94, Rosanne & Don, 24 yrs., Illinois

He sits on my shoulder and "kisses" my neck—I think they are the King of
Lizards.   —interview at herpetological conference

Our iguana [SVL: 15", TL: 3' 11", 4½ yrs.] likes to have the top of his head
rubbed or stroked. He closes his eyes and seems to become very relaxed. If I stop
too soon, he nudges my hand with his head for me to continue.
                                        —I-365, Marilyn, 53 yrs., New York

It pleases me when I study on my bed and my iguana [SVL: 15", TL: 3' 5", 5
yrs.] climbs down from his warm perch and sits on my stomach. I did not expect
him to be as friendly toward me as he is, especially considering that food is often
not his motivating factor.   —I-515, Lynn, 21 yrs., Canada

I didn't expect my iguana [SVL: 13½", TL: 3' 7½", 7 yrs.] to become so
attached. He will look for me when I am in the house, and if I move to another
room he will come look for me in about 10 minutes.
                                        —I-306, Gretchen, 28 yrs., Virginia

A few times she [SVL: 12½", TL: 3' 1", 2 yrs.] has come up to me, stood on her
hind legs stretching up to me to pick her up.
                                        —I-500, Martha, 39 yrs., Oregon

I feel closer to my iguana [SVL: 9", TL: 23", 3 yrs.] when he will take a nap on
the bed with me.   —I-759, Laura, 20 yrs., Pennsylvania

She [SVL: 15", TL: 2' 11", 5 yrs.] runs and buries her head into my chest if she
gets frightened (as when she saw a dog one day).
                                        —I-100, Char, 44 yrs., Illinois

Several times when I've been really upset about something and in tears, my
iguana [SVL: 14", TL: 3' 6½", 11 yrs.] has run to me and climbed on my
shoulder. This makes me feel much better. She doesn't normally do that.
                                        —I-126, Beverly, 30 yrs., Arizona

Curiosity

Iguanas of all ages have a funny kind of curiosity, exploring every nook and
cranny in the house, much like a cat. One of the best things about having an
iguana is just watching it. Young ones in particular rarely stay put when first
allowed to explore your house.

My iguana [SVL: 3", TL: 12"] is very curious about everything. She is always
determined to discover what is on the other side of everything.
                                        —I-468, Jill, 17 yrs., Indiana

Kiss of Death?

People with all kinds of animals as pets, including iguanas, often show affection toward their animals as if they were humans—hugging, sleeping with them, and sometimes kissing them. Perhaps with iguanas we should think twice about the kissing aspect:

I would never let another [iguana] kiss me on the lips. I asked vets whether our human [germs] can be transferred to iguanas and most would not give me an absolute answer. They're not real sure. There's a lot of information that hasn't been looked into with iguanas. All I know is my favorite iguana died shortly after I got the flu for a week. His body was full of virus. That's all we know from the autopsy. Also, one of the other iguanas got ill when I was sick. So whether it's a coincidence, or whether the iguana caught my flu, I don't know, but I don't think it is worth the risk. All I know is my baby, my favorite, died. I'll never put my lips to another iguana again! —I-11, Patty, Washington

My iguana crawls into my "reptile room" and watches the mice run around in their cages. My iguana also often watches the fish in the fish tanks. Let's face it, these guys are characters. —I-203, Greg, Washington

He is very keen and alert. I like the way he watches his environment and never misses anything. —I-722, Andy, California

I love their eyes and how they follow you around the house with curiosity. —I-276, Pam, 45 yrs., Tennessee

He [SVL: 11¼", TL: 2' 10¼", 2½ yrs.] is very curious. When I shut the cats in the back of the house and let my iguana walk around the house, he wants to explore <u>everything</u>! He goes to each place in almost the same order each time: tries to eat the flowers on the rug, kitchen tour, then dining area, down the hall, into the bathroom, tries to jump on the toilet, back to the living room, up the front door screen, then check out the plants, the recliner, and the cats' scratching post. —I-916, Lucretia, 38 yrs., California

While I was building his cage, he [SVL: 13", TL: 3' 10", 3 yrs.] was always following me around trying to see what I was doing. I called him my little helper. —I-773, Rich, 34 yrs., Nebraska

I can relate to Rich's story. When we moved from California to Oregon, I had to reassemble my iguana's large habitat (8 ft. long by 3 ft. wide by 7 ft.

high). As I was doing this assembly, Za (SVL: 14½", TL: 4' 3½", 2¼ yrs.) sat on the edge of the couch and watched. When I started screwing his big basking stick into place, he hopped down from the couch and came into the habitat with me and wanted to hang on my arm as I worked. I finally had to put him back on the couch so I could get my work done.

Another example of Za's curiosity occurred when he was about 1½ years old. I came in from outside and couldn't find him. For about 45 minutes I looked everywhere in the apartment. Finally, I found him in the kitchen near the ceiling, on top of the large wooden frame where I hung pots and pans.

He got up there by climbing on the front handle of the oven, then onto the top of the stove, moving to the wall where I had glued about 100 wine corks (which he used as hand-holds). From there he climbed on the wire-screen food strainers hooked to the wall above the corks, and hopped directly onto the rectangular wooden pot rack. (By the way, I know all this for certain because I caught him in the act, a few days later, repeating the same route!)

This was not a good activity for Za because he could have climbed the stove when it was hot or fallen when he tried to leap from the wire strainers to the pot rack. I stopped this climbing activity by modifying the stove handles.

Thinking back, I remember seeing him on the kitchen floor many times, with his head cocked sideways, looking up at the wooden frame. I should have known it was just a matter of time until he satisfied his curiosity.

Determination

Iguanas frequently get extremely obstinate about a certain place or direction they feel they <u>must</u> go. At first I thought it was just my iguana's behavior, but over time I realized that many iguanas have this stubborn, determined trait.

He can be quite strong-willed at times, and on his bad days he seems to have a temper. He is also very stubborn, and once he sets his mind to do something it can be quite difficult to dissuade him.   —I-799, Rui, 35 yrs., New York

When I let him out of the cage, sometimes he starts trying to jump on top of the front door or go behind his cage. Then it's time to put him back in, because he won't give up and does not like being rerouted from his intended destination!   —I-916, Lucretia, 38 yrs., California

When my iguana wants to go to the curtains to climb, no matter what I do, it will find a way there. Like if I block its normal pattern, it will find a new one.   —I-888, Amy & Howard, 19 yrs., Ohio

He knows what he wants and does not want to be deterred. I'll put him under a warm lamp in the living room, and next thing I know he's marching across the kitchen floor and into the family room, because he's got a particular spot in mind that he wants to go to. Once I caught him raised up and just about to jump from the chair to the bookcase, where he's not allowed. I scolded him, so he lowered his body and relaxed. But as soon as I left the room, I heard the thump as he landed on the bookcase. He is single-minded and determined.

—I-609, Cindy, 37 yrs., Florida

If he gets it in his head to sleep in my closet, even though the door is shut, he will scratch at the door and attempt to find a way to get in.

—I-493, Marcia, 40 yrs., Alaska

BREAKING BARRIERS

It's easiest to love things that are familiar to us. Dogs and cats are easy. For some people, iguanas are less so. But the ability to stretch your acceptance to include creatures very different from you, such as iguanas, enriches your own life considerably. Loving an iguana can be more intense because it takes a deeper level of appreciation and understanding.

CHAPTER 3

Choosing Your Pet

Those who find beauty in all of nature will find themselves at one with the secrets of life itself.   —L.W. Gilbert

I picked one of the brightest green, most alert baby iguanas in the pet shop, and the guy had hell just catching him to put him in the cardboard box. My friend and I were all settled in the car for the ride home, when the iguana threw a giant fit in the box and tried to get out. We just looked at each other, laughing nervously, and I thought, what have I gotten myself into?
                          —I-609, Cindy, 37 yrs., Florida

I'm assuming that if you've gotten this far in the book, one of the following is true (mentally check the box that applies):

❑ I've already read the introduction and chapters 1 and 2, so I have a good idea of the responsibilities involved in owning an iguana. I'm making an informed decision, not an impulse purchase.

❑ I cheated and haven't read anything in this book, but I promise to remedy that right now by reading at least the introduction and chapters 1 and 2.

❑ I have decided not to get an iguana, or I never intended to get one in the first place. I'm simply reading this book because it's so entertaining!

REQUIRED PREPARATION
BEFORE PURCHASE

Before you bring an iguana to your home, there are certain things you need to do. Don't expect the pet-store salespeople to give you all the information you need to properly care for your iguana. You need to learn as much as possible on your own.

Perhaps the best information you can receive will be from a knowledgeable iguana pet care book, such as this one. The more you read and know, the better your iguana's life will be. It's up to you to know what your iguana requires.

AT A GLANCE: Things You'll Need
<u>Before</u> You Buy an Iguana

- Habitat—completely set up and functioning (see Chapter 4, Housing)
- Food—the right kind, prepared properly (see Chapter 5, Feeding)
- Knowledge—gained by reading this and other books, talking to other iguana owners, etc.
- Commitment—to give your iguana the best possible care

I worked as Reptile Department Manager for 1½ years at a local pet shop. One problem I ran into was that customers wanted to keep the cost of purchase down, so they would "wait" to purchase a care book for their iguana.
—I-808, Priscilla, 25 yrs., Iowa

People need to be educated by a well-written book <u>before</u> they make that long-term commitment of being a responsible iguana owner.
—I-790, Cindy, 33 yrs., Texas

Before picking out your first pet iguana, remember that it will not survive in an environment suitable for a puppy or a kitten. You can easily bring these mammals home from a pet store, open a can of food, and let the animal sleep for a while in a makeshift container with some soft bedding.

But an iguana is a tropical reptile that is entirely dependent on the correct shelter, environment, food, and water that you supply. If your iguana is not supplied with these essential things right away, it could suffer severely or die.

Also remember that unless parents are willing to participate with their children in the joint care of the iguana, it's likely that a child-owned lizard may eventually have to be given away or could die through mismanagement.

I think it's important to stress to people that they shouldn't buy an iguana on a whim. They are not pets for everyone, and I think that parents who buy an iguana for their kids, just because the kid wants one, are making a very big mistake. Too many things can go wrong. The animal is not manageable, the kid loses interest, etc.   —I-538, Martin, 37 yrs., Kansas

WHERE TO GET AN IGUANA

Once you've decided to get an iguana and you have the habitat completely set up (see Chapter 4, Housing, to find out exactly what this entails), you have many sources for obtaining your pet. In the old days, everyone seemed to get iguanas from only one place: the local pet store. Times have changed and choices for acquiring iguanas have expanded.

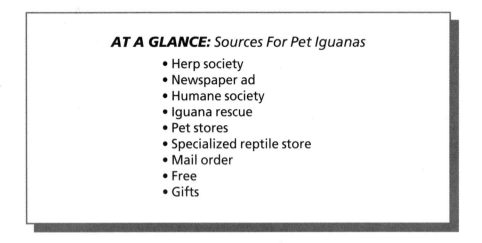

AT A GLANCE: *Sources For Pet Iguanas*
- Herp society
- Newspaper ad
- Humane society
- Iguana rescue
- Pet stores
- Specialized reptile store
- Mail order
- Free
- Gifts

Herp society—Joining a herp society (see Appendix B) has many advantages, among them the chance to get a free or a relatively inexpensive iguana. In one of the herp society newsletters I receive, there are between one and four iguanas up for adoption every month. Another option with a herp society is to trade a pet amphibian, reptile, or other animal for an iguana (instead of cash). Perhaps you can trade a monster for a prince.

It's interesting. I never set out to acquire an iguana. I went out and bought a golden tegu, but after a week I decided there was no way I could live with this lizard (which I was sure was conceived in hell). He attacked unprovoked and eventually the best I probably could have expected was a display animal. So the girl I got him from said she'd trade even for her iguana, and I did it. I had never seen a full-grown green iguana, and I was impressed. My family was, too. Up to this time my girlfriend and my stepdaughter had such a bias against herps that every time I mentioned getting something a fight would ensue. But my iguana proved to be the "gateway" animal with them and they love him dearly. —I-171, Drew, 34 yrs., Minnesota

I traded 20 mice for a 3-year-old iguana. He is now over 8 years old. —I-713, Cindy, 36 yrs., Iowa

Getting your iguana from a herp society member takes the guesswork out of knowing your iguana's life history. You can actually meet and talk with the owner of your future iguana and find out what the lizard has been fed, the kind of care it has been given, possible medical problems, how it gets along with its owner, and some of its personality traits.

But the main reason for choosing an iguana from a fellow herp member may be the best reason of all: It's animal recycling. Getting an iguana from someone who no longer wants it (for whatever reason) means a new home for the animal and, in the abstract, one less iguana ripped out of the jungle. Everyone benefits from this transaction.

Newspaper ad—Depending on where you live and the size of your city, looking through the want ads under "pets" can be a golden opportunity and a nearly effortless way to find an iguana. Here again you get to meet and talk with the owners of your future iguana. When I lived in Northern California there were always iguanas for sale. Even here in Oregon I see ads for iguanas each week.

Three of my iguanas were acquired because the owners couldn't deal with them any more. These iguanas were the lucky ones because their owners cared enough about them to find another suitable home.
> —I-556, Sharon, 40 yrs., New York

Many people need to get rid of their iguana because they are moving, their living situation changes, they've grown tired of the iguana, or perhaps the animal has gotten too big. Frequently, people selling their iguanas are anxious to unload their lizard and its habitat for pennies on the dollar.

We bought our iguana from an elephant trainer who was unable to give the iguana the affections he deserved due to her work schedule.
> —I-661, Chris, 22 yrs., Nevada

Humane societies—When you think of your local animal shelter, probably the first animals that come to mind are cats and dogs. But it's amazing how many different kinds of animals end up there. When I lived in California, the local Humane Society shelter always had an iguana waiting for a new home. Many of the iguanas were free if you could prove to the person in charge that you could take care of the lizard. Showing a copy of this book should be a good start.

I was surprised that our animal shelter had an iguana. He is now my pet.
> —I-882, Jessica, 21 yrs., New Jersey

My iguana was a stray brought to the Humane Society. He was happy to be handled within hours of my taking him home.
> —I-798, Teri, 35 yrs., New Hampshire

The only drawback with an animal shelter is that you don't get to know the background of these usually older iguanas, and many times they have been abused or neglected. Abused animals, like abused kids, need a good home, care, and some love—as well as extra patience. If you have a big heart, this could be right up your alley.

Iguana Rescue—Within the last few years, lovers of iguanas in various cities and states have formed clearing houses for unwanted or damaged iguanas. The first one I heard about was started by some bright, compassionate people in Florida. The number of these rescue operations in different states increases each year.

To find out if there's an Iguana Rescue group in your area, contact your local herp society or veterinary hospital. Iguanas at these rescue operations are usually given away free to caring individuals.

Pet stores—Pet stores are close to the bottom of this iguana source list because (as my introduction states) my main goal is trying to save iguanas that are already here. The first few places to get an iguana get top billing because they recycle these lizards.

Pet stores have been, and probably will always be, the main source of iguanas for the general public. You can find pet stores in just about every town, and often people feel most comfortable purchasing an animal from a store.

Over the years I have visited what seems like millions of pet stores across the U.S. I've seen great stores as well as some that should have their doors immediately nailed shut and all of their animals taken to a healthier environment. Here's how to tell what kind of store you've entered:

• Bad stores—Substandard care, misinformed or uninformed staff, indifference to the well-being of the iguanas for sale—those are some characteristics of bad pet stores. These stores are the ones to avoid when choosing your pet iguana.

The general public believes that the people running pet shops automatically know everything about what they are selling and, unfortunately, sometimes the pet shop people think this is true, too.   —I-493, Marcia, 40 yrs., Alaska

I feel that the pet stores should be more informed about the iguanas they sell. Misinformed or uninformed employees could mean the detriment of the iguanas.
—I-754, Karen, 33 yrs., New Mexico

Again and again I have seen pet stores with minimal or no heating for their iguanas (iguanas need heat!). One such store was located in an indoor mall in Colorado. Because the mall was closed at night and no one would be walking by the pet store, the owner turned all the lights off, including the heat lights for the reptiles, and supplied no nighttime heat.

I mentioned to the owner that on a very basic survival level iguanas need to stay warm so they can digest their food. He was nice for about five minutes, then his plastic smile—the one he must have gotten for Halloween—fell off. He said, "The iguanas were cheap to buy and if some of them die, we'll just get more."

I receive phone calls all the time from people asking for my help with their iguanas. They bought the iguanas from pet stores and now the iguanas don't seem to be doing too well. They all tell me the same things: The pet store told them to feed the iguana lettuce (iceberg) and buy a "hot rock" for heat. They are led to believe that no other form of heat is needed, and lighting of any kind is usually never mentioned. I ask how much time each week they plan on giving the iguana sunlight. They tell me they didn't know it was necessary.

I found that a lot of these people were now on their second to fourth iguanas. I have found myself being very blunt with these people. After we talk for a few moments I kindly tell them that they are killing their own pets out of ignorance.

Pet stores make me very angry. I used to go to pet stores and cry watching hatchling iguanas that I knew were suffering and would probably be dead in less than a week's time. I used to pick pet stores at random and pretend to be interested in acquiring an iguana, asking the basic questions. Very few ever told me anything different than what the people that were calling me said they were told by their pet stores. And it was never suggested that prospective owners buy a book. They acted as if people might change their minds and think it too complicated to care for an iguana if they suggested the purchase of a book.

I probably get very angry because I was one of these people that walked into a pet store knowing nothing and was told everything I needed to know to kill my very own brand new baby iguana. The only difference was that when I realized my iguana was sick I also knew I did not know enough to keep this animal alive, so I took it to a vet. I still have my iguana and it is very much a part of my life.   —I-656, Peggy, 34 yrs., Texas

I have seen too many bad pet stores. The owners of these bad stores act like they've bought a book called "How To Kill Iguanas." For example, they feed chunks of vegetables the size of the iguana's head. Iguanas don't chew their food, so how are they supposed to eat these "boulder" portions? The poor little green guys have to swallow the whole chunk. Or the pet stores offer only lettuce, which has little food value.

The pet store told us to feed our iguana [only] watermelon every three days! Can you believe it? The next morning I called my vet to find out what to really feed our iguana and how often.   —I-530, Kathy, 30 yrs., Florida

I looked for months for a pet iguana, and saw hundreds of malnourished and poorly maintained animals [at pet stores].

—I-629, Theodore, 25 yrs., Michigan

We bought a male iguana from a pet store. He looked like he hadn't eaten in over a month, but was alert. We bought him because the pet store owner was not attempting to feed him or seek veterinary care.
                                        —I-536, Carrie, 22 yrs., Missouri

I have also seen iguanas that were injured and left in the cage to die. Or whose water bowl was a smelly swamp of feces and rotting food. Sometimes an even worse situation is when a young iguana is forced to share a small cage with much larger, more aggressive iguanas. I could go on, but I get so angry I could explode. It's too depressing.

I think there are two basic types of "bad" pet stores. First are the ones that don't know they are doing things wrong and once given the correct information make things right. Sometimes I would give store personnel some helpful hints on how to keep their iguanas healthy and happy. I didn't go into pet stores and suggest how to improve iguana care so that people would pat me on the back. I just wanted their poor animals not to suffer. If I went back to these stores several weeks later and saw improvements, I left the store with a big smile.

The second type of bad pet stores are the ones that don't listen and don't care if their animals die. This makes no sense to me. If these people ran a produce stand, they'd make sure their vegetables were clean, firm, and fresh. So what happens when they sell animals instead of produce? Too often, they are willing to let their iguanas wither away and even die in a cage, to be thrown into the trash like some week-old forgotten sandwich. I seldom go into pet stores any more, in case I encounter something too depressing. These few bad stores are a blight on the reputation of all pet stores.

People need to be aware that bad practices exist. As a potential buyer, you must let the pet store owner know—in constructive, non-threatening ways—that these animals are not up to even the lowest minimum quality standards and that you will find a better place to spend your money. Then take your business elsewhere.

There are pet shops here in town that I will tell people not to patronize because they are either dirty or don't offer reliable information on the animals they sell. On the other hand, I'll pay top dollar at a [good] pet shop that's clear across town.   —I-493, Marcia, 40 yrs., Alaska

Luckily, bad pet stores are not the rule. The good stores can look forward to increased sales because you, as an educated customer, will choose to purchase from them.

• Good stores—One of the many good stores I visited, near San Francisco, was owned and operated by a small family that really cared about its animals.

They had a large (perhaps 4-year-old) iguana, and I asked the price. The owner explained that the iguana had smashed its snout when it was younger and now had a somewhat deformed face. For the rest of its life it would need special care when being fed. The owner said that he would sell this animal only to a person he knew would give the iguana the special lifelong care it required.

Another good store was in a low-income neighborhood in Central California. The manager said he often gave future owners special discounts, or even free iguana-related products, to make sure his animals survived.

Other positive stories abound, but these two should give you the proper feeling. If you are in one of these good stores, you need to let the owner or manager know that you appreciate what they are doing. Good stores need positive feedback, and your comments will spark them to continue their high-quality care. Good deserves good. Spread the word.

Specialized reptile store—Ideally, pick a store that specializes in reptiles and amphibians or one with a large selection of reptiles. You need not auto-

---

SIDEBAR

What Constitutes a Good Pet Store?

The first thing to look for in a pet store is good, healthy animals (see page 137, "Qualities to Look For").

The second is clean, well-lit enclosures. If the cages or store look dirty, turn around and go someplace else. This is just the first physical weak link in the chain of what might have been a good pet store. A store doesn't need to be surgically spotless, but the overall impression should be pleasant and clean.

Often you'll be hit by a strong ammonia smell when you enter a pet store. This does not necessarily indicate a bad store. The store probably sells snakes and other carnivorous reptiles in addition to iguanas. Carnivorous reptiles eat mice and rats, and the rodents' urine gives off that strong ammonia smell. It takes only a few of these rodent "feeders" to smell up a good store. But in the top-of-the-line stores, even this smell will not be apparent.

The cages where the iguanas are kept should feel uncomfortably warm to you. If there are thermometers in the cage, one area should read at least 80°F with another "hot spot" of around 90°F or hotter.

The animals should also have some sort of light during the day that goes off at night (iguanas need a day and night period, just like humans, to remain healthy and happy). But when the light goes off at night, the iguanas should have an alternative heat source.

Check the water bowl to see if the water is clean, without food or feces in it. Be a little forgiving on this point, though, in case an iguana recently defecated in the water bowl and the sales staff hasn't had time to see it yet.

matically disregard a small pet store that has just a few iguanas; I have seen some of the best iguanas in small stores. But the more iguanas you can choose from, the better your chances of finding a great pet. Also, a specialized reptile store is more likely to have a staff more knowledgeable about reptiles.

As I mentioned before, it is important to look at iguanas in at least two stores to compare quality and price. I have seen the full range of pricing: animals priced too high and not worth anything, as well as animals priced high and worth every cent for the extra care they have been given. As you visit more stores, your decision will become clearer.

Mail order—Ordering an iguana by mail—is that possible? Yes it is, and several companies deal exclusively with farm- or captive-raised iguanas. You simply need to look at the advertisements in any of the national herpetological magazines (see Appendix B), then write or call some of these companies for fur-

That is why it's important to visit several different pet stores, a couple of times each—or you might ask them how often they change the iguanas' water.

Knowledgeable salespeople who care about their animals also signal a good pet store. If the people working in the store know how to care for an iguana, the animal you purchase will probably be healthier. The sales personnel don't have to be experts on every aspect of iguanas, but they should have a good grasp of the basics and a caring attitude. For most questions about your future iguana, you can find the answers in this book or in the additional reading in Appendix B.

Lastly, good pet stores will encourage you to come back or call with any questions that may arise. They will also have care handouts and a genuine desire to see that their reptiles are matched with the right owners. (Of course, they get bonus points if they have my book on their shelf!)

After purchasing a healthy iguana and receiving reliable care information from one of these stores, make sure you follow through with what they tell you.

I work part-time at a pet store and over the last year have sold hundreds of green iguanas. The problem is that people do not listen! When you sell them everything—lights, vitamins, etc., including an instruction manual—they always return with a calcium-deficient iguana. They say they ran out of vitamins or didn't have time to feed the iguana properly, etc. I've gotten to the point where I won't sell them or discourage people who I feel won't invest the time to properly care for these wonderful animals.

—I-791, Dan, 20 yrs., Missouri

ther information. They say in their ads that they offer the highest quality available, and their business is built on their reputation. But the Latin adage "Caveat emptor" (let the buyer beware) applies here, as elsewhere.

Free (lucky finds)—Of course, there is also a chance you can get an iguana for free, without even trying.

We have two cats. One is several years old (male) and weighs about 13 pounds. It's very rare that he will catch anything when he hunts, but when he does he usually destroys his prey until it's unrecognizable. The other cat is a 2-year-old female who catches everything and kills nothing. She just likes to bring things back to us as presents.

One Sunday afternoon, my boyfriend and I returned from the beach, and as we stepped into the living room this long skinny green lizard ran out from under the door mat and scurried to the middle of the room. We both screamed, "Lizard!" and it proceeded to run under the couch. The cats were nowhere in sight, but there was evidence of a chase around the room.

My boyfriend carefully tipped the couch forward and stuck his hand out for the lizard to climb on, which it did without hesitation. We checked the lizard out and found that he was very thin, and had a few puncture holes from a cat's claws. The holes were just at the surface (there appeared to be no internal damage), and there wasn't any drainage from the ear. We came to the conclusion that the female cat must have caught this lizard, due to the fact that it was still living.

We decided to keep the iguana because it was tame and obviously didn't belong in our backyard. Besides, if we did release it our male cat might get hold of it next time and then it wouldn't have a chance.

    —I-499, Laurie, 26 yrs., California.

Sometimes choosing the right restaurant for dinner can make all the difference:

My wife and I went to our favorite Italian restaurant for dinner one night. As we pulled into the parking lot I noticed some type of creature hanging on the wooden lattice of the Mexican restaurant next door. I said to my wife, "That can't be an iguana lizard, can it?" I went over and picked it up without a struggle.

We went into the Mexican restaurant to see if someone there owned it. But the people in the restaurant didn't speak English so they had no idea what we were trying to say. So we decided that the iguana was ours (now).

The only thing we had in the car to put the iguana in was a bowling bag. We took the ball out, put him in (he was cold, so he wasn't moving much), put the bag in the trunk, and went and had our Italian dinner.

My wife was very concerned that the iguana would suffocate (I didn't think he would). Needless to say we ate rather quickly! Then we drove to my mother's house where I had a reptile cage from my childhood. We put the iguana in the cage and continued home.

The iguana is still with us and we hope to have him a good long time. The name we gave him is an abbreviation of the Mexican restaurant where we found him originally. —I-534, Dave, 38 yrs., California

Gifts—Birthdays and anniversaries are an ideal time for special presents, as long as you are sure the recipient wants an iguana and will be a responsible owner.

My dad had an iguana when he was a kid. I begged for an exotic pet, and so my dad got me what he once had as a kid—an iguana—for my tenth birthday. It was the best birthday present I ever got. —I-571, Sam, 13 yrs., Oregon

My wife thought an iguana would be a good pet for me, and she bought me one for an anniversary present. —I-872, Dave, 34 yrs., New Jersey

HOW TO CHOOSE THE BEST IGUANA

I drove 80 miles to find my first iguana. I was very picky. I had looked at the area pet shops and did not see healthy enough iguanas. Also, I was looking for a certain personality. —I-793, Lynn, 43 yrs., Michigan

It took more than a year to find the right iguana for me. Originally I wanted an adult, but I all the ones I saw were damaged. This was more than seven years ago, when iguana care was not well understood. Most of the adult iguanas available then had deformed jaws/faces (from previous calcium deficiencies), thermal burns, or missing body parts. In the end I opted for a 3-month-old iguana instead of a damaged adult. Nowadays I see many excellent large adult iguanas for sale. Things are slowly getting better for pet iguanas.

In the next few pages, I outline the qualities and clues that will help you select a great iguana. Remember, you'll be better able to judge iguana qualities if you see a number of lizards at different places.

Armed with the upcoming information in this book and the experience of seeing many iguanas, you will be able to tell what is and what isn't a good iguana choice for you. If you have any further questions or doubts, make sure you discuss them with the person selling the iguana before you make a final decision.

Qualities to Look For

If you see a group of hatchlings in a cage, your first instinct might be to choose the biggest one, thinking it's the best. But this is not always the case. Most of the time, hatchlings arrive over several weeks and often from different sources. As a result, the largest may not be the healthiest or the fastest-growing, it may just be an older iguana that's been around for a while.

Once I saw a slightly bigger iguana in a cage with other iguanas. But after talking with the salesperson, I discovered that the bigger iguana was 6 months older than the others.   —person I met while in a pet store

---

AT A GLANCE: *Qualities to Look For in a Healthy Iguana*

Tail:	fat and plump at its base
Skin:	tight, bright, green
Eyes:	bright, clean, "alive"
Mouth:	no cheesy mucus, not hanging open
Nose:	no mucous discharge
Jaw:	firm, no distortion or swelling
Vent:	clean
Legs:	rounded, not swollen
Stomach:	fat and full
Attitude:	frisky, alert

Tail—Healthy iguanas store fat at the base of their tails (where the tail attaches to the body). The tail should be thick and plump at this point, and you shouldn't be able to see the bones in the tail. A thick tail will indicate that the iguana is eating well and regularly.

Have you ever seen pictures of starving prisoners of war, all skin and bones? I have seen many skin-and-bone iguanas, and this is not healthy! These animals may be stressed and not eating. They might also be harboring parasites inside their digestive tracts that could eventually kill them.

In any case, don't let the salesperson or iguana owner make you believe that a thin iguana will fatten up after you purchase it. It is their responsibility to have a fat, healthy, happy animal to sell. You wouldn't purchase a car with an engine that doesn't start. It's like the owner of the car saying, "Just take the car home; it will start for you." You need to made sure that the iguana you purchase is healthy.

Skin—Do not accept any animal with open sores or blisters. Iguanas in captivity don't deal well with open wounds or sores, and infection can start almost immediately.

The iguana's skin should be tight with no bagginess. Loose skin might indicate that the iguana has not been eating for some time.

A young iguana should have a bright green color. In older iguanas, the green typically becomes more muted, and they may add greys, browns, blues, and other colors as their adult patterns develop. During breeding season, adult males also frequently turn various degrees of orange, especially on their heads, arms, and legs. But they don't call these lizards "green iguanas" because they are black.

The older he gets, the less green he seems to get. Sometimes we notice him an
orangish brown.   —I-940, Linda & Scott, 44 yrs., California

Iguanas' skin color changes depending on various internal and external conditions (but, unlike chameleons, not in response to a change in the color of their surroundings). For example, iguanas' skin often darkens when they're sick, under stress (temporarily or long-term), or to absorb more heat if they are too cool. If you see an iguana with dark, non-green skin, this is a signal to be aware of a potential problem; you may need to delve deeper into the possible causes.

If you're looking at wild-caught iguanas, you may observe one or more ticks on the iguanas' skin. Ticks, little blood-sucking creatures, are rarely seen in farm-raised iguanas. A tick is not a reason to reject an iguana. Ticks can be removed easily (see Chapter 7, Medical Troubleshooting, "Ticks"). In fact, my iguana had a tick that was removed by the owner of the pet store the day I brought him home.

I did find a tick on one of my young ones when it was purchased at a pet shop.
The tick was dead and came right off. I figure the iguana had been given some-
thing for parasites and this also killed the tick.
                                    —I-733, Rick, 34 yrs., Nebraska

Don't be alarmed if the animal's skin looks like it is coming off in torn, thin sheets. The lizard is most likely shedding, a natural, healthy periodic occurrence that starts at birth and ends at death.

<u>Eyes</u>—The eyes should be bright and clear, with no drooping or swollen eyelids and no discharge, tearing, or crusty residue. Iguanas' eyes should have a spunky alertness, and they will probably track and watch you as you move around the room. Remember, these are wild animals and their instincts put them on "yellow alert" when things in their environment change. How do they know you haven't actually come here to eat them?

<u>Mouth</u>—The inside of the iguana's mouth should be a pleasant, healthy pink with no yellow coloring or spongy, stringy, or cheesy mucous discharges. A gaping mouth could indicate a respiratory disease, especially if it is combined with a labored, forced wheezing sound from the iguana's lungs.

To check the inside of an iguana's mouth, hold the nose securely with your thumb and index finger and with the other hand pull down on the very tip of the dewlap, EXTREMELY slowly and gently. Opening a hatchling's mouth is not like raising the hood of a car. Be gentle and delicate, opening it just enough to peek inside and glimpse the mouth color.

<u>Nose</u>—When an iguana is improperly housed, it sometimes tries to get out. In the process of searching for an escape route, it may rub and bang its ros-

trum (nose) against the glass, wood, or wire of the cage. This can cause a rostral abrasion. If an iguana's nose seems like it has excessive damage, don't purchase the animal. Don't start off with a problem pet.

The nose should be free of any kind of runny or mucous discharge. Often, an iguana with this sign of illness will also have other visible illness indicators. You're better off not purchasing this animal

But healthy iguanas do discharge a clear, watery fluid out of their nostrils, in a kind of "snorting" action. When this fluid lands on the glass of the habitat, it dries and leaves salt crystals. Discharging this clear fluid is how iguanas, who do not sweat, regulate their bodies' salt balance.

Jaw—The number-one major medical problem with captive iguanas is metabolic bone disease (caused by calcium deficiency). One of the ways it manifests is as a soft, swollen jaw, often called "rubber" jaw. In extreme cases, an iguana's face can look puffy and grotesque.

Even if an iguana's jaw looks normal, you can check for the first signs of metabolic bone disease by carefully applying a light pressure on the sides of the iguana's jaw. The jaw should feel firm, not soft and spongy.

Be **very careful** when applying this pressure test—you don't want to worsen the problem if the animal is already suffering from early stages of a calcium deficiency. And if the disease is advanced, you might crack the iguana's jaw. Just a light pressure of the thumb and forefinger on the sides of the jaw will tell you what you need to know. Try this technique on several different iguanas to verify your conclusions.

Calcium deficiency can also be seen as a reduced or withdrawn lower jaw. Looking at the iguana's face from the side, the lower jaw does not align flush with the front of the upper jaw, but is drawn back and may also be a little swollen. This is not just a jaw-related problem; it is a malfunctioning of the calcium balance in the iguana.

Do not purchase an iguana with jaw problems, as it may have trouble eating. You don't want to start off with a calcium-deficient iguana. Inform the owners; calcium deficiencies can be corrected if caught early enough.

Vent—The vent is the opening through which the iguana defecates and also where its sex organs are located. To find the vent, hold the iguana vertically (as though it is standing up) about 8" to 12" from your face, looking at its belly. Where the tail attaches to the body is a horizontal slit or fold in the skin, and this is the vent.

There should be no discharge around or anything sticking to this area. A discharge from the vent could be a sign of sickness. As for feces, iguanas are very clean animals and when given the proper habitat space and substrate, they will always clean themselves after defecation. If the iguana is housed incorrectly, it could get feces stuck to its vent and not be sick. If you see signs of anything around the iguana's vent, at least investigate further to assess the cause.

Legs—Healthy iguanas should have rounded thighs and calves. Calcium deficiency problems also appear in iguanas' legs as noticeably swollen or excessively fat-looking legs. In severe cases the lizard may drag its rear legs.

Another very obvious result of calcium deficiency might be a twisted or distorted back (spine). Don't purchase animals like this, and tell the owner that he or she needs to take the iguana immediately to a qualified reptile veterinarian for care.

Stomach—If the iguana has recently eaten, its belly will look full and happy like Santa Claus' belly. The stomach area should not look thin or recessed.

One of the cutest things is to see a hatchling iguana with food all over its face, with that goofy expression they often have. Food on the face usually means food in the belly. If they are eating at the store or their current owner's house, they will most likely eat at your place.

Attitude—When you pick up your iguana it should be feisty. If it relaxes too completely in your hand, it might be sick (unless you are purchasing someone's tame iguana, or perhaps a really mellow captive-raised hatchling).

We picked a little guy that was hiding away from the other lizards because he "looked lonely." In retrospect, I think he may have been sick.
—I-835, Debi, 35 yrs., Oregon

A healthy iguana may try to escape from you when you go to pick it up, or it may squirm for a while in your hand trying to wriggle away. It may even try to whip you with its tail or bite you. Iguanas are wild animals and this is exactly what they do to protect themselves from death. Usually, once held in a gentle manner for a few minutes this feisty animal will settle down a little (see Chapter 8, Domestication, "Proper Handling").

I purchased my iguana, which was wild-caught (that's all there were back then), when he was 3 months old and about 15" in total length (SVL: 5"). He had the attitude of a 10-foot long, 250-pound alligator with Arnold Schwartzenegger muscles. It was so funny to watch, but he had the right cockiness, a healthy survival attitude.

Many people would not purchase an iguana like this for fear that it would be too difficult to tame. But a feisty young iguana will tame down in time, if you work at it. Over time, my iguana settled down into a tame and wonderful pet. These days, most iguanas are captive- or farm-raised and are much tamer from the start.

Different groups of hatchlings respond differently to stress in captivity, from a little nervous to totally insane. If you look in a cage of hatchlings, there might be one iguana that continually bangs into the walls, running around the cage as though Satan himself were on its tail. With pupils as large as dinner plates, the lizard appears constantly spooked.

Many people have written to say that they bought an extremely active iguana like this because they thought it was very healthy, but that the iguana always remained "over the edge." Avoid these hyperactive, out-of-control iguanas, which seem to be "damaged." In my experience, these hatchlings often stay crazy and are not a good choice for a pet.

I bought this iguana because a book had said to get an active iguana so you would be sure it wasn't sick. What this book described as a good choice was really a totally frightened iguana.   —I-764, Diana, 46 yrs., California

<u>Balance</u>—One of the more obscure ways of testing your iguana for health is the balance test. This technique was told to me by one of the big iguana farmers in Central America.

First, hold the hatchling iguana so it's resting in the palm of your hand, with your fingers lightly securing it. Extend your arm away from your body and slowly rotate your hand first to the left, then to the right. A normal, healthy iguana will automatically keep its head level, like a gyroscope. A sick animal will "freak out, start flopping around," the iguana farmer said. He said he is not a veterinarian or biologist, but has found that iguanas who "fail" the balance test often have a heavy parasite problem, or a problem in the brain.

<u>Missing or damaged body parts</u>—Some of the iguanas you want to purchase will not have all of their body parts. It can be a long, damaging road from Central or South America to a wholesaler in the U.S., Canada, or Europe, and then to the individual pet store.

Some wholesalers treat their iguanas with care, while others treat them like disposable diapers. When dealers handle hundreds and thousands of iguanas at a time, sometimes care gets lost in the shipment.

Wholesalers often store iguanas in wire cages. When the wholesaler wants, for instance, 200 hatchling iguanas for immediate shipment, he just grabs a handful and pulls them out of the cage. Sometimes the iguanas hang on to the wire because they are scared. If the person removing the iguanas doesn't use patience and care, and jerks the iguanas out of the cage, the lizard's toes or claws can be broken or torn.

And the wholesalers are not the only people who can cause this type of damage. Unknowledgeable pet store personnel, and even pet owners, can do the same thing. Iguanas may look like sturdy little dinosaurs, but they can get damaged like any other species on this planet if not handled appropriately.

Toes and feet should not be swollen, but a missing toe, if properly healed, will not affect the iguana's health. Iguanas can also have part of their tail missing without causing health problems.

Our iguana's tail was broken off when we got him. It was still an open wound at the time, but dry and not infected. Since then it has regrown about 5 inches. The new growth is very dark-colored, almost black. It does not have the crest as does the original part of the tail and it is blunt at the end. The scale pattern is more irregular in the new growth.   —I-554, Anthony, 29 yrs., Texas

If the tail breaks off, it won't grow back with the same look as the original tail. I know of no statistics on tail regeneration to make an absolute statement, but some evidence suggests that a tail broken within an iguana's first two months or so might grow back like the natural tail. After that time, the tail

---

SIDEBAR

Iguanas' Flexible Phalanges

The natural movements of an iguana's toes and fingers are very different than those of a mammal's! As an example, the rear toes can bend outward (only) as though they had a hinge joint; the exception is the shortest toe. The longest of the toes has three joints that allow the toe to bend at three separate sections. No one has ever given me a good scientific answer for why the toes bend like this, but I speculate that it allows the toes to spread out, covering more surface area—perhaps for better holds or options while climbing.

This could also be the reason why the front toes flop around like pieces of soft spaghetti. These toes don't have the flexibility at the joints like the rear feet, but they do have the ability to spread out. Anyone new to having an iguana as a pet could easily think these "silly" toes are all broken. That is why it is good to look at and handle a lot of iguanas before you make your final pick for a pet.

---

grows back somewhat, but "fully regenerated tails are never so long as unbroken tails" (#29). The new growth forms a stub that is usually brown or blackish in color.

Iguanas with these minor defects are perfectly good animals, you just have to ask yourself if these damaged or missing parts are important to you.

> One of the staff explained that he [the iguana] had been sold to a woman who caught the lizard's tail in the cage lid and broke it off. The woman no longer wanted the iguana because he was "flawed," so she brought him back to the store. —I-866, Kate, 41 yrs., California

Some people love iguanas no matter what imperfections might be present.

> Our latest and largest iguana [SVL: 13", TL: 3' 2", 4¾ lbs.] has a broken toe, is missing one left rear and one right front toe, and has scar tissue on her nose. She apparently suffered these traumas (maybe one big trauma) when she was younger. But they don't present a problem to her at all. They certainly make her look as unique as she is. —I-312, Darla, 39 yrs., Ohio

If minor defects are not a problem, at least try to negotiate with the iguana's owner for a reduction in the price of the animal since it is not the "standard equipped model."

Sick animals—If an iguana has symptoms of any of the major health problems mentioned in this chapter or Chapter 7, Medical Troubleshooting, DO NOT purchase it. There is a good chance it could die within the first month or so. It may sound cruel not to take this sick little guy home, but if this is your first iguana you will already have your hands full with a healthy one.

> *A few years ago I got two iguanas from a pet store and they died within a few days. I did not know much about iguanas and thought that I might have killed them. This was very upsetting and I did not get my next iguana for a couple of years because of it. Now I realize that the iguanas were sick when I got them and there was nothing that I could have done.*
>
> —I-774, Walter, 46 yrs., Arizona

Optional colors, shades, and patterns—Iguanas will vary somewhat in body color, patterns, size, and some minor physical characteristics depending on which country and region they came from. If you know where your iguana comes from, you'll have a better profile of your lizard.

For example, young iguanas from Mexico are a deep, lush green, but as adults this often fades to lighter green with brown and gold tonings. Even in regions within each country, the iguanas can be a little different. While I was doing iguana egg research in Mexico, the researcher who invited me there said that within a half- to one-mile radius, some iguanas had the little horns on their noses, like a rhinoceros, and some didn't.

SIDEBAR

Personal Power

Don't just walk away if you see a sick iguana. It is important to tell the people selling iguanas that you won't buy a sick iguana. But do let the person know about the possible health problem.

Once we start demanding better-quality animals, the people caring for these iguanas will be forced, monetarily at least, to pay attention to proper care. Then there will be fewer and fewer sick and damaged animals.

You can make a difference in the future lives of iguanas, but only if you open your mouth and let them know how you feel. If you don't, the whole damaging process will continue. You have the knowledge from this book, now it's your responsibility to use this knowledge to help correct wrongness. As Jane Goodall, the famous chimp researcher, said one rainy night here in Portland: "You cannot get through one single day without having an impact on the world around you. What you do makes a difference, and you have to decide what kind of difference you want to make."

I've noticed that no two iguanas are ever the same in markings and color. Two of my older males are beautiful with quite a bit of orange, especially during breeding season. The first was green as a baby and as he reached maturity he gradually changed colors. He's now about 7 years old. The other is about the same size and age and was not so green, but not yet so orange when I adopted him three years ago. Both have black stripes on their bellies, like little skeleton costumes.

Another male was already in transition when I adopted him two years ago. He is absolutely beautiful and has a very pretty face and green eyes. He has two small horns on the tip of his nose. I have two females that remained green. Both have white stripes on their bellies. One has brown eyes, the other golden eyes. The new baby I acquired is of course only a few months old and very pea green, with a lime green belly and gold eyes.

—I-200, Dianna, 47 yrs., Washington

One thing most iguana pet owners don't get to choose is their iguana's country of origin, which will determine the color, markings, and even the potential size of the lizard. Pet stores get their iguanas from a wholesaler and the wholesaler gets them from a dealer.

For example, the majority of the hatchlings for sale during one recent year were raised on farms in El Salvador and Colombia. So as a buyer, these were your two main choices. Figure 3.1 shows where most of the U.S. pet iguanas have come from since 1988, according to the U.S. Fish & Wildlife Service. These totals do not include iguanas that may have come into the country under the auspices of the U.S. Customs department, but these numbers are impossible to get.

What usually determines where your iguana comes from (if it's a hatchling) is the month you purchase it. Below is a rough hatching timetable for iguanas, courtesy of an American iguana farmer who has been raising iguanas in Central and South America for more than 10 years:

Mexico: the first of June to about June 15

Guatemala: the latter part of May to the first of June

Honduras: the first of May, give or take two weeks

El Salvador: about the same as Honduras, early May

Colombia: some in the southern part of Colombia hatch around the first of April; the middle of Columbia is around April 15; and the north part is about the first of May

Suriname: starts around November 15

Peru: the first part of November in Iquitos (northeastern Peru)

The iguana farmer told me that hatching times can easily vary by a couple of weeks or more on either side of these estimates. Heat and humidity are the main variables affecting the timetable. If rains come earlier or later than usual, or if it's hotter or cooler than normal, hatchlings will emerge accordingly.

Also, iguana hatchlings aren't always shipped immediately to a pet store

IGUANAS IMPORTED INTO THE U.S.*

	1988	1989	1990	1991	1992	1993	1994	1995	TOTAL
Columbia	1,000	7,120	153,813	129,831	240,505	363,114	341,088	162,224	1,398,695
Costa Rica	0	40	60	21	0	0	0	0	121
El Salvador	500	7,050	19,745	67,908	142,950	334,487	186,561	358,085	1,117,286
Guatemala	0	0	0	0	22,726	55,057	25,026	40,306	143,115
Guyana	4,288	2,378	4,170	4,952	2,556	1,117	302	2,500	22,263
Honduras	54,923	91,881	4,293	0	0	0	0	0	151,097
Mexico	137	2	2	19	12	13	20	203	408
Peru	7,502	7,940	22,786	17,605	7,025	5,100	7,534	60	75,552
Suriname	17,303	21,433	19,596	21,086	18,097	34,324	9,618	2,350	143,807
Others	22	2,000	0	10	15	9,179	143	640	12,009
Total	85,675	139,844	224,465	241,432	433,886	802,391	570,292	566,368	3,064,353

*Raw data of iguana import numbers courtesy of the U.S. Fish & Wildlife Service; compilation by Dunthorpe Press.

Figure 3.1: This table represents eight years of *Iguana iguana* imports into the U.S., as reported by U.S. Fish and Wildlife, which does not track all iguanas brought into the country. U.S. Customs Services also keeps track of iguana imports, but their data is almost impossible to get.

after they hatch. In fact, a few iguana farmers keep their hatchlings an additional four to five months before shipping them to ensure healthier lizards.

FARM-RAISED VS. WILD-CAUGHT

In the past, hatchlings would come into pet stores skinny, sick with diseases, stressed, and running crazy into the sides of the cage. Now that almost all of the iguanas are farm-raised, they come in fat, plump, healthy, and non-stressed.
—pet store owner in Portland, Oregon

As shown in Figure 3.1, the U.S. Fish and Wildlife records show more than 3 million iguanas that have been imported into this country alone since 1988. Until recently, these were almost all wild-caught animals. That means that a group of people (usually local children) went into the jungle where hatchling iguanas were located and grabbed as many as they could, getting paid for each captured lizard. It is estimated that 30% to 50% of these iguanas died in the process from capture to arriving at a pet store in the U.S. or Europe.

Removing wild iguanas for the pet trade is just one way the jungle slowly loses its natural balance of iguana populations. You can help to reduce the numbers of iguanas taken from the jungle by purchasing only captive- or farm-raised iguanas. These should be the only type of iguanas available to the public in the '90s and beyond.

I once heard that for every 100 iguanas taken from the wild, only one lives to make it to the pet shop. Then someone buys it and it survives for two months or so. —I-519, Ellen, 40 yrs., Louisiana

Luckily, in the last couple of years most of the iguanas imported from Central and South America have been raised on farms. In fact, one breeder raised 65,000 iguanas on a single farm in one year. As the name implies, farm-raised iguanas are raised somewhat like commercial livestock.

In the future, I envision inspectors who would check the shipments and put an emblem or stamp on the container to verify that it contains farm-raised iguanas, maybe even with a quality rating. This way, as purchasers of iguanas we won't have to guess how the lizard was raised. But for now, if you see a plump and healthy one- or two-month-old hatchling, most likely it's farm-raised.

How Iguana Farms Work

The iguana farms have a breeding area and a place for the young iguanas once they hatch (for further details on this topic, read Chapter 9, Breeding). There are two basic ways that these iguanas are farmed:

(a) Gravid female iguanas are caught in the wild and held in free-range pens until they lay their eggs. The eggs are gathered and put in incubators built by the farmers. Once the eggs hatch, the hatchlings are cared for until they are sold. In this scenario, the farmers release the adult females back into the wild. The next year, they find a new group of gravid females and start the cycle over again.

(b) The other option, captive-bred and farm-raised, means that the farmers raise their own breeding stock in captivity, rather than taking gravid females from the wild each year.

This second approach to farming has a more positive impact on the environment. Because no gravid female iguanas are taken from the jungle after the first year, future wild iguana populations can increase naturally. Local people (farmers) can still make money selling iguanas—and people like yourself can still own an iguana as a pet.

To confuse you a little, but not on purpose, there is yet another type of non-wild-caught iguana. Usually these animals are bred and raised by enthusiastic iguana pet owners on a hobby level. It's unlikely that you'll see these hatchlings for sale in a pet store; it's more by word of mouth at local herp society meetings.

As of now, the U.S. and Europe have no large-scale *Iguana iguana* farms. They can't compete with Latin American farms, whose labor costs are very low. Also, Latin American farms don't require expensive supplemental heating, lighting, and humidity equipment, because these regions possess ideal natural conditions for these lizards.

The Advantages of Farm-Raised Iguanas

My female iguana was wild-caught and was loaded with ticks and worms.
                                        —I-791, Dan, 28 yrs., Missouri

There is actually no comparison between a farm-raised and a wild-caught iguana. The only one to consider is the farm-raised.

Because farm-raised iguanas get fed regularly each day and are not threatened (stressed) by predators, they should grow faster than wild-caught iguanas. They are also healthier, not only because of the consistent feedings, but also because they are kept away from jungle problems such as ticks and parasites.

From the people that I have talked with, it appears that farm- or captive-raised iguanas are much calmer and tamer. Some of their "wildness" has been reduced by their captive, controlled environment and their regular contact with humans.

When I was at the Belize Zoo in Central America gathering information on captive breeding, I was told by Tony Garel (one of the researchers there) that the iguanas they raised in captivity were very tame. He said, "In the beginning, the small hatchlings would bounce off the walls when we entered the enclosure. But eventually they got to know that you brought food for them. . . .

They were a lot more calm. They would come right up in front of you and feed."

I recently went to a large Reptile Expo where all kinds of reptiles were for sale. One vendor had about 50 hatchling iguanas on display in a (human) kids' plastic swimming pool, minus the water. These hatchlings didn't try to bite or run away and were as docile as ants.

My male and female iguanas mated and produced fertile eggs. When the first baby hatched, I just reached in and picked him up. He stayed on my finger. Even at 3 months old he is still calmer than most iguanas of the same age.
—I-326, Mark, 26 yrs., California

Each year, iguana farmers seem to devise better systems of shipping their farm-raised lizards to minimize the death rate during export. In the old days, a 50% death rate was considered low. I was talking recently to one experienced farmer who said that in the last three or four shipments, he had zero death losses; another farmer reported a death rate of less than 1%.

As a side note, in 1993 there were some beautiful South American farm-raised iguanas with bluish markings that all seemed to die soon after arriving in the U.S. One importer told me that the farmer who raised these iguanas was new to the business and fed the hatchlings the wrong type of food, which caused them to die. Someone else said that the hatchlings died because they were left too long on the tarmac in Quito, Ecuador, at high altitude and cold temperatures, and got respiratory disease. The lesson here is that all aspects of iguana farming are important—not just breeding, hatching, and feeding.

SIZE OPTIONS: HATCHLING, JUVENILE, ADULT

Now that you know where and how to choose a healthy iguana, the next step is to pick the size iguana you want. It will be easier to discuss iguanas if we put a label on the different sizes that are available. Throughout this book, I'll use the following terms for size classifications: hatchling, juvenile, and adult. I didn't invent these terms; this is how people dealing with iguanas have been labeling them for a long time.

There was a 3-year-old iguana advertised in the paper here for $100. I went to see it . . . it looked like a hatchling!! It lived all of its life in a little terrarium.
—I-519, Ellen, 40 yrs., Louisiana

One thing to keep in mind is that the size of an iguana is not always an accurate measure of age. Iguanas of the same age can vary dramatically in size. My iguana at every age looked huge to most pet owners and veterinarians. It's not that he was huge, it's more that other pet iguanas his age were extremely small because of inadequate care. The truth is that he probably followed about a normal growth pattern for a healthy iguana living in the jungle.

Scientists doing research with iguanas use the measurement of "SVL," or snout (nose)-vent (where they defecate) length, which is the actual body length of the lizard. At any point in an iguana's life, it can break part of its tail off, thus reducing its overall length. So SVL provides an absolute measurement, a fixed point without variables, for an iguana. It establishes a good, solid reference for describing and comparing iguanas' sizes.

For us pet owners, another reference when talking about our iguanas is the tail length, a measurement from the vent to the tip or end of the tail. Whatever the SVL, the tail is usually about twice that length—if it hasn't been broken.

The final measurement is the total length, or "TL," a combination of SVL and tail length. The total measurement is used mostly by pet owners, not by scientists.

But remember that pet iguanas' living conditions can vary extremely from place to place, making the SVL for captive pets at best a ballpark figure for determining age. What the SVL can be used for is to determine if an iguana is a hatchling, juvenile, or adult.

Hatchling

"Hatchling" is the proper term to describe what most people call a baby iguana. Any iguana just out of its egg up to a few months old could be considered a hatchling. The SVL varies with the iguana's health and genetics, but a good guess for the average SVL for a newly hatched iguana is about 2⅔", or 6.76 cm (#30).

Hatchlings from the same clutch can have extremely different personality traits, but they all look about the same, with very intense light, dark, and phosphorescent green coloring; large, alert space-creature eyes; a head that seems a little too big for its body; and a goofy, silly, kind of sweet look on its face. In this stage, they all are small and cute, like puppies or kittens (this analogy is for all you mammal fans just getting into reptiles for the first time).

In the hatchling stage, iguanas should be fed twice a day. If your iguana is already eating when you purchase it, then there's an excellent chance it will continue to eat for you when you get it home. As with any animal, the younger the iguana, the easier it is to tame and adapt to your needs. Remember, though, that any animal in this "baby stage" can get diseases, stress, sickness, and can die more easily than an adult animal.

Raising an iguana from a hatchling or juvenile is exciting because they grow and change so rapidly in these stages. In his first year, my iguana almost doubled his size. He always showed some sign of change, whether in size, color, personality, attitude, or preferences. I also noticed the progressive refinement of his temperament, such as his lack of body tension when I picked him up (indicating his growing trust of me).

Reality Check

In case you missed my point earlier, this cute little creature that begins life with an SVL of less than 3 inches could end up measuring 20" SVL and 5+ feet long overall and weigh 13 pounds (in five to eight years). The question is: Are you willing to accept this responsibility?

Iguanas' defense systems vary depending on their size. Hatchling iguanas can move with warp speed: One blink of the eye and your hatchling can be on the other side of the room. Because hatchlings are so small, running away is their main defense against becoming an iguana burger for some predator. Adult iguanas, in contrast, are much slower but can defend themselves using their large, thick tails as a whip, their strong jaws and razor-sharp teeth to bite, and their needle-like claws to scratch and gouge.

Juvenile

The juvenile stage lasts from when an iguana leaves the hatchling stage until it reaches adulthood. Juvenile iguanas are fragile and their personalities are still pliable. How you handle and take care of them in this stage will help determine their future personality and health.

If an iguana is not cared for properly and is subjected to bad experiences as a juvenile, it could be a problem as an adult—just like humans. Among the hundreds of iguana questionnaires returned to me over the years, I've seen numerous instances where iguanas do remember good and bad experiences. And they just plain remember a lot of different "things." Fill your iguana's head with good "things" as soon as you can.

> *I obtained my iguana from an individual who bought the iguana for his son, who never treated it right and could never get the animal to calm down. I had to work with the iguana a lot, and eventually it did calm down, but oddly enough when these same people came to visit one day, many months later, the iguana flipped out, and it was pretty tough calming him down.*
> —I-557, Roy, 32 yrs., Texas

Juveniles can be jumpy and skittish, like juveniles of most species going through a rapid growth period. This is the adolescent or teenage stage for an iguana. Their sexual hormones are also beginning to develop, which makes all creatures a little crazy.

Juvenile iguanas are starting to feel more powerful than when they were

SIDEBAR

Reminder: One Iguana Per Household

Iguanas prefer their own company.   —I-626, Gail, 48 yrs., New York

Here is an important point that will come up in several different chapters in this book: **Iguanas are very territorial!** This has to do with food, heat, and sex (sounds like a basic plot line for many of the movies we see nowadays). This territorial attitude continues throughout an iguana's life. Adult iguanas (especially males) will fight, sometimes to the death, for dominance of their territory, especially during breeding season.

When a clutch of iguanas hatches, the first hatchling in its territory that gets the most food and the proper heat gradient (for digesting this food) grows the fastest. This iguana, with its larger body, will find it easier to keep the other clutchmates away from the food or off a particular tree limb that offers access to the best heat.

When iguanas become sexually mature, the females typically choose to mate with the largest males. Our bully who has hogged the food and heat resources will probably be first in line as the female's breeding partner.

Animal behaviorists have known for a long time that the density of animals within a given area affects their social interactions. Researchers have found that if territorial animals, such as iguanas, feel that there are too many others of their kind nearby, they organize into a hierarchy. The dominant individuals typically try to make the less dominant animals leave, often through aggressive behavior.

By putting two or more iguanas in the same, too-small environment, you in essence increase their density. What then happens is that your iguanas shift into this hierarchical mode, which can entail aggressive, hostile interactions.

A recent year-long scientific experiment studied juvenile iguanas' reactions to the presence of adult iguanas. One aspect of this research looked at possible health problems related to stress when juvenile and adult male iguanas are housed in close proximity:

Over the long term, social stress may also lead to depressed immune function and increased susceptibility to infectious agents.
—Allison C. Alberts, iguana researcher (#35)

Because of iguanas' natural reaction to increased density and the aggression problems associated with territorial control, **I recommend only one iguana as a pet per household**, whether hatchling, juvenile, or adult.

Other books don't address this problem. Some books even say you can have as many iguanas as you like. One herp publication recommended (wrongly, I believe) getting several iguanas because this would encourage them all to eat better.

After six years of research, reading hundreds of returned iguana questionnaires from across the U.S., Canada, and Europe, and seeing many iguanas in people's homes, I'm convinced that iguanas don't get along well together in tight living conditions. It's very apparent to me that more than one iguana (except for those people who want to breed their iguanas and have a huge habitat space) will cause the owner and iguanas nothing but trouble in the long run.

I got both of my iguanas when they were about 6 months old. They are now 4 years old. Both _males_. It's very stressful for the both of them. They always have to be in separate rooms or they will immediately start to fight. They are my babies; I can't give either one away. I wish someone would have told me about the potential problems with two iguanas when I bought mine. I would have gotten only one. —I-605, Laura, 31 yrs., Canada

If you still think iguanas get along together, take a look at some of the vivid personal stories in Chapter 4, Housing, "Cagemates," and Chapter 9, Breeding, from iguana owners with two iguanas. Iguanas don't need other iguanas for companionship. They are not pack animals like dogs.

small, vulnerable, afraid little hatchlings. Sometimes, they test how powerful they are around you. They may turn up the threat factor by whipping their tail, moving quickly, or lunging at you as though they are going to tear you apart. Part of this is practice in controlling their "space" (properly termed "territory"). Sometimes they may even bite, but the bite of a juvenile iguana is more disconcerting than damaging.

Now is the time to stand up to their power plays. If you let them have control now, you will have problems later. Just like with that teenage kid in your house, if your juvenile iguana gets its way completely, your life in the future will be a living hell.

Adult

In the wild, iguanas typically reach sexual maturity (adulthood) at 2 or 3 years of age. In captivity, where living and growing conditions are often minimal at best, age is not a good reference point. The true gauge of the transition from juvenile to adult is the SVL.

As I mentioned earlier, iguana researchers use the SVL because it is a constant, reliable measurement. Unfortunately for my attempts to simplify terms, however, researchers use different words than pet owners do to classify iguanas' life stages.

Dr. John A. Phillips of the Center for Reproduction of Endangered Species (CRES), Zoological Society of San Diego, has done a lot of research with iguanas over the years. As a research scientist, he describes an iguana as an "adult" when it is capable of reproduction.

A female green iguana at 250 mm (10″) SVL or larger is large enough to breed successfully. A male iguana can breed, and therefore be considered an adult, when his SVL exceeds 160 mm (6″)—unless it is subordinate to a larger male. This subordination is accomplished by intimidation from the larger male nearby, which causes stress in the smaller one. This stress essentially wipes out the smaller iguana's sex drive, at least until he can find his own territory to control.

Researchers such as Dr. Phillips use "non-reproductive" as the term that encompasses hatchlings and juveniles. For green iguanas, this would include females with SVL less than 10″ or males under 6″. Thus the "reproductive" category replaces the more common "adult" term for most researchers.

This way of describing iguanas as reproductive and non-reproductive is exact and scientific, but I don't think after all these years that iguana pet owners, wholesalers, distributors, and retailers will adopt these terms. They are accustomed to saying something like, "Hey Charley, Acme Pet store wants five adults, three juveniles, and 10 hatchlings." But I believe that knowing how the scientific community categorizes iguanas can help you gain a deeper level of understanding of your iguana.

Now back to the semi-science world of pet iguanas. Technically, for an iguana to be an adult it must be sexually mature. But remember, this is a function of SVL rather than age. If your iguana hasn't reached the designated reproductive length, it's not an adult and is not capable of breeding.

Variations in care (food, heat, UV light, cage size, being housed alone, non-stress, etc.) can accelerate or hinder an iguana's growth to adulthood. As an example, imagine two iguanas born on the same day but given different levels of care. At 5 years of age, one might be less than a total length (TL) of 2' (SVL: 8") and the other as long as 5' TL (SVL: 19").

In extreme cases, I have seen 4- to 6-year-old iguanas that still had the body size and physical characteristics of a juvenile. In these situations, the immaturity was caused by improper care or by being housed with larger, dominant, aggressive male iguanas.

People are always asking me if I can guess their iguana's age. There is no way that I or anyone else can accurately tell how old your iguana is by its SVL or by any other measures. My iguana had an SVL of 15½" at 2½ years old, while the oldest iguana I saw, at 29 years old, also had an SVL of 15½". Same size, but more than 26 years difference in age.

If you didn't raise an iguana from a hatchling, or have reliable information from a previous owner who did, you'll have to settle for guessing your iguana's age. Just remember that the passage of your iguana to the adult stage—regardless of your iguana's age—is crucial to note, so you can be prepared for the special challenges you'll face as the owner of a sexually mature iguana.

Other Characteristics of Adult Iguanas

By the time an iguana becomes an adult, it has cemented most of its habits about food, life, and being a pet. For example, if you allow a hatchling or juvenile to develop picky eating habits, you'll have an adult that's a picky eater. That's why I always stress providing a variety of food for iguanas. And iguanas need a variety not just of food types and textures, but also of life experiences, to keep them flexible and fulfilled.

SIDEBAR

Owners of Female Iguanas: Take Note

The SVL at which female iguanas become sexually mature should be treated as a red flag by pet owners. This measurement is a countdown to when your female might begin producing eggs, which they do whether or not a male iguana is around. Female iguanas face potential health hazards at this time, including egg binding and calcium deficiencies. If you know approximately when your female is sexually mature, you can help reduce some of these problems by being prepared (see Chapter 9, Breeding, for more details).

If you purchased your iguana as a hatchling, as an adult it should be sweet and nice. It will have gone through the rough growth and assertive stage of a juvenile and will be settling into its life as an older iguana.

When an adult iguana gets around 3 or 4 years old, you're going to see a change. He's going to get a little lazier and quieter and more dependent on you. But he's not going to get meaner, not in the least little bit. If anything, you'll be able to do more with him. He'll just be a limp rag when you pick him up because he'll trust you and love you so much.   —I-11, Patty, Washington

They really calm down with age and size. I think they feel less threatened as they get bigger. I'd say major calming down by 2 years old.
—I-775, Karen, 37 yrs., Arizona

By the time my iguana, Za, turned 5 years old, he would just melt into my arms when I picked him up and would be happy to settle there all day. (But an adult iguana doesn't always stay settled into this Mr. or Ms. Sweet persona. During the breeding season, iguanas—especially males—can offer weeks of grief to us pet owners. See Chapter 9, Breeding, for some chilling real stories.)

Not all iguanas are as lucky as Za, with great food and care. But even if an iguana had a substandard life as someone else's pet and has developed a bad attitude, you can still turn this situation around when the iguana becomes your pet. Iguanas often show positive changes for people who improve their lives.

At first she [SVL: 16", 6½ yrs.] had to get to know us. She had to overcome abuse, abandonment, shelter shuffles, and an air ride. So understandably she was very frightened. I talk to all of my animals, and within a week she had settled into our home. She came in as a 20 on your [1-to-50] tameness scale, and almost immediately, in six days, turned into a 1. No lie. But this is because I give a lot of love and care to my animals.
—I-635, Andrew, 38 yrs., Wisconsin

One of the physical characteristics that comes with age in iguanas (depending on what country it came from) is that they tend to lose their bright, intense green color in exchange for light brown and gold tinges, especially on their arms and legs, as I have mentioned before.

When he was young he was just bright green. After he shed, he was almost fluorescent. As he has gotten older [now 3 yrs.] he has gotten more and more brown. Now he is sort of in-between brown and green. His belly has remained bright green, though.   —I-724, Robby, 14 yrs., Utah

Another characteristic of older iguanas is that males often have huge heads and jowls, which make them look powerful and assertive even without aggressive behavior.

Something that is not obvious until you own an iguana is how rare it is for an adult iguana to still have a full-length tail. Once your iguana gets into the adult stage, keeping the tail intact can be a full-time job. Nearly anything and everything can damage the tail. Za at more than 5 years old still had a completely intact tail, the result of extreme vigilance (and luck) on my part when he was out of his habitat.

I know of one iguana who was exploring the owner's living room and had part of its tail cut off in a fan accident. Another iguana had the tip of its tail bitten off when the lizard lay across the top of a pet gerbil's cage. If you are considering adopting an older iguana that's missing part of its tail, remember that a full tail is not a prerequisite for good health; it's only as important as you feel it is.

Many of the adult iguanas for sale now were probably raised in captivity as a hatchling or a juvenile, not wild-caught as an adult. In the dark "old days," more wild adult iguanas were brought into the country for sale. But today you almost never see large wild-caught adults because there are fewer left in the jungle. The larger an iguana is, the easier it is to spot in the trees. These are the ones that some of the local Latin American people kill for food. In addition, if humans can see the iguanas, birds of prey and other predators can also see them easily.

Capturing a large adult iguana now requires longer trips deeper into remote parts of the jungle. This takes too much time, and often the adult will die from stress in transport back to "civilized life." So it is a self-defeating process.

Even with extra doses of love and care, an adult iguana—wild-caught or captive-raised—with an aggressive, nasty, assertive attitude might not be tamable for a long time, or at all (see Chapter 8, Domestication, for further details). There are basically two kinds of adult iguanas for sale: "sour" and "sweet."

Sour Adult

The most common adult iguana for sale is the monster from hell, because most owners don't want to give up a great iguana. Perhaps the monster from hell's owner got tired of the lizard slowly over the years—stopped handling it and providing special care. One day, the owner decides to dump the iguana.

I got my iguana [SVL: 11", TL: 3', 4 yrs.] at about 3 years of age. Rated 25. She did not bite, she was just frightened and not trusting. After a couple of months things changed considerably. She was quite trusting and got frightened only on occasion. She is no doubt a 1 at this time [one year later]. Extremely tame.
　　　　　　　　　　　　　　　　　　　　—I-322, Marty, 22 yrs., Ohio

My iguana [SVL: 16½"] was around 6 or 7 years old when I got him and was a wild monster from hell. I rated him at 50 [the top # for being wild]. Not longer than 1¼ years later he was a 20. Special hand-fed treats like dandelions helped. He soon allowed me to pet his head, but I never forced myself on him.

If he did not want to be petted, he would turn his head away, and I would leave.   —I-364, Lynda, 30 yrs., Maryland

A large majority of the older iguanas that I have seen and heard about can adjust and be a fine pet even if they didn't get a lot of handling when they were younger. But it's not the iguana that makes the change as much as the new owner. Certain people just have the touch, and to them it's not "uphill" but an experience "upward." They make wild animals feel safe, and that is the foundation of domestication. If you don't have this magic touch, a monster from hell <u>is not for you.</u>

My iguana [SVL: 13³/4", TL: 3' 4¹/4", 2¹/2 yrs.] bit its teenage owner and she no longer wanted him. He was not handled except for the few occasions when they removed him from the tank for cleaning, and then with gloves only. He'd had very limited human contact, and he feared touch at first. The cure: consistent handling, touching, trying to earn his trust, and letting him see it wasn't a bad experience. I turned my iguana loose in the downstairs bathroom, where he began to trust and climb upon me. He soon would paw at his cage to be held or let out to interact.   —I-798, Teri, 35 yrs., New Hampshire

The first time I met our iguana was the most painful for him and me. His owner at the time offered him nothing other than food and water, and the iguana had almost no outside contact for almost six months. I couldn't resist the challenge of handling and taming him. I asked if I could remove him from his cage and was warned that it would be at my own risk. I didn't start to realize how bad this was going to be until I opened the lid and everyone standing around stepped back, far back.

At first the iguana was friendly—"at first" being equal to about 3 seconds. Then he bolted up his branch and from his cage. I caught him in mid-air much like a football player catches the ball above his head with one hand and pulls it in close. At that point he began slashing and scratching and lashing and biting. My right arm absorbed nearly all of this to the point of looking much like a block of cheese that had been grated. He even broke a nail on me.

But eventually he settled down and after about 15 minutes I had him cradled like a baby with his eyes closed and his claws being trimmed by his at-the-time owner. A couple of weeks later he was our newest adopted child. He has tamed considerably and occasionally still enjoys a cradling and belly rub.
                    —I-661, Chris, 22 yrs., Nevada

An older woman, Dorothy, who loves iguanas, told me this story:

One day I was in a pet store and asked if I could handle the adult iguana in the cage. The owner was very nice and polite but said that no one could touch or handle the lizard; it was too wild. I kept asking, so the owner said OK. He came

back with some leather gloves to protect me. I said, "Oh, I don't need those things." I stuck my hands in the cage and the iguana emerged without a struggle and settled into my arms. The owner couldn't believe what he was seeing. I said, "All it needed was some love and gentle caring."

Some people purchase adult iguanas because they want a full-grown iguana—now. For these people time, patience, and adjustment to a sour iguana could be a long-term project, but worth the wait.

My female iguana [SVL: 12½", TL: 2' 8", 3 yrs.] was acquired when she was almost full-grown (rated 50—wild!). But she is so nice now you could not imagine it. —I-537, John, 22 yrs., Louisiana

I did not expect him [SVL: 18", TL: 3' 1", 8 yrs.] to respond as quickly as he did to me. I thought I would be bundling him up in a towel for the rest of his life to change his cage. He also did not seem to have a good personality at first, but he grew to like and trust me, and I grew to like and trust him. He has developed a regal, but likable, personality. —I-364, Lynda, 30 yrs., Maryland
[AUTHOR'S NOTE: Wrapping a towel around an iguana is one way to secure a squirming or thrashing iguana for temporary situations such as trimming their nails.]

Of the people I've heard about who help make the change in these wild iguanas, nearly all are females.

The store tried to talk me out of purchasing this large adult male. They said he was too wild. By the second night I was able to hand feed him, pick him up, and pet him. Four months later I would rate him a 1, loving and affectionate. —I-454, Tina, 26 yrs., Illinois

Women tend to move slower and talk more gently than men. Women are natural nurturers. Their more soothing actions allow the iguana to relax into its new situation more easily. But gentleness is only one part of the taming formula (see more in Chapter 8, Domestication).
I want to make it clear that to try to tame an unruly adult iguana can be a major undertaking. It's a very trying daily task. Unlike hatchlings or juveniles, who are more likely to pretend aggression, an adult iguana means business. If the lizard is mad, it's best to leave it alone until it settles down. A large adult iguana can inflict great pain with the whipping action of its tail. A large 4- to 5-foot, 15-pound male iguana can be a kick-ass, focused, fighting machine!

We had our male iguana for a long time, but when we got our dog we got rid of our iguana. Every time the dog would come in barking and making a ruckus the iguana would get upset and would lash its tail. One day the iguana broke

some furniture with his whipping tail. We found a new home for the iguana.
                    —I-539, Darlene, 26 yrs., Mississippi
    [AUTHOR'S NOTE: I think I would have gotten rid of the raucous dog.]

An adult iguana has teeth like a serrated bread knife that can shred you like a shark, down to the bone, if it gets really mad. Remember this if you have a hatchling or juvenile now—make friends with and train your lizard when it is young and small to avoid the more difficult situations an adult can pose.

I received my iguana [SVL: 14", TL: 3' 6"] as an adult from a friend after the iguana had bitten him rather badly. The iguana has, by the way, never tried to bite me.   —I-556, Sharon, 40 yrs., New York

The older sour adult can usually be tamed, but the degree of tameness depends on how wild it is now and how patient the new owner will be. No matter how you cut it, it takes the patience of Job and the love and caring of Mother Theresa to make a good pet of these animals. You either have what it takes, or you don't.

Sweet Adult

The other type of adult iguana is rarely seen in a pet store and more likely found in a newspaper ad or by word of mouth at, for example, a herp club meeting. Of the half-dozen cases I've seen of "sweet" adult iguanas up for adoption, most were the result of changes within their human owner's family unit. More often than not, the family wanted to start raising captive-born human offspring (the common term is "raising a family" or "raising children").

For most of these owners, it's a gut-wrenching decision to give up their sweet adult iguana. They love their iguana dearly but feel that once the human baby is born they won't have enough time for their pet.

Our iguana [SVL: 17½", TL: 4' 3", 7 yrs., 10 lbs.] was given to us through our vet. His other parents raised him from a baby to 5 years. They had to move back up north and didn't want to subject him to the cold. They did a great job taming him. He loves to be petted and will follow you through the house.
                    —I-786, Miriam & Wolf, 28 yrs., Florida

These owners of sweet adult iguanas are not going to let just anyone have their lizard. You will probably have to tell them your life history and give promises about your future plans for the iguana.

Getting one of these sweet creatures provides the chance to own a large iguana instantly. The iguana may have been well fed and housed in a great environment, and now all it needs is a new loving caretaker. You don't have to wait years for it to grow up; it's here now.

Remember, you should never be in a hurry to purchase an iguana. Check the temperament of your potential pet, which may take several visits. If the iguana happens to take food from the owner's hand, you should also try doing this.

Iguanas can get very territorial in their habitat, and if you try to touch it in there it may behave more assertively. Have the lizard taken out of the habitat so you both are on "neutral" ground and so you can interact with it. (Your future iguana should be accustomed to coming out of its habitat on a regular basis.) Make sure the owner lets you handle the iguana at some point in your visits—don't take any excuses. Sooner or later, you need to know how it reacts with you, and you definitely need to know before you bring the iguana home. The real proof is when you handle the lizard.

In the perfect scenario a friendly iguana will be docile and relaxed, will enjoy being held, and may squirm only a little at first to get settled on your arm. As a helpful note, if you are nervous about handling the iguana, it can get nervous, too. So just relax.

Many people make sure that their iguana is only "their" pet by not allowing other people to touch or hold the iguana. In the long run, I believe this restricts the animal from full participation in the real world. If the owners are the only ones that have handled your new iguana, it may not be comfortable with you right away.

I always tried to let my iguana be touched by all kinds of people: children, adults, Boy Scouts, TV reporters, other iguana owners, and even government officials. So Za was relaxed everywhere I took him. Even during the few weeks of breeding season when he was a pain in the butt at home, he was a perfect gentleman at the schools I visited for show-and-tell. Kids touched him and he'd stay completely relaxed—never a hint of meanness the whole time we were there. I believe that this tolerance for a wide variety of people and situations is a healthy goal for your iguana.

MALE VS. FEMALE

People ask me which gender makes the best pet. There are pros and cons to both male or female iguanas. You should read Chapter 1, Iguana: The Species, "Male/Female Physical Characteristics," and Chapter 9, Breeding, to get a clearer picture of what each gender offers.

Remember, though, you will be able to choose your iguana's gender only if you get an adult iguana. With a hatchling or young juvenile, you won't know if your future iguana is male or female; it's pretty much the luck of the draw.

In the end, the best animal is the one that gets along best with you.

HOW TO GET YOUR IGUANA HOME

There are bits of key information and some quotations that I keep repeating over and over throughout this book. This is not the result of poor editing or a memory lapse, it's just that certain pieces of information are really important for your iguana's health and survival.

One of these repeated ideas is that before you can take your iguana home you need to do what first? . . . That's right. You must set up the iguana's habitat and make sure that all the equipment is fully functioning.

Now that you have a functioning habitat, we can talk about transporting your iguana home. Your iguana's transition to its new environment should be as calm and stress-free as possible. Undue stress may disrupt the iguana's eating for a day or two, or even cause it to stop eating completely.

There are many options for transporting your iguana, depending on how large it is. For hatchlings to small juveniles, I prefer a linen bag. Linen is lightweight material and has plenty of space between its fibers for air, but the iguana can't see out. The bag acts much like a peregrine falcon's hood over its head or a horse's blinders—what they can't see can't scare them. It keeps them calm.

If you need a bag, you can create it easily with a sewing machine or by hand. Here are sample dimensions for making your own bag: For an iguana 5" to 6" SVL and 15" to 18" overall, the bag should be 20" long and 24" in diameter. For a larger iguana, extrapolate from these dimensions. As an option, you could use a pillowcase. Tie the end of the bag with string or rubber band.

The pet store where I purchased my iguana gave me a linen bag for transporting my iguana home. Find out from the person you are purchasing your iguana from if they have such a bag or have another technique that worked for them.

When I brought my iguana home from the pet store, I had to keep feeling to see if there "really" was an iguana in the bag, because he was so small (TL: 15") and lightweight. To see the bag move was actually a relief.

Pay attention! Sometimes it's hard to tell with a small hatchling where it is in the bag, and which side is up. It's important that the bag stays flat on your lap so the iguana doesn't get tangled inside. Make sure when you tie the bag closed that no iguana parts are getting tied up as well. It can easily happen.

Also, bring some paper towels with you in case your lizard gets overexcited and defecates on the way home. When an iguana gets suddenly stressed or is jostled around, it may defecate. The Boy Scout motto—"Be Prepared"—applies here.

A linen bag should not be used to hold an iguana that is more than 2 feet in total length. One option for iguanas over this size is the same linen bag but now just made into a kind of hood to cover the iguana's head.

Some adult iguanas are trained to ride in the car like a cat or a dog. Just remember, transporting an iguana safely really requires two people, one to drive the car and the other to make sure that the iguana is secure on the passenger's lap. Ask the owner if your future pet is comfortable riding in a car, or how they transport it. Better yet, if their iguana rides in the car, have the owner bring the iguana to your home.

A word of caution about car transport: I read a newspaper article about a problem that arose with an iguana riding loose in the car, and this is not some far-fetched, one-in-a-million type of accident. Any animal loose in a vehicle is like a time bomb ready to explode.

A pet green iguana leaped onto a driver, causing him to lose control of his car, which crashed into another car stopped at a traffic light. A third collided with the first two. The three drivers and one passenger were slightly injured.
—from *Derrick*, a newspaper in Oil City, Pennsylvania,
26 April 1993

I had my iguana in the car one day. He wandered around and crawled under the gas pedal, and as I was trying to get to him, I hit a curb.
—I-393, James, 19 yrs., California

ONCE HOME (OVERVIEW)

I noticed about 4 months after owning my iguana that she began pooping two or more times a day, and she had never pooped more than once a day before. I took a fecal sample to the vet, who found that my iguana was full of parasites. The vet gave me medicine to get rid of them.
—I-706, Melodie, 41 yrs., Tennessee

Once your iguana is home and settled, take its first feces to the veterinarian to test for parasites. Make arrangements with the veterinarian ahead of time and call around for prices, which vary greatly. The majority of pet stores do not test their iguanas for parasites. It's too difficult for them to keep the iguanas parasite-free, with new—possibly infected—iguanas arriving all the time.

Dollar for dollar this simple test will save you a lot of money in possible veterinarian bills, and of course keep your iguana healthy. Iguanas can actually die from an overload of parasites (see Chapter 7, Medical Troubleshooting, "Worms"). And don't put this test off until another day. Do it immediately or you will just keep postponing it until it never gets done. I see this procrastination—tomorrow, tomorrow—all the time. Like the Nike shoe ad says, "Just Do It."

Give your iguana a few days or weeks to feel at home in its new environment before you start to interact. This will also give you time to think of a name for your iguana. If you're stumped for ideas—or if you want a good laugh—check Appendix C for more than 500 names that owners have already given their iguanas.

Once you start handling your iguana, keep it to a minimum until the lizard has adjusted to its home. Also, it is important to have a hide box (see Chapter 4, Housing, "Hide Box") or equivalent in the habitat so your animal can periodically retreat to a place where it feels safely hidden from the stress of the world.

This chapter has given you a wide range of knowledge on choosing the right iguana and the right places to find your future pet, or perhaps helped you decide against even getting an iguana. It was my hope in writing this chapter to improve your ability to make the best possible choices. The final decision is now yours.

CHAPTER 4

Housing

Simplify, simplify. —Henry David Thoreau

GENERAL HOUSING CONSIDERATIONS

Lots of people don't realize how much room an iguana needs.
—V-136, Dr. Michel, 38 yrs., Washington

Use the Wild as Your Guide

In an ideal world, everyone who is about to purchase an iguana could travel to a Latin America country, see how these animals live in their natural habitat, and apply that knowledge when building their own iguana's habitat ("the environment in which an animal or plant lives or grows," according to the dictionary definition). Luckily you don't have to leave town, because I've done the travel and research for you. In this chapter, I will relate this information to you so you can create a wonderful home for your lizard.

As an example, when I was in Belize, Central America, I canoed on rivers where iguanas basked in trees 125 to 150 feet high, with just a few iguanas per tree. They all had their own territory. That's one reason why I don't recommend more than one iguana per household—iguanas need their space.

Iguanas in their natural environment live in wide-open spaces. Sadly, most of the pet iguanas I see are living in small fish aquariums. These tanks are for fish, so why stick an animal that is arboreal (tree-dwelling) and accustomed to acres of open space into inches of space? Perhaps if these pet owners had to live in a room the size of a broom closet instead of their normal house, they might have more compassion for their lizard pets and provide larger habitats.

When you think of habitat size, think past your 12" hatchling. In one year, this small lizard could double in size. At 1½ years, my iguana was 3' 4" long. Many iguanas eventually get 3 to 4 feet long and some even reach 5 feet or more (see Chapter 2, Iguanas as Pets, Figure 2.1, for a surprise look at how quickly iguanas can grow). When designing or choosing an iguana habitat, allow for vertical as well as horizontal movement. And like any other animal, your iguana will grow better mentally and physically when the environment is spacious and enriched.

You'll also need to provide the proper heat in the habitat. This is crucial. As humans, if we get cold we can warm up by putting more outer coverings on our bodies or adjusting the heat in our living space. Our bodies also have some natural warming devices, such as shivering. Some animals (mammals) have fur to hold their heat in, others have layers of blubber. But an iguana is a cold-blooded (ectothermic) animal that can't generate its own heat.

An iguana is at the mercy of its environment to achieve and maintain the temperature it requires—which is at least 85°F to digest its food (see Chapter 5, Feeding, "Digestion: Special System" for details). In the wild, an iguana controls its body temperature by moving in and out of the sun, perhaps under a tree limb or bush.

The concepts behind ideal iguana habitats, plus details for how to implement these concepts, will be explained throughout this chapter.

Plan Ahead, Act Now

Make sure people realize [having an iguana] is a commitment. Anyone who is not willing to take the time to set up a good environment should not own an iguana.   —I-551, Frank, 41 yrs., Arizona

Because a correct environment is so critical to an iguana's survival, the habitat must be completely built and operating properly <u>before</u> you purchase your lizard. If you are lax at this initial stage of basic care, your animal will only go downhill, with death the final resting point. Remember that your iguana is a captive and you are its guardian.

I spent much more money than I thought I would to set up my iguana's habitat.   —I-825, Chris, 22 yrs., Illinois

The only thing that I don't like is the amount of money that it took me to set up my habitat. By this point I have put in at least $350. I actually didn't expect to spend as much money as I did. But after having him this long, it was really worth it and I don't mind.   —I-817, Matthew, 24 yrs., New York

An important note to remember: The cost of the habitat almost always exceeds the cost of the animal itself. Most people don't realize this until they are at the cash register of the pet store. A pet store probably isn't trying to sell you more than you need; exotic pets require special care and equipment. It will cost several hundred dollars to purchase or build an effective habitat.

Creating and setting up a proper habitat is much like establishing a watering system for your yard. As an example, your neighbor may put in underground sprinklers and a timer to water his lawn and shrubs, all of which entails a lot of time and money.

Some people might think, why not just use a hose when things need watering? Those who hand-water remain tied to their lawn and garden's need for water, and they will spend countless hours each year moving hoses around the yard. But this summer and the summers afterward, your neighbor with underground sprinklers and timers won't spend another minute watering or worrying about his plants.

Initially setting up an ideal habitat for your iguana presents a similar situation—time and money. You can either spend one chunk of time and money building and installing all of the right equipment, or you can be a slave to your lizard's temperature fluctuations and light requirements (e.g., getting up early on a Sunday morning to turn on the heat and lights for your iguana, or rushing home from work to turn off the lights at night). The way I see it, you can pay once or pay forever.

Many pet owners find themselves purchasing several habitats as they try to solve the problems arising from an iguana's rapid growth. One solution is to build the Ultimate Iguana Habitat™ (described later in this chapter) and be done with the whole thing. The Adult Ultimate Iguana Habitat, once built, could be the last habitat your iguana will ever need.

Whatever housing approach you decide to take, the information in this chapter is intended to help you create a happy, safe, and healthy place for your iguana to live.

HABITAT OPTIONS

If you fail to provide the basic elements in a habitat, then eventually you will lose your lizard. These lizards have an amazing ability to compensate for a suboptimal environment for extended periods, then they will suddenly die after a very short illness or even without any warning.
—V-69, Dr. Alynn, 39 yrs., Mississippi

Husbandry is a term applied to the overall care of an animal, in this case an iguana. One of the most crucial components of husbandry is the home or habitat that you create for your lizard. Habitat options include size (i.e., for a very small hatchling to a large adult), shape, style (including "non-traditional" designs), or a specific design for a special location in your home. Habitats can be constructed of wood, metal, glass, plastic, or any combination of these materials.

No matter which design and materials you finally decide to use, make sure the habitat conforms to the basic requirements, which are stated throughout this chapter. Refine any of the details if you feel you have a better solution, as long as it accomplishes the same basic goals.

Terrarium (Aquarium): For Hatchlings Only

When books say to keep iguanas in aquariums I have to laugh. Because iguanas grow so fast when young, they very quickly outgrow that space. Also, it doesn't give them any climbing room.   —I-548, Eric, 17 yrs., Oregon

Please talk about how to take care of an iguana as a larger animal. Many books refer to them in terrarium tanks and caged constantly. I do not see this as practical or humane for an adult iguana.   —I-554, Anthony, 29 yrs., Texas

The terms "aquarium" and "terrarium" are almost synonymous among most "herpers" (slang for herpetologists—people who study reptiles and amphibians—or herpetoculturists—people who keep these animals as pets). People who own fish call it an aquarium, while most people who own reptiles and amphibians call it a terrarium. In each case, the term refers to a cage with all four sides made of glass or Plexiglas®. A terrarium is fine for small frogs, for instance, but is not appropriate for iguanas.

When people tell me they have their iguana in a terrarium, I get very irritated. It's like a human having to live in an 8' x 10' jail cell the rest of his or her life. Terrariums should be used solely for hatchlings, and then only for a couple of months. For details on setting up a temporary terrarium habitat for a hatchling, turn to Appendix G.

Terrariums were the standard iguana cage for years. I believe it's an outdated concept, especially with today's new technology and environmental systems. I have included a terrarium design in this book only for small hatchlings and <u>only for a few months</u>. If you decide you need a terrarium as a very temporary cage, try to purchase a used one and save at least half the original cost. Start looking in the newspaper for one before you purchase your iguana.

If your iguana is any larger than 4" SVL, it's too big for a terrarium. Skip the terrarium and go directly to the Juvenile Ultimate Iguana Habitat design, or some other habitat you can purchase or make. The Ultimate Iguana Habitat is a double-walled, insulated wood cage with a glass front so the iguana can look out and humans can look in. The version for juvenile iguanas will hold an iguana up to about 3 feet long, while the adult version can comfortably house a full-size adult iguana, probably for its lifetime.

I didn't expect them to grow so fast. If I had known this in the beginning, I would have started with a cage like the one I'm using now, which is the third cage they have been in.   —I-807, Gerry, 26 yrs., California

Ultimate Iguana Habitat™

One of the most common requests I've received over the years has been for a set of step-by-step plans for building a great habitat. I wish there were more designs that I could offer or recommend, but after six years I have honestly not seen even one available commercially. That's why I am offering the design of the habitat my iguana used all of his life. I call it the Ultimate Iguana Habitat because I believe it is just that.

If any of the concepts or building hints presented here seem useful, please use them. It goes without saying that you are not required to build the Ultimate

---

SIDEBAR

Terrarium Troubles

DO NOT try to heat your tank by leaving it in the sun.
                         —V-69, Dr. Alynn, 39 yrs., Mississippi

DANGER: Be very careful <u>where</u> in your house you put a terrarium. Do not leave it near a window, because sunlight coming through the glass can magnify the temperature in the terrarium to dangerous levels surprisingly fast. And the opposite can happen in the winter. Windows are usually the coldest part of the room and can suck heat from the terrarium. The following quotation illustrates the danger of having an all-glass cage next to a window:

My iguana died Sunday from heat exhaustion. I loved him so much and feel so guilty. Please warn others of the risks of leaving their terrarium next to windows that have full sun exposure, for this is how my iguana died. The temperature had climbed so drastically from the sun's exposure. I was not home at the time and I know he was greatly distressed before he died. It sounds like common sense, I know, but I was so preoccupied that morning that I didn't think when I opened the blinds on the windows.   —I-475, Mary, 22 yrs., California

---

Iguana Habitat design. But you are required to create an environment for your iguana that meets the lizard's basic needs.

If you want specific instructions on the construction of the Ultimate Iguana Habitat, please turn to Appendix D. But first, let's look at some of the general principles you should follow in creating a habitat, whether it's the Ultimate design or another option.

Design Principles of the Ultimate Iguana Habitat

During my 20 years as a professional union carpenter, I learned a wide range of building techniques, from conventional to esoteric. I have incorporated many of these ideas into the design of the Ultimate Habitat, not only for efficiency but also for the aesthetics of the habitat.

I feel that the Ultimate Habitat, whether juvenile or adult size, is a great place for your lizard to grow and spend relaxed, happy days. It's simple to build, not outrageously expensive, disassembles easily, holds heat, has lots of room, and it may be the last habitat you will ever have to build for your iguana.

Iguanas need a large habitat, but it doesn't have to be some ugly structure stuck in the back room of your house. A creatively designed habitat, made out

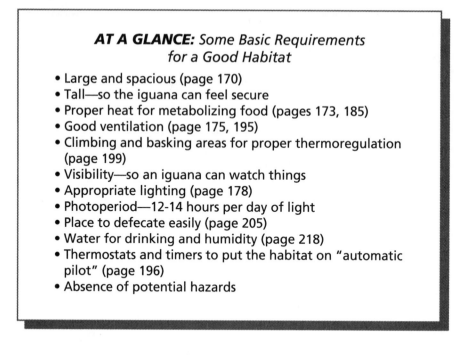

AT A GLANCE: *Some Basic Requirements*
for a Good Habitat

- Large and spacious (page 170)
- Tall—so the iguana can feel secure
- Proper heat for metabolizing food (pages 173, 185)
- Good ventilation (page 175, 195)
- Climbing and basking areas for proper thermoregulation (page 199)
- Visibility—so an iguana can watch things
- Appropriate lighting (page 178)
- Photoperiod—12-14 hours per day of light
- Place to defecate easily (page 205)
- Water for drinking and humidity (page 218)
- Thermostats and timers to put the habitat on "automatic pilot" (page 196)
- Absence of potential hazards

of good materials (and perhaps painted to match the color of the room), can add life and dimension to a living space (see photo section). It provides not only a beautiful habitat, but also a moving, breathing piece of natural artwork—like a live diorama—to enjoy every day. And to fulfill your iguana's visual needs, the Ultimate Habitat has plenty of glass for your lizard to watch and be watched.

I need to emphasize that I am not trying to shove this design down your throat, and you are welcome to come up with a better design. This Ultimate Habitat design is included for all of those people who don't have a clear concept for a habitat, or who want to blend some of their ideas with my design concepts. Once again, refer to Appendix D for all the construction details.

Size

> *Size of habitat: In getting an iguana as a pet, you should be prepared to provide a cage big enough to comfortably house a lizard that will become 3-4 feet in length (or longer). You may be able to start with a small tank, but a baby iguana will outgrow even a 30-gallon aquarium tank within a few months.*
> —V-69, Dr. Alynn, 39 yrs., Mississippi

There are two sizes of Ultimate Habitats: juvenile and adult. Both share the same design and construction; the only significant difference is the size. If you start with the Juvenile Habitat and it's time to upgrade to the Adult Habitat, you can sell the juvenile version and use that money for the construction

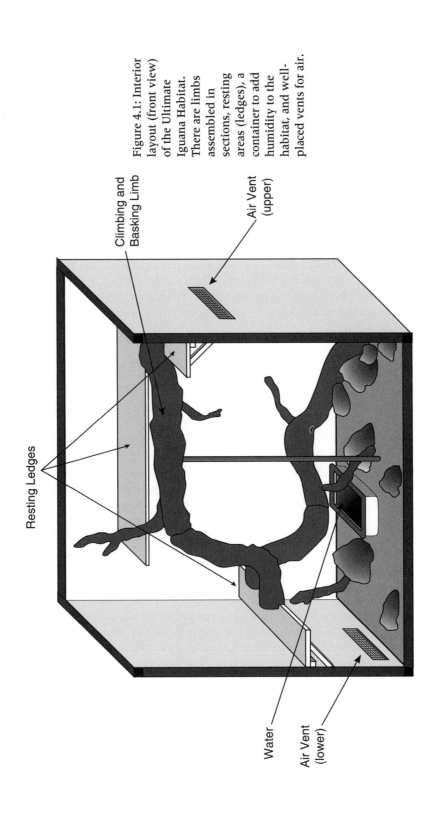

Resting Ledges

Climbing and
Basking Limb

Air Vent
(upper)

Water

Air Vent
(lower)

Figure 4.1: Interior layout (front view) of the Ultimate Iguana Habitat. There are limbs assembled in sections, resting areas (ledges), a container to add humidity to the habitat, and well-placed vents for air.

of the new habitat. No money is lost, and perhaps some is even gained; and someone else gets a great, smaller habitat.

An iguana with an SVL up to about 8" can easily stay in the Juvenile Habitat, but any larger needs the Adult Habitat. My iguana at over 5 years old, 5' 5", and 13 pounds had plenty of room in the Adult Habitat (partly because of the ledge systems, which are discussed later). To expand his living conditions, he was frequently allowed to come out of the habitat and join the household.

Looking at a 12" long hatchling iguana, it's almost impossible to believe that it can easily double its length in a year—and that several years down the road it could reach 4' to 5' in length and perhaps 15 pounds in weight.

This seems like something out of an old Star Trek episode. You know the one: Checkov finds some bizarre but cute or fascinating creature just as they are about to beam up from the strange new planet. The whole crew loves the creature, but by the time they get to the next planet it has engulfed the entire Starship Enterprise with its size. Only Captain Kirk can save the day. But in real life, you can save the day before things start getting out of control. When you see a tiny hatchling or juvenile iguana, think <u>huge</u> and plan your habitat size accordingly.

The iguana should have a cage at least two iguanas [lengths] long, one iguana wide, and one-and-a-half to two iguanas high at all stages of its life; permanent cages should be purchased or built with adult size in mind.
                                    —I-515, Lynn, 21 yrs., Canada

Even after hearing the large size requirements for iguana habitats, some people who have seen the Ultimate Habitat design on paper are still surprised by how big it is in person. But this large size allows room for your lizard to move about for exercise and thermoregulating. It also makes it easier to remove and feed your iguana, clean the habitat, and perform other "housekeeping" activities.

In the next few stories, pet iguanas are communicating in their own special way that they need lots of space. The Ultimate Habitat will help accomplish these desires.

I received this iguana from a friend who was going away to college. The lizard was kept in an aquarium, which he had outgrown. He was about 3 years old when I got him and I would rate him a 35 [on your 1-to-50 tameness scale]. When he became my pet, I put him in a cage six times the size of the one he had. Within a week he was a 20. He would let me pick him up and would lean toward my hand and raise his back to be petted.
                                    —I-764, Diana, 46 yrs., California

My iguana had kind of a small cage. For a week he was in a very large cage because I was on vacation. Before, in the small cage, he used to always whip his tail and fight me when I took him out. For the whole week in the large cage, I could take him out and hold him several times a day without a fight. Then the day my vacation was over he went back into the small cage again. When I went over to pick him up, you guessed it, he whipped and puffed up and tried to jump out of the top of the tank. —I-744, Karen, 34 yrs., Pennsylvania

Our iguana has broken his big toe on his back foot and pulled out two finger-nails scratching to get out of his small cage.
—I-849, Amie, 22 yrs., Oregon

She [SVL: 15", TL: 3' 11¾", 4½ yrs.] was not eating when I first acquired her. She was in a small tank [cage] and very stressed. She was given to me and placed in a large cage and soon began taking food from my hand.
—I-653, Justin, 19 yrs., Maryland

An important component of size is height, and whenever possible have a tall habitat. If not, place the habitat on something stable and tall so your lizard can look down. Even a small temporary habitat can sit on a high stand.

I truly believe that iguanas love to look down.
—I-626, Gail, 48 yrs., New York

The habitat your iguana resides in should echo the lizard's natural environment, and in the jungle iguanas are high up in trees. To test this natural inclination, let your iguana out in an open area in your house. True to its arboreal nature, it will most likely seek the highest spot in that room.

Heating the Whole Habitat

I believe that a properly designed habitat—one that is enclosed, insulated, and correctly ventilated—is the first step in properly heating your iguana.

SIDEBAR

Placement of the Habitat

Ideally the habitat should be in a room where your lizard can see outdoors and where people come by frequently. There are also a few places the habitat should <u>not</u> go. For example, don't place it near or in front of room heaters, air conditioners, or floor heat vents that could cause too many fluctuations in the habitat temperature. They could also wreak havoc with any automatic temperature control systems you might be using in the habitat. And never place the habitat directly in front of a window that gets direct sun, which could cause the lizard's home to become dangerously hot.

Research has proven that iguanas prefer a high body temperature, so why not just start off with a warm habitat?

Most habitats have wire screens covering part or all of the top, a design I call an "open habitat." Any heat you may have created by various heating systems in these habitats escapes out the top and is wasted. Because the Ultimate Habitat has a solid top and walls ("enclosed habitat"), it locks in much of the heat that may be generated. With the enclosed habitat your heating bills will be lower and your iguana will more likely remain at the proper temperature. Another benefit is that your lizard isn't tethered all day by an invisible chain to a single hot spot, as with some other cage designs.

> *You will be surprised how difficult it is to maintain the optimal temperature range in a normal tank. An enclosed tank constructed out of wood will hold the heat much better than a glass tank.*
> —V-69, Dr. Alynn, 39 yrs., Mississippi

> *Our iguana's cage was open at the top. It was also in a room that had a lot of windows that got hot during the day and cold at night. It went down to even the 40s one night. I forgot to turn on my iguana's heat light. He died soon after this terrible mistake.*   —I-518, Karen, 28 yrs., Texas

In the Adult Ultimate Habitat are three 4-foot, full-spectrum fluorescent lights that come on in the morning. (The Juvenile Ultimate Habitat has one or two of these lights.) In addition to providing light, they heat the habitat slowly, simulating the sun's heating. It's not the bulbs that create the heat, but the ballast, a device built into the fluorescent light fixture. The ballast is basically a piece of metal with a lot of copper wire wrapped around it. It doesn't get red hot, just warm. These fixtures generate enough heat to keep the Ultimate Habitat at around 90°F near the top all year round. As a side note, fluorescent lights are among the most economical forms of lighting.

If you look at the photo in the color section, you will see glass windows above the habitat door. This is the area that retains the heat created during the day. This warm air "pocket," along with air vents located on the sides of the habitat (not on the top), distinguishes the Ultimate Habitat from most other habitats.

If for some reason your iguana wants to be cooler, the Ultimate Habitat design enables the lizard to move to the next level (ledge) down (at 85°F), or go to the bottom and be at 80°F.

At night when the full-spectrum lights go off, the habitat has a supplemental night heat source that doesn't disturb the nighttime darkness. The habitat also has fans, which keep it from getting too hot on warm days. All of this will be explained further in this chapter and in Appendix D.

One optional feature you can use with the Ultimate Habitat is a new self-regulating heat system called the Iguanamometer™. This device was designed at my request by an engineer friend; see page 194 for an overview and Appendix E for specific instructions on how to build and use it.

Double-Wall Construction

A significant design feature of the Ultimate Habitat is its double-wall design with insulation, similar to how the walls of your own house are constructed. It's a very efficient way to hold heat for extended periods of time. I have never seen or heard of another iguana habitat with double-wall design. I explain this in detail in Appendix D.

Lights

The Ultimate Iguana Habitat uses overhead full-spectrum fluorescent lights that bathe the habitat in pleasant "daylight" for 12 to 14 hours each day. As a bonus, the fixtures of these lights also provide almost all the daytime heat needed in the habitat, as mentioned earlier.

Ventilation

When I first tell people of my closed habitat design they usually start to panic and say, "How can the iguana get any fresh air if the top of the habitat is sealed up? Won't the lizard get overheated?" I reassure them that the design takes care of that.

If you turn to Figure 4.1 on page 171, you will notice that the vent on the left side of the Ultimate Habitat is low and the one on the right side is high, but not higher than lowest part of the upper window (the heat envelope area). This venting allows fresh air to circulate through the habitat (with the help of fans), while trapping most of the heat at the top.

The heat at the top of the habitat naturally causes cooler air to be drawn in from the lower vent—much like smoke flows upward in a chimney and draws cooler air behind it (hot air rises, cold air follows it). This convection process also gently stirs the air in the habitat to ensure fresh, not stale, air. Whenever I opened the habitat door and put my head inside, it smelled clean, never stuffy, which is a sign of a well-ventilated habitat.

When the temperature drops below the level you pre-set on the thermostat, a ceramic heater (described on page 186), with its internal fan, comes on. And if the temperature goes above the desired heat setting, two small computer fans come on to bring the temperature down. Because the fans and heater come on briefly throughout the day and night to keep the temperature in the correct range, the habitat enjoys an additional supply of fresh, circulating air.

Climbing Objects

In the wild, iguanas climb onto various limbs and branches, often to help themselves thermoregulate. The Ultimate Habitat includes one large limb up high for basking and resting, another that gets the iguana to the middle ledge for a slightly cooler temperature or a change of scene, and yet another that gets the lizard to the bottom of the habitat to defecate or to exit through the door (See Figure 4.1 on page 171 for a drawing of this set-up. This drawing also shows the ledge layout described in the next paragraph.)

One unusual feature of the inside of the Ultimate Habitat is the long and wide ledges that wrap around the upper part. The ledges span the back and side of the habitat, thus extending the area your iguana can stretch out in. As a result, you have more usable space inside the habitat.

The ledges make it easy for your lizard to relax comfortably all day, because they are in the heat envelope area, which maintains a constant 90°F temperature. Your iguana is also close to the full-spectrum lights.

Iguanas spend most of their days basking or resting, so having a variety of sticks, limbs, and ledges is useful for creating an enriched environment (see page 199 for more details on limbs).

Automatic Operation

The Ultimate Habitat is fully automatic, giving you the freedom to never again worry about turning on lights, heaters, or cooling fans. Doing all of these operations by hand every day quickly gets tedious, and there's always a risk you'll forget or be away from home at a crucial time. Even if you don't use the Ultimate Habitat design, at least take advantage of all the labor-saving devices offered (see page 196, "Sensors," for details), notably timers for the lights and thermostats to control heating and cooling devices.

Getting a Habitat Built

For those who can't make an iguana cage, there are several options. The simplest is to take this book to a carpenter or cabinet maker who can then do all the work. All you have to do is pay for the materials and labor.

For those people who have the ability but not the required tools, try taking a cabinet-making class at your local high school or college. This way you can use their tools and get some help from the instructor. If for some reason you can't get into the class, talk to the instructor and see if one of the students can build your iguana habitat as a project.

If you don't have a lot of money, you might consider bartering your time or talents with someone who can build all or some of the habitat. I put myself through college and didn't have a lot of extra money, and often I bartered my talents and hobbies for things I wanted.

Alternative Housing

I use an old greenhouse that has been repaired. It is 15' long by 9' wide by 10' high. Yes, feet! —I-794, Andrés, 30 yrs., California

Creative cages can often substitute for more traditional versions, if they are done correctly. I met a kid at a reptile show in 1991 who told me he gave up his clothes closet to create an iguana habitat. He took out all of his clothes and changed the door so it was part Plexiglas (for viewing) and part screen (for ventilation). He added a heat source, full-spectrum lighting, some ledges, and several thick branches, and his iguana had a new home. I forgot to ask him where his clothes found a new home. . . .

SIDEBAR

Inexpensive Building Supplies

With some smart shopping, you can dramatically cut the cost of building your iguana's habitat. Purchasing used material can save you sometimes 60% to 70% off the original cost.

Most big cities have salvage yards that carry materials taken out of a house or office before demolition or remodeling. Glass from windows and shower doors is usually cheap, with a huge selection of sizes and shapes. Salvage yards also have used wood, plywood, and metal trim. They sometimes get truckloads of "seconds" in wood building materials, which you can purchase at rock-bottom prices. Go into these places and let your imagination soar.

When you need glass for your habitat, ask local glass companies if they have tempered glass, at odd sizes, that they would like to get rid of at a discount. (Tempered glass is like the glass in your car windshield, which breaks into little square pieces that won't cut you.) Tell them you are building a cage for your reptile. From my experience, when you say that the glass is for a reptile rather than a human structure, the price comes down quickly. Find out what sizes they have and design a habitat around them, as tempered glass can't be cut.

Another option is to ask for used regular glass (often called "salvage glass"). The savings are the greatest here because most of this glass comes from broken or replaced windows. Don't worry about a broken edge on the glass; the glass shop can cut this off. They can also cut these pieces to the size you require.

Her habitat is not really a cage but a recessed wall closet (10' x 8' x 8') that was converted into an iguana room. I bought a glass shower door that replaces the original closet door, then I built up the walls and ceiling around it. I laid down tiles with a drain and put Formica (it's a stainless, water-resistant coating) on the walls. Heat lights are recessed in the ceiling with a thermostat to control the heat. —I-843, Brandon, 20 yrs., Georgia

Let your imagine run wild for habitat ideas. One person even used a broken console TV and replaced the front with regular glass. Small enclosures like this are possible temporary solutions for hatchling iguanas only.

Andy and Helen (I-478, 37 yrs.) of New Jersey converted an extra bathroom into an iguana habitat. They put a big limb in the shower and added a heat light and full-spectrum fluorescent light. Another woman here in Oregon had a two-bedroom apartment; her iguana had one room for himself. For guidelines to set up your habitat, look back on page 170, "AT A GLANCE: Some Basic Requirements For a Good Habitat."

I built a partition dividing off the end of a small bedroom for my iguana's habitat.   —I-773, Rick, 34 yrs., Nebraska

Our three iguanas live happily in a room (average-sized bedroom) of their own. Each lizard has its own shelf (ledge), 5' long, which are 5' above the floor of the room with free climbing access to each shelf. Full-spectrum lights and heat are on each individual shelf, plus the room is very warm.
                    —I-734, Rusty & June, 24 yrs., Massachusetts

The large iguana indoor cage is made of glass with a wood frame built into the corner of a room. It has an outside screened window that can be opened and closed according to the weather, which also allows direct sunlight for my iguana.   —I-774, Walter, 46 yrs., Arizona

The two girls [iguanas] live on the porch. We made one-third of our porch into a cage, which is about 6' x 4' x 6'.
                    —phone conversation with iguana owner from Florida

HABITAT EQUIPMENT

I bought my iguana because it was cheap (so I thought). The pet shop didn't tell me how many accessories are needed to keep it healthy and happy.
                    —I-807, Gerry, 26 yrs., California

After the purchase or creation of your iguana's habitat, you still need to add things inside so it will function correctly. Most of the items covered in the next few sections will also make life for your iguana much more enriched.

Lights

The proper illumination for health and reproductive success for any species of herptile is subject to more debate and controversy than any other physical parameter addressed in captive husbandry.
                    —Kevin M. Wright, DVM (in *The Vivarium*, Vol. 6 No. 4, January/February 1995)

Everyone agrees on a few basic principles of light for iguanas:
• Iguanas need 12-14 hours of "daylight" and 10-12 hours of darkness every 24 hours.
• Ultraviolet light—specifically, a range called UVB (which is found in sunlight)—is probably necessary for iguanas to maintain the proper calcium levels and avoid metabolic bone disease.

- Iguanas should be exposed to sunlight—unfiltered by glass, plastic, or other barriers—whenever possible.
- Artificial lighting in a habitat is necessary, but most commercial lights do not emit much UVB.
- "Full-spectrum" fluorescent lights are usually preferable to incandescent light bulbs or "regular" fluorescent tubes.
- For UVB to work its "magic," iguanas also need sufficient body temperatures and sufficient calcium intake.

From these points of general agreement, the whole subject gets very confusing. As with nutrition, knowledge about lighting's role in reptile care is undergoing rapid change, with new research emerging all the time. My discussion is intended to provide the most up-to-date information and opinions available at this time and to prepare you to evaluate future research as it comes out.

Photoperiod

We recommend a consistent photoperiod of 14 hours of light and 10 hours of
dark.   —V-3, Dr. Jeffrey, California

Iguanas are diurnal (active during daylight) and need a regular photoperiod, or cycle of light and dark. Both phases are needed to keep your animal healthy. Keep an iguana in total light or total darkness and it will exhibit crazy behaviors, just like a human would. In a 24-hour period, your iguana should ideally have a photoperiod of about 12 to 14 hours of light and the rest darkness.

Sunlight

Sun is one of the best and healthiest things your iguana can receive each day!

Ultraviolet light: If your lizard were in its natural habitat [in the jungle] it would be spending the better part of every day basking in the sun. Ultraviolet light is crucial to maintaining normal metabolism in your iguana. Ultraviolet light is necessary to convert vitamin D to its active form, and the active form of vitamin D is needed for calcium absorption. Lack of or a deficiency of UV light in your lizard is setting it up for certain nutritional and health-related problems in the future.   —V-69, Dr. Alynn, 39 yrs., Mississippi

Natural sunlight produces a wide band of radiation. "Visible" light, the range humans can see, is 400 to 700 nanometers (nm) in wavelength. Below 400 nm is the ultraviolet (UV) range, which humans can't see. UV light can be further broken down into UVA (wavelengths of 320 to 400 nm, which can be transmitted through glass), UVB (usually considered to be 290 to 320 nm, which does not go through glass), and UVC (200 to 290 nm).

Both UVA and UVB are important parts of the light spectrum for your lizard. UVA may help your iguana see its food better and is most likely tied to reproductive behavior.

The more controversial one is UVB. In your iguana's skin, UVB wavelengths trigger the chemical synthesis of the active form of vitamin D3, and vitamin D3 is necessary for your iguana to metabolize calcium. Without proper amounts of vitamin D3, your iguana will almost surely suffer from metabolic bone disease, a disabling and potentially fatal medical condition. See Chapter 7, Medical Troubleshooting, for details on this disease.

Exposure to direct sunlight is the best and most natural way to make sure that your iguana gets the vitamin D3 it needs to maintain strong, healthy bones. Direct exposure means without obstructions such as glass, plastic, or other clear or semi-clear materials.

Nothing compares to direct sunlight. When he [iguana] is placed in direct sunlight, his entire complexion changes. Sometimes when placed in direct sunlight, his general color becomes a deep olive green. He also gets a very glossy or waxy appearance—he almost appears to be wet. Other times, his patterns become much more distinct and pronounced. Direct sunlight is the only lighting that has this effect. —I-508, Bryan, 27 yrs., Kentucky

IMPORTANT: All the UVB in the world won't maintain your iguana's calcium balance without two other conditions: sufficient calcium intake (through food or dietary supplements; see Chapter 5, Feeding, "Calcium") and sufficient heat.

The heat-dependent aspect of the synthesis of vitamin D may be particularly relevant to the care of captive herptiles, which are of course cold-blooded. . . . The herpetoculturist who is using UV radiation to promote endogenous vitamin D synthesis in captive herptiles should take into consideration the body temperature of the irradiated specimens.
—"Vitamin D and UV Radiation: Guidelines for the Herpetoculturist" (#37)

If you follow the guidelines presented in the "Heat" section of this chapter, you'll also meet your iguana's minimum heat requirements for vitamin D synthesis.

How Much Sunlight is Enough?

One of the most common questions people ask me is: What is the minimum number of sunlight hours that an iguana needs to stay healthy? This is an important question, but unfortunately I am not aware of any long-term scientific research that can answer it definitively.

There is little experimental data on the metabolic or behavioral requirements for natural sunlight or full-spectrum light in maintaining captive reptiles and amphibians.
        —Scientific research paper on light (#31)

The easiest and least expensive [way to provide] . . . adequate exposure to ultraviolet light . . . is to ensure that lizards have access to natural sunlight, ideally for at least 30 minutes a day.
        —Allison C. Alberts, iguana researcher (#39)

If you can expose your iguana to direct sunlight for half an hour a day, that's half an hour better than nothing. Catching a few hours here and there adds up to a bunch of hours by the end of the month.

Ideas for Giving Your Iguana Direct Sunlight

Whenever your region of the country warms up, you can open a window and let your iguana sit in the screened opening (the screen blocks only a small amount of UV light). It's important to note that the screen requires <u>additional</u> securing from the outside to make sure that the iguana can't push the screen open and escape. <u>Secure the outside of the screens to the window frame of the house</u>.

Just two nights ago I had such a scare. My iguana somehow pushed the screen out of the window and got out. I was HYSTERICAL. We finally found him on top of the bush outside the window. —I-814, Lori, 40 yrs., New Jersey

My iguana spent most days in my office, on an antique stuffed chair next to a window. In warm weather, I opened the window to give Za direct sunlight through the screen. When my office window was closed, and all through the winter, Za could still get a dose of the proper UV light because I installed a special greenhouse glass that allows UVB light to come through.

Large greenhouse suppliers are the first people to contact to try to get you this glass (often called UVT). Ask for the glass (or "plastic glass") that allows both UVA and UVB light to come through. Tell them you want it to allow the UVB wavelengths 290 to 320 nm. Don't settle for any other options, as they won't give the results you need. You might have to call around because many companies don't want to be bothered with such a small sale.

If you get this type of glass, install it in a window in your house that gets a lot of sunlight. Build a ledge on the window sill or put a limb near the window so your iguana can bask comfortably.

A special UV-transmitting Plexiglas can often pass more than 80% UV at ⅛ inch thickness. —from Herp-Net on-line bulletin board

Recently, a new manufacturer began selling a plastic glass through herp magazines and at reptile trade shows that reportedly transmits the appropriate

UVB wavelengths. I talked with the manufacturer and he said he had scientific tests performed at an independent laboratory proving that his "glass" does work.

There is one drawback to these UV-transmitting types of glass: Cloth materials near these windows, such as carpets, upholstery, drapes, etc., will fade and deteriorate faster than with normal glass.

Another way for your iguana to receive direct sunlight is in an outdoor cage made of a wire-type product that allows sunlight to enter. This is described in detail on page 253. If you can't get your iguana into direct sunlight, you'll have to deal with artificial lighting.

Artificial Lighting

Recommendations for artificial lighting raise more questions than answers, because not enough is known about iguanas' light requirements.

Lights That Emit UVB

UVB, as discussed previously, is important for vitamin D3 synthesis and calcium metabolism in iguanas. The only kinds of artificial lights that emit high amounts of UVB are fluorescent sunlamps, sometimes called UVB sunlamps. But these lights are impractical because the UVB rays can seriously damage human skin and eyes, and probably iguanas', as well. Besides, these lamps aren't even available to the general public.

Full-Spectrum Lights

When I first bought my iguana, I wasn't informed about full-spectrum lighting. My iguana turned a real dull color because of that, but when I installed the full-spectrum light his color was back in about a month. Now I use full-spectrum lights in both cages.   —I-807, Gerry, 26 yrs., California

"Full-spectrum" light is a term created by Duro-Test Corporation, the originators of indoor lights used for reptiles, for their light called Vita-Lite®. Because they originated the product, the term caught on. To differentiate their products, other manufacturers of this type of light invent their own catch phrases. But the common term used in articles and many books is full-spectrum, so I will use it here to simplify matters.

Despite their manufacturers' claims, full-spectrum lights do not emit much UVB, but they are probably still useful to create natural-looking visible light in the habitat.

Except for fluorescent sunlamps, the UVB irradiances from fluorescent lamps, including black lights, is low compared to natural [sun]light.   —William H. Gehrmann (#3)

Natural sunlight has a much higher UVB irradiance than most commercial sources of low-intensity, full-spectrum lamps. Commercial

full-spectrum light sources, such as the Duro-Test Vita-Lite, have
UVB light irradiances about 100 times lower than natural sunlight.
                                                —James C. Ball, light researcher (#31)

Over the years, iguana owners have written to me and said that after
adding full-spectrum lights their iguanas ate, looked, and acted better. Often
iguanas with medical problems got better, too. These people didn't run rigorous
scientific tests; they just observed changes. But judging from a lot of anecdotal
information, good things seem to happen when the lights are used.

*Before I got full-spectrum light she spent much of the day sleeping, or just rest-
ing. She's more active now and her color is much brighter.*
                                                —I-428, Danielle, 21 yrs., Virginia

My iguana had a general malaise until I got the full-spectrum light.
                                                —I-626, Gail, 48 yrs., New York

*My iguana did not shed for about 6 to 7 months. The second week with a [full-
spectrum light] he shed.*   —I-716, Thomas, 26 yrs., New Jersey

---

AT A GLANCE: Hints for Full-Spectrum Lighting

• Find lights that emit UVA and UVB wavelengths
• Look for a color rendering (CR) index between 90 and 100 (true
  daylight is rated 94.5 CR) to create "daylight" effects (CR index
  has nothing to do with UV output)
• Set them up with nothing (e.g., plastic covering) between the
  bulb and your iguana
• Install them so the distance from the iguana is about 8" to 18"

Within the last few years, entrepreneurs have seen the demand for full-
spectrum lights, and now the marketplace is being flooded with new brands.
They all have their special "edge" to make them stand out from the crowd, and
even the experts have trouble figuring out which light brand is the best. I talked
with someone who is trying to get a big light manufacturer to produce a new
reptile light. It is a fluorescent-type light that might emit more UVB than current full-spectrum lights on the market, though not enough to harm humans'
or iguanas' eyes or skin. It's still in the experimental stages, and rumor has it
this new bulb will even be affordable. Keep your ears open for this one.

Because there is still much left to understand, the role of ultraviolet light in the health and behavior of lizards will undoubtedly
remain one of the most exciting areas of herpetological research
for many years to come.

—Allison C. Alberts, iguana researcher (#39)

Black Lights

Fluorescent black lights (BL) are considered by many people to be in the
experimental stage for use with herps. Some brands of BL produce more UVB
than full-spectrum lights, and they all emit huge amounts of UVA and just a little in the visible light range. Some people use these lights in conjunction with
full-spectrum or regular fluorescent tubes (for more natural-looking daylight)
for their iguanas.

Black light blue (BLB) bulbs are nearly the same as BL except they emit no
visible light and are about four times more expensive. BLB lights were the
"black lights" used in the '60s to make "pop art" posters come alive.

Plant "Grow Lights"

*Neither a cool or warm gro-lux [plant "grow light"] will support the UV needs
of any reptiles that require it.*

—Mark Miller, director of Herp-Net electronic bulletin board

Reptile owners often buy the lights designed to help indoor plants grow,
thinking they'll help their indoor iguanas grow, too. Plant "grow lights" do not
supply proper UV light because they are designed for plants. Don't purchase
these lights for your iguana.

"Regular" Fluorescent Lights

Household fluorescent tubes emit visible light only. They don't produce
any UV light, but they do get rid of darkness.

Incandescent Lights

Incandescent bulbs produce no UVB, only visible and infrared light. The
infrared wavelengths produce heat, which is why many people use these light
bulbs as a heat source to keep iguanas warm.

Lights for Night

In the old days, pet owners used regular household light bulbs to heat their
iguana's habitat 24 hours a day. But iguanas need a dark period as well as light,
as I mentioned earlier.

When the main lights of your iguana's habitat go off, you will need an
additional heat source. See page 186 of this chapter for a nighttime heat source
that won't disrupt your iguana's necessary darkness.

SIDEBAR

Save Your "Used" Full-Spectrum Lights

Recent research indicates that full-spectrum lights may emit their full range of wavelengths for only a few months or a year. Even when they "expire," don't rush to throw away these rather costly tubes. Save them and place them in other fixtures in your house.

In my office, I have two fluorescent ceiling fixtures that each hold four 4' full-spectrum tubes (eight tubes total). This bathes my office in pleasant "beach" light, even in the dead of winter here in Portland—a much more pleasant light than the standard fluorescent tubes.

Alternative to UV: Dietary Supplements of D3

Iguanas get the D3 they need for calcium metabolism from a chemical reaction in the skin triggered by UVB, as already discussed. Other animals get D3 directly in the food they eat. Unfortunately, no one knows for certain whether iguanas' bodies can use dietary D3.

To read more about this controversy, see Chapter 5, Feeding, "Manufactured Vitamin D3."

Heat

Unfortunately, in haste, we purchased a little iguana before properly temperature-testing the cage, and the poor little creature died from lack of warmth for proper digestion. We did not know about the importance of heat then, but we're quite motivated to provide proper heat for our new iguana.
—I-855, Paul & Meredith, 15 & 47 yrs., Oregon

As I repeat frequently in this book, proper heating is absolutely crucial to an iguana's health. In the wild, iguanas thermoregulate—they move in and out of the sun—to attain their desired body temperature. In the Ultimate Habitat, the iguana thermoregulates by moving higher or lower in the habitat.

Specimens from this colony . . . showed well developed thermoregulatory behavior. Until their cloacal temperatures reached 32°C [90°F], they basked by inflating their bodies vertically, inflating dewlaps, and orienting themselves at right angles to sun radiation. At the same time their color was conspicuously darker than usual. They discontinued basking and their color became lighter when cloacal temperatures reached 33.6 to 34.4°C [92.5 to 93.9°F].

When cloacal temperatures passed 35°C [95°F], they oriented themselves parallel to sun rays and their color turned still lighter.
—"Observations on a Captive Colony of *Iguana iguana*" (#6)

Notice that the report states the iguanas' colors were dark then got light
when their temperatures were raised. You will see this in your own iguana. The
iguana darkens in color to absorb more heat and lightens to reduce absorption.

In whatever type of habitat you provide, you will need to create ways for
your iguana to thermoregulate. Your iguana basking under a heat source is
doing more than spending a relaxing day at the beach. Basking is serious business, especially when you remember that iguanas need a minimum of 85°F to
properly digest their food. Juvenile iguanas in the wild have been shown to
prefer even higher body temperatures than adults—31.0°C to 39.0°C [87.8°F to
102.2°F].

Use of supplemental heat was directly related to increased digestive efficiency and decreased transit time, suggesting that digestive
capacity and efficiency both increased with elevated body temperature. . . . [Also,] in their rapid growth phase, young iguanas
tend to select higher body temperatures than adults.
—John A. Phillips, iguana researcher (#9)

If you want more in-depth information on the importance of supplying
your iguana with the proper heat, skip ahead to Chapter 5, Feeding, "Digestion:
Special System." Now that you know how important heat is, I will cover some
of the options that iguana owners can use to provide heat for their lizards.

As you will recall, however, the design of the Ultimate Habitat generates
and maintains its temperature as a result of its insulation and the heat generated by the full-spectrum light fixtures. As a result, with this design you need
to provide supplemental heat only at night and during particularly cold temperatures, at which time the supplemental heater comes on briefly during the
day to maintain the proper heat level.

As a side note, it's important to have thermometers at different levels of
your habitat so you can see what the temperature really is. Don't rely on your
own sense of what feels hot or cool; your iguana's idea of comfortably warm is
quite different than a human's (this is covered on page 197 of this chapter).

Ceramic Heater

One of the best approaches to heating is to heat the entire habitat to a comfortable temperature, with variations in ledge heights for thermoregulating, so
the lizard can move wherever it wants to in the habitat. This new and exciting
concept is an integral part of the Ultimate Iguana Habitat design, but you can
also incorporate it into your own designs.

A ceramic heater is the best device that I have found so far for heating an
<u>enclosed</u>, large habitat at night. It produces no light, so your lizard can sleep in
darkness at night and still be warm. Day or night, whenever the temperature in

SIDEBAR

Too Much Heat = Death

Temperature above the optimum is just as unhealthy [as below] and can be
quickly lethal.   —V-69, Dr. Alynn, 39 yrs., Mississippi

Even though enough heat is an important factor in iguanas' digestion and well-being, too much heat for too long can kill them. And too much time could be as little as 10 minutes if they are abruptly overheated. One research project (#26) found that iguanas start panting to cool their over-heated bodies at 41.4 to 41.5°C (106.5 to 106.7°F); another researcher (#6) found the temperature to be 42°C (107.6°F). In addition to panting, over-heated iguanas may draw their tongues back into the mouth a little and arch the middle of the tongue.

Two iguanas were used in a lethal thermal experiment in San Blas, Mex-ico (#26). In these experiments, one iguana died at 46.4°C (115.5°F), the other at 47.0°C (116.6°F). You are forewarned not to let your lizard get close to these temperatures. For more information on overheating, see page 255.

the habitat drops below your pre-set temperature, the heater comes on for a minute or two. Mine was set at 80°F because that was my adult iguana's night-time habitat temperature.

Having the habitat drop about 10°F at night (to about 80°F) is healthy for your juvenile or adult iguana. Eighty degrees may seem very hot, but the morn-ings I held my iguana (before his lights came on), his body felt cool or even cold. This was after being at 80°F all night.

You can purchase a ceramic heater at most major hardware stores. It's only about 6″ square, lightweight, efficient, attaches easily to the roof of your iguana's habitat with "home-made" brackets, and puts out good, steady heat at a pre-set temperature that you can choose.

Choose a ceramic heater with a built-in thermostat (many of these heaters don't have one), unless you have some way of converting a heater to operate with a thermostat. With the built-in thermostat, all you need to do is set the temperature control selector knob to the temperature you want in the habitat, and the thermostat will maintain that pre-established temperature by cycling the heater on and off. When adjusting the thermostat setting, make very small changes with the knob, as it responds enthusiastically.

Some of the ceramic heater models have a fan to blow the heat around, which could be an advantage. The heater I purchased had a two-speed fan, which I set on the lowest setting. Make sure you point the body of the heater away from the sensor probe for the cooling fans. Any sudden burst of heat could unintentionally signal the cooling fans to come on. Then both devices would wage a never-ending battle of "hot or cool."

Even though I discussed the ceramic heater's operation specifically for the Ultimate Habitat, it will work well for most enclosed iguana habitats. Always try any new device or system without your iguana in the habitat for a few days, so if any problems do arise your iguana doesn't suffer any negative consequences.

To fully appreciate the benefits of the ceramic heater, I'll outline some options that people have used in the past to heat an iguana's habitat—and some things to watch out for.

Heat Bulbs

Here is the standard way that people have heated an iguana's habitat for years: A big limb or log is located directly under a heat bulb at one end of the habitat. This creates a "hot" area (basking site), while the other end of the habi-

---

SIDEBAR

Heat Safety and Burn Protection

- Use only UL-approved electrical equipment
- Secure heat receptacles so they can't be knocked over
- Keep heat sources away from combustible materials
- Don't have dangling or loose cords that an iguana can get tangled in
- Use metal wire mesh around heat sources to protect your iguana from being burned
- Place heat lights and heaters where your iguana cannot get on top of them

Dozens of snakes, lizards and turtles were rescued from a burning building in Napa [California] on Tuesday after an iguana tipped over a heating lamp and ignited a fire in a two-story, wood-frame residence.   —*The San Francisco Chronicle*, February 1, 1996

When my iguana was 3 years old I put a light bulb in his cage. When I came home from work he had burned his stomach very badly. It healed over time with no complications, but he kept the scar forever. When he died at around 13 years, the necropsy revealed that the burn was so bad that a scar had penetrated all the way to his ribs.   —I-519, Ellen, 40 yrs., Louisiana
[AUTHOR'S NOTE: See a photo of this animal on page 190.]

IMPORTANT: I have seen and heard about too many iguanas getting severely burned from light bulbs. Follow all the points listed above—posi-

tat is a cooler area. Theoretically, the lizard can go closer to or farther from the heat source to establish the temperature it requires. The goal is to achieve a temperature of 95 to 100°F (35 to 38°C) at a specific hot spot.

Most of the habitats with bulb-type heating devices also have an open habitat top with wire screen to keep the lizard from escaping. What definitely escapes, however, is the heat created by the light. As a result, the lizard is often in a mostly cool habitat with only a single warm spot, directly under the light. Because the lizard instinctively knows it must keep warm to avoid illness and to digest its food properly, it rarely leaves the basking area. What a sad existence. This is the old approach to keeping your iguana warm.

Incandescent Light Bulbs

The standard incandescent bulbs produce light by heating a filament inside the bulb until it glows. A great deal of the energy needed to produce the light

tion heat bulbs out of reach, secure bulbs so they can't fall over, etc.—to keep your lizard safe from bulb burns. One of the best preventive measures is to place a protective wire cage made of ⅛" to ¼" hardware cloth (wire mesh) around the light, large enough so the bulb isn't touching the wire.

When people tell me their iguana is ignorant or stupid because of something it has done, such as getting burned, usually it's that the owners are unaware of the natural instincts and physiology of their pets. For example, iguanas are not built like humans to be able to feel heat instantly on their skin. Because they don't feel the heat, it's easy for them to burn themselves on light bulbs and other heat sources. It's not the lizard's fault that it gets burned—it's yours. Protect your iguana from any heat source.

> The problem is they don't have . . . skin heat receptors. . . . Their heat sensor is at the base of their brain, so until the heat . . . in the blood has been transferred to that heat sensor they don't get out of the sun [or a hot light]. . . . As soon as [the lizard's] head realizes what temperature it is, [the animal] will get out of the sun [or heat source]. [But] there is a delay relative to skin temperature. Their core temperature is not like yours, where it is the same all the way through. [The lizard's] skin can be very much hotter than the core temperature.
> —John A. Phillips, Center for Reproduction of Endangered
>   Species (CRES), San Diego Zoological Society (#14)

Figure 4.2: The permanent "branding" mark on this iguana is the result of an unprotected heat light that fell on it. Don't let this happen to your iguana. Photo: courtesy of Ellen Broussard

is converted into heat, so these lights work adequately well as a heat source or basking light.

Infrared Bulbs: Alternative Night Heat Source

> *A heat lamp [infrared] positioned [properly] will distribute heat evenly all over his surroundings.*   —I-200, Dianna, 47 yrs., Washington

Some infrared bulbs are like the bulbs used in restaurants to keep food plates hot before a waiter comes and picks them up, or in some bathrooms to warm the room quickly. These lights have a kind of reddish glow and kick out a lot of heat, fast. For about a year, I used this type of light as a back-up in the Ultimate Habitat at night, when the main heat-producing fluorescent fixtures went off. I later found a better source of supplemental night heat in the form of a ceramic heater, described earlier.

One well-known iguana researcher told me that infrared (heat lamps) should be used <u>only as a booster,</u> not as the main heat source, because light at this wavelength dries out iguanas' skin and can lead to shedding problems if used too frequently or for too long a time.

"New" Heat Lights

In the last few years, there has been a deluge of heat-type lights supposedly created for reptiles or amphibians. Many of these are OK, and many have slick advertising claiming that they are the best heat source in the world.

Because this field is changing so rapidly, I hesitate to recommend any one type. But I can say I am pleased with the one I used for the Iguanamometer, which is discussed in Appendix E. Keep an open but skeptical mind about all of the heat-type "bulbs." Ask friends at your herp society which brand they use and why. Don't get sidetracked by pretty packaging or entertaining advertisements; read what the bulb is supposed to do.

Hot Rocks (A Commercial Product)

"Hot rock" is often used to describe any number of commercially made synthetic "rocks" with a heating element inside. The idea is that an iguana can lie on this rock and get warm. But this is not the natural way that iguanas get warm.

A desert lizard gets most of its heat from lying on the hot desert sand or rocks (belly heat). This is the opposite of green iguanas, who spend their time in bushes or trees, getting heat from above by the sun. Capillaries running down the back of the iguana are where most of the iguana's heat transfer takes place. This basic physiological difference makes it obvious why hot rocks do not serve iguanas' heat needs.

Do not depend on "hot rocks/sizzle rocks" to provide your lizard the heat it needs. This is a one-dimensional heat—it is heating only the lizard's underside and is not providing adequate heat. Do not be fooled into thinking this rock is adequate because your lizard sits on it all day long (your lizard is just COLD!). You must maintain a habitat temperature within the optimum range and not just one small hot spot. —V-69, Dr. Alynn, 39 yrs., Mississippi

---

SIDEBAR

Plan Ahead

No matter what type or shape "bulb" you decide to use, it's a good idea to use an indelible marking pen to mark the base with the date you first start using the bulb. If the package the bulb comes in says how long the bulb will last (approximately), you can replace that bulb weeks ahead—so it won't fail some cold winter day when you are not home. Always have some back-up bulbs on hand in case the original one burns out when stores are closed.

Hot rocks are dangerous. They can sometimes fluctuate wildly in temperature, getting hot enough to easily burn an iguana. I have heard of two iguanas that received first-degree burns on their stomachs from lying on these devices. I do not recommend hot rocks for iguanas, under any circumstances. Following are some stories about hot rocks, which I hope will help discourage their use.

I don't trust hot rocks. A lizard can get burned on a hot rock. Also, he may absorb the heat but his surrounding air will still be cool, therefore subjecting him to colds or pneumonia.   —I-200, Dianna, 47 yrs., Washington

I discovered that my iguana's hot rock may have been shocking her. I cleaned the cage with just socks on and when I touched the hot rock I got a shock. I removed the rock and forgot to tell my husband that it was bad. He put it back in the cage. The next day I sprayed my iguana with water and she climbed onto the hot rock and "flew up to the ceiling." I don't recommend these barbaric heat contraptions.   —I-518, Karen, 28 yrs., Texas

My iguana got some thermal burns from a defective hot rock in her cage. Because of this, half of her dewlap was burned off and she has scars on her chest. The hot rock has since been removed, but the scars are permanent.
        —I-747, Stephanie, 22 yrs., Illinois

NEVER EVER use a hot rock!   —V-68, Dr. Daniel, 32 yrs., Missouri

Heating Pads

Heating pads used properly and monitored closely work well for special situations, but I don't recommend a pad as the prime or even secondary source of heat inside the iguana's habitat.

Heating Pads Designed for Humans

A heating pad is a good alternative source to boost an iguana's heat <u>outside</u> the habitat, but it requires continual adjustments to the heat settings in response to the lizard's temperature and to any temperature changes in the room. To test for proper heat, slip your hand under your iguana's belly as it rests on the pad. If the lizard's belly feels too hot, it's too hot; lower the pad's temperature.

Even with a heating pad, your iguana should not be out of its habitat for any extended time if the room temperature is less than 70°F. Any day my office temperature was above 70°F, my iguana sat on "his" chair near the window, atop a heating pad, and watched the animals outside. I loved having him in my office; it made every day special.

On warm days, I had to be doubly alert to my iguana's body temperature. Sitting near the window on a sunny day could easily raise his temperature quickly. Some days, I had to turn the pad off for a while. Heating pads allow your lizard to share time with you, but it's absolutely <u>imperative</u> that you pay close attention to your pet's body temperature.

Heating pads for humans come in standard and extra-large sizes. I used the extra-large pad so my iguana had plenty of heating surface. This also meant I could turn the temperature lower because the heat was more evenly distributed over my iguana's body as he sprawled out on it.

The cloth covering that comes with most pads is made of a thin material, like a T-shirt, and after a couple of washings it is too thin. I got my mother to make a replacement covering for the pad out of a thicker material. The new covering added a softer texture as well as an extra layer of protection against being burned.

> *My iguana was treated for thermal burns that she got from her heating pad,*
> *which I no longer use.*   —I-662, Sharman, 22 yrs., Wisconsin
>   [AUTHOR'S NOTE: This is a good example of what can happen when you don't check your iguana's belly temperature.]

Heating pads work great if you <u>constantly</u> keep an eye on your iguana's body temperature. If you can't do this, don't use the pad.

Metal Heat Pads

New products are continually being created for the herpetoculturist ("herper"). The metal heat pad was created for under-tank (terrarium) applications at night—so for that reason, I discuss it only as an option for your temporary hatchling habitat. When the lizard's basking light goes off at night, this pad supplies supplemental heat until morning, when the basking light comes back on. Both the pad and the bulbs should be placed on a timer so when one goes off the other comes on. Do some test runs before you bring your iguana home to see what overnight setting is necessary to keep the terrarium at the correct nighttime temperature.

These pads come in several different sizes and should be placed under the tank, where heat from the pad will warm the bottom of the terrarium. Locate the pad at the same end of the terrarium as the basking light so your hatchling will always associate this area as warm. The pad should not take up more than one-third to one-half of the terrarium floor space. More than this and your hatchling will not be able to thermoregulate. Most pet stores carry these metal heat pads.

Heat Strips, Cables, and Tape

These devices work best for ground-dwelling lizards and snakes, which routinely receive belly heat in the wild. They are not a proper heating system for arboreal lizards such as iguanas, for the reasons I have already mentioned.

In the old days, before the new crop of heating devices came out, many people used these types of products. With today's new heating options, heat strips, cables, and tapes are outdated products.

"Self-Regulating" Heat—The Iguanamometer™

If you really want to jump to the next advanced level of heating, let me introduce you to the Iguanamometer.

Over the years, I have read a few obscure research papers on iguanas and their temperature demands. Even though 90°F is 5°F over the minimum for digesting their food, there may be times when an iguana wants or needs to get even hotter. Perhaps after eating, the lizard wants to raise its temperature to 100°F or more for a few minutes. The Ultimate Habitat could not provide this raised temperature. Any heat bulb used as a "hot spot" that stayed on all the time in the Ultimate Habitat design would disturb the carefully created temperature balance. As a result, I needed an advanced heating system that would come on only when the lizard needed extra heat.

I had a couple of design ideas in which an iguana could walk to the end of the upper ledge in the habitat and step on "something" that would turn on a heat source. When the lizard had received enough heat, it would walk off that "something" (to get away from the heat) and the heat would automatically go off. This, I thought, would be a great system.

The question was, could an iguana learn to turn the heat source on and off? One day while reading a scientific paper ("Thermoregulatory set points of the eurythermic lizard *Elgaria multicarinata*" #24) I came across my answer. Bruce A. Kingsbury, who wrote the paper, mentioned how he had trained his lizards (not iguanas) to regulate their heat requirements by seesawing on a board that turned a heat light on and off.

According to Kingsbury's article: "After a brief period of exploration, lizards established a heating-cooling routine comprised of regular shuttles to turn the lamp on and off. Between these shuttles, the lizards were usually stationary." This indicated to me that an iguana could learn such a process if it was simple enough.

Dr. Kingsbury sent me a sketch of his thermoregulating seesaw that showed how he used a set of springs and a balancing point to activate the lights. It was a great start, but because iguanas come in varying weights and sizes I needed a different kind of mechanism.

Because I am not an engineer, I turned to my old rock-climbing pal of 15 years, Cris Schiebold, in California. He runs a small engineering consulting firm called, appropriately enough, the Schiebold Consulting Group. I sent Cris some ideas, drawings, and possible solutions. My requirements for this device were basic: something that worked, inexpensive, with simple construction and parts that were readily available.

In less than a week Cris sent me the solution with all the necessary details and an actual working model. What makes this great is that it's cheap to make (less than $20 for all of the parts), easy to assemble, and elegantly simple in design. Cris even offered a name for the device: the Iguanamometer™.

The Iguanamometer can be used in many other locations besides the Ultimate Habitat. The herp community is an ingenious group of people who historically have had to create many of their own products when they were not otherwise available. If you are one of these people, feel free to steal this automatic control device idea. Just make sure you tell people where the original idea came from. The details for how to assemble the Iguanamometer are in Appendix E.

Cooling

Most of the time we worry about maintaining a warm environment for our iguanas, especially during the bleak winter months. But eventually spring and summer come along, and with them more heat and light.

It's important to note that in hot weather, a well-insulated habitat can actually get <u>too hot</u> for your iguana's health and safety. I found that it was <u>absolutely necessary to reduce unwanted heat in the Ultimate Habitat by installing small fans</u> like the ones used to cool computers. I purchased my computer fans at a large general electrical parts store that had a specific section for computers.

I placed two fans side-by-side inside my iguana's Ultimate Habitat in front of the upper ventilation hole (right side), just below the upper resting ledge. The fans were hooked to a thermostat so that they turned on automatically any time the temperature in the upper habitat exceeded 92°F. Appendix D includes an explanation of how to connect these fans.

Computer fans come in different sizes; my two were each approximately 5" x 5" x 1½" wide, moved 110 cubic feet of air a minute (CFM), and were 110 volts, 0.34 amps, and 24 watts. I prefer two smaller fans because they distribute the air more evenly, unlike the hurricane produced with one large fan. I originally started with one small fan, but it took too long to cool the habitat down to the desired 90°F temperature.

I found that the two-fan solution worked great in the Ultimate Habitat, <u>assuming that the room temperature didn't get much over 80°F</u>. That was about the limit of what the computer fans could overcome.

IMPORTANT: Unless you want an iguana with a short tail, you must locate your cooling fan in a place where your lizard can't accidentally stick its tail into the spinning propeller blades. Under the iguana's resting ledge is a good out-of-the-way spot. To be extra safe, and especially if you have a large iguana with a long tail, put some wire screen (e.g., house window screen) around the front of the fans for protection.

Whether you use the computer fans or create something else, <u>a thermostatically controlled fan is required in an enclosed habitat</u>. For the Ultimate Habitat, the sensor probe for the fans needs to be on the right side wall, about 2" from the ceiling.

Ventilation

Proper ventilation is achieved in the Ultimate Iguana Habitat design through proper location of air vents, as explained on page 175, and by the small computer fans. Even though the fans' main purpose is to reduce the heat in the habitat, they also circulate air at the same time. Below are a few general comments on ventilation that apply to any kind of iguana habitat:

- Use your nose as a guide. If you think the habitat stinks or smells stuffy, it does.
- The habitat should not be drafty—large temperature fluctuations could cause respiratory disease.
- An open-topped (with a screen) habitat wastes heat.

A greater volume of air (ventilation) is achieved by increasing the size of the vents. There is a natural balance: Too little ventilation makes the habitat stuffy and potentially unhealthy; too much ventilation makes supplemental heat work too hard and can create a drafty habitat.

Humidity

Iguanas in the wild live in a very hot and humid environment, but in a captive situation (which is not a natural environment) too much humidity can cause bacterial and fungal growth. This occurs in a small space that doesn't get adequate air circulation. As an example, in your bathroom after a shower with the door closed, walls and mirrors become moist. After several showers without proper ventilation, black mold may start to form on the walls and shower curtain. This is the same problem with a too-humid cage environment—it can easily turn smelly and dank.

At the same time, however, your iguana requires a certain level of humidity for proper shedding and for keeping its respiratory system from drying out. So there's a fine line between too little and too much humidity in an iguana's habitat.

Here's a test: If you spray a lot of water on the inside of the habitat to increase humidity, moisture will often form on the inside glass. If this moisture stays for more than about two hours, the habitat is too humid. The standard cause of lingering moisture is inadequate ventilation.

Ways of adding humidity safely and easily:

- Put a container (e.g., plastic tub used to wash dishes) on the bottom of the habitat and fill it with water.
- Directly spray your lizard several times a day with water from a spray bottle. Do not do this just before the habitat lights go out at night because there is a chance the moisture won't evaporate from your lizard, which could pose health problems.
- Spray the branches, ledges, rocks, and walls of the habitat the same time you spray your lizard. This increases the overall humidity of the habitat.

Sensors

Without a thermostat, the heater in your house would never come on. Without the automatic timers for the lawn sprinklers, your lawn would not get watered (except by hand). Sensors of all types make life easier and safer.

This is also true when it comes to your iguana's habitat. With thermostats and automatic timers, you can leave the house and not worry about whether your iguana has the proper temperature or if the lights are on or off. Make life easy: Put your iguana's habitat on "automatic pilot"—use the sensors described in the following sections.

Thermometers

When I first began visiting iguanas at their owners' houses I would ask the owner what the temperature was inside the iguana's habitat. The reply would be, "Very hot," which was all the owner could say because there was no ther-mometer in the habitat to provide an accurate temperature reading. After checking the temperature inside the habitat with a thermometer (which I always brought with me), I found that it was usually cool (70°F or lower).

The first thing I had the iguana owner do was purchase two thermometers, one placed near the basking light and one at the opposite end of the habitat. In the Ultimate Habitat, I put thermometers at the top, middle, and bottom of the habitat. This way I could see that the habitat was maintaining the optimal tem-perature ranges of about 90°F at the top, 85°F in the middle, and 75 to 80°F at the bottom.

With thermometers installed, you can see what the temperature is and make corrections to the heating if necessary. Many of the medical and dietary problems I have seen with iguanas were from a simple lack of the minimum temperature. Guessing at the proper temperature each day is not an option.

Thermostats

A thermostat is an electronic device that will maintain a specific tempera-ture, which you determine. Once your chosen temperature is achieved, a ther-mostat will automatically turn the heat on if it gets too cold, or turn fans on if it's too hot.

A common type of automatic thermostat is the one that operates the heater in your house. For more than five years, I used one of these simple house ther-mostats that I converted for use in my iguana's habitat, to operate the fans and the supplemental heat source. I made this device because at the time there was nothing available on the market.

Now, however, there are commercially available thermostats designed specifically for reptile use that can be ordered through many of the herp mag-azines. They are already wired correctly for immediate use. This is what you should look for.

Automatic Timers

Convenience is one of life's simple pleasures. A timer to control the lights in a habitat is a must with the busy lives we all have, and it also ensures that your iguana will get the right photoperiod. You can use the kind of timers designed to turn the lights in your house on and off when you are on vacation.

All you do is plug the lights into the automatic timer box, set the time you want them to go on and off, and plug this into the wall electrical outlet.

Environment System Controllers

The best approach to sensors and thermostats is to purchase a system controller, which acts as a "brain" that runs your cooling fans and supplemental heat source. Many also have automatic timers, to turn lights on and off in the habitat. Simply plug the heat, fans, and lights into the system controller and it runs them at specific times or temperatures. Like a great department store, system controllers provide everything you need in a single, convenient place.

At this time there are only a couple of manufacturers, and they can be found in most herpetological magazines. System controllers cost around $100, but it's money well spent for peace of mind and freedom. Each model has its special advantages. Talk to the manufacturers over the phone or write for the companies' brochures. Tell them what you have in your habitat to make sure their device works for your set-up. Also ask friends in your herp society for their opinions of these products.

Multi-Plug Device

A multi-plug device, often called a power strip, consists of a single narrow metal box with many electrical outlets built in. These power strips plug into a normal wall outlet and supply two to 10 additional, usable electrical outlets (depending on the type of unit).

If you are serious about safety, you will purchase a power strip for its built-in fuse. If one of the electrical devices or connections gets overheated, the fuse "pops" and your house doesn't burn down. This device is a must for all herp habitats and can be found in almost every major hardware store.

HABITAT ENVIRONMENT

My iguana nearly died as a hatchling in the first two weeks. He wouldn't eat, only licked water. I attribute the cause to . . . less-than-perfect cage conditions.
                                         —I-685, Julie, 36 yrs., California

Did you ever live in an apartment or house that you didn't like? Perhaps it was too small, had too few windows for light and ventilation, or the building was damaged somehow. Coming home to this place was more out of necessity than desire.

Don't make the mistake of creating a habitat for your lizard that is like your worst housing nightmare. I have already talked about the different housing options, and now it's time to discuss the things that go inside the habitat to make it more livable. The following sections will help you create a "user-friendly" atmosphere for your iguana.

Climbing and Resting Areas

As arboreal animals, iguanas are born to climb and be high up in trees. An iguana's body has evolved over the years for climbing, with sharp claws, low center of gravity, and a long tail for balance. Having a habitat without something to climb on is neither comfortable nor natural for an iguana. With a little thought and imagination, you can make sure your iguana's habitat combines great climbing and resting areas. Climbing up and down branches and limbs also gives iguanas some exercise.

Limbs and Branches

The sticks I added were a big hit; as a matter of fact I haven't seen them [iguanas] on the ground much at all lately.   —I-400, Brian, 23 yrs., Ohio

People have written to me stating that when they didn't have branches or limbs for their iguanas to climb, the lizard's toes started to sprawl. After the owners installed a series of limbs for the iguana to climb up and around, the lizard's toes started to function normally again.

Iguanas' feet are not designed to be only on flat surfaces day after day, year after year. In the wild, iguanas move around in the trees and are constantly "gripping" limbs or bushes with their feet and hands.

Branches are good for your iguana's health, but as a bonus they also make the habitat look realistic, natural, and dramatic. In addition, they can be used for rubbing off shedding skin, dislodging stuck-on food, itching body parts, or rubbing tired eyes.

What Makes a Good Climbing Limb?

The following are a few characteristics of good climbing limbs, along with brief explanations of how to achieve them.

* Variety and Sufficient Width

A large horizontal piece of driftwood near the top of the habitat is a perfect basking or resting area. This basking limb should be one to two times the diameter of your iguana's body—larger is even better. A really relaxed iguana will often "ride the pony" with its legs dangling on each side of the limb for balance. I have seen my own iguana, other people's pet iguanas, and iguanas in the jungles of Mexico and Central America do this. It's the ultimate expression of feeling safe and relaxed.

You can also use a combination of semi-vertical and horizontal limbs to create a pathway from the bottom of the habitat to the various landings above (see Figure 4.1 on page 171). Iguanas like a variety of angles of limbs to lie on, so add a few limbs that aren't just horizontal. Try angles from 10 to 45 degrees.

* No Pests, Poisons, or Resins

I brought a branch from a friend's yard for my iguana's habitat, and my lizard got small red mites from the stick.   —I-620, Suzanne, 34 yrs., New York

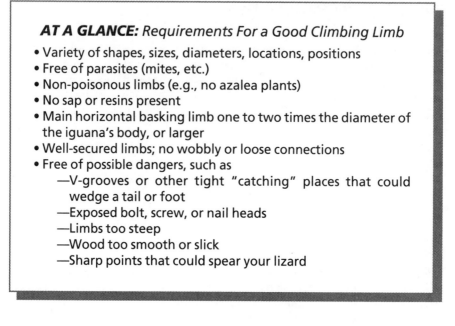

AT A GLANCE: *Requirements For a Good Climbing Limb*
- Variety of shapes, sizes, diameters, locations, positions
- Free of parasites (mites, etc.)
- Non-poisonous limbs (e.g., no azalea plants)
- No sap or resins present
- Main horizontal basking limb one to two times the diameter of the iguana's body, or larger
- Well-secured limbs; no wobbly or loose connections
- Free of possible dangers, such as
  - —V-grooves or other tight "catching" places that could wedge a tail or foot
  - —Exposed bolt, screw, or nail heads
  - —Limbs too steep
  - —Wood too smooth or slick
  - —Sharp points that could spear your lizard

I cut some large apple branches from our back field for my iguana's habitat. My dad sandblasted them to get any fungus, loose bark, and bugs off them.
                                    —I-703, Renee, 22 yrs., New York

Limbs should be clean, without any splitting bark (which could harbor pests) or leaking resins. Some limbs, especially pine or some fruit trees, may exude sticky sap for many months. These are not a good choice.

* Texture

The best branches are not smooth and sterile like manzanita, which is often found for sale in pet stores. Smooth limbs may sound good, but in reality they are very hard for an iguana to climb, especially if its claws are trimmed regularly. It's like trying to climb up a greased pole. Ideally, a limb should have a somewhat rough texture, and any bumps, knobs, pits, valleys, twists, and turns are a bonus. But make sure there are no sharp points that could spear your iguana.

I believe that the driftwood found at the ocean makes the best branches or limbs. The months of sloshing around in the water "tenderizes" the wood so an iguana's claws dig in easily. Driftwood is also aesthetically beautiful, with its twisted, bleached look. The second-best limbs are found along rivers, for the same reasons.

If the only wood you have is extremely smooth, you can take a hand saw and cut ⅛" to ¼" deep saw cuts or slashes at different angles on the limb to create little grooves for the iguana's claws to grip for easier climbing.

* Created Limb Shapes

When people see my iguana's habitat, they often say, "Where did you get that cool limb?" Simple. I created "it" from several different limbs, picking the best parts and putting them together. Look at Appendix F for how this is done.

* Well Secured

Branches are intertwined through his cage. The larger branches rest near the top of the cage to provide optimum basking sites. They are attached to the wooden cage frame by metal anchors and screws.

—I-690, Irene, 34 yrs., Texas

Because your animal will be moving around a lot on these limbs, make sure they are well secured. Secure the limb to something permanent in the habitat, such as the wall or ledge, for added overall rigidity and strength. Remember, loose limbs = possible injuries, which = veterinary bills = $$ out of your pocket + an injured or damaged lizard. Recess the heads of any fastening devices so your iguana won't catch or tear any of its body parts on them.

* No Dangers

Try to eliminate the possibility of any of the limbs crossing each other and forming an "X" or a "V". In such crossings, the lizard's tail could get caught and wedged. A wedged animal could get frightened and go into a full-body panic trying to release itself, thus increasing the chance of breaking its tail or even its spine. If your limbs cross in an X or V, fill the area with wood putty or a wrapping of cloth to create a rounded surface that can't catch and hold any of your iguana's appendages.

Just last year an older, sweet iguana I knew died when it got caught in the branches of its habitat. The owners felt that the iguana probably panicked, flailed about wildly, and broke its spine. The lizard had been in the same habitat for several years. If things aren't laid out correctly, over time the dangers inside a habitat can get compounded. Please pay attention to this note. I don't want your iguana to get injured or die.

Artificial Limbs

I put a 6" PVC pipe covered with carpet in her cage. It's her favorite!
—I-840, Lorraine, 32 yrs., Ohio

Limbs don't always have to come directly off trees. Artificial limbs can be created from lumber material (2x2, 2x4, 4x4) or large-diameter PVC plastic pipe (2" to 12" in diameter). The outer covering could be burlap or scraps of free carpet from your local carpet dealer, glued in place. One problem with new carpet is its overpowering smell; it takes time for the dyes and glues to evaporate. A solution is to assemble the limb and let it stay outdoors for a week or more until the smell disappears.

SIDEBAR

Wood Putty Fumes

If you decide to use wood putty on limbs to fill cracks or smooth out dangerous limb crossings, make sure that your iguana is not in the habitat when the putty is applied and that it doesn't return until the smell is <u>completely gone</u>. Use an extra fan if necessary to speed the drying process. Wood putty contains acetone and as the product dries the acetone vapor disperses temporarily into the habitat. Read the label. Another option is to mix builders glue with sawdust. This method fills the space just as well (it takes a bit longer to dry), but no fumes are created.

Several people have described how they got the discarded cardboard rolls that house carpeting comes on and wrapped and glued several layers of burlap (from a yardage shop) around this tube. These tubes are free at carpet outlet stores and come in diameters of 4", 6", and 8". They can be up to 15' long, so bring a hand saw to cut it to your desired length.

For a softer limb, some people first put padding around the tube, then wrap that with three to eight layers of burlap. This whole thing can be sewn together or held in place with glue from a hot glue gun. Make sure, however, that the material is secured; if the material comes off, so does your lizard.

Not everything is appropriate for an artificial limb. I purchased a sheet of thick, soft, natural cork bark from an advertisement in a herp magazine, thinking it would be a good covering option. I cut pieces of cork off the sheet and attached them with hot glue onto a PVC pipe. My iguana climbed much more easily on this than anything else I had tried before.

But as time passed, small pieces of the cork broke off and fell to the bottom of the habitat. One day I saw my iguana eat a piece, and I was afraid that if he continued to eat the cork, even occasionally, it might cause intestinal problems. I don't recommend using cork bark.

Then there are those people with great imagination who want to combine artificial and real to make something very special:

Following a bad thunderstorm, my husband and I went to a nearby park, which is well wooded, and got a very large branch that broke off a tree. We used it to build a 6-foot climbing tree for our iguana. The tree is mounted to a wooden base, 24" by 24" and 2" thick. The wooden base is covered with a grass carpet and is held in place by several medium screws and one very large screw in the center of the base. It has five branches and one large T branch at the top.

—I-841, Bonnie, 23 yrs., Texas

My mother made my iguana a macramé ladder out of cotton rope, which hangs as a bridge between the ledges in the cage.
                                           —I-703, Renee, 22 yrs., New York

Ledges and Platforms

Captive iguanas don't always like to rest on tree limbs. When my iguana was in his habitat, he spent about 90% of his time on the uppermost ledge (see Figure 4.1 on page 171), which provided a shelf or flat area for him to lie on. A ledge can be made out of plywood or other similar material and needs to attach securely to the wall of the habitat. See Appendix F for details on making and securing ledges in your iguana's habitat.

Ramps

When my iguana was just over 5 years old and 13 pounds, he seemed to have difficulty climbing up the limb from the bottom of the habitat to the first ledge. To make life easier for him I removed the lower limb and replaced it with a ramp made of ¾" plywood that was 9" wide and about 4' long.

When I first put the ramp in the habitat, Za would start to walk down or up it and then just stop. I noticed that he slipped a lot on the smooth plywood surface, which probably accounted for his reluctance to walk on the ramp. To solve the problem, I cut out about 30 pieces of screen molding and glued and nailed them on the ramp for better traction. After that, Za went up and down the ramp much smoother and easier.

Plants: Real vs. Artificial

Plants provide a dramatic way to make a habitat look more like a real jungle environment. In the beginning, I thought only lazy pet owners used artificial plants instead of real plants in their iguana's habitat. My experience, plus that of others, has shown that few real plants can survive shared living quarters with an iguana. As with most items in an iguana's habitat, there are pros and cons to both real and plastic plants.

Real Plants

We have all but given up on trying to keep house plants because one of our iguanas used them as a buffet table. Currently, the only plants that we have are hanging or protected in some way.   —I-554, Anthony, 29 yrs., Texas

Real plants add an extra natural dimension, but the plants need to be placed where your iguana can't get to them. Even if you place the plants in a far, high, isolated corner of the habitat, curious iguanas may eventually find a way to reach the plant. One day when my iguana was just over a year old, he somehow got on a plant that I had thought was unreachable. I came home and there he was, dangling precariously from the plant in his habitat.

Don't stick just any live plant in your iguana's habitat. The list of poisonous plants for turtles, which is the standard plant guideline that many veterinarians use for iguanas, is as long as a football field. Even if you use the turtle plant list as a guideline, turtles are not iguanas, so the list may not be completely accurate. I wouldn't let my iguana touch any plant I didn't know for absolute sure was safe. "Better safe than sorry." Your state Department of Agriculture or local poison control center can usually provide guidance for specific plants you have doubts about.

An important note is that if you purchase a plant for your iguana's habitat or have house plants and your iguana is free to roam, you can still have problems. The plant may be safe but the soil could be dangerous, as explained in "Miscellaneous Things That Can Hurt Them" on page 247.

> *I used to keep live plants in the cage but she [iguana] would knock them over or eat them.* —I-662, Sharman, 22 yrs., Wisconsin

> *At first I put in a small hibiscus plant, which after about three days looked like it had been caught under a lawn mower.*
> —I-773, Rick, 34 yrs., Nebraska

Real plants in an iguana's habitat are destined to get crushed, stomped, chewed, and destroyed. You would have to have a habitat the size of a large bedroom to eliminate this problem. This, along with the worry of problem plants, causes me to not recommend real plants for most iguana habitats.

Artificial Plants

> *Yes, I do have plants in her cage. All of them are silk because she always tramples real plants to death. The cage contains three silk fan palm leaves, two silk vine-like plants, and two silk broad-leaved house plants.*
> —I-806, Tiffany, 14 yrs., Texas

Most artificial plants are made of cloth, silk, or plastic, but they look and feel so real that many iguanas will munch on them—which isn't good. Do a test run by leaving one of these plants in your iguana's habitat—but only when you are there to see what happens. Then you can make the decision whether to keep the plant or not. Often after a few trial bites the iguana will leave these non-real plants alone.

> *We had a small plastic plant with material leaves. Unfortunately, it looked too real and the iguana ate the leaves. We were lucky that he passed them because the leaves were quite large.* —I-434, Karen, 39 yrs., New York

A grouping of plastic plants in front of a ledge in the iguana's habitat can create a "safe area" or privacy area. My iguana had plastic plants (birds nest ferns and tall grasses) on the side where he slept, rested, and occasionally hid. The plants got beaten up a lot because he was always lying on top of them or poking his head between them. He seemed to have fun playing in the plants. Because they were plastic they bounced right back, but after about six months they sometimes started to break down into small pieces of green plastic death. Before that happened I would replace them.

Almost all artificial plants have a thin wire running inside for support. Over time the plant can break and this wire could be exposed and accidentally stick your iguana's eye or body. Again, you need to be alert as to the condition of these artificial plants. If they seem worn, replace them.

One good source for plastic plants is a tropical fish pet store. There are also stores that actually sell nothing but silk or artificial plants. I went to one huge craft store here in Oregon that had almost as many artificial plants as a real nursery has live ones. Look in the phone book for one of these places in your area.

These plants can be attached in the habitat with 5-minute epoxy glue—or even quicker, use a hot glue gun. For a few of the plants, I drilled small holes in the guard rail on the side of the ledges so I could group the plants more closely for a denser look. Then I filled the hole with hot glue and stuck the plant in the hole. Immediately, the plant was secured.

I really love the jungle look that the artificial plants help create in my iguana's habitat. To enhance the artificial plants, I hired a student from a local art college to come over and paint a jungle scene on all three interior walls of my iguana's habitat. I drew a rough sketch of how I wanted everything laid out and the artist made my ideas come alive. The combination of the artificial plants and painted plants gave the habitat a three-dimensional look, especially with the real limbs in the habitat.

My iguana's habitat is in our living room, and it's a beautiful part of the decor (see the photograph section).

As an alternative to painting, many herp magazines carry ads selling large jungle scenes on paper. For a few dollars, you can create a jungle that requires little or no upkeep.

Substrate Options

"Substrate" is just a fancy word for the material that covers the floor of your iguana's habitat to help absorb and contain your lizard's defecation.

Because an iguana expels liquid and solids at the same time when it defecates (like a bird), it's good to have a substrate that can absorb all or some of the fluid, to prevent a small, smelly lake from forming. In the wild, iguanas don't need to worry about where they defecate; but as pets, they need a system that prevents any possible feces contamination.

One person I talked to on the phone said that iguanas are very dirty animals. I asked what she meant by that. She said, "My iguana always walks in its mess." I asked what kind and how large was the iguana's habitat. The answer was the typical substandard terrarium (fish tank). I told her that putting her iguana in an enclosure of that size was equivalent to her living in a phone booth.

AT A GLANCE: *Qualities of a Good Substrate*
- Won't injure iguana; no sharp particles or objects
- Doesn't create any type of dust
- Absorbs fluid from the defecation
- Helps reduce feces odor
- Good "wipability" (iguana can wipe its vent on it)
- Easy to clean up
- Environmentally friendly
- Doesn't have any strong or overpowering odors
- Low cost

I said, if you lived in a phone booth and had to defecate at least once a day, would you ever step in your "mess"? She hung up.

Iguanas are <u>very</u> clean animals and don't like to have any of their feces or urine on them. In the wild, they step around their poop without touching it and wipe their vents clean on a nearby patch of dirt, tree bark, or other substance. Don't get mad that you have to clean up their feces every day, because if the lizard had its way it would still be free, pooping out in the jungle with many miles for its feces to get lost in. Your iguana can't poop freely now that it is your pet, so give it the courtesy it deserves by cleaning up its feces <u>daily</u>—not a little later, not tomorrow, but now. (See the sidebar in Chapter 6, Special Care, "Cleanliness," for important information on iguana feces and salmonella.)

> *I thought that I would not like to change the paper in his cage, but I use it as an excuse to handle my iguana more. I look forward to it now.*
> —I-825, Chris, 22 yrs., Illinois

The #1 complaint I saw on my iguana questionnaires from pet owners was having to clean up their iguanas' feces. To me it's much easier than the 3-pound logs my Alaskan malamute (dog) would leave once or twice a day in the back yard. I had to dig a deep hole in the yard to get rid of those huge boulders. Iguanas' feces are nothing in comparison.

> *He [SVL: 14½", TL: 4' 6", 3 yrs.] scratches to get out of the cage to defecate, and he will wait to go outside so as not to soil his cage.*
> —I-619, Deborah, 38 yrs., Florida

You can actually train your iguana to defecate in a specific place in the habitat (see Chapter 8, Domestication, "Defecation"). Once they learn to defe-

AT A GLANCE: *Which Substrate To Use*

	Yes	OK	Never
• Ultimate Substrate	✓		
• Newspaper		✓	
• Inkless newspaper		✓	
• Brown paper bags		✓	
• Commercial substrates	✓	✓	✓
• Hardwood chips			✓
• Sawdust			✓
• Pine shavings			✓
• Cedar or aspen shavings			✓
• Orchid bark			✓
• Alfalfa (rabbit) pellets		✓	
• Ground corncobs			✓
• Carpeting (indoor/outdoor)		✓	
• Astroturf (plastic grass)		✓	✓
• Gravel (of any size)			✓
• Sand			✓
• Dirt			✓
• Potting soil			✓
• Cat litter			✓
• Water			✓

cate in a specific spot, my number-one recommendation for substrate would be the Ultimate Substrate, which is discussed in the next section.

For many owners, finding the right substrate becomes a frustrating (and sometimes dangerous) game of trial and error. There are pros and cons to all of the substrate materials suggested in this section. I have tried and formed my opinion on all of them. I've also included quotations from other iguana owners, some of whom have different reasons for choosing or rejecting particular substrates.

Some substrates are OK, but some are downright dangerous and should not be used. If you don't want to read about all the various options, my choice is the Ultimate Substrate, which is explained next.

The Ultimate Substrate

This substrate—folded paper towels taped to newspaper—is my own creation and seems to be the best all-around substrate solution. It blends newspaper's easy accessibility and cheapness with the absorption and "wipability" of paper towels. The urine soaks into the paper towels, whose soft surface also makes it easy for the lizard to wipe its vent clean, while the newspaper keeps the moisture from leaking through and adds more surface area in case the iguana hits the edge of the paper towels. This combination of characteristics is not offered by any of the other substrate options.

The only drawback is it's not pretty, and it doesn't look like part of a natural setting. But after six years of testing possible substrates and seeing the problems associated with each option, I am convinced that practicality of a substrate is the number-one priority over the long haul and that the Ultimate Substrate is the answer.

To make this substrate, take two full newspaper sheets and fold them where they naturally bend in the middle. Take three paper towels, stacked on top of each other, and masking tape the towels to the middle of the newspaper. Make up several of these at a time for convenience. The two newspaper sheets and three paper towels is an average. If you have a large iguana, you may want to increase the number of towels and layers of newspaper.

Once an iguana defecates, the soiled substrate should be removed and replaced with a fresh one. This substrate is not designed for multiple defecations. Adult iguanas usually defecate once a day, and hatchlings and juveniles often go twice a day. There will be a location in the habitat where your iguana typically defecates, and this is where you place the Ultimate Substrate.

Newspaper

I recommend newspaper because it's easy to clean up, doesn't cause ingestion problems, doesn't get wrapped around toes, and doesn't harbor parasites or large amounts of bacteria.   —V-36, Dr. John, Connecticut

By building staggered, overlapping layers of newspaper, you can protect the whole bottom of the habitat. When your lizard defecates you can remove just the soiled sections.

When an iguana is finished defecating, it drops its butt and presses its vent to the substrate to clean any remaining feces. Even though many pet owners love newspaper because it is cheap or free, it has a couple of flaws: It doesn't absorb much fluid and is too slick to wipe your iguana's vent clean. It's OK for small iguanas, who don't defecate in large amounts, but it's not as good for adults that poop "big time." But add some paper towels to the newspaper and you have the Ultimate Substrate (see previous description).

Inkless Newsprint

Unprinted newspaper or butcher paper is a very good substrate.
                    —V-117, Dr. Dale, 38 yrs., Texas

Almost every town or city has some type of local newspaper. These places regularly have left-over paper they can't use and will often give it away to polite people. So if you want inkless newsprint, you might be able to get it for free by simply asking.

Brown Paper Bags

We use brown paper bags as our substrate. We are satisfied with it but it probably isn't the most comfortable for the lizard! He goes to the bathroom every day so it becomes expensive to use other substrates.
                                    —I-849, Amie & Ian, 22 yrs., Oregon

I use paper bags cut up into the size that fits the bottom of my iguana's cage.
                                    —I-682, Dylan, 14 yrs., California

Brown paper bags used for an iguana's substrate are typically just old grocery bags. These bags are free and easy to come by, but they don't absorb moisture from the feces, so you can end up with a puddle after your lizard defecates. Also, the wipability of these bags is very low.

Commercial Substrates

In the last couple of years, there has been a huge increase in the number of commercial substrate products available on the market. They range from recycled paper to by-products of ground-up plant material. A couple I have tried seem great, and a couple could possibly cause problems for your lizard.

Don't be tricked or fooled by the fancy, colorful, and exciting descriptions and packaging of these products. If they say it has been tested to be safe, find out what kind of tests were performed, how, and by whom. Advertising and marketing departments of companies are like Houdini, Penn & Teller, Doug Henning, and David Copperfield. They often create something out of nothing. Just because a company says a product is safe for iguanas doesn't mean it's necessarily true.

Be smart and be wary. Check each product's characteristics against the qualities of good substrates in the "AT A GLANCE" on page 206. If in doubt, don't take a risk with your lizard.

I have seen many iguanas that have ingested particle-type substrates, which aren't good.   —V-117, Dr. Dale, 38 yrs., Texas

If you find a commercial product that meets the criteria for good substrates, don't waste it by spreading it all over the habitat floor. Instead, put the substrate in a cat litterbox, a standard plastic tub used for dishwashing (cut down to 2" high), or a similar container. This way the mess is isolated to one area and you use less of the product, which saves you money.

When the animal defecates into the product, simply take a paper towel and scoop out all of the feces and wet material plus some of the surrounding substrate to make sure the area is clean of contaminants. Then replace the scooped substrate with new material and **wash your hands thoroughly**.

With a little help, your lizard can easily adapt to using this type of container. One way to get your iguana to use it is to leave a small amount of the lizard's feces in it to "prime the pump."

Hardwood Chips

I don't recommend these for a substrate. They are hard chunks of wood that offer no absorption but provide a great breeding ground for germs.

Sawdust

NEVER! As the lizard moves through the sawdust, it can inhale dust particles and develop breathing problems. Over time, if enough sawdust particles collect in the iguana's lungs, they could possibly kill your pet. BAD STUFF!

Pine Shavings

I don't like shavings. I don't like animals to be able to eat their substrate and I feel owners often don't clean enclosures as often as they should when they use shavings.   —V-134, Dr. Chris, 40 yrs., Washington

I never recommend pine shavings.   —V-68, Dr. Daniel, 32 yrs., Missouri

I used to love this stuff because it was a fantastic absorber of fluid, it helped neutralize the feces odor, and it had good wipability. I used pine shavings as my iguana's substrate for more than three years without any problems. One reason it worked was that my iguana lived at the top of his Ultimate Habitat and came down to the bottom only to defecate (or to come out of the habitat), then he went right back up to the top again.

One day, though, I saw a small piece of the shavings go into Za's vent after he defecated. The piece got stuck to his hemipenes as he defecated and was taken into the cloaca as the hemipenes retracted. It caused no problem because I removed it the next morning while he defecated. Then about a month later I had to extract a small flake of pine shaving that got trapped in his nostril. Neither event was life-threatening, but I didn't like the idea of what could happen over time.

This substrate is a good example of how things can start off good and go bad all of a sudden. You need to pay attention to all the items in your lizard's habitat because many things can suddenly switch from benign to dangerous. After those two incidents with Za, I switched to the Ultimate Substrate.

I've heard claims that pine shavings are bad because pine is an aromatic wood (like cedar), but the people I talked with said that the particular pine used in pet substrates wasn't a bad aromatic.

Cedar or Aspen Shavings

Don't use either of these two woods as substrates. They are considered aromatic woods and the odor they emit could cause health problems for your iguana. Also, do not use cedar or aspen woods for any of the building materials in the lizard's habitat.

My iguana suffered a cloacal prolapse, and when my vet was operating on him she removed one fine sliver [of cedar bark chip] from the colon tissue. Because

that may have been the initial problem, when I got home I stripped his vivarium, cleaned, and disinfected everything before I brought my iguana back into it. —I-852, Debi, 35 yrs., Oregon

The substrate was changed from one type after several years to aspen shavings. The iguanas seemed to dislike it and scratched endlessly without defecating until I got it out of the cage.
—I-369, Michelle & David, 31 & 36 yrs., Virginia

Orchid Bark

This is found at plant nursery stores and is used as a medium for growing orchids. There are several grades, from fine to large, but it doesn't matter because this stuff is potential trouble as a substrate. Once the bark pieces get wet from the feces or moisture in the habitat, you have a great breeding ground for germs. The product is basically chips of semi-soft wood that have little scratchy fibers on the outside that can break off easily and lodge in your iguana's eye or vent. This product is not recommended.

Alfalfa Pellets (Rabbit Pellets)

Newspaper is considerably easier than rabbit pellets. Rabbit pellets were disgusting after four days. —I-862, Dawn, 23 yrs., Wyoming

Alfalfa pellets are sold at many pet and farmer supply stores. Purchased in bulk, they are very inexpensive. The pellets are nutritious because they are made for rabbits and are good food for iguanas in small amounts.

I tried the pellets for a while as a substrate in my iguana's habitat, but I didn't like them. Of the lesser problems, the smell they emitted in the enclosed habitat was overpowering. Several times I crawled into my iguana's habitat and could hardly breathe because the pellets' smell was so strong. When the experimental test period was finished I was glad to get the stuff out of the habitat.

A more serious problem is that any liquid (which includes wet feces) that comes in contact with the pellets will make them fall apart, creating a soggy, ideal breeding site for germs. Iguanas might also eat the pellets as food, which is not good because of possible feces contamination. I also found little flying creatures coming out of the pellets when I opened one of the bags. Many people recommend this substrate, but I don't. You know the pros and cons; it's your decision.

Ground Corn Cobs

NEVER! Corn cob material starts off lightweight and dry with sharp edges, but once wet it expands. If the iguana gets any of this substrate material in its digestive plumbing, it could get clogged up. At the low end of the problem scale, you may have hefty veterinary bills; at the high end, you could have a dead pet. No corn cobs as substrate!

I bought my iguana from a private owner. Along with the iguana I got the cage. They used shredded corn cob for bedding, and it was really nice and convenient to use, so I started using it, too. Little did I know that it was a killer. One day about 2½ years later, my iguana stopped eating, so I took him to the vet. Well, he died before morning. They autopsied him and found him totally impacted with corn cob. <u>I never saw him eat any of it</u>, but maybe some pieces stuck on his food or whatever and over two to three years it just built up, since it's indigestible. His death was a major devastation to me.

—I-312, Darla, 38 yrs., Ohio

Carpeting (Indoor/Outdoor)

This looks like regular house carpet, except the weave is tighter and shorter (flat) and held together with weather-resistant glue. It has a flat mat so there are no threads that might catch an iguana's claw or that your lizard could accidentally eat. This kind of carpet can handle getting wet, unlike regular house carpeting that eventually falls apart. Indoor/outdoor carpeting is not the same as Astroturf, which is described in the next section.

You will need at least two of these carpets: one in the habitat, and one to replace it when the first one gets soiled. Take out the dirty one, clean (using soapy water with bleach), and allow it to air dry. Meanwhile, the extra carpet is already back in the habitat.

Because you will have to do this replacement routine every day, you may even want to get three or more replacement pieces of carpet. That way, if one section takes longer than a day to dry you can still replace your iguana's substrate with a clean one daily. The negatives to using this is the work involved in cleaning them every day. This product can be purchased at carpet outlets and some of the major discount home improvement centers.

Astroturf® (Plastic Grass)

On first observation, Astroturf (also called grass carpet) appears to be the space-age 21st century substrate. It must be a durable product, if every week football players beat their brains out on it. But there are some potentially deadly side effects of this substrate.

The terrarium set-up came with an Astroturf flooring, which looked nice for the first few months but then began to "shed" blades of "grass" and was removed. I see this type of substrate as potentially hazardous to an animal's health. When the Astroturf begins to shed, an animal could track bits into its food dish and ingest them accidentally, or try to eat the bits believing they were food.

—I-866, Kate, 41 yrs., California

I used to use Astroturf, but found that this was easily ingested plastic. I discontinued using it.   —I-605, Laura, 31 yrs., Canada

One of the potential problems with Astroturf is the broken ends (blades of grass) of the cheaper-made brands. In time, from being washed and used, these green plastic pieces of "grass" fall out. According to one person who worked in a large reptile store, age is the weakness of Astroturf. Once the blades get old and brittle, they can break off.

If these broken green pieces lie on the floor of the habitat, an iguana will surely flick them with its tongue to test if the green substance is food. Once those hard, sharp, indigestible plastic pieces get into the iguana's digestive tract, they could scar or puncture delicate tissue or clog things up inside, perhaps eventually killing your lizard. Some of the products have softer blades of "grass," but if these break off the same problem is created.

I quit using Astroturf because I didn't want my iguana to eat the frayed ends by accident thinking they were pieces of grass or something edible.
                                        —I-680, Catherine, 21 yrs., New York

Another problem is that over time Astroturf's backing can unravel, especially on the ends, if you have to cut it to fit your habitat. Some of the newer products have the ends sealed and are cut to various sizes so this won't happen as easily.

There is a kind of Astroturf where the blades of grass are not single strands sticking up, but rather folded-over loops. I have heard of iguanas who got their claws tangled in the loops and ended up breaking their toes. You have to remember that this turf was created originally for human use. If you buy the kind created for humans, you will have more problems. The ones designed for reptiles are usually a little safer.

I know someone that had a problem with the reptile carpet (besides the iguana's claws getting stuck in it). The iguana also lost a toe end because of a fiber that got wrapped around it and basically acted as a tourniquet.
                                        —I-707, Donna, 28 yrs., New York

To properly clean the turf, scrub the pieces and rinse them like you would do for the floor mats of your car, except add some bleach to the soapy water solution. Hang the turf up to dry overnight in a warm place. Do not put a wet turf section back in the habitat, as it's a potential breeding ground for germs.

Astroturf is not a bad product if you faithfully get rid of it long before it starts to fall apart and you have several pieces as back-up. Also, get only the better-made product for reptiles, with stronger grass-like blades instead of loops.

I think Astroturf is a reasonable substitute, provided extra pieces are available that have been pre-cleaned and sanitized and are ready to immediately replace the soiled piece.   —V-116, Dr. Richard, 37 yrs., Tennessee

Small Gravel

I've sworn off gravel many years ago as this can get stuck on food and if swallowed will block your pet's intestines and kill it.
                                        —I-200, Dianna, 47 yrs., Washington

Aquarium gravel is the worst substrate I have ever seen for contributing to intestinal obstruction and should be avoided.
            —Dr. Patrick J. Morris, veterinarian and former teacher at the
                University of Tennessee College of Veterinary Medicine

I don't recommended gravel as a substrate. One iguana I know ate small amounts of gravel over a period of time. The gravel stayed in the lizard's digestive system and finally prevented the lizard from defecating. The problem was solved by removing the gravel from the cage, then giving the iguana a laxative (under a veterinarian's instruction) over several months to help remove the gravel from its intestines.

Another owner had ⅛" diameter gravel on the bottom of the habitat to help stabilize temperature. It was covered with a plastic membrane, but the iguana broke through and filled himself up with the gravel. Many months and veterinary dollars later the iguana is OK. Using gravel is a good way to rack up expensive veterinary bills or to kill your iguana.

Gravel, sand, and soil should be avoided as they are commonly ingested, leading to impaction.   —V-31, Dr. Jeffrey, California

Sand

Not recommended. Just like gravel and ground corn cobs, sand can compact in your iguana's digestive tract.

I've seen too many fatal impactions with soil, sand, or pea gravel to recommend any of these as a substrate.   —V-135, Dr. Debra, Washington

I put sand in the cage bottom for my iguana, but it caused his rectum to become external [pop out]. The vet had to stick the rectum back in and stitch it up. A lot of unnecessary trouble.   —I-642, Janine, 21 yrs., New York

Dirt

Definitely not dirt. Just mix with food scraps, feces, and water and you have an unsanitary condition.   —I-694, K.L., 29 yrs., Kansas

Stay away from dirt due to the risk of bacteria, molds, and parasites.
                            —V-3, Dr. Betsy, 28 yrs., Arkansas

The regular dirt that you find in the backyard of your house could bring a lot of unwanted "things" (pests) into your iguana's habitat. I agree with the veterinarians and the pet owners; I don't recommend dirt as a substrate.

Potting (Sterilized) Soil

Many of the new potting soils for house plants have added perlite or vermiculite (little balls of Styrofoam-like material) to improve aeration. Some of the even newer potting soils have pumice (jagged pieces of volcanic rock) or small pea gravel for aeration. Perlite, vermiculite, and pumice are great for plant soil, but are a potential death sentence for iguanas because they can cause impaction.

In addition, one pet-store owner said that mites appeared after he put potting soil in the iguanas' habitat. Potting soil is fancy dirt and has all of the negatives associated with dirt. I don't recommend any type of potting soil as a substrate for your iguana's habitat.

Cat Litter

Never use this product for an iguana. There are many types of cat litter on the market. One type has a clay base that could potentially clog your iguana's intestines. The clay also produces a fine dust that can lead to respiratory problems if an iguana inhales it.

Even if you don't use cat litter in your iguana's habitat, it still might be a problem. If you own a cat and allow your iguana to run free in your house, you need to move the cat box to a place where your iguana can't get at it. I have been told by many iguana owners that their lizards often take mouthfuls of the cat litter. Clay, dust, and cat feces are all bad stuff to be ingested by a lizard.

Water

He uses the kitty litter box filled with just a little water to defecate in. I didn't train him so much as it just evolved from his using a small plastic container filled with warm water that was originally placed in his cage for bathing.
—I-493, Marcia, 40 yrs., Alaska

Some people place containers of water (e.g., a small plastic dishwashing tub) in their iguana's habitat to increase the humidity, which is a good idea. To their chagrin, they find that their iguana also uses this tub as a toilet. For iguanas in captivity, water is a natural defecation cue.

It might seem logical to encourage your iguana to use the humidifying container as an in-habitat toilet, but I don't recommend this practice for the following reasons:
- If this is the only water source in the habitat it could be fouled, leaving the lizard no source of fresh, clean water to drink.
- It's too much work to clean the container (diluted bleach solution required each time you clean the container each day).
- The iguana could step in the water, thus contaminating itself and the next person who holds the lizard.
- You might accidentally spill the whole mess on yourself.

I don't like emptying the litter box after he has pooped in it, because of the water sloshing about. I have nightmares of slipping and dumping it all over me.
—I-493, Marcia, 40 yrs., Alaska

I still recommend using a tub of water to humidify an iguana's habitat—but use some kind of platform or pedestal to raise the container off the floor high enough so your iguana can't climb into it easily and use it as a toilet.

Rocks

Rocks on the bottom of the habitat make the environment look more natural, are a good way to hold heat, and help your iguana to shed. But I am talking about rocks 3" to 10" in diameter, not pea gravel or any kind of substrate material that iguanas can accidentally eat.

The number of rocks depends on the size of the habitat and the appearance you want. You need only a few rocks, not a rock garden. In addition, rocks that are stacked in piles are a sure way to cause physical damage to your lizard sooner or later. In a large habitat, place big rocks far enough from any wall so that your iguana can't wedge any of its body parts as it walks around among the rocks.

You can't simply drop rocks on the bottom of the habitat and think that everything will be OK. When you first put the rocks in the habitat, you need to watch how your iguana moves around them, then adjust the position of any troublesome rocks so your lizard flows around the rocks without stumbling.

Rocks with perfectly flat bottoms are the safest because no part of an iguana's body can get caught under them. Rocks should be used **only** in large enclosures like the Ultimate Habitat design, where the iguana spends nearly all its day in the upper part. They should not be used in small or terrarium-type cages where the iguana is constantly on the bottom. The odds are too great that the lizard eventually will get injured.

Another option besides rocks are cinder or building blocks, which can be purchased at building supply stores. Their rough, sandpaper-like surface can help remove shedding skin as an iguana rubs against it.

Hide Box

I have a hiding area for my iguana. He goes to the spot at 5:30 p.m. (one hour before the lights go out). —I-685, Julie, 36 yrs., California

A hide box is a created space or container that you should provide for your iguana when it first comes home with you. When your lizard (especially a hatchling) is put into a new habitat, it will often be scared and unsure of its surroundings. It may need a place to retreat so it won't be exposed to any perceived threats. By having an area to hide for a while, your lizard will feel safe and secure and start to relax.

A hide box can be created out of just about any material. The box should have a hole to crawl in and be large enough for your iguana to get its whole body into and be able to turn around easily. The box or area should be warm like the rest of the habitat interior. If the hide box is not made of a fire-resistant

material, make sure it is not close enough to the basking heat source to possibly catch on fire.

I do not have a hide box for my iguana now. A hide box was offered (hollowed
bark) when I first acquired my iguana, but it seemed to promote anti-social
hiding for long periods of time. The iguana showed no signs of stress when the
hide box was removed.   —I-892, Steve, 22 yrs., Illinois

Leave the hide box for the first month or so, or until your lizard doesn't use
it in the daytime. Also, remove the hide box if your iguana stays in it all day for
more than a day or so. If an iguana has a properly created habitat and good pet
owners, it will soon outgrow its need for the hide box. When I first brought my
iguana home, he used his hide box a couple of times in the day and at night.
After about two weeks of him not using it, I removed the box.

Instead of a hide box, I use plastic plants placed so that my iguana can hide
within them.   —I-825, Chris, 22 yrs., Illinois

When the hide box is removed you can create a screen of plastic plants or
bushes, which I call a "hide area." Or, if you are getting an older iguana that has
been someone else's pet, you can eliminate making a hide box and go straight
to creating a hide area. The area should be on the upper ledge and located at the
end farthest from the heat source. In the Ultimate Habitat this area is on the far
right side corner wall, at the front of the ledge.

Once in a while, my iguana would hide behind his "wall" of plastic plants
for an hour or so. He reminded me of Snoopy the cartoon-character dog, hiding from life in his dog house. More often, Za would peek his nose out of the
plants, as though I couldn't see him. Still other days, he'd relax directly on top
of the plants.

See "Plants: Real vs. Artificial" in this chapter for some interesting ways to
create a hide area. Iguanas are just like every other animal: Some days we all
need a relaxing place to escape from prying eyes and the stress of life for a
while.

I've tried hide boxes numerous times with poor results. I've heard that hide
boxes are good and that they increase the animal's sense of security, but my
iguana abuses and depends on it. When there is no hide box, he is fine.
   I have more than 100 plants in my room, and I keep a huge philoden-
dron on top of his cage that hangs down on two sides and conceals his favorite
resting ledge. In my opinion, he now knows that the whole cage is his domain
and that any part of it is safe (not just the box!).
                                     —I-703, Renee, 22 yrs., New York
[AUTHOR'S NOTE: No book can give you all of the answers for
every possible situation. Renee used common sense and creativity to
solve her iguana's hiding problem.]

Food and Water Containers

You might think that all you need to do is simply place a food and a water dish on the floor of your iguana's habitat. Unfortunately, as with nearly everything else about your iguana, food and water container considerations are more complex than that.

Food Dish

There are two possible places to feed your lizard in a large enclosed habitat. The best is just to leave the bowl of food on the top ledge; it shouldn't take the iguana more than 10 to 15 minutes to eat. The bowl should be heavy or secured in a way that it won't be knocked over or off the ledge.

The second place you might feed your iguana is the middle ledge of the habitat, as long as this area is large enough for the iguana to eat comfortably. I don't recommend feeding your lizard on the bottom of a habitat.

Of course, everyone who has a small terrarium-type cage has only one place to feed their lizard, and that's on the bottom—yet another argument for why a tall cage such as the Ultimate Habitat is the best for your iguana. Keep food and feces as far apart from each other as possible.

Water Dish

You need at least two water containers in your iguana's habitat. In the Ultimate Habitat set-up, I attached a small water dish to the upper basking stick for drinking. Place the dish near where your iguana spends most of its time. You can get a shallow bowl (e.g., the kind used for dipping sauce and sold at import stores and Asian markets) and epoxy (5-minute type) a bolt, thick nail, or wooden dowel to the bottom of the dish. Then drill a hole into the upper basking limb, put epoxy in the hole, shove the dowel into the hole, and you have an instant "drinking station."

Iguanas usually have to learn to drink from this container. If you put a large leaf of kale, collard green, or romaine lettuce in the bowl on a regular basis, the iguana will eventually understand that the bowl is a source of "snacking" food and water. After the first week reduce the size of the green leaf by half. Two weeks later, reduce by half again. Two months later, have just the water or leave a small piece of food for a treat in the afternoon.

There's a spill-proof water bowl for drinking water (which is changed daily or at least every other day).   —I-703, Renee, 22 yrs., New York

Always have a container filled with clean water for your iguana to drink, especially during breeding season. The water container should be cleaned daily with a water-and-bleach solution. Be sure to clear-water rinse the bowl several times to remove all bleach residue.

Put a second water container on the bottom of the habitat (raised off the floor to discourage your iguana from defecating in it). I used one of those plastic containers used for washing dishes, as explained under the subtitle "Humidity" earlier in this chapter. This second container adds humidity and acts as an emergency back-up water source.

Enriched Environment

They get really attached to an environment and places they like.
—I-687, R., 53 yrs., Canada

It's been demonstrated that animals of all kinds, from rats to humans, that are brought up and live in an enriched environment are healthier, more intelligent, more creative, more adaptable, and generally better off than those subjected to less optimal conditions.

What is an enriched environment for an animal? It's one that not only provides the minimum requirements of food, water, shelter, and safety, but also allows the animal to reach its full potential. For birds, an enriched environment may include lots of things the birds can use to entertain themselves, such as bells, mirrors, ropes to climb on and hang from, or time spent with their human caretakers.

Scientific experiments have proven that enriched environments actually affect brain development. Marian Diamond, a researcher at the University of California at Berkeley, found that rats' brains varied in size and the complexity of their brain-cell connections depending on the experiences the rats were exposed to. (One summer, I took a seminar on the brain with Marian Diamond—she's fascinating, and we got to "play with" a real human brain.)

Brain cells communicate chemically using dendrites, hairlike filaments that send messages from one brain cell to dozens or thousands of others. In his book *Ageless Body, Timeless Mind* (Harmony Books, New York, 1993), Deepak Chopra summarizes Marian Diamond's important research:

> Rats confined to small cages and deprived of social interaction with other rats began to develop shrinking cortexes and a loss of dendrites. On the other hand, if an old rat was put back into rat society and given lots of stimulation, its brain expanded and grew new dendrites.

Iguanas are extremely smart for reptiles. They respond to their surroundings, they can learn things about their world, and they can adapt their behavior in response to the demands in their environment. For these reasons, it's perfectly reasonable to assume that iguanas can benefit from enriched environments.

Once you've set up your habitat, watch your iguana in it. Does the iguana seem comfortable and happy, or is it restless, lethargic, or otherwise showing signs of discomfort? Figure out the source of the discomfort (e.g., maybe there is no basking ledge, maybe the habitat is too small or facing a blank wall) and fix it.

Entertainment: Terribly important, yet often overlooked, and is necessary to relieve stress and restore the iguana's joie de vivre. (I really believe in this— stress can kill.) Here are some of the things I have done to entertain my iguana:

- *Visible but not accessible non-threatening animals, like a bowl of gold- fish or birds at a birdfeeder (my iguana's favorites—hours of fascina- tion).*
- *Large rubber cat or horse grooming brushes that are too sturdy for igua- nas to eat pieces of—smell interesting, nice colors, good to bite or sit on.*
- *Jungle gym of ropes or wood; milk crates for small iguanas.*
- *Colorful picture—no pictures of other iguanas or green lizards, as it may seem to the iguana that they are infringing on its territory.*
- *Other things that appeal to the senses (especially vision), or things to climb on or go through.*
- *Food that is presented in a different fashion than usual: pots of home- grown grasses, rolling grapes, and other curious, edible things.*
- *Games for older iguanas, such as "follow the rope around."*
- *Someplace safe to dig or swim.*   —I-515, Lynn, 21 yrs., Canada

Iguanas enjoy the strangest things, and they seem to be attracted to weirdly shaped objects. My iguana would make a point when he was in my office of sprawling across my computer keyboard or the "track ball" (a kind of upside down computer "mouse" where the ball is on top rather than underneath the device), or stretching out on the answering machine or telephone. These jaunts across my desk happened so often that I figured this was part of his "play time" for the day.

At the other end of the "strange objects" spectrum, I placed some of my old socks, stuffed with rags, in Za's habitat for him to lie on. Perhaps they were like large, long, soft limbs to him. I moved these socks around to different places on his upper ledge, sometimes stacking them across each other in a big pile. Almost immediately after I moved the socks, Za would purposefully lie on top of the whole stack, "testing" the new configuration, sometimes stretching out like a human on a bed.

In his sleeping area, I always left one of these socks in the same place. At night he would often rest his head on the sock, or his whole body. I have told many iguana owners over the years about the socks, as something they might want to add to their iguana's habitat. Those who wrote back said how their iguana fell in love with these soft "limbs."

Iguanas are visually oriented animals. That means they get most of their cues about their environment from what they see, not so much from smell or hearing. They like looking at anything and everything. Everyone who has owned an iguana for any length of time will tell you they have the feeling that their iguana is always watching them—and it is.

When my neighbors in California were remodeling their house, my iguana would get on his big basking stick, turn his whole body toward the neighbor's house, and watch the builders every day. After the remodeling was finished, he

Mirrors

One thing that <u>doesn't</u> help create an enriched environment is to place a mirror near your iguana.

Only a few animals besides humans can recognize themselves in a mirror. Many people have written to me and said that their iguana is so vain because it seems fascinated by its reflection in the mirror. But current data indicates that iguanas have no self-awareness. When an iguana looks at a mirror, it "thinks" it sees another iguana staring at it, and this makes it tense that another iguana is in its territory. This is especially true during breeding season, so all reflecting surfaces should be removed from their sight. One male iguana in breeding hit a mirror so hard trying to get the "other" iguana that he cracked the glass.

I put a mirror in the cage to see what would happen. My iguana seemed to get real aggressive toward his image. He bobbed his head up and down and hissed. He even started lunging at the mirror, and I had to remove it so he wouldn't hurt himself. —I-807, Gerry, 26 yrs., California

As a side note, if you find that your iguana is head-bobbing excessively or banging into the glass of its habitat, it might be because the iguana sees its reflection in the glass and thinks there is another iguana just outside the habitat.

If this is the case, you need to move something in the habitat to create shadows, which will disrupt the reflection. If the habitat is well-lit and the room where the habitat is located is dark, this increases the reflection inside the habitat. If your male iguana gets extreme, try putting bits of paper on the glass to block the images of himself.

---

never again sat in that same place and odd position. For him, the "show" was over, and he went back to watching birds and people from a different place in the habitat.

It's important to have a large portion of your iguana's habitat designed so your lizard can look out. Being stuck in a box with four blank walls is a sentence to hell for these green guys.

One person told me that her iguana watched so much television—probably fascinated with the motion—that she bought the iguana its own 10" TV to watch in its habitat. She said the lizard liked only cartoons—probably because of the rapid movements.

Taking your iguana out of its habitat and allowing it to roam free (with supervision) is another way to expand and enrich its existence. The first time your iguana ventures into a new space is exciting to watch. Your iguana will explore much like a cat, looking at and touching (by flicking its tongue) new objects.

Swimming is good for exercise and as a change of routine. If you want your lizard to swim, there is an option that's better and safer than in a chlorinated swimming pool. If you have an enclosed yard, buy a small wading pool (for human kids) and fill it with water from a garden hose (fill it well before "play time" so the sun will naturally heat the water to a comfortable temperature).

Many iguanas seem to love the swimming pool, although my iguana never appreciated it. Za mostly preferred to sit on the rim of the pool or wander around the enclosed yard. I guess for him it was more "fun" to explore the back yard than to swim. It wasn't the water itself Za objected to, because he loved taking baths inside the house. Maybe outdoors he had to be on guard for predators, so he couldn't relax in the water. Who knows?

Safety, Security, and Cleanliness

Some of the information about safety, security, and cleanliness has been repeated in this and other chapters, but I feel it's important to discuss it again here with more specifics. If an iguana has to sit in or smell its own feces, this is not a happy or healthy situation. Also, if your lizard moves around in the habitat and periodically some supporting branch, ledge, or platform comes loose, your iguana will get stressed, and stress leads to mental and physical health problems. Loose supports also pose an immediate risk of injury to your iguana, which is clearly not the way to enrich its life.

Safety

Everything in an iguana's habitat needs to be secured. If something can fall over, separate, and leave dangerous gaps, it will in time. Move your hand through your iguana's habitat as if it's a lizard climbing around. If any limb traps or pinches your finger, if anything moves or falls down, correct the situation with nails, screws, or wood filler, or rearrange them.

Also, look at the "negative space" (i.e., space between objects) where an object, such as a cinder block or rock, sits in relation to a wall of the habitat. Ask yourself, is this negative space going to trap a toe, leg, or most likely a tail, and injure or break it off? Think, think, think. But don't get so afraid that you strip the habitat of limbs, rocks, and other features. A sterile habitat is not natural or good.

Security

Two iguana owners from the opposite U.S. coasts had an iguana with the same name—Houdini—because the iguanas were so skilled at escaping. Security means making sure your iguana can't get out of its habitat. In some cases it also means preventing children from getting into the habitat.

SIDEBAR

Swimming Pools

By now, you know that iguanas in the wild usually live near water and are excellent swimmers. Many people, in an attempt to give their iguanas a treat, permit the lizards to swim in their outdoor human swimming pools. Unfortunately, however, a swimming pool is not a place for your iguana to be, for the following reasons:

* Hundreds of people drown accidentally in backyard swimming pools every year, and so can your iguana. The water level in most pools is lower than the pool's edge, so an iguana can't get out when it needs to. The iguana can get tired and if no one is around the lizard will drown.
* Chlorine or other hostile chemicals can burn their eyes.
* Water may be too cool (even on hot days), slowing the iguana's metabolism so that it can't swim even if it wants to, then drowns.

Before we knew what kind of lid to put on our iguana's house we just placed a piece of unsecured screen on top. One day I came home from work to find the top of the screen tipped inside the cage, and my iguana was gone! The cats had jumped on top of the screen and it caved in. I think the noise might have scared the cats away, and the iguana climbed out on his own. I couldn't find my iguana so I yelled at my cats for a while (hysterically). One of the cats ran out of the house, but the other one looked at me, meowed, and walked over to the cabinet that the TV sits on top of. Underneath the cabinet was my iguana, sleeping, unharmed!! I think we should change his name to Lucky.
—I-499, Lorie, 26 yrs., California

I had a cage for him at first made out of wire mesh with each square about 1". I didn't think for a moment that he could get out of this cage, but he did. I was very lucky to find him!   —I-624, Debbie, 40 yrs., Florida

Security from natural disasters is also important. If you live in earthquake country like I did, secure the habitat to the floor and wall with metal L-bracket clips. I lived only a few miles from the epicenter of the Loma Prieta quake in 1989 and my iguana's Juvenile Habitat almost fell over because I hadn't secured it.

Cleanliness

An iguana is an extremely clean animal in the wild. If you leave your lizard in a cage that is not being cleaned regularly, then you are not providing a healthy environment.   —V-69, Dr. Alynn, 39 yrs., Mississippi

As I have said before, iguanas are clean animals, and only when their environment shrinks to something less than their natural habitat does a cleanliness problem arise. A larger habitat is the first step in solving a cleanliness problem.

Your senses of sight and smell are the best indications of a clean or unclean habitat. If you see poop in the habitat, the habitat is unclean. Stick your head inside the habitat and take a whiff. If it stinks to you it's even worse for the iguana, because in its confined space everything is magnified.

> *I don't like that my iguana defecates in the cage and sometimes smears it on the*
> *cage walls.*   —I-882, Jessica, 21 yrs., New Jersey

I am always surprised that pet owners think it is OK to clean their iguana's habitat very few days or once a week. Iguanas' defecation needs to be cleaned up as soon as you see it, not later. If it is not cleaned up right away your lizard may walk through the mess and spread it all over the habitat and itself, making a bigger mess for you to clean up. Besides feces, clean up any bits of food or shed when you see them in the habitat.

If you are using the Ultimate Substrate, all you have to do is pick up the newspaper and toss the mess in the trash. If you are using the right number of paper towels and newspaper you won't have to clean up any more than this. With other substrates you may also have to use a disinfectant on the floor surface to make sure the area where your lizard defecated is sufficiently clean and sanitized.

Don't use any products such as Pine-Sol® or other pine-scented cleaners in your iguana's habitat, as they may adversely affect your lizard's breathing. You can use a diluted solution of household bleach (one tablespoon of bleach in a cup of water), purchase some Nolvasan from your veterinarian, or get one of the disinfectant products advertised in the herp magazines.

Whenever you handle any kind of animal, whether dog, cat, or reptile, you should always wash your hands afterward. And after cleaning up these animals' defecations, cleaning your hands thoroughly should be second nature. In the last year there has been an increase in the number of articles about salmonella related to reptiles. Chapter 7, Medical Troubleshooting, has a special section devoted to salmonella, and Chapter 6, Special Care, has a sidebar in the "Cleanliness" section. **These are required reading for every iguana owner right now.**

As mentioned earlier, the glass of your iguana's habitat will periodically need to be cleaned. Every so often, your iguana will "snort" salty fluids from its nose, which helps regulate the lizard's body chemistry. This is normal and natural. As the fluid dries, salt crystals will remain, and over time they build up. To clean the salty build-up from habitat glass, use plain water and a paper towel. Special window cleaners contain harsh cleaners that your iguana might lick, causing possible problems.

Keeping your iguana clean is as simple as keeping yourself clean. There are certain things that need to be done every day and we just do them.

CAGEMATES

There are two possible types of cagemates for an iguana: another iguana, or a different animal species. The following section will explain the problems with both types in detail, but if you want to skip the details, the message in a nutshell is simple: **Don't get more than one iguana and have <u>no</u> other animal in the habitat with your lizard.**

Another Iguana

I don't like keeping them separated, but they fight if they are together.
                                        —I-807, Gerry, 26 yrs., California

One woman I know owned an iguana whose entire front leg was bitten off by another iguana.   —I-467, Kris, 32 yrs., Florida

I know of many iguanas that have killed their iguana cagemates, even of the opposite sex.   —V-85, Dr. Sue, New York

Iguanas are not like wild dogs that like to live together in packs. Iguanas are very territorial, especially during the mating season. In the wild I have seen iguanas basking together in the same tree, but each iguana had its own space, or territory, on the big tree limb. Any time an iguana gets into its neighbor's space, head-on confrontation can be expected. Also, the highest iguanas in the trees are usually the biggest and toughest. Like the hierarchy in an office, the boss is on the top floor with the largest space and best view.

I don't recommend more than one iguana per household. I am very strong on this point. I feel this is very important, so be prepared to read some version of this theme many times throughout the book. I came to this conclusion because of iguanas' strong assertive and aggressive attitudes toward their territory (see Chapter 1, Iguana: The Species, "Aggressive Behavior"). When they are housed in a small living situation, these attitudes are magnified. Over the years I have received handfuls of stories from iguana owners that reinforce my conclusion.

My new iguana was housed with an older dominant male iguana, who would not let the new iguana eat. I finally separated them. A few days later the new iguana started eating again.   —I-766, Jeff & Sue, 39 & 37 yrs., Illinois

Territorial animals such as iguanas are better off by themselves. Iguana cagemates at the minimum will tolerate each other. One iguana—especially a male—will be dominant and may control the habitat through aggression. The iguanas might not actually fight, but the subordinate lizard is likely to limit or refuse food because of the constant intimidation by the dominant lizard. The end result could be the death of the subordinate iguana.

An extreme negative example of providing an iguana with a cagemate is a story where one woman loved her iguana so much that (about eight months after getting her first iguana) she bought another one, "to keep it company." The older, established iguana killed the new one almost immediately. In the case of an iguana, if you love it, let it live by itself.

At the other end of the spectrum, however, a male and a female iguana I know would eat together without fighting for control of the food bowl, which is almost unheard of. But this tender example is extremely rare, perhaps one of a kind.

Year after year I tell people, "Only one iguana." But some people still end up with two. It seems so hard for some people to believe this point, until they experience the trouble firsthand. Things seem fine for a while, then one day the pet owner writes or calls and says that the iguanas are attacking each other. Perhaps the following stories will help you learn from others' mistakes.

Both my iguanas were initially peaceable cagemates, but as the weather warmed the older one began vigorous head-bobbing whenever the younger one was on a favored branch, at the food dish, etc. The young one would always give up the branch without a fight. The head-bobbing escalated into biting on the older one's part, at which point the younger one would retreat to the other end of the cage, again without fighting back. Episodes seemed to be worse after both iguanas had been out of the cage for exercise.

A few weeks ago, the violent episodes culminated in the worst fight ever after both had been out of the cage for exercise. With a difference this time. The younger iguana was resting on the screen top while I went to collect the older one. The moment I put the older one on the screen top, she began vigorous head-bobbing at the younger one—at which point the young one came across the screen top, completely berserk, bowled the older one over, and began biting her. I separated them, and they behaved fine later, but that was the episode that decided me on giving one away.   —I-866, Kate, 41 yrs., California

Here are the details you asked for on how my older iguana killed the baby iguana. The baby was no more than 5 to 6 months old and about 5" SVL. My older iguana [SVL: 12", TL: 3', 3½ yrs.] did not seem to behave aggressively toward the baby at first, but she did watch the little one from above in the habitat. The baby did not seem frightened of the older iguana, but the baby did not approach the older one during my periods of observation. After approximately three weeks, my husband went in to look at the iguana cage and found the older iguana with the baby headfirst in her mouth. She dropped him when I ran in and yelled at her, but the baby was already dead. I purchased a second baby and kept it in a separate cage. My older iguana would charge this baby through the glass when she was out of her cage and could get near the baby's cage. In my opinion, iguanas have definite territorial instincts and I believe that the reason she attacked the first baby was that it climbed onto "her" shelf [her territory].   —I-4, Ardith, 41 yrs., California

When I purchased my iguana, he had a severe infection in his joint fluids, especially in the toes and limbs. The primary infection probably came from a scratch or bite from another animal, as he was housed with many other adult iguanas, prior to my ownership. An X-ray showed that the joints (which looked swollen) were completely separated in most of his toes and his wrists, elbows, and knees. As a result, all of those joints are now fused together, making it difficult for him to move around (especially climbing).

—I-561, Karen, 23 yrs., California

My new iguana was under a great deal of stress when caged with my older iguana. The new iguana's personality changed. He spent most of his time flattened out on the bottom of the cage, hiding under the newspaper, or frantically trying to escape from the cage. After he was attacked and injured by my older iguana, he was placed in a separate cage.

—I-685, Julie, 36 yrs., California

You definitely don't want two sexually mature males together. For one thing, there will always be an alpha, or dominant, male trying to control everything in the habitat.

When specific environmental resources are limited, male iguanas establish dominance hierarchies within one month after hatching. Competitive interaction among males results in disproportionate use of defensible heat resources, which ultimately leads to a divergence in growth rate. —John A. Phillips, iguana researcher (#9)

Several of our male iguanas have broken their arms or legs as a result of fighting. —conversation at a local herpetological conference

Most people seem to have the misconception about iguanas always being very peaceful toward one another. Iguanas do fight on occasion, as do many other lizard species. Serious injury and even the death of one of the animals is a possible result.

Our iguana (B) had always tolerated (A) but apparently one day he lost his temper. I had just arrived home for lunch when I heard a commotion on the back porch. When I investigated I was horrified to see (B) biting and shaking (A) violently around the midsection. Blood sprayed everywhere. What amazes me is that these two iguanas had lived together for several years and nothing like this had ever happened before. I got (B) away from (A) and, since I was working for a vet at the time, I rushed back to the clinic. It was so bad that his entrails, still attached, were completely outside of his body.

Fortunately the doctors had yet to leave for lunch, and one donated his lunch hour to put (A) back together again, with an incision running the full length of his body. But remarkably, he did recover. Apparently we had two males whose rivalry eventually caught up with them.

—I-467, Kris, 32 yrs., Florida

There are still a few of you out there thinking, "Oh, my iguanas will get along, I'll just give them lots of love and attention and they will be good friends." For those of you who harbor thoughts like this, please read on. Everyone else—who understand that iguanas should not be cagemates—can take the day off from class and skip to the next section.

My newest iguana started to become aggressive toward my older yet smaller iguana. One day I was petting the older iguana, when the newer one attacked. He broke two legs, ripped off two and a half toes and the end of the older iguana's tail, then he forced the older iguana's side against a stick and the stick went through him. He died.   —I-783, Leanna, 22 yrs., Washington

Our two iguanas were raised together. (A) was the dominant male and always stressed (B). (B) didn't eat properly and there must have been psychological stress as well. Even though both were finally separated, (B) hasn't caught up to (A)'s size. But I did see a big improvement in (B)'s whole attitude after I got (A) out of the habitat.   —I-237, Diane, 44 yrs., Texas

One of my male iguanas bit the other one so badly on the forepaw that he now has no muscle control in those fingers.   —I-273, Bill, 34 yrs., New Jersey

I have cited more than enough examples to show that two iguanas should not be an option. The only reason for having more than one iguana (one male, one female) should be for potential breeding, and then you are required by the laws of nature to supply these two creatures with a huge living space, about the size of a small bedroom.

Non-Iguana Cagemates

Some herpetological magazines and books are very relaxed on the idea of an iguana sharing a habitat with other animal species, but I am not. I don't recommend having any other animals in the same habitat with an iguana, ever. In the wild, certain animal species interact with each other all the time with few if any problems because their living space is so large (acres). But if you put two animals in a 4' x 6' cell, eventually something bad will happen.

Each type of potential cagemate presents a different set of problems. The following examples encompass cagemates other than iguanas, with comments and quotes about potential trouble:

Other Lizards

The only unusual experience we had was when we had to place an anole in our iguana's cage (the anole's cage was damaged so we put it in there temporarily). At first the iguana didn't seem to mind at all. I took the iguana's water dish out to refill it and left the cage open. I got slightly side-tracked and took a while returning dish. All of a sudden we heard a "bang, bang, bang" against the side

*of the habitat. The iguana had the anole in her mouth head first and was bang-
ing it against the glass. We took the anole from her mouth—the anole was a little shaken but is still doing fine.*   —I-628, Yvonne, 29 yrs., California

*My iguana had a green anole as a cagemate. I was gone over the weekend and
when I got back the anole had disappeared. Later I found bones in the iguana's
fecal matter.*   —I-180, Dave & Katherine, 50 yrs., Michigan

*My daughter caught a small horned lizard (about 3" long) and for lack of a bet-
ter place to put it off it went into the cage with our iguana [TL: more than 5', 5
yrs., 18 lbs.]. About 2 or 3 hours later, there wasn't a trace of the horny toad
left.*   —I-379, Russ, 32 yrs., Utah

NOTE: I am convinced that the iguana didn't eat the lizard for food in these
cases, but did so to remove the other lizard from its extremely small living
space. To get these lizards completely "out of sight" they were eaten. Gone in
the stomach is gone out of the habitat. . . .

At the other extreme, it's a bad idea to house iguanas—especially small
ones—with monitor lizards, which are aggressive carnivores. Enough said; the
dangers should be obvious.

Turtles

I once saw an adult iguana housed in a habitat with a large turtle. Because
there was no high basking area for the iguana, he had to stay on the bottom of
the habitat with the turtle. For half an hour I watched the turtle walk over the
iguana. The owner of the iguana said that the turtle had bitten part of the
iguana's tail off, probably thinking it was food. I asked the iguana owner, "Why
do you still keep them together after the iguana was injured?" He said, "I don't
know." Sometimes I think that humans are not very bright.

On the other hand, sometimes it's the turtle that must be careful:

*He [iguana] often sits on his chair and watches the box turtle run around on the
floor, but if it ever goes near him he swats his tail at it.*
        —I-788, Trevor, 19 yrs., Oregon

Snakes

Never put an iguana in the same habitat with <u>any</u> kind of snake. Not even
for a second. <u>NEVER! NEVER!</u>

*Never ever let an iguana see a snake, especially boas, which can eat small igua-
nas. I know someone who thought he could keep the two together until one day
he walked in to see only the tail of his iguana hanging out of his boa's mouth.
Yuk! Poor iguana! I was once on an outing with one of my iguanas and met up
with a boa person. When my iguana got a look at that snake she went berserk
and I had to take her away.*   —I-200, Dianna, 47 yrs., Washington

By not having to deal with another pet, you can spend more quality time caring for your iguana. This will also help tame your lizard faster and build a stronger bond. As your iguana gets older, the benefits will be easily recognized.

OUTINGS

If you treat an iguana as something on display in a small pen, you'll never have a good pet. I believe they should be part of the family. They are really no different than a cat in their behavior.
—I-358, Pamela, 31 yrs., Michigan

"Outings" has two options. The first option, "Loose in the Home," is when an iguana is allowed to temporarily come out of its habitat and spend time with the family. The second option is called "Non-Caged Habitats" and refers to an iguana that has no enclosed structure at all. In this case, its habitat is essentially the whole house, or restricted parts, with specific areas designated for sleeping, eating, and defecating.

Loose in the Home

If I let her loose in the house she [SVL: 11", TL: 3', 4 yrs.] loves to explore, but always "checks up" on me on a regular basis, about every 15 or 20 minutes. She will be with me for a few minutes then leave and go about her business.
—I-322, Marty, 22 yrs., Ohio

My female likes to follow the sun [southern windows] around our apartment.
—I-620, Suzanne, 34 yrs., New York

Once your iguana is tame—and the day will come if you do the things I have outlined—a whole new level of enjoyment can be achieved with your iguana "loose in the home." The decision as to how much freedom, and when and where, is up to you. <u>But with the freedom of the lizard to be in a specific room or the whole house comes the responsibility of the pet owner to make sure that the lizard is safe and warm at all times.</u> As you read through the sections coming up, you will see that this is not an easy matter.

Why

My feelings are that living in a cage your whole life is a prison sentence, and although these guys are safer caged than having free run of the household (too many possibilities of damage or injury), I feel it's been unfair of man to deny them their natural habitat. So I try to make up for it to them by giving them as much as they need of freedom in the summer. They do enjoy it immensely.
—I-200, Diana, 47 yrs., Washington

Some people say it is safer and better for the animal if it stays in a cage all its life—that there are too many things that can injure or hurt your iguana when it is out in the house. It's true that every house has potential dangers, but you can reduce the risks by understanding the possible problems and situations your iguana can get into.

I believe that an iguana develops into a better and happier pet when it can have some free range in the house. After my iguana got used to being out of his habitat, he looked forward to this time. When I first got home from work, Za would walk down to the middle ledge in his habitat and wait until I removed the front door of the habitat. Then he would crawl onto my arm and I would put him in the living room to roam for a while. Once he got a taste of being out, he was enthusiastic about getting out. Restricting out-of-the-habitat times is also a useful training aid, and I used it frequently to fine-tune my iguana's behavior (see Chapter 8, Domestication, "Training").

Requirements During Outings

"Rat-proof" your house so your iguana won't get lost or stuck in any hole or vent or behind any household furniture or equipment.

Under supervision only, all three of the "kids," as we call them, are allowed to roam, run, and raise hell in the bedroom during some evenings and weekends.
—I-661, Chris, 22 yrs., Nevada

Iguanas need to be watched constantly, especially when they are young and small and can hide so easily. If your iguana is free in the house you should be there, too. "Free" is not the exact term, as you will be controlling the places and amount of time your iguana spends out.

For example, after about three or four months of owning my iguana, he became tame and was allowed out to explore the living room of my small apartment at his leisure (my eyes followed him everywhere for his protection). Over a six-month period, Za scouted every inch of that room on the ground, and as he got bigger he expanded his explorations to things off the floor, such as a little recessed bookshelf, plants, etc.

When he was walking on the floor, he would often turn his head and look up at things higher in the room. I frequently saw him stare at the top of a shelf, looking as if he were trying to figure out how to get up there. And if not then, later he would use many combinations of climbing techniques to get to the spot he had stared at earlier. Sometimes his curiosity rivaled that of a cat.

Being a rock climber, I appreciated Za's great combination of moves and determination. But using his tail as a hydraulic jack was cheating as far as I am concerned! One day he couldn't quite reach the bottom of a bookshelf, so he just made his tail stiff at the base and boosted himself up a couple of inches until he could reach the edge of the shelf.

Another time, when Za was about a year old, I watched him climb up a 5-foot antique brass floor lamp to get access to the next level, a tall bookshelf.

There was nothing to dig his claws into, just metal. He got up by shimmying, knees and arms pressed against the metal. He wanted to get to the bookshelf, and nothing was going to stop him. It didn't look like a natural lizard movement. I don't believe this particular move was in the "Iguana Climber's Manual"; it had to be some technique he invented.

A large, older iguana is easier to have loose in the house because it can't hide as well. Also, when an older iguana knows its territory, it doesn't roam around as much as a hatchling—it's usually happy to be in a warm, sunny window where it can watch something outside. Even though the next section is called "Non-Caged Habitats," much of the information in there also applies to "Loose in the Home."

Non-Caged Habitats

Both iguanas are free in the house and climb on various pieces of furniture. The 7-year-old likes to lie on a bed located near a window. This area receives large amounts of sun and she lies there and looks out the window. (It is an unusual sight for passersby outside.) The 3-year-old seems content to lie on a dining room chair.   —I-554, Anthony, 29 yrs., Texas

In a non-caged habitat the iguana no longer is confined to a specific enclosure. The lizard now has a room, rooms, or the whole house in which to explore and move about freely on its own. In this scenario there is always a place for the lizard to go to warm up (some sort of heat source), a place to defecate (newspaper or something comparable), a sleeping area, and a permanent place where food and water are located.

Some people in colder areas of the country have written and said that their iguana not being caged worked well, until it started to get a little cold. One person found her iguana hiding behind the drapes next to the window, dead after a two-day hiding incident. This is not an isolated story; I have many more I could tell. As a side note, any time you don't know where your iguana is, go find it immediately. If it's hiding, bring it out from wherever it is. Sometimes they hide behind a couch or bookshelf, get cold, and eventually are physically unable to move.

There are many dangers and problems that can come up even when your iguana is out for only an hour and you are watching it continuously; full-time non-caged habitats magnify these potential problems by 24 hours. I don't recommend this type of lifestyle for the typical iguana owner; I've included it only to show the full spectrum of iguana "lifestyles." It works only with older and tame iguanas in warm regions of the country, and with especially aware iguana owners. A young iguana should never be allowed unlimited range, even under the perfect conditions.

I have owned an iguana for three years; we got her as a hatchling. I started her out in the "classic" dwelling, a 20-gallon long tank. After she became accli-

AT A GLANCE: *Prerequisites for Non-Caged Habitats*

- Warm region of the country (e.g., Florida, Texas, Southern California)
- Warm/hot house
- Older iguana (2+ years old)
- No children or other pets in the house
- Owner(s) devoted to iguana's life

mated, I started allowing her to roam outside of the tank onto a "tree" I had built in the corner of my apartment. Every day she would climb out on a ladder, and spend the afternoon sunning on her tree.

The bigger she got, the less she liked the tank, and as it was going so well, I decided to try to let her [SVL: 15", TL: 3' 11", 3 yrs.] live uncaged. I made an additional resting area in the tree out of the rolls that carpeting is stored on, which I covered with burlap. There is also a shelf, water and food bowls, a heat lamp, plus a heating pad high up.

She will cruise the kitchen if her bowl is empty, and amazingly enough, will walk to the bathroom to shit every day. I am grateful, as it is much easier to clean up than the carpet! —I-620, Suzanne, 33 yrs., New York

Requirements

Many of the serious environmental concerns you had to consider when creating the proper enclosed habitat for your iguana are still necessary when your lizard is allowed to roam free. Whether it's a short-term outing or a long-term non-caged situation, certain things must be taken care of.

Temperature

I see a lot of larger iguanas that begin having problems due to them outgrowing their aquariums and their owners allowing them free run of the house. The iguanas are usually not provided with a heat source and ultimately develop anorexia problems and other metabolic problems related to the lack of a "basking" heat source. —V-117, Dr. Dale, 38 yrs., Texas

Temperature is a critical element in raising a healthy iguana. Either side of the ideal temperature can put your lizard into temporary or permanent health dangers. Also, if it's too cold your iguana often won't eat.

* Too Cool

As soon as we got him warmed up and the heat was constant [they built a habitat for him], we had no problem with his appetite.

—I-690, Irene, 34 yrs., Texas

Three years ago in New York I left the windows open in my apartment and forgot. It was autumn. My iguana was out of his cage, sitting on his favorite plant in the house when I left. I went to a party and decided to sleep over, forgetting I had left the windows open in the apartment. It was freezing the night I left him alone. When I got back the next day, my lizard was in suspended animation. I took off my shirt and put him against my body, then near his heat light. Luckily he came back fine.   —I-576, David, 23 yrs., New York

Two winters ago it was 70-something degrees. Within an hour and a half it was 30 degrees. We were away from home. When we got back I checked the animal room and couldn't find my large iguana. I eventually found him between the blinds and the window glass—the blinds aren't venetian, they are a solid bamboo. He was pretty well frozen and I thought he was dead. I brought him in, wrapped him in a blanket, and put a heating pad near him. When he started warming up he kept flopping around—sort of like whipping his tail, but his whole body was involved. Maybe they were a form of seizure, or neurological damage of some sort. I pretty much kept him wrapped up for almost a week. It took probably a week to 10 days for him to get completely back to normal.
                                                —I-237, Diane, 44 yrs., Texas

The first basic challenge in making an iguana part of your household is maintaining a warm enough temperature. A cool house is not a place for an iguana to roam free. Pick up an iguana that has been out in a 70°F room for a while. The lizard's body will actually feel cold to your touch. Remember, 85°F is a nice temperature for an iguana. A 70°F room might feel good to you, but that's 15° cooler than the iguana likes. Would you feel comfortable in a room that started at 70°F and dropped to 55°F (15° cooler)?

A warm house (at least 75°F) is OK if there is an additional heat source (e.g., lamp, heating pad, Iguanamometer) located in a designated spot that the iguana can always go to when it needs to warm up. Cold air settles, so this heated area needs to be off the ground, preferably up high. As a side note, most of the thermostats for house heaters take their temperature readings about halfway up from the floor. If your iguana is on the floor, it could easily be 5° to 10° cooler there.

Even though a heat source is provided for your iguana, it doesn't mean the iguana will always use it. Many times when an iguana starts to get cool it just stays in that cool place and gets colder. As it cools its metabolic rate drops, reducing its ability to move. As you know by now, eventually the lizard can't move even if it wants to.

Even warm-blooded humans experience similar cooling problems. I did a lot of long-distance open-water swimming in the San Francisco Bay, which is usually pretty cold (40s to 50s°F). Once when a group of us swam the length of the Golden Gate Bridge, some people nearly drowned—not because they were tired, but because they were so cold that their bodily functions started to slow down. They had trouble even moving their arms to swim. One person tried to call for help but could hardly get the words out of her frozen mouth. Even the people who completed the swim walked around afterward like shaking, frozen popsicles, babbling incoherent sentences to each other until their bodies warmed up.

* Too Hot

It may seem hard to believe that a tropical lizard can get overheated in a home, but I have seen it dozens of times. For example, in a short period of time in front of a hot, sunny window, your iguana can become dangerously over-heated. It's like leaving a glass of water next to a window with the sun coming through. A couple of hours later, you have a glass of hot water.

When my iguana was just a year old this experience happened to him. The first clue that he was overheated was that he opened his mouth wide, like a dog does when it is overheated, and when I felt him he was like a hot rock. I imme-diately removed him from the window.

It was strange, because over the months I had seen him move around the house to get warmer or cooler. Why on that one occasion did he stay in the window and get overheated? Perhaps he would have moved eventually, but I wasn't going to take the chance. I made sure he got out of the heat. This is yet another reason you need to keep an eye on what these lizards are doing.

What was helpful in this situation was that several months before, I had read a number of scientific papers dealing with iguanas' temperature. Vivid in my mind was the fact that in many cases, the first sign of overheating is that the iguana opens its mouth like a panting dog.

UV Light

Besides heat, a source of sunlight or artificial UV light is necessary. In a free-roaming situation, UV light exposure can be "catch as catch can." Make sure that wherever your iguana spends most of its day, it has access to good-quality UV light. (Remember, little or no UV—in the right spectrum—passes through the average house glass window.) If your iguana "hangs out" in a spe-cific window every day, you could install a special glass that allows the appro-priate spectrum of UV light to pass through (see page 181 for details).

Problems

The problems that can scare, stress, injure, or kill your iguana when it's loose in your house are too many to list. And of course there is the added chance of damage to your home and belongings.

He [5 yrs., 8 lbs.] has to be watched closely when he's out of his cage or he'll (accidentally) destroy things by knocking them over.
                                                    —I-476, Marie, 23 yrs., Virginia

I recommend not to keep an iguana or any other lizard loose around the house, as they are arboreal by nature and you may return home to find your curtain rod down and your drapes torn.   —I-200, Dianna, 47 yrs., Washington

As I have mentioned, iguanas tend to climb to the highest point they can reach in each room. If you have drapes, the iguana will use them as a ladder to get to the top. In time, the drapes will be shredded rags. My iguana was trained not to climb the drapes and other tall items; your lizard can be, too (see Chapter 8, Domestication, "Off the Plants and Curtains").

Injured

Watching your iguana climb all over the house and furniture can be very entertaining, but you must be ready to intervene. It's fun to see an iguana jump to a ledge or a piece of furniture, or wedge its body into any object that can help it on its way to its goal. Iguanas perform these acrobatics naturally, but they can also get hurt (e.g., wedge a leg and fall, or snap a tail).

Lost

When my iguana was about 5 months old, I left the room for a minute. When I came back, he was gone. I looked for an hour in all his favorite places, but couldn't find him. I sat down on the couch to think where he might be and happened to see some movement out of the corner of my eye. There, in a large pot of golden pathos plants, sat Za, relaxed and blending in with the greenery, just staring at me. He wasn't permanently lost, just temporarily displaced.

Escaped

One day I had one [iguana] escape. I accidentally left the door open. After frantically searching everywhere, I just called it quits. I told everyone my ordeal. After about one month, my gardener called me over to show me a lizard. I couldn't believe it. He had found my lost iguana. My yard is huge and full of shrubs and trees. Even now I can't believe it.

—I-794, Andrés, 30 yrs., California

One of the most common problems with your iguana out in the house, besides it getting cold, is the chance that it will escape permanently. Iguanas can easily escape through an open door, or any of a million other ways, when someone is not paying attention. Remember, if your animal gets away from you in the winter, it will die. In some areas, even the summer evenings get cool and your iguana could die, or at the very least develop a serious respiratory infection. Then there are the dangers of neighborhood dogs and cats and wild animals. Make sure your lizard doesn't escape.

Automatic screen doors are notorious for closing but <u>not latching</u>. All an iguana has to do is push on the door and it's gone. Adjust the screw on the closure (marked "sweep" on the top of the closure) so the door closes more tightly.

Home Electronic Machines

An iguana roaming the house may not intentionally be looking to join the Information Age, but be warned that without some attention on your part, you could be in for some real surprises with your home electronic equipment.

* _Phone_

On several different occasions while my iguana was wandering around on my desk, he stepped on my telephone. The phone has a button to turn it on, which he must have hit as he headed for a sunny spot on my desk. As a result, my phone was "busy" until I noticed it and turned the phone "off."

* _Answering Machine_

A couple of other times, he walked across the answering machine, and one time he stepped on the button that starts taping phone conversations. I came home to a full 45-minute tape of Za shuffling around on my desk.

* _Computer_

For some reason, Za seemed to love lying across my computer keyboard. Several times, I made the mistake of leaving a document open on my computer, only to come back to it and find that Za had moved or deleted entire sections with some pretty creative keystrokes. On another occasion, my girlfriend came into her office and found Za stretched out on her computer keyboard, with about 30 pages of typed gibberish on her computer screen.

I learned to disconnect my keyboard from the computer any time I left my office with Za roaming around in there. The things we do for our pets.

DANGERS

Dangers

I have had many experiences [with my iguana], and I know for a fact that if there is a place where iguanas have a chance of getting hurt, they will go there. Such as between dresser drawers, under beds, crawling up blinds, and climbing in light fixtures (fortunately, it was turned off). If you have an iguana, you have to expect the unexpected.   —I-719, Lucas, 14 yrs., Indiana

An iguana that becomes a member of the family can be one of the most rewarding experiences, <u>but it also poses one of the most dangerous times for your lizard.</u>

Danger comes in many forms. As I have said before, you need to keep your eyes, ears, and mind alert when your lizard is out of its habitat. There is no way I can list every item and object that can injure or kill your iguana when it is loose in the house. If there is a chance for something to hurt your iguana, it may in time, if not corrected.

One time I was gone for a month in Mexico on an iguana research trip and I left my iguana in the hands of his excellent caretaker, Kendal. Kendal came over to the house every day, fed Za, and cleaned up his feces. Because Za was in his breeding season and very restless, I created a special door to his habitat so he could come out when he wanted and explore the entire living room, and therefore not feel trapped in his habitat.

All the doors to the living room (where the habitat is located) were closed, and before I left I removed the large house plants, knick-knacks that might fall on him, and everything else I could think of to make his wanderings absolutely safe. All the heat vents in the house were closed except the ones in the living room—so Za had a toasty 80°F when he was out of his habitat.

Kendal came to the house one day and found Za in the back bathroom off the kitchen, and he was cold, dark in color, and frightened. It was the middle of a cold winter, and he was in an unheated part of the house. Kendal handled the situation perfectly: He got a towel to pick up the scared and possibly aggressive Za, put him back in his habitat, made sure he warmed up, called the veterinarian just to be sure there was nothing else he should do for Za. Essentially, Kendal did everything I would have done if I'd been there to take care of the situation myself.

Za must have pushed open the heavy, solid swinging door from the living room to the kitchen (which is amazing, because it's hard for us humans to push the door open). In three years of living in the house, we'd never seen Za try to push the door open, but he had seen us go through it thousands of times. Za's tail was also slightly smashed from the escape, which I assume happened as the door swung shut on it.

Luckily, Za hadn't eaten yet that day, or else the cold temperature might have caused any food in his digestive tract to go bad. I returned a couple of days later on schedule from my trip, and I showered Za with extreme love, care, attention, and special treats. It was a long process to save the tip of his tail, but several months later the tail was fine.

The moral of this story: I did everything possible to make Za safe while I was gone, and it was still not enough.

Below is a list of a few places and things that can endanger your iguana when it's loose in the whole house, to help you become aware of potential problems and correct or avoid as many as possible. These stories are only to give you a look at the "tip of the iceberg" when it comes to possible dangers an iguana can get into when out of its habitat.

Floors

• Under foot

The floor is perhaps the most dangerous place for your iguana to be. Even big iguanas are small in relation to people and room sizes. Also, iguanas' coloring blends well into the floor. An iguana getting stepped on seems very likely. The more people in the house, the more dangerous the situation becomes. Iguanas move through the house slowly and don't make much noise.

If there are a lot of people in your home, I don't believe an iguana should have free run of the house. Perhaps restrict it to one room only, which reduces the odds of it getting stepped on. In our household, there were only two humans, and when Za came out of his habitat we both knew it and remained alert.

• Chemicals

The harsh chemicals used in floor-cleaning detergents need two clear-water rinses to reduce or eliminate their potential to cause problems. Iguanas tongue-flick just about anything on the floor, so pay attention to these products. Other household products to be aware of are carpet spot cleaners and waxes on floors and tables.

One person moved into an apartment that had to be fumigated for cockroaches (these critters live even in nice homes). He took his iguanas to work to protect them from the fumigant, which was very smart. When he brought them back they showed no ill signs. But soon afterward they started to go downhill—they stopped eating and finally died. He figured the fumigant must have been absorbed into the wood of the habitat. Even simple over-the-counter flea foggers can be dangerous.

• Carpet (loop-type)

My iguana started catching his claws on the carpet.
—I-852, Debi, 35 yrs., Oregon

Loop-type carpet is thick, rich, and dangerous. Hundreds of fibers are twisted together to form a single strand, and this strand is formed into a loop. Hundreds of thousands of these strands make up the carpet. If an iguana happens to get a claw in this loop, then makes a turn of 180° (back from where he came from), the loop can essentially cinch up like a hangman's noose on the claw, and the iguana is trapped.

Several people have written to tell me how their iguana ripped its claw out or broke a toe on this type of carpet. As the iguana panics from being captured by the carpet, it jerks or runs to get away. Sometimes just regular threads in the carpet can tangle around an iguana's toes. If you aren't paying attention, the thread can eventually cut the blood flow to the toe, forcing it to be amputated.

Things They Can Get Behind

- **Stereo**
- **TV/VCR**

One day one of the baby iguanas was on my shoulder and decided to take a mad dive. It ran through the room looking in every direction and ran right into the VCR and got stuck. We had to take the VCR apart. The iguana was OK, but the VCR never recorded again.   —I-786, Miriam & Wolf, 28 yrs., Florida

- **Couch**

July 19, 1988, my iguana was somehow suffocated in the couch. When discovered, she was limp and non-responsive. Because I'm a registered nurse, I couldn't accept this and did "Infant CPR" on her. Slowly she came around.
                                                        —I-95, Pat, Missouri

Iguanas, especially smaller ones, hide easily behind pillows or cushions of couches, and you can unknowingly sit on your live animal. One iguana hid for several days before its owners found it under the couch. Even though the iguana had turned black from being too cool, it somehow survived. Roll up towels or cut out cardboard to plug the spaces behind and beneath couches.

We let our iguana [SVL: 13", TL: 4', 2½ yrs., 4 lbs.] wander in the house. Last winter she wandered behind the couch where there was a cold draft and she got pneumonia. I took her to the vet but she was weak, wouldn't eat, and her tail was soft and limp. She died that night.   —I-650, Helen, 31 yrs., Ohio

Remember, iguanas can't be left out to hide all day. As I've mentioned before, get your lizard out from under or behind couches, beds, etc. the minute you notice they are hiding. If your house is cold and drafty, your iguana should stay in its own habitat for safety. Even on warm days (to humans) an iguana left away from a heat source for an extended period of time faces extreme danger.

- **File cabinet**
- **Desk**
- **Refrigerator**
- **Stove**
- **Bookshelf**

When I'd had my iguana for about a month, she got away from me and got under the bookcase. I ended up unloading the bookcase and carefully moving it as she wasn't coming out. I was shocked and worried to find her entire body a dark, drab, olive green. I thought she'd run; instead, she acted frozen, comatose, though her eyes were open. Even when I placed her back in her cage, she remained frozen, actually holding one leg up in the air. It must have been 15 minutes before she began moving and returning to her more vivid green and blue tones.   —I-706, Melodie, 41 yrs., Tennessee

My iguana used to have the run of the house, until once when she got stuck between a bookshelf and an outside wall when it was –20°F outside. I found her (almost dead) the next day—cold, stiff, mouth and tongue blue, etc. I wrapped her in a heating pad and gave her warm water with an eye dropper until she started to move around and become more alert (over an hour).
                    —I-383, Tammy, 27 yrs., Wisconsin

• Heater

Once my iguana burned himself around his stomach. He managed to squeeze himself behind a radiator, and it was really hot. It was ridiculous trying to pry him out; he was definitely stuck. I thought I would break some of his ribs try-ing to pry him out. Luckily, only a little of his skin where the radiator touched him seemed discolored.   —I-576, David, 23 yrs., New York

One day our cat was chasing my iguana (it was small then), who tried to hide behind the electric heater along the wall. Well, she was stuck. I panicked and ended up ripping the heater completely off the wall to get her out. I was really scared. I didn't even care about the heater.
                    —conversation with a pet owner at a herp conference

My radiator has been safely encased so my iguana can't crawl behind or under and get stuck or burned (ouch!).   —I-200, Dianna, 47 yrs., Washington

Any time you find your iguana behind something, <u>you can be sure it will go back to that spot again at another time</u>. Do whatever you can to change the configuration of the object so your iguana can't get behind it again.

Things They Can Get Into

One time my iguana got loose in the house when she was small. We finally found her in the children's toy bag. She was so still she looked like another toy animal.   —I-268, Peggy, 32 yrs., Florida

• Closets

You have to keep an eye on your iguana at all times. Once I lost my iguana, but was sure she was in my closet. I looked again and again. Finally I thought to look between my clothes and there she was, hanging on my dress.
                    —I-183, Mary, 24 yrs., Massachusetts

- **Drawers**
- **Toilet**

When your iguana is out loose in the house, make sure that the lid to the toilet is down. Iguanas are very curious and they stick their faces and bodies everywhere—much like what a cat or kitten might do if introduced into a new home environment. If your iguana happens to get into the toilet, with the slick ceramic sides, it might not get out. The faster it tries to get out, the more tired it gets, and it could eventually drown. The other scenario is that the iguana goes for a dive to see what is on the bottom. There is no bottom, only death. Keep the lid closed. [Men, note: Women of the house will love you for doing this.]

- **Shower**
- **Heat vent**
- **Rugs**

Throw rugs that are not completely flat on the floor form nice tunnels of death for your iguana to hide in. The stories go something like this: Your small hatchling finds the dark, secret place in the rug and feels safe. You come back from grocery shopping in a hurry and step on the rug as usual, except this time you have an iguana with a broken back under it.

A hatchling is the hardest size of iguana to protect. They just disappear into everything. That's why I believe that small iguanas should come out only for short, supervised times in small rooms (e.g., a bathroom). When you have an iguana loose in the house, you have to start creating the awareness of a Zen master to prevent injuries to the lizard.

Things They Can Climb Onto

- **House plants**
- **Drapes**
- **Chair**

When my iguana was about 6 months old, he liked to sit atop one of my antique spindle-back chairs. The chair's eight long, fancy carved wooden spindles are spaced about $1\frac{1}{4}"$ apart at the top and narrow to $\frac{3}{8}"$ at the bottom. I worried that if he learned it was OK to climb the chair, he might topple it when he got bigger. But a more serious, life-threatening problem came up instead.

On the very day I decided he should no longer climb the chair, he nearly died doing it. I walked around the corner and saw Za with his head stuck between two of the spindles, his hands trying to grip the smooth spindles for support. He was sliding downward, with the space for his back and neck getting tighter and tighter.

I ran to the chair and supported his body weight, moving him up and out of the spindles slowly so he wouldn't panic. If I hadn't been there, Za would have slid down until his neck was crushed between the spindles, or he could have panicked trying to get out and in his wild flailing broken his back.

Needless to say, I immediately began a program of intense behavior modification to avoid any repeats of the spindle incident. After a few weeks, he never got on the chair again. This story is just one more reminder that almost anything can harm an iguana loose in the house.

- **Anything high or tall**

Everything that is high off the floor, iguanas want to be on. More than once I found my iguana when he was about 1½ years old on my rock climbing rope and rack of climbing equipment that I hung from the apartment wall. Even though I enjoyed watching him climb on the equipment, it had to stop. He was getting too big and I didn't want him to "learn" it was OK to climb in the apartment. I gave him lots of other fun things to do, but climbing in the house became a no-no.

Things They Can Eat

Jungles don't always have to be green, humid, and in Central America to be dangerous. I had to be especially careful of things that might drop on my office floor by accident, including staples or paper clips. Your iguana may not intend to eat a staple, but could be curious and flick it with its tongue. The staple could easily stick to its moist tongue, and down goes a barbed weapon of death.

- **Staples**
- **Paper clips**
- **Bits of paper**
- **Rubber bands**
- **Tacks**
- **Pieces of plastic**

One time I noticed something bright orange in his feces. Upon further investigation I discovered that it was a plastic wrapper from a TDK D-90 audio tape.
　　　　　　　　　　　　　　　　　—I-508, Bryan, 27 yrs., Kentucky

- **String**

Both iguanas will eat thread, strings, or ribbons. Once we walked in, and there was yarn spread all over the room. I assumed it was tangled around one of our iguanas, because the yarn led under the dresser. Worried, I moved the dresser to find that the string led into her mouth. She [SVL: 17", TL: 3' 6", 7 yrs.] had apparently started eating the string and couldn't bite it off (thank goodness). I gently pulled about two and a half feet of string back out of her. She was very cooperative, but choked and gagged as it came out. It was not a pleasant experience for either of us. Our male iguana [SVL: 13", TL: 2' 5", 3 yrs.] has also eaten a ribbon. He passed it out with feces and was a mess. Now we are very careful about leaving these sort of items around. This might be something you would want to warn others about.　　　—I-554, Anthony, 29 yrs., Texas

It's not that iguanas really want to eat the material, it's that once they flick it to see what the substance is, it gets caught on their short, sharp teeth, and their natural response is to swallow. This string story has a very powerful message about how easily an iguana can get in trouble being out of its habitat.

• Nylon stockings

Not long after receiving the string story, I got a letter from an iguana owner whose lizard almost choked to death on her nylon stocking. Iguanas can't spit things out easily, and they can't use their hands like humans would to pull objects out of their mouths. If an iguana gets a bit of a nylon stocking in its mouth, the rest of the stocking will follow.

Soon afterward, I caught my iguana (he was about 2 years old) in my girlfriend's closet (looking for what, I don't know), and he had just flicked and bitten one of her stockings. He shook his head as if he wanted the object out of his mouth, but it wouldn't come out, so he ate some more. I could see that it was caught on his tiny teeth, so I quickly but gently removed the stocking from his mouth. The woman's warning letter helped me be on "red alert" to this nylon stocking problem. I hope this section on potential dangers helps you in the same way.

• Cat litter

If you have a cat, make sure it's impossible for your lizard to eat cat litter when it is loose in the house.

One day I was letting my iguana [SVL: 12", TL: 3' 9", 3 yrs.] walk freely through the house and found her eating litter out of the cat box.
—I-747, Stephanie, 22 yrs., Illinois
[AUTHOR'S NOTE: One month later the iguana died. They didn't do a necropsy (animal equivalent of an autopsy) so they didn't know the cause of death, but they guess it was related to eating out of the cat box over a long period of time.]

• Hair/fur

Shortly after I started living with my roommate, who has two cats, my iguana defecated out a hairball. This sounds quite amusing, but I guess it could have pretty serious implications, because they could get an impaction from hair. I figure it is related to her tendency to taste everything, especially in corners the vacuum doesn't see often. —I-795, Dawn, 24 yrs., Ohio

My iguana ate some cat fur off the floor once, then had a fit trying to get it out of his mouth. —conversation at pet store

My iguana once flicked some human hair off the floor, and it was sticking out the corner of his mouth (I pulled it out before he swallowed it). Another time, I noticed him rubbing his eye on some furniture and pawing at his head with his rear foot. Upon close examination, it was a human hair on his eye, which I removed. Sometimes hair can kill an iguana:

Dr. Thomas D. Morganti, DVM, from Avon Veterinary Clinic in Avon, Connecticut, recently reported his findings that a 3½-year-old iguana was strangled to death by human hair.

The iguana was presented dead on arrival. Necropsy revealed, among other findings, a clump of human hair (2x2x2 cm) inter-twined with vegetation in the stomach. Two strands of hair extended up the esophagus and encircled the epiglottis.

The iguana had been allowed free run of the apartment for 2 to 3 hours per day and had been observed chasing and attacking dust balls, although he had never been seen ingesting one. The owner had found evidence previously of fur and hair ingestion in the animal's fecal material.   —Story in a herp newsletter (#26)

[AUTHOR'S NOTE: Dr. Morganti listed airway obstruction and slow strangulation as the cause of death, although there were other contributing factors.]

• Miscellaneous non-food items

Anything on the floor is fair game for an iguana to try to eat. Having an iguana certainly forced me to have a cleaner house, so no dangerous items would be left on the floor.

He [SVL: 14¾", TL: 3' 7", 12 yrs.] has consumed some strange items. More than once, I have found Styrofoam packing material in his feces. Another time, I found a hard piece of white plastic with rather sharp edges. I have no idea where he got it.   —I-508, Bryan, 27 yrs., Kentucky

Things That Can Fall on Them

As iguanas explore a house, it's not uncommon for them to knock things onto themselves. Items with cords attached are frequent problems. It's not that an iguana is clumsy—in the wild they climb easily—but the inside of a house is a foreign landscape with unfamiliar and often lousy climbing materials (slick painted surfaces, waxed tables, Formica shelves, etc.).

When she was almost two years old she pulled a small fan off a shelf on top of her and it broke her pelvis. The break healed fine, although she has a large bump on her lower back and she is much clumsier at climbing; she falls easily. I don't let her do much climbing nowadays because of that accident.
—I-903, Marty, 37 yrs., Wisconsin

About a year after I got him, he was out of his cage and I was on the phone. I heard a crash. I went over to see what happened. My iguana was on the ledge of a window (inside) and next to him was a broken pitcher. When he walked he did so on three legs. His front right arm was up and his wrist dangling. He didn't want to put any pressure on it. Well, $350, three visits to the vet, a brace, and two x-rays later, it turns out he had a fractured wrist.
—I-576, David, 23 yrs., New York

Your pet can knock books or various things off shelves and get bonked on the
head and knocked out if he's loose without constant supervision from you.
                                    —I-200, Dianna, 47 yrs., Washington

Miscellaneous Things That Can Hurt Them

• Plants

House plants can be toxic, even deadly. And don't think if your iguana
hasn't touched a certain plant that it never will. Your iguana might think,
"Wow, what a great plant to eat, but those humans are giving me that funny
look again. OK, I'll be cool, I'll just walk by and ignore it and when they get
relaxed to the situation I'll just burst my stomach with mouthfuls of those
sweet-looking leaves."

I have said this before; it's reminder time again: Another long-term danger
is not only the plant but also the potting soil. A large percentage of all commercially sold house plant soil contains vermiculite or perlite (the same basic
stuff, just different names), bits of white, round material that feels like Styrofoam. It's added to the soil to allow the plant to drain and absorb oxygen more
easily.

If your iguana starts to eat the soil (and they do like a little taste once in a
while) they will also get the Styrofoam balls in their digestive tract. If enough
is eaten, this could impact them and eventually kill them. I had to go through
my jungle of 23 house plants and change all of the soil.

Don't cheat and think you can just cover the old soil with new clean potting soil. With each watering those white balls of death rise to the surface of the
soil. I know, because that's what I tried the first time. You have to make a complete soil change. Another option is to cut a circle of cardboard with a hole for
the base of the plant to stick through (cut the circle in half for easy removal for
watering).

• Fans

My iguana was out in our house on a hot day and the last half of its tail swung
into the fan that was cooling the room. The tail got chopped off.
                                    —I-88, Garold, 54 yrs., Kentucky

• Doors

My iguana's left leg (femur) was broken when a door was opened onto him and
his leg was caught between the door and the floor.
                                    —I-508, Bryan, 27 yrs., Kentucky

Most doors fit tightly when closed but have a gap underneath them when
opened into a room. One day, I was towel drying my iguana on the bathroom
floor following his daily soak, when the last 3″ of his 3′ tail swept under this
door gap.

He didn't realize it yet, but his tail was stuck, so I had to work fast. I yelled for my girlfriend and she came in and petted him while I put a big screwdriver under the door to lift it just enough to release the tail. If Za had realized that his tail was caught in the door, he might have freaked out and tried to pull the tail out. This would probably have wedged it further, and he would most likely have broken part of the tail off.

This is another example of how even the most innocuous household items have the potential to cause harm to your iguana. Watch out for open doors wherever your iguana might be.

I have actually heard very few stories about iguanas and door accidents. It seems as if there should be a lot more.

• Window screens

My small iguana has broken off some of his claws. This was caused by letting him crawl on our window screens when the windows were open. (I wish somebody had told us about this; we had to learn the hard way!) Some of the nails have grown back, but only to a certain extent. They are like short, rounded nails.   —I-774, Walter, 46 yrs., Arizona

• Roller skates

I have three children and they usually have friends over and it's not unusual for a child to come in the house on roller skates. All this would be hazardous if my iguanas were out loose at this time.   —I-685, Julie, 36 yrs., California

With Other House Pets

About 3% of my business is injuries caused by other pets' interactions with owners' iguanas.   —V-18, Dr. Patty, 49 yrs., California

Dogs and cats frequently injure iguanas [that are] allowed free access in the house.   —V-117, Dr. Dale, 38 yrs., Texas

Any time you mix an iguana with other animals loose in a house, there are potential problems. Only you, the owner of the iguana, can mitigate or stop problems from happening. Awareness and an understanding of the potential problems is the solution. The following are some real-life stories to help get this point across.

Dogs

In general, iguanas do not like dogs. You might even say they hate dogs, perhaps because dogs are big, move too quickly, their barking is too threatening, and they have fur. Someone I met in a jungle in Central America said that one of an iguana's predators in the wild is the coatamundi, which has fur and is about as big as a medium-size dog. So maybe the iguana has a built-in negative reflex toward dogs—but that's only a guess.

Iguanas don't like dogs; everything else seems OK.
—I-733, Linda, 37 yrs., California

Having said that, I've heard the full range of iguana-dog interactions from iguana owners. For balance, I've included examples of everything, from iguanas controlling the dogs in their territories to iguanas being maimed or killed by dogs. Just remember, the "happy" interactions are extremely rare, so I believe iguanas and dogs should not be together. Here are some iguana owners' stories:

We have five well-trained dogs. Our large male iguana [SVL: 12", 5 yrs., 5 lbs.] enjoys drinking out of the dogs' water bowl. They hate it and he knows it. Otherwise our iguana ignores the dogs. The dogs are afraid of him.
—I-237, Diane, 44 yrs., Texas

The dog is afraid of the lizard. One day the dog and iguana got into it. The dog left running with the "Mark of Zorro" across its nose.
—I-638, Jennifer, 23 yrs., California

When my iguana was about 2 years old, one of my dogs attacked her for no apparent reason. Until this happened the dog had always been very docile towards my iguana. So be forewarned: NEVER trust other pets around your iguana, no matter how well they seem to interact.
—I-467, Kris, 32 yrs., Florida

Our dogs must have knocked or jumped against the bathroom door (where both the iguanas live), because it was open when we got home. Our wild iguana must have freaked to see two 75-pound Akitas crash through the door. I'm sure he ran into the living room. The other iguana in the bathroom probably never moved from his perch. I don't think the dogs ever saw him. I found the wild iguana DOA on the living room floor. He wasn't chewed up or anything. He had one or two puncture wounds to his chest from dog teeth. That's obviously what killed him. One of the dogs must have grabbed him around the thorax and bitten down too hard. The dogs had no wounds at all, but were scared and hiding when I came home. Needless to say, we installed a second "bolt latch" three-quarters of the way up the bathroom door to stop this problem from ever happening again.
—I-775, Karen, 37 yrs., Arizona

Cats

As with dogs and iguanas, cats and iguanas can experience the full range of interactions.

Once when my iguana was smaller he leaped off my shoulder onto my cat (she's old, grey, fat, and doesn't move much). I think he thought the cat was a rock for sun basking. I'll never forget seeing the poor scared cat run off with my iguana

still on her back. Now she's terrified of the iguana and he ignores her (mostly). Luckily the cat was too frightened to hurt him.
       —I-753, Kelly, 26 yrs., Pennsylvania

Our "psycho kitty" once jumped on our iguana [SVL: 16", TL: 4' 2", 6½ yrs.]. Our iguana quickly put kitty in her place with a well-placed lash of her strong iguana tail along kitty's side.   —I-635, Andrew, 38 yrs., Wisconsin

When the iguana was small the cats were pretty interested in him as a snack, and we kept them separated until the iguana grew larger. One cat tried to play with his tail once and the iguana gave the cat a quick pop to the head with his tail. Now the iguana is quite large [TL: 3' 5", 3½ yrs.] and likes to climb the carpeted cat condo and claim it for his own. It's not unusual to see our iguana and one of our cats curled up on the top tier.
       —I-690, Irene, 34 yrs., Texas

My large male iguana [SVL: 14", TL: 3' 3", 3 yrs.] interacts with my room-mate's cat. The cat is full-grown but fears the lizard. Probably because one day the iguana was roaming the living room and ran into the cat. A few minutes later the lizard came back to his cage with a chunk of fur in his mouth! The cat stayed clear of all lizards from that point on.
       —I-525, Kimberly, 21 yrs., California

Almost all of the veterinarians who returned my veterinarian question-naire made comments about how cats can injure or kill hatchling or juvenile iguanas.

I have seen several cases where the pet cat has eaten or chewed on a loose iguana.   —V-134, Dr. Chris, 43 yrs., Washington

Many iguana owners' stories echo the veterinarians' experiences.

I have always had my cats while having my iguanas. The very first iguana that I had escaped from its tank and my cats found it. When I found it, it was a mess.   —I-817, Matthew, 24 yrs., New York

I had another iguana, but he was killed by a cat. The cat crushed the iguana's lungs. I had the iguana on medication for one or two months, then it died. I'm still sad about his death; in fact, even as I'm typing this up on the computer, I feel very sad for him.   —I-571, Sam, 13 yrs., Oregon

I've heard stories about how some <u>large</u> iguanas have made "friends" with a very few select cats. Again, though, this is not the norm. If the interactions with cats can work at all, it happens <u>only</u> when the iguana is larger than the cat. It's hard to eat something larger than yourself. When the iguana is small it is just food or a toy for the cat.

Now that you know the dangers, **don't let your iguana interact with your cats**. This is the safest approach. There is a good chance that your cat could kill your young iguana, or that a big iguana could injure your cat.

Both Dogs and Cats

I have a cat and a dog. They've learned to just leave my iguana [15 lbs.] alone. He tolerates the dog, but will intentionally jump the cat whenever he gets the opportunity.   —I-137, Tim & Debbie, 33 & 30 yrs., Texas

I didn't expect him [SVL: 14½", TL: 4' ½", 3 yrs.] to get along with my cat as well as he does. He is more friendly toward my cat than he is to me. However, my iguana is afraid of the dog, which is smaller than my cat.
                                              —I-746, Mark, 19 yrs., Indiana

Dogs and cats are natural enemies [of iguanas] and I'd never trust them alone together.   —I-200, Dianna, 47 yrs., Washington

It's common for cats to severely injure iguanas that are small. Dogs would also kill them.   —V-18, Dr. Patty, 49 yrs., California

Birds

Even though birds seem like innocent animals, an angry bird could peck into the eyes or bite a chunk out of your iguana. Using caution with <u>all</u> animals that might come near your iguana is always the safest situation.

One of our iguanas has an intense dislike for green birds; all other colors he ignores.   —I-237, Diane, 44 yrs., Texas

My iguana [SVL: 12", TL: 2' 11", 7 yrs., 5½ lbs.] hates my Amazon parrot and has from the beginning. He will charge at the parrot from across the room if the parrot is not in its cage. I heard that Amazon parrots eat iguanas. My iguana pays no attention at all to the cockatiels or macaw parrot. In fact, the cockatiel used to share the heat lamp with the iguana.
                                              —I-283, Susan, 44 yrs., Washington

The cockatiel bit off the tip of both of my iguanas' tails. Our parakeet (tiny Amazon parrot) sometimes chews on the iguanas' spikes or picks on their loose skin shed.   —I-11, Patty, Washington

A macaw that I have had for 20 years is very jealous of the attention my iguana gets. The iguana got out of his cage one day and was climbing on the bird's cage. The bird didn't like it one bit and put a hole in the iguana's palm, crushing his second finger. The vet had to stitch up his palm and amputate his finger.
                                              —I-764, Diana, 46 yrs., California

There was a store in Seattle that sold only exotic birds, but the store owner also had a large, 12-year-old iguana that had free run of the place when the customers were gone. The owner said, "The iguana will often go to the cages of the birds he doesn't like and shit on their heads." Perhaps there is justice in the world, after all!

Snakes

It's very simple: **DO NOT** have <u>any kind</u> of snake near your iguana— <u>EVER</u>!!!

We also have Burmese pythons. When our iguanas see the largest python, they all run and hide under the couch.   —I-401, Kathryn, 21 yrs., Illinois

My iguana froze in place when he saw my large boa constrictor strike a rat. He watched with a worried look on his face while the snake killed and ate the rat.
                              —I-283, Susan, 46 yrs., Washington

Small Furry Mammals

The following example sums up concisely the interactions between iguanas and small furry mammals. <u>Don't</u> let them get close together!

My iguana lost about an inch of his tail while sleeping on top of a hamster cage with his tail hanging within reach of the hamster. Also, I do not trust the iguanas around small animals such as birds or rodents. I believe that an iguana, given half a chance, may attempt to attack this type of pet. I sure don't want to find this out the hard way, so I never permit my iguanas to mix with other pets of this kind.   —I-467, Kris, 32 yrs., Florida

Fish

Iguanas love to watch everything and are easily entertained by the colors and the slow, fluid movements of fish. Many people have told me how their iguana loves to watch the fish swim around in their home aquarium. The only real danger with an iguana around fish is from the iguana falling into an open or poorly secured aquarium top. If you have an iguana and fish, make sure that the aquarium top is secured and "bullet proof."

Sometimes my iguana tries to claw at the fish swimming by or even tries to get into the aquarium.   —I-724, Robby, 14 yrs., Utah

One owner's iguana actually fell into the tank trying to swat the fish as they swam around (the top of the tank was open). The iguana got out with the help of the owner, who was watching, but the lizard could have easily drowned. A secure top for a fish tank is a must when you own an iguana.

To Sum Up . . .

This was by no means a complete list of the dangers and problems iguanas can get into when loose in the house or apartment, with or without other pets. The stories and ideas are to get you thinking of the potential dangers before they happen and, with luck, avoid them.

OUTDOOR CAGES

When I first acquired my iguana he was having seizures and his bones were getting soft. His jaw was out of alignment and his left arm was twisted. I took him to a local herp society meeting where it was my good fortune (and my iguana's, too) to meet two folks from our local zoo. They took one look at my iguana (who was having a seizure) and said, "Too much lettuce and dog food— not enough sun." Well, I began the long process of fixing that, starting with exposure to direct sunlight.   —I-283, Susan, 46 yrs., Washington

When my schedule permits, I take the lizard outside to bask in natural sunlight. When the lizard has had a few days of natural sunlight he really turns a brilliant green and has quite the attitude! Rather aggressive and full of spunk!!
—I-638, Jennifer, 23 yrs., California

The main reason for having an outdoor cage is to provide a simple way of providing your iguana with its daily dose of wonderful, healing, stabilizing, natural sunlight (see page 179 about the importance of sunlight).

The region of the country where you live will dictate the design and the amount of time each year the outdoor cage can be used. Certain parts of California, Florida, and the South have temperatures where an iguana can be outside more often. Kris (I-467) lives in Florida and her iguana lives in a screened-in porch (12' x 12') most of the year. Most of us aren't that lucky.

He has two cages: an indoor and outdoor cage. After he uses the litter box we carry him to the other end of the house to his "outdoor" cage. This consists of a walk-in closet with a window that connects to an aviary-wire open air cage suspended from the house's overhanging eaves. The outdoor cage measures approximately 48" x 30" x 40" tall.   —I-600, Don, 69 yrs., California

Design Options

The design requirements for an outdoor sunning cage are much simpler than for the indoor habitat, which needs additional heat and fans. But as with the indoor habitat, certain things are required for your iguana's safety, health, and comfort.

AT A GLANCE: *Requirements for an Outdoor Cage*

• Large size
• Proper caging material
• Designed so that one area provides complete shade
• High off the ground, or away from potential animal attacks
• Protected from bird attacks from above with window screen
• Basking limb, ledges, or both
• Water available at all times for drinking and soaking
• Place for food snacks (kale, collard greens, nasturtiums, etc.)
• Place to defecate easily
• Escape-proof door

Building an Outdoor Habitat

The simplest design is a rectangular frame with a solid plywood floor and framing members of 2x2 wood. The sides and top can be made entirely of hard plastic netting (see "InterNet" plastic netting in Appendix B), or can include some plywood for protection against wind and sun, or to provide an area your lizard can go to feel safe. The plastic netting I am talking about is <u>not</u> that flimsy type used for plants to grow on. This is thick, sturdy, well-constructed, commercial-grade material.

> *All my iguanas have had a broken finger at one time or another. The most common way they do this is by jumping [onto the wire screen] and catching themselves by one hand, sometimes one finger. The weight of their body will twist the finger, which cracks the bone. The finger will swell at the break.*
> —I-764, Diana, 46 yrs., California

One danger of a mostly all-wire cage is that iguanas climb the wire and can injure their toes or fingers. If you supply enough good climbing and basking limbs inside the cage, your iguana will most likely climb these branches instead of the wire.

The legs of the cage should raise the structure off the ground high enough that any roaming animals can't get to your lizard. Having the cage 4' off the ground is a good starting point. Depending on your situation, you may need it to be higher, or it might be that the cage is placed in an area that is already high off the ground, such as a second-floor deck.

Once the cage is finished, give it a shove, as if a big dog had jumped against it. If the cage wobbles or starts to fall over, fix it so it doesn't do this. Perhaps a board nailed to the top of the cage, which in turn is secured to the house, will solve this problem.

Some people have mounted their outdoor cage on rollers so it can easily go out on the patio or deck. Others, in colder climates, assemble their cage each summer and disassemble it for easy winter storage. This design presented here is just to stimulate your own concepts.

Proper Size

The size of the cage depends on the size of your iguana and the size of the area you want the cage located. The cage doesn't have to be as large as the indoor habitat if your lizard is out in the "sun" cage for only short periods some days. If you live in a climate where the iguana can spend more time outdoors, the cage needs to be made larger to compensate for longer time spent in it.

Proper Interior Layout

The interior of the outdoor cage should include a solid bottom as well as the features discussed in "AT A GLANCE: Requirements for an Outdoor Cage" on the previous page.

Precautions

An outdoor cage (or an indoor sunning window) presents many of the same caveats as indoor habitats. They are few, but important.

Protection From Excessive Heat or Sun

Here in the South, it's good and hot much of the year. In their habitat, the iguanas have sun and shade to choose from. I bring them inside when the temperature drops below 75°F at night.   —I-519, Ellen, 40 yrs., Louisiana

One couple in California had a year-old iguana that they loved dearly. They left their lizard out in a screened-in porch many times without any problem. One day the iguana was in the porch area when it was exceptionally hot outside. When they went out to check on the iguana, it was dead from the heat. The problem was that the lizard had no shade area to escape the relentless heat of the sun's rays.

It rarely dawns on people that iguanas, as tropical animals, can't take a lot of heat. As mentioned earlier, there were some experiments done with wild iguanas that were tied up in direct sun until they died (science can be just wonderful, can't it?). The researchers wanted to know the temperature at which an iguana dies from too much heat, and for this experiment the critical temperature (core body temperature) was 46.4°C (115.5°F). They also found that at 42°C (107°F) an iguana opens its mouth and pants like a dog to help reduce the heat. If you see your iguana with its mouth open and it's hot, immediately get your lizard to a shady, cool area.

It's not so much how hot the day is as whether the iguana can move to a cooler location if its internal core temperature starts to increase dangerously. In the wild, if an iguana gets too hot it obviously moves into the shade of the trees or will descend to the ground for a while. If your iguana is locked into one place (in its outdoor cage), you need to provide shade and water so your iguana can't overheat.

Shade

This can be created with a plywood roof that covers one-quarter to one-half of the top of the outdoor cage. Be sure to position the cage so there's always a combination of sun and shade areas inside the cage.

Water

Water should always be available in the form of a drinking bowl. Leaving some edible greens (collard, dandelion, romaine) in this separate water bowl will help make the connection that this water is available for drinking.

You will also need a large container for your lizard to soak in, if the iguana happens to overheat. The first few times you will probably have to put your iguana in the tub of water until it learns for itself what to do.

Protection From Wind and Cold

Wind can cause sudden temperature changes, especially dangerous for an iguana trapped outside in a cage. You always hear about the wind chill factor on weather reports, and depending on its velocity, wind can dramatically reduce perceived temperatures. Often winds pick up in the late afternoon, so you may want to consider this when placing the outdoor cage in the yard.

I live in Florida and the winter brings very unpredictable weather conditions. It can be 80°F for a week and then suddenly drop to 40°F the night that you least expect it to. Twice my iguanas were exposed to [cold weather] unintentionally because of this. No long-term effects were experienced by either, although at the time their metabolism slowed to the point where they lost the ability to grip and actually fell out of the tree that they had been sleeping in at the time. Once they warmed up after this they were fine, although I recommend that iguana owners pay attention to these kinds of small details that can possibly kill your iguana. —I-467, Kris, 32 yrs., Florida

Protection From Animals, Birds, and Insects

Whenever your iguana is left in an outdoor cage, you must also think ahead and prevent intrusions or attacks by both wild and domestic animals, including birds and insects.

Animals

I bring my iguana in the house from the enclosed porch at night. I am afraid a raccoon or opossum might get her. —I-899, Barbara, 49 yrs., Texas

If you have cats or dogs in your neighborhood, it makes having your iguana outside a little problematic. But if you build the proper "fort" you can

SIDEBAR

Sunlight Problem: Trigger for Behavior Changes

Sunlight is by far one of the best ways to make your iguana healthier, but along with the benefits there is one possible drawback. Many people say that their iguanas get aggressive in the sun, sometimes even trying to bite.

My iguana, who was definitely a very assertive iguana most of the time, didn't get out-of-control crazy in the sun like some other people's lizards. Still, he had a predictable quirk whenever he had been outside in our enclosed yard and had absorbed enough sun (or maybe it's not too much sun that makes an iguana aggressive, but just plain overheating).

He would walk very fast toward me where I sat on a lawn chair, with his mouth open ready to bite my leg. Sometimes I would push his head aside just before he got to my leg. Other times I would let him run into my leg. In either case, he never bit me. As soon as he had stopped at my leg, he would crawl up and sit on my lap like a puppy instead. Odd behavior, from looking aggressive to completely docile.

Each iguana responds differently to everything, and a predictable behavior today could change tomorrow. If your lizard gets aggressive in the sunlight, approach with caution and stay away from the biting end of the aggression until the lizard settles down, which it will. The benefits of sunlight outweigh any temporary inconvenience of aggression. With this aggression in mind, it's a good idea to build a large cage door to make it easier to remove a possibly temperamental lizard.

My iguana gets crazy when exposed to the sun. Outside, he tries to bite and escape [if he's not in his cage]. This stops as soon as he's brought back indoors.
—I-273, Bill, 34 yrs., New Jersey

She [SVL: 14½", TL: 2' 10½", 1 yr. 10 mo.] turned into a 50 (top of your scale of wildness) when I put her outside in the garden [in sunlight].
—I-687, R., 54 yrs., Canada

My iguanas are docile in the [house] cage, but can get quite nasty when first approached in the outdoor cage.   —I-714, Roger, 36 yrs., England

keep the animals away. The best solution is to place the cage where these animals can't get to your iguana in the first place, such as an outdoor porch or courtyard.

Birds

Where I live, there are a number of hawks and crows, both smart and assertive hunting creatures. Designing half the cage top for sun protection should help your lizard hide from potential attacks from above. And covering the rest of the cage with sturdy plastic netting should keep your iguana safe.

Insects

One person wrote and said that she arrived home one day to find ants crawling all over her iguana, who was in its outdoor cage. The owner said that her iguana was jumping all over the cage to get the ants off its body and seemed to have a crazy, berserk expression on its face. Ants in great numbers can kill an iguana. They gather at the eye, the softest part of the animal, and start eating. It's a gross concept, but it's necessary to tell you this so you do not let it happen to your lizard.

When I raised rabbits as a kid (as part of a Scouting merit badge program), I knew that on hot days ants would try to come into the rabbit hutch to drink water. Once there in number, they would crawl on the rabbits. I put the legs of the rabbit hutch in tin cans filled with soapy water to stop the ants from climbing into the hutch. The soap breaks up the water surface tension so the ants can't walk on it. To protect your iguana, you could try the same thing with your outdoor cage.

Protection From Escape

> *I could not bear to lose my iguana—he couldn't be replaced.*
> —I-682, Dylan, 14 yrs., California

One of the biggest potential problems occurs when the door of the cage doesn't latch securely. Many people have written and said they knew the cage door didn't close or latch properly and they had planned to change it, but their iguana escaped before it was done. When your cage is finished, pull hard on the door. If it opens, it's not escape-proof.

If you have children or neighbor kids you might want to put a padlock on the door. Also, make the door large enough for easy removal of your iguana, especially for those days when your lizard doesn't feel like coming out of the cage.

> *My iguana was gravid and diagnosed as being egg-bound. Her appetite dropped to almost nothing. She struggled to escape her large indoor tank to the extent that she badly scraped away the tip of her nose. She seemed to be driven by extreme discomfort.*
>
> *We put her in an outdoor reptiliary [like an aviary, but for reptiles] with*

*an artificial tunnel and egg-laying chamber. She spent hours in the under-
ground chamber but was still restless.*

*On October 19, 1991, she dug a hole over 15 inches deep through sand
and dirt down to the coral rock bed. Then, she continued with a horizontal
tunnel of about one foot under the wall of the reptiliary. Finally, she dug up,
out, and escaped. She had dug out from a corner of the reptiliary in just two or
three hours on that sunny afternoon.*

*We looked everywhere and notified all our neighbors, then we gave up. On
the up side, it was a very mild winter in Miami, and we have a number of
yards in our neighborhood with gardens and fruit trees.*

*On February 25, 1992, we came home to find a note on our door to call one
of our neighbors. We did, and he said he had captured an iguana using a large
plastic garbage can. He said another neighbor, an older lady, had called him
when she saw the iguana on her back lawn.*

*We went immediately to the neighbor's house and there was our iguana.
She had no broken bones and was alert, but had turned a solid dark brown.
We thanked our neighbors and took our iguana home. She ate a lot and drank
even more.*

*We took her to our vet the next day, and he said our iguana needed to
regain some muscle and fat mass and confirmed by x-ray that all the eggs had
been laid sometime during the four months she had been loose.*

*By late June 1992, she weighed 3.7 pounds and her color returned, except
for the tail tip. After a few months of eating everything we gave her, she has
become a little picky, as usual. We are keeping her indoors until she becomes
gravid again. We have prepared for this by digging a trench all around the
reptiliary down to the coral rock bed, then filling the trench with wire mesh and
concrete.*

*We are very happy to have our iguana back, and to have learned from our
mistake.*   —I-268, Peggy, 32 yrs., Florida

*Last year my small iguana and the larger 5-year-old iguana escaped from their
outdoor cage. Both were excellent specimens and were a big part of our family.
We live on a 20-acre wooded lot and they probably thought it was heaven. Two
weeks later while I was working in our driveway, the smaller iguana came
out of the woods towards me and offered no resistance when I bent over to pick
him up. The other lizard was never seen again. To this day I still get a sick feeling when I think of him and the many years of having him as a pet.*
—I-395, Bill, 35 yrs., Virginia

Using a Window

You can either build a cage or do the simplest thing possible: Use an open
window. Find the window in your house that gets the longest hours of sun
during the day. If it's a double-hung window (one that opens at the top and
bottom), wedge a stick in the window as a safety precaution to prevent the

window panel from accidentally slipping, sliding, or falling down onto your iguana's body or tail.

Put a towel on the window sill to make it more comfortable for your lizard to lie on. Place a chair (or something) near the window so your lizard can reach the window sill easily, any time it is out of its habitat. As a side note, one family here in Oregon remodeled their house and put a sliding window in their son's bedroom. All the kid's iguana has to do is step from the bed into the window.

IMPORTANT: The window must have a screen and the screen must be secured from the inside with normal window hardware and also nailed or screwed to the house from the outside—or use some other technique that makes the window screen escape-proof. When it is secured, push hard from the inside; the screen should not give way. This window set-up works well for warm weather only.

For an all-around sun room, replace the standard glass in your window with UV-transmitting glass described on page 181. (Normal window glass does not allow the proper UV light to enter.) Even on cold days when the windows must be closed, the UV-transmitting glass will expose your lizard to UV light. You may also need to offer supplemental heat (e.g., put a heating pad under a towel) to keep your lizard warm while in front of the glass in the winter.

A FINAL WORD ON HOUSING

Housing is a huge chapter because it covers information that's fundamental to a captive iguana's health and happiness. Much of the information included here has never been discussed in other iguana books, or has been given only minimal attention.

Even though I purposely put a lot of detail into this chapter and the associated Appendixes, there is no way I can solve all possible situations you might encounter. Iguanas are very complex living creatures, which makes them both exciting and challenging. Many things will come up that you will have to think about and solve yourself. I hope that these pages have given you a little insight and eliminated many of the common potential problems you might have encountered.

CHAPTER 5
Feeding

Tell me what you eat, and I will tell you what you are.
—Anthelme Brillat-Savarin (1755-1826)

GENERAL FEEDING CONSIDERATIONS

Hippocrates, considered the father of modern medicine, said, "Let food be your medicine, and medicine be your food." This must be true, because an improper diet is a major cause of iguana medical problems. A nutritionally deficient lizard is also more susceptible to diseases and other problems.

Improper and careless nutrition will always result in a slow, torturous death for an iguana. Kidney (renal) failure, gout, osteo problems (soft bones) are all common problems associated with poor nutrition. . . . When proper nutrition and heat are provided, problems rarely come up.

—I-11, Patty, Washington

Food Debates

People will always argue about the optimal diet of any animal, including humans. Do we need meat? If we eat enough vegetables, can we still have fries with our burgers? One year nutritionists say that margarine is better for you than butter, then two years later they say butter isn't so bad after all and margarine might be worse.

There has long been controversy about how much protein we [humans] actually need. . . . [It was] estimated late in the 19th century that we need about 120 grams of protein per day. It was not until 1902 that the dean of American physiological chemists, Russell Chittenden, halved this figure. The World Health Organization . . . has established 40 grams as an adequate daily intake [now].

—Food research scientist (#33)

With so much debate over proper human nutrition, it's not hard to believe that there's disagreement about what constitutes a proper diet for an iguana.

Every iguana book has its own interpretation of the ideal diet for iguanas in captivity. No wonder iguana owners are confused about what to feed their lizards. I also have opinions; however, mine are based on what iguanas eat in the wild, on reading scientific research papers on iguana diets, and on veterinary reports on problem foods.

Iguanas are Herbivores

The green iguana (*Iguana iguana*) is one of the relatively few species of lizards living solely on a diet of vegetation throughout its life. . . . The natural diet of the green iguana consists of leaves, flowers, and fruits.
　　　—"Digestion in an Ectothermic Herbivore, the Green Iguana
　　　　　　　　　　　　　　　(*Iguana iguana*)" (#8)

Previous pet-care books have called iguanas insectivores (i.e., eat primarily insects) or omnivores (i.e., eat both plant- and animal-based foods), but all the recent research confirms that they are herbivores (i.e., eat plants). Specifically, they are "folivores," which means herbivores that specialize in leaves rather than fruits or seeds. I feel strongly that you should feed your iguana a diet appropriate for its herbivorous nature.

An amazing bit of information is that the green iguana is the only lizard that both lives in trees and feeds on trees (eating leaves, flowers, and fruit). The only animal-based foods iguanas eat in the wild might be an occasional insect crawling on a flower or leaf that they accidentally swallow.

DIGESTION: SPECIAL SYSTEM

If you understand how an iguana eats and digests its food, it will be easier to understand what and how to feed your lizard.

The Hindgut and the Importance of Temperature

Hindgut fermentation appears to be very important to the digestive physiology of herbivorous reptiles.
　　　　　　　　—*Iguanas of the World* book (#16)

Iguanas and all other true herbivorous lizards "share one significant morphological adaptation . . . found in no other living lizards; all have a distinctly enlarged, partitioned colon" (#16), inhabited by bacteria able to digest the cellulose in plants. This morphological adaptation is known as the hindgut.

The hindgut is a pouch-like appendage between the small and large intestines. It has valves or partition walls inside and is filled with microflora (small organisms that in this case include bacteria and possibly protozoa) that can digest cellulose, or the "fiber" in plants. The partitions help slow food down so the microflora can more easily break down the cellulose, which enables the iguana to extract more nutrients from the passing food than they could without the hindgut. Richard H. and Virginia H. McBee, iguana researchers, estimate that ". . . the green iguana may obtain 30% to 40% of its energy from this hindgut fermentation" (#16).

> It appears to me that the evolution of colic compartmentalization [hindgut] is the key character complex both necessary and permitting total herbivory.
> —"Adaptations to Herbivory in Iguanine Lizards" (#16)

The previous quotation is one of several that reaffirms that iguanas are herbivores.

> Factors that may affect the fermentation rate [in the hindgut], other than amount of food intake, [include] body temperature . . . and would be the highest when iguanas were basking.
> —"Hindgut Fermentation in the Green Iguana" (#16)

As I mentioned throughout this book, iguanas need a minimum of 85°F (29°C) to properly digest their food (research by John A. Phillips, Center for Reproduction of Endangered Species [CRES], San Diego Zoological Society [#14]). That's because this is the temperature that activates the microflora in the iguana's hindgut so they can do their digestive work.

To accomplish this in the wild, iguanas move in and out of the sun to adjust their internal temperatures. When they are in captivity, you must create conditions so your lizard can reach this minimum temperature for proper digestion (see Chapter 4, Housing, "Heat," for how this is done).

> *Our first little iguana died from lack of warmth for proper digestion. We did not know about the importance of heat then.*
> —I-885, Paul & Meredith, 15 & 47 yrs., Oregon

My iguana was always the largest iguana that I saw for his age, and I have seen hundreds over the years. Genes might have been part of it, but I believe he grew well because his habitat supplied the proper temperature to digest his food every day (as well as enough ultraviolet light).

Chop Food for Better Digestion

> Iguanas swallow fruit, flowers, and leaves whole or in very large pieces and little digestion occurs in the stomach.
> —A. Stanley Rand, iguana researcher in Panama (#25)

An iguana's mouth, jaw movements, and teeth are not designed for chewing. In the wild, an iguana will often bite and pull whole leaves into its mouth. For larger leaves, the iguana will use its teeth to perforate the leaf, creating manageable pieces that tear off easily, like the sections on a roll of paper towels. An interesting note: If the lizard is unfamiliar with a new food item it may flick its tongue on a perforated edge to pick up fluids that might provide clues about whether or not the food is safe to eat.

Unlike human saliva that helps in the digestive process, an iguana's saliva contains no digestive enzymes; therefore, it swallows food items essentially intact. Instead, an iguana's digestive process really gets going in the hindgut.

Reptiles, compared with most mammals, only minimally reduce food particle size, and large particles are digested at significantly slower rates.
—Wouter D. van Marken Lichtenbelt, iguana researcher (#8)

As an iguana owner you can improve the hindgut's functioning by pre-conditioning the food offered to your lizard. Food chopped or shredded into smaller pieces (explained in detail on page 306) means less up-front work for the iguana's digestive system. This also allows an iguana to eat more food per meal, and thus receive more nutrition.

WHAT TO FEED YOUR IGUANA

Feed a balanced diet from the beginning. Don't let them just eat their favorite foods (you wouldn't let a child eat only potato chips).
—V-18, Dr. Patty, 40 yrs., California

Iguanas in the wild eat leaves, flowers, and fruits from the trees found where they live, as I have mentioned before. In captivity, we have to bridge an iguana's wild food preferences with our "human" food the best we can.

It's important to point out that the research on the diet of an iguana is still evolving, and all of the details necessary to make good decisions for your iguana's diet are still being worked out. By comparing everyone's input over many years, a diet profile slowly develops.

Sadly, much of the information comes from iguanas that have died from ingesting a particular food source or group of foods that wasn't good for them. That's why I strongly advocate feeding iguanas a wide variety of foods.

Anyone who is not willing to take the time to provide them a varied diet should not own an iguana. —I-551, Frank, 41 yrs., Arizona

Until more is really known about the complete dietary needs of iguanas, it's safest to give them a variety of foods as recommended in the Iguana Food Pyra-

SIDEBAR

Correcting an Old Myth

Now that you have read how an iguana's digestive system works, let's get rid of one old "iguana fable."

One of the books I read said that iguanas need gravel to help them digest the vegetable matter they eat. This made sense to me since I knew that birds needed small stones in their gizzards to grind up food. I took my iguana to the vet one time because I was afraid she was egg-bound. The vet X-rayed her and saw the gravel in her system. He said it wasn't a wise practice to offer gravel to my iguana. —I-554, Anthony, 29 yrs., Texas

I saw two cases where an iguana died from eating gravel and three other situations where the lizard required months of intensive care. The idea that iguanas need gravel to help digest their food is a misconception that continually circulates. Iguanas don't have gizzards.

While researching the diet of *Iguana iguana*, scientists in Panama examined the stomach contents of 31 wild iguanas and "found no sand or gravel [in their digestive tracts]" (#25). After reading about an iguana's hindgut, I hope you now realize that gravel has nothing to do with an iguana's digestion—and that you won't let your lizard eat any kind of gravel or sand.

mid (see Figure 5.1). A diet consisting of primarily one food type is not sufficient. For example, a particular food thought to be fine now may turn out in future years to be bad for your iguana. A variety of food choices reduces the potential that any single item will cause a problem.

Feeding only selected items will cause your lizard to become "addicted" to those items, and the chances of a nutritional deficiency occurring will be increased. —V-69, Dr. Alynn, 39 yrs., Mississippi

Another reason for making sure you offer a variety of food items from the start is that iguanas in captivity are like little children: They will often single out just one type of food and eat nothing else. If you offer variety from the beginning, they will get accustomed to eating a wide range of food items. Iguanas are also creatures of habit, so the more choices they are offered when they're young, the more flexible their eating habits will be as adults.

Also like children, iguanas will often eat foods that are not healthy for them. As an example, they love lettuce because it looks and feels like their natural food—a leaf. But lettuce has almost no nutritional value; it's mostly water.

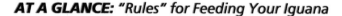

AT A GLANCE: *"Rules" for Feeding Your Iguana*

- Strive for variety, variety, and more variety
- Emphasize vegetables, especially leafy greens
- Offer only small amounts of fruit
- Use lettuce as a treat or training aid only
- Avoid live animals, dead animals, or meat as food
- Chop food finely
- Aim for an overall calcium/phosphorus ratio of 2:1 (see facing page for details)
- Provide food every day
- If possible, feed your iguana in the late morning
- Add calcium supplements (see page 279)
- Expose your iguana daily to unfiltered sunlight or UV light
- Maintain a habitat temperature of at least 85°F

Iguanas can die from a diet of only lettuce. As pet owners, it's our responsibility to give iguanas what they <u>need</u> for optimal health.

I have to think up new food combinations for her to eat so she doesn't get bored with her food.   —I-803, Tiffany, 14 yrs., Texas

Vegetables

It's nice to feed them directly from the refrigerator and not have live food around the house.   —I-632, Rosanne, 44 yrs., New York

I don't feel like a murderer when I feed my iguanas—they are vegetarians.
                                        —I-502, Karen, 23 yrs., Florida

Because iguanas are herbivores, most of their food can be purchased at your grocery store. You don't have to make a special trip to the pet store to purchase mice, worms, bugs, or any other living creatures for them.

If I approach my iguana with a plate of collard greens and yellow squash, he will leap at the plate.   —I-749, Charles, 27 yrs., California

The Calcium/Phosphorus Balancing Act

The best diet should consist of vegetables that are higher in calcium than in phosphorus.   —V-69, Dr. Alynn, 39 yrs., Mississippi

Many of the foods offered to captive iguanas have too little calcium, and many (such as fruit) have too much phosphorus. Calcium and phosphorus—which are incorporated into the bone's mineral matrix—must be present in the correct ratio (about 2:1) to promote normal bone growth.

This complex balance can be thrown off by:

- too little calcium in the food offered
- too much phosphorus
- too many foods containing oxalates or phytates (see page 270)
- lack of vitamin D₃, which is needed for calcium to be absorbed into the bloodstream

The best way to make sure your iguana gets the right amount of vitamin D₃ is to expose it to unfiltered sunlight or the right kinds of UV light (see Chapter 4, Housing, "Lights," for more details).

One way to visualize the importance of the calcium/phosphorus ratio (abbreviated Ca:P) is to see it as a balancing scale with the calcium on the left, phosphorus on the right, and the iguana in the middle. When the scale balances with two (2) parts calcium to one (1) part phosphorus (2:1 ratio), the iguana is healthy. If the balance gets thrown off for an extended period of time, serious physical problems can occur.

Iguanas that don't get enough calcium can suffer from metabolic bone disease, which will show up in a wide range of physical problems including muscle tremors, rickets, soft or "rubber jaw," low bone density (causing bones to break easily), spine curvature, or other deformities (see Chapter 7, Medical Troubleshooting, "Metabolic Bone Disease," for more details).

And these maladies don't show up overnight. Your iguana might look good, but if the calcium balance is off for long periods of time, detrimental changes can be taking place inside your lizard.

Feed Plenty of Leafy Greens

As shown in the Iguana Food Pyramid (Figure 5.1), at least 30% to 45% of your iguana's diet should consist of leafy greens, including the following:

LEAFY GREENS	
collard greens	escarole
mustard greens	turnip greens
dandelion greens and flowers	carrot tops
nasturtium greens and flowers	parsley
hibiscus leaves and flowers	leeks
green onions	bok choy*
spinach*	kale*
Swiss chard*	beet greens*
Chinese cabbage*	

*see page 270 ("Oxalates and Phytates" and "Cruciferous Foods") for more information

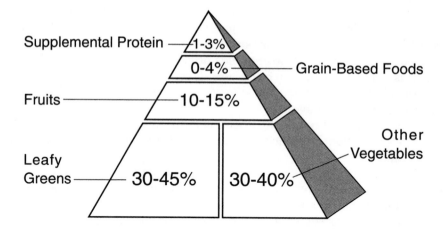

Figure 5.1: Iguana Food Pyramid. Plant percentages (except Grain-Based Foods) courtesy of Robert Ehrig, President of International Iguana Society. He also has more than 15 years of experience breeding and raising iguanas in captivity.

Mix two, three, or more of these items in every meal. This is one category that you don't have to be afraid of "overdoing"!

Please note that all food percentages given throughout this chapter are in <u>volume</u> of food, so it's easy to eye-ball the proportions on the food dish. And don't kill yourself trying to be scientifically exact in the measurements. These percentages are meant only to act as a guide.

Other Vegetable Foods

In addition to the leafy green vegetables, another 30% to 40% of your iguana's diet should come from other veggies, such as:

VEGETABLES

green beans	peas
yellow wax beans	okra
zucchini	carrot (grated or finely chopped)
yellow or crookneck squash	celery
sweet bell peppers	rabbit pellets (i.e., alfalfa)

sprouts (e.g., alfalfa, sunflower, clover)
legumes (cooked—e.g., black beans, garbanzos, pinto beans)
frozen mixed vegetables (thawed to room temperature—carrots, peas, green beans, corn, lima beans)

Sprouts

I have been eating and growing my own sprouts for more than 15 years. (They are a great addition to salads.) When I got my iguana, he also shared this tasty and nutritious food. Sprouts are easy to grow, and most "natural" or health food stores carry the seeds and the kits to grow them.

Sprouts offer a good level of protein and other nutrients. They are also far more nutritious than the seeds from which they were sprouted. For example, a normal pea contains more water than a sprouted pea, which results in a dilute concentration of nutrients per weight. The types of sprouts are nearly endless, including alfalfa, clover, and sunflower.

The main disadvantage of sprouts is that they have a lousy Ca:P, so don't let them be a primary food source, and compensate by adding calcium-rich foods or calcium supplements when you use sprouts.

Rabbit Pellets (Alfalfa Pellets)

I ran out of rabbit pellets and it took me two or three weeks until I got more. When I came in the room with the bag, I thought my iguanas were going to come through the door to get it.   —I-518, Karen, 28 yrs., Pennsylvania

[AUTHOR'S NOTE: The iguanas weren't starved for two or three weeks; they just didn't have rabbit pellets as part of their meals during that time.]

Rabbit pellets can be purchased at many pet stores or agricultural feed stores. Bought in bulk, this food is ridiculously cheap. If you look at the back of many of the new commercial iguana foods, the first ingredient listed (which means it accounts for the largest amount by volume of what's inside) is alfalfa meal, which is essentially ground-up rabbit pellets.

Some iguanas love alfalfa pellets; mine was not overly enthusiastic about them, perhaps because of their strong smell. He ate them only when they made up a minuscule percentage of his food. One way to serve them is to moisten the pellets with a couple of drops of water, then mix them with other food.

One brand of rabbit pellets I saw had 16% protein and a Ca:P of about 2:1, as well as a whole bunch of ingredients besides alfalfa meal. Use the pellets to add variety, not as the main food source.

You are also encouraged to read the back of all food packages. One bag of rabbit pellets said: "Reminder: Store in a cool, dry place. DO NOT feed old or moldy feed to livestock as it may cause illness, abortions, or death." Old or moldy pellets may look and smell fine, so be careful that you keep them dry until serving them to your iguana and that you toss them out if they've been hanging around too long.

As a side note, some people use rabbit pellets as a substrate in their iguana's habitat. I don't recommend this, and the "Reminder" reinforces my opinion.

Go Easy on Some Veggies

Although spinach is packed with calcium and iron, it also contains high levels of oxalates, substances that bind these and other minerals and prevent their absorption by the digestive system. Oxalates are found in many foods, but are highest in spinach, beets, beet

greens, chard, rhubarb, tea, cocoa, and coffee. Spinach contains roughly 600 milligrams of oxalate per serving; by comparison, asparagus contains 5 mg per serving, kale contains 13.
—from a newspaper article by Mark Bittman, New York Times News Service, 1995

Oxalates and Phytates

One wrinkle in the Ca:P equation comes from oxalates and phytates, naturally occurring chemical molecules found in certain plants, unfortunately including many that have high levels of calcium. When humans eat foods containing oxalates or phytates, these molecules bind to calcium molecules, thus preventing the calcium from being used by the body.

It is believed that the same thing happens in iguanas, although no long-term research has been done specifically on iguanas or other animals with hindguts. Some people have suggested that cooking food can reduce both oxalates and phytates, but I've seen no evidence to prove this one way or the other.

For now, the safest thing is to assume that foods containing oxalates do bind up a percentage of the calcium in the foods that iguanas eat. For that reason, use the following foods but don't make them a large part of what you feed your iguana:

VEGETABLES WITH OXALATES AND/OR PHYTATES		
spinach	rhubarb	dock
chard	whole grains	sorrel
beets	beet greens	

Cruciferous Foods

Another class of vegetables that might cause problems <u>in excess</u> are the so-called cruciferous vegetables. Members of the cabbage family, cruciferous vegetables got their name because of the cross shape that's usually visible when you cut the stem and look at the cut end. Cruciferous vegetables contain substances (goitrogens) that can inhibit iodine absorption, which in turn can lead to goiter. Vegetables that are cruciferous include the following:

CRUCIFEROUS VEGETABLES		
kale	broccoli	Brussels sprouts
cabbage	cauliflower	bok choy

As with foods containing oxalates and phytates, go ahead and include cruciferous vegetables, but keep them to a small percentage of any single meal and include them in your iguana's food only once or twice a week.

Low Ca:P

Some vegetables have too much phosphorus in relation to calcium to be considered frequent food items for your iguana. You don't have to ban these items from your iguana's food dish, just make sure the rest of the meal has plenty of calcium-rich foods to compensate. Here are just a few examples of vegetables with low Ca:P values; remember, the goal is a Ca:P of about 2:1 (Ca:P values are adapted from a handout based on the 1975 Agricultural Handbook #456 Nutritive Value of American Foods in Common Units):

VEGETABLES WITH LOW CA:P		
corn (1:33)	potato (1:8)	Brussels sprouts (1:2)
yams (1:3)	asparagus (1:3)	cauliflower (1:2)

Fruits: Use Sparingly

Fruits should not be a regular food item, but may be offered occasionally (most fruits are very low in calcium and high in phosphorus).
—V-69, Dr. Alynn, 39 yrs., Mississippi

Raspberries are a treat that he would like more often than is good for him.
—I-749, Charles, 27 yrs., California

In the wild, fruits constitute a small percentage of an iguana's diet because most fruits are seasonal. That is one reason that iguanas in captivity should be offered only a small amount of fruit. But a stronger reason is that many fruits contain a large amount of phosphorus. As mentioned previously, iguanas need to maintain a Ca:P that's ideally 2:1. Too much fruit can throw this balance off. Overall, fruit is OK but should account for only 10% and no more than 15% of the total.

When you offer fruits, here are some to try (make sure you remove any pits, seeds, or tough skins, such as from an apple or peach):

FRUITS		
blackberries	blueberries	cherries
mango	apple	grapes
papaya	pear	figs
kiwi	banana	plum
peach	apricot	strawberries
melon (e.g., cantaloupe, honeydew)		

Grain-Based Foods

There are a number of plant foods based on grains that are good to feed your iguana, either as a regular part of the diet or once in a while to add variety. They might contribute 0% to 4% to the overall diet. For example, you may toss some cooked, chopped rice or pasta in with your mixed veggies once or twice a week.

Pasta

When they lived out of their cages you could not sit down with pasta or they would attack you. They knew when you were cooking it. They would go crazy over it. —I-11, Patty, Washington

Pasta is a grain-based food that can be offered once in a while. Mix <u>cooked</u>, finely chopped pasta in with your iguana's regular food that day, or on top of the food for a special treat. For visual variety, try pastas of different colors, such as green (spinach), orange (carrot), or red (beet). No spaghetti sauce! Remember, iguanas are reptiles, not humans.

Rice

The other day my iguana [SVL: 15", 5 yrs., 5 lbs.] climbed up on my lap and ate my supper—navy beans and rice. —I-237, Diane, 44 yrs., Texas
        [AUTHOR'S NOTE: I don't believe that animals should share food bowls with humans, but this story shows the culinary preferences of one iguana.]

Because I eat rice in some form several times a week, my iguana also got it in his meals. I found that if I left the rice intact, some kernels would pass through his digestive tract whole. Once I started chopping the rice a little finer (or putting it in the food processor) before adding it to other foods, I never again saw it in his feces.
    A bit of rice mixed with other foods adds a new, slightly nutty flavor and lightens the consistency of the food. Try any kind of cooked rice, including white (long or short grain), brown, or basmati.

Bread

Occasionally, my female iguana [SVL: 15", TL: 3' 11", 3 yrs.] steals crusts of bread from my children's sandwiches.
                                —I-620, Suzanne, 33 yrs., New York

Bread (whole grain—no white) adds bulk, texture, and some additional vitamins and minerals for your iguana's diet. Small amounts of bread (no more than 10% of any day's meal) can be offered once or twice a week.

Cream of Wheat®

Cream of Wheat is a wheat-based (wheat farina and wheat germ) hot cereal that has an ideal calcium/phosphorus ratio of 2:1. It also offers some protein, carbohydrates, and other vitamins.

This is one of the hot cereals I ate as a kid before I went to school in the morning. For my iguana, I cooked (according to the directions) the smallest amount described on the back of the box. While it was still warm, I placed it in an empty ice cube tray and allowed it to set up in the refrigerator. Once it set up (it looks like cubes of rubber), I placed the cubes in a Ziploc plastic food bag. This allowed me to have individual, easy-to-use "blocks" that kept fresh for about five to seven days in the refrigerator.

Once or twice a week, I offered my iguana a meal consisting of chopped vegetables supplemented with some Cream of Wheat (less than 15% of the total meal). Because I fed my iguana only a small proportion of the total amount I prepared, I gave the rest to other iguana owners in the area.

The first time I offered the mixture to my iguana, he walked away from it with a disgusted look on his face. So the next time I added only a tiny bit with the vegetables. This he liked, and over time I increased the amount of Cream of Wheat until I arrived at a level he would eat.

Supplemental Protein

An iguana gets most of its protein from its regular meals. Supplemental protein is protein you can add to the diet, but not often. The Food Pyramid's recommendation of 1% to 3% supplemental protein refers to high-protein (plant-based, not animal-based) food sources. The subject of protein is a source of great confusion and controversy when it comes to iguanas, and the kinks are being worked out a little more each year.

Please note that the Food Pyramid applies to adult iguanas. Hatchlings and fast-growing juveniles have higher protein needs, so you should increase this supplemental protein during these stages.

Foods that fall into the supplemental protein category might include the following:

SUPPLEMENTAL PROTEIN
monkey biscuit
tofu
commercial iguana food
a low-fat, meat-free dog food formulated for old dogs

How often is "not often"? For example, feed your adult iguana one monkey biscuit (softened in water), or one chunk of tofu, or one portion of commercial iguana food or low-fat senior dog food, every 3 to 6 weeks. Of course, if you want to drive yourself crazy, you could add a tiny morsel of supplemental protein to every meal so it makes up 1% to 3% of the food in the dish.

The point is, your iguana's basic need for protein will be supplied by the leafy green and other vegetables and legumes that make up 80% to 90% of its diet.

The Protein Controversy

I don't care for the current recommendation (mostly from vets, it seems) in the U.S. regarding protein intake (mostly for Green Iguanas). It just doesn't make sense nutritionally, given the gastrointestinal anatomy, nutritional heritage, and food preferences of these animals.

—Susan Donoghue, VMD, DipACVN, Nutrition Support Services, Inc. (#28)

There has long been controversy regarding the amount of protein an iguana should get. Consuming too much protein, especially animal protein, is thought to cause serious health problems in iguanas. In the years I have been researching iguanas, the amount of protein recommended has dropped dramatically. The lowered amounts make sense when you recall that iguanas in the wild eat only leaves and fruits to get their daily protein.

Protein is most important for fast-growing hatchlings. Luckily, iguanas hatch in the "wet season," when everything is growing rapidly. The new plant growth is tender and more digestible, making it easier for the hatchlings to extract more protein and other nutrients they need.

If you follow the recommendations of the Food Pyramid (Figure 5.1), you shouldn't have to worry about whether your iguana is getting the proper protein. For instance, legumes, peas, alfalfa (including rabbit pellets), kale, collard greens, dandelion greens, mustard greens, parsley, spinach, sprouts, and turnip greens all contain significant amounts of protein.

The Dangers of Too Much Protein

My iguana died today from calcification of the kidney, intestines, and aorta. The vet said it was from excess protein for too long a time period. Please let others know of this possible problem.   —I-808, Priscilla, 25 yrs., Iowa

Iguanas in captivity sometimes have a strange and powerful attraction to protein, which may stem from their difficulty in finding it in the wild or the long process of extracting it from leaves. Perhaps when they get access to high levels of protein in an easily digestible form, their instinct drives them to load up on it, much as a squirrel hordes nuts for the winter. Iguanas' instincts might tell them to "chow down" on high-protein foods when they are available, in case they don't get any for a while. But their bodies can't take the long-term effects of large protein intake.

For example, captive iguanas offered cat food, which is high in protein, often gobble it up. The biggest source of protein addiction I have witnessed over the years is a product called monkey chow, in biscuit form. In the peak of breeding, when my iguana's appetite dropped to zero for nearly everything, he would devour monkey biscuits if given the opportunity.

As I have said before, hatchling iguanas grow rapidly and need more pro-

---

SIDEBAR

Protein: Animal vs. Plant

When it comes to offering a protein source to iguanas, there are basically two camps: animal-based and plant-based. <u>Protein does not necessarily equal meat</u>. It's a misconception that these two are synonymous. There are some books and magazines that recommend a lot of animal-based protein for iguanas. I am very militant about offering only plant-based protein sources to iguanas.

Iguanas are not designed to eat meat. Animals that eat other animals (carnivores) usually have teeth that can rip or shred flesh, or crunch bones and tendons. Chewing is one way to break down the tough, fibrous flesh. Iguanas can't chew; their teeth are extremely small and not anchored securely into their jaws, like meat eaters. Also, an iguana doesn't have the digestive juices or system needed to process meat. Its system is made for plant foods.

In addition, iguanas are not physiologically adapted to chasing down prey, and they simply don't do this in the wild. A few years ago, many people said that hatchling iguanas were insectivores. Recently, though, researchers have shown that iguanas are herbivores their whole lives.

Nature has not equipped iguanas to capture or eat flesh, so why do pet owners persist in feeding their iguanas things such as mice or crickets? Perhaps some people are unable to believe that any animal can exist without meat (animal protein), or perhaps they don't understand that iguanas' physiology does not meet the requirements for being a carnivore or omnivore.

---

tein than adult iguanas. But a problem arises when iguana owners continue to feed large amounts of protein (and too often animal-based protein) to their adult iguanas, who require very little protein. It appears that many of these lizards are now starting to die much earlier than they should because of the high protein intake.

In iguanas, the medical problems associated with too much protein include the following:

- Gout, which can lead to swelling and severe pain in the joints and inflammation of organs such as the liver, kidneys, and heart
- Mineralization of tissues
- Urinary bladder stones

An iguana I owned from approximately 1982 until 1983 developed a fairly severe case of gout. This disease takes its victim in subtle degrees over time. In the end, the animal had a "steroid" appearance: His limbs were very stout. I was force feeding him large amounts of water, but the animal was just too far gone. When he died, he could barely move.   —I-508, Bryan, 27 yrs., Kentucky

In a colony of research animals at the National Zoo, some of the 25 iguanas that have been maintained for 4 years predominantly on a 25% protein diet developed evidence of renal gout and soft tissue mineralization. One theory is that high dietary protein levels may predispose some reptiles to gout.

—Iguana nutrition researcher (#13)

Research is currently being done on the effects of too much protein in iguanas. They are also trying to find out what levels or percentage of protein iguanas in captivity should be fed. Until we know for sure, it seems the best thing to do is keep the protein levels down. Even if your iguana loves protein, you need to offer it only in the levels previously recommended.

Please, please, please, stress this in your book and let people know that although a high-protein diet will cause young iguanas to grow quickly, in the end it will shorten the life of their pet. The very best they can do for the pet is a varied VEGETARIAN diet.   —I-780, Carl, Florida

Commercial Diets

One evening some friends of mine, Ted and Deb, came over to see photos of one of my recent iguana research trips. While talking about the trip, I mentioned that it was common practice among Latin American people to eat iguanas for food.

Later that evening, I wanted to show them the progress of my book. There on my desk, beside a prototype of the book cover, were three metal cat-food-sized cans stacked on each other. On the outside label of each can, in tall, bold, green letters, was the word "IGUANA." The background of the label showed a close-up of iguana scales.

My friends knew how much it hurts me to see live iguanas sold in the market for food. They both had this perplexed, contorted expression on their faces. Ted said, "You didn't actually buy ground-up iguana in cans when you were in Mexico. . . . did you?" "No, Ted," I said, "it's commercially manufactured food for iguanas to eat!" We all shared a big laugh—and a sigh of relief.

My iguana does not like the formulated diets that I have tried. Even though I tried several different liquids (water, juice, broth) for soaking them (per instructions), he will eat the formulated diets only if they are sprinkled on the food in their dry form.   —I-690, Irene, 34 yrs., Texas

Entrepreneurs are out trying to make money and perhaps help feed iguanas a little better and more simply. Commercial iguana foods are quick and easy, almost like feeding a dog or cat. Some of the commercial diets have a base of alfalfa (like in rabbit pellets), others use corn, and another one is based on collard greens. Just open a can, bag, or jar; use straight or add water or other vegetables.

Many companies will tell you that their product is the only food you will ever need to offer your iguana. Most of them are new companies with little long-term data on what happens if iguanas eat their product exclusively. All are based at least partly on guesswork, because no one in the scientific community has definitively answered all the questions about the ideal diet for either wild or captive iguanas.

One concern is that some makers of commercial feeds use research by a special iguana farm in Costa Rica to set nutritional levels. But the goal of this iguana farm is to raise big animals as quickly as possible for release into the jungle to reestablish native populations. By growing faster they may survive better initially, but perhaps at the expense of a shorter life span. As a result, many commercial formulations may not promote longevity in pet iguanas.

Another concern is that gaps in knowledge about iguana diets are filled in with data taken from other animal species, including horses and cows. These animals are herbivores, but their physiology is different from iguanas. For instance, horses and cows don't climb or live in trees, they are mammals (not reptiles), they have different digestive systems, and their natural diet consists mostly of grasses.

When you see some of the glossy ads for commercial iguana foods in herp magazines, they really suck you in. The ads use powerful words, such as "formulated," "tested," "veterinarian approved," "just like natural food," and show beautiful pictures of great-looking iguanas.

Even against the power of Madison Avenue-type advertising, I still advocate using a variety of food for an iguana's diet. One compromise is to limit commercial foods to small portions once in a while—or to consider them a "protein supplement." That way, you won't be "volunteering" your iguana as a test animal for the long-term effects of a single food source. For example, it took more than five years to find that too much protein might be killing iguanas, because the effects were slow to appear. Are you willing to bet your lizard's life on a single food source?

Feeding your iguana out of a can or jar is so simple that many people might succumb to the convenience of commercial foods. Slowly, over time, it might be the only kind of food they offer their iguana.

On the other hand, your iguana may not even like the commercial foods. Mine didn't. I first stared testing the acceptability of these foods on Za when he was about 3½ years old. He wouldn't eat any of them straight. It would work only if just a little of the commercial food was mixed in with his regular food.

It's very exciting to see research being done into the diet of iguanas, as well as the new food products that are being introduced. Perhaps in time, commercial foods will be able to replace fresh food, like dog and cat food did for those animals. But I think more long-term independent research is necessary before we hand over our iguanas' lifetime health to any single product. Until then, I advocate fresh food, variety, and once-in-a-while commercial food as the safest bet for now.

VITAMIN AND MINERAL SUPPLEMENTS

Supplements are additional vitamins and minerals added to compensate for possible nutritional deficiencies in the iguana's food. There are two approaches when it comes to adding supplements to food—not only in the iguana community, but also the human community.

As in other species, a proper [iguana] diet does not necessitate supplements.
—V-36, Dr. John, Connecticut

The soils [Llanos, Venezuela] don't even support tree life in many of the areas. That's important for iguanas because iguanas eat vegetation and the only nutrients in vegetation are what the plants can pull out of the soil.
—Gordon H. Rodda, iguana field researcher (#27)

One group says that if you eat the right foods you don't need any additional vitamins or minerals. The other side says that foods nowadays are nutritionally incomplete because they're grown in soil deficient in the proper balance of nutrients (caused by not rotating crops, using chemical fertilizers, etc.)—and that to compensate, we need to add vitamin and mineral supplements to our diet. Some people also suggest that cooking foods either kills vitamins or minerals or leaches them out into the cooking water.

When it comes to an iguana's diet, there are some nutritionists who even doubt that we can replicate iguanas' natural food intake using grocery-store food items. There are a lot of strong opinions on these issues, all based on different evidence and beliefs. Researchers have written thick, technical scientific papers on the function of calcium, vitamin D3, and UV light, and there's still a great deal the experts don't know or that they argue over.

Much of what we know about iguana nutritional needs comes from sick and dead pet iguanas. Necropsies performed on dead iguanas have pointed to the dangers of certain food types. Checking the internal organs and bones after death, then talking with the owner of the lizard about the food and supplements supplied, adds to the data base of knowledge. With this information, iguana researchers and veterinarians work backward to adjust the recommended amount of a particular supplement or food type that was suspected as a cause for the medical problem or death.

These records of nutritional "failures," along with anecdotal reports from iguana owners, guesswork, chance, and using herbivorous mammals as the baseline, help determine the vitamin and mineral recommendations for iguanas.

For iguanas, I believe in supplementation of calcium, low amounts of vit-amin D3, and some other nutrients, especially in fast-growing hatchlings or gravid females. But here's the problem: No one knows for sure how much an iguana needs of any nutrients, and that's why it's really difficult to recommend dosages. It's much like people who argue over a simple thing like how much vitamin C humans should consume each day. The government sets one stan-dard, but other groups argue it's not enough.

The information on supplementation is not complete or exact, but it's the best we have for now, and over the years it has improved the lives of iguanas.

Calcium

In captive iguanas, calcium deficiencies are among the most common health problems. Calcium is essential for an animal's bone growth and main-

---

SIDEBAR

Oversupplementation

One <u>very important</u> general note on supplementing: It's better to underestimate the amounts of supplements you add than to add too much. Many of the nutrients can be harmful or even fatal in large doses.

It's easy to think that if a certain amount of supplementation is good then just a little more is be even better. Wrong! This action could possibly kill your iguana, with the likelihood of intense suffering before it dies.

A barely perceptible dusting with a reptile multivitamin is all that is required (once or twice a week). Don't oversupplement.
            —V-137, Dr. William, 64 yrs., Wisconsin

As many problems can be caused by oversupplementing as by undersupple-menting. Sprinkle a small amount of a balanced vitamin/mineral supplement on the food each day in the young iguanas and twice weekly in the adults.
            —V-69, Dr. Alynn, 39 yrs., Mississippi

Problems can also arise if you feed your lizard commercial iguana foods more often than as occasional "treats." Many of these commercial products add vitamins and minerals directly to their products. If you also add sup-plements to your iguana's food on a regular basis, you may be "double dos-ing" the days you offer commercial foods. Pay attention to the ingredients, particularly the vitamin and mineral contents listed on the side of the pack-age or container.

tenance and is also crucial for proper muscle function. An iguana's calcium requirements change as it grows, with fast-growing hatchlings and young juveniles needing higher levels of calcium to build strong bones.

The main source of calcium for your lizard should be the food it eats daily, but providing adequate amounts can be difficult when you don't have access to foods rich in calcium. This is when calcium supplements may be important. Supplements can bump up any meal that is deficient or low in the calcium your iguana needs.

Important: Calcium intake alone can't prevent calcium deficiencies and the resulting metabolic bone disease. The following elements are all crucial for calcium metabolism:

- proper ultraviolet light exposure (see Chapter 4, Housing, "Lights")
- proper temperature (see Chapter 4, Housing, "Heat")
- proper balance between calcium and phosphorus (Ca:P)

One situation where you almost certainly need to use calcium supplements is when a sexually mature female iguana starts to produce eggs. Females can produce eggs during the breeding season with or without a male iguana around, much like a chicken. If the female is low or lacking in calcium, her body will get this needed calcium wherever it can. If her food doesn't supply enough calcium, the lizard's body can turn on itself and draw calcium from her bones. This will make her bones soft and easier to break. It's a dangerous situation.

> *At one year old, I thought my iguana was probably a male. But he turned out to be a she. In her pre-egg-laying frenzy of digging, her arm bone snapped. I took her to the vet to fix the broken arm and he said that the arm broke due to lack of calcium in the month prior to egg laying.*
> —I-100, Charlene, 44 yrs., Illinois

If your female is sexually mature you may need to supplement with more calcium. Check with your herp veterinarian, who will figure out how much additional calcium may be required and for how long.

Types of Calcium Supplements

> *I use only calcium. My favorite brand is Osteoform. It is inexpensive and animals don't object to the taste.*   —V-18, Dr. Patty, 40 yrs., California

There are many kinds of calcium supplements available, including formulations designed for reptiles.

Here are some guidelines for calcium supplements:

- Choose one with no added phosphorus (which defeats the purpose of adding calcium by throwing off the calcium/phosphorus ratio).
- The best calcium sources are calcium carbonate and cuttle bone (scraped to produce a powder or pulverized in a food processor).
- Avoid calcium lactate as iguanas aren't set up to handle lactose, a milk product (see page 290 for further discussion of iguanas and milk products).

- Also avoid calcium supplements that have added vitamin D3 and/or vitamin A if you plan to combine the calcium with a multivitamin supplement, which will also contain D3 and A (both these fat-soluble vitamins can be harmful in large doses).

Natural Vitamin D3

Since vitamin D is a positive regulator of calcium metabolism, an organism that has a deficiency of vitamin D will have abnormally low levels of calcium.   —Matthew Moyle, reptile researcher (#37)

Another important factor in maintaining your iguana's proper calcium balance is vitamin D3. Vitamin D3, along with sufficient temperature, is believed to be necessary to metabolize calcium.

Some animals get their vitamin D3 primarily through their diet. For example, carnivorous animals get vitamin D from eating whole prey (including bones). Because plants offer little or no vitamin D3, iguanas—as herbivores—are out of luck getting it from their food. Instead, iguanas depend on a chemical reaction in their skin that is triggered by ultraviolet light, specifically UVB (see Chapter 4, Housing, "Lights," for more details).

This biological synthesis of vitamin D3 happens when an iguana is in direct, unfiltered sunlight. In the wild, iguanas bask in and out of sunlight all day, which is the natural way for iguanas to regulate their temperature for food digestion and to receive vitamin D3. An iguana sitting blissfully in the sun is like a small chemistry set at work as the light striking the lizard's body causes vitamin D3 synthesis to take place in its skin.

In the wild most animals do not have a dietary need for vitamin D, as sufficient vitamin D can be synthesized in the skin upon irradiation by sunlight containing ultraviolet light in the biologically active B range.   —Mary Allen, nutritionist (#51)

Iguanas in captivity are too often denied access to unfiltered sunlight (i.e., not through glass). As I'll repeat many times throughout this book, one of the best things you can do for your iguana is to expose it as often as possible to direct sunlight. When that is not possible or practical, and whenever your iguana is in its habitat, provide an artificial light source that emits UVB wavelengths from 290 to 320 nanometers (nm); again, see Chapter 4, Housing, "Lights."

Manufactured Vitamin D3

Given the limited UV output of most artificial lights, it may be necessary to provide a dietary source of vitamin D to iguanas [kept indoors].
   —Conference on Nutrition of Captive Wild Animals (#13)

The standard approach to iguanas not getting the appropriate UV radiation is to add a dietary supplement that contains the activated form of vitamin D3 to the lizard's food. But there are at least two problems with D3 supplements:

- "... no acceptable dosage schedules for vitamin D supplementation have been experimentally determined for any species of herptile" (#37), and
- too much vitamin D is toxic.

However, a <u>weekly</u> dose of 100 IU of vitamin D per kilogram of your iguana's body weight is generally considered safe to avoid overdosing (#37). (For the "metrically challenged," 1 kilogram is about 2.2 pounds. So if you have a 5-pound iguana, 200 IU of vitamin D per week should be safe.)

AT A GLANCE: *Hints for Vitamin D3 Supplementation*

- You won't find vitamin D3 in a jar on its own; it will be one ingredient in a multivitamin mix, a calcium supplement product, or added to commercial feeds.
- Make sure you get vitamin D3 (also known as cholecalciferol) and <u>not</u> vitamin D2 (ergocalciferol), which your iguana can't use. If the label doesn't clearly say D3 or cholecalciferol, or just simply mentions "vitamin D," don't give it to your iguana.
- Don't exceed 100 IU of vitamin D3/kg body weight per week.
- Use D3 supplements only to "hedge your bets," not as a substitute for UVB light (especially sunlight) exposure, sufficient calcium intake, and warm temperatures.

Another, more recent, concern is whether iguanas' bodies are even capable of using dietary vitamin D3 for calcium metabolism.

> UVB irradiation appears to be a critical factor in preventing the development of metabolic bone disorders in the green iguana, even when dietary sources of cholecalciferol [i.e., vitamin D3] are available.   —Joni Bernard, nutritionist (#50)

<u>Remember, the natural method for iguanas to synthesize D3 is by the chemical reaction in their skin that's triggered by UVB radiation.</u> The details about UV radiation are still being worked out in the scientific community.

In the meantime, I advocate throwing in a low dose of vitamin D3 as a dietary supplement to play it safe. It may or may not do any good, but the dose is low enough that it won't do any harm. Only time will tell if it is necessary and if so, the exact dosages.

The sun provides a spectrum of radiation, including ultraviolet light of the wavelengths required for biological synthesis of vitamin D.
—Conference on Nutrition of Captive Wild Animals (#13)

In any case, though, you can <u>not</u> rely on dietary supplements to take the place of regular exposure to direct sunlight or good full-spectrum lights, or of adequate calcium intake. I know I have repeated these same points over and over from different angles, but I want to make sure they sink in.

Multivitamins

Multivitamins are mixes of a number of vitamins and some minerals, but not necessarily including high amounts of calcium. They are available as dry or liquid supplements that can be sprinkled or dropped onto food and mixed in. Several years ago, the only multivitamin available for reptiles was a bird vitamin. But in the last few years, the proliferation of iguana products has included multivitamins.

Each brand of multivitamin has its own mix, dosage, and special selling "catch." The problem with multivitamins is that there has not been enough long-term, independent, and reputable scientific research in this area for iguanas. If you decide on multivitamins, be sure you don't get one that's too high in vitamin D or vitamin A (they're both toxic at high doses). And don't get any product that's designed to be put in your iguana's water. Iguanas drink water, but not predictably enough to use this as a way to deliver vitamins.

SIDEBAR

Warning—Excessive D3

If you decide to supplement your iguana's diet with vitamin D3, be very careful because too much can cause harm. Results of vitamin D toxicity include the hardening (mineralization) of various body tissues.

Be especially careful about "hidden" sources of vitamin D. For example, many calcium supplements include added D3. If you combine these with a multivitamin that also contains D3, you can easily exceed safe dosages. Similarly, many commercial iguana feeds or prepared chows (for other animals) contain vitamin D in one form or another, to varying degrees. It all adds up in your iguana's body, so make sure you check the label before feeding anything to your lizard. If you are offering any of these commercial products, you may not even need to add any extra D3 to your lizard's food.

Dosages for Supplements

As part of the research for this book, I sent detailed questionnaires to a number of herp veterinarians across the country, all of whom were recommended. One of the questions I asked the veterinarians was whether they recommended vitamin or mineral supplements for iguanas, and if so, what kind and how much. The answers that came back ranged from "I don't recommend supplements at all" to significant amounts of supplements every day of an iguana's life.

It's not that these people are uninformed, it simply indicates that knowledgeable people will come to quite different conclusions as long as there's so much unknown about iguana nutrition. I synthesized all the responses from veterinarians, along with every other reputable source I could find, to try to come up with a safe middle ground for dosage and frequency recommendations if you decide to use them.

I gave my iguana multivitamins only for his first 1½ years. Theoretically, iguanas fed the proper amount of calcium in their food, including the right Ca:P, <u>and</u> given adequate exposure to UVB and maintained at the proper temperature thrive without vitamin and mineral supplements. In the real world, iguanas often don't get enough calcium and UVB to meet their nutritional needs. If you suspect that's the case, and if you decide to supplement, here are some options:

- Call your herp veterinarian and ask his or her opinion about the specific needs of your iguana.
- Keep reading the herp magazines (articles, not ads) to find out the latest information on nutritional supplements.
- Talk to others in your herp society and try to reach consensus on the best approach (good luck!!).
- Get an "all-in-one" calcium and vitamin/mineral product that has significant amounts of calcium; choose a brand with appropriately low amounts of vitamin D_3 and vitamin A.
- Purchase a powdered bird or multivitamin and mix it in equal parts with an all-calcium powder (e.g., calcium carbonate) that contains <u>no</u> added vitamin D_3 or A.
- Choose a calcium supplement that has no added D_3 (i.e., you decide not to supplement D_3).

Below is the latest semi-scientific "guess" for how much to supplement your iguana's food (in each case, sprinkle the powder over the food; you can mix it in or not, depending on what your iguana will eat). I used this system when I offered my iguana multivitamins and/or calcium. The idea of a "pinch" may seem archaic, but that's how everyone does it.

- Hatchlings and Juveniles: one pinch (or a barely visible dusting) once a day.

- Adults (sexually mature): one pinch per kilogram (2.2 pounds) of body weight once or twice a week.
- Gravid females: one pinch per meal while gravid and for a few days after laying eggs. Better yet, take your female iguana to your veterinarian, who will determine the exact amount and number of days supplements should be used.

WATER

I have read in several books that iguanas are never seen drinking water, but I have seen mine get down from a branch and go directly to the water bowl for a nice big drink. —I-322, Marty, 22 yrs., Ohio

Some of the older iguana pet-care books said that iguanas don't drink water, but to keep some around anyway. I say <u>always</u> have fresh, clean water available because, contrary to popular belief, iguanas <u>do</u> drink water.

In the jungles, iguanas lap up standing water, such as in the little cups formed by bromeliad leaves. Also in the wild, they will tilt their heads back and drink water as it rains on them if they are thirsty. When I was paddling up one of the rivers in Belize, my guide said that he had seen iguanas come down to the river's edge to drink water, but only during breeding season, when their food intake is reduced. It was breeding season then, and he showed me a set of iguana tracks that proved his point.

One topic I feel needs to be addressed is the iguanas' consumption of water. The early information I read said that they get enough water from their food sources and that the iguana is rarely seen drinking water. My iguana loves to drink water. At three months old, he took water from a soft plastic pipette . . . something I was experimenting with one day. Now I offer water in a dish, so he can drink it when he wants to. Sometimes he'll go as long as 3 months without wanting any directly from me, and sometimes he'll gulp several ounces a week.
—I-727, Sharon, 34 yrs., South Carolina

Plan on changing the water daily, and also consider using bottled water if your water is chlorinated or fluoridated.
—V-69, Dr. Alynn, 39 yrs., Mississippi

I've noticed that my iguana drinks quite a bit of water since it has been eating this dry commercial iguana food. —I-895, Julie & Jim, 25 yrs., Texas

Although iguanas get most of their moisture from the food they eat, if their food is low in moisture—especially the new dry commercial iguana foods—water is required. Sexually mature iguanas also frequently reduce their intake of food during breeding season. If food is reduced, so is moisture (water). It's especially important during this time that water be available and always easily accessible.

Another time your iguana may need additional water is when it is on medication (e.g., antibiotics). During a three-week antibiotics series, my iguana frequently drank from a spray bottle. A week after the antibiotics were stopped, Za also stopped drinking from the spray bottle.

> *My iguanas like to drink from the water bowl. They often submerge their snouts, "pump" up several mouthfuls of water, then raise their heads and forequarters and let it "drain" down into their stomachs.*
> —I-541, Mark, 33 yrs., Maryland

Iguanas will drink standing water once they're trained to do it (see Chapter 8, Domestication, "Drinking Water," for how this is accomplished). It took six months before I actually caught my iguana drinking out of the upper water dish of his habitat. After that first time, I frequently saw him drink from the dish. That's one of the exciting things about iguanas—their habits and desires seem to unfold slowly over time.

> *She kind of "smacks" when she's thirsty.*
> —I-903, Marty, 37 yrs., Wisconsin

[AUTHOR'S NOTE: This is how my iguana indicated that he wanted me to give him water from a spray bottle during two separate breeding seasons. The next breeding season he ate more so he didn't require any extra water.]

I purchased bottled water (sold at grocery stores) for my iguana. It's pure, cheap, and a gallon will last practically forever.

Lapping, sipping, and deep sucking are a few of the ways iguanas drink water. I have seen iguanas drink from a bowl, cup, spoon, spray bottle, and other devices. The following stories from iguana owners emphasize that iguanas do drink water, and from many sources:

> *Our iguanas taught themselves to drink water out of a bottle like guinea pigs use.*
> —I-364, Lynda, 30 yrs., Maryland

> *My iguana [SVL: 10", TL: 2' 9", 2 yrs.] loves to drink water right from the spray bottle I humidify his cage with. I squirt it directly into his mouth until he pulls his head away [indicating he has had enough]. He drinks like this every day.*
> —I-744, Karen, 34 yrs., Pennsylvania

> *I have witnessed all three of my iguanas drinking from pans of water in their cage. They will perch their two front feet on the edge of the pan, dip their mouths in the water, and raise their heads high in a swallowing motion.*
> —phone conversation with pet owner

I have a large water dish that my iguana will lap water from. Sometimes he drinks out of my glass when I am drinking.
                                        —I-633, Lynne, 29 yrs., Michigan
    [AUTHOR'S NOTE: Don't share food or water with your lizard. It could cause possible health problems for either of you.]

He likes to drink water from the faucet before he takes a soak in the bathtub.
                            —I-530, Bryan & Kathy, 30 & 27 yrs., Florida

PROBLEM FOODS

I define a problem food for an iguana as anything that doesn't contribute to the lizard's optimal health. As I've said before, the best hedge against nutritional problems is to offer a variety of foods. At the same time, that doesn't mean you should offer <u>anything</u> in your quest for variety.

There are some foods that, for various reasons, should be avoided for iguanas. The first category of these foods, "Not Recommended," are foods that may cause problems if fed too often or in large quantities.

The second category are labeled as "Dangerous," and these are the foods that could kill your iguana or make it extremely ill. My urgings are less gentle here: <u>Do not</u> feed your iguana anything in this category.

Not Recommended

Most of the "not recommended" foods have the potential to create medical problems over time. A number of these foods—such as lettuce or monkey biscuits—are well-liked by iguanas and can become addictive. It's up to you to limit your iguana's exposure to these foods by not offering them on a regular basis.

Chows: Monkey, Fish, Dog, Etc.

Chows are commercial foods formulated for other species but often fed to iguanas. In general, they are very high in protein, vitamin D, and fat. If you use these types of foods offer them only as supplemental protein (see page 273).

Monkey Chow Biscuits

Judging from the overwhelming letters and calls I've received from iguana owners, and feedback from veterinarians, monkey chow biscuits can be overly attractive to iguanas. Monkey biscuits are not a "forbidden" food choice, but they need to be offered in a <u>restricted</u> way because of their potential to cause long-term health problems for iguanas.

We used to feed him a lot of monkey chow, but were told too much protein would stress his liver, so we weaned him.
                                —I-705, Paul & Linda, 45 yrs., California

I made an extremely __bad__ discovery of monkey chow, which was sold to me as iguana chow. My iguana loved it! He refused to eat anything else—and he became __very__ sick. Now, after literally six months of nursing, praying, etc., he receives a varied diet with very little monkey chow.

—I-852, Debi, 35 yrs., Oregon

An older iguana was brought into the animal hospital where I worked for treatment of metabolic bone disease. It is my understanding that the iguana was fed a diet of monkey biscuit exclusively, which was the cause of his problems.

He was admitted because he was having a difficult time walking and all four limbs were quite swollen and most of his fingers twisted. He was not able to stand normally and movement of the limbs was minimal.

Since he was only accustomed to soaked monkey biscuits, the nutritious diet that we offered to him was refused continuously. I started to mix this diet with monkey biscuit, deleting it gradually until he was eating his vegetables/fruits on a daily basis. This process took nearly a month.

He has shown gradual improvement and now 10 months later seems to be fully recovered.   —I-690, Irene, 34 yrs., Texas

My 3-year-old iguana died from being fed too much monkey chow in its diet. The monkey chow diet was advised by a vet whose heart was in the right place as far as iguanas go, but not very knowledgeable.

—I-586, Joanne, 44 yrs., Florida

Unfortunately, I listened to a misinformed vet and fed my iguana monkey chow exclusively for over 1½ years. My new vet showed me the 17 stones from my iguana's necropsy. So I am sure this is the reason for its death.

—phone conversation with iguana owner

Notice that the most dangerous effects are when an iguana is fed a diet consisting mostly of this product. It reinforces my original assertion that variety can eliminate the potential for specific foods to cause problems.

Monkey biscuits are made of ground corn, wheat, and soybean meal, with a lot of added vitamins and minerals, and formulated for the dietary needs of monkeys, as the name implies. The biscuits are soaked in warm water before serving.

Monkey chow was part of my iguana's diet all of his life, but a very small amount, only once in a while, and always mixed with his regular meal of greens and other vegetables. The amount of biscuit depends on the size of your iguana. The biscuits can be cut into halves or quarters if that's all you need.

Lettuce

I babysat a pathetic example of an iguana for a friend of my son. At 1 year, this lizard was the size of the hatchlings I have now. It was being fed 3-inch long

pieces of iceberg lettuce. It ate so much at our house that it had this huge bloated stomach, which contrasted with its spindly little legs. I hear that the lizard is now growing and doing better with the change of diet.
                                            —I-685, Julie, 36 yrs., California

For years I have seen and heard so many cases of iguanas suffering and dying on lettuce diets that I don't recommend it as a food source for your iguana. It's not that lettuce once in a while is bad, it's that too often it becomes a major component of the iguana's food—and that's when the problems come up.

I operate an iguana rescue program here. Addiction to lettuce is a very common problem. Once they are addicted, it is very hard to change that.
                                            —I-730, Brigitte, 32 yrs., Arkansas

The typical problem I see with iguanas in my practice is metabolic bone disease from strict lettuce diets.   —I-46, Sue, 32 yrs., New York

Several years ago, a new iguana owner asked me what foods he should offer his iguana, and I told him, stressing the use of lettuce only sparingly. Six months later, I went to his house and saw a malnourished, sick lizard. I asked what he was feeding his iguana. At first he said a variety of food, but he finally admitted that the lizard was fed a diet entirely of lettuce. Furious, I asked why he would do such a thing, after I had explained before about what foods iguanas require. He said it was because his iguana loved the lettuce so much. In this case, he almost killed his iguana with love.

Lettuce looks and feels like food that iguanas eat in the wild—leaves—so iguanas are likely to eat it enthusiastically. They can easily get addicted to eating lettuce as their main food source, ignoring all other food. Uninformed pet owners go along with feeding their lizard lettuce because the animals eat it so voraciously.

Dark-leaf lettuces such as "ruby red" or romaine types do have some good vitamins and minerals, but lettuce is mostly a water-based material. Never use "head" (iceberg) lettuce; it was created for shipping across the country, so it's sturdy, but it has little food value.

Lettuce (romaine or redleaf) is great as a training aid, but in small amounts and only occasionally (see Chapter 8, Domestication, "Training"). I'm hoping that now you can see the possible danger of too much lettuce, you'll refrain from using it as a main food source.

Insects, Bugs, Worms

In the 1960s, several papers stated [that] juvenile iguanas eat insects. The reasoning was, "They're little lizards, they must eat insects." There is no evidence from the field that they eat anything but herbaceous material.
                                            —Gordon H. Rodda, iguana field researcher (#27)

I also found no basis for earlier speculation that *Iguana iguana*
exhibit an ontogenic shift [i.e., a change as they get older] from
carnivory to herbivory. —John B. Iverson, iguana researcher (#16)

For the longest time, people claimed that hatchling and juvenile iguanas
naturally ate insects. Even now, you see books and ads in herp magazines rein-
forcing this idea, so it almost becomes real.

When I was in Mexico doing iguana egg research, I asked the researcher
who invited me there if it's true that iguanas eat insects. She had watched
iguana eggs hatch at the same spot in the jungle for several years in a row and
said the first thing the hatchlings ate were young shoots of nearby plants. She
said that there were plenty of insects on the plants, but the hatchlings didn't
seek them out.

When an iguana is eating a leaf, a flower, or a piece of fruit and there is
some kind of insect or worm on the food, the iguana eats the item "as is." An
occasional insect might make it to the iguana's stomach, but not because the
iguana ate it on purpose.

Many respondents to my iguana questionnaire said that they feed their
iguanas crickets or various types of worms (mostly waxworms and meal-
worms). Part of this is probably due to the sales people at the pet store (who
have these creatures for sale), and part can be traced to old, recycled misinformation on iguana diets. What's most frustrating to me are the articles and books
that explain how iguanas are herbivores and have a special digestive tract
designed for plant materials, then go off on some tangent about how to raise
crickets and worms as iguana food. I don't get their logic.

They [iguanas] obviously eat insects, dog food, and many other
things in captivity which they don't get in the wild. Horses will eat
sugar cubes until they're sick and horses never eat sugar cubes in
the wild.   —Gordon H. Rodda, iguana field researcher

In the jungle I have observed iguanas surrounded by bugs, making no
attempt to eat them. Insects, bugs, and worms are animal foods that I don't
recommend under any circumstances for iguanas.

*Crickets have been introduced but were met only with confusion ("what is that
thing?") and anxious body language ("get this bug off my leg!").*
                              —I-754, Karen, 33 yrs, New York

*I've offered crickets before, but he [iguana] is afraid of them and runs to the
other side of the cage and tries to hide under the substrate.*
                              —I-630, Robert, 22 yrs., Wisconsin

Dairy Products

Some people have indicated on their iguana questionnaires that they give
milk products (such as yogurt, cottage cheese, and regular cheese) to their

iguana, because milk products contain calcium. On the surface it sounds like a good idea, but milk is a food source produced for infant mammals by adult female mammals. Young mammals have a special enzyme (lactase) to help digest the sugars in milk (lactose). Reptiles are not mammals, and they don't have this enzyme.

Even though milk products contain calcium, I don't recommend any milk products for your lizard. An iguana's digestive system is not designed to know what to do with this "foreign" food type. There are plenty of plant-based calcium options for your iguana that are more natural and better for your reptile than mammalian milk.

Eggs

In a few articles and books on iguanas, people list eggs as a food choice. The calcium/phosphorus ratio in an egg is almost 1:50, which is way out of balance for an iguana (where the ideal ratio is 2:1). Eggs are also high in fats and cholesterol. Also, raw eggs should not be consumed by iguanas or humans because of possible contamination with salmonella.

One person wrote and said that he boiled the whites of the egg, which are a better option than whole hard-boiled eggs. My personal feeling is that eggs don't need to be fed to iguanas. There are plenty of plant-based protein options available.

Acidic Foods

Most iguanas don't like eating acidic foods (e.g., oranges, lemons, tomatoes, pineapple, grapefruit, limes, kiwi fruit), even when mixed with other foods. Because an iguana's saliva doesn't contain any digestive enzymes to break down foods, perhaps the acidity is too caustic for its mouth. I don't recommend acidic foods as a food item for iguanas because there are so many other, better food options.

I mixed a variety of foods together. He picked one piece of tomato, chewed three or four times (testing the food), then let it drop out of his mouth. The other three pieces in that meal were picked up and set off of his plate.
—I-379, Russ, 32 yrs., Utah

I have offered acid foods like tomato, orange, etc., and was very surprised at the results. She acted rather neurotic and her feces were horrid—very runny and quite odorous. Never again! —I-843, Brandon, 20 yrs., Georgia

I offered my iguana pineapple once. He licked it and looked a little shocked. Then he smacked his lips and stuck his tongue out a lot. Kind of funny. He had kind of the same look humans have when they bite into a lemon.
—I-576, David, 24 yrs., New York

Dog Food

If you look at the ingredients on a can of premium dog food, it may have some of the same ingredients you are having for dinner tonight. That's because both dogs and humans are omnivores—eating both plant-based and animal-based foods. The problem is that dog foods often have too much animal-based protein and fat for iguanas. They also contain vitamins and minerals in amounts designed for dogs, which are too high for iguanas.

Dog food (except in rare instances) should be fed to dogs, not lizards. One exception is dog food for senior or older dogs that contains no meat (usually a cornmeal base), is low in fat, and has little or no extra vitamins. This type of dog food can be considered under "supplemental protein" for iguanas.

Dangerous

The foods in this "dangerous" category may harm or even kill your iguana. Avoid these foods underline in your iguana's diet.

Wild Foods

On February 2, 1995, two young iguanas housed together were offered freshly picked, pink flowers from an azalea. The older iguana refused it, but a ten-month-old iguana (total length of 45.7 cm) ingested a small flower. Within minutes the iguana appeared extremely alert and anxious, and the respiratory rate accelerated. After several minutes, the mouth opened widely and stayed open, and the lizard appeared to be panting. It dropped from its perch to the floor of the cage and remained motionless for 20 minutes. The entire flower was then regurgitated and the lizard appeared to become stiff and bloated. It slowly crawled to one corner of the cage and buried its head beneath the substrate. After this, the lizard's movement was restricted to slow, deep breathing. The color of the iguana changed from green to brown within 30 minutes from the time of ingestion, and to nearly black by 60 minutes after ingestion, at which time the mouth closed again, almost as if the animal was too weak to hold it open. At this point supportive care in the form of oral fluid supplementation was administered, but there was little change in the condition of the animal for approximately five hours, after which the condition appeared to slowly improve. By 11 hours post-ingestion, the lizard appeared normal clinically and in color.

Certainly, in this instance, the vomiting of the toxic flower may have saved the lizard's life.

—Bulletin of the Association of Reptile and Amphibian Veterinarians (#38)

SIDEBAR

Eating Dirt

"Pica" is the word used to describe an abnormal craving for non-food items, such as clay, sticks, rocks, sand, etc. Even some humans get these cravings. There are many theories about the cause of pica, but some people believe that iguanas eat dirt because they are looking for minerals that are missing in their food. Perhaps this is just an example of an iguana just exploring its environment.

Outside in my enclosed back yard, I would see my iguana attempt to put small pieces of dirt, weeds, and twigs into his mouth. Most of the time he would just spit them out. I always stopped him from eating anything in the yard.

When it comes to eating dirt, most of the people I've talked with said that their lizard didn't want a big mouthful, just a couple of tiny bites or samples. One big problem is that strange objects swallowed by your iguana could end up obstructing your iguana's digestive tract, resulting in everything from small veterinary bills to death. Don't let your lizard eat anything like this outdoors, or even the dirt from plants in the house.

As the story above illustrates, the leaves and flowers of azaleas are potentially toxic to iguanas. Azaleas, as well as all rhododendrons (azaleas are a type of rhododendron), are just one example of a common garden plant that can kill your lizard.

Wild food can be described as any food found growing in your yard, garden, woods, or other outdoor areas. Don't give something to your iguana just because the flowers or buds look or smell pretty, or because the leaves seem appealing. Death has many forms, including stunningly beautiful colors and sweet, tasty flowers.

Be afraid of everything you don't know for sure is a safe plant. Call a local herp veterinarian or county poison control if in doubt. Most herp veterinarians have lists of all the plants and flowers that are dangerous or poisonous for turtles and use this for iguanas (no lists exist specifically for iguanas), and the list is long.

Some people also use the livestock toxicology table as a guide, but be wary of assuming something is safe for iguanas just because it's OK for some other species. As one knowledgeable iguana owner (who also has a sense of humor) said to me:

Livestock and tortoises can't climb trees and so may not regularly eat tree foliage or vines often accessible to iguanas. Iguanas confronted with the task of getting nutrition from the arboreal environments may have adapted mechanisms to deal with the toxic components of some plants, but we don't know which ones in your backyard.

Humans, dogs, and cats are very different from iguanas in the make-up of their digestive systems; ruminants [animals with four-chambered stomachs, such as cattle, goats, deer] and chelonians [turtles or tortoises], less so. Even so, chelonians tolerate much higher levels of veterinary medicine than do reptiles. The table [of poisons] may not apply in some areas. It is probably valid to issue some warning about plants, however, especially those containing dangerous heart stimulants such as foxglove and lily-of-the-valley.

—I-515, Lynn, 21 yrs., Canada

Meat

Any kind of meat is not real food for an iguana. As mentioned earlier in the chapter, an iguana is not a carnivore and is not designed to capture and consume live animals.

While my iguana was riding around on my shoulder in the house one day, I was preparing lunch for some of my turtles. You know how nosy [curious] iguanas can be. Anyway, I was cutting up some chicken liver for the turtles' lunch. My iguana kept trying to get to the food so he could have a taste. I said fine, if you want a taste, go ahead. So I put him on the counter beside the tub of liver. He leaned over it and stuck his tongue in. You should have seen the look on his face. He pulled back away from the dish, looking like he was trying to spit the awful stuff out. And the look he gave me—he was not a happy camper.

—I-773, Rich, 34 yrs., Nebraska

My vet said he has seen large iguanas that had been fed significantly high portions of animal protein, but said this shortens the iguana's life.

—I-754, Karen, 33 yrs., New York

He [4½ yrs.] ate meat sometimes in his first couple of years. He liked chicken, turkey hot dogs, and smoked turkey lunch meat. He died this year. These foods probably contributed to his death. If I were to start over with another iguana, I would not offer meat products.

—California iguana owner (name withheld as a courtesy)

Pinkies, Mice

We offered one iguana we had mice, which he ate on a regular basis in addition to the usual diet. He died at about 1½ years of age. Our vet wonders if the protein in the mice was too much for him.   —I-536, Carrie, 22 yrs., Missouri

I go against many books by saying that I don't think iguanas should ever be offered pinkies, mice, or rats as a food source, at any stage of their lives. To me, the scientific evidence is perfectly clear that iguanas aren't meant to eat mice or pinkies (baby mice so young that their eyes aren't open yet and they have no hair).

There is no pinkieburger fast food outlet in the jungles. And iguanas aren't built like jaguars, whose bodies are designed to chase down, attack, and digest animal prey. Still, some people continue to feed their iguanas mice or pinkies. Several people who have fed their iguanas mice stopped after they felt their iguanas were getting excessively hostile.

> *We offered pinkies to our iguanas in the past, but noticed much more aggressive behavior. We had one medium iguana who would only eat mice and refused to eat anything else. This iguana was very aggressive and only my husband could handle him. We had to sell this iguana.*
> —I-786, Wolf & Miriam, 28 yrs., Florida

I've noticed that many of the people who feed their iguanas mice also have snakes or carnivore lizards as pets. When I ask these people why they feed their iguanas mice or pinkies, they often say because the iguana likes them. An iguana owner might say, "I'm offering only mice for dinner tonight." And the iguana might think, "These mice sure don't taste like leaves, but it's better than an empty stomach tonight." If you offer a baby human a handful of marbles, it will often stick them in its mouth thinking they are food. But that doesn't mean babies should eat marbles. You are responsible for monitoring the food intake of your iguana.

> *I have only one iguana who relishes mice. He was caged with a water dragon by his previous owner and seemed to learn this eating habit from him. My other five iguanas avoid them [mice] like the plague.*
> —I-556, Sharon, 40 yrs., New York

> *When offered a pinkie, my iguana will shake his head as if saying no and then turn away.*   —I-833, Donna, 36 yrs., New York

Cat Food

> I would . . . caution on the use of cat food in the diet. Cat food has a very high fat and liposoluble vitamin content (A and D) and could result in kidney damage and difficulty in digestion.
> —Thomas Ryan, DVM (#28)

Cat food should be avoided entirely. Cats are carnivores, and commercially prepared cat food is formulated for the particular nutritional needs of a carnivorous diet. Extra protein, vitamins, and minerals are added for the proper balance.

These foods also often contain large amounts of animal fats. When iguanas eat cat food, its high levels of protein and minerals can cause mineralization (hardening) of an iguana's internal organs. In some cases, too much cat food could kill an iguana.

There was a time when I got a call or letter nearly every month about someone's iguana dying from eating too much cat food. The sad part is that all of these iguanas were over 3 years old. Sometimes unhealthy food takes a while to rear its ugly head. Cat food should <u>never</u> be offered to an iguana. This applies to both the canned (moist) and box/bag (dry) types.

Even though you may not feed your iguana cat food on purpose, if you have cats in the house, watch out. If you feed your cat or dog on the floor, you need to make sure your iguana can't get access to the food.

> *Our iguana eats the cat's food when out in the house. Our other iguana died from eating this type of food. I didn't know it was eating that much. The vet said it died of too much cat food [protein].*
>   —conversation with person at pet store

> *Many times I would find my iguana on the floor eating out of the cat dish.*
>   —I-43, Taryn, 27 yrs., Alaska

This section presented the minimum list for dangerous foods for iguanas. In time, with all of the new research being done on iguanas, the list probably will grow. For now, be cautious of all outdoor plants, stick with the recommended diet of 100% plant-based foods, and use a variety of food items as a buffer against possible food problems discovered in the future.

WHEN, HOW OFTEN, AND HOW MUCH TO FEED YOUR IGUANA

Once you've figured out what to feed your iguana, the next obvious questions are: when, how often, and how much food to give your iguana?

When to Feed

Try to feed your iguana at about the same time each day. Iguanas in captivity follow routines quite easily and seem to like them.

The best time to feed your iguana is in the late morning, after it has had time to warm up, but well before its lights go out at night. Morning feeding gives the lizard all day to absorb the heat in the habitat to help digest the food. According to field observations of iguanas in the wild, "feeding bouts were . . . most common in the late morning and early afternoon" (A. Stanley Rand, iguana researcher, #25).

How Iguanas "Tell" You They're Hungry

Many first-time iguana owners wonder how to tell when their iguana wants to eat. Quite simply, you don't have to decide if your iguana is hungry or not; all you need to do is establish a set place and time to feed your lizard. A healthy iguana will eat almost every day.

Once your iguana has been your pet for a while, it will often let you know when it is hungry and what it thinks about the food it has been offered. All you have to do is pay attention to the cues. Following are some interesting observations by pet owners about "reading" their iguanas' signals.

If their breakfast is late, as it is on the weekends, they [both 2½ yrs.] will first sit in the food bowl, then move it around to get my attention. (The habitat is next to my bed.) If that doesn't work, they both move up right next to the glass on the side near my bed, and glare at me until I feed them.
                                   —I-412, Christina, 24 yrs., Indiana

He [SVL: 8", TL: 2' 9", 2 yrs.] usually begins scratching the ground in the location of the food dish around the time I usually feed him (noon).
                                                —I-44, Peter, New York

My iguana [SVL: 6¾", TL: 19¾", 1 yr. 3 mo.] spends hours contemplating his food dish if I have forgotten to feed him.
                                   —I-822, Julie, 23 yrs., North Carolina

When my iguana [SVL: 9½", TL: 2' 5½", 1½ yrs.] is not fed on time, she poops on her floor.   —I-729, Renée, 30 yrs., Canada

These stories are of tame iguanas who have developed their own special personalities and have adjusted well to their lives in captivity. If your iguana is still wild, it may not show any of these signs, yet. The best advice is to feed your lizard every day at a regular time.

How Often to Feed

[It's] estimated that [*Iguana iguana*] spent 96 percent of the day inactive and only 1 percent feeding.
                         —Beverly Dugan, iguana researcher (#16)

[In your questionnaire you asked:] "Does your iguana [SVL: 17", TL: 4' 6", 4 yrs.] ever not eat?" Not in this lifetime.
                                              —I-682, Dylan, 14 yrs., California

Your iguana needs to be fed every day, no matter how chaotic your life may be. Never let the next story happen to you:

My iguana bit me once. It occurred during the summer when she eats every day. I had been very busy and hadn't had time to feed her for almost a week. She was on the side of the cage at the top. I had removed the lid of her cage so I

could remove her food bowl. As I lowered my hand into the cage she bit me. She hadn't given me any warning signs that she was mad.

—code number, name withheld for privacy
[AUTHOR'S NOTE: No excuse for not feeding for such a long time. Yes, the iguana was angry, and I can't blame her for biting.]

Rapidly growing hatchlings and younger juvenile iguanas should be offered food twice a day, ideally.

"Iguanas probably feed every day, but spend little time feeding," according to a scientific paper called "The Diet of a Generalized Folivore, *Iguana iguana*, in Panama" (#25). In this experiment, scientists reported that their group of observed iguanas' eating time "varied from 3 seconds to 17 minutes, most lasting 1-5 minutes."

> *It seems she [8 yrs.] either eats the food right away or doesn't eat it at all. Rarely will she eat food that's been sitting out for 4-5 hours.*
> —I-593, Judy, 35 yrs., Oregon

I was lucky because in the more than five years that I fed my iguana, from hatchling through adult, he never took longer than about four to five minutes to eat. This worked well because all the food was consumed at one time and nothing had to be left in the habitat that might dry out.

Because an iguana's habitat needs to be quite warm, food left in the habitat can quickly dry out, eventually making it unappetizing or unhealthy. The ideal way to feed your lizard is to present the food once (for adult iguanas) or twice (for hatchlings and juveniles) a day for a set period of time (e.g., 15 minutes, one hour), then remove it. They will adapt and "learn" to eat all of the food in this time period.

If you want to leave some food for your iguana to nibble on between feedings, put pieces of torn collard, mustard, or other greens, or sprouted sunflower seeds, in their upper water dish, where the water keeps the food moist all day. Remember, though, not to load this container up; it's not a dinner table, just a snack bar.

A Justification for Daily Feeding

> *Always offer food. Some books say automatically only feed 2-3 days a week. This is a joke. Some days they [male, SVL: 12½", 5 yrs.; female, SVL: 13", 5 yrs.] eat much less than others, but they have never quit completely!*
> —I-626, Gail, 48 yrs., New York

You may have heard or read the "rule" that hatchling iguanas should be fed daily, but that adults (2 years and older) need to be fed only every two or three days. I'll say right up front: I completely disagree with this concept. Offer your iguana food every day, whether it's 8 months or 20 years old.

I feed my iguana [SVL: 9", T: 2' 6", 2 yrs.] every day. Recently I read an arti-
cle that says adult iguanas need to be fed only two or three times weekly, but I
like to feed my iguana every day. That way he can eat whenever he wants.
Some days he will eat a lot of food, especially if I give him something he really
likes or something he has not had for a while. He eats so much that he gets full
and does not eat for a day or two.   —I-806, Shelly, 20 yrs., Pennsylvania

I didn't pay attention to this notion with my iguana because the concept
made no sense. The reality was that Za, even at more than 5 years old, still
packed down a lot of food. So why should anyone stop or reduce feeding an
iguana as it gets older?

Perhaps the practice began as a way to control food portions, for fear that
adult iguanas would eat too much. People reasoned that captive animals typically are less active than if they were free in the wild, so they burn fewer calories and could become obese.

But as the scientific report stated earlier, iguanas in the wild spend about
95% of their day resting. They literally live in their food source (trees), so they
don't have to travel far to eat. Iguanas don't even burn up calories running
away from predators in the wild; more often, they simply hide. Every time I
went into the jungles to do research on iguanas, when they saw me they hid on
the opposite side of the tree limb or branch. Only if I got very close would they
drop into the water and swim away or run into the undergrowth.

So for iguanas, captivity probably has little effect on activity levels. I believe
the danger of iguana obesity comes not with the frequency or amount of food,
but with the _types_ of food offered. A natural diet for an iguana doesn't and
shouldn't include fatty foods. Of course, offering junk or incorrect food will
surely damage an iguana, just as a wholesome, balanced diet will improve your
iguana's health.

Scientific evidence indicates that iguanas know when to stop eating:

**The capacity of the green iguana to process food is, among other
factors, set by the size of its digestive tract. Food intake is probably
set by stomach capacity and bulkiness of the food.**
—Iguana digestion research (#8)

I can't make a pattern or come up with any reasonable explanations; sometimes
he [SVL: 12", TL: 2' 6", 6 yrs.] just isn't interested in eating. I'd say he fasts
probably two days every month (not in a row). There are also some days when
he will just "pick" at his food, probably about 5 days per month (not in a row).
He always regains his appetite and has never refused food for more than two
days.   —I-703, Renee, 22 yrs., New York

It's not unusual for an older iguana to eat a lot of food one day, then take
a day off, but <u>don't</u> you be the one that controls or tries to restrict its daily
intake of food. Let your iguana decide whether it wants to eat each day, and
how much.

Even though an iguana typically should eat every day, there are some situations when this may not happen. Look in Chapter 7, Medical Troubleshooting, "Appetite: Stopped or Reduced," for some reasons that an iguana might reduce its daily food intake and some possible corrective measures.

Where to Feed Your Iguana

Just as a routine feeding time works well for your iguana, so does a specific location. Ideally, create a feeding station halfway up in the habitat or even better at the top on the resting ledge, where it simulates eating up high in trees, which is natural for them. If fed on the bottom of their habitat, they could inadvertently eat small amounts of substrate, which in time could clog up their digestive system. Eating on the bottom of the habitat also means eating in the same area where they may have defecated, which is not healthy.

In addition, put your iguana's food in a container, not dumped on the floor of the habitat; they're not pigs. A heavy ceramic bowl is a good choice, and it's easy to clean. A container with a rounded bottom (as opposed to one with straight sides and a flat bottom) makes it easier for their pointed faces to pick up the food.

> *When food is placed into the cage, my male will sometimes warn off the female so that he can eat first.*   —I-772, Andy, 32 yrs., California

If you have two iguanas in the same habitat (which I don't recommend), there should be two separate food dishes so the dominant iguana won't hog all the food and cause stress for the other lizard. In addition, an iguana's food should be served at room temperature, not straight out of a cold refrigerator.

How Much to Feed

> *Usually my iguana cleans his plate, as much as he is able to without [the aid of] lips!*   —I-379, Russ, 32 yrs., Utah

How much to feed an iguana? Every iguana eats different amounts, depending on the age and size of the iguana, its mood, the time of year, and other variables. After you have fed your lizard for a month or so, you will start to see a natural pattern for the amount it will eat at each meal. It's better to offer more food than not enough.

> [If you are an iguana,] the main problem in your life is how to avoid being eaten. This concern of theirs with predators is so overriding that an iguana that's been taken from the wild will often refuse to eat if there is any type of disturbance at all in its environment, even if it is sitting in a bowl of nutritious greens.
> —Gordon H. Rodda, iguana researcher (#27)

A young or newly acquired iguana often won't eat the first day you bring it home, especially if it knows it is being watched. In this case, just leave the food in its habitat and don't hang around watching all the time. My iguana didn't eat in front of me for several weeks after I brought him home.

The graph on page 302 shows the daily food consumption of one male iguana over about a five-year period. It shows the full range of consumption, from a couple of teaspoons a day as a hatchling through adulthood, when he packed in almost 60 teaspoons (1¼ cups). It also shows the dramatic fluctuations of food consumption during his breeding season. In this one long case study, all the food was finely chopped (1/16" to 1/8" pieces) or put in a food processor, making it extremely dense. For this reason, the actual nutrition and calories consumed is greater than in the same volume of coarsely chopped food.

For another "snapshot" look at food quantities, here's a list of one iguana owner's feeding amounts for her different iguanas (food chopped coarsely, not finely):

> *Here's what I feed my iguanas, according to their size:*
> *5" SVL iguana—2 to 4 tablespoons*
> *7½" SVL iguana—3 to 6 tablespoons*
> *8" SVL iguana—5 to 8 tablespoons*
> *12" SVL iguana—2 to 3 cups*
> *13" SVL iguana—2 to 3 cups*   —I-764, Diana, 46 yrs., California

Preferences and Picky Eating Habits

> *I don't appreciate having to throw away perfectly good food just because he's in one of his moods or doesn't like the color that particular day. He will sometimes pick out only the orange or green food and leave the rest. This is maddening.*   —I-493, Marcia, 40 yrs., Alaska

Iguanas, like many other animals, often have strong food preferences and may want to eat only a favorite food item—even to the extreme of not eating unless that food is offered each time. Or they might take a strong dislike to a particular food (perhaps something you feel is good for them) and refuse to eat it or any meal containing it. As a pet owner, you must not cave in to your lizard's desires if they interfere with proper nutrition.

It's tempting to feed your iguana only what it seems to prefer. For example, offering a single favorite food makes you feel good because your lizard loves it and the feeding operation becomes quick, easy, and predictable. But once hooked on a single-food "life style," it is a long, time-consuming path trying to wrestle your iguana back to healthy variety.

> *My iguana goes through spells of favorites [foods]. One day he may eat something and the next day refuse it.*   —I-605, Laura, 31 yrs., Canada

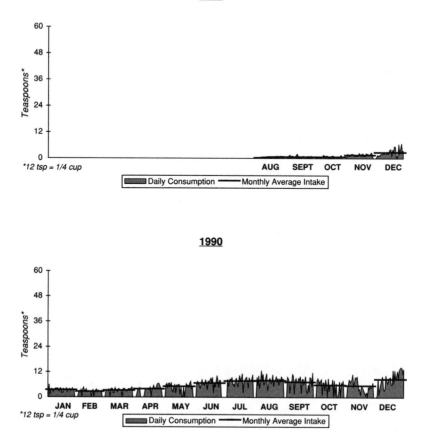

Figure 5.2: Iguana Food Consumption (one case study, above and facing page). The study began when the subject male iguana was about 3 months old and lasted until he was just over 5 years old. The graph shows the many changes an iguana can go through over time, such as the drop in food consumption during the breeding months.

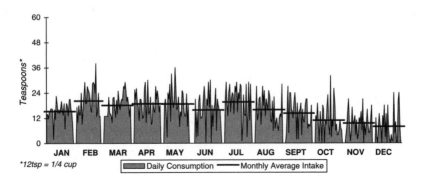

1991

*12tsp = 1/4 cup

Daily Consumption ▬ Monthly Average Intake

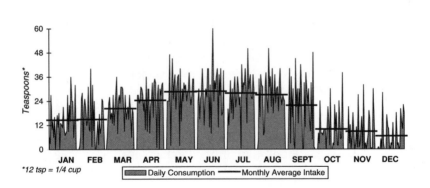

1992

*12 tsp = 1/4 cup

Daily Consumption ▬ Monthly Average Intake

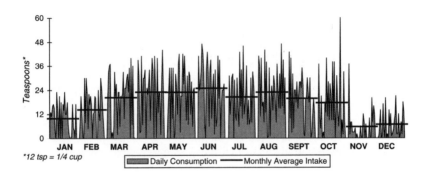

1993

*12 tsp = 1/4 cup

Daily Consumption ▬ Monthly Average Intake

I find that she will fixate on one or two food items for as long as a month, then suddenly they will change and something else will be a "favorite."
—I-754, Karen, 33 yrs., New York

Don't give up on any particular food item that your iguana may not like. Food preferences flip-flop over time, even in a single week. For six months my iguana loved yellow squash, but then for the following six months he wouldn't eat it knowingly (I hid it in with the rest of his food). You might try hiding less-favorite foods amongst other foods, but iguanas quickly catch on and sometimes start picking it out or eating around it. Bring in the food processor for a while, which melds favorites and disliked items into blended harmony.

My iguana has the habit of picking through his meal and eating only those items he likes and leaving the rest.   —I-690, Irene, 34 yrs., Texas

Overcoming Picky Eating Habits

To get an iguana to eat a new food item that it doesn't like, mix a small amount of the new food with some favorites. Gradually increase the proportion of the disliked food until it's at the level you feel is right for your lizard.

An iguana can be hungry and still refuse to eat. Once in a while at meal times, my iguana would come over to the food bowl, stick his head inside, look up at me as though the bowl was empty, then walk backward away from the bowl. He was hungry but didn't like what was offered, or the way it looked, or something.

I found a quick cure to this problem. When he refused the food, I would go to the kitchen and reorganize the food into two or three separate stacks, or one big pile. I also made a lot of noise in the kitchen, as though something was really happening. When I returned with this "new" food, he would often gobble it up. I learned this trick from a woman who went through the same problem with her 2-year-old (human) child.

Her [SVL: 15½", TL: 3' 5¾", 4½ yrs.] favorite food is variety. If not she tends to get "bored" and does not eat as well.
—I-653, Justin, 19 yrs., Maryland

Iguanas can get bored with food items presented in the same manner. One solution to this type of pickiness is to present the food with different textures: grated, chopped, blended, or zapped in food processor. Also try combining different foods into one big mixture. Firm vegetables can be grated into soft, long strands. One person wrote to say that after she started grating the food, her iguana was more hungry at dinner time. Another option is presenting individual food types separately.

Another way to generate interest is to place a couple of pieces of leaf (e.g., kale, collard green, mustard green) on top of the food to attract your iguana's attention. Another trick is to put the leaves underneath the rest of the food, with only the edges sticking out, to encourage your lizard to stick its face into

SIDEBAR

"I Don't Like This Food!"

Iguanas have very dramatic ways of letting us owners know what foods they don't like.

If he [SVL: 9¹/4", TL: 2' 9¹/4", 2 yr. 6 mo.] isn't pleased with his food he will turn the food dish completely upside down.
—I-421, Darren, 22 yrs., Canada

My iguanas [both 5 years old] will rush at me if a favorite food is coming. They may even jump on me [no aggression, just excited about the food].
—I-626, Gail, 48 yrs., New York

My iguana refused her "new" food last week by backing away from the food. If she really doesn't like a "new" food and accidentally eats it, she will spit it out. —I-680, Catherine, 21 yrs., New York

[AUTHOR'S NOTE: This as one of the standard behavior patterns of captive iguanas, as I discovered in my iguana questionnaire research. As the iguanas back up from the food, they look as though whatever is in the food bowl is the most disgusting thing they have ever seen. It's a very funny sight.]

When she doesn't like her food, she promptly shuts her eyes and puts her head down. It's her way of telling me she doesn't want the food.
—I-725, Marie, 23 yrs., Maryland

the food. Pre-cooking some of the food items just a little can bring out different flavors. For example, carrots often taste sweeter when cooked. Be inventive, and keep your iguana on its toes.

FOOD PREPARATION

The only thing I dislike about having an iguana is the time it takes to prepare his food to ensure that his diet is balanced, and his food is always fresh. Considering that most people hate to cook for themselves, and often eat out of cans and fast food restaurants for weeks when they live by themselves, I think this is understandable. The necessity of always having fresh fruit and vegetables in the house does, however, have a good influence on my own diet.
—I-515, Lynn, 21 yrs., Canada

Whether your iguana's food is chopped and served as separate food items or all mixed together, it must first come to room temperature. Cold food is fine for some human meals, but not for iguanas. You can leave the food out in a plastic Ziploc bag until it comes to room temperature or speed the process by putting the bag in warm water. Also, rinse vegetables to get rid of any possible contaminants.

Many vegetables have more nutrition if not cooked, while others (e.g., carrots) get sweeter and more appealing if steamed for a few minutes. Be inventive; try cooking some vegetables once in a while to perk up your lizard's appetite.

Chopping/Shredding

There is nothing I dislike doing for my iguana. Sometimes chopping his food into small pieces can be a bit of a pain, but so is doing the ironing.
                    —I-505, Sheila, 30 yrs., Canada

Remember in the beginning of this chapter I said that iguanas don't chew their food; they just bite and swallow it. Also, their digestive system works best when the food is presented in small pieces rather than big chunks.

All vegetables from the grocery store or garden need to be chopped, grated, shredded, or put in a food processor or blender to accomplish this goal. The smaller the food size, the more vitamins, minerals, proteins, and carbohydrates go into its growing body. It's almost like pre-digesting the food before your iguana gets it. The following is a perfect example of why chopping the food finer can help iguanas:

Doug Brust, who did this study for a degree, found that the average passage time for these animals [wild iguanas in Venezuela] in

---

SIDEBAR

Food Processor

If the thought of standing at a cutting board, knife in hand, chopping veggies and fruits into tiny bits for your iguana doesn't appeal to you, perhaps a food processor is the answer. I used mine frequently and have nothing but good things to say about it as a time-saving tool for preparing food.

If you don't think you will ever use one of those big, expensive food processors, they now have mini processors for about $35 that do the same job for less money and space. Do some research into which brand name to purchase. The one I bought is not the well-known, expensive brand, but the review I read rated it better—and it cost much less.

this population was 6.9 days, almost an entire week! Now, that seems slow, but their food is not very digestible; it takes a lot of breakdown by bacteria to break up all that plant material.
—Gordon H. Rodda, iguana field researcher (#27)

<u>Never</u> offer large chunks of food. I chopped all of my iguana's food very fine (into bits of about ¹⁄₁₆″), until he was 2' long. When he exceeded this length, I chopped the food into pieces of about ⅛″ to ³⁄₁₆″. The only drawback is that food dries out much faster when it is chopped this finely. If you feed your lizard at a specific time each day, your iguana will probably consume all the food for that meal at one sitting, so drying out isn't a problem.

I have already started chopping her food into smaller pieces as you recom-mended, and she does seem to like it better.
—I-818, Donna, 38 yrs., Texas

The only exception to the "always chop finely" rule is with leafy greens, such as dandelion, mustard, or collard. These are like the foods iguanas eat in the wild, except they are tender enough to eat unchopped. If you have one huge leaf, you can tear it into more manageable mouthfuls, or take the leaf and roll it into a loose ball in your hand, then straighten it out for the iguana to eat. This technique breaks down the rough fiber in the plant, making the leaf easier to swallow. If a leaf has a thick stem running down the middle, it's best to cut this section out.

Separate vs. Mixed

When I first got my iguana (at about 3 months old), I always offered veg-gies and fruits as separate items on the food plate. My iguana seemed to like mostly vegetables and would only nibble on the fruits. Remember, their food preferences vary with nutritional requirements, temperature, season, age, and moods. Often I mixed fruits and veggies together so everything would be eaten.

Iguana owners often ask which is the best way to present an iguana's food: as separate items or all mixed together. If the food items are separate, you get a chance to see your iguana's likes and dislikes. I suggest starting off with this method the first few days after you acquire your iguana. It's a great way to learn your iguana's food preferences—but it also could allow your iguana to simply pick out one or two favorites and not learn to eat the rest.

More realistically, the easiest and fastest approach is to mix several food types together. That way, no particular food the iguana might dislike will be left uneaten, and less time is wasted fussing with individual piles of food. The main problem with this method is that food could become contaminated if left out too long in the habitat. Sometimes one food item, perhaps a fruit, will go bad quickly and contaminate the rest of the food. If your iguana eats its food right away, there should be no problem. In addition, mix the food just before you

SIDEBAR

The Dangers of Large Food Chunks

Besides aiding digestion, small-size food portions might also keep your lizard alive. Iguana owners have told me how their lizards choked on food because the pieces were too large. One person told me that his iguana actually got a piece of food caught in its throat. Luckily, the lizard got the piece loose by shaking its head violently back and forth. Here is one more story:

The last episode at the vet's was an emergency. My iguana had some yellow crookneck squash for supper and a piece lodged in her throat (she was 4 years old at this time). She was making the most awful noises (for an animal that never utters a sound except for sneezing, we knew this was serious), so we phoned our vet. The office was closed but the vet asked that we meet her as soon as possible. The effort to get my iguana into the car and the trip there must have jarred the squash loose, as the noise stopped by the time we got to the vet's.
—I-124, Joan, Florida

feed your iguana each time, rather than mixing a week's worth of food at a time, which could go bad.

Tips for Obtaining Vegetables

Some food items are difficult to find in the grocery store, or are not available certain times of the year. To compensate for this, I made a special food garden for my iguana that was about 2' x 6'. In this small space outside my office window, I grew enough kale, mustard greens, nasturtiums (leaves and flowers), and dandelions (leaves and flowers) for several iguanas. In addition, when my iguana was allowed out in the enclosed yard, he would often go and eat freely from "his" garden. There's nothing like watching your iguana eat straight out of the garden.

This winter I've grown mustard and collard greens in the house under the [plant grow] lights. The mustard grows really well in the house. I will try to grow more for next winter. I've got a spare bedroom that I'll make into a little greenhouse room. It's a lot of work, but I try to do the very best I can for my babies [iguanas].
—I-605, Laura, 31 yrs., Canada

Many iguana owners grow food in their yards, patios, or even in pots. For example, Janice (I-289) has her own garden of vegetables, fruits, and flowers.

Her iguana especially loves rose and carnation petals and nasturtium leaves. Because Janice grows them herself, she knows for sure that her plants have not been exposed to poisons. It's very important that you feed your iguana home-grown foods that have NOT been exposed to pesticides, fungicides, or other poisons.

People in Florida, Southern California, and the Southern states who have the right climate can offer their iguanas hibiscus flowers and leaves, which are excellent food for iguanas. When I was on an island off the coast of Belize, I met a woman who had a pet iguana that she brought to the island. As we walked around the island talking, she would stop periodically in front of the naturally growing hibiscus bushes to let her iguana have an afternoon snack.

Dandelions, which are considered a weed in most lawns, are great iguana food (but be very careful when picking neighbors' dandelions, which may have been sprayed with insecticides). Their calcium/phosphorus ratio is about 2:1 (ideal) and iguanas can eat both the leaves and flowers.

In the summer I started my iguana's day by picking up to 100 nasturtium leaves (and occasional flowers) from our yard (we understand these are great for calcium—and he loves them).   —I-705, Linda, 46 yrs., California

Nasturtiums thrive on neglect, so can be stuck anywhere, even in flower pots on the porch or in a sunny window. They grow beautifully colored, delicate flowers from a vine-like stem and will survive outside until the first frost. Both the leaves and flowers can be eaten by your lizard.

Salad Bar

Salad bars are available in many grocery and delicatessen stores, with salad often sold according to weight. It's a cheap and efficient way to feed your lizard and a great place to find a wide variety of vegetables.

Salad doesn't mean a plate of lettuce for your iguana—and of course no dressing. I found salad bars with several kinds of vegetables plus various legumes (e.g., kidney beans, garbanzos, small white beans) and fruit. Once home, I rinsed the vegetables (many stores put a chemical agent called sulfites on green vegetables to preserve their freshness) then put all the salad bar items, along with leafy greens, in a small food processor and chopped it fine. I fed this mixture to my iguana once a week, and it was always one of Za's favorite food days.

Free Food

I get most of my iguana's food free from a local grocery store that lets me have it for free if I help collect it at the end of the day.
                                                                        —I-650, Helen, 31 yrs., Ohio

Sometimes you can get free bruised, broken, or overripe fruits and vegetables from your grocery store. They don't have to be perfectly shaped; any damaged or spoiled parts can be cut out.

Frozen Foods (Occasional)

I stress fresh vegetables, but in many parts of the country it's hard to find fresh produce in the winter. A good temporary substitute is frozen mixed vegetables (brought to room temperature), which can be used as a base for adding whatever fresh vegetables are available. But remember, frozen vegetables should not be a replacement for fresh foods, primarily leafy greens.

WHEN YOU'RE AWAY FROM HOME

We have a summer home and our iguana [6 yrs.] makes it hard to go away on the weekends. We schedule ourselves around him because I do worry about him when we are not there. —I-654, Bill & Kathy, 25 & 27 yrs., Illinois

Most people take vacations at least once a year and often like to get away on the weekends once in a while. When you leave even for a short time, your lizard still needs to be fed and its feces cleaned up.

Finding an Iguana Sitter

If you have a dog or cat and you leave for several days, it's easy for a neighbor or friend to feed them. If you go away for several weeks, dogs and cats can be boarded and well cared for by professionals.

It is hard to find a house sitter for my iguanas [3½ yrs. & 1 yr.] who will give them the care and attention that I do. —I-774, Walter, 46 yrs., Arizona

Finding a professional place to board your iguana safely and happily is almost impossible in most parts of the country. When I lived in Northern California, there was a huge reptile store and also a few veterinary hospitals that boarded iguanas, but that's an exception. Before you leave your iguana at one of these places, be sure the cage it will stay in is an appropriate size and that it has proper heating.

To find someone to care for your iguana at your home, try your local herp society—another good reason for joining such a group. As for friends and relatives, many people are afraid of reptiles. You might find that your friendly neighbors, who would gladly watch your cat while you're gone, will have elaborate excuses for why they are unable to care for your iguana.

I made numerous trips to Mexico and Central America gathering information for this book and had to leave my iguana home. However, I could not have found a better caregiver for Za than Kendal (the illustrator of the iguana drawings in this book). He did everything right, and I was very lucky.

Arrangements Depend on Time Away

The level or depth of arrangements you make for the care of your lizard will depend on how long you'll be gone. Below are some general guidelines and ideas.

One Day

The iguanas don't require as much daily affection and attention as other animals. If I need to go away for a day or two, as long as they get fed, they're OK.
                                         —I-685, Julie, 36 yrs., California

Fill up the lizard's water and food bowls with its favorite food the morning you leave (if that is a time it usually eats or will eat a lot). Or you can feed your iguana the day before you leave with this favorite food, which will guarantee a full stomach for at least a day. Make sure that you leave plenty of water and perhaps some dandelion or sprouted grasses in a dish with a little water to keep it fresh. I never left my iguana alone for more than a day without someone coming in and taking care of him. (Because he would defecate on command, I would poop him just before I left that morning so he didn't have feces in his habitat all day.)

Up to One Week

You will need someone to take care of your lizard any time you're gone longer than a day. A week is a very manageable commitment for most caregivers.

I went away for one week and left my iguana [SVL: 12", TL: 2' 11", 7 yrs.] at a friend's house. When I returned and brought my iguana home he followed me around the house, or would find me and sit beside me for long periods of time.   —I-283, Susan, 44 yrs., Washington

My iguana will become un-littertrained if I am not home for a week or so (he is usually left in the care of a roommate). He will also become much more restless, knocking many more things over than usual and climbing up into places that he normally does not go. Near the end of the week he will find someplace to hide, usually under my bed.   —I-515, Lynn, 21 yrs., Canada

More Than One Week

The first time I went to Central America for three weeks, I left my iguana (about one year old then) and his Ultimate Juvenile Habitat (which I took apart and reassembled) at the house of a fellow herp club member, Wanda. I trusted her completely with Za's care, so I never worried about Za while I was away. Trust and reliability are the two important considerations when looking for an iguana sitter, and they are the hardest values to find.

Za was well cared for by Wanda, but after one week of eating normally, he dropped to about half his regular food intake for the next week, and the last week he ate only sparingly every other day. When I picked him up and reassembled his habitat back home, Za ate like a pig for a couple of days. We were both happy to be home again.

> *All three of my iguanas quit eating when I went on vacation and they were boarded. Also, the skin on one of the iguanas turned black (normalized when I took them home).*   —I-650, Helen, 31 yrs., Ohio

It's not uncommon for an iguana to go "off feed" if someone else is taking care of the lizard or if it is moved to a new place to live temporarily. Iguanas don't like their routine or security disrupted.

Taking care of <u>anything</u> for more than a week requires special, exact details and a special person. Start looking now for one of these special people, because they are hard to find. Perhaps you can train your next-door neighbor kid to do the job. To test the person, start with simple overnight care, then a couple of days, and keep increasing the time and responsibility until you know you can trust and rely upon this person.

You will need to write down an exact list of what is required of your iguana sitter. Include the phone number of your veterinarian and/or helpful herp friend as a back-up. Have the sitter come to your house several times before you leave to get familiar with actually feeding, handling, and cleaning up after your iguana. This process will also give your iguana a chance to become familiar with someone new feeding and holding it, while you are still around to provide the feeling of security. This familiarity may prevent your iguana from going off feeding when you actually leave.

When I was growing up, my neighbors went to Canada each year for a week to 10 days. I was a little kid, but I took care of their two cats while they were gone. They had exact details of what they wanted done each day and paid me what I considered a huge sum of money. But what I really liked was that two adults left their favorite pets in my care. I loved the responsibility, and it made me feel special. Perhaps you can let your neighbor kid feel special and have your iguana cared for, all at the same time.

CHAPTER 6

Special Care

Cleanliness is, indeed, next to godliness.
—John Wesley (1703–1791)

Every animal has its own distinct set of needs that require attention. Although some things become a real chore at times, there is nothing that I really dislike. All of these are necessary and were an understood part of owning an iguana when I purchased mine. —I-772, Andy, 32 yrs., California

After the initial set-up of your iguana's habitat, you will still need to perform daily, weekly, and monthly care tasks for your lizard—as you would with any pet. These tasks are not exceptionally time-consuming but are absolutely necessary for the overall health and well-being of your animal.

I am amazed at how many people have iguanas and how many people don't know how to take care of them. —I-183, Mary, 24 yrs., Massachusetts

Scattered throughout the chapters in this book, I describe a variety of care needs for iguanas. In this chapter, I concentrate in greater detail on a few specific care requirements, because of their importance.

CLAW TRIMMING

Her sharp claws!! Unbelievable—I have so many scars.
—I-183, Mary, 24 yrs., Massachusetts

I don't like the sharp claws when he tries to sit on my head. When they are small it's cute, but now at 10 pounds. . . . ! ! !
—I-786, Miriam & Wolf, 28 yrs., Florida

When I first thought about getting an iguana as a pet, I wanted its life to be as natural as possible in captivity. But by the time my iguana, Za, reached 8 months old, I couldn't stand his claws digging into my arm any more. From simple daily handling, my arms looked as if they had been attacked by a lion.

Another problem with iguanas' claws is that, because pet iguanas are usually confined to a much smaller space than they enjoy in the wild, they can end up sticking themselves with their own, extra-sharp claws. For example, I have seen several iguanas with small pinholes in their dewlaps inflicted by their own claws. And there's always the potential for other problems to occur.

The biggest problem was when I didn't keep my iguana's toenails trimmed well enough. They would curve and catch on things (especially the wire cage), which occasionally pulled out a toenail (they always grew back) or pulled the joint badly. A few toes on each foot were slightly deformed for years as a result of this. Cure: trim the nails!   —I-519, Ellen, 40 yrs., Louisiana

I realized I needed to achieve a happy medium between my iguana's natural state and his captive lifestyle. The solution was to trim Za's claws just enough to eliminate their "icepick" points. With the dulled claw points, I could now handle him without discomfort, which encouraged me to handle him more, and he was still able to climb the limbs in his habitat. We both benefited. He also seemed to be a little less aggressive with shorter claws.

If your iguana is accustomed to climbing objects in your house, you should be aware that trimming its claws may increase the lizard's risk of falling. By dulling the sharp points of the claws, you are reducing your iguana's extra climbing security.

We have found that if we blunt [trim] his nails, he has a hard time climbing on his branches.   —I-690, Irene, 34 yrs., Texas

To compensate for my iguana's duller claws, I modified the climbing objects in his habitat. I installed larger-diameter limbs with side branches that acted as ladder rungs, or hand holds, to make climbing easier and safer. I also used a hand saw to cut deep, ¼" wide grooves at angles into the climbing branches to give him a better grip.

I know people who have suspended big limbs from the ceiling of their houses for their iguanas to climb and rest on. I don't recommend high limbs like this for pet iguanas, especially those with trimmed claws, as it's too easy for them to fall and be injured. In fact, one iguana lost his grip, fell, and broke his back.

I usually clip only the sharp needle points off the tips of the claws so the lizards can climb and I can handle them and not get torn up.
                        —I-200, Dianna, 47 yrs., Washington

Because of Za's rapid growth during the hatchling and juvenile stages, I had to trim his claws about every two weeks. At around 2 years old his rapid growth slowed and so did the number of required trims per month. By the time he reached 4½ years old, it was a good four to five weeks between trimmings (it took only about 10 minutes for all his claws).

How to Properly Trim Claws

The first time you trim your iguana's claws, you will probably feel nervous and unsure. That's OK; in fact, you should be, but the more times you practice the process of claw trimming, the more confident you will become. It just takes some getting used to holding the lizard and performing the proper cuts.

Most iguanas don't enjoy being restricted while their claws are being trimmed, and if you ever happen to cut or hit a nerve in the claw, the lizard will remember and put up more of a fight the next time. If your iguana is a hatchling, it's easier to train it to tolerate claw trimming. Older iguanas will put up some initial struggling until they learn that nothing bad is going to happen to them.

SIDEBAR

Claw-Trimming Tools

There are a number of tools available for trimming your iguana's claws, and each has its own special functions and problems.

- **Large toenail clippers for humans**—tend to "crush" rather than cut the claw
- **Human scissors**—cutting blade too long; incorrect leverage
- **Reptile claw clippers**—the best if you get the right brand (see below)
- **Dog clippers**—too large and improper cutting angle
- **Bird clippers**—often have a spring-loaded device that holds the claw in position while cutting; danger of pulling the iguana's claw off if the lizard jerks its foot or hand suddenly
- **Hot-wire cutters**—designed for birds; exposed hot cutting wire can be dangerous for both the cutter and the "cuttee"

I have tried all of the tools listed here and like only one type. Throughout this book, I have tried to avoid recommending specific brand-name products. New iguana products emerge all the time, and something I recommend today may be obsolete tomorrow.

Having said that, for now I recommend Four Paws® reptile claw clippers. The Four Paws clippers have a stainless-steel cutting blade that is super-sharp and holds its edge. They also won't rust and the blades cut cleanly without crushing the claw. If you find a cutting instrument that works better than this for you, by all means use it.

Because my iguana went through the trimming process frequently when he was young and never experienced pain, he usually sat quietly as I trimmed his claws. As he got older, the process got easier and easier. Of course, some days he would put up a fuss, but it wasn't the claw-trimming process that was the problem. He just didn't want to be controlled that day.

There are many claw-trimming techniques that work for iguanas. I have included my preferences for the sake of people new to iguana ownership, to provide at least a starting point. If you already have a technique for trimming your iguana's claws and it works, stay with it. For everyone else, consider some of the ideas described in this section.

AT A GLANCE: The Claw-Trimming Process

• Designate a specific area for trimming your iguana's claws
• Relax the iguana beforehand on a heating pad
• Cut one claw at a time, in a routine pattern
• Trim the proper amount
• Be prepared in case of bleeding

Proper Place

Before you start trimming your iguana's claws, you will need to designate an area where the task can be done safely and comfortably. Choose a room with bright light and minimal disruptions—a bathroom or small bedroom is ideal.

This area could be the same place you help your lizard with shedding and medical first-aid treatments. By having an established place, your lizard gets familiar and feels safe with the routine here. As an example, if your iguana has a piece of dried skin dangling above its eye that is driving it crazy—and you take the iguana to its special-care location and gently remove the source of its discomfort—your iguana will remember good things about this room, and about you.

Another way of conditioning your iguana to being comfortable in its special-care location is to offer it a small food treat before doing the required procedure. At the end of your session, offer a food treat again and touch the lizard's body in a reassuring, non-medical way.

Relax Your Iguana

Allow your iguana to rest in its designated area on a human heating pad for about 10 minutes before proceeding with claw trimming or any other care treatment. The heat will make the lizard relaxed, docile, and less inclined to squirm around. Start the pad on low and manually adjust the temperature until the lizard's stomach feels warm but not hot.

Much of the fuss an iguana puts up during claw trimming is from being held too tightly, being restricted, or not feeling secure and settled while the process is taking place. You need to have the lizard's whole body balanced and secure before you start trimming.

Routine Cutting Pattern

Establishing a pattern for trimming your iguana's claws will greatly simplify the process. It's easy to forget which claw you just cut, and a routine will help. Either start with the "thumb" working to the "pinkie" claw, or the other direction, and stick with this order every time.

Take one claw at a time and hold it gently but firmly away from the other claws. Once the claw has been trimmed, immediately move your cutting tool to the next claw in the proper order. If you need to move your iguana's claw or wrist to get a better angle, do it slowly and the lizard is less likely to resist.

Pay close attention to all aspects of claw trimming; anything can happen. One time I was very focused on the claw I was cutting and didn't notice that one of Za's other fingers had gotten in between the handles of the clippers. As I pressed down on the clippers, I cut the claw perfectly but by accident I pinched that other finger. My iguana jumped and opened his mouth in an aggressive manner. I learned that lesson quickly.

Often my iguana would, in a blink of an eye, jerk his hand away from the cutting tool for no apparent reason. If you feel this happening, just let the cutting tool fall to the ground as the iguana's hand retreats. If you hold tightly to the cutters you could damage your lizard's claw or finger.

How Much to Trim Off

While trimming my iguana's nails, I inadvertently cut more than I should have and she yanked her foot away and bit me on the base of my thumb.
—I-772, Andy, 32 yrs., California

You need to be careful not to trim the claws to the quick, causing bleeding. I've had no trouble, but I've seen iguanas with bone infections via this route. Not good.
—I-775, Karen, 37 yrs., Arizona

In the first year I was trimming my iguana's claws, I inadvertently nicked the vein a couple of times, causing some bleeding. But I quickly learned the right amount to trim off so that he didn't bleed or feel any pain. Once you know the technique, trimming the claws will be a fast, easy, and painless process for both of you.

Each claw has a nerve and blood vessel—the quick—that extends down the middle of the claw, almost to the tip. In iguanas, you can see the quick as a black line through the middle of the nail. Make sure when you trim the claw that you get only the very tip, below the quick, or you will not only make the nail bleed but also cause pain to your lizard.

Look at the illustration on page 318, which shows where to cut the claw.

This recommended trimming point is actually on the conservative side, with a built-in safety margin. I have cut the claws on a lot of other people's iguanas, and the point at which the nail bleeds varies from one iguana to the next. It's <u>always</u> better to undertrim than to cut too much. In reality, I was able to cut my iguana's claws just a little more than the drawing shows, but for beginners the drawing provides a good, safe starting point.

> *My iguana is very wild right now (first owner didn't treat her well) and her long, sharp fingernails tear me up. The vet won't even clip them because my iguana is so wild. The vet says, "Don't clip them, file them." Right. The lizard from hell will sit while I slowly file her nails.*
> —I-249, Linda, 36 yrs., New Jersey

In addition to trimming the nail, some people use a human fingernail file to smooth out any rough edges left by the clipping. This sounds good in theory, but I found that after trimming his claws, my iguana had endured enough of

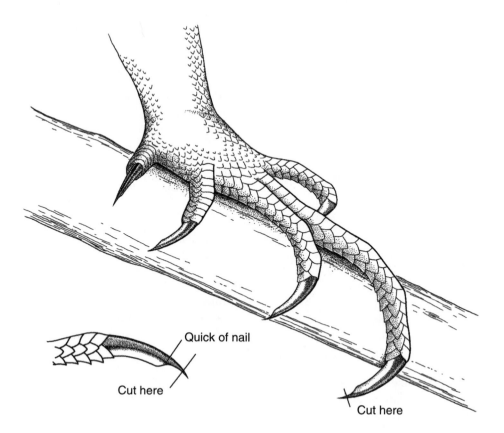

Figure 6.1: For safe claw trimming, take off only the very tip, as shown.
Illustration by: Kendal Morris

the process and didn't want any more, so I never filed his claws. One option is to file the nails smoother another day.

Be Prepared—Bleeding

When trimming your iguana's claws, have KWIK-STOP® powder (or some other, similar coagulant product) handy. KWIK-STOP is a powdered form of the styptic pencils that men use for shaving cuts. KWIK-STOP is made specifically to stop nail bleeding in cats, dogs, and birds. In an emergency you can also use corn starch.

Before you begin trimming the first claw, put some KWIK-STOP powder in the top of the lid (used like a plate) and wet one or two Q-tips® for applying the powder—if necessary—to the bleeding claw.

If you do cut into your iguana's claw and it starts to bleed, dip the moistened Q-tip into the KWIK-STOP and apply the powder to the claw. If a lot of blood is coming out, put the claw directly into the lid with the powder. This will stop the bleeding. This experience should scare you enough to make you pay closer attention for the next cut.

AT A GLANCE: Additional Claw-Trimming Hints

- Pre-soak the iguana (10-30 minutes) for softer claws and easier trimming
- Have help in the beginning to manage your iguana
- Use a control device, such a towel wrapped around your animal (if necessary)
- Have a qualified veterinarian demonstrate proper trimming techniques

---

Pre-Soaking

Just as your own nails are softer after you have taken a bath or shower, so are an iguana's. By pre-soaking your iguana (about 10 to 30 minutes in a bathtub; see page 332, "Bathing"), the actual cutting will be easier. Bathing also tends to relax your lizard, making the trimming process less of a hassle.

Have Help in the Beginning

If you are new to claw trimming, it's best to work with another person until you feel confident about what you are doing. Eventually, though, your goal should be to trim your iguana's claws by yourself.

Once your iguana has settled on the heating pad, you can begin the trimming. If there are two of you, have one person keep the lizard still by applying light pressure of their hand around the animal's back. This "holder" person can pick up a foot and offer one claw at a time for you to trim. An important point: When one foot is picked up, make sure the rest of the iguana's body is balanced and stable, or the lizard will squirm throughout the trimming process as it tries to balance itself.

One alternative approach is for the holder to sit in a chair with a towel on his or her lap and a heating pad on top of that. Then put your lizard on the heating pad and let the other person begin trimming. You can also use the technique of a heating pad on your lap for solo trimming. In fact, that's typically how I trimmed my iguana's claws when he was an adult. The only time I needed help was during breeding season, when he was hormonally crazy.

Use a Towel

My iguana puts up a fuss getting his nails trimmed. Not real bad, but he makes the ordeal more time-consuming. I covered his head with a towel and that solved the problem. —I-798, Teri, 35 yrs., New Hampshire

[AUTHOR'S NOTE: This worked for her iguana, but yours may hate it and might even freak out during cutting.]

When trimming his nails, at first I used a towel to wrap him in. But he came to associate the towel with being restrained, which he hates, so that he would attempt to flee or thrash me with his tail as soon as he caught sight of the towel. —I-493, Marcia, 40 yrs., Alaska

When facing older, unruly iguanas, some people wrap the lizard in a towel like a hot dog in a bun. They pull one hand or foot out of the towel at a time, trim the claws, put it back in, then bring out the next appendage. If possible, use this only as a temporary technique until human and beast feel more comfortable with the trimming process. This is one example of the many possible techniques that can help with the trimming process. Experiment until you find something that works for you and your iguana.

Veterinarian

"Seeing is believing." If you still have doubts or insecurities about the claw-trimming process, one idea is to observe as a qualified veterinarian trims your lizard's claws. Be sure to ask a lot of questions and even try trimming the claws while there, so when you are home and doing it yourself you'll remember what to do and feel more confident.

It's important to verify that the veterinarian has lots of experience trimming claws on <u>iguanas</u>. If the veterinarian says something like, "I've done cats and dogs, and it's about the same," you might think twice before you take your lizard there. An iguana's claws are much more sensitive than—and different from—a dog's or cat's.

A few people have contacted me with distressing stories about how they took their iguana to a veterinarian who claimed expertise in claw trimming, but who turned out not to know the first thing about iguana claws. If you're going to learn claw-trimming techniques from a veterinarian, choose one with specific iguana expertise.

"Scratch Reducers"

Even when they're trimmed, iguanas' claws can still scratch your skin. For those people who are very sensitive to being clawed, there is further help available. By putting a protective covering over the arm you hold your iguana with, you can eliminate all scratches. This can be as simple as a long-sleeved sweatshirt. Nearly any kind of covering will work, but here are a couple of ideas to start you thinking.

To help stave off the inevitable scratches I get from letting my iguana perch on my arm, I bought a pair of neoprene "wristers," basically one-foot long neoprene tubes that slip on over your forearm. I got them when I was fishing in Alaska, where they were used to keep some of the jellyfish slime and other assorted lovelies from burning your arm. One of these tubes makes great protection for your arm, and also gives your iguana something to grip and balance himself with. They were $14 or so in Kodiak, so probably are less in the lower 48.   —Brian, via the Herp-Net on-line bulletin board

These pre-made neoprene sleeves may be hard to find, so one option is to make your own. Purchase a piece of neoprene (the material of wet suits) from a dive shop. Wrap the piece around your forearm so both ends touch or butt together. Secure this butt joint with duct tape, which you can purchase at any hardware store. For more security of the joint, put another strip of duct tape on the inside seam. It's not very pretty, but it may do the job.

Kevlar sleeves are a must for handling thrashing iguanas. They are worth their weight in gold for examining strange or pissed off iguanas.
                                            —I-775, Karen, 37 yrs., Arizona

Another option is to make the same forearm covering except with Kevlar®, the stuff they make bullet-proof vests out of. I have seen butchers, who use a sharp knife all day, using gloves and wrist protectors made out of Kevlar. Perhaps you can ask your local butcher to order some sleeves made of this material for you.

SHEDDING

When he sheds it looks as though the old skin is exploding.
                                            —I-882, Jessica, 21 yrs., New Jersey

An iguana's skin shedding (known scientifically as ecdysis) is an ongoing process from birth to death. Unlike a snake that sheds in one piece, an iguana does it in patches or sections. These sections are often well-defined, with an actual border or starting and ending point. As an example, when an iguana's hand is ready to shed, the wrist is the demarcation point between the hand and the forearm, often making it look as if the lizard is wearing a pair of off-white surgical gloves.

I haven't noticed a pattern except that the whole leg never sheds at once. The foot will go, then some other body part, then the thighs! There's always a very clean line between the shedding zones and the other areas of the body that are not shedding.   —I-862, Dawn, 23 yrs., New York

She [SVL: 9½", TL: 2' 6½", 1 yr. 8 mo.] is always shedding somewhere, though if there is a sequence I can't figure it out.

—I-865, Julie, 46 yrs., California

After six years of talking to iguana owners, I have come to realize that iguanas shed in no particular sequence (head, then legs, etc.). There is no single correct or natural pattern that all iguanas follow to shed properly. Even if an iguana seems to follow an established shedding pattern, this might change over time.

The first sign of an imminent shedding can be a dulling of the skin area—as though a watered-down milk mixture had been spilled on it, like the glove example I gave before.

Sometimes shedding is quick, other times it may take a week or two, but the skin will shed when it is ready. After shedding, the new skin will have a deeper sheen with more distinct patterns.

He sheds more often during the summer than the winter. I figure he grows more during the warmer weather and longer days. The older he gets the more segmented the shedding areas get.   —I-773, Rick, 34 yrs., Nebraska

How often an iguana sheds depends on the lizard's age as well as the time of year. When an iguana is in its hatchling and juvenile stages, it sheds faster and more often than in the adult stage. Like a human child who quickly outgrows its clothes, a fast-growing young iguana sheds frequently to keep up with its expanding body.

Older adult iguanas usually shed only a few times a year because they are no longer in their rapid growth phase. As my iguana reached about 4 years old, his shedding pattern changed. Instead of all the body parts shedding before the next round began, his head would shed two or three times before the rest of his body. Because he was a very dominant male, his head was always getting larger, which I believe was the reason for its multiple sheds. In fact, from age 4 to 5, his belly shed only once.

Older iguanas' shed is thicker and the shedding process is fewer times per year compared to a fast-growing hatchling. I'd say that my iguana [6-year-old male] sheds about once every two to three months.

—I-703, Renee, 22 yrs., New York

My iguana is almost 3 years old and not all his body parts shed each time (i.e., sometimes his head or tail will skip one shed, then be first the next time around or between sheds).   —I-916, Lucretia, 32 yrs., California

Things That Help Shedding

Captive iguanas often have more difficulty shedding than iguanas in the wild. In the wild, it's hot, the humidity is greater—perhaps a light rain will shower on them in the afternoon—and there are all kinds of natural objects to rub against to help remove loose shed. You can aid your iguana's shedding process by re-creating a more natural environment and lifestyle.

Rough-Surfaced Objects

My iguana will rub against the cage or branches to help remove shed.
                              —I-200, Dianna, 47 yrs., Washington

If an iguana in the jungle has a problem shedding a part of its body, it will find a bush, tree limb, or rock and rub against it to help scrape off the loose skin. Many habitats designed for pet iguanas are too sterile for this to happen, so we pet owners need to offer some more options.

Placing rocks, rough bricks, or concrete building blocks on the bottom of your iguana's habitat is helpful because the iguana can rub against them when it needs to. Rough branches placed higher in the habitat also help your lizard shed. Be sure to secure these rough-surfaced objects so they won't accidentally fall on your lizard as it pushes or climbs on top of them.

Soaking

He sheds constantly. I put him in the bathtub a couple of times a week to swim and add moisture to his skin. I think that when he gets wet, the dead skin comes off more easily.   —I-654, Bill & Kathy, 29 & 27 yrs., Illinois

Moisture helps an iguana's skin release (shed) easier. In the wild, high humidity and rain showers help accomplish this, as I mentioned earlier. But if you try to create a damp and humid condition in an enclosed habitat, you run the risk of causing respiratory problems for your lizard. This stems mostly from the lack of fresh circulating air.

A good method to add direct moisture to your iguana is to soak it in a large container of water (usually a bathtub). Besides helping to moisten, loosen, and remove shed, it allows your lizard to swim for a little exercise. (See page 332 of this chapter for more on bathing and soaking.)

Misting

During the summer, when there is no chance of a draft, I mist my iguanas with tepid water once a day. This also aids in their shedding.
                              —I-11, Patty, Washington

Besides soaking, another way to help shedding is to mist your iguana with a plant-type sprayer. Adjust the nozzle to a fine mist setting and spray your pet several times a day. You may notice your lizard raising its head when being misted, because when it rains in the jungle, iguanas often tilt their heads back, open their mouths, and get a drink. These are natural traits that they carry with them into captivity.

Important note: Don't mist your iguana if it's cold, if there's a breeze blowing on your lizard, or if it's close to when the habitat lights go off. These conditions could make your iguana ill.

I've only had a problem [with shedding] with one female. I'd spray her with warm water and wipe her down gently with a soft, damp wash cloth. It seemed to help the shed. —I-200, Dianna, 47 yrs., Washington

Mineral Oil

Iguanas normally shed their skin with little difficulty, but occasionally they might have a problem area. Mineral oil can be purchased at most drug stores and can help shedding skin that seems "stuck."

For example, if your iguana's spines are having trouble shedding, rub a few big drops of mineral oil between your thumb and forefinger, place these oiled fingers on either side of the problem spines, and massage the oil in gently. This can be done several times a day until the stuck shed releases.

For other body parts with stubborn shed, add the oil either directly to the skin or to your hand—whatever works the best. Do not get any of this oil in your iguana's eyes or nostrils, and use this technique only for problem shed areas. (Beginning on the facing page, you'll find more help with shedding specific body parts.)

Hand Picking

She peels easily and loves it when you help take the skin off her. —I-249, Linda, 36 yrs., New Jersey

As I have said, some areas of shed may need your help. But don't get overzealous about removing this skin. It should come off effortlessly. As an example, do you remember a time when you got badly sunburned, and a few days later your skin started to itch and peel? You may have asked a friend to pull some of the loose peel off, but he or she got carried away and peeled too much, ripping "real" skin in the process. The same thing can easily happen to iguanas, but more damage can occur. Never force nature. Just as a rose opens at its own pace, shed comes off at its own pace.

I was helping my iguana with his nose shedding and must have pulled the skin too much around his nostril. This caused the nostril to get inflamed and close. I took the iguana to the vet, who opened up the nostril. But the iguana still has trouble when he sheds in this area. —I-736, Joyce, 36 yrs., New Jersey

When you help your iguana with its shedding, pay attention to the physical clues the lizard gives you. If it really doesn't want you messing around, it will make this desire very clear to you.

I was removing a piece of unshedded skin from my iguana's back and she bit me on my thumb, a warning of what would come if I did not leave her alone. It was nowhere near the kind of bite she is capable of when she's mad.
—I-653, Justin, 19 yrs., Maryland

Themselves

Iguanas scratch at their shed, so I assume it gets itchy for them. My iguana has also rubbed against the palm of my hand while I was stroking her to help stop the itch or help remove the shed. —I-200, Dianna, 47 yrs., Washington

Iguanas don't have hands like ours that can pick at shedding skin, but they do have feet and claws. It's common to see an iguana use its front or back foot to scratch its body, like a dog that has fleas.

Shedding—Specific Body Parts

The following sections describe various iguana body parts and the ease or difficulty with which they typically shed. There are some hints about the special care you can administer to help reduce or eliminate any problem areas.

Feet/Toes and Hands/Fingers

When I first got my iguana, he seemed to have problems shedding on his feet and tail. These parts seemed smaller and I think their growth was restricted by shed that didn't come off. I also feel that this is why he lost toes prior to my purchasing him. Through proper care, his shedding problem went away shortly after I bought him. —I-847, Angie, 31 yrs., Florida

One of the most important areas for shed to come off properly is the toes and fingers. It may appear as though all of the skin has come off a particular appendage, but upon closer examination you may see a little shed "ring" that hasn't sloughed off. This ring acts like a rubber band wrapped around the appendage, which can eventually die from lack of blood circulation. It's especially common in fast-growing hatchlings or juveniles, so keep an eye on these areas. I have removed shed rings from many iguanas whose owners hadn't even noticed the problem.

The way to eliminate any potential problems for these appendages is to be aware that the problem can occur. Each time your iguana sheds its hands or feet, look very closely at the fingers and toes. If you see one of these restriction rings, take a pair of scissors and <u>carefully</u> cut the ring off.

The only shedding problems I have encountered are on the toes of hatchlings. I have seen more than one digit swell from a problem "ring" of shed that required being cut. The swelling will disappear if this is removed in time.

          —I-508, Bryan, 27 yrs., Kentucky

Spines

I watch his dorsal crest to make sure the spines shed with no problem, and I spray him with water or offer him soaking baths.

          —I-609, Cindy, 37 yrs., Florida

Imagine that the fingers of your hand are your iguana's spines, then think about putting a glove on this hand. When the spine sheds, it's like the glove coming off your hand: The shedded spine is hollow inside, just like a glove finger.

Sometimes it's hard to see when the spines are ready to shed. If you look closely they have a duller, opaque look to them. On fast-growing iguanas, these spines come off naturally and easily.

Older iguanas' spines tend to be very long and often a little twisted, sometimes with broken tips that snag the shed and prevent it from coming off. If shed is not removed each time, it will build up layers of dead skin, thus restricting the growth and health of the spines.

The best release technique for stubborn spines is to soak the iguana in water at a depth that will completely immerse the spines. After about 30 minutes, take your lizard out of the water and, starting at the base of the spine, stroke gently upward on the spines with your thumb and index finger, using firm but gentle pressure. Don't force the spine sheds off. If they are ready, they will slip off like fried eggs from a Teflon frying pan. If you have to work at removing the shed, it's not ready.

When my iguana was about 4 years old, he had his first trouble shedding three of his neck spines. Twice these spines got the distinctive ready-to-shed look, but they failed to shed even after special soaks. I began to worry because I knew that each unshed layer would build up and make it even harder the next time.

To help solve the problem, I not only soaked my iguana, but also rubbed mineral oil into the base of the spines several times a day. A few days later I was gently rubbing (not pulling) Za's spines in the bathtub, when suddenly all three of the troublesome spines just slipped off!

The spines are one area where you can't relax and think those unshed spines will correct themselves. If they need your help, take care of them.

Head

Most of the head sheds in small patches, like thick flakes of human dandruff, and rarely is a problem. At one point when my iguana was a juvenile, the shed was coming off so dramatically that if his head had been made of paper it would have looked like an exploded paper sack.

She [SVL: 9½", TL: 2' 6½", 1 yr. 10 mo.] appreciates help with the loose skin on her head (I think it tickles). She indicates a desire for help by first scratching her head with a foot or hand (she's done both), rubbing her face against my right thumb, and then looking up at me as if to say, "Well?!" I gently flick the loose stuff off and then she goes about business-as-usual.
—I-865, Julie, 46 yrs., California

She always gets really grumpy right before her head sheds and sometimes actually seems to enjoy me peeling the loose skin off.
—I-620, Suzanne, 33 yrs., New York

Once in a while, my iguana would shake his head as if something was crawling on it. Also during these times, he didn't like me to touch his head. I soon recognized this as the first phase of Za's head starting to shed, although his skin showed no sign whatsoever of a shed in progress. Sure enough, two or three days later, the shedding process would begin.

Jowls

Usually, when the jowls are ready to shed the whole area comes off in one thin piece, with cellophane-like thickness and texture. Sometimes the cheek scale of a big adult will come off in separate pieces, following the patterns of the jowl scales. I've never seen or heard of the jowls as a problem area for shedding.

Nose

The outside of an iguana's nose sheds, but even stranger is that the inside of the nostril does, too. Each nostril sheds as a completely independent unit—it just pops off like a bottle cap, a little perfectly formed hole. It's a very funny-looking piece of shed, especially on big iguanas.

The shed from the flat area below the two nostrils, called the rostrum, is thick and feels just like a piece of hard, clear plastic. It, too, comes off as an independent section, almost always without a problem.

Ears

An iguana has external ears, whereas humans have internal ears. On iguanas, the ear membrane is right on the surface. It may look impenetrable, but it's actually very delicate and should be treated with great care.

Iguanas' ear membranes do shed, typically at the same time as the head, and are usually not a problem. You will first notice a dullness over the membrane, then maybe it will pull away just a little at one edge, looking like a torn pocket on a shirt. As I said before, this is a very delicate area; let it shed by itself!

Eyelids

I have helped them remove the shedding skin from around their eyes, which bothers them a lot, and they seem grateful when it's gone.
—I-626, Gail, 48 yrs., New York

The upper and lower eyelid is usually the most sensitive of all the shedding areas for an iguana. Shed from other areas of the body feels mostly like different thicknesses of plastic, but the shed from the eyelids is thin and soft, about the feel and texture of sunburned, peeling human skin.

Once in a while, eyelid shed may need a little assistance. For example, the shed can come partially off and get in the lizard's eyes, driving it nuts. But <u>don't</u> pull it off. Instead, carefully and slowly remove the loose, hanging skin with your fingernails, being careful not to pull any skin that is still connected. People with long fingernails have the best tool for this process.

Many times I removed this type of irritating shed from my iguana. When the onion-skin thick shed was removed from his face, he was so happy that if he'd been a cat he would have purred. Za would stay perfectly still and let me move his head into any position I needed to accomplish the task. Allowing me to get this close and fuss with his face was one of the turning points in developing a tamer animal (bonding), building trust and confidence.

The process of helping Za shed his eyelids began by first noticing that he was shedding and that it was irritating him. Next, I petted and stroked his head with my hand slightly cupped, my fingertips and thumb on both sides of his eyes. When I stroked him slowly I found that he would press either his left or right eye into my fingers. I would stop moving my hand and let him use my fingers as a "scratching post." This way, he controlled the amount of pressure he needed to remove the shed without injuring his eyeball.

Legs

On hatchlings and juveniles, the leg area is not typically a problem. But as an iguana gets older, the shed gets thicker and tougher, almost like thin leather, and your iguana will most likely need soaking to help remove it.

Stomach

As an iguana gets older, its stomach skin also gets thicker, stiffer, and tougher. By the time my iguana was about 4 years old, his stomach skin felt like a piece of canvas. The solution to easier shedding in this area was longer and more frequent soaking during the actual time of shedding. The stomach area typically sheds in a few big sheets.

Vent

The vent does not shed separately, but usually sheds with the leg area. It's mentioned here as a separate item because it can be a minor problem.

A few people have written and said that the area around their iguanas' vent only partially shed, and it hung like an open bag between the iguana's legs. Somehow when their iguana defecated, this hanging bag filled up with feces because it was right below the vent. <u>Yuck</u>! So keep an eye out for an open bag waiting to be filled. The best way to inspect this area is to stand your iguana vertically, stomach facing you, with its feet resting on the floor or a table.

One person called and asked if I could look at his iguana to see if it was healthy. Upon examination, I saw loose shed around the vent (again formed like a sack) that had filled with feces. The owner didn't even know that there was a problem. I took a pair of tweezers and gently pulled the shed, which was ready to come off, away from the vent. If the shed had not been ready, I would have cut the "poop bag" off so it wouldn't be a collector any more.

At the end of the procedure, I rinsed the iguana off and washed my hands and the tweezers with antiseptic surgical soap, and the owner learned another thing to inspect during shedding—the underside of his lizard.

Gentle is the key word when removing shed near the vent. The shed actually goes inside the vent a little. Remember, scissors or sharp objects around an iguana—especially near the reproductive and "sewage pipe" areas—is a delicate procedure that requires you to remain very safety-conscious.

Tail

The tail is another one of those areas that can be difficult to shed, especially in older iguanas. If the tail shed does not come off when it is supposed to, it can act like a patch on a tire. When the next shedding cycle occurs on the tail, this unshed area may build up an additional layer (patch) of skin, compounding the difficulty of future sheds.

An unshedded tail tip is the worst section of all. Like unshedded skin on an iguana's finger, it can act as a tourniquet and choke the blood supply to the tail tip. The tail section can die or get a form of gangrene that works its way up the tail, killing the tail as it goes. I know of several iguanas whose tails had to be amputated because of this "choking ring."

There haven't been any problem areas except for the tip of his tail. He gets a good soaking in the tub about every week. If there is any stubborn skin, I pick it off gently. —I-773, Rick, 34 yrs., Nebraska

Soaking, awareness, and special attention to the area are the solutions to any tail-shedding problems. When Za's tail began shedding, I soaked him in the bathtub for half an hour or so, took him out of the tub, put a wet wash cloth loosely around his tail, and slid it down the full length of the tail. Usually, the shed came off like wet paper.

Mineral oil rubbed directly onto the problem skin also helps. Apply the oil in the morning, then later that day let your lizard soak. If the whole tail is a problem, run your oiled hand down the full length of the tail until the dead skin comes off. Depending on how well attached the shed is, this may take several lubrications and soakings.

Reminder: The scales on the tail are laid down in one direction, with the "one-way street" going from the vent to the tip of the tail. Running your hand up the wrong way will cause the sharp scales to cut into your hand.

Helping with shedding on the tail can be very important. Don't neglect this special-care task. When my iguana was almost 4 years old, I saw that his whole tail had shed except the very tip (the last half-inch or inch of a 30" tail).

I kept an eye on it, soaked it, and it just didn't come off. Part of the problem was that the tip was a little roughed up from a previous, minor run-in with a door.

When his next tail shed came, I waited and the tip still hadn't come off. I declared all-out war to make sure it sloughed off before the third shed. I was afraid that the tourniquet effect would surely start by then. I could see that the tip of the tail was already being constricted.

Several times each day, I gently rubbed mineral oil into this stubborn tip section. A few weeks later when I was examining his tail with a magnifying glass, the shed just slipped off into my hand. I still have that #@*$!! piece of shed in a plastic bag, like a trophy, to remind me that determination does pay off.

> *The tip of the tail appears to be a problem area for my iguana. About 4 inches of the end of his tail became necrotic last month. The only explanation I could figure out was that the skin at some point had not shed. This also happened to about 2 inches of my other iguana's tail.*
> —I-685, Julie, 36 yrs., California

> *I always help him [SVL: 17", TL: 4' 6", 3 yrs. 6 mo.] with the tip of his tail.*
> —I-682, Dylan, 14 yrs., California

Back

The back shed usually comes off in big patches with no problems. As with other body parts, this area might be a little harder to shed as an iguana gets older and its skin gets thicker and tougher. Soaking and misting are the best approaches.

Injured Body Parts

If an iguana has an injured body part, this could cause simple or serious shedding problems—as with the example I gave of my iguana's tail tip.

> *My iguana's only problem shed area is her scarred nose [trauma from a previous time and owner]. The old skin has to be manually pulled off delicately, at the right time.* —I-312, Darla, 38 yrs., Ohio

My iguana had a congenitally malformed ear that complicated shedding. At its worst the ear distended ⅝" and had to be operated on, which left some temporary external scarring. The ear had protruded so much that the normal flat surface of the membrane crunched together, like a dented fender on a car. These little crevices held the shed from releasing naturally.

After the operation most of the crevices disappeared, but it took an additional 10 months of delicate and deliberate help from me for the ear to shed easily. After that, the old skin just fell off during each new shedding cycle like it was supposed to.

To help shed this messed-up ear I waited until the side of my iguana's head started to shed, then I put mineral oil on and around the ear. Once the shed started to release a little from the side of his head, I used a Q-tip to apply some oil to the opening between the ear and the shed, which helped the shed come off more easily.

It was a very delicate procedure, and I had to use just the right amount of pressure at the exact time in the shed process to allow it to release and not tear the ear. Too much pulling could have torn the ear open.

Patience, patience, observation, and awareness are the keys to helping shed injured body parts. If your animal has an injury that requires you to help with the shedding process, don't be in a hurry. Also, don't make your animal afraid of the time you spend helping with the shed. Make it a non-threatening experience. My iguana would sit in the same place for easily half an hour while I performed my delicate task on his ear. I believe he had confidence (from a long list of past events) that what I was doing was not meant to hurt him.

Your iguana will never have an ear problem like Za's; his was a fluke of a lifetime. But I have included the experience for all of you who may have to provide some other weird, delicate shedding help for your iguana and need a little extra confidence that everything will turn out all right.

Even though I have included a long section on possible shedding problems, don't panic when your lizard starts to shed. Nature does a great job by herself. All you need to do is be aware of any potential problems, and take action only when necessary.

Attitude and Diet Changes During Shedding

Iguanas exhibit a wide range of responses during shedding. They can be mean, irritable, and restless, they can lose their appetite for a day or two, or they can seem completely oblivious to the whole experience. There's no common denominator to these reactions, such as age, size, gender, season, or care given.

The next set of stories are to make you aware of some possible situations that can come up during shedding. These responses are not what the majority of iguanas experience, but they are still "normal."

She acts especially hungry before shedding (about 1 to 2 weeks).
—I-795, Dawn, 24 yrs., Ohio

He gets attitudes when he is shedding his skin: He's cranky and often he will not eat until the next day or night.   —I-890, Kim, 18 yrs., Ohio

She's usually grouchy during face-shedding, but the other parts don't bother her.   —I-865, Julie, 46 yrs., California

When he is shedding he seems more wild.
—I-716, Thomas, 26 yrs., New Jersey

My iguana gets a little moody during shedding.
                        —I-200, Dianna, 47 yrs., Washington

[I don't like] his occasional little snits when he doesn't like to be touched, especially around the time he is shedding. I never know if he'll carry out his threat displays and bite or attack. I'm 95% sure it's all bluff, but the larger he gets, there's that 5% that's in the back of my mind.
                        —I-493, Marcia, 40 yrs., Alaska

CLEANLINESS

I like how clean iguanas are!   —I-687, R., 54 yrs., Canada

Feces

Cleanliness starts with a large enough habitat so your iguana isn't forced to step in its own feces as it moves around. In the wild, iguanas are clean animals. It's only when we, the pet owners, reduce an iguana's range of living space from several acres to several cubic feet that contamination comes into play.

It's also important to supply a substrate material in the habitat that helps reduce fecal contamination (see Chapter 4, Housing, "Substrate Options"). In addition, feces should be removed every day, not every other day or when you get around to it. Any time you start to get lazy about cleaning up the daily mess, ask yourself how you would like living in the same room with your feces for several days. Feces not only smell bad but can be a vector for diseases.

Bathing

She has problems shedding on her feet and paws so I soak her in the tub and the skin comes right off.   —I-622, Sharman, 22 yrs., Wisconsin

One way to keep your iguana sparkling clean is to give it regular baths. Bathing also helps remove loose shed, dried food, etc. that may have accumulated on its body. Bathing your iguana is simply the process of using water to clean your lizard and can be done once a week or more, depending on how dusty or dirty your lizard is or if it is shedding. It can range from a quick rinse to a more leisurely soak.

He [SVL: 18", TL: 3' 4", 2 yrs. 8 mo., 10 lbs.] has been in the shower, but I don't take showers with him because of fear the soap will damage his skin. Also, he kind of leers at me.   —I-705, Linda, 46 yrs., California

No soap should be used for these clean-up sessions, unless your lizard has feces stuck to its body. Even in this case, it's best to try to remove whatever

SIDEBAR

Iguana Feces and Salmonella

While I was writing this book, a number of mainstream newspapers and magazines began running stories on the potential for reptiles, and in particular iguanas, to infect humans with salmonella. Salmonella is a bacterium that lives in the intestines and feces of many animals, including iguanas, turtles, and chickens. (See Chapter 7, Medical Troubleshooting, "Feces Problems," for a sidebar with more information on salmonella and iguanas.)

In humans, salmonella can cause intestinal problems such as diarrhea and vomiting. While it's mostly a minor ailment for healthy adults, salmonella poisoning can be fatal to members of high-risk groups, which include very young children, the elderly, chronically ill people, pregnant women, and others with a weakened immune system.

The September 1995 issue of *Health* magazine ran a short story on salmonella and reptiles, quoting Fred Angulo, a medical epidemiologist with the Centers for Disease Control and Prevention (CDC) in Atlanta and an expert in food-borne and diarrheal diseases. According to Angulo, the increasing popularity of reptiles as pets is causing the rate of salmonella infections in humans to rise sharply.

Salmonella poisoning can occur when people handle their iguanas, get feces on their hands (usually in amounts too small to notice), then either prepare food or touch their lips with their fingers. Owners don't even have to handle the iguana to get sick, however. As the *Health* article states: "The same people who rightly scrub cutting boards and wash their hands after handling raw chicken to avoid salmonella contamination, Angulo says, may think nothing of cleaning their snake's cage in the kitchen sink or mixing up a bottle of baby formula after playing with a pet lizard."

What does this mean for current or potential iguana owners?

First, *Health* reports the CDC's recommendation that "live-in reptiles are a bad idea for child-care centers and homes with children under five years old." For others, "Angulo urges common sense and good hygiene. 'Conduct yourself,' he says, 'as though you'd just handled dog feces.'" In other words, "Wash your hands. Wash your hands. And after that, wash your hands" (#34).

might be caked on with water alone, gently dislodging the gunk with your fingers. If you do use soap, be very careful to keep it out of your lizard's eyes or vent.

The easiest place to soak your lizard is in a bathtub, but if no tub is available, invent something. When my iguana was less than a year old, all I had in my apartment was a shower. I put one of those large, flat rubber stoppers over the drain and filled the water up to the edge (about 1½" deep). Another option was that once or twice a week during the summer I took my iguana to my girlfriend's house, where she had a tub. Do the best you can with the soaking container you have available.

Water Temperature and Height

The first step is to fill the tub or container with the right temperature and height of water. The water should be warm, not scalding hot and not cool. Remember, an iguana's body temperature becomes that of the water. As the water cools during the soaking time, it will need to be reheated with new warmer water. When the hotter water comes into the tub, don't let it hit your iguana directly; blend the new hot water and the cooler tub water with your hand so there are no hot spots to burn your lizard.

> *I put in a little more water than is strictly recommended (two-thirds of its body height in the deep end).* —I-795, Dawn, 24 yrs., Ohio

The height of water in the tub depends on the design of the tub. A good basic rule is that the deepest part of the water should not be more than the height of the lizard when it is lying flat on the tub's bottom. For the first few times, do not fill the tub with much water, to reduce the chance of your iguana getting scared. Over a period of several days or weeks, increase the water level until you reach the desired height. There should also be a shallow area in the tub where your iguana can retreat. In most cases, the deep end is where the drain is located and the shallow area is at the opposite end of the tub.

Introducing Your Iguana to the Tub

> *I let both of my iguanas [about 7 months old] soak in the bathtub for a few minutes. One loves this and he is quite a swimmer. The other one doesn't like being in the bathtub but will relax and soak as long as I sit and talk to her. The second I leave, she flips out.* —I-725, Marie, 23 yrs., Maryland

Because the tub is such a new and foreign place, few iguanas in the beginning come running to get into it. They're more likely to put up some kind of a fuss, most of which disappears once the iguana gets used to the water. But some iguanas can actually freak out when the water touches them.

> *He hates taking a bath or having his skin misted.* —I-815, Janice & Jimmy, 40 yrs., Alabama

Introducing your iguana to soaking should be a slow, easy, non-threatening process. Have the water already in the tub before your iguana gets in, otherwise it might get scared of the "falling" water from the faucet. Because soaking helps an iguana on so many levels, it is worth your time and patience to help change a resistant iguana's attitude.

One approach is to start by adding only enough water to get your iguana's feet wet, then drizzle handfuls of warm water on its back. The next step is to let your iguana sit on the palm of your hand(s) and lower the lizard slowly into a tub that has more water in it. The first time an iguana goes into the tub it's often a little apprehensive, so it might just sit on your hands or try to climb up your arm to get out. Let your iguana stay in your hand(s) until it decides to swim off on its own. It might even come back to your hands, like a swimmer resting on the side of the pool for a while.

Safety and Comfort Considerations

Iguanas seem to freak out if their feet can't touch some part of the tub bottom. Another problem is that once their feet do touch, the lizards get frightened because they slip and slide on the smooth ceramic bottom. Perhaps they feel uncomfortable, as if starting to fall off a tree limb. One solution is to use a rubber non-skid mat on the tub bottom, like the ones humans use to keep them from slipping while taking a shower. This mat will give your lizard both traction and peace of mind.

You also need to safety-proof your tub so your iguana won't accidentally get hurt. For example, women often leave their shaving razors on the edge of the tub for easy access. But if a razor falls into the tub, your iguana could cut itself. Also, remove shampoo, hair conditioner, soap, and any other foreign objects that look innocent but could potentially hurt your pet.

As a precautionary warning, I know of one iguana death from soaking in a tub. The female iguana was around 19 years old (this was back in the days when an iguana living to one or two years old was a big deal) and had just laid some eggs that day. The owner told me that he put the iguana in the tub for moisture and relaxation like he had done many times before. But this time the iguana was unusually exhausted from the egg-laying process. The owner needed to go to the store and was "gone only a few minutes," he said. When he got back, his iguana was dead.

He guessed that the lizard had panicked and wanted out of the tub. She probably tried climbing out of the tub, but because she was weak, she couldn't get out like she normally did. As she crawled up the smooth ceramic side she kept slipping back into the tub water. Finally she most likely ran herself into extreme exhaustion and slipped into the tub, drowning in just a small amount of water. Don't think this is a fluke case and that it could never happen to your iguana. Everything happens to iguanas that you don't think can. Perhaps a rubber mat, like I mentioned earlier, could have saved her life.

With or without a rubber mat, however, never leave your iguana soaking in a tub if you're not able to see or hear the lizard. Under no circumstances should you leave the house while your lizard soaks. It's not worth the risk.

Time to Come Out?

He [SVL: 18", TL: 3' 4", 2 yrs. 8 mo., 10 lbs.] goes into the bathroom, scram-
bles to get in the tub, sometimes succeeding, and waits for us to come fill the tub
with water. He often spends long periods of time in the tub—we warm the
water from time to time.   —I-705, Paul & Linda, 45 yrs., California

The amount of time an iguana soaks depends a great deal on how the iguana reacted to the experience of being in the water the first time. If it really likes the water, start with about 15 minutes and work up to 30 minutes. I believe 45 minutes is the maximum time an iguana needs to relax and soak. An iguana is not a boat or a fish.

I have received several letters and phone calls about iguanas that soaked long periods of time each day and developed skin problems. In one iguana, the tissue area around where the claw originates swelled and began to "rot" away. Once the daily long soaks were cut short, the nail healed. Another iguana got an irritation around the vent from too much soaking. Learn from others' mistakes—45 minutes a day is enough.

Many iguanas set their own time limits in the tub. From 2 to 3 years old, my iguana would not stay in the water more than about 50 minutes. From age 3 to 4 his time was about 40 minutes, and from 4 to 5 years old it was about 30 minutes.

When he was small and wanted to come out, he would claw and splash in one corner of the tub until I removed him (my office was only 20 feet from the bathroom, so I could hear when he was ready to come out). As he got older and bigger, he would climb out on his own. I purchased an extra rubber tub mat and hung it upside down over the edge of the tub, thus creating an excellent climbing ladder. Having it upside down exposed the little rubber suction cups, which he used as small, flat hand-holds to climb out more easily.

By the time Za reached 4 years old he was so big and strong that he didn't even need the mat, but I left it for safety reasons. Also, I never left the house when he was in the tub, again for safety reasons. When he tired of being in the tub, I could hear him splashing around, then he climbed out and I would go directly to the bathroom for his next treat.

He always got towel dried. This kept him from dragging water all over the house and from becoming cold. I loved to spoil him with extra care. Running the towel over his body also helped removed any loose shed. It's amazing how 30 minutes in the tub could make most stuck-on shed just slip right off.

Most Iguanas Enjoy Soaking

As you will see in the upcoming soaking stories, at a certain point bathing for cleanliness turns into an ideal relaxation break. Many iguanas seek out a bath to soak for what we can only assume is a pleasurable experience.

We let her use the bathtub because she gets warmth, moisture, and exercise (swimming). She [TL: 3' 11", 5 yrs.] sometimes sits in the bath for an hour. She scratches on the side of the tub when she wants to get out.
—I-124, Joan, Florida

After Za turned 4 years old, he had free run of the house (warm weather only, and he was always supervised). Sometimes I would find him outside the closed bathroom door waiting for someone to let him in. When the door was opened, he would crawl into the tub and wait for a human to add some warm water for him. I would have thought this was strange or even special, except that I have received many letters from iguana owners with similar experiences.

He [SVL: 15", TL: 3' 4", 3 yrs. 6 mo.] likes to sit in the shower and let the warm water "rain" on him. Sometimes when he wants a shower he will go into the bathroom and sit in the shower, and wait for me to turn on the water. I don't allow him to shower with me. —I-704, Marilyn, 40 yrs., Maryland

After a warm swim in the tub he usually thrashes around and tries to get away from me when I try to take him out of the water. He always throws a big thrashing fit when it's time to get out of the tub, whatever the reason.
—I-609, Cindy, 37 yrs., Florida

One morning I couldn't find my iguana [SVL: 15½", TL: 4' 4", 3 yrs.]. I looked all over the house and finally found him sitting in the empty bathtub, patiently waiting for me to run the water for his soak and daily constitutional.
—I-493, Marcia, 40 yrs., Alaska

Water as a Defecation Cue

Sometimes he goes [poops] in the tub while he is soaking.
—I-773, Rick, 34 yrs., Nebraska

Water is one of the environmental cues that stimulates your iguana to defecate. Because your iguana might poop in its bath water, it's best to start your iguana in just a little water (one to two handfuls). The lizard will probably defecate right away. Remove your iguana from the tub, then clean the mess by removing the feces with toilet paper and flushing it down your toilet. Rinse your iguana under the tub faucet, then lift the lizard out. Clean and scour (with bleach) the tub twice, and rinse thoroughly with hot water. Now you can refill the tub with fresh water and put your iguana back in for soaking or relaxing.

IMPORTANT: In the beginning of this section, there was a sidebar on salmonella. If you didn't read it before, do so now. Any time you handle your iguana or anything its feces may have touched, you need to thoroughly clean your hands with warm, soapy water. Also clean objects that may have had contact with feces; use a diluted bleach solution followed by clear-water rinses.

EXERCISE

The books I have read say that iguanas need exercise, but exactly how do you get them to exercise? Is running around in the cage enough, or should we be doing laps around the living room floor?   —I-609, Cindy, 37 yrs., Florida

Do iguanas need exercise? Many years ago there was a short article in one of the herpetological magazines that brought up this subject. It didn't really answer the question; it was more of a tongue-in-cheek joke. But I have received so many questions from people over the years about whether their iguana should exercise that I decided to address the question here.

You need to go back and look at how iguanas live in the jungles to get a baseline for "normal" iguana activity. As I have mentioned throughout this book, adult iguanas spend most of their life in the trees and move only to regulate their temperature (moving in and out of the sunlight), to eat, to defend their territory, and to mate.

Hatchlings spend time on the ground and in bushes, and are more active than the adults. By the time they become juveniles they stay in the trees, not only to eat but also because they're safer from predators. There are a few minor exceptions to these statements, but this is their basic lifestyle in the wild. Some researchers estimate that iguanas spend 95% of their time resting. So these animals don't move around a lot.

If we know that iguanas don't chase down their food (they eat leaves, fruit, and flowers) and don't wander long distances for this food, you can assume they don't need much exercise even as a captive pet. What you have to worry about more than exercise is not to fill your iguana with a lot of junk food and fats that they normally wouldn't eat in the wild. This way there's no excessive fat to be burned off—just like with humans.

Instead of asking if your iguana needs exercise, perhaps a better question is: "Do iguanas need some activity or movement of their bodies during the day?" The answer is yes; they should be able to move about in their habitat, and that is one of the reasons I stress having a large habitat. If the habitat is too small, what is the point of the iguana even trying to move about? Also, allow your iguana to have some freedom in your house, whether it is in one designated room or the whole house. If given the opportunity to be out of the habitat, your iguana will move around the house, exploring.

Soaking your iguana is also good because they often swim a little. That doesn't mean you have to fill the tub to the top and paint lane lines on the bottom so your lizard can do 500 yards of back stroke and 200 yards of butterfly each day. It just means some simple body movement to maintain flexibility and muscle tone.

Iguanas need to be taken out of their cages and exercised once a day.
                                        —I-605, Laura, 31 yrs., Canada

Try to let your iguana "swim" in a tub at least once weekly. It will provide some exercise.   —V-69, Dr. Alynn, 39 yrs., Mississippi

SUNLIGHT

Many pet owners I come across do not seem to understand their iguanas' need for direct sunlight several hours a day.   —I-780, Carl, Florida

I took my iguana outside to get sun as frequently as I could because he had bone problems. His skin would turn from pale silver to black as he soaked up the rays. After 10 to 15 minutes we'd come back in. Soon he began to seek the sun himself (he tried to get out of it at first). His seizures are gone and the bones are solid now.   —I-283, Susan, 46 yrs., Washington

After being involved with iguanas for all these years, I've seen one thing that stands out as a master cure and maintainer of good health for iguanas, and that is direct sunlight. Not through windows, but the good old natural sun, unfiltered and without any restrictions.

I have never seen any scientific research that gives the minimum time an iguana needs to be in sunlight for the most beneficial effects. If you can get your iguana 30 minutes a day, that's a good start. Of course, the longer the better.

To get a complete understanding of the light requirements for your iguana, see Chapter 4, Housing, "Lights." In this section, you'll find a discussion of all the different lights your iguana needs, including the topic of "Sunlight." **Sunlight can't be over-rated; it's the greatest thing you can possibly give your lizard every day.**

SLEEP

Iguanas sleep soundly at night. Unlike some other reptiles, they have a very definite sleep state, and they usually sleep at the ends of branches, preferably in a place that is overhanging water because the only thing that will disturb them is something walking out on that branch, an opossum or something like that. If that happens, the iguana will fling itself off the branch and into the darkness.   —Gordon H. Rodda, iguana field researcher (#27)

Iguanas are diurnal—that is, they are active during the day and sleep at night. Sleep is as important to an iguana's health as it is to yours or mine.

Dark and Light Photoperiod

Iguanas retire to their sleeping perches [in the wild] . . . shortly before to shortly after sundown, but typically while it is still light. They do not leave before dawn, usually remaining until well after sunrise. —Gordon M. Burghardt and A. Stanley Rand, iguana research in Panama (#42)

They want it dark when they sleep. Should I forget to turn out the light, they get under their towels (in the cage). —I-798, Teri, 35 yrs., New Hampshire

Just like humans, iguanas need a dark and light cycle—and like humans, if this cycle is taken away, the iguana will suffer. Proper cycles of light and dark keep animals' circadian rhythms (the body's internal clock) healthy.

If you want to see a human go crazy, take away the night. Keep the room bathed in light and after a while the human will hallucinate and start to crack up. Keep certain animals only in light and they become neurotic, their eating habits and food choices change, and their natural breeding desires are lost. Your iguana needs both a night and a day period.

You can create this cycle for your iguana by a simple automatic timer purchased at a hardware store, like the kind often used in a house to turn a light on and off when you are away (see Chapter 4, Housing, "Sensors," for more details). This timer, connected to the iguana's habitat lights, will turn the lights on for the desired number of hours, then off for the night.

What is the right balance of "day" and "night"? As with other aspects of care, look to where iguanas live in the wild for the answer. In the tropics where they are found, days and nights are about equal in length and vary little from season to season. So a good rule of thumb is about 12 to 14 hours of light and the rest darkness in every 24 hours.

Some people say for every degree of latitude (from where your iguana originally came from), add or subtract an hour or two of light to mimic seasonal changes. This might be important if you intend to breed your lizard, but in reality if you have to worry about 1 hour of light to make sexual things happen, you don't have all the right conditions to start with. So for 99.99% of iguana owners, don't worry about adding or subtracting this time.

Remember, when the lights of the habitat go out at night, there still needs to be a source of heat for your lizard. Chapter 4, Housing, has a section on "Heat" that will give you some ideas for alternative night heat sources.

Iguana Sleep Stories

Below are some interesting stories about iguanas and sleep. Even though most of these stories are about my iguana, they are typical of other iguanas that are tame, allowed to be free, and are spoiled. I will give you a little hint: Iguanas don't sleep like you would expect lizards to.

I feel closest to my iguana when he stays up past his bedtime and falls asleep on the tree we have for him in the front room. I then go and pick him up to put him in his cage, and those eyes open for a minute and then he falls asleep in my hands. It's like putting a sleepy little kid to bed and it's so cute.

—I-841, Bonnie, 23 yrs., Texas

During the winter months, I had my iguana [SVL: 15", 4 yrs.] sleep on a heating pad (on low) in our bedroom, because [his normal sleeping area was] too cold. The first winter, this arrangement worked very well. However, starting this winter, the iguana began climbing out of his sleeping spot and into our bed. Even though we repeatedly put him back in his sleeping area (which is warm and covered with a piece of fleece), he continued to climb into our bed. Finally, we started allowing him to sleep at the foot of our bed under the covers, an arrangement he's very happy with. Lately, he has started to sneak up toward where my husband and I rest our heads on the pillow.

—I-704, Marilyn, 41 yrs., Maryland

Pillows

Several owners, including myself, have placed pillows in their iguana's habitat so the lizard could rest its head at night. I have received several photos from various pet owners proving this to be true (see photo on page 342). One person took her iguana's pillow out of the habitat one day to clean it and forgot to put it back. That night, her iguana paced around in its dark habitat for some time. The owner heard the noise, remembered the missing pillow, and returned it. Once the pillow was replaced, the iguana went right to sleep. Tame iguanas have many mammalian qualities.

Curtains

When my iguana was about a year old, he liked to climb to the top of my bedroom curtains and fall asleep at the end of the day. Sometimes Za preferred the curtains to his open and waiting habitat. I had to take him down from the curtains and put him in his habitat the days he did this.

The first time I carried him to his habitat he woke up. The half-dozen other times, he slept through the whole experience of being taken off the curtain and returned to the habitat. He felt heavy and completely relaxed at these times, like a baby kitten, not like a lizard. I believe the reason for this relaxed attitude was that he felt safe in this environment and he trusted me.

I stopped Za climbing the curtains by closing my bedroom door so he couldn't get in the room. Closing the door didn't bother him; he adjusted by going to sleep in his habitat, like he should have.

Childlike Sleep

One time when my iguana was about 10 months old, a friend asked if I could bring Za down to his furniture store so he could see him. I arrived at about 5 p.m. and stayed much longer than I had planned. All the time I was in the store

Figure 6.2: "Rexina" hugs her favorite pillow, as she does every night as she sleeps. Sounds more like a human activity than lizard behavior. Photo: courtesy of Char Nemec

I had Za draped across my forearm in my typical holding position. At 6:30 p.m., a half hour past Za's regular bed time (at that age), he fell asleep on my arm. No transition, he just flopped his head on my hand and his body went completely limp, like a small child kept out past bedtime. (And this is a reptile?!)

My girlfriend got a small blanket out of my car and I wrapped it around Za to keep him warm. On the walk to the car he woke up just enough to raise his head, then went completely asleep again. When I got home I put Za in his habitat on his sleeping ledge, and he fell right asleep.

Sound Asleep

The experience that makes me feel closer to my iguana is kind of weird. What touches my heart the most is nighty-nighty time. He's so cute and vulnerable—looking all sacked out in his sleeping area. —I-609, Andy, Florida

When pet iguanas are deep in slumberland, they often fold their arms straight back at their sides, with their palms facing up toward the sky. Sometimes their eyes will seem to bulge slightly out of their heads. Once asleep, iguanas seldom move if they feel safe in their habitat. I have talked with several eye witnesses who have seen sleeping iguanas in Mexico tumble out of trees onto people, the ground, or roofs of buildings. Boy, can iguanas sleep!

"Wild" Sleep

An average of about 2 hours before dusk, they [iguanas] begin moving back into the trees [in the wild] and to the place where they will eventually sleep.
—Gordon H. Rodda, iguana field researcher (#27)

Here's a story about wild iguanas and their sleep patterns. It adds a bit of contrast to the stories mentioned previously. An iguana research scientist I talked with said that he had gone out in the wild to observe iguanas sleeping. He found that if he just walked around and caused no major disturbance, the iguanas he observed would return to the same tree on subsequent nights. One night he used a flashlight to look at some of the sleeping iguanas in more detail. These iguanas did not seem to stir under the light of this observation, but the next night they did not return to that tree.

"Cat Nap"

Throughout this book I mention some similarities between house cats and iguanas. Another similarity is that older adult iguanas take afternoon naps, just like cats. But unlike cats who go dead asleep, iguanas will often pop their eyes open if they hear or feel an unusual vibration.

I used to catch my iguana (between age 4 and 5) taking naps in the afternoon in his habitat. If Za knew I was staring at him, he would open his eyes quickly as though they had closed for only a second. But in reality I had been watching him for quite some time while his eyes were closed. Za never seemed to like being caught asleep.

Sometimes iguanas share their nap times with humans, as the following stories show:

Our iguana loves to snuggle up to my husband under a blanket, and they nap together, too.   —I-200, Dianna, 47 yrs., Washington

My female iguana [12 yrs., owned 4 yrs.] follows me around the house and likes to sit on my lap to be petted. She always ends up falling asleep on or very close to me.   —I-322, Marty, 22 yrs., Ohio

My iguana [SVL: 12", TL: 3' 3", 1¾ yrs.] is special to me when he cuddles up to me and goes to sleep.   —I-731, Stephen, 14 yrs., Canada

If I let my iguana [SVL: 6½", TL: 18"] sit on my chest while watching TV, he goes right to sleep.   —I-707, Donna, 28 yrs., New York

Routines

For three years Za slept in the same spot in the habitat, and in almost exactly the same position, every night. I've heard from other iguana owners that their lizards do the same thing.

Another example of routine was Za's reaction to his habitat lights. The lights went off at the same time every night, and eventually he began to anticipate—even expect—"lights out" at 7:00 p.m. sharp. Often, about 15 minutes before the lights went off, he would flick his tongue or paw at the lights.

A few times he started this pawing at around 6 p.m. If he persisted for five minutes or more, I turned his lights off manually because I figured he wanted to go to sleep early. On those few occasions when I turned the lights off early, he actually moved to his sleeping area, put his head down, and stayed there until morning. Perhaps some days he needed extra sleep.

Every night before I went to bed, I would look at Za in his habitat (until his death at just over 5 years old). There he would be, sound asleep in his usual sleeping corner, head on his pillow, arms back, palms facing up, and looking so innocent and nothing at all like a lizard, more like a large cat. He was a very beautiful and personable creature, and it was a warm and pleasant experience to see him each night—something I always looked forward to.

CHAPTER 7

Medical Troubleshooting

Common sense is in medicine the master workman.
— Peter Mere Latham (1789-1875)

As a little kid, I seemed to find every sick and injured animal in the neighborhood. I even took a hummingbird out of the death grip of a local cat and repaired some body damage. In two days the bird was well and I set it free.

I wanted to be a veterinarian when I was growing up, but I got awful grades as a student. My parents always joked that I might try being a quack veterinarian because of my strong desire to help animals. But I am not going to pretend I am a veterinarian and tell you how to cure the really complicated problems your iguana might encounter. A good herp veterinarian can mean life or death to your iguana.

On the other hand, there are many basic things that pet owners can and should do for their iguanas, such as watching out for signs of problems, as well as some basic first aid. These will be explained throughout the chapter. I will also give some guidelines on when to call in a veterinarian, because simple problems can quickly become life-threatening in iguanas.

For those people who have experience treating their own iguanas, there are some veterinarian-oriented medical books listed in Appendix B that might give you more in-depth help. A note of caution: Sometimes doing your own herp medicine can be as dangerous as doing none at all.

OVERVIEW OF MEDICAL PROBLEMS

It should be stressed to iguana owners that knowledge of husbandry is crucial. Ninety-five percent of [iguana] illness is due to poor husbandry.
— V-135, Dr. Debra, Washington

Most of the problems I have encountered have stemmed from ignorance of the most basic biological facts about their animals.
— Dr. Patrick J. Morris, veterinarian and former teacher at the University of Tennessee College of Veterinary Medicine

345

In the wild, iguanas do just fine on their own, without medical care. It's when they are captured, stuck in a cage one-thousandth the area of their natural range, kept indoors, and fed "strange" human food that problems arise.

The point of this chapter is to provide you with a better understanding of some medical problems that can happen to your iguana, and some ways to identify and solve the problems before they escalate. Not knowing what is happening to your iguana when it's sick makes you feel scared and inadequate. I hope the information presented here will help you feel less stressed and more in control of your iguana's health.

The Green Iguana, Iguana iguana, *is one of the most frequently purchased reptiles and consequently one of the most commonly presented to the veterinarian. Sadly, their diet and husbandry requirements are inadequately explained to most new owners, leading to their early demise in a high percentage of animals. This accounts for the pattern of problems and diseases seen clinically.*
—V-31, Dr. Jeffrey, California

Through proper diet and husbandry (see Chapter 4, Housing, and Chapter 5, Feeding, for details), you can avoid the vast majority of medical problems in iguanas. But even if you feed your iguana the proper food, and provide appropriate housing, there are still many little things that can go wrong. It's an inevitable part of living in captivity.

Don't wait until your pet is sick to establish a veterinary care plan. Your veterinarian cannot change what has already gone to hell. Iguanas deserve, indeed require, a check-up with an experienced veterinarian the day they are brought home. Waiting only leads to trouble, often irreversible.
—V-132, Dr. Willard, 55 yrs., Washington

Please have pet owners come in with their iguanas for initial exams after purchase. Don't wait until the iguana is too sick to save.
—V-79, Dr. Lonnie, 37 yrs., New York

As I have mentioned earlier in this book, get a sample of your iguana's feces and take it to your veterinarian to see if your lizard has parasites. This is one of the best preventive medical things you can do for your new pet. Do this the first or second day after your iguana arrives home, before you get busy and forget about it.

For example, my iguana looked healthy and ate well when I first got him. I took him to the veterinarian for a general check-up and decided to have his feces tested at the same time, just as a precaution. I could not believe it, but my iguana had worms. The veterinarian treated him with medication, and the worms went away (see page 373 for more details on eliminating worms).

Owners should be advised to get familiar with the smell and appearance of normal iguana poop, the feel of a pinch of iguana skin (hydration), appearance of the scales on the lizard (spacing, color—especially through the shedding cycle, etc.), and color of the inner mouth. An educated iguana owner should be able to tell the difference between poop produced from plant matter and that from animal matter. We all probably really don't spend enough time examining our iguanas, and this is the first step in prevention—knowing what your iguana is all about when it is healthy. If you know what a healthy lizard looks like, deviances from this can then be brought to the attention of a trained professional, a veterinarian. —I-515, Lynn, 21 yrs., Canada

The best way to keep an eye on your iguana's physical well-being is by daily handling. Each time you pick up your lizard, give it an overall physical check. Begin at the head and go to the tip of the tail, feeling all your lizard's body parts, looking for cuts, abscesses, swollen or discolored areas, foreign objects in the eyes, or anything amiss.

After a while, your hands and eyes will get familiar with what is "normal" for your iguana, so when something unusual comes up you will see and feel it. Another advantage of touching your lizard in this "medical" way is that your animal will get used to it. During real medical examinations by a veterinarian, your lizard will be more relaxed. Whenever you get a chance to handle other people's iguanas, do this same examination, as this will give you valuable comparisons with your lizard.

LOG BOOK

It's important to keep records on diet, elimination, weight, length. Often, iguana owners do not remember when their sick iguana last ate, had a bowel movement, shed, used all four legs, broke its tail, etc.
—V-3, Dr. Betsy, 28 yrs., Alaska

Along with physically observing changes in your iguana, make sure you put any pertinent information down on paper so it won't be forgotten. You can't be expected to remember everything from day to day.

It's also important to observe your iguana's diet, elimination, routines, changes in normal behavior, or symptoms that may signal the need for veterinary care. A log book helps keep a record of these things. For example, during the big Northern California (Loma Prieta) earthquake in 1989—my Los Gatos apartment was a few miles from the epicenter—everything was so chaotic I couldn't remember the last time my iguana had defecated. By checking the log book, I knew that it had been two days and took corrective action.

By entering information about your iguana daily, you will have a profile of your pet. If you have to take your lizard to the veterinarian for medical care, you won't have to rely on memory to describe symptoms or changes. I kept a detailed record on my iguana for more than five years, which helped assist my veterinarian in tracking and explaining problems.

Instead of loose pieces of paper, choose a bound notebook as a log book so you'll have a permanent record. Try to keep the record-keeping simple, or it may become a chore and be discontinued. I had a pretty elaborate log book, but then I like details and keeping records. To simplify record-keeping, I typed out all of the points to be covered each day, with space below each heading for comments. I made several hundred copies of this and put the copies in a three-ring binder so I wouldn't have to write the headings every day.

The log book items listed below are basic and necessary for a clear picture of your lizard's life.

Initial Set-Up: Background on Your Animal
- Name or some type of identification for your iguana
- Male or female
- When and where purchased and for how much
- Captive bred or wild caught
- Identifying marks—As your iguana gets older these become more apparent (for example, my iguana had a hole in his dewlap from a self-inflicted claw penetration at 3 years of age)
- Snout-vent length (SVL), tail length, total length (TL), weight, age at purchase (if possible; or your best guess for its age)

Daily Record
- Date—Month, day, year
- Defecation—Length, width, height, color, consistency, time; unusual things in it; when and where deposited
- Out-of-habitat time—Include any unusual experiences when out
- Food—Time, amounts given & eaten; eating enthusiasm (I used a scale of 1-10); dietary supplements, if any
- Water—Date the bowl is cleaned and new water added
- Soak time—Duration, location
- Sun time—Duration, location, time of day
- Shed—Body part(s) shedding; start and finish date; unusual areas that don't shed properly
- Miscellaneous observations
    * Unusual behavior (e.g., good way to document beginning of breeding or egg-laying phases)
    * Special medical notes (e.g., injuries, medication given [include dosages, time, etc.])
    * Comments (if applicable—could be details that don't fall into other categories, or "summary" comments)

Long-Term Observations (every 3 months)
- Date—Month, day, year
- Body measurements—SVL, tail length, TL, diameter of the tail base, body weight, and any other specific measurements you want to track

- Attitude—Overall impressions of the past three months, taken from daily observations
- Overall health—Highlight any specific problems or concerns
- Miscellaneous—Anything else of note that you want to add or track

Prevention and early detection of diseases and disorders can often be accomplished by daily observation of your iguana. Sometimes the changes are subtle, but if observed early enough, corrections can be made to improve your lizard's health or save its life. The first sign of an ailment is often a change in your iguana's behavior and/or appearance.

I think that the time I spend observing my iguanas is very important. I can tell a lot about them by the way they act. Hopefully if anything goes wrong with them I would be able to spot it right away.
                                —I-680, Catherine, 21 yrs., New York

FIRST AID

If there are any unusual changes, whether in behavior, appearance, or color, seek veterinary care immediately. Don't wait for a problem to be out of control to contact a vet. Use common sense. If it doesn't make sense to do to your children, don't do it to your iguana! Common sense goes a long way in reptiles.
                                —V-18, Dr. Patty, 40 yrs., California

First aid is the science or art of knowing how to comfort and aid an animal (or human) without aggravating the condition until knowledgeable help can be obtained (if necessary). It is also the art of knowing when to consult a veterinarian—by phone or in person—or when a "bandaid" will suffice. Do what you can and leave the rest to the professionals.

First-Aid Kit

"Be Prepared"—Boy Scout Motto

First-aid kits offer more than just the supplies to fix an injury; they give the mind a sense of safety and security, a kind of mental edge against disasters. Everyone should have a first-aid kit in their home and automobile—and, of course, one created and designated specially for your iguana.

The contents for my iguana's first-aid kit evolved over time. In the beginning, it was just a good-quality magnifying glass to examine my iguana's congenitally deformed tympanum (outer ear covering) and some tweezers and a flashlight to see things more clearly. I stuck these few items into a Ziploc plastic bag and placed it on top of his habitat for quick access. As time went along, I got more things for the first-aid "bag" and eventually transferred all the items to a small plastic lunch pail. I used this first-aid kit dozens of times, and it was well worth the time and money it took to create it.

AT A GLANCE: *When to Consult Your Veterinarian*

<u>Most important, never guess! Always consult your veterinarian when:</u>
1. You don't know what you are doing.
2. Your iguana is not breathing or is unresponsive.
3. A cut or wound won't stop bleeding.
4. A wound is moderate to large in size.
5. Your iguana fell and is limping on an injured arm or leg.
6. An eye shows signs of infection.
7. You observe swelling, lumps, lesions, diarrhea, constipation, oozing, redness.
8. A small wound doesn't look better in 24 hours.
9. Your animal is obviously stressed by trauma.

The items listed below are a good starting point for a basic first-aid kit for your iguana. By having these supplies on hand, you can solve minor problems or get your iguana stabilized and ready to see your veterinarian. To keep all the items in one place, you might use one of those plastic food storage containers with the snap-on lids. Then label the top with a felt pen "<u>Iguana First Aid Kit</u>" so everyone knows its purpose. Leave the kit near or on top of your iguana's habitat so you can always find it easily.

<u>Item</u>	<u>Use</u>	<u>Where to Purchase</u>
Magnifying glass (good quality)	Improves ability to see the medical problem	Cutlery or scientific supply store
Pen light (Maglite®) (small, intense beam)	Helps you see what you're doing	Outdoor store
Sharp scissors (good quality)	Cuts tape, shed, etc.	Drug or cutlery store
Nail trimmer	Cuts sharp points off claws	See Chapter 6, Special Care, "Claw Trimming"
Nail file (board or metal)	Smoothes rough edges of claws after trimming	Drug store
Tweezers (flat—safest and most effective	Removes objects that fingers can't reach	Drug store

Item	Use	Where to Purchase
Disposable rubber gloves	Ensures a more sterile contact when body fluids are involved	Drug store
Mineral oil	Helps loosen stubborn shed	Drug store
Tape—variety of widths	Holds splints, bandages, loose appendages	Drug store
Bandages: gauze, compression, etc.	Protects wounds; keeps ointments in place	Drug store
Second Skin®	Secures minor skins separations (see sidebar on page 353 for details)	Drug store
Q-Tip®	Simplifies application of ointments, cleaning agents, or KWIK-STOP®	Drug store
Cleaning agents (some options) Nolvasan® Betadine® Hydrogen peroxide	Washes out wounds	Veterinarian Drug store Drug store
Topical antibiotic cream (Polysporin® ointment)	Promotes healing for small cuts, blisters, infections	Drug store
Sterile saline (contact) lens solution)	Washes out eyes or cuts	Drug store
KWIK-STOP®	Helps stop minor bleeding from nails trimmed too close	Pet store
Small notepad and pen	Organizes notes of medical problems to be reviewed later with your veterinarian and entered into log book	Stationery store

Here are a few other items that you should keep handy, though not necessarily in the first-aid kit itself:

- Towel—for handling or stabilizing your iguana during nail trimming or transport to the veterinarian.
- Human electric heating pad—for your iguana to lie on to keep warm while you apply first aid or trim nails. It can also help calm your lizard.
- Hot-water bottle, empty soda bottle, and/or zip-lock plastic bags (double bagged)—to hold warm water to keep your iguana warm as it's being transported to the veterinarian or elsewhere.

In addition to assembling the first-aid kit, you can also become familiar with first-aid techniques. CPR is the modern version of the old mouth-to-mouth resuscitation technique for saving humans who are unconscious and can't breathe. Three people wrote to me that they saved their iguana by breathing into its mouth.

July 19, 1988, my iguana was somehow suffocated in the couch. When discovered, she was limp and non-responsive. Since I'm a registered nurse I couldn't accept this and did "Infant CPR" on her. Slowly she came around.
—I-95, Pat, Missouri

CHOOSING A VETERINARIAN

It is important that clients seek out a DVM [Doctor of Veterinary Medicine] with interest and experience with reptiles or go to a DVM who is interested and willing to coordinate or consult with someone who works with reptiles regularly. Expect that the [veterinarian] might charge a consulting fee, which would possibly be an additional cost to the client. Realize that our knowledge of reptile care and medicine is in its infancy; no one will have all the answers. Look for someone willing to research, consult with others, and, if no explanation is forthcoming, is willing to say "I don't know." Expect to pay more for the office call, treatments, medications, etc., because everything takes more time (e.g., often a pill or injectable medication can't be taken off the shelf—it needs to be crushed and suspended in a liquid or diluted).
—V-135, Dr. Debra, Washington

My vet is top of the line, very knowledgeable, compassionate, and caring, and is on a first-name basis with several reptile experts throughout the country.
—I-543, Bill, 40 yrs., Mississippi

Veterinarians, like doctors for humans, have to spend many years in school and many dollars on veterinary hospital equipment. To work with reptiles (or amphibians), a veterinarian also must master an additional level of knowledge and skill in areas such as proper husbandry practices, diagnoses, treatments, drugs and dosages, and rehabilitation techniques, to name a few.

SIDEBAR

Second Skin®

Second Skin is the brand name of a product to prevent and treat blisters and other skin irritations in humans. My girlfriend always takes this in the pack when we go hiking because of her propensity for blisters. It's a liquid, but when it dries it forms a flexible seal, kind of like a liquid plastic coating.

I used Second Skin on my iguana for an ear problem. Za had a hole in his ear from surgery, and I needed to seal up this hole so it wouldn't become infected. To do this, I soaked a small piece of Za's old shed in Second Skin, then placed it over the hole. I applied gentle pressure to the shed for a few minutes, and it stuck like a patch on a flat tire. For the next three days, I added a thin layer of Second Skin to build up more of a protective layer. This worked like magic, and by the next shed, the ear was healed.

Because Second Skin creates a good protective coating, it can also be used on minor abrasions or superficial cuts on your iguana. But it should never be used for deep or bleeding cuts, for fear it might enter the bloodstream. Also, water tends to dissolve Second Skin, so skip soaking the affected area of your lizard while the product is in place.

Finding a Good Veterinarian

While cat and dog veterinarians are in abundance, there can be difficulty in finding a knowledgeable reptile veterinarian.
—I-690, Irene, 34 yrs., Texas

Finding a good herp veterinarian can be difficult. Often the money for establishing a veterinarian hospital goes toward setting it up for the needs of more common, money-making, and abundant animals, primarily dogs and cats.

Perhaps the best place to find a well-qualified veterinarian is through a herpetological society in your area. A herp society with many members will most likely have tried all the different veterinarians in the area and have arrived at one or two that are the best. Another way is to call several pet stores; if they all give the same doctor's name, then that could be a good recommendation.

I spent some time researching before I found a vet who specialized in reptiles, and I'm glad I did!
—I-825, Chris, 22 yrs., Illinois

I drove my sick iguana 350 miles (one way) from home to find the best herp vet.
—I-605, Laura, 31 yrs., Canada

My vet is the only one I have ever gone to. I did my research before selecting a vet. His prices are very reasonable and he loves lizards (he has an adult male iguana and adult female Savannah monitor in his office). I'm satisfied with his services and his availability. I highly recommend him.
                                        —I-749, Charles, 27 yrs., California

My first vet is much closer to my home, but although he probably knows what he is doing medically, he gets such a low (like negative) score on the human scale that I'm willing to drive half an hour (one way) out of my way to deal with someone who treats my iguana (and me) with the respect due any sentient being.   —phone conversation with iguana owner

Once you have narrowed the choice of prospective veterinarian, you need to ask questions such as:
* How many iguanas or other reptiles are seen each month?
* Does the veterinarian receive regular medical updates on the latest herp medicines and techniques?
* Does he or she attend continuing education classes in reptile veterinary care?
* Does he or she know other herp veterinarians to contact if more information is needed on a particular case?
* Finally, ask yourself, do you get along with the veterinarian and feel comfortable with this person?

I got a great vet recommended by a friend. He seemed knowledgeable in handling a large reptile [SVL: 15", TL: 3' 11", 3 yrs., 6 lbs.]. He teased me pleasantly about all the scratches on my forearms and said he could tell I had a large lizard just by looking at me.   —I-620, Suzanne, 33 yrs., New York

As with your own doctor, sometimes the final choice of a veterinarian comes down to how well he or she relates to you and your iguana. For example, the first veterinarian I chose was highly recommended by a number of long-time iguana owners in my area. I took my iguana to this veterinarian, but was not happy with how roughly he handled my iguana.

Unsatisfied with my initial choice, I started taking Za to another highly recommended veterinarian about an hour away. What a difference! This veterinarian seemed to take a genuine interest in Za and handled him gently but firmly, which made Za very relaxed.

When I moved to Portland, one of the very first things I did—before finding out where the grocery stores and hardware stores were located—was to find a new veterinarian for my iguana. I again turned to a highly recommended local veterinarian and took Za in for an introductory meeting. During this first encounter it didn't seem like the chemistry worked, but the veterinarian was very competent. By the second meeting, whatever had happened the first time was gone, and Za and I found him to be an excellent veterinarian in every respect.

You also need to find out additional information, such as whether the veterinarian can be contacted after normal working hours, and if not, if there is a back-up veterinarian for emergencies. When I lived in California, my regular veterinarian had no back-up service, so I made sure I had another veterinarian I could call for possible emergency situations.

Don't choose the veterinarian according to who is the cheapest, and don't be surprised by what some of the medical costs might be. Reptile care can be expensive, but if we take animals out of the jungle and into our homes we have to accept the responsibility of seeing that they get proper care. Iguanas are exotic animals with many sensitive needs. As a pet owner, you need to understand that a qualified veterinarian is the best solution to your iguana's health problems.

A $25 office visit is a small cost to ensure that your animal is growing healthily.   —I-749, Charles, 27 yrs., California

The medical bills are higher [with iguanas] and that's if you can even find a vet who looks at reptiles.   —I-183, Mary, 24 yrs., Massachusetts

I spent $900 on vet care for my iguana because I refused to give up on him. He died anyhow, but I never regretted spending that money. He was worth the effort.   —I-200, Dianna, 47 yrs., Washington

Preparing for Your First Appointment

Ideally, you should research and choose a veterinarian before you bring your iguana home. Schedule a visit with your new-found veterinarian as soon as possible after the iguana joins your household. The veterinarian can check for any possible problems and establish a baseline for what your pet looks like, and you can begin to build a relationship with the veterinarian, just as you would with a doctor who treats you.

Before you go in for that first appointment, write down any problems or symptoms your iguana may have, as well as any questions you want to ask the veterinarian. That way, everything will be clear and you won't forget any important points.

Taking my iguana to the vet was pretty interesting. I felt kind of out of place because everyone else had mammal pets.   —I-846, Bobby, 19 yrs., Texas

As I sat in the waiting room at the veterinarian hospital with my iguana, I noticed other patrons waiting with their pets: an older couple with a cocker spaniel, a mother and daughter with Fluffy, their cat. And here I was kissing and cradling my iguana close to me. It was quite an amusing scene.
                                    —I-853, Eva, 25 yrs., New Jersey

SIDEBAR

Some Statistics on Iguanas as Patients

This information was compiled from questionnaires I sent to herp veterinarians across the U.S. in 1994 and 1995. Of those veterinarians who responded to the questions represented below, I extracted a low, high, and average value for each topic. It's not a rigorously scientific survey, but it gives a snapshot of iguanas' prevalence in veterinary practices.

Number of iguanas seen per year
- Low: 24
- High: 500
- Average: 190

Iguana patients (% of clientele)
- Low: less than 1%
- High: 20%
- Average: 1-2%

Change in % of iguana patients over recent years
- Low: no change
- High: 400% increase
- Average: 120% increase

Once your veterinarian appointment date comes up, you will encounter another problem—transporting your pet to the veterinarian's office or hospital. To make life easier, look at Chapter 3, Choosing Your Pet, "How to Get Your Iguana Home," for some transportation ideas.

Receiving the best possible care for your iguana requires you to cooperate with your veterinarian and respect his or her efforts. Unfortunately, reptile owners as a group have a less-than-glowing reputation among many veterinarians. You can counteract this negative stereotype by showing up for scheduled appointments, following directions for follow-up care, and paying your bills (remember, if veterinary bills will cause financial hardship, you shouldn't own an iguana).

The standard joke amongst veterinarians who treat reptiles is that if a check is going to bounce, it will be a reptile owner's check, or if you end up admitting the reptile there is a very high likelihood of never seeing the owner, or any money, again. Veterinarians need to be compensated for their work on reptiles just like they need to be compensated for their work on dogs and cats.

—veterinarian name and code number withheld as a courtesy

Be considerate in keeping your scheduled appointments. I hate to generalize, but reptile owners, as a group, are the worst at missing appointments without calling to cancel or reschedule.
                    —veterinarian name and code number withheld as a courtesy

The Bad, the Good, and the Outstanding

Be forewarned that not all veterinarians who say they work with reptiles know what they are doing. That's why it's good to ask the questions mentioned on page 354 and to get leads from people who have found good veterinarians.

Going to the vet one time with my iguana turned out to be a funny incident. My iguana had been acting under the weather for a few days, so I made the appointment to have her examined. The vet, it turned out, was not at all experienced with reptiles, even though he claimed to be. He decided to "check the iguana's reflexes"—with a hemostat [a clamp-like instrument used in surgery]! The vet got down on the floor with my iguana and pinched her toe with the hemostat. This is not the sort of thing I'd recommend doing to an iguana, even a sick one. I'm sure that my iguana was convinced that the doctor had boldly approached her and bitten her, and she did the only thing that can be expected. She leaped up off the floor and bit him back. The poor doctor had blood running

---

SIDEBAR

Helping Your Vet Help Your Herp

Iguanas take lots of time [for veterinarians], as a great deal of reptile medicine is actually teaching basic husbandry. No, the animal cannot run loose in your home [if you live in a cold climate]. No, he can't live on just lettuce and ground beef. No, you don't get enough UV light through a window. Yes, the animal needs extra warmth, and humidity.
                    —veterinarian's name withheld as a courtesy

I have heard comments similar to the one above from many veterinarians across the U.S. Let veterinarians serve you best by offering medical care, not providing basic information that you should have already acquired before purchasing your iguana.

It's not the responsibility of the veterinarian to explain every detail of basic care for your pet. It's your responsibility to find out! By all means, ask your veterinarian for clarification, pointers, and discuss any areas where you have questions or concerns, but take it upon yourself to learn the basics of iguana care. By reading this book, you're well on your way!

---

down his hand, but my iguana decided that this wasn't enough. She chased him out of the examining room and would not permit him to come back in. We had to catch her and confine her before he could safely re-enter the room. His diagnosis? Her reflexes were just fine. As to the rest? He had no idea. Fortunately, since this incident we have located an excellent vet.

—I-467, Kris, 32 yrs., Florida

Don't get me started on vets that are not qualified. I would have lost my iguana if not for our own research and knowledge. I believe the vet I went to provided false information as to his experience with reptiles. He was unable to spot calcium deficiency (metabolic bone disease) even with telltale signs—soft jaw, sore and swollen limbs, etc. Had this been my child I'd have more recourse. I understand all vets have to start somewhere, but I don't feel it should be at the cost of my pet. My situation could have resulted in the loss of my iguana if it hadn't been for my action. I paid this man of so-called knowledge and experience to do this for me; he was the professional. I'm upset, and it shows.

—I-798, Teri, 35 yrs., New Hampshire

Despite the previous unfortunate experiences, I've received far more positive and even glowing stories and recommendations from pet owners about their herp veterinarians. The good ones are invaluable, and the outstanding ones make you feel pleased to know that such people are around.

In my opinion, a 10 would not do my vet justice. He is an all-knowing guru when it comes to reptiles. He works closely with a top university nearby, and he is the professional that the professionals from three different zoos consult. He takes the time to make sure that I understand completely what is wrong with my reptiles when I bring them in, he makes sure that I understand exactly what the cause was, and exactly what I need to do to make it well again. He charges $15-$18 for any type of a visit (if medicine is prescribed, it's extra, but I've never paid more than $5-$8 for medication) no matter what he has to do, even if he looks at two of my animals in one visit. The going rate for other vets is $30-$40 [1994 prices] just to look at the animal, and most places will not treat reptiles. I have NEVER asked him a question that he could not immediately answer completely and comprehensively. Every time I see him, he has xeroxed some articles out of his various monthly medical journals for me to read. He also has convenient evening and weekend hours. Last Memorial Day when I had a minor emergency with my 12-foot Burmese python, he was checking her out an hour after I called. My vet is an hour from where I live, but I would drive twice that distance to see him.

—I-703, Renee, 22 yrs., New York

This man gets 10+ in skill, bedside manner, and going the extra yard. He spent lots of time checking out new research on my iguana's problems and was very clear and patient explaining what was going on and both the advantages and disadvantages of different treatments.   —I-865, Julie, 46 yrs., California

My vet is great! He is informative and spends quite a bit of time with me. I would rate him a 9. You don't get that assembly-line feeling that you get from many vets. —I-680, Catherine, 21 yrs., New York

ADMINISTERING MEDICINE

Choose a DVM who treats reptiles and establish a client/doctor relationship immediately. Have a post-purchase examination done and trust and follow the advice given. I can't tell you how many post-purchase exams I've done, tried to educate clients about proper care, diet, etc., only to have instructions ignored or poorly followed and seen the animals six to eight months later with metabolic bone disease and/or near death from improper care!
                                          —V-116, Dr. Richard, 37 yrs., Tennessee

SIDEBAR

Why Become a Herp Veterinarian?

Ever wonder why someone would become a reptile veterinarian? This is one of the questions I asked on the questionnaire I sent to veterinarians. The next group of quotations are meant to give you a more personal feeling for the medical professionals who treat iguanas—a little glimpse beyond the clinical demeanor to the person wearing the DVM badge.

I grew up with lots of birds and reptiles as pets and could never find a veterinarian able to help me whenever they were sick. All pets need competent care, whether mammal, avian, or reptile. —V-117, Dr. Dale, 38 yrs., Texas

Before my DVM training, I worked in pet stores and bird specialty stores and developed a fondness for them; I kept snakes as a youngster. I also realized the need in the veterinary field for people willing to provide health care for them, as the number of vets who (a) knew anything about them, and (b) wanted to work with them, was limited. —V-116, Dr. Richard, 37 yrs., Tennessee

Working with iguanas is an interesting diversion from more common pets, and there is a great need for DVMs in reptile medicine.
                                          —V-135, Dr. Debra, Washington

I've been fascinated with herps since I was a kid. I always had turtles, frogs, salamanders, etc. I would have gotten a Ph.D. in herpetology if I hadn't become a vet. —V-136, Dr. Michel, 38 yrs., Washington

Medications to treat or prevent illness will work only as well as the iguana's body can "cooperate" with the medication. When humans get an infection, their body temperature increases naturally (i.e., they get a fever) to kill the invading bacteria, virus, etc. (As an additional note, see the sidebar on page 372 for a scary look at what a virus is.) Iguanas don't have this physiological response; they have to move to a warm source to raise their body temperatures.

The immune system of reptiles is very dependent on temperature. Even medications might not have the desired effect unless the iguana is warm enough. If your iguana is sick, make sure the habitat temperature is 90°F. Your lizard may also need to spend more time under its basking heat source to further increase its temperature.

In addition, any time your iguana is sick, don't let it wander around in the house; it needs a warm, controlled environment at this time. Also, if you have two iguanas in the same habitat (NOT recommended at any time), the sick or injured iguana should have its own habitat to get well in. This is no time for the extra stress that a cagemate can create.

When your iguana is sick, there are several ways that you or your veterinarian can administer a possible treatment: topical, oral, subcutaneous, intramuscular, and intravenous. Sometimes the veterinarian will instruct you in one or more of these methods, so you can treat your iguana at home to help reduce your medical bills.

The following sections contain a mixture of stories and information to get you familiar with some of these medication concepts and terms in case one day you need to know them.

Topical Medicine

"Topical" is just what the word sounds like, something put on top. Topical ointments are used for small cuts, abrasions, and blisters to speed healing, and they often include an antibiotic ingredient.

Oral Medicine

Oral medicine usually consists of pills, capsules, or liquids. If you put your iguana in a "head lock" and try to jam the medicine down its throat, the situation can easily become an ordeal—especially if this scene is repeated several days or weeks in a row.

The best solution is to slow down, take things easy, and work with your iguana to get it to take the oral medicine required. See the section on "Force Feeding" on page 409 for some ideas on opening your iguana's mouth safely.

Giving medication orally is lots of fun! First, hold the animal securely in place around the neck and the base of the tail, positioning the iguana's head away from your body and the tail towards your body so that you can tuck the tail up

SIDEBAR

Medication Instructions

Encourage pet owners with sick pets to take the animal to a veterinarian specializing in exotics. I have worked for many pet shops and two veterinarians, and the most frustrating thing to me is when I try to help someone and then find out later that they didn't follow up on the advice given. They then come back to buy another iguana to replace the one that died.

—I-467, Kris, 32 yrs., Florida

IMPORTANT: When the veterinarian says to give a certain frequency and dosage of medication, especially antibiotics, give the amount prescribed—no more, no less, and exactly as directed. Don't take matters into your own hands, perhaps thinking, "Well, my iguana looks better today, I can stop now."

Every time I've been on antibiotics, the doctors always stressed, "Take **all** of the pills I have prescribed." This is also true for your iguana, unless your veterinarian explicitly directs otherwise. If you don't complete the full course of antibiotics, you may leave the strongest bacteria (the ones that didn't die during the first few doses), which will multiply and could create a super-strain of bacteria that's more difficult to kill.

Similarly, if the veterinarian tells you to give the medicine at a specific time of day, that's what you should do. Ask questions to find out the reasons behind specific instructions if you have doubts. A good veterinarian should make sure that you understand every aspect of your iguana's home health care before you leave the office.

under your arm for your own safety. Then wrap a towel around the body snugly with the iguana's legs pointed back toward the tail and give the medication. Another way to give medication is to gently pull downward on the dewlap; this will cause the animal's mouth to open and medication can be inserted. After any treatment of this kind be sure to offer the animal a few moments of gentle stroking and calm talk to soothe it and let it know you are still its friend. —I-11, Patty, Washington

She was given medication used normally for dogs. It came in capsule form, so I had to cut them open with scissors, then try to squeeze the contents into her mouth. Trying to pry open her tiny jaws didn't work because I could have easily broken her jaws. TLC worked! I would put honey sugar water drop by drop on her nose (not in the nostrils) and when it got on her lips, she'd soon start licking it off. Once she started that, I could open the capsule and try to get a few drops on her lips. A liquid via eyedropper would have been better, but the vet only had dog and cat medicine to try! Anyway, it worked.

—I-100, Char, 44 yrs., Illinois

Injectable Medicine

Medicine can be injected through a number of methods: subcutaneous means just under the skin; intramuscular means into the muscle; and intravenous means into the vein. Different medicines require different injection sites; your veterinarian will know where your iguana's medicine needs to go.

If long-term injections are required, there may be another option besides going to your veterinarian's office each time. You and your veterinarian need to get together and decide if you can accomplish the injections at home. If you both agree, this will eliminate daily drives to the veterinarian's clinic and save money on office visits.

The money and time savings mean nothing, however, if you are not willing or are unable to give injections properly. I am not going to explain how to give injections to your lizard because there are many specific details that need to be shown in person. Also, people with a little knowledge about injections, thinking they know it all, could seriously injure their iguana. Your veterinarian is the best person to explain and demonstrate how to give injections. But I will include some helpful hints.

As they say, "It's always easier to shoot a sitting duck." An iguana can be an active, kicking, squirming animal and difficult to stick with a needle. Some squirming is OK, but with certain kinds of injections a sudden movement can break the needle. Ideally, work with another person to give an injection.

You might want to use a towel to get better control over the iguana. Wrap your iguana in the towel with its arms and legs pinned against its body and only the injection site (e.g., leg) left out. One drawback with using a towel is that the iguana can freak out because it is being restricted and struggle more than if you didn't use the towel. Another possibility is that the iguana will learn to associate towels with being restricted and stuck with needles. Later, the mere sight of a towel can make them freak out. Each iguana reacts differently to the towel option. My iguana hated it.

If you don't use a towel, hold the iguana only as firmly as necessary to get it into the proper position for injection. With my iguana, I found that if I pinned him to the couch so he couldn't move, he wound up struggling the whole time. He wasn't used to this kind of "abuse." Keeping a firm but easy hold worked best with him. Your iguana may have to be pinned down. Find a level of firmness at which, after some wriggling, the iguana settles down enough for you to give the shot.

In my iguana's case, he was put on the back of the couch, where the full length of his body was supported by the padding and we had easy access to him. My girlfriend had experience in injecting animals, so all I had to do was keep Za calm and controlled during the injection. I put one hand on his shoulder area to protect me or my girlfriend from accidentally being bitten by Za during the actual injection. My hand was flat against his neck to reduce the area that could be bitten. My thumb came around the front of his neck to help hold him in place, if necessary.

Za was injected in the rear leg. For the month of shots, we alternated between his left and right leg each day so that one leg didn't become a "pin cushion."

Once the injection is completed, talk softly to your lizard and offer a leafy food treat (e.g., kale, collard, mustard green). Pet and talk to your iguana gently for a few minutes, trying to communicate that the injection is not a punishment.

I also made a point of never giving my iguana injections in any of his secure or "safe" areas, such as in his cage or on "his" chair in my office. If the medicine you're injecting can be given at any time of day, try to choose different injection times each day so the iguana doesn't come to associate a particular time of day with "shot time." Unfortunately for my iguana, his antibiotic injections had to be done at about the same time every day for several weeks in a row.

Za's injection time was about 5 p.m. If I picked him up anytime after about 4 p.m. or so, he got very upset. The rest of the day before that time, there was no problem. These lizards are very smart, and it didn't take Za long to figure out—and get upset—when injection time drew near.

The location of the injection—back leg, front leg, tail, etc.—can be important, again depending on the type of medication being injected.

Virtually all reptiles [including iguanas] have a renal portal system, which means that the circulation in the back half of the body goes right through the kidneys first. So your priorities for injection site are a) where is it easy to inject, and b) is it damaging to the kidneys? If the drug can damage the kidneys, you're forced to inject into the front half of the body no matter what; convenience is going to take a back seat in this case. If it won't harm the kidneys, and it's a drug that needs to be injected deep into a muscle group, you may be forced to the back legs or the base of the tail, where there are some beefy muscles.
—V-151, Dr. Mark, 35 yrs., Oregon

If you do your own injections, make sure you discuss with your veterinarian exactly where the needle should go, and why. If you have any doubts at all, let the veterinarian handle the injections.

COMMON MEDICAL CONDITIONS

It's important to realize that from a scientific point of view, we are in our infancy in iguana (and reptile) medicine, and unfortunately, money for research is very limited. Much like with exotic birds, we are far behind in general knowledge when compared with other animal species. Much of what we

know and how we practice has been learned slowly, often painfully, but has been freely shared through the years. Often we're "flying by the seat of our pants," so to speak. Inroads have been made, knowledge has been gained by those dedicated people, professional and lay persons alike. But medicine is not an exact science. No guarantees can be made as to any condition or treatment.
—V-116, Dr. Richard, 37 yrs., Tennessee

Detection

It takes iguanas a long time to get sick and a long time to get well.
—V-18, Dr. Patty, 40 yrs., California

Unless your iguana is bleeding profusely, limping badly, or has some other obvious injury, it is frequently difficult to detect a medical problem.

Don't expect to always see a dramatic physical manifestation if your iguana gets sick. In the wild, weakened animals have to hide the fact that they are sick or injured. Any sign of weakness could attract an otherwise hesitant predator. Because of this instinctive tendency, it is sometimes hard to tell that your animal is sick until it is too late.

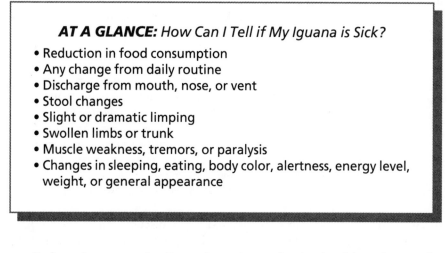

AT A GLANCE: *How Can I Tell if My Iguana is Sick?*
- Reduction in food consumption
- Any change from daily routine
- Discharge from mouth, nose, or vent
- Stool changes
- Slight or dramatic limping
- Swollen limbs or trunk
- Muscle weakness, tremors, or paralysis
- Changes in sleeping, eating, body color, alertness, energy level, weight, or general appearance

By knowing your animal's routine you can often notice things that may be a little off on a certain day. As an example, one day I saw my iguana rubbing his eye with his back foot. The log book showed that he had just shed, so this was not a possible cause for irritation. I looked at his rear foot and his eye but did not see anything wrong.

The next day I took him out into the bright sunlight and saw a glint in one eye. It was a human hair, which I had to get out quickly before it disappeared behind the eyelid. I ran and got the first-aid kit and removed the hair <u>delicately</u> with tweezers. Luckily, one end of the hair was sticking outside of the eye, so it was easy to grasp. Because all my iguana's first-aid supplies were in one box and located in a specific place, I didn't have to run around the house trying to find the tweezers.

As a side note, using tweezers near the eyes is not recommended for anyone who doesn't have a steady hand and previous medical interactions with their lizard. You also need to have an iguana that remains calm in situations like this. Eyes are a delicate structure. As an extra hint, when examining your iguana use the brightest light you can find—sunlight is often the best.

In general, the most effective tool for knowing when your lizard may have a medical problem is by paying attention to anything you feel is different from what your iguana normally does. If you think something is wrong, don't wait to take your iguana to the veterinarian.

Waiting only leads to trouble, often irreversible.
    —V-132, Dr. Willard, 55 yrs., Washington

Many of the iguanas that I see are gravely ill by the time they are brought in.
    —V-101, Dr. Kimber, 42 yrs., Oregon

The rest of this chapter lists various medical problems that might affect your iguana, including a definition of each problem, its likely symptoms, possible causes, and potential solutions. These sections should help alleviate two of the scariest things about owning an iguana: How do I know if something is wrong with my iguana, and what do I do next? This is a pet-care book, not a veterinary medicine textbook. The descriptions and treatments are included here simply to give you some comfort and clues for identifying potential problems. The real hero for solving many of the medical problems listed will be your qualified herp veterinarian.

Metabolic Bone Disease

75% of the iguanas we see are in for a metabolic bone disease problem.
    —V-22, Drs. Doug & Richard, 40 & 38 yrs., California

I see about 50 to 60 iguanas per year. Nearly all of the iguanas I see are calcium deficient.   —V-136, Dr. Michel, 38 yrs., Washington

What Is It?

Metabolic bone disease (MBD) is the most common medical problem in captive iguanas. In the questionnaire I sent to veterinarians, the respondents said that metabolic bone disease makes up about 80% of the problems they see with iguanas. It's a serious problem that is preventable with proper diet and lighting, but that if left untreated can deform, cripple, or even kill your iguana.

Symptom(s)

Knowing and recognizing the symptoms of metabolic bone disease has helped me to get help for my [iguanas] before [the disease] gets out of hand.
                              —I-200, Dianna, 47 yrs., Washington

Early signs of metabolic bone disease can include some or all of the following:
- "Rubber jaw"—a softening of the mandible (jaw) bones; the jaw also feels "spongy" to the touch
- Broken or fractured bones, which usually happen only when bones are weakened by decalcification
- Swollen back legs, which are often mistaken for "fat" healthy legs (sometimes only an experienced herp veterinarian can tell the difference)
- Softening of the leg's large femur bones
- Muscle twitches or tremors, especially in the arms and legs
- Dragging the back legs or whole body as it moves, instead of lifting the body off the ground
- Lowered appetite
- Weight loss

If your iguana breaks a bone, you can almost be sure it has a calcium deficiency. Iguanas in the wild fall out of trees all the time, with no broken bones. I have talked with a surprising number of people who said that, while they were on vacation at Mexican resorts, an iguana fell on top of or near them—and got up unharmed and ran away. Every captive iguana that I have seen over the last six years with a broken bone had a calcium deficiency, which was diagnosed either before or after the bone was broken.

When I bought my iguana last year, the woman who owned him said that one day the iguana broke his back and no one knew how it happened. Since then I have learned about these injuries and their cause. My iguana's back is fractured in several places down his spine and tail from metabolic bone disease. IMPROPER food and lack of ultraviolet light. He gets around pretty well now that I have corrected his diet and lighting.
                              —I-680, Catherine, 21 yrs., New York

My iguana had metabolic bone disease when he was purchased from a dumb teenager who didn't take care of him. I took him to the vet. The iguana had a swollen, very rubbery jaw and two of his legs looked like Popeye's arms from the curve in the bones. He had to get vitamin, calcium, and antibiotic shots and seems to be doing better now, except that I think his growth has been stunted.
                              —I-650, Helen, 31 yrs., Ohio

One symptom of a calcium deficiency might be an involuntary twitching of the toes and fingers, which sometimes progresses to twitching arm and leg muscles. The lizard will often seem to have trouble using its hind legs. Other symptoms might be general listlessness and a soft lower jaw. Careless handling at such times or a fall from a branch could cause bone fractures. These symptoms are of great importance to recognize. —I-200, Dianna, 47 yrs., Washington

More advanced signs of metabolic bone disease can include the following:
• Bent spine or tail
• Swollen, deformed jaw
• Lethargy
• Withdrawal of the lower jaw (causing a permanent "overbite")
• Paralysis, such as in the hind legs or forearms
• Convulsions or seizures
• Death

As a general rule, bone problems with MBD (e.g., receded lower jaw, curved spine) tend to show up in younger iguanas whose bones are growing rapidly. Muscle or nerve problems (e.g., tremors in the hands or feet, seizures) are more common in adults.

My iguana's previous owner reports that as a hatchling, the iguana had a calcium deficiency. This is apparent from her jaw. It has a lump on the right side. The lump is hard, not spongy. It is a misshapen bone, not an abscess. Her legs appear well-formed. —I-685, Julie, 36 yrs., California

He developed metabolic bone disease, which resulted in a soft jaw. After I changed his diet and lighting and saw a veterinarian, my iguana's jaw did solidify, but it never grew at the same rate as the rest of him. He's got a bad overbite to this day, which hampers his eating somewhat. He also tends to get plaque deposits on the exposed gum area.
—I-273, Bill, 34 yrs., New Jersey

Possible Cause(s)

Metabolic bone disease is typically the result of a lack of calcium, which the body needs to maintain strong bones, for muscle contractions, to conduct nerve impulses, for blood clotting, and for other important body functions. More precisely, the problem is an incorrect balance between calcium and phosphorus. If your iguana doesn't have the correct calcium/phosphorus ratio (i.e., Ca:P of 2:1), and if this imbalance continues for an extended period of time, it's at risk for metabolic bone disease. In addition, ultraviolet light (sunlight is the best source) is necessary for the calcium to be absorbed into the iguana's body.

If your lizard were in its natural habitat it would be spending the better part of every day basking in the sun. Ultraviolet light is crucial to maintaining normal metabolism in your iguana. Ultraviolet light is necessary to convert vitamin D to its active form, and the active form of vitamin D is needed for calcium absorption. Lack of or a deficiency of UV light in your lizard is setting it up for certain nutritional and health-related problems in the future. You should provide a

normal "day" of ultraviolet light by using artificial lighting (or direct sunlight with available shade) for at least 12 hours daily.
—V-69, Dr. Alynn, 39 yrs., Mississippi

Once the iguana's blood level of calcium is low, it will compensate by pulling calcium from its own bones, which will leave the bones soft or brittle. If untreated, iguanas eventually die a slow death, preceded by deformed and swollen limbs and, presumably, a great deal of pain.

Sexually mature female iguanas, who can produce and lay eggs with or without the presence of a male iguana, are especially prone to calcium imbalances. See page 427 for the section on "Calcium Deficiency" under "Female Iguana Medical Problems" for more information.

Possible Solution(s)

- See your veterinarian <u>first</u>.
- Handle your iguana gently and as little as possible until MBD is diagnosed and treated.
- Alleviate specific physical symptoms (e.g., treat broken bones).
- Expose your iguana more frequently to natural (unfiltered) sunlight and/or proper wavelengths of UV light (see Chapter 4, Housing, "Lights," for more details).
- Add calcium supplements to your iguana's food, as directed by your veterinarian.
- Change the diet to emphasize foods rich in calcium, and limit foods high in phosphorus.
- Eliminate animal protein from your iguana's diet, and limit overall protein intake.

We finally found the source of my iguana's tremors in his back and front legs. Upon doing a blood test, my vet found the calcium/phosphorus ratio was 1.43 calcium to 6.00 phosphorus. [It should be about 2:1.] And the vet said the underlying cause was not a deficient diet, but not enough UV lighting for the calcium to be absorbed. After aggressive supplemental force feeding and proper UV light, within 3 days the tremors were almost gone. Five days, no more tremors noticed. Since then, my iguana has been tremor-free. Blood tests were taken again 2 weeks later and the calcium was 2.16 and phosphorus was 2.70. Much closer to normal. —I-605, Laura, 31 yrs., Canada

Your veterinarian can often diagnose metabolic bone disease by a physical examination and radiographs (X-rays) and confirm suspicions by using the dietary history from your log book.

If you suspect that your iguana has MBD, or if it shows any of the symptoms listed earlier, be very careful when you handle the lizard. If it does have MBD, you could break a bone, cause pain, or worsen a symptom. Pick your lizard up only when necessary, and be extremely gentle.

Unfortunately for pet owners, preventing metabolic bone disease isn't as simple as piling on calcium supplements to your iguana's food. Calcium is regulated in a delicate balance with phosphorus and with vitamin D3, which is necessary for iguanas to absorb calcium. (Humans need calcium, too; our deficiency is called rickets.) In the wild, iguanas bask all day and soak up plenty of vitamin D from the sun, which helps their bodies metabolize calcium. I've seen some beat up, scrawny iguanas in the wild, but never one that showed signs of metabolic bone disease. This is a problem associated with captive animals.

The ways to prevent metabolic bone disease include proper lighting and controlling the amount of calcium, phosphorus, and vitamin D3 your iguana takes in. But as with so much else about iguanas, the scientific and medical world has yet to determine a fool-proof formula for this balancing act. So in the absence of "rules," we need to settle for understanding as much as possible about how and why iguanas become calcium deficient, how to recognize the early signs, and what to do to prevent and treat this serious condition.

In addition to correcting the diet and getting your iguana out in the sun as often as possible (aim for 30 minutes a day, weather permitting), your veterinarian might also prescribe calcium and/or vitamin D3 supplements or injections. You might also need to treat specific symptoms of metabolic bone disease that have already manifested themselves. For example, your veterinarian may need to set broken bones, and if your iguana's jaw is soft or painful, you might need to feed it mushy food until the jaw heals.

The effects of MBD can be stopped if you catch it early enough. But be forewarned that if the disease is extremely advanced before you begin treatments, you might be too late. It's a very serious medical problem, and I urge you to be aware of the signs described earlier and to seek veterinary help when necessary.

About 2 months ago, he got very lethargic and couldn't move like he normally does. He stopped climbing his favorite wall sculpture and became too weak to eat and drink on his own. He would drag himself along surfaces, developed lumps between his hind legs, got a rubbery jaw, and held his front paws in strange positions (almost as if he hadn't the strength to straighten himself up). Also, his feces got softer and grayish in color, almost the consistency of clay, very soft and watery. We took him to the vet, who diagnosed metabolic bone disease and gave him a variety of shots.

At home, we were told to give Neocalglucon every day (orally) as well as manual feeding, since he was too weak to eat or drink. He was given water orally and fed finely chopped food every day. During this period he had to be almost force-fed, since he had very little appetite. He was also given access to natural sunlight (UV light) every day. His appetite gradually improved and by the following week, upon his third visit to the vet, he was in great shape and the additional calcium shot was not deemed necessary. He hasn't had any problems since.   —I-799, Rui, 35 yrs., New York

We switched to liquid Neocalglucon, which gave noticeable results almost immediately. It took several months, but she's doing great now with only a lit-

tle swelling left in the thigh bones, which are continuing to heal. She loves to climb (anything—everything—she heads straight for the top). It was very interesting watching the healing process. At first, she could hardly move, but every time the swelling lessened, more mobility returned, her eyes got brighter and rounder, and she got more active. We did a graduated "physical therapy" program involving short walks, then low climbs on gradual inclines, etc. (with me underneath to catch her if she slipped), all accompanied by lots of cheering and applause. This seemed to help keep her spirits up. Now she can climb vertical parrot ladders.   —I-865, Julie, 46 yrs., California

Respiratory Problems

Respiratory problems used to be more common for iguanas a few years ago, before people knew the basic principles of proper housing for their lizards.

What Is It?

It's important to distinguish between a medical respiratory problem and your iguana's normal "snorting" of salty fluids out of its nostrils (see Chapter 1, Iguana: The Species, "Nostrils"). As in any animals, a respiratory problem can affect breathing and so must be taken seriously.

Symptom(s)

- Difficulty in breathing (rapid or labored)
- Mouth open wide for extended periods of time
- Excessive mucus in the mouth
- Foamy, liquid discharge around the nose area (not to be confused with the salty residue from "snorting")
- A wheezing sound when your iguana breathes
- Decreased or no eating
- Reduced normal activity

I think my iguana may be sick. Up until now she has been healthy. I keep her in an extra bedroom that I have turned into an "iguana room." I keep the temperature in the room above 80 degrees at all times, and there is also a lamp for her to bask under. The problem started late this summer when the baseboard heater in the room quit working, and the iguana was left without heat for several nights, until I realized the heater no longer worked. She developed severe diarrhea at this time and lost her appetite. After the baseboard heater was fixed the diarrhea went away, but her appetite hasn't returned and she discharges a fluid from her nose constantly.

—from the Herp-Net on-line bulletin board

The lizard I purchased from a pet store already had a respiratory disease. When it breathed, its throat would blow up. It's getting better, but very slowly.
—I-764, Diana, 46 yrs., California

Possible Cause(s)

- Prolonged exposure to cold temperatures
- An excessively humid habitat with too little ventilation, which can breed pathogens that cause respiratory infections
- An excessively dry habitat, which can dry mucous membranes and make the lizard more susceptible to infections

Possible Solution(s)

- Raise the habitat temperature (assuming it's too low).
- If the inside of the habitat smells damp and musty, increase ventilation and control the humidity.
- See your veterinarian, who can culture any discharge to determine what course of action might stop the problem (e.g., antibiotics, changes in the habitat).
- Make sure water is available and your lizard is drinking it. If mucus is being discharged, hydrating your lizard is important.

He raised his head and pointed it straight up, and he wouldn't eat or move around. His throat would bulge with air and he'd gape with his mouth. I was worried. Then one night I opened his mouth and it was "slimed." He had a respiratory infection. I elevated cage temperature to 95-100°, 24 hours a day. He was well in three days without an antibiotic.
                    —conversation at a herpetological conference

The iguana in the previous quotation was extremely lucky that it didn't die without antibiotic treatment. If you think your iguana has a respiratory problem, see your veterinarian immediately! Respiratory problems can go from bad to death in a short period of time.

Even though this person didn't take his lizard to the veterinarian, he did do one thing right by increasing the habitat temperature. See page 360 for a discussion of the importance of temperature for a sick iguana.

Gout

Gout is a painful joint disease traditionally blamed, in humans, on too much rich food, drink, and inactivity. For instance, novels of the 19th century often featured one or more wealthy men characters afflicted with gout. It turns out that many reptiles get gout, too—and diet is frequently to blame.

What Is It?

Gout is a disease that shows up most often as swollen and painful joints (arthritis), especially in the hands and feet. This type of arthritis is the result of too much uric acid in the bloodstream or tissues; uric acid is a chemical product of protein digestion in the body. The uric acid forms crystals that lodge in tissues such as joints, lungs, kidneys, and liver.

SIDEBAR

Virus: The "Terminator"

"A virus is a small capsule made of membranes and proteins. The capsule contains one or more strands of DNA or RNA, which are long molecules that contain the software program for making a copy of the virus. A virus is a parasite. It can't live on its own. It can only make copies of itself inside a [host] cell using the cell's materials and machinery to get the job done. All living things carry viruses in their cells.

"Viruses may seem alive when they multiply, but in another sense they are obviously dead. . . . Some biologists classify viruses as "life forms," because they are not strictly known to be alive. Viruses are ambiguously alive, neither alive nor dead. They carry on their existence in the borderlands between life and nonlife.

"Viruses are molecular sharks, a motive without a mind. Compact, hard, logical, totally selfish, the virus is dedicated to making copies of itself—which it can do on occasion with radiant speed. The prime directive is to replicate. A virus makes copies of itself inside a cell until eventually the cell gets pigged with virus and pops. . . . If enough cells are destroyed, the host dies."   —From *The Hot Zone* by Richard Preston. Copyright © 1994 by Richard Preston. Reprinted by permission of Random House, Inc.

Symptom(s)

- Swollen joints, especially fingers and toes
- Other swollen tissues, such as the eyes
- Lethargy, inactivity, general "sick" appearance
- Unhealthy-looking skin or scales

Possible Cause(s)

Gout in iguanas is almost always the result of eating animal protein. As herbivores, iguanas are not designed to handle animal protein. Many of the cases I've heard about were the result of iguanas eating a steady diet of cat food, pinkies, or mice. Gout is also more likely to occur in lizards that don't take in enough water.

Possible Solution(s)

It's pretty easy to prevent gout in iguanas: Don't feed your lizard animal proteins, including cat food (which is formulated for carnivores). Iguanas don't need and shouldn't be fed animal-based foods. If you've read this far in this book and you're still not convinced that iguanas are herbivores, all I can do is urge you to re-read the pertinent sections of Chapter 1, Iguana: The Species, and Chapter 5, Feeding, until you see the light.

If your iguana already shows signs of gout, see your veterinarian. Treatment will probably include both medication and an immediate change in diet; it might also require surgery. Also make sure that your iguana always has access to fresh water to drink. If it's too late to prevent gout, at least try to catch it early. Even with the best veterinary care, your iguana will probably suffer from permanent pain or loss of mobility if the gout is too far along.

PARASITES: WORMS AND "BUGS"

Parasites are organisms that feed and live on or in another organism, without benefiting the host and often causing harm. Parasites can cause disease and other medical problems for animals, including reptiles, and are frequently seen by herp veterinarians in their practices.

Worms

When my iguana was 3 years old I happened to take a close look at his feces and saw worms. The vet said they were iguana-specific roundworms. TESTING OF YOUR IGUANA WITHIN THE FIRST WEEK FOR PARASITES IS A MUST.
—I-519, Ellen, 40 yrs., Louisiana

What Are They?

Iguanas can get a wide variety of worms, but the ones usually seen are pinworms, roundworms, and tapeworms. They live inside the iguana's body and can feed off the lizard's blood supply, take up physical space and cause compaction in the intestines (like too many cooked spaghetti noodles stuffed in a jar), and steal nutrients from the food in the digestive system. If these parasites are left alone, they can multiply and spread quite rapidly, causing illness, disease, and even death.

Symptom(s)

- Loss of appetite or refusal to eat
- Reduced daily activity or lethargy; malaise
- Mucus in the feces
- Worms visible in the feces
- More frequent than usual defecation

Possible Cause(s)

Some worms enter the body of the host when worm-infested flesh is consumed. Because iguanas are herbivores, if you feed them the proper diet you can eliminate this avenue of entry. Feces are typically the main transport mechanism of worms into an iguana.

If you bought your iguana at a pet store that has many reptiles housed together, it only takes one infected animal to infect the rest. Infected feces can get on the food or in the water bowls, and contamination spreads quickly. The infected animal may have originally gotten infected at the iguana farm where it was raised, perhaps from bird droppings or contaminated soil in the holding pen.

Possible Solution(s)

All [iguanas] should be checked for worms, as it is a very common finding.
—V-149, Dr. Eddie, 38 yrs., North Carolina

I have a fecal sample checked each year the same time I get my dogs checked.
—I-34, Dale, 36 yrs., Indiana

I took my iguana to the vet. They did a fecal exam and determined he had worms. He was given medication, which we had to give him by mouth for a couple of weeks. Also the vet gave him a shot of vitamins because he was a little run down from the worms.   —I-790, Cindy, 33 yrs., Texas

The simplest solution is to immediately attack the "would-be" worms. Take a sample of your iguana's feces to your veterinarian for examination. The office staff will tell you how much to bring and other specific requirements. This sample should be brought in the first day your iguana defecates in its new habitat.

First exam after purchasing my iguana revealed hookworms and pinworms. Treated by the vet with Panacur then re-treated two weeks later for possible eggs hatching. Checked three weeks after that and still was free of worms.
—I-493, Marcia, 40 yrs., Alaska

If it turns out your iguana has worms, the veterinarian will give the appropriate injections or pills to rid your lizard of its wiggly pests. Oftentimes the medicine is spread out over a specific period of time so any worm eggs can also be destroyed.

After being dewormed, my iguana has doubled his weight in two weeks and eats three dishes of food on the same day.   —I-656, Peggy, 34 yrs., Texas

If your iguana is found to have worms, you <u>must</u> thoroughly scrub and clean the habitat to remove any infected feces. In addition, each time your iguana defecates, the feces need to be cleaned up immediately. You don't want potential worms or worm eggs lying around in the habitat, ready to re-infect your lizard. The veterinarian will tell you when you can relax this fecal clean-up alert.

My iguana was misdiagnosed at first as having strongyles [another type of worm] and was given Ivermectin, which should have worked, but I wasn't told to clean the environment. Once pinworms were diagnosed, I cleaned the environment with 1:30 bleach/water mixture. After the worms were gone, he seemed to have more appetite than ever before.
—I-840, Lorraine, 32 yrs., Ohio

My iguana had a heavy infestation of pinworms and was treated with Panacur and repeated in two weeks. I immediately began to see live worms in his feces and was very diligent during this time about cage sterilization. His weight during this time went from 61 grams at initiation of deworming to 79 grams in two weeks. I really began to see a big difference in growth after deworming.
—I-511, Deborah, 41 yrs., Virginia

Bugs

In the previous section, we encountered unwanted creatures inside the iguana; now we will discuss "bugs" trying to have a free lunch on the outside of an iguana's body, at the expense of the lizard. The two creatures that "bug" iguanas most often are ticks and mites, which will be explained separately. As a side note, many people call ticks and mites bugs or insects, but in fact they are in the class of vertebrates known as arachnids, which makes them relatives of spiders.

Ticks

Humans and iguanas share a common blood-sucker: ticks.

What Are They?

Ticks are slow-moving, hard- or soft-bodied parasites that stick their hose-like beaks into an iguana's (or human's) skin and suck up blood. When ticks first start to suck blood they are very small, but in a short period of time their whole body swells up like a balloon full of water—except they are full of blood.

Not only do ticks deplete an iguana's blood supply, but they also can be a source of disease. And like any crawling and biting "thing" on a human, the experience is irritating and stressful to an iguana, too. The greater the number of ticks, the more stress, fatigue, and possible disease must be endured.

Symptom(s)

- Excessive scratching
- Possible listlessness
- Any change in eating or normal activity
- Shedding problems (too much or not enough)
- Irregular or damaged scales in a localized area
- Small, ugly creatures crawling on or stuck to the surface of an iguana, especially under scales and in skin folds

Possible Cause(s)

Ticks are seldom seen on iguanas because most iguanas are now farm-raised. In the old days, when all iguanas were wild-caught, it was almost standard procedure to check for ticks. Also standard procedure when I was exploring the jungles in Mexico and Central America was to tuck the legs of my trousers into my socks, then duct tape the top of the socks to the pants. If I didn't do this, the ticks would be sucking blood from my legs by the end of the day. When I got my iguana (wild-caught hatchling) seven years ago, he had a big fat tick on his stomach, which the owner of the pet store removed for me.

Ticks are not just in the jungles of Mexico and South America. They are also found all over the United States. Where I lived in Northern California we had to make sure we stayed on the hiking trails during the summer months because ticks were supposedly waiting for us in the bushes and grasses. It was true, because often my dog would get them when he ran off the trail chasing imaginary foes.

Possible Solution(s)

First, you need to identify that your lizard has ticks. If a tick is engorged with blood it will be easier to see, as it will be much larger than normal. Some of their favorite hiding places are around the eyes, vent, and armpit of the iguana. They need to get under a scale to the soft part of the iguana's body to suck blood.

The easiest way to rid your lizard of ticks is just to pick the creature off your iguana. But a tick buries its head and mouth parts into the skin of its victim, so if you pick it off too quickly, there is a good chance the head will snap off in the victim. This could possibly lead to infection.

When I was a Boy Scout (more than 35 years ago), they told us to "unscrew" a tick (can't remember if it was clockwise or counterclockwise) if you discovered one on your body. Years later, I found out that ticks don't have a direction to unscrew, so this was pretty stupid advice. The safest way to remove the tick is gently and slowly with your fingers or tweezers. Grab the tick as close to the iguana's skin as possible, where the tick's mouth parts are embedded in the lizard. The tick will feel the slow pull and will finally "let go."

If you spot a tick in a hard-to-reach place, such as inside the nostril, your veterinarian will probably have to do the job.

Because the skin has been irritated by the bite of the tick, clean the area with an antibacterial agent such as Betadine or Nolvasan. Complete the first aid with an antibiotic cream (these products can be found in the First-Aid Kit on page 349).

If you just purchased your iguana with a tick and then removed it, no further action is necessary. But if your iguana gets a tick while in its habitat, the dwelling needs a thorough cleaning to kill any tick eggs or young ones that may be living there. This step is more often a nightmare than a reality.

Mites

Unlike ticks, mites are something that humans are less likely to encounter.

What Are They?

Mites are not much larger than the dot over the "i" in the word "mite." For such a small creature, it can cause much grief. I wouldn't wish mites on my worst enemy. By the time you see these dreadful creatures, you probably have hundreds more hiding on your lizard and in its habitat.

A friend of mine went down the Amazon River and said that when he was in the water, often a piranha would nip at his flesh. He said it wasn't even much of a nibble, at that. But my mind still reels at seeing a scientific movie where a dead cow was put in a river that had hundreds of piranhas in it. It seemed that once the piranhas attacked the cow, the water "boiled" with the aggressive fish. In about 5 minutes the only things left were the bones floating to the surface of the water. Mites, like piranhas, get their strength and killing power from numbers. They reproduce faster than a thousand happy rabbits. You don't want mites on your iguana—they suck blood and can transmit disease.

Mites spend most of their time under an iguana's scales (where it's easier to suck blood and hide at the same time). In your iguana's habitat, the biggest problem is that these little bastards hide in the places most difficult to clean, and their eggs thrive at the same temperatures as your iguana.

I had a big problem with mites. At first I saw a few little bugs, and I thought nothing of them. But then there were more of them. The pet store said they were mites. Then I got worried. The mites were tiny little red bugs usually, though every once in a while I'd see a brown or black one. They were anywhere from one pinpoint to five or six pinpoints. I would see them in between the scales on the iguana's hind legs and around those round, pointy scales on the neck. They would move. Sometimes I'd just see the little buggers scurrying around on him.

I bought some stuff from the pet store to get rid of the mites, but it didn't work very well. Sometimes they would go away for a month and then come back. Luckily they brought no diseases.

Finally, I got rid of them. The main thing you must do is "Never Give Up." They are hard to get rid of. Even when I totally cleaned my iguana, and changed him from a 30-gallon aquarium to his new cage he is in now, the mites came back. I hated the mites.   —I-724, Robby, 14 yrs., Utah

Symptom(s)

Mites are commonly found around the mouth, eyes, dewlap, and vent of an iguana. The symptoms of mites are generally the same as for ticks (see the previous section). Sometimes, the mites will do such a good job of hiding and blending in with your lizard's skin that you won't see them there. Instead, you might notice dead mites as little specks, like black pepper, in your iguana's water container. Or you might see or feel tiny crawling dots on your hands or arms after handling your iguana.

Possible Cause(s)

If your iguana never had mites in the past and has never had another cage-mate, it will probably never get mites. If mites appear, they usually come with the lizard, from wherever you purchased it. Because they are so small, mites are not usually noticed until they are out of control in large numbers.

> *Mites—they came home from the pet store with us.*
> —I-822, Julia, 23 yrs., North Carolina

> *I did not have any mites for four years, then I left my bird at another house for a week. The day after I brought the bird home I noticed red dots on the cage walls. I examined the iguanas and sure enough, they had mites from the bird.*
> —I-764, Diana, 46 yrs., California

> *Both my iguanas had mites at various times, mostly due to my having imported ball pythons [snakes] around.*   —I-237, Diane, 44 yrs., Texas

Possible Solution(s)

Wiping out all the mites in your iguana's habitat is a must. If only two mites are left in the habitat and they are a male and female, the couple will breed like an out-of-control nuclear reactor and the problem comes back immediately. Examine your iguana closely when you first purchase it so you don't bring mites into your iguana's new home, which will be hell to clean up.

Getting rid of mites is a big problem for such a small speck of a pest. There is only one formula to get rid of mites: robust eradication procedures applied with tenacity and vigilance.

First, remove and kill all the mites on your lizard. Several pet owners have said that they have put their iguanas in warm water baths for half an hour or so (mites can't hold their breath that long and die). But some of the smart mites move as fast as possible to the iguana's head and survive. And of course there are mite eggs that can hatch later.

> *Mites . . . always a problem. My roommate's iguana (now deceased) became infested with them when some wild-caught spiny lizards were added to his terrarium. These lizards were infested and subsequently the entire collection became infested. His iguana later died from complications from that infestation. My pair, however, were very resistant and I had not noticed any mites. Once they did come down with it I did everything imaginable to eradicate them. I have noted that if you cover the iguana in vegetable oil, it smothers and kills the mites and acts as a temporary barrier to reinfestation.*
> —I-772, Andy, 32 yrs., California

Other pet owners suggest putting a thin layer of baby oil on the iguana for a couple of hours, then rinsing it off. Repeat this process once a week for three or four weeks. One veterinarian wrote and said that he used a flea spray that's safe for kittens (3 to 4 weeks old). This is sprayed onto a towel and rubbed lightly over the iguana's body once a week for a month; the iguana is then rinsed off under running water.

By spraying the towel instead of the iguana, you get more control—and therefore safety. A small washcloth works the best, because you can reach into tight places like the iguana's armpits while avoiding the eyes and mouth. Start at the iguana's head and end up at the tip of its tail.

There are also many new commercial mite-eradication products on the market. Look in the different herp magazines for advertisements of these new products. Beware, though, that there is not always truth in advertising, and many products contain insecticides that can harm your iguana. Ask your veterinarian or friends in your herp society what specific products they have used, and how they worked. If you have any doubts at all, take your iguana to your herp veterinarian for advice on getting rid of mites safely and effectively.

> *My iguana got mites twice by introduction of new lizards. I got rid of the mites, then I scrubbed the cage (and all corners), as well as the cage furnishings, with disinfectant.* —I-650, Helen, Ohio
>
> [AUTHOR'S NOTE: NEVER use the disinfectant with the brand name PineSol® in an iguana's cage. It could cause breathing problems for your iguana.]

After you rid your iguana's body of mites, remove the substrate from the habitat, then scrub the entire habitat completely and thoroughly. Mites (and their eggs) hide in the hardest-to-clean little nooks and crannies. If not completely eradicated, they'll keep coming back. And that's an understatement. Put new substrate in every day until the mites are gone.

For heavy infestations, your iguana may need treatment with a product such as Ivermectin (discuss this with your veterinarian). The lizard might also need treatment for secondary problems resulting from the mites, such as anemia. Regardless of how your iguana is treated for mites, you still need to clean the habitat thoroughly as described above.

Now that you've heard how dreadful mites can be, I can give you the bright side: I have only seen or heard of a handful of cases of mites in all of the hundreds of iguanas I have encountered over the years.

INJURIES

When I was in the jungles of Belize, my river guide said that he once saw a very large male iguana with its front paw missing, but still alive. Iguanas are tough, determined animals and when the desire to live is strong, they often beat the odds against a bad medical condition.

Broken Bones

About 15% of our business with iguanas has to do with fractures.
                    —V-22, Drs. Doug & Richard, 40 & 38 yrs., California

What Are They?

A broken bone can range from a simple hairline fracture to a compound break where part of the broken bone sticks out of the iguana's skin.

Symptom(s)

- Limping on or "favoring" the suspected limb
- Swelling in suspected injured area
- Unusual or unnatural bending of a limb
- Pain expressed by iguana
- Part of a bone sticking out of the skin

Yesterday I noticed that she had apparently broken a finger and it's sore, because she waves that hand around when she stubs it, as if it hurts.
                    —I-805, Kenneth, 40 yrs., Idaho

Possible Cause(s)

Our iguana had a broken front leg at about 1½ years. The vet told us his bone walls were too thin due to insufficient calcium. We gave him calcium supplements and natural sunlight daily for a year after that. He seems fine now.
                    —I-705, Linda & Paul, 45 yrs., California

As I have mentioned before, if iguanas can jump or fall out of trees in the wild without getting hurt, they should be able to do the same in captivity. In almost every case where an iguana breaks an arm or leg, it's a reflection of improper diet, specifically a lack of calcium, and inadequate exposure to sunlight or artificial ultraviolet light. This complex balancing act is described in a previous section called "Metabolic Bone Disease," on page 365.

We have an exposed cross-beam ceiling in our front room. I carpeted it so my iguana could climb easily and be high, like in the jungle. One day he fell. He was in almost a full-body cast for 3 months, and he hated it.
                    —I-43, Taryn, 27 yrs., Alaska

Breaking of small bones such as toes is often a function of a captive life style. In a habitat that's too small, every possible problem is magnified over time—such as gaps and crevices in tree branches, limbs, or ledges where claws can get stuck. And then there are all the dangers associated with an iguana that is allowed to roam freely in your house.

Possible Solution(s)

About a year after I got him, he was out of his cage and I was on the phone. I

heard a crash. I went over to see what happened. My iguana was on the ledge of a window (inside) and next to him was a broken pitcher. When he walked away he did it on three legs . . . his front right arm was up and his wrist dangling. He didn't want to put any pressure on it. Well, $350, three visits to the vet, a brace, and two x-rays later . . . it turns out he had a fractured wrist.
—I-576, David, 23 yrs., New York

Feeding your iguana the proper diet, and making sure it gets direct sunlight, minimizes the major causes of broken bones. But accidents do happen, and if you think your iguana has broken or fractured a bone, the best person to see right away is your herp veterinarian.

The veterinarian can determine the severity of the break and apply the proper restriction, from a simple wooden splint to a plaster cast like humans use. Depending on what is broken on the iguana, the veterinarian might require that you remove any climbing limbs from the iguana's habitat until the lizard fully recovers. And if the break is the result of metabolic bone disease, you'll need to correct inadequacies in your iguana's diet, calcium intake, and exposure to UV light.

If you don't see your veterinarian soon after the break, it will start to mend in whatever position it's in, which might be twisted. Your veterinarian has the experience and skills to treat your iguana's broken bones correctly.

Our iguana broke a toe when he was about 6 months old. Cause unknown. It had to be surgically reset and put in a cast. (By the way, I've never seen anything more stupid-looking than an iguana in a cast, but he seemed to get around just fine with it.) —I-830, Elisa, 27 yrs., New York

Two months of having her arm wrapped immobile along her side had no bad effect on the arm. The moment the bandages were off, she walked and climbed with no difficulty or "limp" at all! The vet was very surprised. But the spines along her back grew to a permanent curl from being bandaged.
—I-100, Char, 44 yrs., Illinois

Abscesses and Bites

My very first iguana after 4 years got an abscess. By the time I realized that she was sick, she was blinded in one eye. When I took her in to the vet, we tried a few medications to no avail. After four months of treatment and no positive results, I found her all crippled, twisted, and round like a snake. I asked the vet to put her to sleep. We thought for all the pain she was in that this would be best. —I-794, Andrés, 30 yrs., California

[AUTHOR'S NOTE: Iguanas' health problems can escalate so fast, it's unbelievable. Observe your animal daily. Don't drift off—pay attention to the smallest changes!!]

What Are They?

When you have more than one iguana in a habitat, there is a good chance your lizards will fight, which can result in bite or scratch wounds. What may look like a minor bite or puncture wound on an iguana can quickly become infected. Bites to iguanas from other animals, such as dogs and cats, are usually fatal, so they won't be considered in this section. I have grouped bites and abscesses together because a bite wound from another iguana frequently turns into an abscess.

This is a strange type of infection, where the body reacts by locally sealing the infection so it can't spread. This localized infection grows internally because it is sealed off and the natural agents in the body that kill invading bacteria can't get to the problem. The infected area gets larger and larger until you see it as a rounded, swollen lump on the outside of the iguana's body.

Symptom(s) of Abscesses

- Unusual localized swelling or lump
- The material in the swelling feels solid
- The iguana may experience pain when the lump is touched

Possible Cause(s)

Abscesses are usually a secondary problem created when a bite from another iguana gets infected. Abscesses can also be caused by claw scratches or any open wound that is in contact with "bad" bacteria, as you will see in one quotation under "Possible Solution(s)."

Abscesses need to heal from the inside out, which eliminates the need for stitches in most cases.

> *Iguana bites (to each other) are dirty and usually result in infections that often lead to abscesses [if not cleaned out immediately].*
>
> —I-11, Patty, Washington

Possible Solution(s)

If there is only one iguana in a habitat, it's hard for your lizard to get an abscess. Wounds of any kind should be immediately flushed out with one of the agents listed in the First-Aid Kit (on page 349). With prompt disinfection, your iguana might avoid getting an infection or an abscess. Also, if it were my lizard, I would take it to the veterinarian to see if any antibiotics or other treatments were necessary. In general, reptile wounds heal more slowly than wounds in mammals.

> *My iguana had an abscess on the top of his nose. When he was little, he used to run into the side of his glass tank frequently when I would stick my hand in to pick him up. I assumed the bump was nothing more than a bump much like a human would get. For a couple of weeks, I noticed the bump getting larger and*

starting to look very tender. I rushed the iguana to an exotic pet specialist that a friend recommended. The doctor diagnosed the bump as an abscess, drained it, shot antibiotics in it, and instructed me to give him shots for 4 weeks. The trip was well worth any money, because my iguana is healthy and alive and barely sports any scar at all from the "bump."
—I-853, Eva & Scott, 25 yrs., New Jersey

As I said earlier, in an abscess the infection is sealed off and will continue to grow until it's treated. If it's a large infection, your veterinarian will cut the abscess open, remove the material inside, and thoroughly clean the wound. Antibiotic ointment will usually be put in the opening, which will be left to heal from the inside out. The veterinarian might also give injectable antibiotics and/or pills.

I've had experience with iguana abscesses, which tend to be somewhat common. Your vet will have to remove the abscess, which will leave a wound that you must keep clean. The hole will close up and heal within days. Occasionally a lump can be a tumor and not an abscess; that's why it's important to see your vet. —I-200, Dianna, 47 yrs., Washington

Bleeding from Cuts

My iguana fell from the top of the closet once and cut himself on his back. It swelled and I was afraid it was infected. I took him in and the vet said that their thick skin makes healing difficult. There is still a scar, but the swelling is gone. —I-554, Anthony, 29 yrs., Texas

What Is It?

Many abrasions, punctures, tears, or gashes in an iguana's skin cause bleeding. There are two levels of cuts that cause bleeding: superficial and deep.

A superficial cut is any cut that is shallow, on the surface of the skin, and in which bleeding stops by itself. A deep cut is when you can look into the wound and see several layers of "flesh." A deep cut is sometimes difficult to stop bleeding. You might get the wound to stop bleeding temporarily, but any sudden jarring starts it up again. Of course, the depth of the cut determines the course of the treatment. If you can't get a cut to stop bleeding, you need to seek veterinary help quickly.

In addition, a wound left unstitched takes an extra-long time to heal. This situation could cause the wound to get infected. Iguanas don't deal very well with infection. They can get sick and die. See your veterinarian.

Symptom(s)

An open wound somewhere on an iguana's body where blood is present indicates a cut.

Possible Cause(s)

Just about anything you can imagine can cut or wound your iguana enough to make it bleed.

Possible Solution(s)

When you find a cut on an iguana, clean and soak the affected area with hydro-gen peroxide (diluted 50/50 with water) until the fizzing action dies down, then apply mercurochrome. If the area remains swollen, or if the animal refuses to use an injured limb, see your veterinarian for antibiotics or further help.
                                        —I-11, Patty, Washington

For a superficial cut, first clean the wound of any foreign material, then apply one of the topical cleaning agents found in your iguana First-Aid Kit (see page 349). Put an antibiotic cream on the wound to help the healing process, until it is healed completely.

Depending on the location of the wound, you may need or want to cover it with some sort of simple bandage to keep it clean. Try to keep adhesive tape off your iguana's skin. Check the wound daily to make sure it is healing properly.

If you see any redness around the cut, <u>immediately</u> take your lizard to the veterinarian. Redness is an urgent indicator that an infection might be devel-oping and that the veterinarian needs to start some kind of antibiotic treatment.

A deep cut warrants a trip to the veterinarian, but before you leave for the hospital at least clean the wound with Nolvasan, Betadine, diluted hydrogen peroxide, or a similar cleaning solution to prevent any possible infection. Take some gauze out of the iguana first-aid kit and wrap it around the wound to keep it clean until the veterinarian sees it. <u>Don't</u> wrap the gauze so tightly that you cut off the circulation to the injured area!

For profuse bleeding, slightly elevate the injured area if possible, and apply firm direct pressure to the wound. Put something, such as a clean cloth, between your flesh and the wound, or use rubber gloves, if necessary. Get to the veterinarian immediately.

Claw Pulled Out

What Is It?

The claw is pulled completely out of the iguana's foot or hand.

Symptom(s)

Bleeding from the tip of a finger or toe is a good indication that a claw is broken or missing.

Possible Cause(s)

If an iguana's habitat is not prepared and maintained properly, over time problems can arise. If your lizard is allowed out of its habitat, then additional problems can come up, even for owners who are careful about their iguana's safety (see Chapter 4, Housing, "Loose in the Home," for help in avoiding potential trouble).

For example, one day I allowed my iguana (then about 1½ years old) to explore a new area of my apartment. All of a sudden, he started climbing one of my tall file cabinets.

Above the file cabinet was a bunch of sports stuff, including all of my rock-climbing gear and a large poster of El Capitan in Yosemite. It seemed perfect. The file cabinet was a mountain and Za was the expert climber. But solo climbing for humans or iguanas can be dangerous. Za was climbing up by hooking his claws over the cabinet's drawer handles. He had almost made it to the top when he started to lose his balance, and in one panic leap he stuck one claw into the metal bracket that holds the file drawer name. He fell and as did the claw pulled completely out (stuck in the metal bracket).

When he hit the ground, I was right there. He bled profusely from the finger where his claw had been ripped out.

Possible Solution(s)

In Za's case, I immediately took him to his designated "treatment area," put him on his heating pad to relax him, then applied direct pressure to the wound. That didn't stop the bleeding, so I put KWIK-STOP (a product that stops minor bleeding; it was in Za's First-Aid Kit) on the wound and applied pressure again for 10 minutes. The bleeding stopped.

During this whole ordeal, Za didn't freak out or panic but sat quietly on the heating pad as I worked on him. He even let me move and touch his injured, bleeding finger without the least resistance. My feeling was that he trusted that whatever I was doing was good for him.

At the end of the day I washed off the KWIK-STOP with Nolvasan and applied Polysporin ointment. Just before he went to sleep I coated the end of his finger with Second Skin (two coats) to protect it in case he jostled or rubbed the wound as he slept.

Yes, I admit I was very stupid to allow my iguana to climb up the front of the file cabinet in the first place. After that experience, I taught Za not to climb anything in the house, except in his habitat and certain "approved" pieces of furniture. Amazingly, the claw grew back normally within a few weeks.

Tail Break

A big piece of his tail broke off last year when he knocked over a flower pot onto his tail. About 5 inches has grown back.

—I-705, Paul & Linda, 45 yrs., California

What Is It?

A broken tail is when any part of an iguana's tail breaks away and is no longer attached. Chapter 1, Iguana: The Species, "Tail," will give you more details on the tail.

When an iguana's tail breaks, it is not like an arm or leg that gets put into a cast. If an iguana's tail breaks, it separates from the rest of the tail and the two parts can't be connected again. Tail breaks happen more frequently to hatchlings and juveniles than to adult iguanas.

My one-year-old iguana had its tail broken off (previous owner). Two years later it has regrown about 5". The new growth is very dark colored, almost black. It does not have spines on it like the original part of the tail has. Also, it is blunt at the end and the scale pattern on the new growth is more irregular.
—I-554, Anthony, 29 yrs., Florida

Symptom(s)

- Some portion of the tail hangs at an unnatural angle
- One day your iguana has a full tail; the next minute part of its tail is no longer connected

Possible Cause(s)

I swear to the iguana gods that I did not grab my iguana by the tail. I had her by the chest, keeping her front legs pinned down, and went to grab her back legs around her back. I touched her tail and POP! off it came, wiggling and spurting blood and everything. I had owned her for only hours, and I am sure that she was stressed out from moving to a new house, which just aggravated her sensitive tail. And who knows? She could have bumped it on the move over. I just know that I did not "pull her tail off." It has grown about two inches since the "tail incident" and it grows in spurts. Sometimes it doesn't grow for months, then all of a sudden I notice, "Hey! Her tail has grown ¼ inch! Wow!"
—I-908, Amy, 26 yrs., Arizona

Even wild iguanas lose their tails; it's part of having to drag a long, fragile appendage behind them all day. The letters I have received over the years indicate that people grabbing their pet iguanas by the tail is the major cause of tail breakage or loss in a captive iguana.

Another cause is when an iguana is struggling full-force to escape from being held. When an iguana gets into this "over-drive" mode, it throws its whole body into the escape. The quick, jerky motion of the tail lashing about often breaks the tail.

Possible Solution(s)

If your lizard starts to run away, <u>never grab its tail</u> for something to hold onto. This one action will prevent the vast majority of tail loss. In addition, if you support your iguana properly, it will be less likely to struggle crazily and thrash its tail about. (See Chapter 8, Domestication, "Holding Your Iguana," for details.) But if the tail does break off, take your iguana to the veterinarian, who will administer the proper treatments to make sure the tail heals properly.

ENVIRONMENTAL CONDITIONS

By now you should understand that your iguana, as a reptile, is dependent on the temperature of its environment to achieve and maintain its own body temperature—and that the correct temperature is crucial for your lizard's health and survival. You can prevent a number of common medical problems simply by paying close attention to the temperature of the habitat, room, or other areas where your iguana spends time.

Too Cold

Oftentimes, what you feel as warm and comfortable can be too cold for your iguana.

What Is It?

Too cold for an iguana means that its temperature is below what is necessary for it to function normally (see Chapter 4, Housing, "Heat"). An iguana that gets cold and stays cold is in a dangerous situation. The longer the lizard remains in this condition, the more problems can occur (e.g., weakened immune system). I know of three iguanas that died after being left out in the house overnight.

Symptom(s)

One extremely hot day I put a large house fan on low in front of my iguana while he was out in the house. The problem was that it was blowing directly on Za. After no more than 30 minutes, I saw that he had a black head and a dark, muddy-green body. He had lost a lot of body heat simply from the fan being on him for half an hour. It was the wind-chill factor we hear so much about that created the cold condition. Remember, reptiles <u>can't produce their own heat.</u>

Iguanas will generally darken in color in an attempt to absorb more available heat. (An exception to this cause of dark coloring is when your iguana may be sick or under stress, when it is also likely to darken.) When cold, your iguana will also slow down, perhaps to the point of no movement and loss of motor skills. One person wrote and said that their iguana was left in an outside enclosure and got so cold it lost its grip on the tree branch and fell off.

Sometimes it seems as if the lessons on iguana care are never-ending.

Possible Cause(s)

The typical reason an iguana gets cold is from lack of attention by the pet owner. Even when the weather appears warm to you, an iguana could be too cool in that same environment. For instance, 75°F usually feels warm to a human, but not necessarily to an iguana. Also, if there is no thermometer in the iguana's habitat, how can you know what the temperature really is?

Possible Solution(s)

Have several thermometers in the habitat (i.e., at the top, middle, and bottom) so you can see the temperature. Whatever your house thermometer reads, remember your iguana crawling around on the floor will be colder (heat rises, cool air sinks). So if the temperature reads 75°F in your living room, it's a good guess that the floor might be 70°F or less. This is not a good temperature for an iguana.

Wind can reduce the perceived temperature (remember the wind-chill factor). Don't let your lizard sit in an open window when the wind is blowing hard, and don't have a fan blowing directly on your iguana, like I did.

If your iguana is dark in color from being cold, or feels cold to the touch, you need to bring the lizard back up to its normal temperature, but not too rapidly. One method is to wrap your iguana in a heating pad on a low temperature, then wrap that in a thick towel or blanket. Another approach is to put your iguana in a bathtub with warm (not hot) water. Because your iguana may be going through severe shock, you will need to hold or support your lizard the whole time it is in the water. If you have to leave the bath area for any reason, the iguana must come out of the water! Once your iguana starts to move about or its body feels warm, towel dry the lizard and put it immediately back in its warm habitat.

If your iguana was out overnight or you feel your lizard was extremely stressed by being too cold or cold for an extended period of time, be sure to see your veterinarian, who will monitor it for possible respiratory problems. Also, keep your lizard caged for several days so it can rebuild some strength and resistance.

Overheating

> *I had the wrong kind of heat in his cage in the beginning and nearly parboiled him.* —I-685, Julie, 36 yrs., California

What Is It?

With the high temperatures that iguanas love, overheating seems like an unlikely proposition. But every creature has its threshold of heat, including iguanas. An iguana overheated for too long will <u>die</u>.

Symptom(s)

> *Once I saw our iguana dehydrated because the room was too dry and hot. The iguana had its mouth open. I gave it water.*
> —I-734, Rusty & June, 24 yrs., Massachusetts

[AUTHOR'S NOTE: This is a typical sign of overheating, not dehydration. But giving water is <u>important</u>, as is taking your iguana out of the overheated area.]

One of the first signs that an iguana may be overheated is if it opens its mouth wide, like a panting dog that has been running loose in the street.

If your lizard gets too hot, it will lose some of its bright color, taking on a somewhat faded appearance. This is a response of the lizard's body to reduce the amount of heat it absorbs. Your iguana may also defecate an unusual number of times in a short period of time while it's overheated.

Possible Cause(s)

My iguana died Sunday from heat exhaustion. I loved him so much and feel so guilty. Please warn others of the risks of leaving their terrarium [cage] next to windows that have full sun exposure, for this is how my iguana died. The temperature had climbed so drastically from the sun's exposure. I was not home at the time and I know he was greatly distressed before he died. It sounds like common sense, I know, but I was so preoccupied that morning that I didn't think when I opened the blinds on the windows.

—I-475, Mary, 22 yrs., California

The most common cause of overheating is when your iguana is left without escape routes in an area that's too hot. An iguana's habitat should have enough safeguards, such as thermostatically controlled cooling fans, to keep the lizard from overheating on hot days.

As an example of a house-related problem, one day my iguana was on his big basking stick that was in front of my 6' living room window. It was early morning and wasn't yet hot in the room. But glass can intensify light and often will hold the heat around a window if there is no breeze in the house.

Luckily I always kept an eye on Za when he was outside of his habitat. All of a sudden, Za's jaw dropped open and his tongue raised up inside his mouth. He appeared to be panting like a dog. I ran over to him, not knowing what was happening to him until I picked him up—he felt like a hot metal pan just out of the oven.

Possible Solution(s)

For this particular situation, I put Za on the couch and sprayed water high above him from a plant sprayer, creating a light mist. You don't want to put a hot lizard in cold water all of a sudden—that would be like putting a hot jar into ice cold water. After the misting, I offered him water from a spoon, which he sucked down immediately.

Several months later, I saw him do the same thing with his mouth, but this time he got off the stick and went immediately to his habitat. On the way, he walked through the tub of water in his habitat, then directly into his (cool) hide area, where he stayed until the next morning. Za knew what he had to do to normalize his body temperature. He probably got stressed out, and needed some time to regroup in the cool box. He never again went through this overheating experience in the house. So why did one time he sit overheated until I moved him, and another time move himself out of the heat? He was only about 10 months old the first time; perhaps he needed one experience to learn from.

What is frightening is that most people are not aware of the potential for their lizard to overheat and don't know the symptoms to watch out for.

Thermal Burns

When I got my iguana her lip was black. About three days later the black part sloughed off, leaving a bloody pink mess and some exposed teeth. So the "interesting coloring" was more likely a thermal burn, possibly from the exposed and too easily accessible heat lamp at the pet store. I applied Neosporin to the lip, and she has also been treated with an injectable antibiotic so the lip wouldn't get infected. The vet said it may never look normal, but it continues to get better every time she sheds.   —I-865, Julie, 46 yrs., California

What Is It?

Several years ago, thermal burns ranked right up there with metabolic bone disease as common medical problems for captive iguanas. Back then I got a phone call or letter several times a month from pet owners who had inadvertently burned their iguanas from improperly protected or placed heat lamps. Now that more herp magazines are being sold that instruct about proper iguana care—as well as new high-tech heating devices for iguanas—incidents of this sad type of injury have been drastically reduced.

But for those people with iguanas who have missed this warning, I will repeat it. Thermal burns are usually caused by three sources: hot rocks, human heating pads, and heat lamps.

Symptom(s)

Hot rock and human heating pad burns are on the belly of an iguana because they lie on these devices. If you don't handle your iguana often, you won't be able to notice if the iguana has been burned. A burned lizard will probably respond with pain as you pick it up. Burns on any other part of the body (mostly from heat lamps) will be easy to notice. The burned area will look discolored, more or less depending on the degree of burn. In severe cases, the skin may appear blistered or blackened.

Possible Cause(s)

All the thermal burns I have seen on iguanas were from unprotected heat lights and what people call "hot rocks." A hot rock is a synthetic "rock" made out of plastic or other materials, with electrical wires embedded on the inside. They often "whack out," causing the temperature of the rock to get so hot that it can burn an iguana severely.

Heat lamps burn iguanas when the lamps are not secured and fall down on the iguana, or when they are put in a place where the lizard can reach or get on top of the hot device.

One other less-common source of burns is human heating pads. I have only heard of two such cases and it's usually a function of not paying attention to the iguana's stomach temperature. I used a human heating pad for my iguana for more than five years and never had a problem. But I never left it on "high," and when it was on "medium" I was always in the room checking my iguana's heat level. In addition, the room temperature was high enough that my iguana wasn't stuck in one spot to keep warm. He could also go back to his habitat, which was always an ideal temperature, whenever he wanted to.

Za's pad was usually on "low," but I still checked his body temperature frequently. Don't just feel the top of your iguana; slip a hand under and feel its belly, because that's where the heat is being generated and where the possible problem could arise. Any heating device can be a problem if not closely monitored.

Turn now to Chapter 4, Housing, "Heat," if you haven't already read it. It will fill you in on all the considerations for providing heat for your iguana.

Possible Solution(s)

The main solution is not to use any type of hot rock. This is not an appropriate way for an iguana to keep warm in a habitat, and neither is a heating pad. Heating pads are used as an additional temporary heat source when your iguana is out of its habitat. If you use a heat lamp of any kind, put it in a place your iguana can never touch or climb on top of, and further protect your lizard by wrapping the bulb with ¼" hardware cloth (wire mesh).

If your iguana does get burned, a minor burn can be handled at home by first cleaning the burned area with Nolvasan or Betadine. Pat the area dry with a clean cloth and then apply a thin coating of Polysporin (antibiotic ointment).

Secondary infections occur if the burn is deep or is not treated promptly. If you have any doubt as to the severity of the burn, see your veterinarian, who can speed your iguana's recovery with advanced care techniques.

My iguana was treated for a thermal burn on her stomach. The vet gave my iguana a cherry-flavored antibiotic fluid, some topical antibiotic ointment, and iodine pads. I gave her the antibiotic fluid twice a day, soaked her with iodine pads, and put the ointment on once a day. She refused to eat [because of the trauma associated with the burn], just like the vet said would probably happen, so I mixed her food up in a blender to make it easier for her to eat. She recovered fully after 3-4 weeks. But she still has the scars on her stomach.
—I-662, Sharman, 22 yrs., Wisconsin

The only serious injury my iguana sustained was a thermal burn from a heat lamp that he pulled down on his tail and rear leg. I was only out of the room for 5-10 minutes, but it was enough to produce a second-degree burn that blistered the area and took many months of intensive treatment to properly heal. There is still a faint scar more than a year later and he has difficulty shedding in this area. I use debridement cream (Derma Clens) and kept the area moist *and clean. Once the area was <u>completely</u> healed, I used a soft bristle scrub brush to encourage a complete shed over the wound area.*

—I-493, Marcia, 40 yrs., Alaska

Dehydration

Iguanas get the majority of their fluids from the foods they eat. But as I've said before, and despite what you may read in other books, iguanas <u>do</u> drink water.

What Is It?

Dehydration is the loss of fluid in a body. Iguanas, like humans, can experience minor loss, such as an athlete involved in vigorous sports activity, or major loss, such as a person lost in a desert for several days without water. If the percent of fluid drops below a certain level, organs start to fail and death can occur.

Symptom(s)

How can you tell if your iguana is dehydrated? Gently "pinch" some of the iguana's skin together. The best testing areas are on the arms or legs. The skin should snap right back to its original position. If it stays up for a few seconds or so, the iguana may need more fluids.

Possible Cause(s)

- Habitat temperature too high
- Fresh water not available
- Overheating when outside
- A combination of lack of water and food low in moisture content

Iguanas need extra water whenever their food intake drops—such as during breeding—and any time their diet consists of lots of dry foods, such as commercial iguana food.

Possible Solution(s)

Make sure that the possible causes mentioned before don't happen. Dehydration is a dangerous condition for a pet. Your iguana can't tell you that it is dying of thirst. It's up to you to <u>always</u> have clean, easily accessible water available for your iguana to drink at any time.

Iguanas usually need to be taught how to drink standing water, and this is covered in Chapter 8, Domestication, "Drinking Water."

As mentioned in a previous section, an overheated iguana will open its mouth and sometimes "pant." If your iguana opens its mouth wide and feels very hot to the touch, spray water gently into your iguana's mouth to help cool it and also add moisture back to its system.

Please be aware of any subtle body language that might indicate thirst. In the advanced stages of dehydration, only your veterinarian can save your iguana with replacement fluids. Don't let the situation get that far.

BEHAVIORAL CONDITIONS

Iguanas react to particular situations or environments with characteristic behaviors. Some of these behaviors are perfectly normal and healthy, while others require action on your part. The next few sections outline a few of the common conditions that cause behavioral changes, as well as some of the behaviors themselves, to help you sort out the benign from the worrisome.

Stress

Stress is a part of living, whether you're a human or an iguana.

What Is It?

Dr. Hans Selye, who is one of the great pioneers in stress research, says there are basically two types of stress: negative and positive. Dr. Selye says, "Stress is not always the non-specific result of damage. Normal activities—a game of tennis or even a passionate kiss—can produce considerable stress without causing conspicuous damage."

For us humans, winning a million-dollar lottery is a positive stress. A low-grade negative stress might be the experience of being trapped in bumper-to-bumper traffic, watching the minutes tick by as a scheduled appointment time slowly slips away.

Covering stress under troubleshooting for a reptile may sound a little strange, but iguanas are creatures deeply responsive to and affected by their environment, and stress is part of their lives. Again, Dr. Selye says, "Stress reactions do occur in lower animals and even plants, which have no nervous system." Mild stress can induce uneasiness; prolonged stress can create dis-ease (i.e., disease).

For your iguana, moving it from a 2' x 2' x 2' cage into a 6' x 6' x 6' habitat would be a positive stress. Moving your lizard from the large habitat to a smaller one would be a negative stress.

There are two basic components of stress: physical and mental. For an iguana, physical stress could come from being bitten by another iguana cagemate. Mental stress may result from the fact that this overly large, dominant, biting male cagemate is still in the same habitat and won't go away. Caged with an aggressive male iguana, your iguana is likely to feel some distress from the situation, which can create a series of negative reactions, including not eating.

Over time, the body of a negatively stressed animal, or human, can suffer a suppression of its immune system. This is like taking the steel plating off a tank. At that point, any simple thing can cause great problems.

Symptom(s)

- Iguana's body turns a dark, muddy color
- Reduces or stops eating
- Defecates more frequently or not at all
- Hides
- Has trouble sleeping or sleeps too much
- Appears "zoned out" or even catatonic; unresponsive
- Conversely, runs around frantically and chaotically
- Shows signs of illness
- In severe cases, death

If an iguana gets "maxed out" on negative stress, it might just close its eyes, or its eyes might get super dilated, wide open like a deer in front of a car's headlights, but without showing any recognition. During this "blank" mode, iguanas might run full speed into habitat walls or other objects in their path. They either don't see the objects or think they can go right through them, and this banging and running continues until they "run out of gas."

> *While cleaning house, I ran the vacuum under my iguana's cage. He bolted, slamming himself into the walls, back and forth, FREAKING OUT. He slowly calmed down. He didn't eat for 4 days. Then he was fine.*
> —I-494, Jim, 25 yrs., California

When I was a carpenter, there was a guy that, every time we were assigned a complicated and urgent project, would run to the portable toilet on the job site and make a stressful deposit. Iguanas are often the same way. Wild-caught iguanas will often defecate on their captors from the stress of being held and transported against their will.

> *She is not terribly fond of being restrained or having her nails trimmed. We have a true power struggle. Afterwards, she sometimes goes straight to her litter box and defecates, even if she's gone earlier that day (more frequent defecation is her typical response to major stress times).*
> —I-706, Melodie, 41 yrs., Tennessee

> *When my iguana gets stressed (like when I vacuum) he turns kind of brownish. When the stress is removed the brown goes away.*
> —I-680, Catherine, 21 yrs., New York

Possible Cause(s)

There is a full smorgasbord of potential stressors for your iguana, from cagemates to vacuum cleaners—too many to list. Just simple over-handling or rough handling can cause your animal to "shock out" for a while, which might mean it stops eating or sleeping normally.

They can become stressed out if handled improperly.
                                        —I-11, Patty, Washington

My dog attacked my 2-year-old iguana one day. Luckily she survived the attack,
which thankfully was more a stressful ordeal than a physical one. She did seem
to go into shock when this happened and remained in a coma-like state for
nearly an hour before coming around.   —I-467, Kris, 32 yrs., Florida

During the 1989 Northern California earthquake, my apartment in Los
Gatos got trashed. My iguana didn't get hurt in the quake, but he went into
what I would call semi-hibernation. His body temporarily shut down, perhaps
to compensate for the overload of physical and emotional stress that the earthquake created. His eyes were closed, his breathing was very shallow, and he
wouldn't open his eyes even when touched. I just left him alone, and made
sure that all the basic needs were there for him—heat, food, water, and a hiding area. I kept a close eye on him, and the next day he came out of his hiding
area and ate a little food.

Not too long after I got my most "wild" iguana [SVL: 10", TL: 2' 7"], he got out
of the cage and ran across the floor into the corner. When he saw me coming
after him, he freaked out and frantically scrambled around and tried to climb
up the wall and was generally terrified. When I caught him, he went into shock.
He was completely paralyzed—only his eyes moved. So I thought if I put him
into a tub of warm water, it might help. Well, when I released him, he sank to
the bottom of the tub. I really believe he would have drowned had I left him
there. He was incapable of moving his body at all. So I put him in a cage for a
while, and it wasn't long until he was moving around and seemed to be OK. He
doesn't appear to have suffered any lasting ill effect and acts like usual. My vet
explained it as like a brain overload from too much stress and the brain shuts
the body down temporarily.   —I-312, Darla, 32 yrs., Ohio
   [AUTHOR'S NOTE: Never put a "shocked" or unresponsive iguana
in water.]

Possible Solution(s)

When he does get stressed out I let him stay in his enclosure without noise or dis-
turbance for a couple of hours. He seems to do well with this method of stress
relief.   —I-638, Jennifer, 23 yrs., California

Watch for aberrant behavior and see if this behavior ties into a certain
event or experience that happened near your lizard, then make sure that the
stressful event doesn't happen again, if possible. Even better, recognize potential stressors before they happen, and prevent them. Over time, it will be easy
to see which things stress your iguana negatively.

One of the best ways to prevent negative stress reactions is to expose your
iguana routinely to new experiences. By slowly, carefully, and safely allowing

your iguana to see all the diversity that life can offer, you'll help your lizard cope more comfortably with a wide range of situations. This is what I did with my iguana, and over time nothing seemed to phase him very much.

Color Changes

A chameleon lizard can change its color to match whatever it is sitting on or near, such as a leaf or branch. An iguana can't do this, but it will get lighter or darker depending on a variety of factors, from temperature to sickness to mood. Although color changes were covered in the previous sections "Too Cold" and "Overheating," and in Chapter 1, Iguana: The Species, it is included here for clarification and to reinforce the concepts.

Turns Darker Color

When they [iguanas] are cold or scared the whole top of them turns black. I saw one iguana that had gotten loose at a pet store turn totally black by the time it was caught.   —I-764, Diana, 46 yrs., California

What Is It?

Your iguana might turn a darker hue of its normal color, or its skin may take on a dark brown, grey, or even blackish color.

Symptom(s)

The iguana's whole body starts to darken in color.

She seems to turn a dark color, almost black (her whole body), when she is upset or cold or when she gets real hot from sitting in the sun a long time.
                    —I-662, Sharman, 22 yrs., Wisconsin

Possible Cause(s)

There are a number of reasons an iguana turns darker, but frequently this is a sign that is something is wrong and that some action is required right away.
   • In the sun, temporary darkening is normal.
   • The iguana is scared or stressed.
   • The iguana is ill.
   • As mentioned before under "Environmental Conditions," iguanas can turn a dark color if they are too cold. They might be trying to absorb more heat to get warm faster, or it might be a stress reaction to being too cold.
As an example, some people I knew let their iguana stay under their couch all afternoon, and when they finally decided to get him out, the lizard was black in color and very cold. If you see that your iguana's color has darkened, pick up the lizard. If it feels like a cold, black banana, it needs to warm up.

Possible Solution(s)

If your iguana happens to be left out in the house and gets too cold, don't just stick it in a fire to warm it up. Turn a heating pad to low or medium and put your iguana on it. Place a large bath towel, doubled in half, on top of your lizard to trap some of the heat from the heating pad, thus speeding up the warming process. Don't turn the heater to "high"—low or medium provides the gradual transition temperature you need. And don't just walk off, but monitor the iguana's body heat as it warms up. Continue this until your iguana feels pleasantly toasty.

An iguana should never turn dark (cold) in its habitat. Don't guess at the temperature. Have several thermometers located at different levels (heights) in the habitat to monitor heat. If you need help with understanding heat in a habitat, read Chapter 4, Housing, "Heat." The stress of being too cold weakens iguanas, and if it happens repeatedly they could get a respiratory disease or other medical problems.

If your iguana turns a dark color and it isn't in the sun, and it isn't too cool, there's something else very wrong. The lizard is either severely stressed or sick.

Muddy Color

A muddy color is usually a sign that your normally green iguana is sick.

What Is It?

Your iguana's body takes on a brownish appearance. It's very apparent that something is wrong.

Symptom(s)

Your iguana has an overall muddy color, or just in the chest area.

Possible Cause(s)

Nearly any kind of medical condition can cause this muddy color, but most likely the lizard is suffering from stress, sickness, or infection. My iguana once fell and the stress of the accident caused him to turn a muddy green on the upper part of his body.

Possible Solution(s)

Call your veterinarian if the muddy color persists, and especially if it is accompanied by other symptoms.

Turns Pale

Turning pale is usually a temporary condition that can be corrected quite easily.

What Is It?

An iguana's body gets pale, as if the color has been washed out of it.

Symptom(s)

My iguana's head would lose its bright color and become pale whenever he was scared or stressed. For example, this happened the first few times he visited his new veterinarian.

Possible Cause(s)

General draining of body color typically indicates stress or overheating.

Possible Solution(s)

Just as an iguana will darken to absorb more heat, it may become lighter in an attempt to deflect heat when its body temperature is too high. If the iguana is overheated, remove it from the heat source and allow it to cool down (see page 388 for more details). For dealing with stress problems, refer to page 393.

Moving Disorder

If anyone still thinks an iguana is just an inert, dull, lifeless creature staring out blankly from its habitat, just try changing its surrounding environment and see what happens!

What Is It?

When an iguana's perception of how its environment should be is changed, it reacts.

Symptom(s)

When he is stressed by moving from one house to another, he eats less.
                              —I-665, Molly, 17 yrs., Oregon

If you move the whole family and the iguana to a new home, the lizard can manifest its confusion about the new situation by eating less, inactivity, mood swings, and even going to a corner of its habitat and hiding. Such temperamental creatures!

Possible Cause(s)

He was very quiet for about 3 days after we moved, but then he perked right up and has been fine ever since.   —I-476, Marie, 23 yrs., Virginia

If the environmental change is for the better (e.g., a move to a larger habitat), it won't take more than a day or so for your iguana to snap back to its old self. But if the change brings a lesser quality of life (e.g., a smaller habitat), your lizard will probably take longer to adjust, or may not snap out of it at all.

Possible Solution(s)

Back in April, when we moved to where we live now, my iguana was stressed. She would bite and defecate when we took her out of her cage. But we continued to take her out and introduce her to her new surroundings. She now seems happy.   —I-622, Sharman, 22 yrs., Wisconsin

I have moved a number of times since adopting my iguana. I think that these moves put a lot of stress on him. His eating habits would fluctuate and he would become quite temperamental. My last move, over a year ago, has proved to be the best environment for both of us. The iguana's temperament improved almost on the day we moved in.
—I-853, Eva & Scott, 25 yrs., New Jersey

You don't need to be afraid of moving your iguana's habitat across the room, across town, or to a new state. All you need to know is that there are some common reactions to these moves, so don't panic. In a short time, life will again be "normal" for both of you.

Hiding

An iguana that hides for too long or too frequently is an unhappy lizard, and this behavior can worsen if it is not corrected.

What Is It?

An iguana prefers to hide part of its head or its whole body from "life."

Symptom(s)

My iguana hides under the newspaper substrate.
—I-586, Joanne, 44 yrs., Florida

If the iguana hides under the substrate in its habitat (especially with a newspaper substrate), sticks its head in the corner of the habitat, or spends most of the day in its hide box (an enclosure designed for occasional reprieve from life—see Chapter 4, Housing, "Hide Box"), you probably have a hiding problem.

Possible Cause(s)

- Iguana still getting used to its new living space
- Habitat too small
- Needs to escape from being looked at too much (usually new iguana)
- Has a cagemate that intimidates it
- Sick, ill, or injured

Possible Solution(s)

Hiding or retreating periodically is a natural response to life for iguanas (and humans). Newly acquired or recently moved animals frequently hide more than usual as they adjust to their new surroundings.

However, excessive hiding is a sign that something is not right. First, make sure your lizard is not sick. Then go down the list of possible causes and correct the ones that may apply to your particular situation.

Nose Rubbing

My iguana had a problem with her nose. She would get excited to come out of her cage and rub her nose on the metal screen door. She rubbed it so hard that it bled. I applied an antibiotic cream, which seemed to help because now it has scabbed over and is almost well.   —I-662, Sharman, 22 yrs., Wisconsin

What Is It?

It's hard to believe, but it seems that an iguana doesn't make the connection that it can't go through glass to escape from its habitat. So in an effort to get free, the lizard will constantly push its nose against the glass (or wire) of its habitat. Sooner or later, its nose will be worn down and start to bleed. Sometimes in a crazy effort to escape, the iguana will also run full-force at the glass, increasing the damage to its face.

Symptom(s)

- Pacing back and forth in front of the glass or wire of the habitat
- Charging or running at the habitat's glass or wire walls
- Worn or bloody nose

Possible Cause(s)

The cause of nose rubbing is that the iguana wants out of its habitat and will do anything to accomplish this goal. Here are a few reasons that the iguana might want to escape from its surroundings:

- Habitat is too small
- Habitat is too hot or too cold
- Habitat is too bright or too dark
- Habitat is too sterile (i.e., walls and nothing else)
- Iguana has another iguana as a cagemate
- Iguana is in breeding (in males, mating hormones can make them restless; in females, might be looking for a place to deposit eggs)
- Iguana sees its reflection in habitat glass

If you find that your iguana is bobbing its head excessively or banging into the cage glass, it might be because the iguana sees its reflection in the glass and thinks there is another iguana outside (they don't see their reflections as themselves, but as another iguana).

Possible Solution(s)

If the rubbing (often called rostral abrasion) and running at the habitat glass or wire isn't stopped immediately, your iguana could have a permanently scarred face. I have seen cases where the nose was so damaged that it didn't grow back correctly and the iguana had trouble eating for the rest of its life.

Some of the easier solutions to the problem could be:

- Make sure the habitat has the proper heat and lighting

- Make the habitat more inviting—and remove any cagemates
- Move some of the "furnishings" or lights in the habitat to create shadows so the lizard will perceive the glass as a barrier
- Take a black felt-tip pen and draw bars or grids on the outside of the habitat glass to create a visual barrier, or blacken out a section of the glass with dark paper
- Erect physical barriers so the iguana can't get to the glass
- Let the iguana out to have some controlled free time in the house

The best solution is often a larger habitat for your lizard. Most of the iguanas I have seen over the years with rostral abrasions have been kept in a "prison cell" existence: four walls and a ceiling that are too close together. Judging from the experience of people who have written to me asking for corrective measures, enlarging the iguana's "home" is the one solution that works most often. The next most effective solution is a fake plant barrier (see Chapter 4, Housing, "Artificial Plants," for some ideas).

Don't use regular wire screen (hardware cloth) as a cage material, because it's likely to damage the iguana's nose or face. Instead, use the hard plastic netting I recommend in Appendix D, "Door."

If you have a sterile habitat, add climbing limbs, plants (real or artificial), rocks, and ledges. All these things create more natural surroundings and make the iguana feel more at home—and less likely to want to escape.

During breeding, while my iguana was whacked out on sex hormones, he would launch himself against the glass of his habitat in an attempted attack of anyone walking by. I couldn't stop his hormones, but I did place a black strip of paper on the inside of the habitat, in front of the area where he was hitting the glass, to prevent him from seeing us walk by. In this particular case, the paper was put on the inside of the habitat to eliminate any possibility of Za seeing us or his reflection in the glass.

Medical Solutions

If your iguana has already suffered rostral abrasions or other injuries from face rubbing, in addition to preventing the behavior, you also need to treat the injuries.

For minor damage: Wash the area with Betadine solution, then apply an antibiotic cream or ointment (the kind used for minor cuts). For major damage: See your veterinarian, who can give antibiotic injections and perhaps a stronger prescription antibiotic cream.

DIGESTIVE SYSTEM PROBLEMS

Iguanas can suffer from a full range of digestive disorders. While some digestive problems are caused by disease, iguanas are also extremely sensitive to their environment, and disruptions can cause them to reduce their appetite or suffer digestive troubles. It's also important that you understand fully the relationship between proper heat and your iguana's digestive system (see Chapter 5, Feeding, "Digestion: Special System," if you have any questions).

Appetite: Reduced or Stopped

Not eating is the ultimate in picky eating by your iguana. Lack of appetite is not a disease, but rather a symptom of something else.

What Is It?

Often you will hear the medical term "anorexia" used when an animal (or human) lacks appetite or stops eating on its own. If an iguana stops eating, something is wrong. Healthy iguanas eat every day. Contact your veterinarian if this continues longer than a couple of days. An exception is if your lizard is obviously sick or injured, in which case you should see the veterinarian right away.

Another exception is when your sexually mature lizard (male or female) is in breeding season. In this case, you can relax a little on the two-day minimum. Breeding and the effects on appetite are explained later in this section and in Chapter 9, Breeding.

Symptom(s)

Your iguana refuses to eat, reduces its food intake dramatically for more than a couple days in a row, picks at its food (unless it's an unfamiliar or disliked food!), or consistently backs away from its food. The key impression is that your lizard shows a noticeable break in its <u>normal</u> eating patterns.

Possible Cause(s)

There is always a reason your iguana stops eating.
                                        —I-775, Karen, 37 yrs., Arizona

Every once in a while he [SVL: 11½", TL: 2' 10½", 2½ yrs.] will refuse food for a day or two—not enough to concern me, though.
                                        —I-916, Lucretia, 32 yrs., California

Habitat Temperature Too Cool

Lower ambient temperatures severely inhibit digestion.
            —Behavior & hormone interactions research project (#7)

. . . when they [iguanas] succeeded in raising their body temperatures to about 30°C [86°F] by basking, they would also eat some food.   —H. Mendelssohn, iguana researcher (#6)

So many times I have had calls, "My iguana hasn't eaten in two weeks and it is very lethargic." And most of the time by then the iguana usually doesn't make it. One case the iguana only lived one hour after I was called. By the time

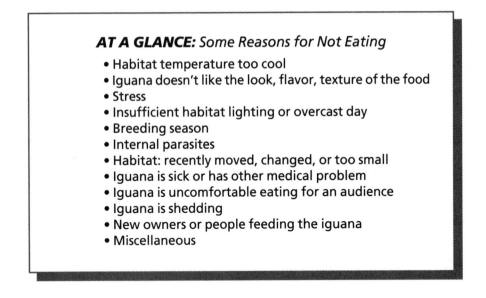

AT A GLANCE: Some Reasons for Not Eating
- Habitat temperature too cool
- Iguana doesn't like the look, flavor, texture of the food
- Stress
- Insufficient habitat lighting or overcast day
- Breeding season
- Internal parasites
- Habitat: recently moved, changed, or too small
- Iguana is sick or has other medical problem
- Iguana is uncomfortable eating for an audience
- Iguana is shedding
- New owners or people feeding the iguana
- Miscellaneous

I got hold of the vet the iguana was dead. The problem was the iguana had been cold and he did not have adequate heat after two weeks of not eating. The iguana got an upper respiratory infection and died. If the owner would have called on day 3, we could have saved this 8-pound, 5-year-old male iguana. If they stop eating, there is a reason and something needs to be done.
—Florida Iguana Rescue

In colder weather they tend to eat every other day, especially when it's cloudy.
—I-780, Carl, Florida
[AUTHOR'S NOTE: This pet owner lives in southwest Florida and keeps his iguanas in outdoor cages.]

He [SVL: 14½", 3 yrs. 2 mo., 6 lbs.] seldom eats on cold or rainy days.
—I-619, Deborah, 38 yrs., Florida

These quotations are all great arguments for why your iguana needs a temperature-controlled habitat. See Chapter 4, Housing, "Heat," for suggestions on how to make this happen.

Iguana Doesn't Like the Look, Flavor, or Texture of the Food

I have found that often when they do not eat, it is because they do not have a taste for what is in the bowl, especially in winter. After adding a favorite food to the mix they will often start eating. Usually once they start eating they will eat more than just their favorite food. —I-764, Diana, 46 yrs., California

One person called and said his iguana was not eating much food. One of the problems, it turned out, was that the food was presented in pieces that were too big. He called me back the next day all excited because his iguana had doubled the amount it normally ate. The food, now chopped and grated into smaller, more easily swallowed pieces, was "gobbled up."

Stress

Occasionally he will skip eating a day (especially if there is unusual, increased activity around his cage).   —I-46, Sue, 32 yrs., New York

After Northern California's 1989 earthquake, my iguana did not eat for a day. I would guess that his not eating was a result of the violent shaking of my apartment (and his habitat) during the initial 7.1 magnitude shock and the significant aftershocks that continued through the next day. In fact, the first jolt was so strong that it almost knocked Za's habitat over. No wonder he lost his appetite!

A more chronic form of stress that can thwart an iguana's appetite is having to share a habitat with another iguana, especially a larger or more dominant animal. See Chapter 4, Housing, "Cagemates," for further explanation.

Insufficient Lighting or Overcast Day

He [SVL: 14½", 3 yrs. 2 mo., 6 lbs.] seldom eats on cold or rainy days.
                    —I-619, Deborah, 38 yrs., Florida

An iguana identifies its food by seeing it. If the light is too dim, your lizard might miss or skip meals. If the habitat has the proper lighting, it shouldn't matter if it's overcast outside, unless your lizard has free range in your house. If this is the case and your iguana misses a meal, make the lizard stay in the warm, lighted habitat the next day until it eats.

Breeding Season

He never refuses to eat except during breeding season, when his other head does all the thinking.   —I-791, Dan, 28 yrs., Missouri

I also discovered that my male iguana will barely pick at or refuse food during mating season, which begins around early November and ends in mid-January.
                    —I-200, Dianna, 47 yrs., Washington

During breeding season both male and female iguanas can either reduce the amount of food consumed each day, skip several days, start eating again, or any combination of these, or just plain come to a screeching halt and refuse to eat. You can offer your lizard its favorite food, stick it right in its face, and the iguana will often look at the food like it's invisible.

In the wild, iguanas change their eating habits during breeding season, so it's not surprising that they often do the same thing in captivity. A couple of times my iguana did not eat for three days, then maybe on the fourth day he would eat a little or a lot. Even so, he lost very little weight, because all year he had been eating and storing fat for this time of year.

For more information on feeding habits during breeding, look at Figure 5.2, a graph of iguana food consumption, in Chapter 5, Feeding. From this one case study, you will get a feel for the normal daily food intake of a male iguana over a five-year period. Look at the breeding months (October through January) on the chart and you will notice that when the iguana became sexually mature, his food consumption dropped dramatically during these months.

Breeding season also affects sexually mature female iguanas' appetite. They can produce eggs with or without a male iguana, and as the eggs get larger they take up space inside the female that's normally reserved for food and digestion. If your lizard is sexually mature and it's breeding season, read Chapter 9, Breeding, for what you might expect.

She [SVL: 17", TL: 3' 6", 7 yrs., 8 lbs.] quit eating for at least six weeks before she laid eggs. After laying the eggs her appetite returned.
—I-554, Anthony, 29 yrs., Texas

Our female iguana [SVL: 16½", TL: 3' 11½", 3 yrs., 5½ lbs.] stops eating when she is about to lay her eggs—usually about 3 weeks before they are laid.
—I-616, Jonathan, 27 yrs., Connecticut

She quits eating about 4-6 weeks before laying eggs.
—I-509, Troy, 30 yrs., Missouri

Internal Parasites

My lizard had been a very finicky eater. I took him to the vet and it turns out my iguana had worms. Now that he is finished with the deworming medication, he is starting to eat like normal again. —I-918, Kay, 48 yrs., Wyoming

My iguana stopped eating for 8 days when I was getting her dewormed for her pinworms. The veterinarian said to let her get hungry and she will eat. Boy, did she!! —I-840, Lorraine, 32 yrs., Ohio
[AUTHOR'S NOTE: Often an iguana will go off its daily routine a little when on medication, but this is too long without eating.]

An iguana's reduced food intake is often caused by internal parasites. Be sure to read the earlier section on "Parasites: Worms and 'Bugs'" in this chapter.

Habitat: Recently Moved, Changed, or Too Small

Iguanas don't like change. Routines and familiarity make them feel safe and secure. As I said earlier, if your family moves to a new house, or you move your iguana's habitat a long or short distance from its original position, your lizard may stop eating for a day or two. Also, if you put your iguana into a smaller habitat, your lizard will probably reduce or stop eating. Putting your lizard into a smaller habitat is <u>not</u> a good idea.

Below are some normal experiences that iguana owners have related to me over the years about their iguanas "going off feed" because of habitat changes.

> *He became anorexic for four or five days after I brought him home from being boarded for 2 months. Also I had moved, so that he was unfamiliar with his surroundings. I took him to the vet and she gave him an injection of calcium and vitamin B to stimulate his appetite. He began eating the next day.*
> —I-493, Marcia, 40 yrs., Alaska

> *When I first got my iguana he stopped eating. He was moved twice in as many days and didn't eat the first day I had him. He adjusted quickly and ate the next day.*
> —I-749, Charles, 27 yrs., California

> *When we went on vacation we took our two juvenile iguanas to a friend's house. Over a period of 2-3 days they ate less each day until they weren't eating anything. When we brought them home they resumed their normal habits.*
> —I-523, Ron, 26 yrs., Illinois

> *My iguana has quit eating for a day or more on a few occasions. I am a college student and live in an apartment near campus with my iguana. When I go home for Christmas or summer break, I take my iguana with me. He usually goes off food for the first few days after he is moved. Feeding always resumes afterward.*
> —I-892, Steve, 22 yrs., Illinois

Iguana is Sick or Has Other Medical Problem

When any animal is sick, including humans, appetite is often the first thing to shut down. Our bodies are letting us know that healing is taking place and food needs to be skipped or reduced. If your iguana stops eating and you don't know why, pay attention and find out if your lizard is sick. Work through all the common iguana medical problems listed in this chapter, and see if any of the descriptions fit. Call your veterinarian if you need additional help.

> *She had surgery because she was egg-bound. Two clutches of eggs were removed as well as her ovaries. It took her 3 weeks of care to begin eating normally again. I brought her home for "personal" care rather than leaving her at the vet's.*
> —I-899, Barbara, 49 yrs., Texas

> *My iguana refused to eat. I took him to the vet and the iguana had an abscess inside his mouth that was removed. With antibiotics, the lump got smaller every day and was gone in about 4 weeks. [Because of his mouth problem] I had to force feed the iguana with an eyedropper for 3 weeks.*
> —I-703, Renee, 22 yrs., New York

My iguana quit eating for two or three days when he was fighting a cold. Time, plus a shot from the vet, and he started eating again.
                                            —I-371, Brent, 32 yrs., Minnesota

Iguana Uncomfortable Eating for an Audience

He [iguana] is fairly nonchalant about human presence except when he's hungry.   —I-508, Bryan, 27 yrs., Kentucky

Iguanas usually prefer to eat in private when you first bring them home, until they feel safe in their habitat. This is especially true of hatchlings. Once they feel safe, iguanas eat like hungry pigs whether people are around or not.

Iguana is Shedding

One of the things I asked pet owners on my iguana questionnaire was whether their iguana had any problems during the shedding process. Only a handful of the people who responded said that their iguana would modify its eating habits during this time. Change in eating habits is definitely a minority response, but worth mentioning, especially if it's happening to your lizard. Most iguanas go through the shedding process with no change in any behaviors.

He [SVL: 7", TL: 2', 1 yr.] perhaps eats a bit less during his shedding time or just before.   —I-855, Paul & Meredith, 15 & 47 yrs., Oregon

He [SVL: 17", TL: 4' 4", 5 yrs.] stops eating once in a while when he's shedding heavily. He won't eat for a day.   —I-476, Marie, 23 yrs., Virginia

See Chapter 6, Special Care, in which the section on "Shedding" covers everything you ever wanted to know about the process and your iguana's possible reactions to this natural occurrence.

New Owners or New People Feeding Your Iguana

She didn't eat for a week when I left her at the vet's while I was gone for 10 days.   —I-899, Barbara, 49 yrs., Texas

As I have said before, change an iguana's routine or surroundings and the lizard's behavior can slowly unravel for a while. This includes not only a new home or location, but also different people supplying the food each day. The good thing is that they adapt to these changes eventually.

Miscellaneous

Sometimes things come up that don't fit into any category of basic problems.

At one point my iguana stopped eating regularly and acquired diarrhea. This went on and off for 2 or 3 months. During this time I changed his diet, excluding some watery food products and adding dry products. I also had his stool

checked for parasites and checked the red color-coated light bulbs in his habitat to make sure they were not Teflon-coated. I kept the heat in the cage way above 88°F (but not above 100°) for 10 hours each day; misted him with warm water twice a day; changed water dishes once every 12 hours instead of every 24 hours; and increased his time spent out of doors in actual sunlight.

He did not have parasites and nothing I did made any difference. I was very frustrated and concerned with dehydration. I increased the vitamins and went back to giving him very watery food products.

By now I was in tears and very sure that I had created the problems and because of my ignorance could not figure out what I needed to do to correct the situation. So as a last resort (which should have been my first) I sat down and thought very hard: <u>*What has happened or what changes have I made to the iguana's life immediately before this started?*</u>

One of the things I remembered was that I bought him a new basket to go inside his cage. I buy baskets that you would put plants or fruit inside to decorate your home. I turn them upside down and cut a hole in each side and use it as a hiding box for my iguana in the cage. As with anything made of wood, I soaked it in hot water and put it in the oven on a low temperature to sterilize it.

Well, I have a very hard time smelling because of allergies, but every once in a while when I got in the iguana's cage I could smell this unusual smell. I finally decided that the smell was coming from his basket. I took it out and examined it. I noticed it had been coated with something to make it shine. Sure enough, whatever they coated this basket with was toxic when heated up. I found another basket made of natural material with no coating on it to replace the toxic one.

He went back to eating regularly almost immediately, and the diarrhea gradually stopped within about 2 weeks.   —I-656, Peggy, 34 yrs., Texas

[AUTHOR'S NOTE: I love people like this. They encounter a problem and just don't let anything stop them from making sure their iguana doesn't suffer or die. Remember this story, because there may be odd problems you will have to solve by yourself that are not covered in this or any other book.

A great help in problem-solving is the daily log, which I talked about toward the beginning of this chapter. Just a little note each day: "no changes," "normal day," "I added a new shiny basket today," "my iguana seemed to walk more on its left rear foot than the right one," etc.]

Possible Solution(s)

An iguana that stops eating can continue this pattern for a long time. It's as though they forget how to eat. All the solutions to the individual problems are grouped together here because most solve themselves in time (i.e., moving, breeding, shedding, owner on vacation, etc.). But a few specific problems that need solving are addressed individually.

• Medical problems (internal parasites, sick, etc.)—Because you will be going to a veterinarian to solve the medical problem, make sure the veterinarian also addresses your iguana's not eating and gives you instructions for correcting the specific situation.

- Temperature—read Chapter 5, Feeding, "Digestion: Special System," for the importance of proper heat for your iguana's digestion and appetite.
- Food—it sounds simple, but make sure you're offering your iguana the right food, in the right form, at the right time of day. Again, see Chapter 5, Feeding, for details.
- Habitat—besides the right temperature, make sure it provides the proper lighting, space (including height), ventilation, and privacy. Review Chapter 4, Housing, for all the elements you need to consider.
- Stress—find the cause and eliminate it. Also re-read page 393 on "Stress" for helpful hints.
- Cagemate—remove any cagemates from your anorexic iguana's habitat and set each animal up in its own habitat.

Here are a few additional solutions that may help increase your iguana's appetite.

Warm Baths

Half an hour or so in a warm (not hot, not cold) bath can sometimes stimulate a lethargic appetite.

Direct Sunlight

Unless the weather doesn't permit it, get your anorexic iguana out in direct natural sunlight for 30 minutes to an hour, or more, as often as possible. Sunlight is great not only for your iguana's appetite, but also for its general health.

Force Feeding

I had to force feed him with a syringe [without needle] for 2 weeks.
                              —I-638, Jennifer, 23 yrs., California

If your iguana quits eating, you and your veterinarian may decide at some point that force feeding is necessary to get your iguana's eating patterns back on track. (Be aware that there might be instances, such as during breeding season, where it's perfectly all right for your iguana to go for some time without eating.) The mildest form of force feeding is simply to put the food bowl up to your lizard's face to entice it to eat.

The next level up is having to gently open the lizard's mouth and stick in some finely chopped food. The easiest way to do this is to roll the finely chopped food in a soft leaf of kale, collard green, or romaine lettuce, like a burrito. Hold the leaf in front of your lizard and let the iguana bite off sections. This "burrito" technique is to "prime the pump," to get your lizard interested in food again—the taste, smell, and feel of real food.

If the iguana won't open its mouth to even test this food, you need to take control. To get an iguana's mouth open for force feeding, pull down slowly on its dewlap (close to the end of the chin)—so slowly that you can hardly see anything happening. This is NOT a quick or jerking motion, just slight pressure downward. At this slow pace, the iguana will not feel threatened and will usually relax its jaw. If you pull too fast, the iguana might jerk its head away. Make sure you are not near the lizard's throat, but out near the chin. Remember, all parts of an iguana's body can be injured if roughly handled.

Once the lizard's mouth is open, use the free hand to offer the burrito. Keep your fingers outside of the iguana's mouth at all times. As the sign says above the power machinery, "Keep your hand clear of all moving parts." Many people have told me how they were severely bitten, accidentally, while opening their iguana's mouth to force-feed or give medication.

> *I used to use my fingers to get her mouth open; now I follow my vet's advice and use a credit card. I slide it in flat, then gently turn the card and the mouth opens*
> —I-795, Dawn, 24 yrs., Ohio

If the burrito technique doesn't work and your iguana still won't eat, it's time for real force feeding. You will need to ask your veterinarian if he/she recommends force feeding your iguana (with a syringe minus the needle). If yes, get him or her to show you exactly how to do this. Force feeding is another one of those situations (like giving injections) where words may not be enough to completely explain how the process is done. There are also a few possible complications that could come up, which the veterinarian can explain.

> *At first it was time-consuming force feeding my two iguanas, but I got it down to an art. It took about 10 minutes to force-feed both iguanas when they were sick.* —I-605, Laura, 31 yrs., Canada

> *Right now I am force feeding my iguana. It's stressful for her and sometimes her teeth bleed from biting on the syringe.*
> —I-183, Mary, 24 yrs., Massachusetts

To prevent an iguana from accidentally biting down onto the hard plastic of the syringe, some veterinarians attach a small rubber hose or tubing to the end of the syringe. The food is pumped from the syringe through the tube and into the iguana's mouth, where the tube can rest comfortably. It is important that the tube fit tightly over the syringe so it doesn't come loose and fall down your iguana's throat.

Have your veterinarian demonstrate how to do force feeding and correct anything you might be doing wrong. The veterinarian will also explain what foods and supplements, if any, need to be included in the food formula. But don't let your iguana be fed this way any longer than absolutely necessary, as they can get addicted to this force feeding routine and only accept food this way. In a week or less, they should come around to eating on their own.

He had stopped eating so I was force feeding him, but before long he would open his mouth for the food and seemed to enjoy this pampering very much.
—I-434, Karen, 39 yrs., New York

My iguana became so dependent on my giving her food via eyedropper (mixture of sugar, mashed guinea pig pellets, cream of wheat, vitamins, and honey made into a liquid mixture to go through the eyedropper) that she refused to eat on her own for several weeks after the bandages were removed. She would not take solid food unless I gave it to her with my fingers! Gradually, I got her to take some food on her own when I gave her favorites (e.g., cantaloupe) right in front of her.
—I-100, Char, 44 yrs., Illinois

Prolapse

Since we are discussing digestive system problems, now is a good time to talk about the other end of the digestive tract. Even here at the cloaca (vent), problems can occur.

What Is It?

"Prolapse" is just a fancy word for "the falling or slipping out of place of an internal organ, as a uterus or rectum" (*Webster's New World Dictionary*). If you see soft-looking tissue hanging out of an iguana's cloaca (vent), it could be part of its intestines. This is called an intestinal prolapse.

An intestinal prolapse should not be confused with the normal observation of a sexually mature male iguana's hemipenes extending from the vent, especially if it's breeding season.

Hemipenes look like globs of soft flesh, but are actually the male iguana's two penises. The hemipenes normally come out during sexual intercourse, masturbation, or sometimes at the final push of defecation. The important point is that if they come out during these normal activities, it should be for only a very short period of time (a few seconds for defecation, maybe a minute or so for masturbation, and no more than half an hour for breeding). I knew a couple of iguanas whose hemipenes stayed out of their bodies all day, and this is another kind of prolapse called "hemipene prolapse."

Symptom(s)

You can physically see flesh hanging on the outside of the iguana's body at the vent.

Possible Cause(s)

As one veterinarian told me, if an iguana's hemipenes come out and stay out, there has to be a reason. Hemipene prolapse is not common and it appears that no one is sure what causes it. One iguana I heard of had a hemipene prolapse and ended up having cancer in this area. Was the prolapse a reaction to the cancer? There's no way to be sure—and not all prolapsed hemipenes are cancerous. But don't ignore prolapsed hemipenes.

For an intestinal prolapse, the cause might be internal parasites, a bacterial infection, constipation, or straining during defecation.

About a week after I obtained my iguana, I noticed that she had a cloacal prolapse. I took her to the vet and he said that prolapse was often caused by internal parasites. He checked a fecal sample, found worms, gave medication to get rid of them, then repaired the prolapsed cloaca and put a few stitches to hold everything in place until healed. The stitches were taken out in two weeks.
—I-846, Bobby, 19 yrs., Texas

Possible Solution(s)

My iguana had an intestinal prolapse. He had this thing out of his rear, so I called around and this one receptionist knew what I was talking about. Apparently this is not uncommon in iguanas. The vet pushed it in, put in two sutures, and we applied ointment. Three weeks later he's eating and defecating and has gained 4 grams [of body weight].
—phone conversation with pet owner

For a hemipene prolapse, a hemipenis that is sticking out for more than a few minutes up to, say, half an hour needs to be returned back inside the vent. Returning the hemipenis to its internal, natural position is a delicate procedure that <u>should be performed by a veterinarian who has done it before</u>. I have done the procedure, and another time the veterinarian and I worked together, and it's still difficult. It can't be stuffed back in like clothes into a duffel bag, because it will just pop out again and you could injure the delicate tissue. A hemipenis rolls out of itself. It's kind of like if you rolled your sock down your leg. In order to get the sock back up your leg again, you have to reverse the process.

It becomes more difficult the longer the hemipenis is left out. In time, the hemipenis, which is soft, moist tissue, can become swollen, inflamed, and dry, making it extremely difficult to "roll" back into the iguana's body. Keeping the hemipenis moist while it is outside the iguana's body helps it from drying out and swelling. Spray water on the hemipenis until you can see the veterinarian, but don't wait long.

If a prolapsed hemipenis can't be rolled back properly because of swelling and dryness, it may have to be amputated. Obviously, this is a task for the veterinarian to handle.

But the biggest question you need to answer is, "Why did this happen in the first place?" It's a signal that something isn't right. Perhaps by reviewing your iguana's log book and talking with your veterinarian, you can find and solve the underlying problem.

My iguana [SVL: 10", TL: 2' 9", 2 yrs.] suffered a prolapse. Fortunately I was home so I got fairly prompt help for him. The prolapse could not have hap-

pened more than 20 to 30 minutes before I noticed. I immediately got a box to transport him, lined it with a towel, misted the towel and his prolapsed tissue, and set out for the vet. He went through the minor surgery and anesthetic pretty well considering he was already weakened.

—I-852, Debi, 35 yrs., Oregon

For an intestinal prolapse, the solution depends mostly on how long the intestines have been hanging out. That's why it's important to handle and examine your lizard every day. Only a veterinarian can solve the problem. He or she will usually re-insert the tissue and secure it in place with stitches. This solves the immediate problem, but as with the hemipene prolapse, you still need to get to the root cause of the prolapse to make sure it doesn't happen again.

Regurgitation and Vomiting

I used to hear that an iguana could not regurgitate or vomit because of the structure of its mouth and throat. But I have seen it firsthand and know that they can, although it's not common.

What Is It?

Regurgitation is the voluntary or involuntary process in which your iguana brings solids and/or liquids from its upper digestive tract back out of its body through its mouth. Vomiting specifically refers to the expulsion of food (partially digested) from the stomach through the mouth.

Be aware that lizards don't regurgitate or vomit easily, and when they do, it's often a sign that they are seriously ill. The one iguana that I saw do this died a few hours later.

Symptom(s)

You see fluid and/or other material being expelled from your lizard's mouth, or you find the material near the iguana or in its habitat.

Possible Cause(s)

Theoretically, a number of situations could cause an iguana to vomit. Possible causes could be rough handling of the lizard just after it has eaten, low habitat temperature, tumors, abscesses, eating poisonous or foreign material, or bacterial or parasite infection. I have been gathering information on iguanas for many years, and I have heard of only two cases of iguanas regurgitating.

Possible Solution(s)

If regurgitation or vomiting happens other than in response to low habitat temperature or after handling, improper feeding, or eating too much at one feeding, call your veterinarian at once for advice and help. It may be that your lizard has eaten some bad food, has worms or other intestinal infection, or has eaten some object in your house that isn't iguana food (paper clips, clothing, buttons, etc.). It's also possible that your iguana is in real trouble and needs immediate medical care.

FECES PROBLEMS

You may not like the homework assignment for this section, but it's required to pass the class.

A minimum of twice a week, when your iguana defecates, take a long look at the color, structure, consistency, length, diameter, and smell of its feces. You don't have to stick your nose in it, just notice any odors it may be emitting. Ideally, if you check your lizard's feces each time you clean out the habitat, you will start to see a pattern for what's normal for your iguana. Once you know what your iguana's feces normally look and smell like, you have a baseline from which to judge changes.

An iguana's feces construction is much like that of a bird: Solid and liquid comes out all at one time (one orifice for excretion). The urine is not watery like humans', but more solid, soft, and creamy colored. The feces of an iguana are usually brown and semi-solid, but the color and consistency can be affected by what foods the iguana eats.

> *I gave my iguana red chard <u>once</u>. My girlfriend came home and saw the lizard shitting—she was convinced the iguana was bleeding internally and was rather hysterical about the "blood" mingled in the shit.*
> —I-762, Brian, 33 yrs., California

Runny Feces/Diarrhea

As I said earlier, iguana feces are normally solid rather than liquidy.

What Is It?

The difference between runny defecation and diarrhea is the frequency and number of defecations per day.

Symptom(s)

- Fluidy, loose stools
- Frequent, runny defecations

Possible Cause(s)

The most common cause for runny feces is recently eaten food that contained a high percentage of water (such as fruit). The problem is compounded if foods like these are eaten several days in a row. Diarrhea is usually the result of infection by a bacterium, virus, or other organism. Some other possible causes include:

- Temperature in the habitat too high

- Temperature in the habitat too low (food not properly digested)
- Drastic change in the diet or a poor diet
- Eating contaminated food
- Parasites
- Disease
- Stress

Possible Solution(s)

If your iguana gets soft feces once in a while, don't worry. What you are concerned about is runny feces occurring frequently. To stop runny feces, tear a piece of fresh bread into little crumbs and add some of the crumbs to your iguana's food. This will add bulk to the meal and help absorb the fluids.

If you believe your iguana has diarrhea, get your lizard checked by a reptile veterinarian as soon as you can. He or she may have to prescribe some medication to stop an infection or get rid of parasites. In addition, you can review what you are feeding your iguana to make sure its diet is appropriate.

Having been to Latin American countries many times, I have personally experienced "Montezuma's Revenge" firsthand, where the diarrhea (with a capital "D") never seemed to stop. Many people and animals can get very dehydrated from such frequent defecation, so fluids need to be replaced. This can be done by drinking more fluids or, in extreme cases, by intravenous (IV) replacement. Your iguana can die from being dehydrated too long, which is why it's important to see your veterinarian if the cause of the diarrhea is something other than overheating or a meal of overly watery food.

Smelly Feces

P-U!!!

What Is It?

What's smelly to you may not be smelly to someone else, though in general all feces emit an odor. But there is a certain odor level that everyone could agree stinks! If your lizard's feces have always had a certain smell and then suddenly they really stink, check to see what food was offered the previous day or several days before.

Symptom(s)

Your iguana's feces smell significantly stronger or different than normal.

Possible Cause(s)

The food source is almost always the cause of smelly feces. "You are what you eat," after all. When my iguana had black beans or other vegetable-based proteins, his feces would often smell. Individual humans react to certain foods by producing extra-smelly feces—and it's the same with iguanas. Perhaps your iguana reacts unfavorably to corn, for instance.

Salmonella—Protect Yourself

IMPORTANT!! For your safety and health, wash your hands with warm, soapy water before and after handling an iguana, its bedding, feces, or body fluids and after providing any medical care. Your iguana may be carrying salmonella bacteria.

> The U.S. Department of Agriculture has said that 4 million Americans become sick each year and up to 3,000 people die from poisoning from meat and poultry contaminated by the salmonella and campylobacter bacteria. —Reuters News Service, March 1996

When you hear the term salmonella poisoning, you probably think about someone eating undercooked meat or eggs. But in the last couple of years, there has been an increase in the number of reports of iguanas being the source of salmonella contamination in humans. (By the way, when an animal has a disease that can contaminate or infect humans, it is called a zoonotic disease.)

In humans, salmonella poisoning is mostly a minor ailment for healthy adults, producing symptoms such as abdominal pain, vomiting, or diarrhea. But for high-risk groups—including very young children, the elderly, chronically ill people, pregnant women, and others with weakened immune systems—salmonella can be fatal. Even if you're not at high risk, you don't want to get this type of bacteria in your body.

With iguanas, the main culprit for transmitting the salmonella organism is the iguana's feces. If your iguana has salmonella and it steps in its feces and then accidentally scratches you (opening your skin), you could

---

The second possible cause could be a "bad bug" affecting the internal organs.

Possible Solution(s)

Again, first look at your iguana's log book to see what foods have been offered in the previous three days. Track any suspicious food for a while in the log book. If any come up as "smell creators," reduce them at the next meal.

There is a very slim chance that the cause is a virus or bacteria. If this is the cause, other symptoms will usually occur, such as lack of appetite, listlessness, and changes in normal behavior patterns. If these other factors come into play, contact your veterinarian for help in determining the source of the problem.

become infected. If you clean your iguana's substrate and touch the fecal matter, and later pick up something to eat without first washing your hands, you could become infected.

Any time you handle your iguana or anything it has touched (food, water bowl, substrate, etc.), you need to thoroughly wash your hands and other body parts that your iguana or its habitat items may have touched. This is a sensible and intelligent thing to do, even if your iguana doesn't have salmonella.

You can have your iguana's feces tested to see if it has salmonella, but because of the nature of the organism it may take several tests at different times to verify the results positively or negatively.

If your iguana has salmonella, most of the time it won't affect the lizard. As of now, there doesn't appear to be a medicine or treatment to wipe out the salmonella organism permanently from an iguana. But there is always hope that future research will produce something.

Douglas R. Mader, DVM, a renown herp veterinarian and a contributing writer for *Reptiles* magazine, wrote an article that appeared in the April 1994 issue of that magazine about salmonella and pet reptiles. This was his concluding statement:

> To put this whole problem in perspective, herpetologists and pet reptile owners are at a greater risk of contracting Salmonellosis from uncooked chicken than they are from handling reptiles, if good hygiene is practiced. A conscious effort at maintaining sanitary animal quarters, with proper attention to personal hygiene, will minimize the risk of infection with *Salmonella* bacteria.

Constipation

Some people have written to me and said that their iguana may not defecate every day—some to the extreme of not defecating for more than a week. If your iguana is eating normally every day but doesn't defecate, it is constipated.

What Is It?

What goes in must come out! If your iguana eats every day on a regular basis, it should defecate every day.

Symptom(s)

Your iguana does not defecate on a daily basis, as is normal.

Possible Cause(s)

Our iguana began ingesting gravel and dirt and had a blockage, which was cleared with Laxatone (the stuff used to get rid or hairballs in cats). This was given to her via a plastic syringe (no needle attached!) by our vet.
—I-724, Joan, Florida

Some of the sources of constipation can be related to food, temperature, stress, infection, blockage by foreign objects (e.g., improper substrate material, objects on the floor of your house), or internal parasites. One owner reported erratic feces in his iguana, then none for a couple of days. It turns out that the lizard had been eating the small gravel on the floor of the cage (substrate) and the gravel was building up in its digestive tract.

Possible Solution(s)

First, try to pinpoint the source of your iguana's constipation. As mentioned in the section on parasites, worms multiplying over time in your iguana can form a blockage in the intestine, which can hinder normal defecation. Take a fecal sample to your veterinarian to check for parasites.

Temperature is crucial to normal digestion in iguanas. Iguanas have natural microorganisms in their hindgut that work properly only at around 85°F. Make sure your lizard's habitat is the proper temperature (see Chapter 4, Housing, "Heat," for help).

With all of the new dry commercial iguana foods available, there are more opportunities for your lizard to become constipated. As I stressed in the food chapter, don't use commercial iguana feeds as your lizard's only source of food. And whenever you do use these commercial foods, make sure your iguana drinks plenty of water so the dry food doesn't clog up the digestive system.

For minor constipation, your veterinarian may prescribe one or more of the following:
- Increase the habitat temperature
- Warm bath soaks (can stimulate defecation)
- Fecal testing for parasites
- Exposure to natural sunlight
- Laxatives or other medication

Warm baths work wonders on my iguanas' constipation. I find it triggers them to defecate almost always.   —I-605, Laura, 31 yrs., Canada

A while after I got my iguana she went through a "constipation" phase. I soaked her as is recommended by many vets, and she pooped.
—I-795, Dawn, 24 yrs., Ohio

My iguana stopped defecating and urinating. By the time I noticed, he had
developed a urinary tract infection. The vet took X-rays, dewormed him, and
gave injectable antibiotics. This cured the urinary infection, but he never
regained his defecating abilities. I was shown how to express my iguana [man-
ually manipulate an area on the iguana's body to squeeze out his feces and
urine] by my vet. It's a huge chore to do this every day [forever], but he's my pet.
                                          —I-273, Bill, 34 yrs., New Jersey
        [AUTHOR'S NOTE: I sent Bill a postcard with three gold stars on
it for his big heart. Some people's devotion to their pets and their
responsibility is very admirable.]

        If your iguana defecates like clockwork every day and then doesn't for a
couple of days, call your veterinarian. The reason I urge you to go to the veterinarian so soon is that there may be some obstruction that needs to be
removed. The veterinarian can use X-rays and other techniques to look for
blockages or obstructions in the digestive tract.
        In the case of the gravel-eating lizard, X-rays revealed the problem, which
was solved with a laxative, time, and the skills of a good veterinarian—plus, of
course, a change in habitat substrate. By the way, eating large amounts of
gravel or sand can kill your iguana.
        In another example, an iguana had swallowed a screw (probably on the
floor in the house) and it was stuck in the digestive tract. The screw had to be
surgically removed. Only a qualified veterinarian will know for sure what's
causing your iguana's constipation. Play it safe; see the veterinarian first.

EYES, NOSE, MOUTH PROBLEMS

        I've grouped together medical conditions of the eyes, nose, and mouth
because these anatomical features are all close together on the iguana's head.

Eyes: Problems

        With luck, if your lizard gets any eye problems at all, they will be minor.
The most common eye problems occur when an iguana bangs the side of its
head into something when scared or during breeding season (when male iguanas get a little crazy). Because the eye is such a delicate organ, it's a prime can-
didate for injury. For instance, if multiple iguanas are caged together, fights
can break out and eyes sometimes sustain serious injuries.
        My iguana was unlucky enough to get both a minor and a major eye prob-
lem. On the simple end of the scale was the day Za got a human hair in his eye,
which I talked about at the beginning of this chapter.
        In the category of major eye problems, he had to have a delicate surgical
operation to remove a benign tumor from the corner of his eye. Surgery near
iguanas' eyes is extremely dangerous, because of major blood vessels in the

SIDEBAR

Eating Feces

An adult iguana should not eat its own or another iguana's feces. This is a sure sign that something is not right. Some people feel it signals a lack of vitamins in the lizard's diet, but there is no scientific proof of this. Don't let your lizard do this.

area. My iguana's eye surgery turned out OK, but Za apparently lost a good deal of blood in the process (an unavoidable part of the operation; luckily his veterinary care was excellent).

Iguanas' eyes sometimes swell up and protrude, which lasts only a few seconds. My iguana sometimes did this when his eyelids were shedding, or at random times as if his eyes were itching. At these times, he often rubbed his eyes on a nearby object or my hand. Your iguana's eyes can also swell if you hold the lizard too tightly behind its head, as when you are trying to control or subdue the lizard. Although it's presumably harmless, temporarily swollen eyes following a "power struggle" are a sign that you should grasp your iguana in a different place and with lots less force.

You don't want to do "home medicine" with eye problems your iguana may have. If anything about the eye looks unusual or wrong—e.g., swollen, extremely bloodshot, mucous discharge, runny, pupils unusually dilated or constricted, one eye that doesn't track normally, obviously injured—you owe it to your lizard to call your veterinarian to discuss the matter.

Fluids From Nose

NOTE: The fluids discussed here, which signal a medical problem, should not be confused with the clear, watery fluid that an iguana regularly "snorts" from its nose. This healthy and normal snorting is part of how iguanas regulate their salt balance (see Chapter 1, Iguana: The Species, "Nostrils," for more details).

What Is It?

Thick or bubbly fluids that come out of an iguana's nose are not normal or healthy.

Symptom(s)

Mucus-like fluids—or clear but foamy fluids—come out of the nostrils or are visible on the nose.

Possible Cause(s)

One reason for the discharge may be related to a habitat that is too cold or an iguana allowed to roam freely in a home that's too cold. There are too many other causes to list, but basically the animal is sick and needs immediate care (for some ideas, see a previous section on "Respiratory Problems").

Possible Solution(s)

See your veterinarian so he or she can identify the specific cause (e.g., bacterial or viral infection) and prescribe appropriate corrective measures (e.g., antibiotics). Don't assume your iguana "just" has a cold and ignore it. For example, iguanas can get pneumonia, which can be life-threatening. Get prompt veterinary help before your lizard gets really sick.

Mouth Rot

Mouth rot used to be one of the more common medical problems an iguana would get, but nowadays it is seldom seen.

What Is It?

Mouth rot, also called infectious stomatitis, sometimes looks like a cottony substance inside the mouth or a crusty yellow substance on the edge of the iguana's jaw or gum. Mouth rot is not a direct cause of death, but the infection often makes an iguana's mouth sensitive and soon it can't eat. If it can't eat, the lizard will eventually get stressed or even die from something that could have easily been cured.

Symptom(s)

Visually, you can see a thick, stringy, cheesy substance around the gum line of your iguana, or a cotton-like growth inside its mouth.

Possible Cause(s)

Mouth rot is caused by an infection, but it happens almost always in stressed lizards. When it is present, many other problems come along with it, and all are the result of improper housing and nutrition. A habitat that's too cool or a poor diet are the most common culprits.

Possible Solution(s)

If mouth rot isn't taken care of right away, it can spread and get out of control, possibly causing skin lesions and destruction of tissue. It can also make it difficult for your iguana to eat, which only exacerbates the problem. Work with your veterinarian on this creepy infection. The veterinarian will probably first scrub the area down with something like Nolvasan, Betadine, or a hydrogen peroxide solution to remove as much of the visible "slime" as possible, then follow up with topical antibiotics.

Once at home, you might be required to do the same thing as the veterinarian did to ensure that the mouth rot doesn't come back. If you have a veterinarian that is up-to-date on the current literature on mouth rot, he or she may also use other aggressive measures.

SKIN DISEASES

Diseases to an iguana's skin (scales) are not common for iguanas in the wild. Most of the diseases I have ever heard of stem in some way from domesticating the animal and putting it in a captive environment.

Black Fungus Disease

I first heard about black fungus or black spot disease in 1992, but I have not heard much about it since then.

What Is It?

Black fungus usually appears on hatchlings or small juveniles, and it seems to be contagious. One person wrote and said she had her hatchling for several months and got another hatchling cagemate for it. The new one had an "odd" skin disease, and the original hatchling also ended up getting it.

Symptom(s)

This disease causes the iguana's skin to turn black, dry, and crusty. This black, dry, crusty skin can spread and cause the iguana's skin to kind of rot or flake off if not stopped.

Possible Cause(s)

I called one of the big breeders and importers of iguanas and asked his opinion on the cause of black fungus disease. He believed it was caused by poor husbandry practices, or lack of understanding of housing and nutritional needs, at iguana farms in Latin America.

Many of the hatchlings were kept in pens that didn't allow the lizards to get off the ground when they wanted to. Consequently, the lizards sat in dirty and sometimes wet and moldy conditions all day long, something they would not naturally do in the wild. This is the theory of how the fungus was supposedly picked up.

The importer I talked to said that the incorrect husbandry conditions have been corrected on most of the farms. This must be true, because I have not heard of the disease for a long time. Because more "novices" are starting iguana farms, I have included this disease in case it starts appearing again.

Possible Solution(s)

Sometimes they can get a skin fungus. If this happens simply apply a topical ointment like Neosporin. They very rarely get any fungus ailments with proper

temperature control, but if one should get a fungus, treat it immediately as they
are contagious.   —I-11, Patty, Washington

Sunlight and a warm, dry habitat are the solutions. One person said that when his iguana finally shed the "black mess" it never returned.

If your iguana shows signs of this fungus, try rinsing the lizard with Betadine or a similar product every day for two weeks. Keep the Betadine away from your iguana's eyes. Be sure to wash your own hands afterward, and after each treatment discard any materials you used to apply the cleanser. Topical antifungal medication is always helpful.

Sunlight is a magical cure for your iguana, so let your lizard get some "naked" sun—unfiltered and natural. With your help, your iguana will eventually shed this fungus off if you follow treatment instructions, but it may take two or three sheds, depending on how far fungus has progressed.

Blister Disease

The name "blister disease" sounds mild, but in reality it should be called something like "leprosy."

What Is It?

This disease starts off with blisters that look like the blisters a human gets after a bad sunburn. At this point, prompt medical care can bring the problem to a screeching halt. If medical care is not applied, the disease can hyper-jump to lesions, ulcers, and destruction of the skin.

I have never seen this disease on any iguanas, but my veterinarian friends always describe it in the most despicable terms. If no corrective procedures are taken, a lizard can die from the disease.

Symptom(s)

I have had one iguana get blister disease. He had water blisters along the bottom of his sides. I thought they were from the spot light. Then I read a description of blister disease. I was sure this is what my iguana had, not burns.
                              —I-764, Diana, 46 yrs., California

• First sign is small, fluid-filled blisters
• More advanced cases exhibit lesions, ulcers, skin destruction

Possible Cause(s)

Damp and unclean habitat conditions are usually the culprit. If your iguana has proper housing, blister disease is unlikely.

Possible Solution(s)

Make sure that your iguana's habitat is clean and that it is neither dry like a desert nor sopping wet like a swamp (read Chapter 4, Housing, for some ideas). Because this disease can escalate to monster-movie proportions, have your veterinarian take care of the problem right away. In addition, remove other reptile cagemates so there is no chance of them also getting the disease.

FEMALE IGUANA MEDICAL PROBLEMS

There is one class of problem specific to female iguanas, and that is egg-related problems. These problems can start when she becomes sexually mature and capable of breeding—i.e., when she is 250 mm (10") SVL or greater (#14).

Egg Binding

She had a teratoma in the uterus (diagnosed as egg-bound) and was spayed to remove.   —I-840, Lorraine, 32 yrs., Ohio

There are many variables that determine the month that a female iguana will start to develop eggs, but a safe bet is to start being alert to this situation around January or February once your female is sexually mature.

What Is It?

I see about three iguanas a year that are egg-bound.
                                   —V-132, Dr. Willard, 55 yrs., Washington

Egg binding, sometimes called egg retention, results when a gravid (pregnant) female iguana cannot pass or expel one or more eggs from her reproductive tract. This is not a normal experience. If these eggs are not passed, the death of the iguana is possible.

Eggs growing inside the female iguana's body put pressure on nearby organs. If your iguana is egg-bound, the eggs might move around inside her body and end up in unnatural places, endangering some of the nearby organs. This is another reason to see your herp veterinarian right away if you suspect egg binding.

Symptom(s)

The first vet I had (highly recommended) was the type to wait and see if it takes care of itself instead of taking time to research and call a few people. He was surprised to hear my iguana was carrying eggs instead of an infected organ. I'm glad I didn't put her to sleep like he suggested!
                                   —I-183, Mary, 24 yrs., Massachusetts

Sometimes it's obvious that your iguana is egg-bound, and sometimes it's not. But as I have mentioned earlier, if your female iguana is 250 mm (10") SVL or greater, she's capable of breeding and therefore of producing eggs.

If she is not eating and looks bloated or expanded in the mid-section, there is a good chance she may be gravid. Noticing that your iguana is gravid is one thing; deciding if she is egg-bound is another matter.

An egg-bound iguana might appear listless, unresponsive, or depressed. If your iguana's body turns a muddy color, that might also indicate that she is having some problems, but by then it may be too late. Her body color at this point is like litmus paper, indicating that she is not well.

Besides having eggs bound up inside her, the lizard may also become calcium deficient due to the extra demands of creating the calcium-rich shell on the eggs. Your veterinarian can also help at this time, perhaps by increasing the amount of calcium your lizard normally receives each day. This will be discussed in the next section.

Possible Cause(s)

The most common cause of egg binding is when one or several eggs are excessively large or perhaps abnormally shaped. This happens more often to females the first time they become gravid, or if the female is not in good health. Below are some additional possible causes of egg binding:

- No proper place for eggs to be laid (see Chapter 9, Breeding, "Female Iguanas: What Problems Might Occur During Breeding Season?," for more details and quotations from iguana owners)
- Stress
- Nutritional problems
- Too many eggs

My iguana's [SVL: 13½", TL: 4' 1", 2 yrs.] pacing at the window and constant scratching about was a sign of her being gravid. Indeed, quite gravid! On Feb. 21 the X-ray revealed the outline of many eggs, so many that they were pressing up into her lungs. —I-706, Melodie, 41 yrs., Tennessee

[AUTHOR'S NOTE: This story continues under "Hysterectomy (Spaying)" at the end of this section, and again in a sidebar in "Surgical Operations."]

Possible Solution(s)

Your safest bet is to have your herp veterinarian look at your female iguana if she is sexually mature (i.e., she's achieved the minimum SVL), she has a bloated or expanded mid-section, she is not eating, and it's breeding season.

An X-ray taken by your veterinarian will show whether she is gravid, as well as the location of an egg or eggs that might be causing a problem. If one egg is found to be causing egg binding, do not let anyone, including a veterinarian, palpate the eggs. Two people I know had an inexperienced veterinarian press on the iguana's stomach area to manually manipulate the "blocking" egg out of the way. In both cases, the "blocking" egg ruptured and the iguana died.

If X-rays show a blockage, you could lubricate the iguana's vent and hope that the egg slips out. Sometimes this is done in conjunction with warm-water soaking. To me, this is too passive for a potentially dangerous situation in which anything can go wrong.

Hysterectomy (Spaying)

Hysterectomy is more commonly referred to as "spaying" when done to animals like cats or dogs. In this case it's an operation to remove the reproductive organs of a female iguana. It is usually not an elective surgery, but one that has to be done in an emergency to save a female iguana's life because egg binding has escalated too far.

Once your iguana is spayed, she can no longer produce eggs. As one iguana researcher I talked with in San Diego said, egg production puts a tremendous strain on a female iguana's body, including her calcium balance. If the operation is done correctly, it should increase the life span of the female by removing the stress of having to hold and lay these eggs every year.

> *We've already done 15 to 20 [hysterectomies] this year.*
> —V-22, Drs. Doug & Richard, 40 & 38 yrs., California

> *I have performed two successful hysterectomies; the third female was induced to lay her eggs.*   —V-117, Dr. Dale, 38 yrs., Texas

> *I've done only two surgical procedures on gravid females. One had eggs in the oviduct, one was entirely ovarian (follicular stasis) and an ovariectomy was done with the rest of the reproductive tract left intact. The gravid female was relieved of the eggs and the oviduct closed but remained intact. Since then, no history of egg laying. [I did] the ovariectomy [because] the owner decided to have surgery because she couldn't stand the behavior any longer!*
> —V-116, Dr. Richard, 37 yrs., Tennessee

> *She [SVL: 16", TL: 5' 5", 9½ yrs.] was gravid too long and didn't deposit eggs. She finally laid the eggs but was "paralyzed" [from this prolonged time period] from the neck down. She wouldn't swallow, etc. for 10 weeks. We force-fed her baby food and calcium supplements until she regained her strength and full recovery.*   —I-509, Troy, 30 yrs., Missouri

> *My vet told me that the eggs would be laid any day, but within 2 weeks. Two weeks later there were no eggs and we returned to the vet. He thought she seemed okay.*
> *On March 18 we returned to the vet again because the eggs still hadn't been laid and she wasn't moving around much at all. I'd begun investigating having her spayed. My vet had not done this surgery and referred us to an expert vet.*
> *Thank goodness I didn't wait any longer! Pre-surgery, an X-ray showed the eggs were still in the ovaries, never having been released to the oviducts. (I*

think they called her condition "follicular stasis.") The eggs on one side had already begun "changing," "on their way to going bad," the surgeon told me. Very soon, my iguana would have been in <u>serious</u> trouble and the same surgery would have been done in emergency circumstances. Her condition would have been already compromised and the outcome of surgery less certain.

There had been 19 eggs on one side and 14 on the other. When the first egg mass was removed, my iguana's heart rate and respiration both increased and improved, the vet reported. Her body had been under great stress. My 3.3 pound iguana came home weighing 2.3 pounds. Quite a difference! Although it had been less than 24 hours since her surgery, she was not at all depressed. She seemed glad to be home, and she was energetic! It's as though she wanted to investigate the entire room and go to all the places she'd been unable to see for the past 6 weeks or so of her pregnancy. She showed little sign of pain.

The surgeon told me that since it's fairly new surgery there's no guarantee on long-term effects. Time will tell. But without surgery, my iguana would likely have died. So whatever the long-term effects, better those than her death.

Also, I recently heard something that you might want to include in your book. The "follicular stasis" (the eggs never being released from the ovaries) more frequently occurs in iguanas that have <u>not</u> been bred. Often the owner, unaware of what is happening, allows it to go on, without treatment, and the iguana dies. —I-706, Melodie, 41 yrs., Tennessee

Calcium Deficiency

For gravid females, at a certain point there is an additional demand for calcium when the shells of the eggs are being formed.

What Is It?

Calcium deficiency is a common problem when iguanas are not properly fed, do not get sufficient UV radiation, or both. Being gravid increases the calcium demands of a female iguana, and thus increases the likelihood of a calcium deficiency.

Symptom(s)

See page 365, "Metabolic Bone Disease," for details.

Possible Cause(s)

If your female iguana is the least bit low in calcium to begin with, the extra demand of building shells on the developing eggs could cause her to become seriously calcium deficient.

Possible Solution(s)

Refer back to page 365, "Metabolic Bone Disease," for an entire section devoted to all aspects of calcium deficiency.

Cloacal Infection

One of my female iguanas some 10 years ago came down with a cloacal infection, similar to [vaginal infections that] female humans get. I've only come across this once. Where or how is a mystery to me, and I'm glad to say it was an isolated incident. It was so long ago and I'm sorry to say I don't really remember the symptoms I encountered, but the treatment was to give her a douche with a solution given me by my vet.

She was a large adult and I, having no one willing to help me, had to turn her on her back, belly side up on my lap, mesmerize her into total relaxation, and hold her steady while inserting a nozzle (not too far up) ever so gently into her cloaca, careful so as not to injure her, and inject the solution slowly. I did this twice-a-day procedure for about a week, if I remember correctly. Can you imagine doing his without having your pet bolt and run? Don't ask me how but I did it to this 4-foot adult and never got bitten. She was successfully cured, I'm happy to say.

—I-200, Dianna, 47 yrs., Washington

Because I have heard of only this one case of cloacal infection, I will just give the quotation, which explains the treatment. It is included here just in case there are more incidents than I have assumed.

MALE IGUANA MEDICAL PROBLEMS

There is one specific medical problem for male iguanas—injuries from fighting with other iguanas—and it happens mostly during breeding season, which usually starts around October and goes through January.

Injuries From Breeding Aggression

If you don't have another iguana in your house, there can't be any fighting with, or injuries from, other iguanas.

What Is It?

All sorts of injuries, ranging from scratches, cuts, bite wounds, and even death, can occur to male iguanas during breeding season.

Symptom(s)

Look at Chapter 9, Breeding, for problems that may occur during breeding season. Much of this information consists of real-life stories from iguana owners. You will also find out that male iguanas can take their sexual aggressions out on human family members as well as other iguanas.

A few weeks in early December, my male iguana was extremely cantankerous and I think the whole family was bitten at least once. In fact, he nipped at my girlfriend while she was just sitting on the couch. In two weeks he was back to his sweet self.   —I-171, Drew, Minnesota

Possible Cause(s)

During breeding season, male iguanas overdose on hormones and run crazy: fighting, biting, and defending territory against other male iguanas. Throughout this book I have stressed the importance of not having more than one iguana. This is especially crucial if even one of the iguanas is male.

Possible Solution(s)

First of all, take seriously my warnings about owning only one iguana at a time. If you do have two iguanas, and especially if one or both are males, separate them <u>before</u> they hurt each other.

Sperm Plug

My iguana at about 2 years of age passed a strange wishbone-shaped length of dried skin (?). It took several days to come out his vent. I looked in a half dozen iguana books and not one mentioned it. Concerned, I sent the dried piece to a friend who raises snakes. He thought it looked like the sperm plug a snake passes when he starts producing semen. For a couple of weeks after that, there were one-inch round splotches of dried white liquidy stuff (which I wondered if it were excess semen). He also passed another plug. Since he was eating and active, I quit worrying about it, and the symptoms have since subsided.
                    —I-609, Cindy, 37 yrs., Florida

What Is It?

A sperm plug looks kind of like a piece off one of those light-colored rawhide bones that dogs chew on, but very small. When my iguana was 3 years old (and going through his breeding season) I saw one of these plugs, which was about ¾" long and ⅛" wide. The plugs can take any shape, it just depends on how the semen dries.

Symptom(s)

The symptom in this case is dried semen that may be observed hanging out of the iguana's vent. It will usually be seen only during breeding season, unless it is a plug that has been caught inside the vent for some time.

Possible Cause(s)

During breeding season, a male iguana sometimes masturbates if there are no female iguanas around to mate with. You can detect this by seeing fresh semen in the habitat, looking like soft melted cheese. When the hemipenes retract after ejaculation, the semen may end up inside the vent area. Once the semen dries, it can be rigid or flexible, depending on the thickness and volume of semen. A couple of large-volume ejaculations could dry and create a sperm plug.

Possible Solution(s)

I observed one of these plugs sticking out of my iguana's vent. I kept an eye on it, and about a week later I found the plug on his basking ledge. It apparently fell out on its own.

The following year I saw anther such plug, but after a week it did not fall out. I had a friend hold my iguana in a standing position on a cloth chair for traction. This way Za's vent was exposed, and I very delicately grasped the plug with tweezers and applied just the slightest pressure downward to see if the plug was anchored or loose. It fell right out.

It's very important that if you do not feel comfortable doing this kind of procedure—don't! If you have an iguana that won't put up with any kind of medical manipulation, don't do this. See a veterinarian for help. Over the years my iguana trusted me to do just about anything to him. This is one good reason to work toward having a tame iguana.

If you decide to manipulate the plug, never jerk or yank on it. The plug might be wrapped around some delicate, soft tissue and your yank could tear the tissue easily. If I had felt any resistance at all I would have stopped.

Sperm plugs are not a common medical problem to worry about, but I felt you should at least have the knowledge for that rare day you might see a strange object dangling out of your iguana. Typically, normal defecation flushes any potential plugs free from the iguana's body.

SURGICAL OPERATIONS

Often, a surgical operation may seem like an easy solution to a medical problem, but you need to be aware that every time your iguana goes under general anesthesia there is a chance of complications or even death.

When we thought we would lose our iguana after surgery, I thought I would die.   —I-736, Joyce, 36 yrs., New Jersey

My iguana was a beautiful healthy green color, easily handled, and things were great. Then one day I noticed a bump on his lower jaw. It didn't appear to bother him and I decided to just keep an eye on it. Well, that thing grew very quickly, so I took him to the vet. They did surgery on him (I watched) and it was a tumor about the size of a marble. It didn't look that large from the outside, most of it being hidden in the mouth. Anyway, he suffered nerve damage from the surgery and wouldn't or couldn't eat. He was extremely lethargic—he just lay there and never even moved. I swabbed out his mouth often because his tongue started to slough off tissue and he was just a mess. My vet went out of

Reminder

In the majority of the medical cases we have just gone through, I have mentioned seeing a herp veterinarian. I didn't do this to avoid giving a full answer, but rather because I believe strongly in seeking expert advice for iguana problems. I was extremely lucky in having superior veterinarians the whole time I had Za as my pet—veterinarians that allowed me to do some care at home and who worked with me to solve Za's short- and long-term medical problems.

I didn't run to the veterinarian every time something a little unexpected came up; oftentimes all it took was a phone call. A good veterinarian is a great security blanket for people with an exotic pet like an iguana.

On a positive note, sometimes medical problems can be the turning point for bonding with your iguana. I have seen and heard stories like these enough times to know that they are real.

When I was feeding him from the medicine dropper he required a lot of handling. He became a lot more comfortable with people after that.
—I-521, Sharon, 35 yrs., New Jersey

We got our iguana when it was about one year old and had some medical problems that took 10 months to correct. We enjoy our iguana's company very much. There is a personal gratification in helping a once-neglected creature reach its potential. —I-690, Irene, 34 yrs., Texas

town, so I took him to another vet. They kept him overnight, tube fed him, had him in an incubator with oxygen and everything, but he never recovered.
—I-312, Darla, 38 yrs., Ohio

[AUTHOR'S NOTE: Iguanas can get injured or sick and just in a matter of days can go downhill and die. Don't delay in calling or seeing your veterinarian, and don't say you can't afford it. In the beginning of this book, I said that iguanas may need veterinarian care, and exotic vet care is not cheap.]

Even if things go well during the operation, post-op care often requires significant time. You may have to change bandages daily, apply ointments, or administer medicines, including shots. You may have to deal with blood, pus, and feces. Operations can be an intense and stressful time for you and your lizard. But sometimes surgery is the only solution.

Then there is the expense of medical care. In the five years I had my iguana, I spent almost $650 on medical care. I don't begrudge one penny spent and it even seemed cheap when you consider what had to be done. Almost all of the medical expenses for my iguana were for one-in-a-million problems. I guess I won the lottery for oddball iguana medical problems.

One problem my iguana had was a rare ear problem. Some years later, a benign tumor was removed from the side of his eye, and he also had to have one hemipenis removed (it turned out later that the hemipene problem may have been caused by cancer). In addition, he had an extensive necropsy (like a human autopsy) after his death.

Post-Operative Care: Za Story

I have included a short story of my iguana's ear operation to give you a feel for the post-operative care that sometimes follows a surgical operation. The ear problem was an infection deep inside Za's inner ear that caused the ear membrane to distend ⅝". During surgery, the veterinarian removed a pus ball from inside the ear.

The whole day of Za's ear surgery I felt restless. This type of surgery had not been done before on an iguana, and exotic animals can die when given anesthesia. When I finally picked up the "green guy" he was alive but completely limp and seemed like no one was home inside his body, just a dull, drugged stare. It was a scary experience to see him like that.

My veterinarian said that it wouldn't be safe for Za to sleep in his habitat because he was still "drugged out" and could fall and cause more complications. A month before his operation I trained Za to sleep in the downstairs heated water bed, where I knew he'd be safe and warm.

That first afternoon I had Za on a heating pad in my office so I could closely monitor him. That evening at about 6 p.m. I took him down to the bedroom, put him in the water bed, and pulled the covers and blankets up to his "neck" with just his head resting on the pillow. For some strange reason, when I first moved the pillow to the side he moved over and rested his head on it. So to make life easier I just put his head on the pillow every night of the week that he slept there.

Once Za hit the pillow in the evening, he was always out like a light and didn't move until morning. The first two nights after his surgery, I came downstairs and checked on him about every hour to make sure he was OK and at the right temperature.

Medical doctors always tell human patients to get plenty of sleep when trying to recover from an illness or surgery. I followed this advice with Za by keeping the blinds closed in the bedroom to let Za sleep in darkness until at least 9 a.m. each day. This gave him about 15 hours of sleep each night.

In the morning it was quite strange to see this lizard asleep with just his head poking out from underneath the covers. When he was awake, I took him upstairs and put him in the bathtub with a little water and he defecated (he was already conditioned to do this). The first time after the operation it took a long time for Za to defecate, but I felt it was important to get him back into normal routines right away, which is often what doctors recommend for their human patients.

I also fed him a little of his favorite foods so he would continue eating and squirted water in his mouth to maintain his fluid balance. The first day after the surgery, when I squirted it in his mouth he sucked in a large volume in a short period of time. I also rinsed him off each day in the bathtub, careful not to get his ear wet. And of course there were specific at-home medical tasks to do for Za's ear, assigned by my veterinarian.

SIDEBAR

Stitch Awareness

This is a continuation of the story on pages 425 and 426 about one iguana's emergency hysterectomy. It shows that operations are not over, like some people say, until "the fat lady sings."

The next day she was quieter and seemed to notice that her belly was sensitive (the incision is a bit over 3 inches). Her appetite returned 3 days after surgery. That's also about the time that her itching began. I thought that she was having a convulsion the first time that I witnessed her raise her belly slightly and then rock wildly, rapidly back and forth, and in circles! [AUTHOR'S NOTE: Having received stitches more than 15 separate times in my life, I notice that toward the end of the healing process the cut area with the stitches often became itchy. Perhaps iguanas also experience this sensation.]

The vets warned me to supervise her activity so she doesn't tear her sutures. She's adjusted well to being more confined than usual. At 3 weeks I'm to take her to have her stitches checked (I check them a minimum of twice daily). They may be removed then, or more likely a week or two later. I understand that, in some cases, stitches are not removed for 6 to 8 weeks. However, the surgeon was very impressed with my iguana's condition, diet, home environment, and he doesn't believe she will take so long to heal.

Update: 4 weeks post-surgery as of tomorrow—the stitches are still in. (Yes, iguanas do heal slowly!) But she seems entirely "normal" now. Eating well, beginning to shed for the first time since January. Back to normal activity and happy in her cage (vs. her discontented confinement to a travel cage for 10 days to prevent tearing open the sutures). This sure has been a learning experience! —I-706, Melodie, 41 yrs., Tennessee

DEATH

Death is usually a reliable symptom of a health problem.
—Sean Eric Fagan, in the newsletter of The Bay Area
Amphibian and Reptile Society (BAARS), September 1994

The only pet I was allowed to have as a child growing up was a cat. One day I came home on leave from the military to learn that Willie, my cat, had died—he was 15 and I was 21. This was a big shock for me, since I'd had him for the majority of my childhood. I cried and felt sad, but my life continued on.

When I was in college, I remember joking to a friend that death was the last frontier. It was kind of my way of laughing, scoffing, belittling death and all that it entails. This was the late '60s and death, peace, love, and war were all tossed around as ideas. As the years flew by, close and distant friends died.

In an ideal world, I would wish that your pet iguana would never die. But birth, life, and death follow a non-changing routine. Saplings grow into trees, which eventually die, and there isn't anything you can do about it. It's all part of the experience we call life.

But knowing that death is inevitable still doesn't lessen the emotional damage that the death of a pet can bring. The death of a pet is real! Some people who have never had a pet or developed a close bond with animals might tell you, "Just get another pet." But it's not like replacing a broken window on your car. The death of your pet is not a replaceable option.

I found that a lot of people were very good about the death of my iguana, while others who I thought to be friends were so rude and cruel. I think the worst was when they would say, "Why don't you just skin it and make a belt out of it?" The thing that upset me the most was that the ones who came out with comments like this had recently lost pets themselves and were overwhelmed by grief. What's more, they meant everything they said to me [about my iguana]. Then they got mad at me when I asked them how they would feel if I told them to make a coat or hat out of their cat or dog.

They got really upset at me when I told them I felt the same way about my iguana as they did about their cat or dog. I said, "My comments really hurt, didn't they?" So the next time someone's animal dies, whether it's a snake, rat, lizard, spider, or hamster, I hope they might be a little nicer, because these pets were loved just as much as they loved their cat or dog.
                                    —I-759, Laura, 20 yrs., Pennsylvania

Years of intense interaction, feeding, nurturing, and caring create a bond locked deep in your heart and soul. The more your pet has become part of your life, the stronger the bond.

I've known people who died and it didn't affect me as much as this [the death of my iguana]. On the day that I picked up his body from the vet, nothing else

in the world made a fucking bit of difference. All I knew was that I had lost a
friend that I'll never be able to replace.

—I-171, Drew, 34 yrs., Minnesota

Between January '92 and this past Mother's Day night, I have made countless
trips to the vet, spent many dollars, administered medicine, took special care, etc.
In the end, he died. I really loved my iguana.

—I-543, Bill, 40 yrs., Mississippi

He [4½ yrs.] took his last few breaths at about 11:30 that night. It's a sad story.
. . . He was special to me and I really do miss him dearly. I still have a hard time
talking about him without having to hold back the tears.

—name withheld as a courtesy

The End

The world rushes on over the strings of the lingering heart making
the music of sadness.   —Tagore, from *Stray Birds*, XLIV

When your pet dies, it leaves a black, cold, silent void where once joy,
warmth, and excitement lived. The void is in your soul and heart, but you feel
mostly an emptiness, an uneasy sensation, near your stomach.

My iguana lived for 4 years and became as much a part of our family as our
dogs. Even my mother, who is against keeping anything but domestic animals,
got pretty attached to her. When my iguana died, there were very few people
who understood the depth of feeling and the grief emotions I was going through.
My vet sent me a sympathy card to let me know that my lizard was the best
taken-care-of iguana in our area. She was also (so far) the second most long-
lived in our area. My work (since it was a pet store) allowed me to take off as
much grieving time as I felt necessary. There were only a couple of people in my
immediate family who understood the grief I was feeling.

I hope people will begin to understand that iguanas are just as much work
and commitment as a dog and when they die, you feel just as great a loss as if
you lost a very dear friend.   —I-808, Priscilla, 25 yrs., Iowa

What To Do After Your Pet Dies

I originally began writing this section several years ago, because of the gut-
wrenching letters I had received from iguana owners whose pets had died.
They all echoed basically the same theme: In terms of loss, it was like losing a
child or a close friend.

I've enlarged this section beyond my original scope in hopes of reducing
the time and amount of pain the death of your iguana can bring. The information and stories won't eliminate all the pain in one day, but I hope they will
help you in some way.

I know firsthand the pain of losing your pet, because my iguana, Za, died at just over 5 years old. From a healthy iguana to suddenly dead, with cancer. It was a bad month for my close circle of iguana friends. First it was Za that died; then the oldest iguana (29 years), which I had visited several years in a row in California; then a close friend's older iguana; and Za's former veterinarian—all within a month of each other. It was a black month for my iguana community.

The first three days after Za died, I just kind of banged around the house. Room to room, chair to chair, thing to thing. I felt restless, but no place I went made me feel comfortable. Even though Za never made a sound, his death made my office feel silent and empty. By the time several months had passed, part of each day I would feel normal, then later I'd again be empty and missing my green friend.

Friends of mine who had iguanas told me that each day I would feel a little better. Contacting other iguana friends is important at this time, especially ones who have lost their iguanas or who have owned one for a long time.

People sent me flowers. I put them on the chair in my office where Za spent his days with me. It was sad but beautiful, and it reinforced that his time with me had been real and that he mattered.

My iguana died this morning around 5:20 a.m., in my bed where I'd taken him for comfort and support. I know he was hurting and his bladder was too far gone to heal, so it was best. But I'm gonna miss him. I guess it's a bad end to the summer of 1994.

I had him out on the porch on my lap Sunday and he snuggled close to me and enjoyed the sun and soft breeze. I talked and chirped to him and kissed his little head. I thought the fresh air made him sleep well. But later that morning, I suddenly woke up at 5 a.m. and felt uneasy. I went to check on him and knew then it was time, so I took him in my bed and held him and told him I'd miss him, but knew that he was hurting. I told him it was time for him to go.

Then he took his last breath and left. I'm so numb I can't even cry yet. That will come later.   —name withheld as a courtesy

After Za died, many friends advised me to have some kind of ceremony to acknowledge his death and celebrate his life—that it would help the grieving process. I'm glad I took their advice, because it did help. That might mean a burial, cremation, or some other ceremony. But I urge you, as my wise friends urged me, to create a ceremony of some kind that has meaning for you and your lizard.

As for the most unpleasant thing I do for my pets, I hate funerals and cremation. I do see that when they are done well, it helps. My iguanas are very much family. The animal gives so much to me in its life that I abhor the idea of just throwing the body into the garbage pail. My pets are not garbage. Animals are so pure of spirit and so unconditional in their love that they deserve the best,

SIDEBAR

Cancer—It Seems to Get Every Species

One of my great surprises about iguanas was when I found out that they can get cancer. It never dawned on me that reptiles could get such a disease. I'm not sure if it's true, but I heard that sharks are the only animals that don't get cancer.

> *My iguana looked really good. But he was in a lot of pain and very sick with cancer. The bone in his left leg was almost completely eaten away and the cancer had spread to his spine. I put him to sleep to stop his pain.*
> —I-929, Tina, 32 yrs., Canada

As with all animals, cancer can strike iguanas in various organs and body parts, from hemipenes to their bones. The symptoms vary, depending on the location of the cancer, and there are no specific "signs" to look out for. Stay attentive to any changes in your iguana's health, behavior, eating habits, or daily activity.

When my iguana got cancer, the only thing that was dramatically different in his life was that he no longer went to the bottom of his habitat to defecate. He defecated on his upper ledge, which he never did before. Also, when he was out in the house he would just defecate wherever he might be resting. Again, he had never done that before.

I had Za checked for worms, changed the inside of the habitat, made sure he defecated in the bathtub each morning—but nothing helped. As it turned out, he had cancer in his hemipenes. I believe that the cancer in that area disturbed his defecation patterns.

> *and mine always get the best. However unpleasant a task, it is a gesture of respect and love as the last thing I can do for him or her.*
> —I-200, Dianna, 47 yrs., Washington

> *I buried my iguana and put up a tombstone. It was just like my son dying.*
> —name withheld for privacy

Dr. Gerald Mann, a wise television theologian, was asked, "How do I get over the grief of my loved one dying?" In this case it was a human, but a loved one is any <u>one</u> you have loved dearly. Dr. Mann said, "Ask yourself, would you rather suffer the grief of the loved one, knowing all of the great and wonderful times you had together, or not have known the person [pet] and not suffered the grief?" Of course, the answer is to have known the person [pet].

He also said: "Focus on all of the good things that you can remember of your loved one, and don't dwell on the sadness." If given a foothold, sadness and grief will wrap around you in layers, smothering all hope and life from your body. Focus on the good, the uplifting—keep yourself free.

A friend of mine's wife died at a very young age, and he was depressed. His mother called and asked if I would come and try to help. I brought a few things: open ears, sensitive heart, boyhood friendship, possible set of directions out of the blindness of grief, and a book by Elisabeth Kübler-Ross, *On Death and Dying*. It shows the stages a person goes through when someone close has died. It's a road map through the long valley of death, to a new beginning at the other end. It might help with your suffering, too.

When I lived in California, some friends who attended the University of California at Davis told me about a group there that gives support for people whose pets have died. Not until I started this section did the group's name pop back in my head. It's called Pet Loss Support Hotline, (916) 752-4200, and they operate from 6:30 p.m. to 9:30 p.m. Pacific Standard Time. They have counselors you can talk with to help relieve some of the burden that a pet's death brings with it. Give them a call if the pain feels too great, or if you think it would help to talk to people who really understand what you're going through. Humans talking with other caring humans is a masterful cure for many ills.

For many of us, especially if we're not sure exactly why our iguanas died, it's important to have a necropsy (what an autopsy is called when it's an animal) done to pinpoint the cause of death.

> *Heart failure recently claimed my third and largest male. Calcification of the aorta and bladder stones, according to the autopsy report. I prefer to know what my pets die from so I can be wiser next time and the vet can gain more insight also. This benefits not only my other pets but someone else's, also. In 23 years of loving, caring for, and sacrificing for my iguanas, I've tried to do my part in contributing to veterinary knowledge about them by consenting to autopsies after death. I love iguanas very much and I guess I feel this to be a way in which the death of one beloved pet will not be in vain. His contribution will help others of his species.* —I-200, Dianna, 47 yrs., Washington

Offering your iguana's body to be cut up for science is not everyone's ideal. For some, it's not a choice. In my case, I had made a decision that I would not give my iguana's body up for necropsy if he died because he was too dear to me. But fate always seems to offer options you never think you would pursue. Because I was writing this book about iguanas, I felt obliged to find out all I could about the quality of care that Za had received over the years.

My intellect won over my heart and I had an extremely detailed necropsy done on Za that took more than two months. Blood samples, organ analysis, bone scans, microscopic examination—just about every possible test. The good word was that the pathologist concluded that Za was the biggest, best-conditioned iguana he had ever seen (except for the cancer). In fact, Za's bones were

Necropsy

If your iguana dies, many veterinarians will do a free necropsy to find out the cause of death. They learn from the experience more about the internal "workings" of an iguana and you might learn how your iguana died—so you can perhaps avoid repeating problems with future iguanas. It's a win-win situation. First call the veterinarian, though; don't just arrive unannounced with a dead iguana. Also find out if it's free or what the cost might be.

We brought her back to the vet the morning after she died and "donated" her to find out what exactly was in there. We found major calcification of the kidneys, intestines, and aorta. There was nothing that could have been done.

Here's why I donated her for an autopsy:

1. I wanted more information on how and why she died. This was the best way to find out.

2. It was winter here and I knew she wouldn't want to be buried where it would freeze every year. I wouldn't have been satisfied had I buried her in the cold.

3. I thought she would be of educational help to my vet.

It was a hard decision, especially since I am aware of what is done with the body after the autopsy. My husband didn't know what is done with the bodies and doesn't want to know. —I-808, Priscilla, 25 yrs., Iowa

so dense and hard (many iguanas' bones are soft from improper diet or too little ultraviolet light) that it took several weeks of soaking in a demineralizing solution before the bones were soft enough to section for analysis.

I told the pathologist that I wanted Za back when all the tissue samples had been gathered. My 5' 5", 13-pound iguana was sent back in a small square box. The pathologist said not to open the box, and I understand what he meant. Za and his box were buried in the back yard with a special ceremony. Words, letters, some of his special food items, and flowers were buried with him. I was surprised that I wasn't disturbed by burying Za in a box that measured a quarter of his original size. But it was nice just to get him back home in any form, to the yard and people who loved him.

To Get Another Iguana, or Not?

I miss my iguana [SVL: 11½", 2½ yrs.] a lot. Right after he died, I didn't ever want another one because it hurt so much to lose him, but now I think I would try again. —I-521, Sharon, 35 yrs., New Jersey

I acquired my recent iguana because I miserably missed my first iguana that died.   —conversation at pet store

At some point, the idea of getting another iguana will probably come into your mind. The first desire for a new iguana may be the wrong one—to fill the void of the dead one. Or it might be that you love iguanas so strongly that you want that feeling to continue without lapse. I felt this shortly after Za's death, but fought the feeling.

For one thing, how important can your dead pet have been if it is replaced the next day? But there is a better reason for waiting. There is a certain flow and time that is needed before the hole left inside of you by death is filled properly. Even once the hole is filled, the scar remaining can be rough and jagged for some time.

Please don't rush into getting another iguana. Let time pass until getting another one really makes sense. At that point, it will be fair to your dead iguana's memory and to the value of the new lizard, which will have its own personality, likes, and dislikes. You'll be able to welcome the new iguana into your household and appreciate it for itself, not as a replacement for the pet you lost.

CHAPTER 8

Domestication

"Men have forgotten this truth," said the fox, "but you must not forget it. You become responsible, forever, for what you have tamed." —*The Little Prince* by Antoine De Saint-Exupery

In the beginning God created the heavens and earth and a "wild-caught" monster lizard from hell: Za, my pet iguana. For about the first three months, he would whip his tail at me, at his food, and at imaginary foes. On his really bad days, he would open his mouth and try to bite me. And he disliked being held! He would flash those black-as-coal eyes and squirm as if someone were trying to steal his soul when I attempted to hold him for even a minute.

And then, transformation. Around four or five months later he was 60% better and at nine months he became sweet, friendly, and unafraid of me, no longer wiggling to get out of my hand. By the end of a year, he was completely tame.

So wild iguanas can change, even some of the worst ones. Iguanas have not been domesticated on a grand scale for thousands of years like dogs or cats. They are wild animals. It's amazing, when you really think about it, that they can be tamed at all.

Since I have had my iguanas they have gone from aggressive and scared to trusting and comfortable. —I-272, James, 26 yrs., Washington

I can't believe how she has become so tame. I did not know they could be tamed. —I-801, Tom, 16 yrs., California

The first part of the taming process starts by simply slowing down your movements in and around the iguana's habitat and avoiding loud noises. This will help your animal feel that it is in a safe place. Remember that fast movements by any animal in the jungle usually signal it's killing, being killed, or trying to escape being killed.

My iguana was very stressed in the first few weeks at home, scurrying for cover every time we approached him. He has since gotten used to our presence and

441

does not react stressfully any more, except getting startled with loud noises or rapid movements.   —I-799, Rui, 35 yrs., New York

First and most important is to keep the stress to a minimum. It is important to have the iguana realize that our presence is not a presence of intimidation.
                    —I-653, Justin, 19 yrs., Maryland

The first few weeks in its new environment, your iguana will be frightened and stressed, so don't force yourself on it. The only close contact for a while should be to offer food and water and to clean up feces daily.

GETTING YOUR IGUANA OUT OF ITS HABITAT

He doesn't like you to reach in the cage and take him out. Once he bit me and drew blood. But as soon as he's out, he's fine.
                    —I-739, Mike & Sherree, 22 yrs., Ohio

An iguana is a wild animal, so it's not unusual for it to bolt, whip its tail at you, and in general act as if it doesn't especially like to be touched when you try to get it out of its habitat. No wonder. Here is this huge thing (hand) chasing it around the habitat for who knows what purpose. But once caught, an iguana usually settles down, probably thankful that the thing with five projections didn't eat it right on the spot. Your iguana will stay aware, on red alert, to see what comes next. That's why it's important to ease up a little on the pressure when you grasp your lizard.

Don't make coming out of the habitat a stressful event. Iguanas will often reflect your emotions. If you get excited, move quickly, act nervous, or speak loudly, they will think something bad is about to happen and will go into "fight-or-flight" mode. Soothe the wild beast with a soft voice and non-threatening, slow, easy movements.

When you take your iguana out of the habitat, <u>don't</u> pick it up from above if at all possible. In the wild, iguanas sit in the tops of trees and bushes, basking and taking it easy. Eagles, hawks, and other birds of prey make meals of the iguanas by grasping the lizards from above and flying off with them. Instinctively, perhaps, iguanas associate "thing grasping from above" with "danger!"— and react accordingly.

I was once foolish enough about a month ago to reach for him from the top when his head was toward me. I put my hand around his back, and he clamped his little jaws right onto the outside of my right wrist. It was just a tight pinch, and since I didn't let go, neither did he! So I pulled my skin out of his unrelenting pinch.   —I-855, Meredith, 47 yrs., Oregon

Also, don't let Mr. Hand chase the iguana around and around in the habitat trying to get it out. If you chase your iguana with the "hand monster" each time you enter its habitat, the lizard will only get more stressed because it will remember the last chase scene.

Stop this negative routine. Do something different: Put your hand into the iguana's habitat, then <u>wait</u> a minute. Your next movement should be slow, smooth, steady, with your hand getting closer and closer to the iguana, hand flat, palm up, close to the bottom of the habitat. In this position, it is hard for your iguana to bite you—and your hand looks less threatening.

The ideal position for picking up a hatchling iguana is with your fingers sliding under the iguana's breastbone. Then turn your hand 90 degrees to the side so your thumb is facing in the same direction that the iguana's head is pointed (forward). Then slowly and gently wrap your fingers around the middle of the animal's body and slowly remove the lizard from the habitat.

This technique gets your iguana completely off guard. Iguanas have no records in their mental survival tapes of being picked up from the bottom in this manner. This technique—with your hand approaching the iguana from below—is almost impossible if you keep your iguana in an enclosure that opens only from the top (e.g., an aquarium tank). That's one reason I don't find this kind of environment suitable for iguanas. (See Chapter 4, Housing, "Habitat Options," for some good design ideas.)

Don't always take your iguana out when Mr. Hand goes into the habitat. Sometimes offer a food treat instead, or just touch your lizard gently. Soon your iguana will think that Mr. Hand is OK. Hands should not be associated with something unpleasant, but rather with things such as food, warmth, and peace.

I think it helped to put our hands in the cage for something other than to grab him—to fiddle with things or just hang there.
        —I-705, Linda & Paul, 45 yrs., California

My iguana scratched my arms a lot trying to get him out of the cage. Then I started petting him while he was in the cage. Eventually he quit running around in the cage. So then I started taking him out and holding him every day for about 5 to 10 minutes. Eventually he calmed down and started to enjoy coming out.   —I-783, Leanna, 22 yrs., Washington

If your iguana is already tame from a previous owner, it might climb onto your hand without the methodical technique described above.

We have had our iguana for only about four months [5-month-old iguana], and it already climbs readily up my arm when I put my hand in its cage.
        —I-830, Elisa, 27 yrs., New York

It's important to note that even though iguanas look like indestructible dinosaurs, they <u>aren't</u>! They have many delicate body parts prone to easy injury. For example, on the way out of the habitat, iguanas often grab onto anything and everything with their grappling-hook claws. Don't jerk them away from an object when they hook on like this. Toes and claws can be broken or even ripped completely off if the animal is pulled or yanked out of the cage too quickly. (Children and impatient adults are the usual culprits here.) Instead, gently lift the specific claw or foot that is hooked.

The tail is <u>especially</u> susceptible to breakage. An older iguana's tail does not have sections that are meant to break off easily for survival, as in some lizards. Even so, it can be broken. **Don't ever grab or hold the tail tightly.** Let me say that again: **Don't ever grab or hold your iguana's tail, EVER!** It can break off!

More than a dozen people have written to me and said how bad they felt when they either grabbed or held their iguana's tail when the lizard was trying to get away, and the tail broke off. One person said that his iguana was running into the kitchen (where it wasn't supposed to be) and he just grabbed the most accessible body part. The tail broke off as the iguana flailed violently to escape.

Once the tail is broken, its growth will be retarded and it will never be long and beautiful again. The new growth will be more like a stub than an original, slender tail and will be brown or blackish with little or no other natural coloring. Without a full-length tail for balancing, your iguana will have a more difficult time climbing.

If you don't pay attention, you can also accidentally sit on the tail or catch it between objects. Iguanas don't make any sounds, so if they are in trouble or pain they won't let out a yelp like a dog to alert you to the situation.

HANDLING YOUR IGUANA

If you don't know how to properly handle my iguana [SVL: 14", TL: 3' 9", 3 yrs.], he will take charge of the situation. He does this with others, not me.
                    —I-798, Teri, 35 yrs., New Hampshire

When you touch your new friend, the first thing you will discover is that your iguana doesn't care about you or about being touched! Of course they run away when you try to grab them. Of course they don't want to be held. They are wild animals forced into a foreign, captive situation, dependent on strange, upright, hairy, non-scaly creatures for their survival.

When first acquired from my daughter, my iguana thrashed around quite a bit. My daughter said she had to wear thick gloves because the iguana would bite her. But I felt she didn't handle him enough because I have not had that experience. He's calm and very docile. I handle him two times a day minimum.
                    —I-586, Joanne, 44 yrs., Florida

My husband has handled our iguana most of the time it has been our pet [3 yrs.]. As the iguana got older he liked only my husband and would hiss at me.

I have been handling our iguana this last year and he no longer hisses at me.
                                      —I-434, Karen, 39 yrs., New York

The only way your iguana will become familiar with you is through handling. The more it is handled, and not hurt or stressed in the process, the more
familiar and confident it will become with you.

But too much handling, especially in the beginning, can be very stressful.
For the first two or three weeks don't try to handle your iguana if it seems
scared. Allow it time to settle into its new home and feel safe. When you can
put your hand into the habitat without your lizard running and hiding, you can
start touching it. Your iguana may even avoid the whole situation by retreating
to its hide box (Chapter 4, Housing, "Hide Box") that you have provided.

Work with your iguana frequently. Winning his trust through careful han-
dling is the only way to tame him. "Working with" also means knowing when
to give the iguana privacy, for excessive handling can cause great stress. Your
iguana's behavior will help you determine how much handling is right. Hyper-
activity and excitability are signs of early stress, while weakness, depression,
and lethargy are often signs of extreme stress.
                                      —I-237, Diane, 44 yrs., Texas

Getting your iguana used to being handled must happen in a series of small
steps. Once you start handling your iguana, do it for about 10 to 15 minutes
once a day for a couple of weeks, then try a couple of weeks of holding the lizard
for about 15 to 30 minutes once or twice a day. After that you can easily double
the length and frequency of your sessions or create your own timetables.

I would spend just a few minutes with them, gradually increasing my exposure
with them until I could spend an hour. After achieving this I would try to hold
them. This sounds a lot easier than it is. In a few months my iguanas became
at ease with my presence.   —I-794, Andrés, 30 yrs., California

Someone told me, "Hold your iguana for a long period of time; let him run
over your hands, back and forth." I had my iguana out for 30 minutes at a time
about three weeks after he became my pet. After that break-in period, I once
held him for two hours while watching TV. He was instantly better, by the next
day. The long time seemed to break him.   —I-494, Jim, 25 yrs., California

When you are handling your iguana, make sure the lizard feels secure. If
the iguana feels like it's going to fall, it will claw deeply into your skin for a
more secure hold. In the wild, an iguana will tighten its grip if it senses that it
might be falling out of a tree or bush. When you hold an iguana, your arm is
like a tree branch to them. If you don't want to get clawed unnecessarily, support your animal properly. Information for correct holding of all sizes of iguanas will be explained in the next section, starting on page 446.

Most wild iguanas will want to wiggle out of your hand to escape. The tighter your grip gets, the more the iguana will want to escape because it feels it's in danger of being killed. Predators in the wild grip tightly before they deliver the final death blow so their prey can't escape. Don't put a death squeeze on your iguana.

If the lizard struggles to get away, let it know that it's not going anywhere by applying a slight pressure on its body with your fingers. Iguanas usually struggle severely for only a few seconds and then kind of give up and relax. That's the time to relax your gripping pressure a little. The key is that when the iguana gives up struggling, you relax your grip slightly. Eventually, your iguana will make the connection that the hand holds tightly only when the lizard struggles.

Gentleness works every time.　　　—I-635, Andrea, 38 yrs., Wisconsin

Iguanas have distinct personalities and they respond to gentle handling.
　　　　　　　　　　　　—I-521, Sharon, 35 yrs., New Jersey

When holding an iguana, exert about the same pressure you would use for a handful of flowers—not so strong as to break the stems, and not so gently that the flowers will fall out of your hand.

Also, try gently stroking the iguana's head and talk softly to it. I don't believe that the iguana at this wild stage really enjoys being petted, as a cat or dog would, but gentle touching shows the iguana that your hands are not "things" that are going to injure or kill it.

HOLDING YOUR IGUANA

There will be many "right" ways to hold an iguana. I present a technique here for those who don't have any idea how it's done, or who would like to try a new approach. All that really matters is that both the holder and the holdee are happy with the situation.

They say that a picture is worth a thousand words, so look now at the illustrations on pages 448 and 449 for one good approach to holding your hatchling, juvenile, or adult iguana.

If you have a hatchling or small juvenile, start by putting the lizard in the hand you use the most, for best control. (The drawings in this book show iguanas held in the human's left hand, because I'm left-handed.) The drawing shows how this should look, but a few extra details might be helpful. By having the iguana's arm come out between your fingers, as illustrated, you have more control if the lizard wants to jump around or off your hand. All you have to do is apply clamping pressure with your ring and little fingers around the lizard's arms.

What you can't see on the other side of the hatchling drawing is that the

---

SIDEBAR

Gloves

A few people who are afraid of being scratched or bitten by an iguana have used leather gloves to protect themselves. For a hatchling or small iguana, this is overkill. For large juveniles and adults, I believe it might be a temporary solution for a specific situation (e.g., giving medicine), but should not be the way to handle your lizard on a daily basis.

If you put on gloves just to handle your iguana, it doesn't take the lizard long to get the connection. The iguana may get more nervous, anxious, or aggressive when it sees the gloves.

With gloves, you also lose the sensitivity of handling your iguana properly. I have handled a number of angry, large iguanas and sometimes thought gloves might help the situation, but I never used them. I felt I would lose the quickness, agility, firmness, and sensitivity the situation required.

There is a quotation in Chapter 3, Choosing Your Pet, about a woman who wanted to handle a large iguana at a pet store. The iguana was considered "wild," and the owner brought gloves to protect the woman from the wild beast. The woman refused the gloves and just picked up the lizard, who immediately settled in her arms. You need to be the judge of your specific situation—gloves or no gloves.

---

iguana's left arm drops between the human hand's thumb and forefinger. If your lizard starts to "get out of control" you can essentially hold the lizard in place by curling your thumb over the top of the iguana's neck and applying some light pressure. For more control, your forefinger can come in tighter from the side. Also, if your iguana turns its head to bite, you can control it with a light pushing pressure with your thumb (if the lizard is trying to bite from the left) or index finger (if the bite is coming from the right).

An extended index finger can also be used as a resting place for your iguana's head. Once your iguana gets used to being held, the next thing it will do is relax, and it will naturally want to rest its head on the finger. Iguanas are silly creatures and this little index finger support trick makes them very happy.

When holding your small iguana, try not to let the iguana's tail just drop off your arm. If you can get the tail to balance on your forearm (and trail back toward your armpit), your iguana will feel more secure. Often I would bring my forearm close to my body so my lizard's tail was supported by the side of my body as well as my forearm. (But don't pin or squeeze the tail.)

Holding a large juvenile or adult is much like a hatchling, except that you support the lizard on your forearm instead of your hand. Your arm is a perfect

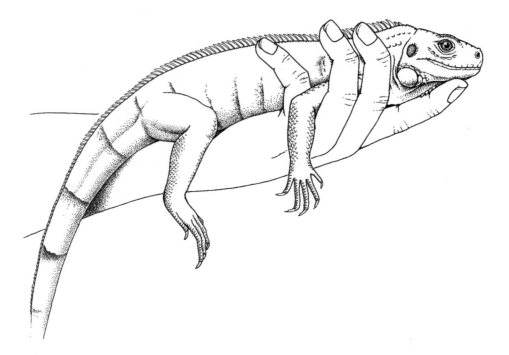

Figure 8.1: One way to hold your small iguana is in your hand, as shown here.
Illustration by: Kendal Morris

resting or carrying place for your iguana. To the iguana, it's like a big tree limb. If your lizard feels secure on this soft limb called an arm, it won't dig its claws into your skin, as mentioned earlier.

For extra support, hold the iguana's tail under your armpit (as shown in the illustration), which also prevents the tail from flopping or whipping about. Even as large as my iguana was at five years old (SVL: 19½", TL: 5' 5½", 13 lbs.), he was very easy to carry in this manner. The holding arm should be your strongest arm, as these lizards can get heavy after a while.

Another way to hold a large iguana is against your chest, flat, like a human baby might be held. After Za turned 4 years old, this was his favorite way to be transported from room to room in the house. His head would naturally rest at the top of my shoulder, his hands and body flat against my chest. In this position, you must also give a supporting hand under the lizard's butt and legs.

Be aware, however, that a few problems might occur when holding an iguana against your chest:

- Your iguana might want to climb from your chest to the top of your head the first few times. <u>Don't</u> allow this to happen (if you don't know why,

Figure 8.2: Large iguanas need more surface area to feel settled when they are being held; using a forearm (shown here from both sides) is one good option. Illustration by: Kendal Morris

read page 486 for the reasons). If your lizard starts climbing up, remove it and put it back on your chest. Also, when your lizard attempts this, say "NO" in a firm voice, so it recognizes that something is not right.

- A sweater or any other open-weave garment could catch the iguana's claws. Not only could the sweater be torn, but your iguana might also get its claws tangled. If the lizard were to fall or jump to the ground, its toe(s) could easily be broken. Just as serious, you could have a wild, crazy, tangled iguana close to your face.

- When the lizard is close to your face, its claws could easily catch an earring. It took my girlfriend only one tangle with my iguana's claws, and the resulting pain, to learn not to wear her earrings when he was close to her face.

It almost pulled my ear off when a claw got caught in my earring. The faster we tried to untangle it the more the iguana got "spooked," causing me more pain.
                                                    —phone conversation with an iguana owner

TAMING

If you want a friendly, responsive pet [iguana], you must put a lot of care and time into it. If you want just a showpiece (as does a zoo), then food, water, and light will do. —I-626, Gail, 48 yrs., New York

Changing the instinctive protective life-support patterns of an animal that has been on the earth for millions of years sounds impossible. For a wild iguana, to be held for an instant is to die—just another meal for a predator. From the moment an iguana cracks out of its egg, its instincts scream, "Run, hide, and don't get caught!" Iguanas are wild animals. To even think they can be tamed seems preposterous. But they can.

In my iguana questionnaire research, one of the things I asked iguana owners was to rate their pets' degree of tameness based on a 1-to-50 scale, with 1 being sweet and 50 being a monster from hell (see Appendix A for more background on this research). Throughout this book, the numerical tameness ratings you see in various quotations from owners are based on this 1-to-50 scale.

When purchased, my iguana would whip his tail at me, feign biting, and run like hell from any hands that came into his cage, including those that held food dishes. He would not eat in front of humans. He would not sit on a person. From my experience with other juvenile iguanas, I would rate his tameness at about 35-40, in that he reacted like any other iguana that had received minimal handling, and was not a predisposed evil personality.
—I-515, Lynn, 21 yrs., Canada

AT A GLANCE: *Things That Will Help Tame Your Iguana*
- Build your iguana's trust and confidence in you
- Handle and touch your iguana daily
- Feed by hand
- Have patience—taming takes time

The act of taming an iguana is not meant to break its spirit, but to expand the perimeters of its life. The basis of taming is very simple: Avoid those things that in the wild would scare your iguana or make it feel vulnerable. Understand that many of their predators attack from above and hold on tight to kill; that iguanas are extremely territorial; that iguanas are most secure when they are at the highest point in an area (this may be a treetop, the top of the curtains, or your shoulder); and so on. Work with the natural instincts of your pet, and the results will amaze you.

Some iguanas, especially at the hatchling stage, need only a little taming.

*I wouldn't call what we did taming him. He took about a week to acclimate
himself to us.*   —I-171, Drew, 34 yrs., Minnesota

*I'd rate my iguana [SVL: 15"; TL: 3' 1", 4 yrs., 6 lbs.] at 40 when I first pur-
chased him. He was very young (approximately 3 months), very fast, and very
small. He showed no aggressive behavior but he did not like to be held and
would hide in his hide box when approached. I really don't remember how
long it took to tame him. I don't remember it taking very long—maybe two
weeks and I had him eating out of my hand and he wouldn't scurry off when
approached. He is now very tolerant and gentle—I would rate him about 10 on
your scale.*   —I-727, Sharon, 34 yrs., South Carolina

Some iguanas may be skittish or act like tough guys in their habitats
because it's their territory they need to defend, or because they are afraid.
Often, once out and away from their territory, they become sweet and gentle.

*He is wild when he is being taken out of his cage. After he is out, he calms
down. He will sit with us for a long time, but he also likes to go exploring.*
                              —I-806, Shelly, 20 yrs., Pennsylvania

The majority of iguanas have had a rough life on their way to your home.
Small hatchlings are often shipped across the planet in cramped containers
with low temperatures. Sometimes little or no food is offered during transit, so
these lizards may retain some bad memories of what humans can do. Older
iguanas may have had several different owners in their lifetimes and might
remember previous mistreatment. Only over time with a good pet owner will
the iguana feel comfortable and secure.

By following a few set procedures a couple of minutes every day, you can
tame an iguana enough not only to be held but also apparently to enjoy it.
When an iguana gets older and bigger it can even become a member of the
household, walking around the house freely much like a house cat (see Chapter 4, Housing, "Loose in the Home").

Building Confidence

Your first priority must be to build your iguana's confidence in being
around you. This will take some time. But, you ask, how long will it take?
Think of the taming process as a journey. How long does it take to drive from
New York to Los Angeles? It all depends on how much time you actually spend
driving instead of just talking about it. Confidence is something that should
grow each day without much effort during the trip.

Below are a number of stories from iguana owners around the country,
representing a full range of interactions between iguana owners and their pets.

No Rough Play

A very important note is that iguanas don't understand or want any part of rough play or teasing, like some dogs enjoy. Iguanas will respond with an aggressive or defensive behavior if treated in this manner. It's not in their nature to understand these kinds of situations. So don't think that over time they will learn to "enjoy" it; they won't.

One time I was teasing my adult iguana and he bit me, but it was my fault.
—I-940, Linda, 44 yrs., California

I never tease or "play" with my iguanas. They do not understand these actions and doing it will only make them fear you and others.
—I-764, Diana, 46 yrs., California

These stories should help you realize that you are not alone with the challenges involved in taming your iguana.

I try to spend as much time with my iguana as I can. The more time I spend with him, the better he behaves and stays calm.
—I-841, Bonnie, 23 yrs., Texas

I bonded with my iguana by handling her every day. If she began to get stressed out while she was being held, I would try to calm her down. If that didn't work, then I would just put her back in her cage and try to hold her again later in the day.
—I-806, Tiffany, 14 yrs., Texas

When purchased at 4 months old, my iguana was rated at 35. He was hard to pick up and would lash his tail wildly and was constantly trying to get away. At 7 months old he sits on my lap or shoulder and does not lash his tail. I would rate him now about a 10.
—I-716, Thomas, 26 yrs., New Jersey

When I first purchased my iguana she was the iguana from hell (the worst on your rating scale). Now she's no different than my dog in attitude.
—I-782, Elizabeth, 16 yrs., New Jersey

Our iguana was wild, about a 45. He disliked being touched; not affectionate at all; aggressive; opened his mouth and showed his teeth; and moved his tail like a whip for defense. Even a strange hissing sound came out of him.

After about a year—no joke—his tameness is much better. He likes having his head rubbed, he will sit on your shoulder, and he will allow you to carry him. It took continued efforts to tame him. We just never gave up, taking time daily to interact. Finally he became less wild. However, he is still not really affectionate. If he is in the mood he will allow himself to be touched. It has to be on his terms and when he's ready.

—I-815, Janice & Jimmy, 40 yrs., Alabama

When I got my iguana, she was probably a 53! (way past your tameness scale's upper limit of 50) because her previous owners were kids and they abused her very badly. I thought I could work with her and tame her. Well, I did, and now she is about a 2. It took about four or five months.

—I-864, Cynthia, 13 yrs., Florida

He attained his current level of tameness—rated about a 5—after about six months. He gets nervous when my 2-year-old son is around (most people get nervous around my 2-year-old).   —I-872, Dave, 34 yrs., New Jersey

If you don't pay attention to your iguana, your iguana won't pay attention to you.   —I-764, Diana, 46 yrs., California

Close Encounters

Remind people that you get out what you put in. I have gotten a lot from my iguana because I have spent a lot of time with him.

—phone conversation with a pet owner

An iguana needs time to adjust to being out in an environment significantly larger than its habitat. Most iguanas have spent too much of their lives in small cages. If you let your iguana out in a big room for the first time, it may run wild hitting walls, furniture, or anything else that's in its way. Perhaps it feels in this big space that there is finally a chance to escape from those damned humans. That's why your iguana's first outside-the-habitat time should be spent in a small room.

Open spaces noticeably made her feel vulnerable in the beginning.

—I-249, Linda, 36 yrs., New Jersey

She was mostly just scared when out in the front room. She'd hide or run (without turning for walls—poor snout!).   —I-865, Julie, 46 yrs., California

Once my iguana is out of my hand, I better keep an eye on him or I may spend half the night looking for him.   —I-702, Kathleen, 22 yrs., Missouri

The best place to start the taming process is in a small room (such as a bathroom or den) to reduce the potential of the lizard getting injured or lost, but you should wait and introduce your iguana to this taming space only when you feel the animal is somewhat tame—perhaps three to four weeks after it joins your household. Too much freedom in a large space in the beginning can be a little overwhelming for your lizard.

Start by bringing your iguana into this room with you for 15 to 30 minutes three to five times a week, but make sure you "rat-proof" the taming space first. Iguanas are great climbers and fast as lightning. Because of this, make sure the iguana can't escape down some vent hole or be wedged, tangled, burned, cut, or injured somewhere in this room. Cover drains, plug holes, secure dangling wires, and prevent doors from opening suddenly with a sign on the outside saying: "Iguana loose inside—Knock first."

> *Daily contact will provide tranquillity. Your iguana will begin to look forward to your daily visits.*   —I-694, K.L., 29 yrs., Kansas

> *We tried to keep her environment as stress-free as possible while she was out of her cage.*   —I-754, Karen, 33 yrs., New Mexico

> *Exposing her to changing environments often, and always allowing her to destress if necessary at these times, is important. She is quite trusting of humans now.*   —I-795, Dawn, 24 yrs., Ohio

While in the room with your iguana, you might bring a book or something to do to help the time pass faster. Sit on the floor and put your iguana on your knee. Let the iguana decide to stay with you or roam around the room. Don't try to force your will upon the lizard, except if it is headed for some kind of danger. If your iguana stays with you, that's OK. If not, don't worry. What usually happens is that the lizard explores all parts of the room, much like a cat. Eventually, it will be get bored and come to visit you. If it does, you can attempt to slowly pet the top of its head. If it acts like it dislikes this, stop.

> *I let my iguanas do as they pleased for one hour each day. In the beginning they ran around, climbed curtains, and didn't even want to be touched. But then they began to trust me. After a while they would know it was playtime and let me hold them and pet them, and they would stay relaxed.*
> —I-317, Todd, 19 yrs., California

This act of freedom really speeds the process of taming. The iguana begins to see you as something non-threatening and as the provider of freedom.

Please note that it's not a good idea to let a hatchling have full run of the house all the time. My questionnaire research indicates that iguanas given too much freedom too early tend not to tame easily. It's much like a human child who is allowed to have all the freedom it wants from day one. You end up with a monster on your hands.

If the size of the training room is expanded slowly (perhaps start in a bathroom, then a bedroom, then living room) along with the length of time out, the iguana adjusts much better.

Petting Your Iguana

Recently, I started taking him [SVL: 5", TL: 18", 1 yr.] to the living room to watch TV or walk around the apartment with him. He is petted daily and seems to like to be stroked around his neck and on his head. He seems to be calm and quiet, and sometimes he even falls asleep. —I-799, Rui, 35 yrs., New York

Make sure you stroke or pet your iguana only in the direction its scales point—the scales lie like the wood shingles on the roof of a house. Petting in the wrong direction will irritate your iguana and can cause you to scrape your own skin on some of the sharper scales.

When you pet an iguana's head, the iguana will often close its eyes, which causes most people to think that the lizard is enjoying the experience. But an iguana encountering an irritating object or sensation will close the eye nearest to the irritating stimulant.

One way to check if your iguana is enjoying being petted is to see if the other eye is closed, too. If it's open, your iguana is most likely just tolerating you. If both eyes are closed completely—and the iguana's body is relaxed, not stiff—your lizard is most likely enjoying the experience. If both eyes are closed and its body is stiff, there is a good chance your lizard is uncomfortable with what is happening to it.

An iguana that seems very aggressive or fearful should not have its head touched for a while. Touching too soon is a quick way to lose its trust and be bitten at the same time. An iguana's instincts tell it that other creatures close to its head signal big trouble or death. You need to build up your iguana's confidence in you before you touch its head.

There are many places and ways to pet an iguana. Iguanas do have definite personalities, preferences, and moods, which are easily noticed. Pay attention. One moment your iguana may want to be petted, the next minute not. Iguanas "talk" loud and clear with body language.

My iguana has bitten me only once. I was petting him and he indicated he was tired of it. Well, I had to do it just one more time! My fault entirely.
—I-916, Lucretia, 32 yrs., California

Za, my iguana, absolutely hated having his neck rubbed for the first year of his life. But I figured that because he bobbed his head so much, the muscles in his neck must be tight and that rubbing this area would be relaxing to him. About one-and-a-half years later, he gave in to this experience and from then on his whole body would just melt whenever his neck was rubbed.

Za also had a strange quirk: He liked his head held somewhat firmly (as a hatchling he would move into my curved hand, then poke his head out between my fingers). This evolved over the years so that he liked my hand wrapped around his head with just his nose sticking out. Even at 5 years old he liked this strange handling.

But he never liked his head petted when he was outside in the yard. Maybe it was because he thought he had to be "on guard" outside and he didn't want anything to block his view or his third eye. "Don't touch my head," he would say with his body language, by kicking his rear leg forward to knock my hand off his head. Pretty straightforward language! He would also shake his head wildly back and forth trying to dislodge my hand from his head. I would always take my hand off when he did this. Za made his desires very apparent to me. All iguanas do the same; just pay attention to them.

Hand Feeding

By hand feeding, the iguana will learn to trust you much faster, and will quickly learn that you're not going to eat it! Daily attention will produce results.
—I-11, Patty, Washington

For the first month, your iguana might not even let you see it eat from its food bowl, let alone take food from your hand. My iguana was still a little shy about eating while I watched, even after several weeks. Don't be surprised if your iguana refuses to eat with an audience for at least this long.

Hand feeding is a short cut in developing trust, which in turn is an important component of taming. Once your lizard lets you watch it eat, then you can start trying to feed it <u>occasionally</u> from your hand. The best food items are leafy greens such as collard and mustard greens, kale, carrot tops, beet leaves, and celery tops (sweet and tender). Also good are dandelion and nasturtium leaves and flowers.

Lettuce (with essentially no food value) should be the taming food of last resort. If you must use lettuce, romaine or redleaf are the best. Head lettuce was developed for shipping across the country and has about as much nutritional value as the cardboard it's shipped in.

Teaching your iguana to take food from your hand requires some patience initially. Hand-fed iguanas are generally more tame and "pet-like."
—I-237, Dianne, 44 yrs., Texas

I think what helped tame him was when I began feeding him treats by hand. At first he wouldn't eat at all, but I was very persistent. When he would flick his tongue, I would shove a leaf in his mouth. He was rated a wild 45 at first; now six months later I would rate him a 3.
—I-783, Leanna, 22 yrs., Washington

There will be a point when your iguana doesn't run from the hand offering the food. The lizard will be curious, flick the food item with its tongue, and most likely eat it.

The hand-feeding technique should be initiated about an hour or so before normal feeding time, if possible. Hold the food in your fingertips close to your iguana's face; hold steady, don't move. If your lizard runs away, try the technique another day.

*She eats from my hand, but any quick or careless movement on my part sends
her into the usual panic flight.* —I-629, Theodore, 25 yrs., Michigan

In the beginning, your iguana may accidentally bite your fingers. When my
iguana was offered a dandelion flower the first time, he got so excited he nipped
my finger a little with his teeth. It was more startling than anything else. He
learned very quickly what was food and what was finger. Soon he would
extend his soft tongue and very delicately pluck the food item from my fingers. It's actually quite amazing that they learn so quickly to distinguish food
from non-food.

*Today she [SVL: 6½", TL: 22", 7 mo.] tried to swallow my index finger, not
realizing I did not have food. I picked her up and put her back in her cage a few
times until she got the idea that I was coming to say hello, not to just bring her
food. I really have to give her more non-food related "attention" in her cage
now, before she grows up and does some real damage.*
—I-725, Marie, 23 yrs., Maryland

If they eat from your hand, it is an indication that trust is developing. Once
the initial trust has developed through hand feeding, you can continue to do it.
Trust has deeper levels, so hand feeding becomes a ritual. Besides, it's really fun
to feed your iguana by hand—just don't overdo it.

Hand feeding once or twice a day, every couple of days, is plenty. Remember, you are not supplying dinner, you're developing trust and bonding with
your lizard. Reserve this technique for specific times, such as when entering the
cage or as a reward or training aid. Otherwise, your animal could become
spoiled and start to eat only by hand.

*When we got our iguana, I made an effort every day to touch her and feed her
by hand (which was perhaps not a great idea because she went through a phase
where she would eat only from my hand).*
—I-620, Suzanne, 34 yrs., New York

This is not just a hypothesis. I have seen at least 15 cases where iguana
owners inadvertently trained their iguanas to eat the main meal out of their
hand because it was such a fun bonding experience. Untraining the lizard from
this very bad habit is a slow, tedious, and difficult task.

Red Flags and Unhappy Cues

*It helps to know the signs of an agitated iguana: inflated body turned sideways,
tail readied for whipping, arched back. Hissing is often evident as well. Knowing these signs could save an owner from a painful lesson.*
—I-726, James, 24 yrs., Pennsylvania

Breaking Your Iguana's Addiction to Hand Feeding

If you start to feed your iguana its main food of the day by hand, it will start to get lazy. After a while, that's the only way it will eat. Some people stick small pieces of food into their iguana's mouth, like a treat given to a dog. But a conditioned addictive response is created when hand feeding is overdone.

When I tell people who are feeding their iguanas in this manner that the iguanas will get hooked, they don't believe it. Often they will call some time later and say they can't go on vacation or be gone from the house during the iguana's dinner time. They ask, "How can I get my iguana to eat on its own again?"

For all those people who feed their iguanas only by hand, it's time to break this bad habit and never start it again. There's an easy solution: Don't feed them by hand any more. But in reality, the conditioning may be so strong that they won't eat any other way.

What you need to do is uncondition them slowly. One way is to put the food on a flat plate and lift the plate up close to their face. They will see your hand and the food, make the connection, and eat the food. Do this for about four days. Then when you bring the food (on the plate) to their eating area, make them come to the plate to eat. This way, they are slowly being broken of a strong conditioning.

Once you feel that your iguana has adjusted to this phase, the next step is to leave the food dish in the habitat but keep one hand about 2" away from the food dish. Then keep moving the hand away in slow increments each day until not only is your hand away from the food, but your whole body is gone.

How long it takes for the complete transition from hand-feeding to the lizard eating on its own is a function of how long the bad conditioning has been going on. It might take several weeks to several months. This sidebar should encourage anyone starting to offer hand-fed treats to be very careful about how often it is done. If you think you're overdoing it, back off.

My iguana will bite sometimes when it is tired of being held. People need to notice signs of irritability early so they can put iguanas down. No one loses face. Trust develops, and domestication grows.

—I-554, Sharon, 40 yrs., New York

Because iguanas don't vocalize, they communicate mostly through body language. If you learn to read the subtle signals they display, you can hear them "talk."

For example, first thing in the morning my iguana didn't like to be touched or fussed with. When he was touched for more than a 15-second greeting, he squirmed as though you had dropped the black plague on him. He would often get a stiff body and swing his head quickly toward my petting hand with an evil eye as if to say, "Get your stinking hand off my body." Perhaps it's that his body hadn't warmed sufficiently to feel comfortable (or perhaps he just wasn't a "morning person"). But in the afternoon he got friendlier, and by evening he was sweet and cuddly. As he got older he maintained this same "schedule."

She snorts and grunts when she wants to be let go of.

—I-662, Sharman, 22 yrs., Wisconsin

Being able to identify some of these cues will help guide your taming sessions and your everyday interactions. If you watch your iguana closely, you may see that many of the "red flags" happen at the same times each day—an additional clue to taming and training your iguana.

The behavioral postures described briefly in the next few pages will help you interpret some of your iguana's likes and dislikes. They are postures used by wild iguanas to ward off, threaten, or manipulate other iguanas. For a more in-depth look at these postures, read Chapter 1, Iguana: The Species, "Common Iguana Behaviors."

Head

When he doesn't want to be petted on his head, he'll shake it from side to side (to get your hand off). —I-171, Drew, 34 yrs., Minnesota

When an iguana shakes, rolls, or bobs its head, it's communicating with you. Male iguanas tend to head-perform more often than females, and males tend to do it more as they get older, especially after they become sexually mature.

A gentle bobbing up and down is generally a greeting to acknowledge your presence and is usually non-threatening. The faster the performance of the bobs and shakes, the more it means that your iguana is in an irritated, aggressive, or assertive frame of mind, especially if it is looking right at you.

Eyes

Eyes tell all in attitude. —I-798, Teri, 35 yrs., New Hampshire

When its pupils are dilated, an iguana's eye looks like a large dot of black ink. Many times a dilated pupil is an expression of anger, like the "evil eye" my iguana gave me when I tried to touch him too early in the morning.

Pupils that dilate several times in succession often mean your critter is not happy. Treat it like a blinking yellow traffic signal: "CAUTION." But sometimes, frequent dilating is a sign of intense concentration or curiosity, as when the iguana is examining some new food or object (as some parrots do). You can almost see the lizard's brain struggling to make sense of the situation. If curiosity is causing the eye to dilate, the iguana's tongue may even come out and flick the object of interest to gather more information.

When you pet your iguana, often it appears that its eyes close from pleasure, like a cat's or dog's would. As I mentioned earlier, if only the eye nearest you is closed, most likely it's an overstimulation response. Perhaps the iguana feels if it closes that one eye, you will disappear. On the other hand, if both eyes are closed and the body is relaxed, that may indicate a relaxed, happy iguana. When an iguana is irritated, angry, or scared, the eyes will be wide open, much like in other animals and humans. Also, when you first encounter an unfamiliar iguana, don't stare into its eyes. Many animals and people see this as a challenge.

Mouth

All the times we got bitten by our iguana we were "warned" by him first, with an open mouth.   —I-171, Drew, 34 yrs., Minnesota

Iguanas don't waste time moving or doing anything for no apparent reason. They really know how to conserve energy. So if your iguana's mouth is open more than about a quarter of its full range, the lizard is most likely giving you a signal that it is agitated. In general, the wider the mouth is open, the more intense the message you are supposed to receive.

One exception to be aware of is that iguanas also open their mouths wide when they are overheated (see Chapter 1, Iguana: The Species, "Panting"). In most cases, it's pretty easy to distinguish between an overheated and an extremely agitated lizard.

When an iguana also raises or arches its tongue in its open mouth, and the tongue looks engorged, the lizard is really mad. I have seen the engorged tongue reaction only from males during breeding season. The full alarm is when it is doing all of the above plus hissing (pushing air out of the lungs). All these together make a very threatening display. Whatever you are doing to or near your iguana—STOP! Your iguana is <u>very</u> upset.

I've never been bitten, but when I first purchased my iguana he would have liked to (the first few weeks probably due to fear). He no longer opens his mouth wide to do so.   —I-798, Teri, 35 yrs., New Hampshire

Another exception to the open-mouth-means-danger rule is when your iguana's mouth is open to just a little slit. Often the lizard will turn its head from side to side at the same time, looking as though it were trying to figure something out, such as how to get up the drapes from the coffee table, or analyzing something totally new in its environment. I saw this hundreds of times from my iguana, always when he appeared to be "calculating," concentrating, or evaluating.

Because nothing ever hurt Za, he was not afraid of anything, not even loud mechanical noises, such as hair dryers, TVs, vacuum cleaners, drill motors, hammers, or ringing phones. True, he would walk up to a new object cautiously and a little defensively, but when this happened I would usually hold him in a gentle way and bring the object slowly to him. He would cock his head and open his mouth ever so slightly as the object came toward him. Once the object was right in front of his face, he'd flick it with his tongue and eventually relax. I guess for him it was another thing conquered in his world for the day.

Dewlap

The dewlap—the skin flap under the chin of the iguana—can be extended by the iguana at will. An extended dewlap can mean several things: The iguana is too hot or too cold, giving a general greeting, showing irritation, displaying dominance, feeling very threatened, claiming territory, or advertising for a mate.

If the dewlap is extended with no head bobbing or defensive body language, it might be performing as an ingenious all-purpose temperature-control device. An overheated iguana can extend its dewlap so that any breeze nearby can cool the blood circulating in the thin wall of the dewlap—much like a car radiator cools the engine as the wind blows against circulating water. A too-cool iguana may extend its dewlap toward a heat source, which warms the blood circulating through the dewlap, like a bank of solar collectors absorbs heat from the sun. When it's being used as a heater, the dewlap will usually turn a blackish color, because dark colors absorb more heat.

If the extended dewlap is accompanied by a gentle head bobbing, the iguana is most likely a male and is greeting you or acknowledging your presence with a little more "pomp and circumstance." But if the head is bobbing or shaking violently or in a quick, jerky movement, the iguana is using its extended dewlap to signal agitation.

Neck

When your iguana is very comfortable and relaxed while being held, its neck muscles will be firm but pliable, like a human biceps in a relaxed position. By stroking your iguana's neck, you can feel if it's tight or relaxed. Tight doesn't automatically mean the iguana's in a bad mood, but relaxed neck muscles do mean a relaxed lizard.

Tail

I really don't like it when my iguana beats the crap out of me with his tail on those occasions when I have to handle him.   —I-780, Carl, Florida

Iguanas in the wild whip their tails as a means of self defense, and so do pet iguanas. A pet iguana might use its tail if it feels particularly scared or threatened—e.g., facing a dog, being given an injection by a veterinarian, being teased, or being held unwillingly.

If your iguana is not yet tame, you'll no doubt get a first-hand look at tail whipping. As the iguana gets ready to whip, its whole body tenses and the reserved energy goes to the whipping tail. The iguana's body can jump forward to help the tail swing better. That jump forward is the part that really scared me the first few times my iguana (as a hatchling) did it—not the actual tail whipping. And it all happens in a split second.

When he becomes irritated or mad, he lifts and tenses his tail so that the base is higher (at about a 20° angle). Then he whips at me.
—I-825, Chris, 22 yrs., Illinois

He will twitch his tail back and forth when he is not in the mood to be touched.
—I-685, Julie, 36 yrs., California

If you are confronting a large iguana that is about to whip you, stop whatever you are doing. Being hit with a large iguana's tail is an experience you won't forget. Even a whip of the tail from a hatchling can cause significant pain, if it's directed at the right spot.

One day when I was taking my iguana [SVL: 6"] out of his cage I had my face too close. He whipped his tail at me and left my eye watering for 10 minutes. I have developed a certain respect for his aggressiveness despite his small size.
—I-661, Chris, 22 yrs., Nevada

If you get startled, scared, and pull away from a hatchling's whipping action, the iguana might think that it has discovered a way of keeping Mr. Hand at a distance. And the first few times that's just how I reacted to my iguana's whipping, until I realized that he wasn't trying to bite, just whip his tail. Once I didn't pull my hand away, he soon stopped doing it.

Just remember, if you think the pain caused by your hatchling or small juvenile is a problem, wait until the iguana becomes an adult. It's better that you correct the problem now (see page 487, "Tail Whipping," to learn how).

Hands and Feet

She was originally rated as 20; she is now around a 5. She does not mind being handled but she does have her moods where she will hit you with her front "hands" if you pet her when she doesn't want it.
—I-653, Justin, 19 yrs., Maryland

If your iguana isn't enjoying being petted, it might take its rear leg or foot and push or kick your hand off. Sometimes the foot comes up fast and sometimes in slow motion, almost comically. The iguana can also use its front arm or hand to push at your hand, but it doesn't have the same impact as the bigger rear foot. Often the lizard's eyes will begin dilating, another clue that the iguana is becoming irritated.

Once your iguana is tame, if it occasionally does this kicking, be considerate and remove your hand. My iguana as a juvenile and adult did this about once a month, so I just removed my hand. If the kicking is done on a more frequent basis, it most likely means your iguana is not yet tame and you need to overcome this reaction by leaving your hand where it is.

Claws

A tame iguana won't use its claws to hurt or injure you on purpose. Scratches from a tame iguana are usually the result of the lizard trying to get balanced on your arm. If you don't want to get clawed, support your iguana properly while holding it. In addition, trimming the very tip of their claws will dull them enough to reduce the possibility of injury. For details on this delicate but effective procedure, see the words and illustrations in Chapter 6, Special Care, "Claw Trimming."

Skin Color

An iguana's skin color will change in response to certain external and internal changes. Some of these changes require action on your part; more often, they indicate mood or temperature changes. For example, some iguanas respond to stress by darkening in color.

One of my iguanas [new animal] in particular doesn't appreciate being held and will quickly darken.   —I-556, Sharon, 40 yrs., New York

My iguana went rigid and turned a brown/gray color. It was several hours before he returned to normal.   —I-727, Sharon, 34 yrs., South Carolina

My iguana will turn a dark brown, almost black, when really pissed off.
                                                    —I-694, K.L., 29 yrs., Kansas

Some situations that can also cause your iguana to turn a darker color have nothing to do with stress: when your iguana is cold and needs more warmth, or if it's physically sick. In addition, some iguanas respond to certain stressful situations by losing color rather than darkening. The first few times my iguana went to the veterinarian's office, his head turned extremely pale, as if he were nervous. Both darkening and lighter-than-normal color can also occur if your iguana has been out in the sun for a long time.

Our iguana is bright green with a tinge of blue on his head. When he is mad or upset, his head turns dark gray, almost black. When he's out in direct sunlight, his body turns from bright green to dull, darkish green with brown spots.
                                                    —I-815, Janice & Jimmy, 40 yrs., Alabama

For more information on what a particular skin color might mean, see Chapter 7, Medical Troubleshooting, "Color Changes."

Breathing

He will now give us a warning, by breathing heavily, to tell us he is mad.
                                   —I-895, Julie & Jim, 25 yrs., Texas

Deep, sometimes rapid breathing usually indicates that your iguana is angry or scared. Another breathing quirk is that they may expel all of the air in their lungs, in one quick movement, creating a sound that some people call hissing. Or the iguana may even hold its breath for a minute or two. This last trick is much like a human child holding its breath while having a temper tantrum. The iguana's chest expands like a balloon, and it lets the air out about a minute later.

People have written to me with stories about their iguanas holding their breath, but I never saw this particular behavior until my iguana was about 3½ years old. Za did this when he wanted, for instance, to go into an "off limits" area of the house, and I wouldn't let him. After I had moved him three times away from this area, I would pick him up and hold him a little while to help break his determined pattern.

He would flail around in my arms, irritated as hell that he couldn't get into the room and that he had to be held and restricted. He would stop flailing and suck in all the air he could, holding it for about 30 seconds. Then the air would rush out and he would suck it back in. He tried this control move for only about a two-month period. Because he was such a big macho male, we often battled in the beginning to see who was in control.

Usually Za liked to establish eye contact with me when he was mad, but during this particular pouting session he would not look at me, perhaps to emphasize his irritation. After a few minutes of this pouting I would say in a soft tone, "Are we going to be a spoiled brat all day long? You will just stay in my arms until you breathe normally again." Three or four minutes of this holding and talking and he would settle down. He didn't understand my words, but I believe he did understand the process.

When he was calm again, I would pet his head and put him on the ground. He would usually walk someplace else in the house, turning back at least once to give me the "evil eye." He thought he won the battle, and I thought I did. Ten minutes later he would be back to his normal self, and if I picked him up his breathing would be normal and he would be relaxed. These creatures are so full of personality and life. And it wasn't just my iguana that acted like this. Other iguana owners have told me stories like this for years.

Swallowing

Swallowing is a non-threatening mannerism that probably indicates your iguana is nervous or upset—like a human who is nervous and has a dry mouth and is swallowing to get more fluid in the throat before speaking.

In addition to the trick of holding his breath, my iguana sometimes swallowed purposefully after he had a battle with me over something he wanted to do and I would not let him (for his safety). As I held him, he didn't struggle to get away but looked straight ahead and not at me. In about a minute he swallowed deeply a few times. He started this behavior when he was about 3 years old and did it half a dozen times over the next two years.

One exception to this experience is if your iguana is <u>not</u> in conflict with you or something else in its environment. In this case, the swallowing might be a medical problem associated with breathing. If in doubt, or if the behavior persists, check with your veterinarian.

Body Movement

An iguana can assume a wide range of movements when angry, irritated, defensive, or aggressive—from showing assertiveness and territorial control by puffing and expanding the body, to exhibiting distrust or irritation by slightly turning away from an object and closing one eye. For example, squirming is the standard reaction of iguanas trying to get away from us humans. In time, with careful observation, you'll learn to recognize and interpret your iguana's various body movements.

Many common iguana body movements are covered in more detail in Chapter 1, Iguana: The Species, "Common Iguana Behaviors." In addition, Chapter 9, Breeding, is filled with real-life stories from iguana owners, including great descriptions of aggressive body movements by male iguanas during breeding season.

Nipping

A nip from your iguana is usually just a warning. It's a small percentage of what a full-scale bite can be. There are basically two types of nips.

With the first type, you can see it coming. The iguana will have black, dilated, flashing eyes, its mouth is sometimes open, and usually the lizard lunges forward to inflict its warning. I would usually leave my iguana alone on the days he would try to nip. He was probably having a bad day and just wanted to be left alone. After my iguana was tame, the only time he ever nipped me was during breeding season.

> *He never bites like he used to, though if he's on the top of the curtains in the front room and I pet him and he walks away or bobs and I still pet him, he'll reach his head back toward my finger, then turn away, then back, and away, finally back, mouth opened, just a little, real slow, and he'll nip me.*
> —I-494, Jim, 25 yrs., California
> [AUTHOR'S NOTE: This is a very common pattern that all iguanas use. It's an indication that you have pushed your luck, and your iguana has made every effort to scare you off.]

The second type of nip is when you don't expect anything. It's usually from a new iguana in your household trying to assert itself, or during breeding season when your lizard (especially male) is being ruled by hormones. During breeding, be on guard and keep your lizard away from your face. For much more background on nipping and biting during the breeding season, turn to Chapter 9, Breeding.

Biting

I want to mention that we never became mad when our iguana bit us. He is merely a scared animal that thought we were dangerous to him.
—I-895, Julie & Jim, 25 yrs., Texas

When I was bitten by my iguana [SVL: 13", TL: 3' 6", 4½ yrs.], he had gotten tangled in a lamp cord while on one of his freedom days in the house. When I saw him tangled I got overly excited while trying to remove him from this potential danger. Consequently, I got bitten. I believe he saw my swift movements as a potential threat and bit me more as a protective mechanism.
—I-772, Andy, 32 yrs., California

Biting is usually the last weapon an iguana uses and the one that can leave the longest memories, especially from a large iguana. The bite of a hatchling is more of a surprise than anything else.

As a hatchling, my iguana bit me during the second week I had him. I work with my hands so they were pretty tough, and I didn't feel a thing. After Za bit me, he looked down at his feet with a strange expression on his green-and-turquoise face. Something like: " Just kidding—I didn't really mean it," "I won't try that again," or like a child caught with his hand in the cookie jar. He never bit me again until two years later, when he was going through his first breeding season.

I almost lost the end of my finger to an older iguana. They're quick and have one hell of a grip. —I-694, K.L., 29 yrs., Kansas

Being bitten by a 1½-year-old iguana is like having a serrated bread knife dragged across your bitten body part. On the other hand, a good bite from a 5-year-old, 13-pound iguana results in a trip to the hospital for stitches. I know, because Za bit me during an extremely irritated time in his fourth breeding season. He let me know he was irritated by all of the red flags I have already mentioned. I didn't feel like listening to his body-language messages that day, but I also didn't want the two stitches I got at the hospital.

Each time I've been bitten by my iguana it was for a reason, not just for the sake of biting. —I-764, Diana, 46 yrs., California

Below is just a sampling of some of the "biting stories" that people have shared with me over the years. I've included them to make you more aware of some of the reasons and ways an iguana might bite. Also, just as in the nipping section, your iguana can bite suddenly and unexpectedly or you can see him get prepared across the room. The stories also suggest ways to reduce or stop the biting. For further details on training an iguana not to bite, turn to page 487 in this chapter.

He has opened his mouth to try and bite my hand but missed. He will do it if he does not want to be touched, like an aggressive gesture.
—I-759, Laura, 20 yrs., Pennsylvania

My iguana [SVL: 6½ ", TL: 22", 7 mo.] has bitten us both on the finger a few times when he doesn't want to be "bugged." It normally won't stop me from holding him. I guess it's the "get back on the horse before he realizes that works" theory. It seems to work for me.
—I-725, Marie, 23 yrs., Maryland

We've all been bitten a few times, but mostly he's completely tame. One thing I would like to mention is that each time we were bitten, our iguana "warned" us first with an open mouth. We didn't pay attention to that and got bitten. The bites were deep and drew a lot of blood. You do need to be careful.
—I-171, Drew, 34 yrs., Minnesota

My new iguana has never even tried to bite me, not even when he was wild. But my first iguana bit my fingers every time he had a chance. That iguana was just a biter and if anyone was in reach, he would latch on.
—I-783, Leanna, 22 yrs., Washington

My iguana threatens to bite me several times a week, when I first pick it up. However, after I have been holding it for about five minutes, it will sit calmly on my hand. —I-685, Julie, 36 yrs., California

I have been bitten only twice by my iguanas, once by the male and once by the female. The time I was bitten by the male, he was very young and we were busy establishing who was the big iguana and who was subordinate. The female bit me while I was trimming her nails; I must have cut into the quick by mistake. —I-772, Andy, 32 yrs., California

I find that most iguanas will bite until they do not find you a threat.
—I-780, Carl, Florida

The only times she bit me was during the time I was taming her. She [hatchling] would open her mouth and I would let her bite my finger. Once she realized she wasn't hurting me and I wasn't going to jerk my hand away, she quit trying to bite. Now I pick her up and start rubbing the back of her neck and she goes to sleep. —I-818, Donna, 38 yrs., Texas

Sometimes biting is really just a mistake. My fault, my thumb. I didn't know that iguanas could distinguish color, and I was wearing red nail polish while hand feeding my iguana. He saw the red, probably thought it was one of his favorite foods (cherry or strawberry), and tried to eat it (my thumb).

—I-769, Yolanda, 20 yrs., Michigan

Inappropriate Defecation

My iguana is new and is a 40 on your scale. He runs away, whips, and defecates on you when you try to hold him.

—I-680, Catherine, 21 yrs., New York

One day I left my iguana in my office while I went downtown for a while. I didn't want him wandering around the house unsupervised, so I closed the door to my office. When I returned a short time later, I found a pile of poop near the closed door.

This happened five other times when I closed the door to keep him locked up. The first two times, I thought his defecations were just a freak accident. But the next times I faked leaving and peeked through the window to see what he would do. Sure enough, during three separate "experiments," Za came down off his chair by the sunny window when I closed the door. He scratched at the door, then defecated next to it!

I believe he saw the closed door and realized, after investigation, that he couldn't leave the room. Because iguanas are curious and stubborn animals, I think Za got mad at his loss of freedom—and expressed his displeasure by defecating by the closed door, even though in each case he'd already defecated before coming into my office.

I solved this particular problem by closing the office door partially when I was still home, leaving it open about 8". Then I went outside and watched him hop off "his" chair and walk to the door. He went through the open door, then turned back into the office and up onto his chair, without defecating.

After the third day of fake departures with the door partially open, he stopped coming off his warm, comfortable chair. I realized that he was happy with the new situation, and from then on I closed the door completely but gently on future trips away. Maybe he thought the door was still open and was too comfortable or lazy to check it out. In any case, he no longer expressed his frustration by defecating near the door.

Another defecation experience happened one day when I "jailed" Za (put him in his habitat) for going to an out-of-bounds area in the house one time too many. I closed the door to his habitat and didn't let him out the rest of the day. He was so mad (I guess) that he defecated in his upper water dish. His whole cage stank and was a mess. He made his point. If you doubt that this was an expression of anger or frustration, consider that he had already defecated once that day, and he never deposited feces in his water dish again. In addition, his body language and large, dilated eyes reinforced my conclusion.

I used to take Za to a lot of schools (elementary through high school) and talk to the kids about the rainforest, ecology, being good to each other, and, of course, iguanas. Each talk lasted about an hour, with between 20 and 300 students attending each time. Za seemed to love sitting on his special heated stand as I talked, and after the talk the kids all got to touch him. But when the group got over about 100 people he would need to defecate, even though he defecated just before we left for the school. Because of the limits of time and space in the building, he usually defecated on a stage—which, of course, the kids loved!

I told the kids not to make any noise as Za defecated on the paper towels I always brought. Afterwards, Za settled in and the talk continued. Stress can create unusual situations for both people and animals. It must have been a minor stress, as he always ate and otherwise behaved normally when he got home after one of these school trips.

I talked with some of the people who catch iguanas in the wild (in Mexico and Central America) to be sold as food in the marketplace. They said that after the iguanas are caught and stuck in a bag, they often defecate in the bag because they are scared.

> *For the first few weeks, if he got nervous he would poop down my neck when he was on my shoulder.* —I-773, Rich, 34 yrs., Nebraska

Yawning

Iguanas yawn! This is not a sign that something is wrong. The first time I saw this, I roared with laughter. A lizard yawns just like a human. By accident, my girlfriend yawned in front of my iguana one morning. He yawned back. Over a two-year period, he would yawn back about 75% of the time that she yawned in front of him. It seemed to work best when she really yawned, instead of faking it.

At this point, you now have enough background information on the habits and natural tendencies of your iguana—as well as the basics of handling and holding your lizard—to actually start the taming process.

Taming Formula

> *I feel that an iguana is tame when you can pick it up almost any time without a struggle and it doesn't try to run away.*
> —I-764, Diana, 46 yrs., California

Some of the key elements in taming your iguana are handling, patience, and consistency. This is the secret formula for soothing the wild beast:

Taming Formula

$$t\,[T + H\,(P + C)] = I_t$$

The Taming Formula symbols translate into the following concepts:
time [Trust + Handling (Patience + Consistency)] = Iguana$_{tame}$

If you apply the basic elements of *trust, handling, patience,* and *consistency,* in *time* you will have a *tame iguana.* Of course, if you can add more elements to the basic equation, the results will be faster and more long-lasting.

The first few months of taming typically are very slow, then you might get a big jump in results, then a plateau for quite some time, then little bits of change thereafter. The rate of success varies with each individual iguana.

Listed below are the basic taming elements with a detailed explanation of what they mean and how to go about implementing them.

Trust

I like the knowledge that my iguana knows me and trusts me.
—I-687, R., 54 yrs., Canada

The most rewarding and interesting thing is the complete trust my iguana [SVL: 14", TL: 3' 2", 3 yrs.] has in me. My friends comment, "He acts as if he is part of the family." And of course I respond, "He is."
—I-407, Ruth, 32 yrs., Ohio

Before starting any type of taming with your iguana, you <u>must first have</u> the trust of your animal. You can't start taming successfully without it.

As discussed in the previous section, one of the best ways to develop trust is to act daily in a non-threatening way around your iguana. That means <u>never</u> hit your iguana; move slowly and non-aggressively; and speak in soft quiet tones. Also, offer good, healthy, varied food and clean up the iguana's poop every day. These may seem like simple requirements, but some people have trouble maintaining them over time. But if you do these things, your iguana will eventually see you at least as a non-threatening entity, perhaps even as something it likes to be around.

On your 1-to-50 scale, he is now a 3. Very tame. Anybody can hold him. He no longer whips his tail or bites. It took from July to November for this. The biggest jump (20 to a 3) was during the two weeks that he was at his sickest. We had to give him a lot of special attention for long periods of time. He learned to trust us.   —I-530, Kathy & Bryan, 27 & 30 yrs., Florida

He [SVL: 6½", TL: 12½", 9 mo.] was mildly afraid of me at first. He would run when approached. It took a couple of months to get him to where he is now. He is about a 5 now. I handled him every day for about an hour. I would talk to him and gently stroke his head and let him walk from one hand to the other. I think a major key is that when you initially approach the iguana for at least the first month, you have to approach it in a non-threatening manner. Move slowly, and if they run, let them hide for a little while before trying again. Don't push them or they just become more stressed. Now he eats from my hand all the time. Sometimes he is still a little leery of me touching him, but not usually.   —I-788, Trevor, 19 yrs., Oregon

When I first got my first iguana [SVL: 13", TL: 3' 6", 5 yrs.] he was about a 20. The second iguana [SVL: 12½", TL: 3' 3½", 5 yrs.], who has always been more highly strung, I would rate as a 25. Yet both ate right away and I was able to approach them without flight right away. I was able to pick up the first iguana after a week. It took the second iguana three weeks. I think it took a complete change of seasons before my iguanas "trusted" me completely. I would rate the first iguana as a 5 today—he's almost like a cat—and the second one is a 10, as she's like a nervous cat now. —I-626, Gail, 48 yrs., New York

It takes time to build trust. If your lizard doesn't trust you, how could it ever think about eating out of your hand, sitting on your lap, or even walking over to you to be petted?

For my iguana it took two or three months for the first level of being tame. Once Za was completely tame and I took him out in the world, he would push close to me when he was not sure of people or things he saw. He seemed to feel more secure pressed against me. This was a dramatic change, considering that in the beginning when he was not trusting of me, he would push <u>away</u> to feel secure. Time! Time is needed to win and secure an iguana's trust.

We learned what she likes and doesn't like. Keeping what she doesn't like to a minimum, she readily calmed down and knew we were not going to hurt her. Now, she thinks of us as her protectors when threatened (such as at the vet's office) or when someone approaches that she doesn't know.
—I-754, Karen, 33 yrs., New Mexico

Handling

[Taming takes] lots of handling and feeding by hand and just keeping the iguana out and around people. —I-467, Kris, 32 yrs., Florida

He was not a pleasant pet as a hatchling. I could hardly hold on to him. Finally, a herp guy advised me that I was just gonna have to bite the bullet and handle him or he would never settle down. So I gritted my teeth and started handling him. I was diligent and resolute about handling him every day and it paid off after a couple of months. I started handling him in his cage—picking him up and [putting him] down. The first bad behavior to go was the biting, then the tail whipping. Now he's pretty easily managed.
—I-609, Cindy, 37 yrs., Florida

People often tell me that they are having trouble taming their iguana and will just wait until the lizard gets older and bigger. That's like saying you will put money in a savings account perhaps in a few years. Don't save today, don't handle today, and you will not have any results tomorrow. The biggest problem with taming your iguana in the future is that each day that goes by, your iguana becomes more set in its wild ways. The future begins now, so start handling your iguana today.

Patience

While she was sick she needed extra time spent on her. It also gave me time to study her while keeping her alive. Almost losing her helps me remember to be a little more patient with her when she's well.
>   —I-183, Mary, 24 yrs., Massachusetts

I am sure that people reading this book will get the impression from all that I have written that I was extremely patient with my iguana. But there were several times where I almost lost my patience and blew up. Like you, on certain days I may be more irritable and stressed than usual, when little things make me blow my stack easier.

When Za was about 4 months old and had been my pet for only a month, I got very angry with him. I had offered him a variety of fresh, finely chopped vegetables, all separated on a plate and looking quite beautiful. As I brought the food into his habitat, he took his tail and whipped the food dish (or my hand . . . who knows). The food went flying all over the habitat, which meant extra clean-up and more food, and I was already late for an appointment. The day had been bad from the start, and this almost pushed me over the top.

Of course, it wasn't his fault that he was thousands of miles from home locked up in some giant creature's house. This realization always helped to neutralize my impatience. I also realized that it was my choice to have an iguana as a pet, so it was my responsibility to make sure that his stay with me was the best it could possibly be every day. But it's amazing how these green creatures can really try your patience. Stick with the plan, even when it's difficult. Remember that your iguana isn't being "bad" when viewed from its perspective. Iguanas do just fine in the wild without human contact.

Our iguana was rated probably a 50 in the beginning. We got her [SVL: 16½", TL: 3' 11½", 3 yrs.] from a woman who kept the iguana in a 55-gallon tank (which was too small for her size). The woman's two children used to poke the iguana with pens and pencils through the screen top. It took my wife and me about a year of patient interaction to bring her as far as she is today. She is now a very loving and trusting part of our family. She is a 1 in tameness now. This was achieved by lots of interaction and understanding and patience.
>   —I-616, John, 27 yrs., Connecticut

Consistency

I try to respond to them in the same way each time they do something negative.
>   —I-764, Diana, 46 yrs., California

Iguanas seem to be happier with consistency and a set routine in their lives, at least in captivity. For example, they appreciate having the habitat lights come on and go off at a set time and being fed at about the same time each day. Iguana owners have told me about how their iguana will push the food bowl around in their habitat if they aren't fed on time.

Similarly, many people have related stories about their iguanas waiting by the door of the habitat at about the time their owners get home from work. As soon as the owners enter their house, the iguana scratches at the door of its habitat to come out. Once out, the lizard is handled and played with.

Iguanas are true creatures of habit in captivity. My iguana slept in the same place and same position every night for almost two years. Patterns. Take advantage of this "habit attitude" to help tame and train your iguana faster. Once they start something they usually keep doing it—bad or good.

Time

In the beginning, both of my iguanas whipped me with their tails, ran away, hissed, and scratched. I would rate them at 50. I would say it took me at least a year, but the time was well worth it. Tameness for both is now probably a 1.
—I-317, Todd, 19 yrs., California

The more time I put into my pet, the more I get out of it.
—I-746, Mark, 19 yrs., Indiana

With time, almost any iguana can get better. If you paint a small section of your house every day, eventually the whole house will be painted. It's the same with taming an iguana. By adhering to the basic elements of the taming formula over time, you can achieve tameness. Any single element of the equation may be difficult or easy each day, week, or month. For example, patience—a key element of the taming formula—is often hard to uphold if your iguana lashes its tail at you every day for a month. But if you handle your iguana regularly, with consistency and as much patience as possible, eventually your iguana will become tame.

It took about seven months to tame him [SVL: 5", TL: 15"]. It was a very gradual process, but now he interacts even with guests or friends.
—I-799, Rui, 35 yrs., New York

He was a 50. He bit, even drawing blood, scratched like crazy. Six months later, he's a 30 . . . still trying.   —I-597, John, 32 yrs., New York

Taming took a couple of months initially, but I consider it an on-going process.
—I-609, Cindy, 37 yrs., Florida

Additional Taming Techniques

The basic formula will get you results. To get faster and more long-lasting results, add as many of the following extra elements to the basic taming equation as possible.

Awareness

Awareness is more than just plain observation. It also involves intuition and conscious alertness to gross or subtle things being observed.

My iguana was 1½ years old when I got her and wild. I could hardly touch her. By accident, I dropped water on her head and she seemed to settle down. Now I take a paper towel soaked in warm water and drip it on her for her bath—carefully. I became aware that she like it dripped on her head. After about three to four weeks, I could use this method to calm her down—sometimes. Slowly she came to realize that warm water dripped on her head felt good and she accepted this daily. Then I began rubbing the warm, wet paper towel on her body—another three to four weeks to accept as OK. She'd keep her eyes closed when you touched her head and open them when you touched her body. Then this led to closing her eyes and totally enjoying her "bath." Bath time was the only time she was nice—opening her mouth at you and getting into the "hit you with my tail" position was decreasing. She also "hissed" at me from the beginning. All this was decreasing, slowly.

—I-249, Linda, 36 yrs., New Jersey

[AUTHOR'S NOTE: I am not prescribing this as a specific technique, but as an anecdote to illustrate awareness.]

By being aware of your iguana's daily activities you can often gain insight into its likes, dislikes, proclivities, or moods, as in the previous example and the example I gave earlier about my iguana not liking to be touched in the morning. In my iguana's case, I moved the touching time to later in the day, which made it easier for both of us.

Being aware of how your iguana acts and responds in normal daily activity can also give you a baseline for spotting any changes that might signal illness or injury.

Flexibility

In our hurried existence nowadays, flexibility is a difficult word, even when it comes to our iguanas. We might have in our mind how iguanas should act or react as our pets. Forget the preconceived notions. Iguanas are very individualistic, and it's hard to stick your iguana into any set mold. You, as the pet owner, must be flexible to the demands and responses of your iguana.

At the same time, however, your iguana also needs to develop flexibility in its new living conditions. If an iguana is sheltered from all life experiences, then as it gets older, life will be a scary place if something new comes up. An inflexible iguana frequently is jumpy and skittish.

With that concept in mind, I allowed my iguana to see and feel as much of life as possible. From the time he was very young, he was exposed to the noise of hair dryers, vacuum cleaners, and power tools; he saw humans talking, laughing, cooking, and brushing their teeth; he met and was handled by all kinds of people; and he heard just about every style of music imaginable. I controlled his exposure to new experiences so that they unfolded safely and peacefully. It was fun to watch his world continually expand.

One time, I had to repair something in Za's habitat. I took the electric drill motor into the habitat and did my work as Za sat on his basking stick and watched curiously. After about a minute of watching and hearing the motor whine, he came over slowly to where I was working. I put my hand on his back and stroked him as I talked softly and brought the drill motor (now turned off) close to his face. He flicked the motor with his tongue and went back to his stick, where he remained watching until I was finished.

Za was rarely startled by anything, because he was flexible. People need to be flexible, and they also need to foster flexibility in their iguanas. It makes life easier and more enjoyable for all involved.

Caring (Love)

Even though caring (loving) is near the bottom of this list, it really permeates every aspect of developing a wonderful pet. The more you show your caring attitude to your iguana, the faster its "wildness" melts away and it becomes the pet you want.

> *When young, it ran wildly inside its lizard house, hiding and "shrinking," shivering. Cure: calm voice, gentle stroking, reassuring her that the noise couldn't come in and "get" lizards. Last 4th of July my iguana was frantic. This year, she watched some of the neighborhood kids' fireworks through the window and didn't seem upset.* —I-865, Julie, 46 yrs., California

> *A strange bond, I know that my iguana [SVL: 16", TL: 2' 6", 4½ yrs.] can sense that I care.* —I-527, Ron, 44 yrs. Illinois

Taking Physical Control

> *I achieved his tameness by constantly handling him and talking to him in a soft, soothing voice. Also, the more he struggled to free himself, the more I hung on until he calmed down. Then I would let him go and feed him treats for good and friendly behavior.* —I-493, Marcia, 40 yrs., Alaska

As mentioned earlier in this chapter, part of handling and taming your iguana is finding the degree of physical pressure that gives you control over your lizard. Hold too tightly, and your iguana will struggle to break free; hold too loosely, and the lizard will be in control. If your iguana persists in struggling, you might have to exert greater physical control over your pet, maintaining a constant grip for a longer period of time and using the "Three NOs" technique, described on page 484. Sometimes taming requires a breakthrough period, like a cowboy breaking a wild horse.

Continue holding your iguana until it relaxes in your hand—but no longer than 10 minutes per session and no more than 10 sessions per week. Remember to relax your grip when the iguana relaxes. Eventually, your lizard should get the idea and quit fighting when it is held. I did this with my iguana when he was young, and it worked. Even when he was more than 5 years old and started to get in one of his pissy moods, I used this technique to settle him down. But he was so well conditioned that I didn't have to hold him more than five seconds in this tighter grip.

Don't do this technique with anger, such as, "You move and I'll squish you, you little monster!" More like, "That's enough wriggling; just take it easy." Also, there are certain days where your iguana is just in a bad mood, or has an "attitude," and this technique should not be used. The longer you own your iguana, the easier it is to identify when your iguana is moody or has a bad attitude. On those days that Za looked like he had to have his way, I didn't even try the technique. Asserting physical control on a day like that only encourages frustration and reduces the technique's overall power.

Standing Your Ground

She [iguana] tried to bite quite often in the beginning. She will try to scare you when you first pick her up, until she realizes you aren't afraid.
—I-628, Yvonne, 29 yrs., California

When a young iguana puffs up, starts bobbing its head, and opens its mouth as if to bite, don't be scared or bluffed—stand your ground. Try not to pull away in panic, or show any signs that the iguana's defense system will work on you. Move in slowly and touch part of the lizard's body gently, then slowly pick it up. If you allow it to scare you and back you down, it will do this all the time and may even get bolder and try to bite. You need to show that you are the boss and in control.

Please note, however, that you can't be so cavalier with an aggressive large iguana, especially a male in breeding season. At these times, hormones take over and make an iguana more likely to attack, not bluff. A bite from an adult iguana can be extreme. See Chapter 9, Breeding, for more details on handling aggressive male iguanas during this trying season.

A youngster [iguana] will sometimes pull pranks or test you now and then to see if he can get the upper hand. They're no different from human children and must be handled the same. Gently but firmly, lovingly let your pet know who's got the upper hand. Never let him get one over on you.
—I-200, Dianna, 47 yrs., Washington

When I put my hand in to touch her, she would try to hit me with her tail [wild iguana from previous bad owner]. She scared me, really! I realized that if I took my hand out of her cage after she scared me, she won and would do it again. The more I persisted at winning (while still being nice to her), the more I won and she settled down.   —phone conversation with a pet owner

I have gone to the homes of several people who said they couldn't pick up their iguana because they were afraid it would whip its tail or bite them. I would put my hand into the iguana's habitat and pick up their lizard, and in only a minute the lizard would be relaxed in my hand. The owners were invariably astonished. I would put the lizard back into the habitat and explain how to take the iguana out of its home correctly. Now it was the owner's turn to be astonished as they took their iguana out of the habitat without any trouble. Immediately, they understood it was not me, it's the technique.

One of the problems many people have is indecision. They start to pick up their iguana, and the iguana inflates its body, opens its mouth, and wiggles its tail. The owners pull back their hand because they are afraid, then try the same process a few seconds later. By this time the iguana is really feeling threatened by the thing that keeps coming at it.

This in-and-out movement is how some snakes attack their prey. Also, as your hand moves in and out, you get more frightened and stressed, and the iguana picks up on your physical cues. By the time you two finally meet, it's like two mouse traps snapping off at the same time. Just do it! Pick your iguana up with a positive, assertive, smooth motion.

Well, I'd honestly have to say there hasn't really been an iguana I couldn't handle, from my very first baby to the largest adult. My affinity with this species and most lizards is very unusual. Most iguanas whose owners can't hold on to them, or who dominate and intimidate their owners, usually submit to me within minutes. Much has to do with your confidence around the lizard.
—I-200, Dianna, 47 yrs., Washington

She would whip her tail and open her mouth as if to bite. I knew I had to do something soon, because she was getting bigger and if I didn't break her of this soon I wouldn't be able to handle her. It took about a month or so, and now she no longer whips her tail or opens her mouth to bite. I would say she is now a 1 rating.
—I-183, Mary, 24 yrs., Massachusetts

An iguana that has bluffed and scared its owners for years, that doesn't get touched, is usually given away. An older iguana like this can be a handful. That's why you need to spend time with your hatchling or juvenile now if you don't want a demon in a lizard suit for a future pet. An iguana that is tame in the beginning is going to be a tame adult, as long as you keep interacting with it.

Our iguana used to be very tame. After two children in the past 2½ years, we have not had time to handle and spend time with our iguana. Now I hate to admit she is wilder than when we first got her. I think it helps to hold or touch your iguana daily.
—I-554, Anthony, 29 yrs., Texas

I need to emphasize again: The only way an iguana will tame down is through handling and time. I know I keep repeating myself throughout this chapter, but this is an extremely critical point. I have received letters from people who said their iguana was still wild after five months and that they handled the iguana frequently. After asking a few questions, this "frequently" usually turned out to be maybe 15 minutes a week. This is not sufficient!

My iguana took about three months to settle down. But after that three-month break-in period, the taming process became faster. The captive-bred iguanas that are available now will be much tamer right from the start. Taming an iguana initially is a labor-intensive activity, but the results are well worth the effort. Talking with lots of people over the years makes me realize this simple point is too easily forgotten. So I keep pounding on the idea.

Who's the Boss?

Koko the gorilla was famous for communicating with her handler through the use of a symbol typewriter. One day Koko typed, "Get lower." If iguanas could type, they might ask the same of their owners. Being up high gives them the feeling of dominance, which they love. Whenever possible, give your iguana a treat. If your lizard is on a chair or ledge, get on your knees so you are below or at the same level as your iguana.

Sometimes when you and your iguana battle to become king of the house, you need to stand up to the lizard, literally. If you are taller and bigger than your iguana, that should show it who is the boss in the family, at least for a while.

> *My philosophy is to show your iguana you are the bigger lizard. In their society, the smaller lizard will always back down in a challenge. At times, I'll open my mouth and let out a long, low hiss from the back of my throat, such as iguanas do when annoyed. This "language" usually tells them I'm the bigger lizard and they calm down. My iguanas are all very tame.*
> —I-200, Dianna, 47 yrs., Washington

[AUTHOR'S NOTE: This works for her but doesn't necessarily work for all iguanas. It could even get your iguana more irritated.]

Sleepy Lizards are Easier to Handle

Some people have written that they handle their iguana close to the time the lizard usually goes to sleep. The owners have indicated that even their wild iguana would go to sleep in their arms or on their chest at night while they watched TV or read. Sleepy animals are less threatening. Iguanas seem more mammalian than reptilian when they sleep: They actually react and feel like a tired kitten at night. Using this sleepiness is another trick for reducing barriers and for taming your iguana without a lot of hassle.

"Facing" Your Iguana

> *When I first had my iguana, his level of wildness was over 50. I handled him every day and as much as possible. He became familiar with my voice and my face. After about two months of this care, his level of tameness is now about a 10.* —I-759, Laura, 20 yrs., Pennsylvania

When your iguana is out of its habitat, pick it up and slowly move it up close to the side of your face, talking in a soft tone. Do this off and on for a couple of weeks. Then move your iguana to the front of your face. Being so close to your mouth can be frightening to your iguana, who assumes that mouths are for eating and biting. Do this technique a couple of times a week for about a month, and your iguana will realize that you aren't going to eat it.

After this time, you will never have to do this technique again. Your iguana will start to be relaxed around all the parts of your body. When my iguana was about a year old he began resting his chin on my chin, if I was lying on the couch. That's about as close to a mouth as you can get without being inside it. He continued enjoying this position even after he was 5 years old, and sometimes he would even go to sleep with his head resting on my chin.

Water as a Taming Device

Humans often take baths to soak and relax. Below is a little twist on this idea:

> *[Taming my iguana] was achieved by handling him frequently (at least once a day) and bathing him—being exposed in the bathtub with no place to hide and no recourse but to come and sit on my hand to relax after vigorously swimming. He would get tired and hold on to my hand for support. I also talked to him and still do in a gentle tone, calling out his name.*
>
> —I-799, Rui, 35 yrs., New York

Outside Help

If you feel your iguana is not taming fast enough, talk to a person that has an older pet iguana. This is where being a member of a herpetological society is useful (see Appendix B). Members can put on their lizard psychologist hats and tell you to hang in there, it will just take some more time. Also, holding one of their tame large juvenile or adult iguanas will help recharge you.

When Za was a monster from hell (partly because he was wild-caught, not captive-raised) and I thought he would never be tame, I went to see an owner of an 8-year-old, 11-pound, 4½-foot iguana. That did the trick for me. That iguana was like a pet dog who waddled like a duck. It actually enjoyed being touched. When they are big, they are so nice to hold. This kind of experience will get you over your down period fast. This difficult time with your iguana could be considered like a child's terrible twos, or the teen years. You think they will never get past it, but they do. But you must stick to your daily handling schedule. No handling, no tameness!! That's a basic, absolute rule.

Fortunately, iguanas only get better with consistent taming. One reward of taming a wild iguana is to see and feel that you are part of this slow, unfolding process. The iguana starts to allow more touching of its head, spines, and the soft pads of its feet. This continuous process of getting to know your iguana proceeds much like most human friendships. Except most humans don't whip you in the beginning of a relationship.

Taming Stories From "The Field"

Below are some real-life taming experiences from iguana owners to let you know you are not alone as you try to tame your iguana.

The devil's own spawn. He dashed about like he was on drugs. He had a mean, evil look in his eye. I would rate him a 100 on your scale of 1 to 50. He opened his mouth as if to bite, hissed or puffed up, clawed, and defecated on me every time I picked him up. He was 3 months old when purchased. Now at 15 months, he's rated a 20 and getting better.

—I-540, Samantha, 38 yrs., Missouri

A 50 when we got him [at about 3 months old]. He seemed terrified of us and flung himself around his cage to avoid our catching him. Now he [SVL: 18", 2 yrs. 8 mo., 10 lbs.] is pretty much a 1, very sweet—and he comes to me for affection when I've ignored him too long.

—I-705, Linda & Paul, 45 yrs., California

Taming the iguana not to whip its tail or resist handling, and to accept the presence of humans (not jump around in its vivarium, eat when humans were present), took about six months. Totally domesticating the iguana (litter training, making it look at you if you called it, making it not close its eyes if you touched it or came very close to it, getting it to accept toenail trimming, etc.) took an additional 1½ years.   —I-515, Lynn, 21 yrs., Canada

My iguana was about 1½ years old when I got her. Her previous owner supplied minimal and inadequate care. She was the monster from hell. She also had a lot of medical problems. She is now so tame that when I pet her, her eyes close and she leans into my hand (like a cat).

—I-249, Linda, 36 yrs., New Jersey

Our iguana rates a 1. No time—no lie. He was an exception. At present, another iguana that we have is still not tame after three years. He has a fairly high-strung personality that requires a little extra work. Plain and simple, we just haven't devoted the required time to do so with him.

—I-508, Bryan, 27 yrs., Kentucky

He's my sweetie. Very tame right from the start.

—I-308, Debby, 33 yrs., Minnesota

Sometimes an iguana coming home from a pet store may seem quite tame, perhaps rating a 10. With better housing and food, it might jump up to a 30. One reason for the increase in wildness might be that the iguana was not well cared for before you got it, and it was too weak to cause trouble. Now that you have made it healthy and secure, it's doing its natural thing. Don't worry; your iguana will become tame much quicker, knowing that where it lives now is a good, safe, and healthy place.

When your iguana finally becomes tame, remember there will still be days when your lizard will put up a fuss about being picked up or petted. We all have days when we don't like to be touched. Respect your tame lizard's moods.

TRAINING

My definition of training in this book is a habit created for an iguana, through repetition, for the mutual benefit of the lizard and the pet owner.

To me, training an iguana does not mean teaching it to do weird tricks, such as jumping through hoops of fire. When I owned an Alaskan malamute dog, all I trained him to do was come and stay—commands necessary for the safety and convenience of us both. Similarly, you might decide to train your iguana for its safety, health, happiness, and definitely for improved personal interaction.

Most people don't believe that lizards can be trained. But my experience, and that of other iguana pet owners, proves that they can. No, they won't perform tricks like a circus animal, but neither will most cats. As a practical example, you can train your iguana not to climb the curtains or certain plants when it's out in your house, or train it to defecate in a designated spot that you both agree upon.

Who's to say what amazing bonding and training achievements can be accomplished with an iguana? The next story is just one very rare example:

> *I had one iguana around 12 years ago who was an exceptional case. I had him registered with [a talent agency] and he'd done commercials, TV shows, and fashion shows with me. He was also doing guest appearances at a local cafe. He was trained to come to me when I knelt and slapped my knees, jump if I'd stand and slap my legs, stand up, walk forward, and stop and sit if I'd hold my hand palm out and say "Stop! Stay!" He was 5 feet long, had big jowls, and was green with orange arms. Very affectionate, too. He would stay in any pose you put him in if I said "Stay"; so photographers loved working with him. It took an exceptional closeness between us, lots of hours, weeks, months of training, and of course an exceptional personality to achieve this. Not all iguanas have it.*
> —I-200, Dianna, 47 yrs., Washington

Training Formula

I'll provide a plan for training that, if followed closely, will work. These techniques work best when your pet completely trusts you and is tame (see the previous section on "Taming").

This trust can develop at any point, but usually happens by the time the lizard is about 8" to 9" SVL (which my iguana reached at approximately 5 months old). This measurement is not set in concrete; it can swing drastically either direction. It depends on the personality of your iguana, whether it was wild-caught or captive-raised, the size of its habitat, and how you have taken care of the lizard, to mention just a few variables. You can start the training earlier, but it might take longer to see results.

When my iguana was about 5 months old, all of a sudden I said out loud, "He is tame; he trusts me." I could put my hand in the cage without being whipped, he would come out of the cage quietly, I could hold him and he wouldn't squirm and wriggle, trying to run away. At this stage, you can begin a simple training schedule.

Training Formula

$$(C + R) \times t = I_{tr}$$

In words, this formula means:

$$(\text{Consistency} + \text{Repetition}) \times \text{time} = \text{Iguana}_{trained}$$

For the first time in any iguana pet-care book, there is now a simple formula for training your lizard. This formula is short and to the point. Even though the terms in the formula seem self-explanatory, I have included some brief comments.

The word *consistency* comes from the word constant, which means not changing, remaining the same, continual. Whatever technique you use, it needs to stay the same, and you need to do this technique over and over again (*repetition*) until your lizard grasps the concept.

Your iguana may learn the specific thing that it was trained to do in a few weeks or several months (*time*). If the trained activity is described in this chapter, it has already been accomplished, either by my own iguana or some other owner's iguana. If you want to try something outside the list, go for it—and let me know the results.

Working With Your Iguana's Instincts

There are two basic categories of training: discouraging behaviors you don't want and encouraging those you do.

To discourage behavior, you'll need to understand that your iguana's undesirable behavior may just be a natural instinct. For example, iguanas naturally want to climb and they need to defend themselves from predators. But in a captive situation you probably don't want your iguana to climb up your drapes or whip you with its tail.

On the other hand, you can use other "natural" behaviors to your advantage to train your iguana to do specific things, such as defecating in a certain place or drinking standing water. In both untraining "bad" behavior and training "good" behavior, which will be discussed in the next sections, you still use the principles of the Training Formula plus a few additional techniques. Stick with the formula and you will be amazed by the results.

SIDEBAR

Discipline

I've owned iguanas for 10 years. All six know their names and what "no" and
"stop" mean.   —I-289, Janice, 43 yrs., Illinois

Never, never, ever hit any animal. There is no situation in which
hitting does any good for the animal, the trainer, or the training. It
teaches only one thing: fear of the hitter.
         —Brian Kilcommons, author of *Good Owners, Great Cats*,
                      renowned animal trainer (25 years), and teacher at
                                   Tufts School of Veterinary Medicine

Before your iguana can be trained, you first need to know how to discipline the lizard for inappropriate behavior. Discipline as part of your training program is absolutely necessary if you want a friendly and tame iguana.
Hitting, however, is not part of any discipline program for iguanas. Iguanas
don't understand the process of being hit for doing something "wrong." If
iguanas are hit, they will either retaliate in self-defense or they will cower
from you. In any case, you will lose the trust that has been built up and you
may have to start over.

Discipline should be applied right at the moment the iguana does
something wrong, never later. Discipline is rather touchy, because iguanas
are sensitive and can become neurotic if reprimanded improperly. Patience,
gentleness, and love will keep an iguana emotionally healthy. Let your
lizard know you're not going to harm it, but that you are unhappy with
what it's doing.

What I like is their different personalities. They are just like people. My female
iguana is really docile and easy to work with, while the male is more aggres-
sive—but yet my favorite because he seems to try to see how far he can push me.
                                        —I-272, James, 26 yrs., Washington

Iguanas respond more quickly to certain people, like the woman whose
iguanas did TV commercials. In addition, iguanas are individuals, and they
differ widely in their reaction to discipline. Regardless of the variables, the
process of changing bad habits does not take place overnight. It takes a
great deal of time and patience, but the results are worth all the effort, as
you will see in the next section of this chapter.

Correcting Specific "Bad" Behavior

All iguanas seem to develop a few specific behaviors that, while normal and natural for them in the wild, cause problems in captive situations. They are "bad" behaviors only in the sense that they are not compatible with living in captivity. Luckily, these behaviors are relatively easy to correct.

A Couple of Helpful Techniques

Whether you're trying to overcome an iguana's natural instinct to climb or to defend itself, I've found a couple of specific techniques that seem to work effectively.

The "Three NOs" and Relocation

Once I caught him [2 yrs.] just about to jump from the chair to the bookcase, where he's not allowed. I scolded him, so he just relaxed. But as soon as I left the room, I heard the thump as he landed on the bookcase. He is single-minded and determined.   —I-609, Cindy, 37 yrs., Florida

Iguanas are very stubborn and single-minded about some things. If he gets it in his head to sleep in my closet, even though the door is shut, he will scratch at the door incessantly to find a way to get in.   —I-493, Marcia, 40 yrs., Alaska

I hear stories like this all the time. When an iguana makes up its mind to go to a certain place or do a certain thing, then that's what it is going to do! By applying the Training Formula—$(C + R) \times t = I_{tr}$—you can correct most bad behaviors.

One specific way to stop an unwanted behavior is to physically move your iguana to a new place far from the problem area. They seem to forget or not care about what they were originally doing.

If they do go back to the same area again, try what I call the "three NOs" technique. Any time your iguana does something you don't want it to do (e.g., gets into a plant), <u>immediately</u> pick it up and say loudly, holding the lizard facing your mouth, "NO, NO, NO" (three times). Remember, saying "NO" works <u>only if your lizard is tame</u>.

He responds to "good boy" and "NO."
     —I-540, Samantha, 38 yrs., Missouri

Your lizard doesn't understand the word "NO"; it's responding to the volume and tone of your voice, your tense and irritated body language, and the firmness of your hand's grip. It's also responding instinctively as it would to the biggest iguana in the jungle, the "alpha." Repeating "NO" three times reinforces the sound and creates a recognizable pattern.

When your iguana is close to your face and sees your big head, mouth, and teeth, it's clear to your pet that you are bigger than it is. At this point, you effectively become the alpha and have more control over the situation. Once the "three NOs" part of the technique is accomplished, relocate your iguana to another place away from the trouble area.

The Habitat as "Jail"

Sometimes stubborn iguanas will turn right around and attempt the "forbidden" activity again, even after the "three NOs" and relocation. Any time your iguana repeats the same forbidden activity three times in a row, immediately put the lizard back in its habitat. If your iguana enjoys coming out of its habitat, caging it for specific bad or improper behavior is a good training tool.

On many occasions after my iguana was "jailed" for an hour or so, he'd come back out and be well-behaved the rest of the day. These kinds of experiences year after year make it easy to believe that iguanas do understand and can be taught simple things.

There needs to be a clear distinction between being put in the habitat for punishment and normal "going back home." When putting your iguana back into the habitat for punishment, repeat the "three NOs" to remind it of its bad behavior. Pick the lizard up quickly, hold it a little more firmly than normal, and walk toward the habitat at a brisk pace. Moving quickly helps to get their attention. The iguana will "feel" that something is different.

Place your iguana safely and securely into the habitat, but with quicker-than-normal movements. Close the habitat door and walk off. Half an hour to an hour later, you can let your lizard out again. In time, your iguana will make the connection that when it misbehaves, it gets put in "jail."

In contrast, the normal way of returning your iguana to its habitat is to walk slowly to the habitat while holding your iguana lightly, pausing in front of the habitat for a couple of minutes, and talking softly (e.g., "good boy/girl"). In this normal circumstance, place your pet slowly and securely inside the habitat, talk to it for a few seconds, then close the door gently and walk off, perhaps looking back a couple of times before completely leaving the room.

> *Animals understand more than we give them credit for. If you can learn the social structure of iguanas and their behavior patterns and body language, then you can communicate more on their level. You have a better understanding of what makes them tick. Also, reassurance, kindness, gentleness, and careful handling are important.*   —I-200, Dianna, 47 yrs., Washington

Off the House Plants and Curtains

Iguanas like to climb and be up high, looking down at everything. It's natural and it makes them feel secure. Curtains in your house, as well as many tall house plants, satisfy these needs. Plants also provide an easy "ladder" to perhaps the highest point in a room and are a familiar part of their wild habitat.

It's unnatural for an iguana not to climb. But over time, your curtains and plants will be shredded from the iguana's sharp claws and weight if you don't stop them. Luckily, you can change this pattern so that you won't have rags instead of drapes and defoliation in place of living plants.

I stopped my iguana from climbing in the very beginning, when he was first allowed to be loose in the house. <u>Every</u> time he began to climb the curtains or any of my many tall plants, I did the "three NOs" technique and moved him to another place in the house. Consequently, he never acquired the habit of climbing the curtains or plants. The technique is pretty simple, just requiring awareness, diligence, and repetition of the discipline technique.

My iguana [SVL: 15", TL: 2' 11", 5 yrs., 9 lbs.] stops if I yell "NO!" when she begins to climb the drapes.   —I-100, Charlene, 44 yrs., Illinois

My iguana knows that if she wants to go sit in the sun, she must climb up the towel I provided for her instead of the curtains. The towel is draped over the window sill so that one end of it is touching the floor. The upper end of the towel is secured to the window sill.   —I-806, Tiffany, 14 yrs., Texas

One owner got tired of her iguana climbing the drapes and rolled up a newspaper and smacked the curtains as the iguana was climbing. The sound must have startled the iguana and it was effective—to the point where any time the lizard was about to climb the curtains, the owner merely picked up a rolled newspaper and the iguana would stop climbing. The owner had this iguana for several years before the problem started, so they had built up a good, solid relationship. This worked for her, but it might cause problems with your iguana. Every iguana is different.

No Head Rest

She always wanted to sit on my head. It was OK until she gained a few pounds! Then I had to put a stop to it.   —I-808, Priscilla, 25 yrs., Iowa

Moving from your shoulder to the top of the head is a natural progression for an iguana. Your head is often the highest spot around. When iguanas are in the hatchling stage, your kids will scream and giggle with happiness when the iguana is on their heads. Adults will also giggle in their own special adult way.

But later, when the iguana weighs a couple of pounds and measures several feet, it's no laughing matter. Even if the claws are trimmed, you will still feel them, especially if your iguana accidentally slides off your head. And if this happens, of course the kids will get angry and perhaps throw the animal to the ground, risking injury to the lizard. Whose fault will it be? The owner's, of course.

While the iguana is still young, it is <u>imperative</u> to stop this head-resting behavior. I taught my iguana when he was about 4 months old not to climb on my head. It took almost two months of using the "three NOs" technique. This was probably the most difficult bad trait to correct. It was non-stop "NOs" and taking him off my head for weeks. Even a couple of times into the training process, when I said "NO" he immediately froze as though he "understood," but then would try to climb again. Eventually, though, it worked. By the time he was more than 13 pounds and over 5′ long, I was glad he learned that it was not OK to sit on my head.

When your iguana starts to get on your head from your shoulder, take the lizard off and put it on your lap or just hold it gently. If it tries to climb up, again say "NO, NO, NO" close to its face and remove it from your head. If it does it once more, send your iguana to "jail" (its habitat) for a while, or move it to another part of the house.

Tail Whipping

A really pissed off iguana makes a cat look tame. Iguanas have one additional weapon over cats—the tail! (Six weapons: mouth, four pairs of claws and a strong tail!)   —I-775, Karen, Arizona

An iguana's first defense against danger is to run away. If it can't run, it will use its tail as a whip. The whip can be used either as a scare tactic or, with accuracy, to hit delicate body parts of the intruder. If the iguana thinks the tail whipping will work, he will continually use it.

If your hatchling iguana whips its tail at you, the best solution is the one I mentioned earlier: Don't jerk away from the whipping tail, and the iguana is less likely use it. But what if you face a large iguana with a huge, thick tail that threatens you with tail whipping?

The tail whipping can work only at a distance, so the solution is to get as close to the iguana as possible. Go in and pick the lizard up quickly and hold it in the manner I described at the beginning of this chapter. Once your iguana is next to your body there is no room for the tail to whip.

I have picked up large iguanas that love to whip, but once next to my side the tail flails miserably in an attempt to strike, and then stops. The hard part is to get in there and grab the big guy. When you have done this a few times, your confidence will make you wonder why you were so afraid of picking up your tail-whipping iguana.

Biting

When I have an iguana that tries to bite when being picked up or opens his mouth in a threatening way, I put food in his mouth. After a few days they usually only let me get one piece in. After a few weeks they seldom open their mouth when being picked up.   —I-764, Diana, 46 yrs., California

As many iguana owners have found out, it's pretty hard to be bitten by your iguana when its mouth is full of food. The technique for training them not to bite works with large or small iguanas. On big iguanas it's better to use a full, long leaf of kale, collard, or mustard green. Think of this long leaf as a green pole to keep a wild iguana at a distance, or as a green distraction. The lizard will usually stop and "flick" the food, take a bite, and get side-tracked. Then you can move in closer to feed or pick the iguana up, if that is what is needed.

Just as with tail whipping, if you cower from an attempted bite attack the iguana will continue to use this potential weapon. Be careful, be smart, but don't let this bad habit continue.

He has never even tried to bite me. In fact, he is one of the few pets I own that hasn't tried to bite at some point in its life.
　　　　　　　　　　　　　　　　　—I-749, Charles, 27 yrs., California

Working With "Good" Behaviors

Juvenile [iguana] behavior patterns are not learned from exposure to adults, but are largely innate and may be modulated by inter-actions among the young as they grow.
　　　　　　　　　　　　—Nancy C. Pratt, iguana researcher (#10)

I found the previous quotation in one of the scientific reports I received on iguanas. Perhaps we as pet owners can take on the role of these other young iguanas to influence the future behavior of our pets. This is all new territory. Who knows what amazing things might develop from it?

Don't expect too much in the way of training results from your iguana, and then what does happen will be a complete joy.

Defecation

I'd just as soon he [iguana] would sit on the toilet and flush than have to clean up his mess in the cage.　　　　　　　—I-379, Russ, 32 yrs., Vermont

In my iguana questionnaires I asked owners what they disliked most about caring for their iguanas. Overwhelmingly, the answer was cleaning up feces. This is a necessity with any kind of pet you might have, from goldfish to lions. If you have no poop to clean, you have a dead animal for a pet. What goes in, must come out.

I felt that if an iguana could learn anything, the most important thing would be to defecate in a specific place and perhaps on command. With a little help, your iguana can be trained to do this, which makes clean-up much easier.

I especially like how easy it is to housetrain my iguana.
　　　　　　　　　　　　　　　　　—I-687, R., 54 yrs., Canada

We didn't like cleaning his excrement in the beginning, but now we've gotten used to it and also it makes it easier that he [SVL: 5", TL: 18½"] has chosen a specific spot to defecate and will not go anywhere else.
　　　　　　　　　　　　　　　　　—I-799, Rui, 35 yrs., New York

My iguana [SVL: 9¾", TL: 2' 9½", 1 yr. 3 mo.] has learned to go to the bathroom only on the one-fourth paper in his cage and not on the three-fourths carpeting substrate.　　　　　　　—I-540, Samantha, 38 yrs., Missouri

I often take my iguanas when I visit friends. When it's time for my iguanas to defecate I will lay down some newspaper and they will go on this. This always makes people say things such as, "Oh, they are not so stupid, are they," or "You wouldn't think a lizard had a brain."
> —conversation with a woman at a pet store

When you first bring your iguana home, it will most likely not defecate in front of you until it feels safe and secure with its new surroundings. So none of the following techniques can be used until your iguana at least feels relaxed defecating in your presence.

From there, you can proceed with techniques to train it to defecate in a convenient spot. To do this, you'll be working with your iguana's natural tendency to return to the same location to defecate (in a captive situation). This works for both inside and outside the habitat. All you have to do is condition them to the spot you both have agreed upon. Iguanas are very habitual in this respect.

In the Habitat

Let's start with the easiest place to train your iguana to defecate: a specific spot in its own habitat.

I got my iguana at 3 months old to defecate on a 4" piece of paper towel. Very easy to clean up. —I-328, Mark, 26 yrs., California

My iguana does his business on a piece of 10" by 12" Astroturf (newspaper around the periphery). —I-494, Jim, 25 yrs., California

He [SVL: 12", TL: 3' 3", 1 yr. 9 mo.] usually does his poo in a metal tray with newspaper in it. —I-731, Stephen, 14 yrs., Canada

The way you paper-train a puppy dog is to cover the whole area (say, a kitchen, where it might stay during the first part of housetraining) with newspaper. Each day you reduce the amount of paper until you are down to one page—preferably the business section. You can work the same process with your lizard. If your iguana defecates twice in the same place in its habitat, leave newspaper (or my favorite substrate, newspaper and paper towels) on that spot only.

Out of the Habitat

She [SVL: 8", TL: 2' 11", 1 yr. 10 mo.] seems almost self-conscious or aware of her preference for not defecating in her cage. No complaints here.
> —I-926, Robert & Virginia, California

Once your iguana becomes a member of your household and is allowed out in specific places in your house, training it to defecate somewhere besides

SIDEBAR

Substrate

I have tested just about all of the habitat substrates available, including commercially produced ones. I have found newspaper and paper towels to be the best combination.

Stack three paper towels together and place them in the center of two full pages of newspaper, folded in half. Tape all the edges of the paper towels to the newspaper with masking tape. The paper towels absorb the fluid and are perfect for wiping the iguana's vent area clean. This system is compact, cheap, simple, effective, easy to clean up, and environmentally friendly. For anyone wanting more choices, look at Chapter 4, Housing, "Substrate Options."

on the $8,000 handmade Persian rug is very important. Equally important is that there isn't a pile of poop somewhere in the house that you might step on in your bare feet in the middle of the night.

To train your iguana to defecate in a specific place in the house, you need to first catch your iguana in the act, just before it defecates, and move it to the designated spot. At this spot, I recommend placing the same newspaper-and-paper towel substrate as discussed earlier.

If your iguana hasn't chosen a defecation site, one way to get it interested in a designated spot is to "prime the pump" by smearing a little of its feces on the paper and showing this spot to your iguana. It might think this is a place it has previously chosen.

You may have to fine-tune the location by spreading paper over a larger area in the beginning if your iguana is missing the bull's-eye. Once your iguana "knows" the spot, reduce the paper size gradually to the size you want it to be. Make sure the defecation area is located someplace out of the main flow of traffic, but easily accessible to your iguana. A second-best option is to find out where your iguana defecates and put the substrate there.

Knowing the number of times your lizard defecates each day, and what time of day it usually does its business, will also help. For example, if your iguana defecates in its habitat only once in the morning, you can be pretty sure it will defecate when out in your house at about that same time. A number of variables might change this pattern, however. For instance, if the lizard gets very hot, such as in a window or on a heating pad, it might be stimulated to defecate again.

It's easy to tell when the iguanas are getting ready to defecate. I'm sure that all iguanas act much the same when it comes to this behavior—flattening the hindquarters against the ground and swaying back and forth slightly. Then they go. What's funny is how they breathe so deeply while they are going, as if it's a big effort to them! When finished, they walk away, being very careful not to drag their tail through the mess. Mine always eliminate on the ground, never from a higher elevations, such as a basking limb in their habitat, as I've heard many other people's iguanas do.   —I-467, Kris, 32 yrs., Florida

In addition, by knowing the signals and characteristics an iguana displays before it defecates, you'll have some advance warning if you need to move your lizard off that expensive rug and perhaps to the designated defecation spot.

When he is ready to defecate, he will circle around, settle in the spot, lower his hind legs and body, and raise up on his forelegs with head and neck stretched up.   —I-916, Lucretia, 32 yrs., California

When he's going to defecate, he reminds me of a dog, with his back legs spread and bent so he can get low.   —I-849, Amie & Ian, 22 yrs., Oregon

Catching the lizard just before it poops is one of the hardest steps of this technique. Here's what to look for: Before an iguana defecates, it often flicks its tongue into the air or at a specific spot, as if trying to find the best place to do its business. It may also look at its surroundings a little nervously, like it's antsy or in a hurry. Then it will stop, plant its rear feet firmly, drop its butt to the ground, and may have a "concentrating" look on its face. This is a good time to pick up your iguana and move it to the designated pooping area.

When moving your iguana to the paper, hold it gently, not in a tight grip that would make the lizard feel threatened. Use soft words, such as "good iggy" (or whatever its name is). If you get excited, your iguana will get excited. Don't move too rapidly or act angry, irritated, or threatening. But do keep moving, as you are carrying a delicate time bomb (or poop bomb); if you move too slowly, it might go off in your hands.

Set your iguana on the paper and either walk away or sit motionless, not looking at the lizard until it is finished doing its business.

The signal that your iguana is ready to defecate is when its rear end gets a little "rumba" action. Sometimes this process looks like a plane trying to land on an aircraft carrier on high seas—bouncy, bouncy. This happens just moments before they actually defecate.

As the iguana starts to defecate, it will lift its hindquarters up so it doesn't come into contact with the poop. After completing the defecation process, the lizard will lift its tail up and move it to the left or right of the poop, to avoid getting any feces on it, and walk forward. Once it has moved away from the poop pile, the iguana will drop its "butt" to wipe its vent clean of any mess. Iguanas are very clean animals.

Concentrate on conditioning positive training reactions while moving your

iguana. If your lizard defecates on the way to the designated spot or in a different location, just relax. If you get upset, or make a big deal about your iguana
pooping on the floor, you will wreck the training progress. It all washes off.
Humans handle poopy human babies all the time. Just make sure to clean it off
and wash your hands thoroughly—twice.

Iguanas' feces are much like a bird's, with liquid and solid coming out the
same hole (the vent) at the same time. When they "go," it often literally pops
and sprays out like a champagne bottle turned upside down, especially if they
have moist food in their diet.

If you want to condition your iguana to be really flexible when it comes to
defecation, you might consider alternative toilets.

Portable "Toilet"—Because I had such a small apartment, I allowed my
iguana the full run of it when I was home. To simplify his time out, I trained
him to defecate in a portable "toilet." This portable toilet (the size of the container varies with the size of the lizard) was a hard rubber dish pan; I cut the
sides down to l" high so my iguana could get in and out of it easily. The pan sat
on the floor of my shower stall, with several moist paper towels on the bottom
of the dish pan. The moist towels stimulated my iguana to defecate.

Here is how the portable toilet evolved. When I first had my iguana, he
defecated in his habitat while I was at work, and I cleaned up the poop as soon
as I got home. As he became more tame and trusting, he actually waited until
I got home to defecate in the habitat. Perhaps he did this so he didn't have to
smell his poop all day. Pretty smart, especially for an 8-month-old iguana.

I used this pattern he had established to expand his defecation to a portable
toilet. First thing when I got home from work, I removed Za from his habitat—
before he had a chance to defecate—and put him in his portable 8" by 8" toilet
located in my shower stall. After no more than four days of this routine I got
him to defecate in the container, even if he had gone already that day. Once he
picked up on the routine, it never took more than 5 minutes for him to poop.

After your lizard learns to defecate in this kind of container, switch to dry
paper towels, which are easier to handle and reduce the chance of contamination. You don't need to use a shower like I did, just find a place your iguana
wants to defecate and put newspaper around the pan for extra protection.

Whatever location works best for you, put your iguana in its portable toilet near the time it defecates, or if you see it's about ready to go. If it's not your
iguana's normal defecation time, the iguana will probably not poop and will
walk out of the toilet.

Once your lizard identifies the portable toilet as its defecation spot, it can be
used in or out of the habitat. You now have a toilet that brings freedom as well
as portability. As proof of how well it worked, one time I took my iguana to my
parents' house, which was about two hours away. I brought the portable toilet,
and when it was around the time of day my iguana usually defecated, he did his
business in about three minutes in the container.

My parents were quite impressed that a lizard could defecate not only in a
specific place, but also on command. I was there for two days and my iguana

never pooped in the wrong place—only in the portable toilet. But for safety, I put the pan on the bathroom floor, just in case he made a mistake.

Za got so consistent with his portable toilet routine at home that one time I accidentally left the lights off in the bathroom, and he walked into the shower in the dark and pooped anyway. And they say reptiles are dumb. Well, a house-trained lizard sounds many notches above dumb, and I have seen so many other iguanas that defecate in a localized spot that I know this is a trainable act.

Water Toilet—An effective technique to help eliminate potential "mistakes" in the house is to "pre-poop" your iguana using water as a defecation cue. When you bring your iguana out of its habitat to spend time in a specific room of your house, first put the lizard in the bathtub or shower with a little warm water. This should stimulate your iguana to defecate (see the sidebar "Cleanliness Reminder" on page 494). Now, with a semi-empty digestive tract, your iguana is less likely to poop in your house.

This technique evolved from soaking my iguana. When Za soaked in the bathtub he would automatically defecate, which made a horrendous mess. I found that if I put him in the tub with just about an ⅛" of warm water near the drain, he defecated in about 10 seconds to three minutes. As soon as he defecated I cleaned up the mess and thoroughly cleaned the tub, rinsed Za off, and washed my hands. Then I put fresh water in the tub for him to soak.

Za was so well trained to defecate in the tub on command that I used this technique to control his pooping in the house. In fact, he progressed out of his portable toilet after mastering water defecation.

I also used this pre-pooping method before I took Za to the veterinarian (animals often get nervous around veterinarians, and it's not unusual for them to defecate on or near the vet), to one of the schools where I gave iguana talks, or in other trips in the car. Za would do this pre-poop any time of the day, even if he had already defecated earlier. It made life much easier and a lot less messy.

Za was certainly not the only iguana on the planet that defecated in this way. I periodically ask other iguana owners if they have ever used this trick, and many of them say yes.

My iguana [SVL: 7½", TL: 2' 2", 1 yr. 4 mo.] is trained to defecate in the bathtub. I started putting him in the bathtub (with about ¹⁄₁₆" to ⅛" of water in it) to get him to defecate there so he wouldn't go when he was loose in the apartment. Now he walks into the bathroom and waits there whenever he has to defecate. I then set everything up for him.   —I-892, Steve, 22 yrs., Illinois

It's important to note, however, that Za was not dependent on me for his pooping. If I was gone for the day or any time he was ready to poop, he would defecate in the habitat on his designated spot.

Outside

When I had my iguana out in our enclosed back yard, I trained him to defecate next to a big boulder. Again, it simply meant working with his natural

SIDEBAR

Cleanliness Reminder

NOTE: <u>Absolutely</u>, for <u>sure, no ifs, ands, or buts</u>—any time an iguana or any animal defecates directly where humans come in contact, the area needs to be cleaned <u>thoroughly</u> with soap, water, and bleach and rinsed clean. Feces often carry potential diseases (see Chapter 7, Medical Trouble-shooting, "Feces Problems"). <u>Never</u> forget to clean up immediately— NEVER!!!

tendencies. The first time Za was in the yard he went to this big rock and defe-cated next to it. So every time he was out in the yard and I saw his butt do the "poop wiggle dance," I would gently pick him up and put him next to the rock. After about six times of moving him to the boulder he caught on.

Whenever he was in the yard after that, the only place he ever defecated was next to the rock. Sometimes if I had to take him someplace for part of the day I would use the rock to pre-poop him—just like using the bathtub, except outside. There are so many options and places for your iguana to defecate. Just remember to be consistent in your training and the techniques will work.

> *I used to be able to hold him [SVL: 11", TL: 3', 3 yrs.] over the toilet, and he would poop after a few minutes, but he doesn't poop every day like this any more.* —I-724, Robbie, 14 yrs., Utah

Come Out of the Habitat

> *I don't like the traumatic experience we have every time I go to take her out of the habitat. There always seem to be a few pregnant seconds of terror for both of us—her fearing my picking her up, and my having to deal with the "strug-gle." Then everything's all right and everybody's happy once she is out.* —I-926, Robert & Virginia, California

Instead of having to struggle to get your iguana out of its habitat, wouldn't it be nice if your lizard emerged easily? With time and technique, you can train your iguana to come out of its habitat on its own, at your command.

When my iguana was a hatchling, I did just that. Za spent most of his time in his habitat on his upper ledge. The technique started with me tapping my fin-gers on his big basking limb, then calling his name to come down. I realize he didn't know his name or what I was up to, but surprisingly enough he did come down. One way to entice an iguana to come down faster is to offer a small piece of kale, mustard green, or dandelion. When the lizard takes the food, you can easily slide your hand under its belly and slowly pick it up (see page 442, "Getting Your Iguana Out of its Habitat"). This technique works only with habitats that don't open from the top.

With Za, he soon realized the freedom that coming out of the habitat offered, so after a couple of months he needed very little coaxing. All I had to do was stick my hand in the habitat near the "conditioned response area" (the big basking limb), and eight times out of ten he would come out on his own. Sometimes he would get so excited about coming out that he would by-pass the conditioned area and go directly to the bottom of the habitat, which was fine.

Several months after he knew the learned the conditioned response process, he made up his own system of coming out—which he trained me to follow. Whenever he wanted out he would walk down the big basking limb to the lower ledge or landing and stare at me. The ledge was about in the middle of the habitat, which was very accessible for me. Any time he came down to this lower ledge and I was in the house, I opened the habitat and let him out. Always! I followed the Training Formula—consistency and repetition. This new pattern he created made life easier for both of us.

The funny part was that Za would make sure he'd made eye contact with me before heading down the big basking limb. I'm convinced—after a couple of non-scientific tests where I purposely avoided looking at him—that he wouldn't make his move until he knew he had my attention. Maybe he wanted to be sure he didn't waste his energy.

This story is just to let you know that there are many possible ways of training your iguana to come out of its habitat, or for that matter to perform any training option. And again, Za wasn't a genius; many iguanas can do these things if their owners work with them. All you need is to be flexible about how to get what you need, and work with the desires of your lizard.

My iguana is trained to leap from the door of his enclosure onto my shoulder when I pat my chest. —I-791, Dan, 28 yrs., Missouri

My young [1-year-old] iguana has been "trained" so that whenever I put my arm into her cage, if she wants out she crawls onto my forearm and I will lift her out. If she doesn't want out, she will walk the other way.
—I-846, Bobby, 19 yrs., Texas

I planned and worked with my iguana to get him to come out of his habitat. Some iguanas like the feeling of being out of their habitats so much that they will make every effort to let you know this. When your lizard indicates strongly that it wants out, do it (unless it has been sentenced to "jail" time for misbehaving).

If he wants out of his cage he puts his nose up to the glass and just lies there and looks pathetic. The other thing he does is claw at the Plexiglas (it sounds like a fingernail on a chalkboard). The lizard usually gets what he wants when he does this. —I-638, Jennifer, 23 yrs., California

It's obvious when he wants out because he walks back and forth along the glass door of his cage and also scratches at the door like a dog to get out.
                                        —I-746, Mark, 19 yrs., Indiana

When my iguana [SVL: 15", 1½ yrs.] wants out he stands at the cage door and has this "funny" look.   —I-594, Daniel, 38 yrs., Virginia

Drinking Water

Dogs, cats, and humans get most of their moisture from drinking water directly. Iguanas get most of their moisture from their food. For that reason, many people over the years have assumed that iguanas <u>can't</u> drink standing water. Wrong! They drink water in the wild, lapping up rainwater on leaves and from rivers or streams, and they often open their mouths to collect falling rainwater.

Most areas of the country aren't humid like the jungles of Central and South America; many homes in the winter are extremely dry; and iguanas frequently reduce their intake of food during breeding season. For all these reasons, it is important for your lizard to have water available at all times. Iguanas will not always drink standing water on their own, so in captivity you need to train them to do so.

Because your lizard spends the vast majority of its time at the top of its habitat, install a water dish there for quick and easy access (see Chapter 4, Housing, "Food and Water Containers," for details). To train your lizard to be aware that water is present, place small amounts of torn mustard, collard, or dandelion greens in the water. Attracted by the food, your lizard learns where the water is. After a while it makes the connection between food and water and starts to drink, but <u>only</u> if this conditioning is done consistently until it understands. It might take several weeks or months for the message to sink in.

Once your iguana learns to drink the water, you can stop putting the food in the bowl, or leave it for a special treat. This technique is also a good way to feed small amounts of fresh greens if you're gone for a day. Just load a bunch of greens in the water, where they will stay fresher longer.

The water bowl should be changed daily, or at least every other day. Beyond this period of time, it begins to have characteristics of a wilderness pond, and your iguana could get sick. Scrub the dish with a bleach and water solution, and be sure to thoroughly rinse all residue of the bleach.

It's also important to note that I specified the upper water dish for drinking, as opposed to a large container of water you may have on the habitat floor for humidity. Often an iguana will defecate in this large water container. This <u>is not</u> where you put the kale or collard greens. This humidity container in the habitat is fine, but you also need the other water source for drinking.

Spray Bottle

In addition to drinking directly from his water dish, my iguana also trained me to give him additional water on command with a spray bottle. This happened when Za was on an antibiotic for a month, during which he increased his consumption of water by about 80%.

When he was thirsty during this time, he would lick his "lips." His tongue did not come out the front of his mouth like a usual iguana flick, but to the side like he was licking his chops. At first I was uncertain what he wanted. I offered him a number of options, then finally I took a regular plant-type spray bottle and adjusted it so the water came out in a solid stream. I put the spray head against the side of Za's mouth and gently pulled the trigger. He started drinking immediately, sucking the water down like he was dying of thirst. Obviously, what he had wanted all along was water.

The next year, two other iguana owners told me that their iguanas also licked their chops when thirsty. So it wasn't just a "Za thing." Remember way back in the taming section, I said you need to have awareness of your animal's daily activities. By being aware of one small change—licking his chops—I was able to deduce Za's desire for extra water. You may need to do something similar. It's not difficult and is kind of fun—like solving a mystery.

One breeding season, Za dramatically reduced his food intake. With less fluid intake through food, he required more water. At this time, he would excitedly drink water from the spray bottle again, like a man who had been out in the desert too long.

I have seen iguanas drink water from cups, spoons, and spray bottles. One person had their iguana drinking out of a hamster water bottle for a while.

My iguana will drink from a water glass if held in front of his face.
—I-171, Drew, 34 yrs., Minnesota
[AUTHOR'S NOTE: This sounds cute, but don't you as a human drink from this glass also—not a healthy thing to do.]

Head and Body—Fine-Tuning, Adjustments

Perhaps you want to photograph your iguana, or have some other reason for needing your lizard's head or body in a particular "pose." Here is one technique for achieving that perfect body position.

If you want your iguana to move to the left and it won't move, you would logically apply pressure to the right side of your lizard. But assertive iguanas will often push against the pressure you apply. Try tricking them by pushing them with gentle, steady pressure from the left side to move them left. They will push against the pressure, then all you have to do is ease up slowly, and your iguana will be where you need it.

The best technique, though, is to make extremely slow adjustments in the direction you want your iguana to move, and usually the iguana won't put up a fight. Za was on several TV shows and photo shoots. I could always get his head, arm, or body into any position by just moving that specific body part slowly to where it needed to be. It's almost as if they aren't aware that anything is moving.

"Tricks"

I have received a large number of photos from iguana owners over the years, but the first time I saw a photo of an iguana sitting up for food, I was really impressed (see the photo on the facing page). And the iguana didn't look stupid, but cute and adorable. After the sixth letter telling of, or a photograph showing, an iguana sitting up, however, I was more astounded than impressed. These letters came from all around the country, not just "Circus City, U.S.A."

Many people are impressed if their dog can sit up for food. Can you imagine what the average person would think if they saw an iguana sitting up for food? "Why, I thought lizards were supposed to be stupid. Must be pretty smart." This might be a good way to change the thinking patterns of the typical "person on the street" about how smart an iguana is.

My iguana will follow you across the room for a specific food treat and beg (like a dog) on his hind legs for some.   —I-171, Drew, 34 yrs., Minnesota

I have trained my iguana to stand up for fruit.
—I-776, Matt, 10 yrs., Ohio

Out in Public

Because many people treat their iguanas like a "normal" house pet, some take their lizards out in public, much as they would a cat or dog. Before you head out with your iguana, however, there are a few things you should consider.

Transporting Your Iguana

Having your iguana ride in your car can be dangerous, so I don't want to encourage it. If that is something important to you, ask another iguana friend or people at your herp society how they do it.

I came across a newspaper article about a person who had gotten in a three-car pile-up because an iguana got loose in the car. Details are sketchy, but supposedly a pet iguana leaped onto the driver, causing him to lose control of his car, which smashed into two other cars. In another instance, a woman in Massachusetts had a 4-foot iguana that got free from its cage—which was a moving car. The escape caused the woman to lose control, and the car fell over a 25-foot embankment. Luckily, both the driver and the iguana received only minor injuries. But anything can happen if your iguana is loose in your car.

We were in the car one day and I wasn't paying attention to my iguana. He crawled under the gas pedal, and as I was trying to get to him I hit the curb.
—I-401, Kathryn, 21 yrs., Florida

One iguana owner told me how his iguana was riding in his truck one day, got under the dash, and would not come out for three days. The owner even

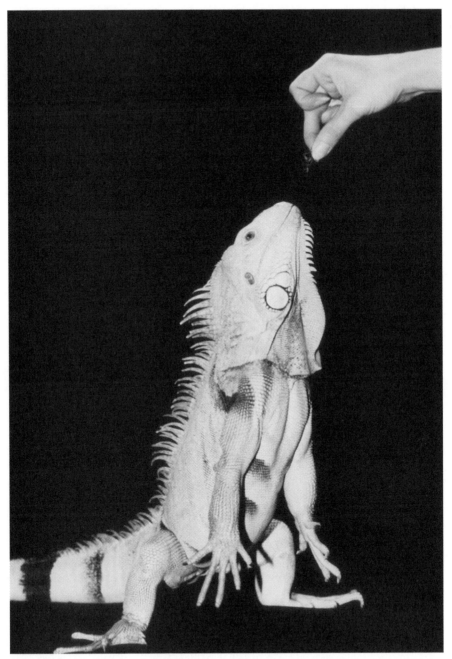

Figure 8.3: Tired of your friends bragging about how smart their dogs are? Teach your iguana to sit up for food. That should stop their bragging. Photo (and "Iggy"): courtesy of Dave and Laura Stinson

took the dashboard apart. Finally he turned on the air conditioner and the iguana came right out.

Possible Hazards of Being Out in Public

Whenever you take your iguana away from the semi-controlled environment of your house, you multiply the number of dangerous things you have to watch out for.

Temperature

The most immediate problem with an iguana out in public is the proper temperature—in particular, making sure your iguana stays warm enough. I describe iguanas' temperature requirements in several other chapters, so I won't detail it here. Just remember to think twice before subjecting your iguana to a stroll in anything other than warm weather.

At the other end of the temperature spectrum, consider that if the air temperature is 90°F, the concrete, rocks, or asphalt could easily be over 100°F. If your iguana crawls on these surfaces, it can get burned.

> *Outdoors in the sun they often "go berserk" and end up in the top branches of the tallest neighborhood tree!* —V-135, Dr. Debra, Washington

In addition, each iguana reacts a little differently to being outside in natural sunlight (some become aggressive). Look at Chapter 4, Housing, "Outdoor Cages—Precautions," for more information.

Escape

Another obvious hazard is escape. Everyone I talk with who lets their iguana outside always says:

- "I'll always be next to my iguana and it will never get a chance to get away."

Let's say you take your iguana out a couple of times, and the lizard doesn't run away. You relax, then one day the iguana gets startled by a new experience and puts itself into fast forward—good-bye iguana.

- "He won't get away," or "It won't happen with my iguana."

Read the next few stories before you take your own iguana outside. Some escape stories end happily, but many don't.

> *I had been letting my iguana [SVL: 11", TL: 3' 5", 3½ yrs.] out into our garden on a daily basis to bask and nibble on the edibles. He rarely moved and I usually stayed a few feet away, pulling weeds or cleaning. One morning we went out and I placed him on a garden bush and proceeded to work about 5 feet away. I checked him every few minutes to see if he moved. Well, he eventually did and I went to check where he went . . . and I could not find him! Within just a few minutes he had totally disappeared from my garden. Our neighborhood is fairly new and the trees have not gotten very large. My surrounding neigh-*

bors have sparse backyards and you would figure he would be easy to locate. That was not the case. For an hour I looked for him before I panicked and called for help.

I had several adults and the neighborhood kids searching. I offered $50 to whoever spotted him first. I went in every backyard down the block and gave my number out to everyone. Unfortunately, we didn't find him. The next day I called the humane societies, veterinarians, local pet shops, and animal control. I put up signs and told the neighborhood security patrol to look out for him. I borrowed binoculars and scanned every tree in sight. Still no luck.

A few days passed and I was feeling pretty discouraged. I could not believe we had not found him. He was fairly large at this time, about 3 feet long. Someone had to have seen him! My only thought was that a neighbor's dog had gotten him—and if that was the case, he was gone for good.

Almost a week had passed and I realized I probably would not find him. I was feeling quite sad and very guilty for losing him in the first place. What if he had injured himself or was found by some unscrupulous kids? I didn't want to think about it.

Suddenly, I got a call from my husband. Our iguana was in our own backyard. He had spotted him climbing down from the honeysuckle bush, not a scratch on him. What a relief! To this day we still have no idea where he was all that week, and of course he is not telling. To say the least, we are more cautious with him now and do not let him out of our sights.

—I-690, Irene, 34 yrs., Texas

AND . . .

I used to take him outside, but one time he got away and ran like a jet taking off at the airport.   —I-793, Lynn, 43 yrs., Michigan

AND . . .

My first iguana ran away when I took it outside for a photographer.
—I-758, Terry, 45 yrs., California

AND . . .

In early April my iguana was riding on my shoulder outside when a car drove by and startled her. She jumped off my shoulder. I looked and looked, but I could not find her. I thought she was lost for sure. A month and a half later my iguana turned up alive in a neighbor's tree.
—I-462, Ben, 20 yrs., Maryland

Dirty Walking Areas

After the first two major problems of temperature and escape, there are still many other problems with an iguana being outside. For instance, have you ever looked closely at the sidewalks or parks you visit? On the ground you might see spit, dog turds, sticks, and paper covered with mold and greenish brown sludge that seems to be alive. It could be an unhealthy situation for an iguana to walk through.

Pigeons and sparrows, as well as other birds, are notorious salmonella carriers, and their splattered feces can be found in most cities and parks. I wouldn't walk barefoot myself in these places, much less put a tongue-flicking iguana on the mess.

Poison Parks

Parks often spray their lawns with chemicals to kill weeds. How are you to know what poisons were used, and when? Often the lawn won't look, feel, or smell different. Unless you know the area where your iguana is going to walk, it's best not to let it roam freely. Remember, as an iguana moves, its tongue comes out and flicks the air and ground. Poisoned ground equals the possibly of a poisoned iguana.

Animal Predators

Not all iguana predators live in the jungles of Central America. Even in your own back yard, a neighbor's cat or dog could suddenly come out and scare your iguana away or attack it. Even though I live only 10 minutes from downtown Portland (Oregon), we have all kinds of critters crawling and flying around. Nature is beautiful, but it can also be dangerous.

Over the years I have seen four kinds of hawks in our trees. In the yard one day, I saw the remains of a bird that one of the hawks killed. The bird looked as if it had exploded from the inside out. All that was left was a beak, a handful of feathers, one leg, and blood. Be on guard all the time.

When I lived in a small town in California, a kestrel hawk smashed into the front plate glass window of my apartment. The hawk was trying to get my iguana as he rested on a big basking stick in that window. You never know what could happen in that split second of inattention.

Iguana on a Leash

My iguanas are all very tame and well-behaved enough for me to bring out for walks. But I don't recommend everyone to try this as iguanas are fast. If you're not so close to that animal as to be actually one with him, knowing every muscle twitch and every eye movement, then you can lose your pet in an instant, only to see him hit by a car or worse. Mine are quite large, well trained, and tame before I attempt an outing. Also I've had 23 years of experience handling them. Still, I always have them in harnesses (that I make and fit securely but not too tight) and on a leash.   —I-200, Dianna, 47 yrs., Washington

Within the last year or so, several leashes for iguanas have come onto the market. These devices also include a harness, which wraps around the iguana's chest area and connects to the leash. You hold the leash in your hand and thereby have a tethered iguana. The idea with this leash set-up is that you can take your iguana outside and walk it like a dog. It's supposedly a way to control your iguana when it is out in public.

With so many iguana products coming out each year, there's no way I can comment on all of them, nor would I want to. You need to make your own choice. Think about how each particular harness on the market works.

AT A GLANCE: Leash-and-Harness Potential Problems

- Entanglement
- Iguanas can escape from poorly constructed harnesses
- Harnesses can break iguanas' spines and damage other body parts
- Harnesses can injure your iguana's throat
- Iguanas often hate wearing these devices
- Some people get scared by seeing big lizards out in public
- All the problems inherent with iguanas being outside (proper temperature; possible escape; dirty walking areas; lawn and garden poisons; attacks from dogs, birds, or other animals)

Entanglement

One owner put a harness on his iguana and attached the leash with a hook to a clothes line. This way, the iguana could move about in the back yard but couldn't get away. One problem is that the lizard could tangle itself in the line. I have seen many dogs on lines like this in people's back yards, and when the owner gets home the dog often looks like a gift-wrapped birthday present. Goats sometimes are secured in this same manner in people's yards to eat weeds. They, too, are notorious for either tying themselves in knots or, more often, strangling themselves to death.

Harness Can Break

If plastic is part of the harness's security system, watch out: Plastic can break. It all depends on the quality of the plastic used. The problem is that you only know the plastic is bad when it breaks and your iguana escapes.

Many producers of iguana products send me their merchandise to try out. Currently, there are no harnesses for large adult iguanas (i.e., weighing 5 pounds or more) that fit or work correctly. When my iguana was 2 years old, all the devices for sale were already too small for him.

Possible Throat and Spine Injuries

Iguanas can be harness-trained for walks, but they lose the spines on their backs from it. —I-317, Todd, 19 yrs., California

The people who use harnesses typically report that the devices wear or break off iguanas' spines. And one <u>dangerous</u> type of harness goes under an iguana's throat. Iguanas have a delicate bone (actually, cartilage) network under the throat that supports their tongue and helps extend their dewlap. Harnesses that go under the neck area could damage or break this bone. <u>EXTREMELY SERIOUS</u>! <u>Do not</u> use this kind of harness.

She did have a reaction to a harness used on her last summer. On her dewlap, which is not prominent, and on her chest (two spots), she developed a discoloration (black) on the scales, which later turned grey/white. These areas remain de-pigmented, and part of the dewlap (approx. 5 mm x 5 mm piece) sloughed off. I can only conclude that there was a sort of pressure necrosis of the skin and scales due to pulling against the leash and harness. I have not seen any appreciable improvement despite subsequent sheddings.

—I-795, Dawn, 24 yrs., Ohio

I have designed a harness that does not hurt the iguana, and it gives them some freedom. It is much easier to catch a six-foot leash than a frightened iguana.

I measure from armpit to armpit on the iguana, then I transfer this measurement to a very soft piece of leather or nylon material. I cut holes just big enough to get their hands through without hurting them. The tabs on the back of the material just touch. Sizing is very important. Too large and the iguana will get away, too small and it will hurt them. I put one hand of the lizard in, then hold that side tight to its body while putting the second hand in, gently working the harness over the elbow. Then I hook this to the leash.

—I-764, Diana, 46 yrs., California

Iguanas Can Hate the Experience

I tried to put a harness on, he tried scratching, biting, and whipping his tail. After the harness was on, he did flips in it. I tried the harness only twice, but it was way too stressful for him. I would advise against using a harness on untamed older iguanas.   —I-759, Laura, 20 yrs., Pennsylvania

The leash-and-harness system seems to work best on hatchling iguanas. Adults often raise hell if one is put on them.

The thing he hates most of all is when I put his harness and leash on him. I always do this if we are going outside for an extended period of time.

—I-773, Rich, 34 yrs., Nebraska

My iguana once nipped me—I was putting his harness on to go out for a stroll in the yard. I had been fiddling too long and he lost his patience. Generally both of my iguanas are very tolerant and forgive my ineptness. (I believe I overheard one iguana say to the other, "Cut her a bit of slack. After all, she's only a human.")   —I-632, Cynthia, 38 yrs., California

Our iguanas walk on leashes only in our yard. The first time out was quite an experience. I never knew they could roll so many times so quickly when irritated.   —I-798, Teri, 35 yrs., New Hampshire

Reactions from Other People

You love your iguana and think it is the most beautiful creature in the whole world. But the problem is that many people feel completely the opposite. If you want to take your iguana out in public, be prepared for people who may become scared or angry with what they think is improper behavior. This is a common reaction, so be on guard not to scare or bother other people with your pet.

Many old-time herpetologists get a little crazy when we "new" reptile owners take our pets out in public. Their concern is that we risk negative experiences with the general public. The reptile (usually a large snake) might scare someone and the police may be called. Then we "herpers" get a bad name. I agree with them on this point.

I also agree that there are pet owners who don't protect their pet from the many potential dangers of the world outside, and I see this lack of responsibility occurring even in the daily care of their lizard. It's not iguana owners as a group that are screwing up, it's only specific people.

Your first concern must be the safety and health of your iguana. There are many outdoor places you can take your iguana and not have crowds of people around. When I lived in California, my girlfriend had a small house with a tall brick wall that completely enclosed the yard. I used to take my iguana over there on warm, sunny days so he could suck up the heat and sunshine. I even had one of those human plastic baby pools for him to play in. He was very pampered, and it showed in his health, personality, and tameness.

If you are going to take your iguana outside, you need to be aware of everything that is happening or could happen, including any clues your iguana might display. Whether you do or don't take your iguana out in public is your own choice. Just be sure you can handle any consequences of your decision.

Iguanas Training Their Owners

Often, as an iguana gets older it will train us to do what it wants. As I have mentioned before, my iguana trained me to give him water when he was thirsty, but that's not all. Za would frequently sit in front of the closed door to the bathroom in our house, turn his head, and look up (with one eye) as if to say, "I want to soak, please let me in." I'd let him in and then put some water in the tub so he could soak. Sometimes he would climb in on his own, but mostly he'd give me that "look" and I'd help him into the tub. Other times he would sit at the kitchen door (closed) with a pathetic look: "I need to look for something in there I left last week." I'd open the door and he would walk with purpose to particular places in the room.

I would take Za (then 3½ years old) out in our small enclosed front yard and let him sunbathe while I kept an eye on him. When he felt he had had enough outdoor time, he would walk to the front door, which was about 40 feet away and required climbing two concrete steps. Once in front of the door, he would look pathetically at the closed door as if to say, "I've had enough, open that door, I want to go in now." I'd open the door and he would walk straight into my office, to his habitat, or to the bathtub. He knew what he wanted and how to get it.

The following are just a few examples of how a well-trained pet owner and pet interact.

He trains me; I don't train him.   —I-918, Kay, 48 yrs., Wyoming

My iguana does not live in a cage, so when he has to go potty he goes in the kitchen (he prefers linoleum). He starts pacing, looking for the right spot, which is usually the same spot every day. He waits for me to get the paper towels ready, then he does his business.   —I-730, Brigitte, 32 yrs., Arkansas

We haven't trained our iguana to do anything. He [oldest iguana recorded at 29 yrs. old] has trained us to put a litter box where he customarily defecates, and not to try to feed him stuff he doesn't like.

—I-600, Don, 69 yrs., California

When I come home he scratches on the glass (cage) until he sees me coming. Then he goes to his favorite log and waits for me to pet or mist him.

—I-769, Yolanda, 20 yrs., Michigan

He's training me (bring him food, put him down when he tires of being held, etc.).   —I-685, Julie, 36 yrs., California

Za continually trained me. I loved Za and it gave me pleasure to do his bidding. Ours was a very special relationship. Your iguana can be special also; just be observant and follow the taming and training methods and formulas discussed in this chapter.

CHAPTER 9

Breeding

The vigorous, the healthy, and the happy survive and multiply.
—Charles Darwin (from *The Origin of Species*)

IN THE BEGINNING

When was the last time you won the state lottery for $10 million? In the past, it seemed that herp hobbyists faced better odds of winning the lottery than successfully breeding iguanas in captivity. Even the major zoos in the world had trouble raising iguanas in captivity, let alone breeding them.

The first gigantic leap forward in captive breeding of iguanas was started in Panama by Dr. A. Stanley Rand, senior scientist with the Smithsonian Tropical Research Institute, and Dr. Dagmar I. Werner, a German-born, Swiss-educated biologist. In 1983, the Smithsonian Institute funded their first-of-a-kind biology experiment to raise iguanas in captivity for future release back into the wild.

To make a long story short: Project support ended after about five years, the political climate changed in Panama, and Dr. Werner packed up 2,400 iguanas and years of research data and headed for Costa Rica in a small pickup truck. The story of getting her animals and truck to Costa Rica is an adventure in itself. All the details on arriving, acquiring the land to raise the iguanas, procuring funding to keep the project alive, and dealing with Costa Rica officials who embraced Dr. Werner and her iguana project deserve a special story some day—but not in this book.

The independent iguana research project now being conducted by Dr. Werner in Costa Rica is partly to release iguanas back into the jungle to re-populate devastated local iguana colonies. But the project is also layered like an onion—returning iguanas to the jungle, creating a stable and nutritious food source for the *campesinos* (peasant farmers), encouraging the growth and retention of more trees, boosting local economies, stimulating ecology awareness, saving the rainforests, and more. Too much to explain in this pet-care book, but this gives you a little insight into Dr. Werner's plan.

I feel that to really know about iguanas you need to pick the brains of the top people in iguana research worldwide. When I was in Costa Rica, I was lucky enough to learn much needed information about iguana breeding from Dr. Werner, sometimes called the "Iguana Mama," and Daisy, her main support person. Other quests for information took me to Mexico, Belize, and the San Diego Zoo, where each time I hooked up with one or more people who added significantly to my understanding of iguana breeding.

Starting on page 521, until the end of the chapter, are many important facts that you need to know about the effects of breeding season on your iguana—whether you plan to breed your iguana or not. For those few people who want to breed their pet iguanas and produce hatchlings, there is information in this chapter for you, too.

ADVENTURES

In the process of researching this book, I've had the opportunity to visit some exciting research sites where people are working at the forefront of iguana research. If you'd like to hear about my adventures in gathering this information, read on! If you're not interested in these adventure stories (starting below), skip ahead to page 518.

Mama Iguana's Place

Every trip I take to Latin America seems to turn into an adventure, and the saga of visiting Dr. Werner's iguana research station in Costa Rica was no exception.

Before I left for Costa Rica, I had sent a series of long letters to Dr. Werner explaining why I wanted to visit her research station (farm). Several months later I arrived with my photographer and Spanish translator (Amanda) in San José, Costa Rica. The next morning, without missing a beat, we were off to the iguana farm, as excited as two children heading for the candy shop with a wad of dollar bills. By midday we'd feel more like we held Monopoly money instead.

The two-hour bus ride from San José to the Pacific-slope town of Orotina was the easy part of the journey. Finding the iguana farm was the first obstacle. In retrospect we were in the center of the bull's-eye and couldn't see the target. We asked several local people where the farm was and each time they headed us in a different compass direction. In Latin American countries it is considered impolite not to help people, and it's bad manners not to give directions when directions are requested. Even when the local people we encountered didn't know the answer, out of politeness they often made one up.

After heading in all the wrong directions for more than an hour, we ended up walking down a long, desolate, dirt jungle road that ended at a heavily fortified steel gate. The sign next to the gate more or less said, "Scram, get out of here, and don't bother us." For the very brave, the sign did have a phone number to call. We retraced our steps back up the road, found a working phone, and called the number.

The person who answered the phone was the "Iguana Mama" herself. Dr. Werner asked what I wanted (probably surprised that anyone would dare to call). I told her about the letters and what I wanted to accomplish. She said she never received any letters, and from there she verbally shredded me like a pit bull at dinner time. She said, "You can't come in . . . you must leave." The innocent, excited child in me sank with a thud. I had been forewarned that Dr. Werner can at times be very difficult (make that a capital D). She said that she is very busy and has no time for outsiders.

I made a last-minute attempt to get permission to see the iguana farm. I said, "When I got into San José I called your office to see if I could come out to the research station, but I got no answer." I wanted to let her know that I didn't just drop by that day and expect people to jump for me. In a biting manner, she asked how I got her office phone number. I told her I got it from Dr. Gordon Burghardt (one of the world's leading iguana experts and co-editor of the classic book *Iguanas of the World*; I'd corresponded with him since starting my own book research).

She said, "You know Dr. Burghardt?" I said, "Yes." She said again, "You know Dr. Burghardt?" I said, "Yes." She seemed very surprised at this concept. I said that Dr. Burghardt had given me much useful research information on iguanas over the years. I was just telling her the truth.

And as though I were caught in a scene from a child's story book, "Dr. Burghardt" was the magic word for the day, like "Shazam" or "Open Sesame." Again she said, "You know Dr. Burghardt?" I said, "Yes."

She said, "Good. Then be at the gate tomorrow morning at 9:00 a.m. We won't wait if you are not there. And you will not be treated special. We have important people coming from Sweden. We will be releasing 1,000 juvenile iguanas into the jungle. The press will be there—and you can come along." And she hung up.

See the farm! See the iguanas! See the "Mama Iguana" and be part of the team releasing iguanas back into the wild! All of the troubles getting back into San José that day didn't even register on the stress meter. We were going to see and be involved in some amazing things the next day.

I am sure that most of you are thinking by now that the "Iguana Mama" appears to be less than a caring mama, essentially treating us like insects. There is no way to describe in 100 words or less Dr. Werner's real contribution to preservation. She is taking on a giant project: to save iguanas, but in the bigger picture to save the rainforests. I know her onion-layered plan and it is well thought-out, correct, smart, and she is going about all the levels in the right way.

She is very focused, like a laser beam. And sometimes things in the path of a laser beam get a little singed. She can't be bothered by anything that could slow her progress. Luckily, I knew what I was up against, so I didn't allow her not-so-pleasant manner to affect me. I see her as a champion. If I had a crucial project and needed some good back-up, I would love to have someone like her on my side.

The *Reader's Digest* version of just getting back to the "farm" the next day was mostly no sleep and waiting for hours at the gate. We arrived very early, at about 7 a.m., to make sure we didn't miss anything. After 11 a.m. we were beginning to think that perhaps the previous day's Central American high heat and humidity had triggered hallucinations that I had actually talked with Dr. Werner. But about 11:30 a.m. we heard cars, then we saw the dust rising in the distance, and then around the corner came a Datsun pickup truck with two cars trailing behind. By the time the vehicles arrived at the gate my body was drowning in adrenaline.

Little did I realize that the difficult task of getting into the iguana farm was not over yet. I ran up to the pickup truck, spotted Dr. Werner, and said I was Jim Hatfield. All she said was, "Open the gate." This adventure to the farm now had all the elements of a Greek tragedy, but written by Mel Brooks.

I ran to the gate and opened it. I stood at attention like a soldier as the three vehicles passed. The vehicles stopped long enough for someone to yell, "Close the gate" (guess who?). I was laughing inside and having one of my best days. Like someone once said, "Attitude is everything."

As I closed the gate, the lead vehicle with Dr. Werner moved ahead. I ran after the pickup and in one smooth leap I cleared the edge of the pickup bed and landed inside the moving vehicle with near-perfect form. We approached the next gate, and before Dr. W. could even open her mouth I jumped out of the moving truck, ran to the gate, and opened it—and of course I stood at attention.

The parade of cars and trucks proceeded without slowing down while I closed the gate, ran and caught up with the moving target, and again the jump into the pickup bed. The Swedish people in the two cars following the lead truck, who were from World Wildlife Fund, were laughing and seemed to be completely entertained by my actions.

One more gate, one more jump, and we arrived at the compound. When the cars stopped, the Swedish people immediately came over and introduced themselves and seemed delighted to meet me. When Dr. Werner got out of the truck I asked her (with a little grin on my face) if I closed all of the gates properly. I was just trying to finish one more line of this Mel Brooks movie that I had invented inside my head. She said, "Yes, it was fine." At the corner of her mouth a slight smile started to curve upward. She also got a twinkle in her eye that she seemed unable to control. As stern as she would like to appear, she was somewhat melted by this bizarre gate experience. Mel Brooks would have loved the way the script turned out.

After that, she seemed to soften toward me with her speech and actions. She was actually very nice. I think she liked the fact that I didn't crumble under her iron rule. That I would, and could, work for her. In fact, later that day I would literally kill for her iguana cause.

She spent some time with me at the farm and then said, "I am sorry, but I must be with the people from Sweden." Daisy, second in command to Dr. Werner, gave me some research information on the farm and showed Amanda and me the iguana compound. There was the research center, breeding stations, and cages for the more than 5,000 hatchling, juvenile, and adult iguanas. Each iguana was beautiful and perfect.

As we toured the facilities everything was clean and spotless—almost Eden-like. But then we rounded one cage of large adult iguanas and found a snake in this iguana paradise. The snake, which looked to be about 4' long, had threaded its body through part of the 1" to 1½" square wire cage mesh. The last 7" to 8" of its body was woven into the wire like thread in a piece of fabric, but its upper body was moving freely toward the adult iguanas in the cage.

I feel that iguanas truly have personalities and physical expressions, and the contorted looks on the two iguanas in the cage was of terror. I yelled at Daisy to tell her what was happening, and she motioned to one of the farm workers. In a split second that 4' snake sprang and extended to 6', stopped no more than an inch from the side of Daisy's neck, then fell to the ground. The only thing that prevented the snake from biting Daisy's neck was that its lower body was still threaded into the wire mesh. It sprang full speed and full length, missing the target by less than the width of its open mouth.

As soon as the snake struck, missed its target, and fell to the ground, Daisy said, "SON . . . OF . . . A . . . BITCH" in this long, drawn-out, adrenaline-filled, breath-catching pace. Then, with an agitated hand motion, she hurried the farm worker to where we were standing. The worker arrived with a rake to hold the snake's head down and a machete for killing the intruder. But he wasn't going to do it, and Daisy wasn't going to do it, either. They both turned and looked at me. The worker, with both arms straight out, held the machete in one hand and the rake in the other. He dangled each tool from just his thumb and forefinger, as if the implements were contaminated. He came closer and pressed the tools next to me. I don't speak Spanish but I do read body language. I thought, "Hell, I don't work here . . . and I don't like killing any animals."

Then I again saw the look of extreme terror on the iguanas' faces and without hesitating I killed the snake. Before the machete made contact, I mentally wished the snake no pain. There was no anger in the deed I was about to perform. I wished the snake the best in the next life, understood it was doing what all animals do (try to survive), but I had a responsibility at that particular moment in the cosmos to protect the iguanas.

When the snake was dead, no one would get close to it. Daisy and the workers thought the snake might be a Fer-de-Lance. That's a snake that once it bites you, you don't even have time to dial 911 for help.

So, like I said in the beginning, trips to Latin America can become epic adventures very easily. It's all part of the challenge of gathering research information. Often the best information is the "stuff" you can only get in person.

One example of the information I picked up at the farm from Dr. Werner was that female iguanas are basically lazy. If you can provide an alternative to them having to dig tunnels for laying eggs, they will easy adapt to that situation. For a practical application of this knowledge for pet iguanas, see the nesting (egg-laying) box in Appendix H. More of the information I gathered and saw at Iguana Mama's research farm is scattered throughout this chapter.

Huevos La Mancha Style

Much of the exact research at the iguana farm in Costa Rica is kept under close wraps. I was lucky to fill in some gaps in my knowledge about a year and a half later in the jungles of Mexico.

This adventure began with a letter from Maria Socorro Lara López, a research student at the Ecology Institute in Xalapa, Mexico. Xalapa (pronounced hah-LAH-pah) is a small colonial-style city about 100 miles northwest of the port town of Veracruz, on the eastern (Gulf of Mexico) coast. Socorro had heard that I was gathering information on iguanas and invited me to come and share some actual, in-the-jungle, hands-on iguana research with her.

After a couple of months of sending letters and faxes back and forth and getting all our equipment and details organized, Amanda (again my photographer and interpreter) and I flew down to Xalapa. At the Institute we met the Director, Dr. Alberto Gonzalez, and Socorro. The next morning we were scheduled to go to a restricted research station called La Mancha on the Gulf of Mexico, and Alberto had to sign some special permission papers allowing me in.

We toured the Ecology Institute in the morning, and that afternoon Socorro, Amanda, and I went into town and assembled all of our food supplies, then packed for our stay at La Mancha. We left early the following morning in complete darkness in a "travel-all" van that belonged to the Institute. With us was Cinco, an entomologist (branch of zoology that deals with insects) doing research at the Institute on the effect of worms on corn production.

I had to laugh to myself about Cinco and Socorro. Here I was riding toward an unknown jungle with a person named "Five" (Cinco) who raised worms and another named "Sorry" (Socorro) who dug up iguana eggs.

Cinco had loaded (I mean loaded) the van with what seemed like tons of concrete building blocks for creating permanent holding areas for worm breeding at La Mancha. As we headed out of town, every time we hit a bump the van bottomed out from the excessive load, and we could smell the burning rubber from the rear tires. I could just see us 100 miles from nowhere and both rear tires blowing out on a steep mountain curve, the van tumbling to the bottom of some desolate ravine.

But this didn't happen because about four miles later we dropped some of the concrete blocks off at Socorro's house to lighten the load. I felt guilty; it's rare that these researchers have access to the van, and because they were taking me and Amanda, they had to leave behind more than 150 pounds of blocks. But as I've found typical in Mexico, people there rarely make you feel guilty about anything. They tend to be genuinely kind and giving people.

The two-hour truck ride to La Mancha was a combination of mountains, greenery, and small, colorful farm villages that ended at the environmental research compound right on the Gulf of Mexico. The compound was originally an attempt by some Mexican entrepreneurs to create a resort on the Gulf, but it failed and the government took it over because of back taxes owed. In time it was converted into an ecology reserve.

Entering La Mancha

As we passed through the locked gate into La Mancha, to the right were the actual compound buildings, straight ahead was the ocean, and on the left was the jungle. In the middle of the jungle was a small lagoon, with hundreds of white heron-type birds squawking so loudly you could hardly hear yourself think. It was the peak of the breeding season and all of the birds were trying to get the attention of a future mate.

Because ecology doesn't get a lot of funding in Mexico, the buildings at La Mancha were a little tattered, but functional. [ADDENDUM: Three years later, funding came through and the whole compound got a face lift and mechanical upgrading. It's now a beautiful expression of Mexico's desire to support more ecology-related research.]

Anything made of wood or cloth deteriorates rapidly in the jungle's high heat and humidity, and La Mancha was about 90°F and 95% humidity every day we were there. One smart idea was that the cabins for sleeping were made of fiberglass so they wouldn't deteriorate in the hot, humid environment. However, their small windows allowed practically no ventilation and trapped excessive amounts of heat, so at night it was like sleeping under a fiberglass camper shell in Death Valley.

Sleep each night remained a distant wish until the building cooled off around 4 a.m.—just in time to get up at 6 a.m. By the fourth day my eyeballs looked like they had been soaking in a bottle of rum, and my body walked through the jungle like a run-down automaton.

Socorro had been coming to La Mancha for two previous years to do her iguana research and found out the lizards laid their eggs in the same general area each year. The area was at the top of a sand dune covered with marginal grasses and small bushes. About an eighth of a mile in front of this area lay the Gulf of Mexico, and just behind was the lagoon.

The lagoon was ringed by tall trees, several of which supported basking iguanas. Around the lagoon were turtles, alligators, the breeding white birds, plus green vines as thick as rope and fragrant, colorful flowers. In the low jungle area beyond the sand dunes were thousands of lobster-red crabs the size of small salad plates roaming through the undergrowth with a distinctive clicking sound. There were so many that the ground itself appeared to be in constant motion. With a volcanic mountain range in the distance covered in a net of camouflage green, this place looked like a perfect location for a Hollywood movie about prehistoric creatures.

Find the Eggs

We spent our first day at La Mancha trying to find the "needle in the haystack"—iguana egg nests. The area on the large sandy dune where Socorro had found iguana eggs in previous years was about the size of a football field. ("Female iguanas typically return to the same nesting sites each year" [#15].) The problem was trying to find the exact spot. Each year it changed slightly.

Iguanas prefer to lay their eggs in a medium that is easy to dig (iguanas would rather bask in the sun than work hard digging holes), and the sand here was ideal for both digging and egg incubation. The top 3" to 5" of the sand was dry, then it turned moist and warm below.

This area was not a barren sand dune, but was covered with strange plants with special protective qualities. For example, the small bushes grew thorny devices that felt like barbed wire or thumbtacks as we crawled across them looking for signs of the iguana nests. Many of these thorny things got stuck in our hands and knees throughout the day. And of course if the outside temperature is 90+°F, the sand was at least 100°F. Our mantras for the day were burn, ouch, burn, ouch, burn, ouch!

A total of five of us—me; Socorro; Amanda; Enrique, curator for the La Mancha compound; and Raul, an ornithologist (bird observer)—spent most of a day crawling on our hands and knees on this football field-sized egg incubator, looking for possible surface clues that the iguanas had deposited eggs beneath a specific spot. But there were literally no signs on the sand to indicate that eggs were buried below.

Perhaps if we could have been at the site five minutes after the eggs were deposited we might have seen some indications. But it rains most days and the winds blow constantly, making the sand smooth and clueless. It was very disheartening to end our first day no closer to finding the eggs than before we left for La Mancha that morning.

The next morning at 6 a.m. we headed for the dunes again. We took the same trail by the lagoon every morning so we could look for iguanas along the way. We never saw any on the trail but heard a lot of animals scurrying about in the jungle underbrush. Near the edge of the lagoon we would always hear the retreat of several animals as we came down the trail, and Socorro taught us to identify the animal by the sound it made as it entered the lagoon. The alligator and the turtle had their own special sounds, but none were as loud as the iguana, which sounded like an overweight child doing a belly-flop at a local swimming pool as it jumped from a tree into the water for safety.

Socorro was excited this morning as three of us (Socorro, Amanda, and I) stood on the sand dune. Socorro felt that it was a special day and we would find the egg nests. In the distance, through our binoculars, we could see adult iguanas basking in the tall trees on the edge of the lagoon. The sky was the blue of a robin's egg, accented with white puffs of clouds. A slight cooling breeze coming off the Gulf brought with it the sweet fragrance of flowers. Indeed, the day did feel special.

We divided the football field area into a workable grid pattern, each of us searching a different section, to make finding the needle in the haystack a little more methodical. As we worked in the sand, Socorro instructed us to be very careful, that the eggs could be anyplace. Iguanas can dig straight down, sideways, or in any combination. Sometimes, she said, your hand would pick up a dug tunnel, and sometimes the tunnel would have collapsed and the eggs would just be "there" in front of your hand under this collapsed sand.

After about three hours I began to think today was not a special day after all, now that cramps had settled into the flexible shovel that I once called my arm. As I was digging into what I thought was a tunnel, Socorro yelled from the distance to be careful because often snakes will enter the iguana tunnel and either lay their eggs or just camp out in the tunnel for a while. The first thing I thought was how the snake at Dr. Werner's iguana farm in Costa Rica had almost sunk its teeth into Daisy's throat.

Digging around in a deep, long tunnel, lying on my side, the sand up to my armpit, I was thinking about how many snakes might be lying in ambush at the end of this tunnel waiting for a warm "gringo sandwich." All of a sudden I touched something and my hand and arm backed out of the tunnel at about 100 miles an hour, accompanied by a scream exploding uncontrollably from my mouth. I felt a little stupid standing there on this desolate sand dune with my one arm hanging limp at my side, the fingers twitching involuntarily. I checked . . . all of the parts were attached, in the right place, and functioning, with no bleeding.

Someone yelled, "What's wrong?" To regain my researcher status I said, "Everything is fine." I saw Socorro and Amanda heading in my direction to see if I needed some help. Because I still had a hand attached to my wrist, whatever was in the tunnel was definitely not something that likes to eat hands. I regained my composure, and my arm disappeared into the sand up to the armpit again.

I touched the thing in the end of the tunnel . . . it didn't touch back. I touched it again. It didn't move. I touched it again and yelled to the sky, "I think it's an egg!" The two women ran over to me at double speed. I told Socorro that I'd feel better if she dug the sand away, as there was a certain art required and she had done it many times before.

Yes, indeed, it was iguana eggs, and Mr. Lucky had found them. Lucky is an understatement. When Dr. Werner first tried to collect iguana eggs in the wild for her iguana breeding program, she and her helpers often spent days digging up an entire nest site, with little to show for their efforts. That was one of the reasons she wanted to breed iguanas in captivity.

I marked the location of the eggs with a stick in the sand and then re-filled the tunnel so it wouldn't cave in when we started to dig the eggs out from the top.

Our next task before we dug the eggs out was to take temperature readings of the air and the sand's surface for Socorro's records. We took another reading halfway down in the sand, and a final one at the level of the nest itself. All of these temperatures are important for the scientific "guess" as to when the eggs will hatch.

We very carefully pulled, not dug, the sand away from the center of the indicator stick. Iguana eggs, unlike the chicken variety, don't have rigid calcium shells. They are encased in a leathery-textured outer covering that can easily break.

When we first saw the tops of the eggs, we all spontaneously stood up and

Figure 9.1: This is the actual nest of iguana eggs that the author found at La Mancha in Mexico. Photo by: James W. Hatfield III

screamed and hugged each other like we had found a golden treasure chest. We all love iguanas and this "find" pushed us over the edge of sanity. Then suddenly we stopped screaming and looked around. No, there wasn't anybody around to commit us to a crazy house.

We dusted off our over-excitement, straightened our research attitudes, started taking temperatures, and measured and weighed all the eggs in the nest. Then we returned the eggs exactly to their original place and position, along with the same sand at about the same compaction that it originally had. Socorro gave a final expert brushing of the sand's surface to erase any evidence of the nest's location. As we headed down the trail back to the compound we were all silent, separately locked into our own visions and fantasies of the day's events.

For the next three days we made nest recordings at about 7 a.m., noon, and 5 p.m., noting air, surface, and internal sand temperatures. After that first day of digging we never removed the eggs again, just the sand covering the top of them. And after each trip we replaced the sand at its original level and swept the surface with broken bushes, to hide any signs that anything had been near the eggs. We did it to prevent potential predators from guessing that there might be something there to eat.

Socorro said that everything looked good for hatching in about a week. Her guess was based on a combination of egg size, sand temperatures, outside temperatures, and humidity. But my time was running out, as I had more research planned about 300 miles away in two days. I left Socorro with 10 rolls of slide film to document the iguanas as they hatched (see the photo section).

Socorro said that each year she usually knows within a week when the iguanas are going to hatch. But because of the very unusual weather patterns (El Niño) the year I was there, the hatching guess was off by about a month— it happened long after I'd returned to the U.S. The last week before hatching, Socorro literally lives at the egg site so she can carefully measure each hatchling as it emerges from the sand.

Socorro surrounds the egg site with ⅛" wire mesh frames to hold the hatchlings, like corrals for miniature cattle, so she can get their measurements and weights. Later, she checks the nest for iguanas that may have died in their eggs. Interestingly, most of the new hatchlings got used to Socorro and quickly became tame.

On page 568 are the temperatures Socorro recorded at La Mancha for 1991 and 1992. [NOTE: In 1993 the funding arrived too late and she was unable to do her usual research.] These temperatures give a baseline for what iguanas in the wild need for hatching. Also, the weights and lengths (see page 578) give you an idea of an "average" hatchling. If you see what's happening in nature it will help you better understand your own captive breeding program—if, indeed, you decide to undertake such a program.

ZooDiego

The next natural progression in my knowledge of iguana breeding was to find a place that raises iguanas in captivity, but on a smaller scale than at Dr. Werner's iguana farm in Costa Rica. One day on television, I saw a five-minute segment about a captive iguana breeding program in Belize, Central America. One of the organizers for the reproductive program was Dr. John "Andy" Phillips, based at the San Diego Zoo's Center for Reproduction of Endangered Species (CRES).

I wrote several long letters to Dr. Phillips explaining that I was trying to gather current information on iguanas, but I never received a reply. It turned out that Dr. Phillips wasn't even in San Diego, he was in Africa doing research and wouldn't be back for another six months.

Because you always get more information in person than you can ever get by phone, I flew to Southern California to meet and talk with Dr. Phillips when he returned from his research trip. He was extremely helpful and proved to be a storehouse of iguana knowledge.

On the steps of CRES he filled my tape recorder with new and exciting information about iguanas not readily available to the general public. Dr.

Phillips also showed me his captive-raised iguanas at CRES and some of the 10 years of research that went along with them, including advanced research to help increase iguanas' reproductive potential. Dr. Phillips is also credited with the research explaining how important it is for iguanas to maintain a body temperature of at least 85°F for proper food digestion and better growth (see Chapter 5, Feeding, "Digestion: Special System").

Dr. Phillips helped add significantly to my iguana information, and he also corrected a lot of widely spread misinformation on iguana care. Much of his advanced iguana information is found in this chapter and throughout the book.

Belize Zoo

The short television segment where I first saw Dr. Phillips was filmed at the Belize Zoo, the site where some of the iguana reproduction research was done. It drove me crazy to think that there was this terrific, small, and highly productive iguana breeding facility in Belize, and that I hadn't seen it. So about two years after talking with Dr. Phillips I flew down to Belize and met with one of the people who helped first create the zoo, Tony Garel.

The Belize Zoo is small, but it has had many write-ups throughout the world because of the quality of life its animals enjoy, largely due to the natural setting in which they are presented. The zoo keeps only animals that are native to Belize and recreates the environment appropriate for each of these animals.

The temporary iguana breeding program was in a small facility attached to the old zoo, which was recently replaced by an updated and even more "natural" setting nearby.

When the breeding program at the Belize Zoo ended, all the adult and juvenile iguanas were returned to the wild. (As evidence of the Belize Zoo's success at recreating healthy environments, some of the released iguanas from the original breeding program have taken up residence at the zoo. No one counts the iguanas among the "official" zoo animals, but Tony can point out where particular iguanas usually hang out.) Much of the information that Tony explained to me about iguanas is incorporated throughout this book.

BREEDERS

Usually, the only real difference between commercial and amateur (pet owner) breeding of iguanas is volume. The techniques are basically the same, but as a pet owner your heart is your guide, and the reward is rarely financial gain.

Commercial

"Farm-raised" is the name given to hatchling iguanas that are raised for the pet trade from eggs on farms, much like chickens. Only a few places in the U.S. raise green iguanas on a commercial level, and the production is very small.

Dollar for dollar, it's more economical in the U.S. to raise other types of reptiles with bigger price tags than iguanas. It's hard to compete with the large iguana farms in Central and South America, where the labor is extremely cheap and no special housing or supplemental heating is required. The number of farms in Central and South America varies with the public's demand for iguanas.

The term "farm-raised" encompasses two different ways of farming. One is to go into the jungle and capture female iguanas that are gravid (i.e., with eggs) and bring them back to the farm. Sadly, in a number of countries you can find markets selling gravid females to people who want to eat the eggs (even though many countries now are making this illegal). Getting gravid iguanas for farming usually isn't a problem if money is offered.

Typically, this kind of farming operation has a holding pen with soft soil so the female can dig and deposit her eggs. The "farmers" dig up, incubate, and hatch the eggs, then feed and house the hatchlings until they are ready to be exported. After the eggs are deposited the farmers release the females and the whole process starts over again the next breeding year. Often these places hold the hatchlings until they grow to the size of a small juvenile for healthier, safer transport to the U.S. and Europe.

The bad thing with this approach is that it requires taking new gravid females from the jungle every year. As a result, the wild population is not allowed to expand as it naturally would. This is not the best technique for maintaining a healthy, balanced jungle.

The other technique is more environmentally friendly. It begins with a few females acquired in about the same manner as described before, but adult males are also captured. With sexually mature male and females, the farm now can create its own breeding "stock." This way, no further iguanas need to be taken out of the jungle. A couple of commercial farmers are doing this now, with more on the way thanks to pressure exerted by environmental groups, the countries that the iguanas are found in, and people like yourself.

Iguana farming requires specific knowledge that not everyone possesses and that is often closely guarded, as I was told by one of the commercial breeders. In the beginning of commercial iguana farming, many people tried it and most failed because they lacked some crucial piece of knowledge.

Raising iguanas is only one aspect of iguana farming. You also need to know how to properly "package" the iguanas so they won't die during shipment. Even if the iguanas are packed properly, other things can go wrong before the lizards reach their final destinations. There were some iguanas coming from Peru some years ago that looked healthy but that died shortly after arriving in the U.S. Some people assumed that the iguanas were fed the wrong food. A big commercial iguana farmer I know told me what actually happened:

"The reason they're dying is that all the shipments have to come through Quito [the capital of Ecuador], which is 9,000 feet above sea level," he said. "And when they bring them [the iguanas] up to that altitude, the temperature is cold, down to 40°F, and most of the people who are shippers there don't have enough sense to keep the hatchlings warm. When the farmers or shippers drop the iguanas off at the airport, if the iguanas have to stay overnight, they're sitting there in that low temperature, and they get upper respiratory disease and they die. And you don't know it until days later, after they've arrived in the United States. They look good when they come in; they're all alive, then they start breaking down, start dying, and nobody knows what's wrong with them."

Pet Owners

I hope to raise quality captive-born iguanas for responsible people.
—I-401, Kathryn, 21 yrs., Florida

One afternoon I got a call at my office and the person on the other end of the phone said something like, "They are starting to hatch . . . ONE IS HATCHING RIGHT THIS MINUTE!" I held the phone, confused, not knowing what was happening or who I was talking to. The person speaking said, "LOOK, THERE IS ANOTHER ONE HATCHING RIGHT THERE!" Of course I couldn't see anything—not over the phone, and especially since the caller was about a thousand miles away.

It turned out the caller was someone I had met at my old herp society (Bay Area Amphibian and Reptile Society, or BAARS) in California. Mark Sanchez was the proud father (I know this is an incorrect term, but at the time Mark's enthusiasm could only be described as "fatherly") of three iguanas, with more hatchlings on the way (see the color photo section for a look at one of his babies). Even though Mark had a mating pair of iguanas and an incubation box, he was still shocked as "his" green monsters came alive in his apartment. By the end of the phone call I felt kind of like Uncle Jim at the hospital baby ward.

I've come into contact with fewer than 10 pet owners within the last six years who have actually bred and hatched iguanas. I think more iguanas will be hatched by pet owners in the future as we learn more about keeping iguanas not only alive, but also healthy and happy in captivity.

The majority of iguana owners I've spoken to don't care about breeding iguanas in captivity, and that is just fine by me. But there is still a percentage of people who want to breed their iguanas for profit, pleasure, or to help reduce the supply of iguanas coming from the wild.

This chapter will help those people wanting to breed iguanas, but more importantly give every pet owner a preview of the many changes your sexually mature adult iguana, male or female, might go through during the breeding season. This is a very important chapter, even if you do not contemplate breeding your iguana. Much of this information has never been detailed in any previous book.

I've always felt that the major barrier to breeding in the "old days" was the failure to meet iguanas' basic need for proper food and housing. If iguanas aren't fed proper food, if they live a shoe-box existence and always feel sick, then sex isn't a high priority.

In the last few years, I have seen great strides in iguana pet care. Because of this new and positive trend in pet-care knowledge, iguanas going into breeding season at home is becoming much more common.

> **AT A GLANCE:** Some Things Covered in This Section
> - Female iguanas lay eggs whether they have mated or not
> - Sometimes female iguanas need physical and nutritional help during egg development
> - Sexually mature male iguanas can be aggressive, mean, and nasty during breeding season
> - Iguanas often go off feeding during this time

QUESTION AND ANSWER

This section presents and answers some of the most-asked questions concerning iguanas and breeding in a simple format.

How do I know if I have a male or a female iguana?

With hatchlings or very young juvenile iguanas, it's essentially impossible to tell from looking at the outside of their bodies for clues. There is nothing physically different to see, as with male and female humans. Because iguanas' genitalia are all internal, it's not always clear-cut, even with adult iguanas. But as iguanas approach sexual maturity, males and females typically begin to exhibit outward differences based on their gender. The basics for identifying the gender of an iguana are covered in Chapter 1, Iguana: The Species, "Male/Female Physical Characteristics."

Not everyone has to rely on visible iguana characteristics to identify males and females. A major zoo in the U.S. uses an X/Y chromosome identification technique to distinguish between male and female iguanas, but this technique is not currently available to the general public. However, a company in California that specializes in DNA-based veterinary applications is trying to devise a safe, easy, and inexpensive test to identify male and female iguanas, even at the hatchling stage. They told me that they are getting closer to the solution and hope to have this test available sometime late in 1996 for about $25 to $30. Until then, we have only simple guessing methods.

What are the months that iguanas breed?

To date, mating between my male and female occurs around the last part of October and ends about the first week of December.
                                        —I-722, Andy, 32 yrs., California

Breeding season here in Arizona is between October and February.
                                        —I-775, Karen, 37 yrs., Arizona

The first of the males starts [breeding] the first of December. He thinks he is the dominant male and seems to be "in heat" into March. Everyone [the iguanas] calms down in April, and just a little aggressive behavior (the usual dewlap display, head bobs, and a little chasing) goes on.
—I-764, Diana, 46 yrs., California

In the wild, male iguanas typically start exhibiting mating behavior around October, peaking around January or February, and this happens only once a year. Female iguanas lay their eggs in the dry season, which is advantageous because the eggs will then hatch at the beginning of the rainy season, when vegetation (food) is most abundant and tender.

In captivity, the majority of iguanas follow the standard breeding schedule, but several people have written to say that their male iguana goes into breeding in May, or during the summer. A few said that their males go through breeding twice a year (May and October).

My iguana's [SVL: 15", TL: 4' 4", 4 yrs.] first breeding season lasted from May to late August. —I-727, Sharon, 34 yrs., South Carolina

Our iguana's mating season behavior lasted from April to August or September. —I-705, Paul & Linda, 45 yrs., California

Some people think that variations in breeding months is tied to the latitude, while others think it's determined by the length of the day (number of hours of light) or how hot and humid the area might be. I think any or all of these have an influence.

Mating always took place between December 20 and January 4, except this year—due to the fact that we moved to a new house and the iguanas got their own room, which offered more natural light and a better constant temperature. —I-714, Roger, 36 yrs., England

The longer you own your lizard, the easier it will be to pick up the often subtle clues that the breeding season has started. As a general rule, October is a good starting time to become aware of the changes your sexually mature iguana might go through. After the peak around the end of December or first part of January, male breeding activity tapers off until you have your "normal," nice iguana again. But as you'll learn later in this chapter, if you have a female iguana, it's crucial that you become aware whether she is in breeding season.

What physical signs would indicate an iguana is in breeding season?

Both male and female iguanas demonstrate certain physical and behavioral changes during their breeding season. In general, the breeding season for males is characterized by an increasing curve of activity, often accompanied by increased aggression and decreased appetite. It's a little more difficult to identify the signs of breeding for female iguanas, especially with younger sexually mature lizards.

> *She seemed to go into breeding close to when she turned 2 years old. She stopped eating for about 10 days and stomped around the apartment a lot as though she were looking for something. She was also extremely agitated and one time clawed at the windows until her knuckles bled. She was certainly wilder during this time and it seemed to last a few weeks.*
> —I-620, Suzanne, 33 yrs., New York

More details of these characteristics will be explained in various sections throughout this chapter, but here's a quick overview of some of them:
- Aggressive or fighting behavior (typically males only)
- Color changes (e.g., bright orange), especially males' arms, legs, and spines
- Increase in head bobbing (males)
- Mood swings
- Irritability
- Roaming or restless behavior
- Femoral pores (the males' will be enlarged or swollen)
- Reduction of food intake (both males and females)
- Digging (females trying to find a place to deposit their eggs)
- Male mounts female

How can I encourage mating?

AT A GLANCE: *Conditions That Encourage Mating*
- Sexually mature iguanas (male and female)
- Male and female of approximately equal size
- Healthy animals
- Long-term excellent diet
- Natural and sufficient ultraviolet light
- Photoperiod
- Space

Sexually Mature Iguanas: Male

"NO MINORS ALLOWED: I.D.s required." One of the first questions that most iguana owners want to know is, "How can I tell if my iguana is old enough to breed?" Age is really not the main criterion, but rather the snout-vent length (SVL). It's important to read Chapter 3, Choosing Your Pet, "Size Options: Hatchling, Juvenile, Adult," for a detailed explanation of what a sexually mature iguana is.

AT A GLANCE: *Signs of a Sexually Mature Male Iguana*
- Hemipenes visible during defecation
- Masturbation
- Femoral pores prominent, exuding a hard waxy substance
- Bulge at the base of the tail
- Color changes (usually orange, sometimes reddish)

Hemipenes

If you have a male iguana, one physical way to see if he is sexually mature is to watch him defecate. Just as the feces hit the ground and the vent starts to close, the iguana will often give one last squeeze to get rid of any remaining feces. In this last squeeze you may see two things pushed out of the vent that look like small pieces of intestine (not to be confused with a prolapse—see Chapter 7, Medical Troubleshooting). These are the hemipenes (two penises) of the male.

For younger sexually mature lizards, this observational technique is more useful during the breeding season only. An older sexually mature male's hemipenes can usually be seen during defecation throughout the year.

Masturbation

When my iguana is out of the cage lately, he frequently gets on the arm of the blue recliner chair and bites it. He then squirms his whole body against it with his tail, slashing wildly. When he's finished he just lays there with his tongue sticking out. If he's not doing some sort of mating thing, which is what it looks like, I don't know what he's doing.   —I-476, Marie, 23 yrs., Virginia

I observed one of the most obvious signs of a male iguana being sexually mature when my iguana was about 1½ years old. Za was in his habitat resting on his big basking stick, when I saw his hemipenes roll in and out of his vent three or four times. A substance the consistency of soft, melted mozzarella cheese came out. He exhibited no expression on his face or any body positioning to indicate that anything special was happening to him. What my male iguana had just done was masturbate.

Over the next several breeding seasons, I never actually saw this happen again, but I did see dried semen in different parts of his habitat. The dried semen looked like the thin, crisp cheese left in a frying pan after you've made a grilled cheese sandwich. The most samples I ever saw in one day was five. Sometimes weeks would go by and I would find nothing. The days he did masturbate he seemed to do it early, around 7 a.m., shortly after his habitat lights came on. It's always a good idea to keep a close eye on the subtle changes that happen in your iguana's habitat, whether it's semen or other strange things that might show up.

Sometimes an iguana gets extra help during these hormone-ridden days.

One time, for a week, I thought my iguana was constipated. He also developed a strange bulge at the base of his tail and seemed depressed. I went to my vet, and he said that the iguana's gonads were enlarged because it was mating season.

Before I could break the good news to my friend, who had been babysitting my iguana, she said excitedly, "Guess what? I cured your iguana's medical problem. I massaged the bulge on his tail, until he went to the bathroom. It was strange, however; I didn't know that their feces were <u>white</u>!" Oops. I hated to break the news to her that she had just masturbated my iguana.

—identification withheld as a courtesy

A female owner (single apartment-dweller) during her monthly cycle found that her male iguana was now sexually mature because he attacked her and ejaculated on the floor, with his hemipenes extended. The owner freaked! She wanted to have him examined, for what reason I don't know. I explained to her the situation, that it's a common occurrence for healthy male iguanas. She wanted to know—in all seriousness—"should I help him when he does that?"

—V-125, Dr. Bill, 37 yrs., Texas

As a side note concerning male iguana reproductive equipment, Dr. Gordon H. Rodda (who has done years of research on iguanas and has published numerous scientific papers) made the following statement during a presentation to the Tucson Herpetological Society on 21 November 1989. As you can tell, he has a great way of mixing humor and scientific information into easily digestible facts:

Now I should point out, for the record, that iguanas have relatively spectacular testes. I have not been able to find a compendium of that statistic in lizards, but it has been well documented in primates, and among primates, the chimpanzee is notorious for having the largest of any primate, and runs about 0.25% body mass. For a male green iguana it is a little over 1% body mass, which are spectacular testes for the animal kingdom.

—Gordon H. Rodda, iguana researcher (#27)

Femoral Pores

Another physical clue to male iguanas' sexual maturity is visible on the underside of their legs. On the inside thigh is a row of about 12 to 20 little round nubs, in a single file, called femoral pores (they are explained in more detail in Chapter 1, Iguana: The Species, "Femoral Pores"). Both males and females have them, but in the male during breeding season these pores swell and exude a hard waxy substance, sometimes extending outward almost like small claws. This substance is thought to leave chemical cues—pheromones—for both foraging and social communication as the iguana moves around (#22). If your iguana has these swollen pores, you can be pretty sure it is a male.

Bulge at the Base of the Tail

Look for bulging at the base of the tail, just beyond where the tail attaches to the body. This bulging, on both sides of the tail, is caused by the male iguanas' swollen hemipenes (this is more pronounced during the breeding season).

Color Changes

Males get more aggressive, possessive, and wild during breeding. Also, my large male turns oranger on his upper legs and side.
                                              —I-289, Janice, 43 yrs., Illinois

During breeding season, a sexually mature male iguana gets dressed in his finest garish attire to attract females. Some iguanas get intense, bright colors (usually orange) on their spines, front legs, and jowl areas. My iguana, who was from Honduras, turned bright orange on his arms and legs—and sometimes his spines were so intense in color, it looked as though someone had melted and dripped orange crayons on them.

Head Bobbing

There is a tremendous increase in the number of head bobs during the period of copulation. We [iguana field researchers in Venezuela] worked out how many extra head bobs a male gives during this period and it works out to be 10,850 extra head bobs. There's a lot of head bobbing going on and nothing like that happens with the females. They continue along at the rate they were going [before breeding].   —Gordon H. Rodda, iguana researcher (#27)

Not every male displays the same degree of head bobbing in captivity. It varies greatly with the size of the habitat, how much freedom your iguana normally gets, how well the iguana has been cared for, its personality, and if other iguanas are in the vicinity. But if you notice a marked increase in your male iguana's head bobbing, and nothing else in his environment has changed to explain it, there's a good chance it's a sign that he's sexually mature and in the breeding season.

Sexually Mature Iguanas: Female

Female iguanas don't have dramatic and obvious outward signs to indicate their gender or that they are sexually mature—unlike males with their two penises and bright breeding colors.

Identifying a sexually mature female from its outward physical appearance is tricky, like the old magic "rabbit out of the empty hat" trick. One minute the iguana is behaving like any normal iguana and the next minute, out of nowhere, it's dropping eggs all over the place. This may sound like an exaggeration, but this is actually how some iguana owners have found out that their iguana is a female. One person had a gorgeous lizard named Rex. After it unexpectedly laid eggs, the owner had to change the iguana's name to Rexina.

The only obvious outward sign to indicate that a female iguana is sexually mature may be a swollen belly as the developing eggs get bigger. Sometimes it's apparent and sometimes not, depending on the age and size of the iguana, as well as the number of eggs developing inside. In any case, the swelling becomes noticeable only toward the end of egg development.

One helpful clue: Female iguanas with an SVL greater than 10" are large enough to successfully breed (#14). When your female iguana gets close to this reference measurement and it's breeding season, keep a closer eye on her abdomen and on her overall behavior.

Additional identification clues can be found in Chapter 1, Iguana: The Species, "Male/Female Physical Characteristics." There are also many more bits of helpful information for identifying female iguanas scattered throughout the rest of this chapter.

Male and Female Equal Size

Remember Darwin's theory of natural selection, where the best-adapted members of a species are most likely to survive and reproduce? This theory applies to iguanas. A female iguana, deep in her genetic memory, wants to produce the biggest and healthiest iguanas to increase the odds that her offspring will survive and also reproduce. The best way to achieve this is for the female to mate with a male iguana that best displays vigor, health, and large size.

If you start your breeding program at home with a male and a female of at least equal size, there's a better chance that the female will go out on a "first date" with that male. If the male is larger than the female, romance will likely be in the air.

In the wild, the larger the male, the better chance it will have to attract females for mating. A smaller male may attempt to breed with a larger female—but the female, interested in a robust mate, will usually resist mating in this case.

Last year I tried to get involved in breeding my female [SVL: 15½", TL: 3' 11¾", 4½ yrs.]. I acquired a male that was smaller than my female. He made

many attempts to breed but every time he had a secure grip on her neck she would toss him off before he could insert a hemipene.
                                        —I-653, Justin, 19 yrs., Maryland

And don't think that the male is always the strongest individual. If a male is smaller he could get his "butt" kicked by a larger female. Or even worse.

Once an adult male attempted mating with a larger female I had, and in the ensuing battle the male was bitten so severely that he later died of infection despite vigorous veterinary care.   —I-282, Tom, 39 yrs., New York

Male and Female That Get Along

In every breeding species, some pairs of potential mates get along better with each other than others. There is always magic in the world; some things fall into place naturally, and some don't.

There is no systematic way to pick two iguanas that will get along. Two iguanas raised together may not be compatible, while introducing a stranger could produce instant harmony. It really comes down to luck or magic. Just remember that you don't have much control over this part of the process. What you need to do is make sure that any iguanas who obviously don't get along are not forced to stay together.

Sometimes if nothing happens when a male and female iguana are brought together, the introduction of a second female can perk up the male's interest. In many breeding colonies, two or more females are available for each male to breed with. Perhaps the male gets more excited because there is more to choose from or because there is more movement in the habitat. But even this may not always work, especially in a small environment or habitat.

There was a case where a male and female iguana, long-time cagemates, got along but weren't mating. A second female was introduced and both of the other iguanas attacked her instantly. The owner immediately removed the second female to save her life. Use this story as an example: Don't put iguanas together and go down to the laundromat for two hours. Watch your iguanas (from a distance) and intervene if dangerous problems arise.

Healthy Animals

This seems such an obvious condition for breeding, but for many years a healthy iguana was hard to find. People who are sick and in the hospital don't want to have sex. Their main, often only, goal is to stay alive and try to get a little more healthy each day. Like the television commercial says, "If you have your health you have everything!" Keep your iguanas healthy, and natural things will more likely develop.

Long-Term Excellent Diet

At this point it might be a good idea to review some of the highlights of Chapter 5, Feeding. Producing eggs puts a heavy strain on a female iguana's calcium balance, and because both the male and female often reduce their food intake during the breeding season, they need to have been eating really well for a long time to build up their fat reservoirs.

I know of one case where the owners let their new but "sickly" female iguana mate with their healthy male. The female died because of the stress incurred during mating and egg development.

Natural and Sufficient Ultraviolet Light

Calcium balance is important during egg development, and calcium absorption is triggered in the lizard's body with natural, unobstructed sunlight (ultraviolet light). In the wild, the sunlight that iguanas receive as they bask all day helps their bodies absorb calcium. In a captive environment you need to re-create this process. Please refer to Chapter 4, Housing, which directly addresses this topic in "Sunlight."

Even though proper habitat lighting is covered in detail in the housing chapter, a few comments are important to bring up now. I have seen too many iguana habitats with the light level of a sleazy bar. When I say an iguana needs 12 to 14 hours of light, I mean light! As an example, in the Ultimate Iguana Habitat described in that chapter, three 4-foot, full-spectrum lights create a beautiful, bright, sunny habitat.

Wild iguanas spend most of their day in the bright light of the tropics. You need to replicate these lighting conditions not only for breeding, but also for your iguana's normal health and physiological processes.

Photoperiod

Photoperiod is the cycle of light and dark in each 24-hour day. Green iguanas come mostly from equatorial regions, where there are about 12 hours of light and 12 hours of dark each day all year round—but with some minor variations as you get further from the equator.

Years ago, when most of the iguanas were wild-caught as older animals, many people felt that proper stimulation of breeding required that an iguana be exposed to the exact number of hours of light that occurred naturally in the animal's country of origin. Now, most iguanas you see for sale in pet stores are farm-raised (typically in Central or South America) and spend only a few months at the farm—not enough time to adapt to the photoperiod variations of the specific country.

The consensus of most iguana authorities is that an iguana in captivity should get from 12 to 14 hours of sun or equivalent light daily, regardless of whether or not you want to breed it. If you establish this healthy photoperiod from the beginning, you shouldn't have to adjust it for breeding.

Space

We worked out how many meters an iguana moves while patrolling his territory keeping out the intruders, and it works out to be a little over 10 kilometers [more than 6 miles] in the course of a mating season. That's spectacular for an animal that normally moves only 100 meters a day [roughly the length of a football field].   —Iguana field researchers in Venezuela (#27)

Space: It's not only the "Final Frontier," Star Trek fans, but one of the special ingredients in the formula for iguana mating. A small space, especially with two iguanas, can cause excessive stress. Add sex hormones to each of these animals, and you have the potential for daily, ferocious "cat fights."

Put two humans in a small space, day in and day out, and see what happens to them. Everyday normal occurrences are magnified, and these magnified experiences can cause tremendous stress, fighting, or even death.

When I visited the Belize Zoo, I found that their iguana breeding program was successful in part because the iguanas' habitat was so large. Free space enabled the lizards to roam and move about, to feel safe while eating, to have areas where they could hide for protection if necessary, and for male iguanas to feel they could control some territory. The Belize Zoo's iguana breeding program found that close quarters or overcrowding caused stress that inhibited, reduced, or even prevented mating.

I've been told by zoo keepers that iguanas, like most wild animals, will not mate in captivity unless they are comfortable in their environment.
                    —I-200, Dianna, 47 yrs., Washington

The ideal breeding environment is huge and outdoors, with natural sunlight, humidity, warmth, and basking sites for thermoregulating. Because the weather in most of the U.S. during the "normal" iguana breeding period (i.e., fall and winter here) is too cold and gloomy, artificial conditions must be created indoors to replicate the warm weather of iguanas' Latin American homelands.

Pet owners in southern Florida live in one of the best places to breed iguanas in the U.S. In fact, many iguanas have escaped or purposely been released and are living a nice, natural "wild" life there. Constant warm, humid weather with lots of sunlight are the key ingredients. After Florida, parts of California and Texas come in second place as potential outdoor breeding sites.

Male iguanas: What problems might occur during breeding season?

Aggressive Attitude

Male iguanas during the breeding season are like single men (humans) in the "bar scene" trying to pick up women—agitated, obnoxious, pushy, and aggressive.   —I-18, Daneen, 25 yrs., California

People need to be made aware of the possible sexual aggression a male iguana can go through BEFORE they purchase an iguana. Otherwise a lot of iguanas are going to end up unwanted and abused. —I-790, Cindy, 33 yrs., Texas

AT A GLANCE: *Possible Breeding-Season Problems
in Males*

- Aggressive attitude
- War injuries
- Female humans singled out for attack by male iguanas
- Reduced or no eating

When I was in the jungles of Belize, I got many close-up looks at male iguanas in breeding. This was especially true when I climbed into the trees where they lived. I could see that they looked and acted just like many of the pet iguanas that I have seen in people's homes, except they had more space.

Our iguana's mating season behavior really pushed us all to the limits of tolerance. He picks on me. I had to really stay on guard. He tried to bite me. When I had to go near him I carried a big flat board to keep between him and me. He came downstairs during our Thursday afternoon music practice and chased me around the room. He chased me around the house. He chased me into the den where I closed the door and couldn't come out because each time I peeked out he was there, ready to lurch at me. He occasionally leapt onto me, spanning several feet from his window ledge. I dodged and ran and sidestepped and called my daughter or husband to help me when I was cornered. He is rarely aggressive with my husband, and never aggressive with my daughter. It was really ridiculous. When he is not in breeding, he has a sweet disposition.
—I-705, Linda & Paul, 45 yrs., California

Breeding season is not always a fun time for the pet owner, especially if you own a healthy sexually mature male iguana—and especially if you are a female human. When your sexually active male gets into the breeding season, your once-friendly pet can turn into a monster for several weeks. Some testosterone-pumped males can even stretch this out to months (like my iguana). My own male had enough testosterone during breeding to jump-start a dead man.

Male iguanas are the worst at this time. He can be a real creep during breeding.
—I-737, Linda, 37 yrs., California

All of the breeding hormones and environmental conditions react in your male iguana's bloodstream, whether he is in a South American jungle next to several females or "HOME ALONE" in the U.S.A. Drugs are drugs, and hormones are powerful. Look how hormones transform nice, innocent teenage boys into monsters. I was once one of them, so I have great sympathy for the male iguana's uncontrolled and obnoxious sex drive.

My male iguana [SVL: 15", TL: 4' 3", 5 yrs., 5 lbs.] has the full run in the animal room (where I have a lot of other miscellaneous animals in cages and terrariums). Last year during breeding season, whenever I went out to that room, my iguana would pay an unusual amount of attention to me. If someone else came out with me, the iguana would get between us. One day my son and I were out in the room fooling around with the snakes and I lay down on the floor on my stomach to pick up a snake that had escaped and crawled under a shelf. My male iguana jumped down from his shelf and got on my back, grabbed my neck in his mouth, and desperately tried to mate with me. My son thought it was a lot funnier than I did!   —I-237, Dianne, 44 yrs., Texas*

During breeding season even some extremely nice male iguanas become vicious monsters.

Early fall, our iguana [SVL: 15", TL: 3' 5", 5 yrs., 5 lbs.] turns into "Igor the Anti-Iguana Unit." He has attacked mirrors so vigorously that he has cracked them, knocked them off the wall, or both. He breaks into vivariums and eats my other lizards, from anoles to leopard geckoes to iguanas. He sits on top of my gerbil cages and tries to bite the gerbils. In the kitchen, he knocks the mirrored toaster around. He makes more patrols of the apartment, and gets much more upset than usual by even slight furniture changes (occasionally defecating on the item of furniture that has been moved; he also defecates on wet shoes or stinky sneakers during this time). He patrols the windows and rubs his nose against the screen when he spots squirrels. The rest of the year he is a gentleman.
—I-515, Lynn, 21 yrs., Canada

He will attack everything and anything that enters "his" room during breeding. He does a real number on the vacuum cleaner.
—I-351, Tim, 36 yrs., Texas

If your male iguana is normally sweet, he may start gently nipping at your hands or feet once in a while as he gets closer to breeding season. This pattern could gain momentum and actually lead to aggressive attacking and biting.

My male [SVL: 14", TL: 4' 3", 3½ yrs.] acts different during breeding season. He gets up on all four legs real tall, arches his back, wags his tail, bobs his head, and walks slowly with real stiff legs. He becomes unpredictable and opens his mouth as if he is going to bite while assuming an aggressive posture. Normally he's the sweetest, calmest iguana I have.   —I-577, Jill, Florida
[AUTHOR'S NOTE: This tail wagging is not like a puppy dog, more like a rattlesnake ready to strike.]

Over his four breeding seasons, my iguana exhibited many different reactions. For the first two breeding seasons, Za seemed to be a complete jerk the whole time. Then all of a sudden, as if he awoke from a bad dream, he was the sweet creature that I always loved—a complete black-and-white transformation. The next two years he seemed to start the breeding season a little later than normal and was less aggressive, less orange, and retained more of his appetite.

Za's changing moods are shown in Figure 9.2, "Male Breeding Behavior: One Case Study," on page 534. Remember, this graph is just one example of male breeding behavior, intended only to give you a look at the daily changes for this animal. But you can see from the graph how a male iguana during breeding can be completely insane one day and a mixture of all attitudes the next. A true Dr. Jekyll and Mr. Hyde personality.

All iguanas have their own personalities and attitudes in and out of breeding. It does appear, however, that the bigger and healthier a male iguana is, the more aggressive he is likely to be during breeding.

He walks around inside his cage as though he were in charge of the cage.
                                        —I-735, Tammie, 31 yrs., Kansas

What an Aggressive Attack Looks Like

During Za's peak of aggression, he would be bug-eyed, as though his eyelids were glued open, with a glazed stare from never-never land. This was the first phase of his attack mode. Sometimes from inside his habitat he would see me or my girlfriend in the house and run so fast trying to get out of the habitat to get one of us that he'd fall from the top of his basking branch to the floor of the habitat, right himself, and haul full speed to get us.

One of his aggressive behaviors out of his habitat was to puff his body up to make himself look taller (this is what iguanas do in the wild). Looking at him from straight on, his body actually was thinner in the middle, compensating for getting taller. His next aggressive move was to fully extend his dewlap to what I call the "full sail" position. Then he would bob his head around like he was a baseball coach giving signals to a base runner (the signal is . . . this is my territory and I am going to shred you to pieces if you don't leave NOW!).

The funniest part to this whole "scene" started during his last two breeding seasons, when he did what I call the princess ballerina act. He got so excited, so amped-up, that he got on his tip toes (tips of his claws) and headed toward you. So here was this tough-looking, green-and-orange ballerina, tall but thin, with an extended dewlap and a glazed, nobody-home look. For an outsider this "look" is scary, but I often saw it as extremely funny.

If he attacked from a distance I waited until he charged, then just as he got to my feet I bent down and quickly picked him up (keeping any of my flesh away from his mouth). For Za this knocked 75% to 80% out of his aggressive attitude. He would often forget what he was up to (this is a common experience among other iguana owners). Then I looked at him, still held in my hands but from a distance for safety, and said, "Are we having a bad day today, you little #@!!*#%@?. . . . You ought to work for a living to see what a really bad day is!" Partly, this loud and aggressive talk showed him that I was the alpha male. It

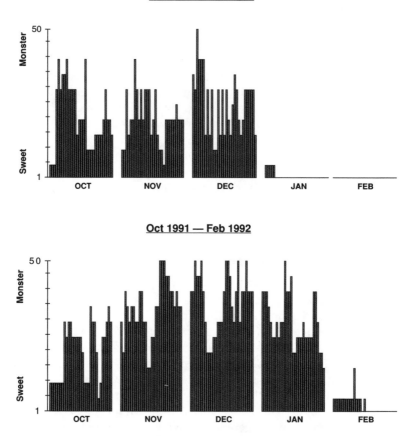

Figure 9.2: This one case study (above and facing page) of a sexually mature male iguana's attitude during breeding season, ranging from "sweet" to "monster," covers four years. One observation is that his nasty breeding attitude peaked a little later each year.

also helped me calm down, because I have to admit some days I got extremely angry that this lizard thought he ruled the house.

His other strategy was to keep moving slowly toward me on his ballerina claws. Once he was at my feet he would often lunge at me. As he lunged I did the same process as above, then I moved him to some other part of the house. If he tried stalking me a second time, I picked him up firmly and quickly, moving toward his habitat (usually calling him several swear names or telling him how I was going to leave him outside on the back porch and let the wolves eat him). Then I quickly put him inside his habitat at the top of his sleeping area. All these actions reinforced that I was in control of him. If you don't assert your dominance, your male iguana will get the idea that he is in control.

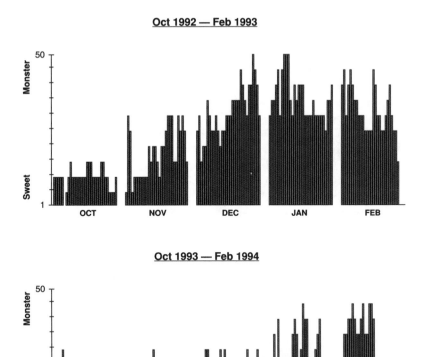

Oct 1992 — Feb 1993

Oct 1993 — Feb 1994

Any time I moved fast taking him to his "cage," talking gruff and mean, he had to feel my anger vibration—or something equivalent on some iguana level. When he was not in breeding and was "normal," I moved him around very slowly and talked softly and sweetly (see Chapter 8, Domestication, "Training," for details).

Za never picked on me again with the same intensity after his first breeding season, but turned his attention to my girlfriend, who had also known him his whole life. The first couple of years she would run out of the room when Za acted aggressively. But then she took a class called "Model Mugging," a self-defense class to give women skills to combat rape and other attacks through physical, mental, and verbal techniques. One technique was to use the power of your voice to prevent assault. The idea was not to say a weak, wimpy, "No . . . leave me alone," but to have the feeling come from the core of your being, confident and powerful. . . . "**NO!**"

One day soon after she had taken this course, Za attacked full speed across the hardwood floor to bite her. Her natural reaction now came spontaneously (from practice in the class) as she yelled "**NO!!**" Za hit the brakes and literally skidded across the floor on his ballerina claws. She picked him up, yelled, "**NO, I DON'T LIKE THAT KIND OF ATTITUDE FROM YOU**," and quickly put him on the couch. He deflated his sail, took off his ballerina shoes, and his head didn't bob. And that is how she handled him from then on. She put him in his place without any physical abuse (iguanas should <u>never</u> be hit—it only registers as an attack to them). It takes some guts to stand your ground. But once you have the confidence and see the results, the threatening attack of iguanas seems less powerful because now you, not the lizard, are in control.

> *My male iguana [SVL: 13", TL: 3' 5", 7½ yrs.] chases my roommate during breeding because she runs away. He doesn't chase me, but I don't run so he just runs into my leg and stops.*   —I-633, Lynne, 29 yrs., Michigan

This whole experience of attack and aggression is simply an iguana's expression of controlling territory or wanting to mate. Every month I used to take Za to different schools and talk to kids about reptiles and rainforests. Even at Za's peak worst breeding month he was sweet during these visits, never getting the least bit aggressive toward the kids or me during the talks. Perhaps because he was not guarding his territory, he could relax.

Another strange variable was that when people came to the house to visit, Za would be very nice, and again during the worst day of breeding he never attacked or was aggressive while the visitors were around. As soon as the visitors left, Za would immediately become a jerk again. There are as many twists to the breeding behaviors of male iguanas as you can think up. I believe that Za was at the extreme end of the scale when it came to breeding aggression because he was so healthy and was allowed out in the house on a regular basis.

Non-Aggressive Males

Have I gotten you scared of male iguanas during breeding? Well, there might still be some hope. From the information gathered in my iguana questionnaires, I discovered that some male iguanas exhibit almost no changes during breeding.

> *Mating season is around January or February and continues until about April. I have seen no difference in the behavior of my iguana [SVL: 13", TL: 3' 6", 5½ yrs.] toward humans during mating season.*
>   —I-626, Gail, 48 yrs., New York

The male does not pick on any humans during breeding season and is in fact much more docile to (human) men while he has a female iguana with him. You can pet him and feed him strawberries by hand at this time.
— I-775, Karen, 37 yrs., Arizona

One male iguana at 8 years old didn't show any signs of breeding. Another person wrote that the only thing different that their 5-year-old iguana does is bob maybe 40 times a day during breeding. Other than that, everything remains the same. I found that story quite amusing, considering that Za typically bobbed 40 times in the first hour of his "normal," sweet, non-breeding days.

Variables

What causes the extremes? The iguanas that showed few if any aggressive signs were usually small for their age, had poor health at some point, experi-

---

SIDEBAR

Sexual Preferences

When the male [SVL: 15", TL: 4' 2", 4½ yrs.] is in breeding he is uncontrollable. He wants to attack or mate with anything in sight during breeding, especially green things. He also attacks and likes to mate with two bean-bag stuffed iguanas we have on display. I have several iguana shirts I can't wear then because he attacks them. Don't wear green near a horny male iguana.
— I-616, Jonathan, 27 yrs., Connecticut

Every iguana is different. The iguana above responded to the color green and to bean-bag iguana toys during breeding, while my iguana had a fetish for hands or feet.

Bill (I-273) has an iguana with a fetish for his plaid shirt during breeding season. Each year the iguana (SVL: 16", TL: 5', 6½ yrs.) attacks this shirt like a pit bull, drags the shirt around the house as if it were a female iguana, and even mounts it. He doesn't react to the shirt any other times. I know this is a true story because I have seen photos of the iguana in action. One group of photos was taken with a motor drive, so it's almost like a slow-motion movie. From the floor of the owner's office the iguana runs, springs into the air like a tiger attacking its prey, pulls the shirt to the ground from the office chair, drags the shirt off, and has his way with it. And the iguana does this only during breeding season.

Iguanas in captivity . . . I have seen and heard so many weird stories that nothing appears strange any more!

enced negative stress, had a small habitat, or lived with multiple iguanas in one habitat.

Iguanas that are allowed to become members of the household also seem to be more aggressive and dominant. Perhaps when they get part or all of the home to run around in, they treat the whole area as their territory during breeding season and feel they have to protect it. People who make an iguana into a true pet—hugging, handling, taking the iguana with them places—make the bond stronger. Could it be that the iguana perceives these people as other iguanas?

Breeding season is a very trying time, especially toward the peak of the season when you are just tired of the whole thing. Close to the end of the breeding season, I was sick of iguanas. Then when breeding was over I "almost" forgot what a daily pain Za was. My girlfriend suggested it's like when women have natural childbirth and experience intense pain. Years later, when they are thinking about having another baby, they often say, "Oh, it wasn't that bad."

If your iguana goes through any of this intense breeding behavior, take a look at the breeding graph once in a while to bring some sanity to your life. Yes, there is life after breeding, but only <u>after</u> breeding.

> *During breeding season, my iguana [SVL: 19", TL: 5' 2³/₄", 6 yrs.] gets very dangerous. I wouldn't say mean, but . . . demented, deranged. Yes, that would be a much better word. He would just pick on me, attack, and try to mate with me. Luckily I wore a thick sweater or he would have done some real damage. I end up locking him in his room.* —I-930, Tina, 32 yrs., Canada

I realize the next story is long, but it gives a great picture of so many of the elements possible with a male in breeding season.

> *My iguana is a 12-year-old sexually mature male. He goes through a complete personality change in his breeding season. The following is a brief history of the development of this behavioral change.*
>
> *The first time my iguana showed indication of this change was around December of 1986. When my roommate or I entered the room, he would raise his head and shoulders up, extend his dewlap, and head-bob. I also observed him walking around the apartment differently. He would drag his hind quarters along the ground. It was during this time that he developed protrusions from his femoral pores. These protrusions were all roughly ½" long and had the look and feel of a hard waxy plastic. I believe this served the purpose of marking his territory. On occasion he would also raise up on his haunches and evert his hemipenes; sometimes he would ejaculate. Shortly thereafter, the attacks began.*
>
> *The ritual usually involved an ambush from atop the sofa. He would take a flying leap as you passed by. Typically, he would end up attacking your pant leg—grabbing hold with his mouth and swinging back and forth. He would*

also twist at times. Sometimes he would climb your pant leg up to about your knee and stop. It was almost as though he would forget what he was doing. But once removed, he would repeat the event.

For the most part, he has always had the run of at least a room. For a short time in 1988 and 1989, he was caged for my roommate's safety. During these periods he would attempt to attack anything that passed his cage. I ended up covering the habitat with towels to prevent him from injuring himself.

As for successful attacks, he has only gotten me twice. The first time was during his second breeding season and he was not a full-fledged terror. It was his ritual to climb up on my bed each morning, walk around me, and head-bob. After a while I began to ignore this, especially when half asleep. One morning, he latched onto the back of one of my upper arms as I was sleeping. He would not let go. I literally squeezed his head as hard as I could to get him to release. Needless to say, it hurt like hell and it was not a very nice way to wake up.

The second time occurred recently while I was giving some visitors a tour of our collection of animals. I was holding him so he wouldn't attack anyone. He was cradled on his back—I let my guard down and he turned his head and bit my biceps. This time he left a scar. He is the size now [SVL: 14³⁄₄", TL: 3' 7", 6 lbs.] that he could undoubtedly do permanent damage. I have several pairs of leather tennis shoes with rips and tears from him. In one encounter, he tore a chunk out of the cover of one of our kitchen table chairs. In addition, our vacuum cleaner has permanent scars.

During one demonstration for some "non-believers," he grabbed hold of a rolled newspaper, shook it violently with everything he had while rolling with it. He bounced off a cage, stopped rolling for a second, but still shaking the newspaper back and forth. He then did another roll and shake combo. The display ended on the other side of the room (20 feet away). A shredded newspaper was on one end of the room and a group of speechless people was on the other. I guarantee this one would have been worth money if I had caught it on film!

An interesting point is that I usually know when he is getting ready to go "bad." The color of his head changes, especially the top of it. This color change always precedes the other changes.   —I-508, Bryan, 27 yrs., Kentucky

War Injuries

So far, I have mentioned only the effects of one male iguana in a household. To double the trouble, just add another sexually mature male.

My two males are in breeding season and are going nuts. They got in a ferocious fight. The smaller male just about had his arm ripped off by the other, bigger male and had to have stitches. If I didn't know better, I would say the injured iguana is hell-bent on revenge. A lizard possessed for sure. He spends his days trying to escape from his cage so he can spend hours bobbing, head-butting the glass cage, strutting, and hissing at his attacker.

—I-43, Taryn, 27 yrs., Alaska

Male iguanas aren't always beaten up by other males. A large female can sometimes inflict serious damage to a male when she gets fed up with the constant biting and mounting antics.

They [male & female, both about SVL: 16", TL: 4', 5 yrs.] were kept together but during the first breeding season they started to fight. The female won and the male needed stitches on his left arm. I separated them after this.
—I-546, Chuck, 32 yrs., California

My female [SVL: 13", TL: 5' 3½", 8½ yrs.] is violent at times with the male [SVL: 16", TL: 5' 5", 9½ yrs.], chasing him around the cage.
—I-509, Troy, 30 yrs., Missouri

Not all of the war victims of breeding season are iguanas. War is hell, and sometimes civilians get in the cross-fire or get pulled into the battle without their consent.

I visited a couple in California who had a 3½-year-old, large, beautiful male iguana named Iggy. Judy was the primary owner and took care of Iggy most of the time; her husband Stan took over when necessary. During the breeding season Iggy was a little testy but got along with both of them pretty well.

One year the couple decided to breed Iggy with a friend's female iguana. Because Iggy had full run of the house, they ended up letting both iguanas run free in the house to simulate natural breeding conditions. But soon the two iguanas wanted everything their way.

If Stan walked near the female iguana, Iggy would step between them and would not let Stan touch her. It was Iggy's first girlfriend and he didn't want Stan "stepping in." Judy, on the other hand, could more or less do what she wanted with both iguanas at any time.

Normally Iggy liked to be petted by both humans, even in breeding. But during this breeding season Iggy played a mean trick by sitting with Stan under the guise of being petted. As soon as the petting began, Iggy turned around and bit Stan, then ran away. I talked with several bird owners who said that this is a practice birds often use to signal possession. I realize iguanas aren't birds, but it at least gives a possible reason for the behavior.

For the whole breeding month the iguanas essentially ruled the house. Iggy was no longer a friendly pet and Stan was completely "shell-shocked." Judy and Stan's vow was, "Never, ever have a female iguana over for breeding again!"

And, of course, there are other people across the U.S. who have also gotten caught in the cross-fire of breeding:

I have three adult male iguanas. During mating season they are always trying to get to each other. If I have handled one iguana and forget to wash my hands and then pick up the other, the second iguana thinks I am the first iguana and

SIDEBAR

How to Remove an Iguana's Biting Grip From Your Body or Clothing

The way a male iguana mates during breeding is by biting onto the female's neck, holding on, and hoping that he can insert one of his hemipenes before she escapes. If your iguana bites you or your clothing and won't let go, here are a few helpful hints:

- <u>Never</u> squeeze the iguana's head or body parts to make him let go. Your anger might interfere, making your muscles add more pressure than your mind had intended—and it doesn't work anyway.
- Don't try to pull your iguana off if it has a <u>strong</u> grip. It's like pulling your leg out of a bear trap.
- When my iguana clamped onto my pants (no flesh caught) and would not let go, I walked with a stiff leg (iguana attached to my pants) to the bathroom. There I put rubbing alcohol on a towel (or any kind of cotton ball, etc. can be used) and placed the moistened towel above Za's nose. He <u>immediately</u> let go! Make sure the towel is <u>not</u> dripping alcohol that could get into the iguana's eyes or nose. All you need is for your iguana to get a whiff of the alcohol.
- Another option is to turn your iguana upside down. Most iguanas don't like this experience. I did this trick with my iguana several times and he let go about half the time. The look on his face indicated that the experience was unnerving or scary for him.

Proper handling of an aggressive iguana is important for your safety. Here is one more helpful protection technique:

They can move very fast when they want to. When picking up an aggressive male, use both hands around the middle and keep their head away from you so they can't bite. If they don't want to be picked up they often will place one arm tight down along their side and roll in your hands and try to bite. You must be very careful. When my iguanas try this I place one hand over the shoulders and one over their hips. I hold them firm to the ground until they relax (this can take some time). Be sure not to hold too tightly or press too firmly, which might hurt them. When I first started doing this they whipped their tails and twisted a lot. Make sure the tail doesn't get stepped on while you are doing this. They have learned my response and fight less each time.

—I-764, Diana, 46 yrs., California

tries to bite me. It seems their taste buds go crazy; just one little taste of another mature iguana and they are ready to fight or mate.

—I-764, Diana, 46 yrs., California

[AUTHOR'S NOTE: The iguanas are probably tuning into the pheromone-emitting substance exuded from the femoral pores, as mentioned earlier in this chapter.]

Males during mating season can get snappy, depending on the individual personality. I've been bitten by a male several times during the season when I got between two males who could see each other from across the room. Mean, nasty bites. Yeow! —I-200, Dianna, 47 yrs., Washington

One iguana during breeding season clamped down on his owner and would not let go. Both parties went locked together to the veterinarian to get disconnected. Both survived. Another owner was bitten by a large male and had to have three stitches in his finger. This iguana normally was ultra sweet, but during the peak of breeding he got a little crazy (raging hormones). The iguana gave plenty of signs to the owner that he was in a bad mood. The owner ignored the signs and got three stitches. The owner now pays attention to the obvious signs the iguana shows.

Female Humans Singled Out During Breeding Season

In the wild, once the female has "chosen" the male she wants to breed with, the male still needs to "protect" her from other interested males in the area. The male does this by aggressive body posturing, lunging, chasing, and even physical attacks if necessary. This may be the same aggressive behavior that happens in your own home during breeding season, perhaps even against you, by your sexually mature male. This aggression is the natural result of breeding instincts.

Over the last few years, I have recorded an increase in the number of female humans being picked on or attacked during breeding season by male iguanas, while others in the family might be left alone. If you look back at the section "Aggressive Attitudes" you will see that most of the quotations are from female humans.

Perhaps one reason for females being attacked is pheromones. In a previous section I mentioned that the femoral pores of a male iguana exude a waxy substance during breeding season that probably contains pheromones. It's likely that a male iguana picks up chemical cues from this femoral pore substance.

One example of pheromones in action happened frequently in my own home. I get many letters from iguana owners and often have to stack them on the floor of my office for more space. My iguana would sometimes go to the stack, knock it over, and select certain letters to flick his tongue on. He would continue flicking incessantly until I removed the envelope from his reach. I believe he was sensing another iguana's pheromones on the envelope. Per-

SIDEBAR

Ways of Reducing Attacks During Breeding

- Leave town during this time! (Just kidding.)
- Be on guard, watch for signs of aggression, and don't put yourself in a position to be bitten.
- Stand your ground; be the "alpha male iguana" in your house. Do everything you can to show your iguana you are not afraid of him and that you are in control.
- One technique I <u>don't</u> recommend is photoperiod modification (i.e., greatly reducing the number of light hours). An iguana needs a certain amount of light to be healthy, and to take this away is unnatural and dangerous.
- Hormone therapy is too new to recommend. There are a limited number of good reptile veterinarians, let alone enough who understand hormone modification.
- Castrate your male iguana. At this time this approach is too experimental for me to recommend. Because not enough of these operations have been done, no one knows for sure the long-term effects, positive or negative. Also, any time you put an exotic animal under general anesthesia there is a chance it could die.

So you are left with being on guard until something better comes along that has proven itself effective and safe. Remember, what you are dealing with are the strong natural instincts of your lizard, and it will be almost impossible to stop them.

haps the owner who sent the mail had just handled his or her iguana. Za never spent time flicking other "business" mail.

Humans also give off pheromones, and some researchers suggest that the pheromones given off by a menstruating human female may trigger some sort of mating urge, or a defense or attack mode, in male iguanas. One woman has been bothered by her aggressive male iguana during breeding for the last three years. The iguana attacks her, but not her husband or young daughter. Now the woman is just entering menopause. So far this year, she feels her iguana is less aggressive toward her. Maybe once she goes completely through menopause her iguana won't attack her any more. Only time will tell.

Perhaps it's not your good looks that drives your iguana crazy during breeding season. Maybe it's your perfume. One iguana researcher I know had a couple of female technicians working with him on experiments. Here's what happened:

My technicians could not wear certain brands of perfume, even if there were no female lizards around, because during breeding season these guys [male iguanas] would be incredibly interested in this particular brand of perfume . . . I can't remember the name. The males would jump up against the screen cages and go berserk as the technicians walked by. I didn't figure out if they were interested in a mating sense, or if the technicians smelled like another male, so they would be in an aggressive state.

—John A. Phillips, Center for Reproduction of Endangered
Species (CRES), San Diego Zoological Society (#14)

Reduced or No Eating

My male is more interested in mating than eating during this time.
—I-539, Daryle, 35 yrs., Mississippi

There is an old story, perhaps Greek, about two (human) lovers whose love was supposedly so strong they didn't need to eat. During breeding season the male iguana is like this, except he is not what we call "in love," but driven by sex hormones. And the urge is so strong that at some point in the breeding season many male iguanas will:

• Reduce the amount of food consumed each day
• Skip several days and then start eating again
• Come to a screeching halt and refuse to eat anything
• Any combination of the above

Our male iguana [SVL: 18", TL: 4' 10", 3 yrs.] quit eating nearly entirely for several weeks when he went into breeding. We took him to the vet, who told us our lizard seemed fine and that he would probably come out of it soon, which he did. —I-705, Linda & Paul, 45 yrs., California

My male [SVL: 13", TL: 3' 7½", 8½ yrs.] eats less as soon as breeding season starts. He eats with the same frequency, but a lot less food at a time.
—I-509, Troy, 30 yrs., Missouri

My male didn't go back to a normal feeding pattern (volume and frequency) until seven to ten days after the females were removed.
—I-775, Karen, 37 yrs., Arizona

My males tend to eat less at this [breeding] time because all of their attention is used to mount the females. The girls eat about the same amount of food.
—I-650, Helen, 31 yrs., Ohio

Turn to Chapter 5, Feeding, Figure 5.2, "Iguana Food Consumption: One Case Study." If you look at the typical breeding season months (October

SIDEBAR

Human Females Singled Out—Non-Breeding Season

Recently, I've received letters from females saying that their sexually mature male iguanas are picking on and overtly attacking them around or during their menstrual cycle, even out of the breeding season.

I have a very sexually mature iguana. The vet told me he was an alpha male, which makes him larger and more aggressive than the average male iguana. There is not a specific month that he acts crazy, but every month a week before and the week of my menstrual cycle he is very aggressive toward me especially. He gets real mean, he is always on the defensive, and he has bitten me once (very badly).   —I-654, Kathy, 27 yrs., Illinois

When I am menstruating my iguana seems extra aggressive, especially when I try to handle him too much.   —I-753, Kelly, 26 yrs., Pennsylvania

All my iguanas [three of them] are aggressive to me during my period.
          —I-734, June, 24 yrs., Massachusetts

This is just an interesting fact: During my menstrual cycle, my iguana gets very aggressive. He won't let me touch him at all, and acts totally wild. If I try to hold him, he whips me with his tail.   —I-783, Lenna, 22 yrs., Washington

through January), you will notice on the graph how food consumption drops dramatically and then slowly resumes its normal pattern after the breeding season. Even though the graph is of only one male iguana, it gives you an idea of the erratic feeding patterns your iguana might experience.

Male iguanas modify their food intake and choices because their main drive is mating, and females reduce their food intake because once the eggs start growing inside them, there is not a lot of space for food. (More will be explained on this topic in an upcoming section devoted to female iguana breeding problems.)

Many pet owners ask what they should do during this topsy-turvy, unpredictable breeding period when their iguana doesn't eat. You need to realize that reduced eating during breeding season is a natural experience for both wild and captive iguanas. When I was on the Oaxacan coast of southern Mexico, I caught, examined, and released several wild iguanas. I noticed that because it was breeding season, the males were very scrawny and didn't have much body weight.

If you have a healthy iguana eating normally all year, it will have been storing some of its calories at the base of its tail and legs as fat. This is the future "lunch pail" for the iguana. Often iguanas will eat more prior to the breeding season to help store more food (fat) for this event. The better fed your iguana is on a regular basis, the better it will be able to withstand any possible food reduction during breeding.

Although my iguana reduced his standard intake of food and even stopped feeding during breeding for a couple of days, his actual weight loss was minimal. One year when Za weighed 13 pounds normally, he only went down to about 12 pounds during the peak of breeding.

If your iguana hasn't eaten in three days, my feeling is try to get them to eat at least a little food. The problem is that even when you offer your lizard his favorite food, he might look at the food as if it came from Mars.

One solution is to wrap a small amount of his favorite food, chopped up very fine, in a piece of kale, collard green, mustard green, or even romaine lettuce (just the soft, dark green part) like a burrito. Because this food looks like a giant leaf (one of their natural foods in the wild), iguanas will often eat it. I could always trick my iguana to eat at least a few of these "burrito" bundles during breeding.

If your iguana stops eating for more than three days and it is <u>not</u> breeding season (read Chapter 7, Medical Troubleshooting, "Appetite: Reduced or Stopped"), it could be a medical problem that needs <u>immediate</u> correction.

Make Sure They Get Enough Water

Iguanas get the majority of their moisture (water) from the food they eat. Because food intake is often reduced or stopped during breeding, <u>it's essential to have water available</u>! Water can be offered in the standard water dish in the habitat (which should always be available), or from drinking cups, spoons, or blasts from a spray bottle directly into the side of the iguana's mouth.

During his third year of breeding, my iguana trained me to give him water from a spray bottle when he was thirsty. For several days during this breeding season, I noticed that the water in Za's upper water dish seemed low, and I figured he was drinking more.

One day he started licking his lips (I know they don't have lips, but this gives you the necessary image) as I walked by his habitat. I took a plastic spray bottle and gave him a squirt in the side of his mouth. He drank it in like a thirsty dog. Every time he did this lip-licking—and only when he did it—he would accept water eagerly from the spray bottle. The next year of breeding Za ate more food and didn't lick his lips for water.

If breeding season causes your iguana to reduce its food intake, supply the extra water that is <u>necessary</u>—whether your iguana "asks" you for it or not. They can also be trained to drink water, which is explained in Chapter 8, Domestication, "Drinking Water."

Female Iguanas: What Problems Might Occur During Breeding Season?

AT A GLANCE: *Possible Breeding-Season Problems in Females*

- Body damage to the iguana
- Moody
- Reduced or no eating
- Egg binding
- Calcium deficiency

Body Damage to the Iguana

My iguana's snout is blunt and flat in front. She [SVL: 17", TL: 3' 6", 7 yrs.] used to have two small horns protruding from the top of her nose, but during the first frantic episode of burying her eggs during breeding, these were scraped off. She used her snout to push sand and it left her with two abrasions. They healed quickly, but the horns did not grow back.

—I-554, Anthony, 29 yrs., Texas

Males beat up females more than I expected.

—I-197, Rebecca, 38 yrs., Massachusetts

Female iguanas usually get their necks chewed up a bit during breeding, but rarely does an infection set in if you clean up the area with hydrogen peroxide or Betadine. —I-11, Patty, Washington

My female [SVL: 16½", TL: 3' 11½", 3 yrs.] had an infection that was caused by my male [SVL: 15", TL: 4' 2", 4½ yrs.] trying to mate with her. He had gotten hold of her toe and had bitten halfway through it. We had to have part of the toe amputated. —I-616, Jonathan, 27 yrs., Connecticut

During breeding season, don't leave a male and female together in a small enclosure, particularly when the female can't get to a place to hide safely from the male. Use common sense. If the female is injured or looks scared about being locked up with a high-octane, hormone-driven male iguana, remove her from the area.

Moody

Males have the crazy sex urge that throws them through many mood swings, sometimes in a single day. When a female is getting close to laying her eggs she, too, can get moody, but usually won't turn mean. One of the main reasons she becomes restless or edgy is that she needs to know there is a safe, secure, and available place for her to lay her eggs. The nesting box described in Appendix H will help alleviate this problem.

She [SVL: 16", TL: 4' 2", 6½ yrs.] withdraws a bit, stops eating, and fluctuates emotionally very similar to human females in the ovulation/period cycles.
—I-635, Andrew, 38 yrs., Wisconsin

My female [TL: 3', 8 yrs.] starts to get a little crazy about Christmas time. She claws and digs maniacally to get out of her cage. When we do let her out, she goes straight to the sliding door and claws at that. I tried putting a cake pan of fine sand in her cage, but she just kicked it all over the place. The second year of "womanhood," she was a bit mellower but still had the urgency to get out. She calms down when she starts to lay [eggs] about the middle of January.
—I-593, Judy, 35 yrs., Oregon
[AUTHOR'S NOTE: A pan of sand isn't sufficient as a nesting box.]

There is just a slight difference in the breeding months of October through January with my iguana. She [SVL: 15½", TL: 3' 11¾", 4½ yrs.] tends to be less tolerant of people in "her room" but she is not mean or wild. She never picks on any one person in particular.   —I-653, Justin, 19 yrs., Maryland

Reduced or No Eating

Like male iguanas, female iguanas often reduce or stop eating for a period of time during the breeding season, but for different reasons. Because a female iguana has only so much space inside her body, she can't have a lot of eggs developing and still eat large volumes of food. As a result, she sometimes reduces or stops eating toward the end of her gestation period. While male iguanas can eat during breeding but sometimes don't, female iguanas physically can't eat.

The next group of pet owners' stories are meant to give you some real-life examples to help you stay calmer when your female iguana modifies her eating habits during this time. These stories are also to reinforce the importance of making sure that your female iguana receives proper care—including nutrition—year-round so she'll be in shape to weather a period of little or no food intake.

Our female [SVL: 10", TL: 2' 10", 5 yrs., 6 lbs.] stopped eating three weeks before she laid 40 eggs in November. She resumed eating after she laid about half of the eggs.   —I-536, Carrie, 22 yrs., Missouri

She [SVL: 17", TL: 3' 6", 7 yrs. 3 mo.] refused all food for four to six weeks prior to laying her 43 eggs. She was huge. Immediately after laying her eggs her appetite returned and she regained much of her weight in a matter of a few days.   —I-554, Anthony, 29 yrs., Texas

Our female [SVL: 12", TL: 3', 4 yrs.] eats voraciously at the start of breeding season. At the end of the season she goes off feeding approximately three weeks prior to laying. Then she resumes her normal intake of food within hours of laying. —I-772, Andy, 32 yrs., California

In case you don't have a male iguana and didn't read the previous section, iguanas get most of their water from the food they eat each day. No food = no water = dehydrated iguana = medical problems. Review page 546 on males not getting enough water for what to do, which also applies to female iguanas.

Egg Binding

She [SVL: 15", TL: 3' 1½", 2 yrs. 3 mo.] laid 18 eggs in January, then within three days 30 to 33 more eggs developed. One egg got ruptured and the vet treated her, but she was too weak to be operated on. We waited 'til morning. . . . We found her dead. The eggs were not fertile, as I don't have a male iguana. —I-692, Dolly, Pennsylvania

A female iguana is egg-bound when she can't lay the eggs she has created inside her body. As I have said earlier, a female iguana develops eggs much like a chicken, without needing the presence of a male. But unlike a chicken, iguanas lay eggs only once a year.

A female iguana 250 mm (10") SVL or more is large enough to breed successfully (#14). So once your female iguana achieves this length, it should be a red flag for you to keep an eye on her during breeding season. This doesn't mean she will necessarily lay eggs when she reaches this length, just that it is now possible.

It's important to be alert to signs of egg binding because it can cause dangerous medical problems for your iguana. The following story is a vivid but sad example of the need to pay attention to your female iguana during breeding season:

[After a gravid female died unexpectedly, a necropsy was done because the owners suspected egg binding was the cause of death.] The female iguana was cut open and two eggs were found fused together and lodged in the uterus (total 49 eggs). The positions of the vital organs were noted, and were even more displaced than would be expected in a heavily gravid animal. The heart was pushed up as far as the neck—whether this had any bearing on the female's refusal to feed for the past 15 days is a matter for supposition.

[We were] not sure whether, or for how long, the female ceased to feed prior to laying, but she gave no immediate cause for concern. [The day before she died] she was still refusing food, and had used up virtually all of the fat reserves in her legs and tail.
—Paul Styler and Roy Cimino, *Journal of the International Herpetological Society* (United Kingdom), March 1993

By the time they noticed the female iguana's distress, which they guessed was due to egg binding, it was too late in the evening to contact their veterinarian. The two authors also mentioned elsewhere in the article that because they didn't expect egg laying so soon, they had not yet set up an egg-laying box. While setting up an egg-laying box will not necessarily prevent your iguana from getting egg bound, inability to find a suitable nesting site can contribute to egg-binding complications.

Causes for Egg Binding

No Place to Properly Deposit Eggs

We see many females that are egg-bound who eventually lay eggs if given a suitable egg-laying site and opportunity.
—V-116, Dr. Richard, 37 yrs., Tennessee

One of the main reasons an iguana will dig excessively in her habitat or around the house is her desire to find the proper place to lay her eggs. If you create an appropriate place for your iguana to dig and bury her eggs (like the nesting box described in Appendix H), this will help reduce some of her stress and the potential problems associated with egg binding.

Joyce (I-736) of New Jersey spent almost $370 for surgery and related pre- and post-medical care for her 3-year-old female iguana that was egg-bound. There were complications with one egg that had already broken, and the rest were all pushed together like a bunch of grapes. The cost and time of providing an egg-laying box seem cheap in comparison.

When we found out she was gravid we put her in moist sand where she laid eggs almost immediately.
—I-509, Troy, 30 yrs., Missouri

Some people are lucky and have no egg problems with their female iguanas.

In the 2½ years I have owned my female iguana [SVL: unknown, TL: unknown, 3 yrs.], she has never laid eggs.
—I-747, Stephanie, 22 yrs., Illinois
[AUTHOR'S NOTE: Perhaps the iguana hasn't reached the minimum 10" SVL for sexual maturity.]

Oversized or Odd-Shaped Eggs

My female was having trouble laying her eggs. She laid most of her eggs around the cage and had been scratching on the floor bottom, as if digging, earlier that day and the previous day, too. She stopped laying and I assumed that was it!! Well, a few days passed and my female was inactive, looking pale, not accepting food, and seemed to be in pain. Her color got muddy and her eyes had dark rings and I realized she may be egg-bound. I was advised by my vet and fellow herpers to lubricate her cloaca with a little olive oil and that saved her life. She

---

AT A GLANCE: *Possible Reasons For Egg Binding*
- No place to properly deposit eggs
- Oversized or odd-shaped egg causes blockage
- Female iguana is too "young"
- Excessive number of eggs produced

---

passed the blocked egg, which was rather deformed and unusually larger than the other, normal eggs. After the passage of that bad egg she laid the other normal eggs.   —I-200, Dianna, 47 yrs., Washington

[AUTHOR'S NOTE: Dianna has years of medical experience with iguanas; what she did <u>should not</u> be attempted by most people. Also, the incessant digging shows the need for a proper egg-laying box. The muddy color often indicates a medical problem.]

I have heard of numerous cases where one egg, which might be oversized or irregular in shape, blocks the vent so the remaining eggs can't get out (see Chapter 7, Medical Troubleshooting, "Female Iguana Medical Problems" for more details).

Usually, this kind of problem can be solved only by a good herp veterinarian. Doing your own veterinary care at this time is very dangerous! If you fiddle around and happen to break any eggs still inside your female, she could die.

Too "Young"

I left them together and my iguana became gravid and laid her first clutch at the age of 2½ years. Had I known better I would have kept them apart at least one more year for her to be one year stronger.   —I-780, Carl, Florida

Many of the problems associated with a female becoming egg-bound occur within the first year or so of her becoming sexually mature. Even though she is sexually mature she may still be "young," and some of her female anatomy may not be up to full operating capacity for the ordeal of developing and laying eggs. You can't control whether she develops eggs, but you can prevent her from mating with a male iguana until she's a bit older and larger.

Excessive Numbers of Eggs

The production of too many eggs at one time is another reason for egg binding. Unlike with many birds, there is no set number of eggs an iguana lays. Between 20 and 60 is typical, with 41 eggs about average (#20). One person wrote and said that his iguana had 100 eggs and that this caused her death—the large number of eggs just got jammed up inside.

Hysterectomy (Spaying)

Over the years I have seen many reports from iguana owners who have had their female iguanas spayed after egg problems occurred. All of them went to qualified reptile veterinarians and all the operations were successful.

My iguana seemed lethargic and uninterested in coming out of her cage, so we took her to the vet. He performed a full examination, including mouth, weight, skin color, etc. He gave her vitamin shots, put her in a nebulizer, took radiographs, and kept her for two days. He consulted with another vet and the conclusion was there were eggs being produced.

We started giving her extra calcium supplements and antibiotic injections (totaling 4 shots) for any potential infections she might have. We continued with the calcium and in a week took another radiograph. This time, eggs were starting to become apparent. Because she was having such a hard time producing the eggs, it was suggested that spaying her might be the best decision. No vets in the state of New Mexico had ever done a procedure like this and were hesitant to try.

We scheduled the surgery for February and flew to Phoenix, Arizona. The surgery went well (just under 50 minutes) and about 18 polyps were removed. She was then flown back the next afternoon (flying with an iguana is an experience all its own!). Due to the slow healing of herps, her stitches will stay in for six weeks.

This story has a happy ending. . . . She is eating better than she ever has, there have been no repercussions from the surgery or flying, and because she is so physically active, I forget she still has her stitches in.

It is common for female iguanas to have the problem my iguana experienced. If not caught in time, the iguana could die.

—I-754, Karen, 33 yrs., New Mexico

There is much more information on this topic in Chapter 7, Medical Troubleshooting, "Egg Binding."

Calcium Deficiency

Another problem for a female iguana during breeding season is the risk of calcium deficiency. When a lizard becomes gravid, she needs more calcium to form the shell of the egg. If she is low or deficient in calcium, her body will steal calcium from wherever it can to build the egg shell. The first choice is the calcium from her own bones, which may lead to metabolic bone disease.

During gestation, increase the amount of calcium in your iguana's diet. The best approach is to go to a qualified reptile veterinarian, who will weigh your iguana and give her the appropriate dose of oral calcium. If she is excessively deficient, the veterinarian might also give an injectable calcium supplement to help jump-start her return to a balanced calcium/phosphorus ratio. If you are unfamiliar with the meaning of the term "calcium/phosphorus ratio," turn back to Chapter 5, Feeding, "Calcium."

She developed partial paralysis and muscle tremors over three days when she should have been putting shells on her eggs. We figured the need to put calcium on her eggs threw her body into calcium deficit. I treated her with oral calcium gluconate as per our vet's instructions.
                                            —I-775, Karen, 37 yrs., Arizona

My iguana quit eating for at least six weeks before she laid eggs. I took her to the vet and he gave her a calcium supplement because she was low in calcium. It was a liquid that she readily took from a medicine dropper. This seemed to give her more energy until after she had laid the eggs. After the eggs were laid her appetite returned.   —I-554, Anthony, 29 yrs., Texas

COURTSHIP

Courtship is an important factor in female mate choice, in facilitating female receptivity, and in establishing bonds of familiarity between mates. . . . The long courtship period prior to copulation may benefit females by providing the opportunity to review several males before being inseminated, to ensure the fitness of a chosen mate.   —Beverly Dugan, iguana researcher (#16)

As I mentioned earlier, during breeding season a female iguana is looking for a male that will ensure a strong lineage for her offspring. One of the main qualities she looks for is a large male.

The male iguana does a great deal of "strutting around" during breeding season, as if he is showing off his physical characteristics to the potential female mate. The male also does an excessive amount of head bobbing (displaying), and the breeding colors on his body often become brighter. Part of this "manly" display also seems to discourage other males in the area from cutting in on his "girls."

In the wild, this is how courtship takes place:

In the most common courtship sequence, the male approached the female from behind, performing a shudder bob (rapid, low-amplitude vertical head movements) before, during, or after the approach. The female then moved the posterior two-thirds of her tail to one side (tail arch). After the tail arch, the male stopped and performed a signature bob.

The sequence (recorded as one courtship bout) was repeated from one to more than a dozen times, with pauses between each approach. . . . a minimum of four weeks of courtship preceded copulation. At least the last two weeks of the courtship period were spent with the male with whom the female mated.
—Beverly Dugan, iguana researcher (#16)

Any time you can mimic the natural instincts and desires of your iguana—whether it's about feeding or courtship—the results will be more effective.

Sometimes it seems that something extra is required to initiate mating, such as the female moving or running off. This seems to stimulate and excite the male into the mating mode.   —I-714, Roger, 36 yrs., England

From my experience, I have learned to bring the female iguana to where the male is.   —I-775, Karen, 37 yrs., Arizona

If your male and female aren't lusting after each other in captivity, try taking the female away from the area for a day or more. Introduce her to the male's territory for a limited time each day. Take her back to her separate housing each night until successful mating occurs.

Another technique is to bring an additional female into the breeding area to stimulate or excite the male. But don't leave them alone, as three separate hormone-driven creatures can do some damage during this time, from biting to even killing one another. Never bring two males to one female; that is a recipe for sure disaster.

THE "ACT" (COPULATION)

After copulating two or three times, the amount of courtship immediately prior to copulation decreased dramatically.
—Beverly Dugan, iguana researcher (#16)

I've observed coitus firsthand and close up. The male will approach her and grab the thick part of her neck with his teeth, then mount her and wrap his arms around her belly and hold on. He has to literally pin her down and sub-

due her. She swats at him with her arms as if she were swatting flies off her back until he's pinned her. Then she will lift her tail so he can slip under and their cloacas [vents] meet, then out come the male organs. It is very strange and fascinating. They stayed interlocked that way for around 15 full minutes.
—I-200, Dianna, 47 yrs., Washington

The mating act in iguanas can be a pretty rough-and-tumble affair, as you have glimpsed in some of the previous sections of this chapter. Remember the movie the "Terminator," where the mechanical creature would not die? It just kept coming back in every scene no matter what was used to try to stop it. That in a nutshell is what a male iguana is like during mating season. The male will constantly chase and try to mount the female. As I have said before, it's important not to lock the male and female together in a small space during this time and leave them alone. Stay near the lizards in case they need to be separated for safety.

At our commercial farm we have found it's not good to leave the male and female together for long periods of time unless you have a lot of space, a lot of hiding area—things that are conducive to preventing the male from aggravating the female to death, and enabling the female to get away from him. The damned old male is running around horny [all the time]. But the females, when they get heavy with eggs, it's just an impossible task to mate.
—commercial iguana breeder in Central America

My iguanas mate like cars in a destruction derby.
—I-502, Karen, 23 yrs., Florida

When our male [SVL: 13", TL: 3' 7½", 8½ yrs.] wants to mate with our female [SVL: 16", TL: 5' 5", 9½ yrs.], she often ends up hiding on the bottom of the cage with her head in the corner (stressed out).
—I-509, Troy, 30 yrs., Missouri

Successful mating in iguanas happens only with the cooperation of the female. Remember, in the wild the female chooses a mate. Even so, it's up to the male to initiate the mating act, and often it requires that he "persuade" the female to cooperate. When a male iguana wants to mate with the female, he uses his teeth to hold her so she can't run away. He firmly bites into her neck to control her.

The bite is not like a tiger ripping the flesh off its prey, but just a firm, constant grip. Even so, females' necks often get cut, scraped, or ripped during the act, if the female tries to get away from the relentless male. "Mr. Terminator" will be back on her in a second if she escapes, and this battle can go on for days.

With the male's teeth firmly gripping the female's neck, the next phase of the act can proceed. The male might use one of a number of possible ap-

Figure 9.3: Iguanas mating in captivity. Photo: courtesy of Alan Messinger

proaches to make copulation happen, including using his legs as levers, or sweeping and pushing with his tail. Once he has control of the female, she will typically lift her tail so he can insert one of his hemipenes into her vent. Hemipenes means two penises—yes, two penises! If the male rolls the female to the left he can insert one hemipenis; if he rolls her to the right he can insert the other one. Either side, he will be ready.

With an initially uncooperative female, the male will try to get her off balance just long enough to position her vent so he can insert a hemipenis. One person told me how her male iguana had been trying for several days to mate with a female that they had brought to their house. The animals were allowed to roam free in the house. The first few days the mating attempts took place on the living room carpet, but the problem was that the male couldn't flip the female on her side to insert his hemipenis. When the male tried to flip the female, she would lock her claws into the loops of the carpet, which helped anchor her.

The male constantly followed the female everywhere in the house. One day they ended up on the kitchen (linoleum) floor. He flipped her instantly on the slick surface and inserted his hemipene. After that successful mating in the kitchen, the smart male iguana would bite onto the female's neck and gracefully waltz her into the kitchen and then—wham!—flip her in a second. It took him only one time to learn that linoleum was the key to his successful mating in this situation.

The copulation time lasts about 15 minutes.
—I-714, Roger, 36 yrs., England

While in the act, the male's head may sway rhythmically from side to side, and he may have a distant, cosmic, glassy, drugged glaze in his eyes. The female seems just to tolerate the situation. Once the male is finished he will release the female, who often leaves the area as fast as she can.

Will he try it again the same day?

They mate a few times a day for a couple of weeks. Then the female doesn't want to mate anymore and gets grouchy.
—I-546, Chuck, 32 yrs., California

Of course there are exceptions to the aggressive, ripping, shredding, crashing rule.

The male was never "mean" or dangerously aggressive toward the female. In my opinion, the male acted like "quite a gentleman" (if you get my drift!).
—I-399, Christine, 32 yrs., Colorado

He stays in active, constant pursuit of his female for most of the daylight hours during the two to three weeks [of mating]. They sound like they are knocking the walls out, but do no damage to each other or the house. The male is apparently a real gentleman to the ladies. He does no physical damage (no wounds or scars) to his dates. He must bite them in the neck very gently. I've heard other "romantic encounters" require an emergency trip to the vet or at least first aid for lacerations. I've not had that experience.

He is protective of his females and will stand with one foot on them if you enter the room. He seems to be waiting to see if I will take his female away and wants me to know he's not done with her yet. When they take little or no interest in each other after two to three weeks, I separate them.
—I-775, Karen, 37 yrs., Arizona

I have a sexually mature pair of iguanas. I have never seen the male aggressive or wild. There is much ritualized head bobbing and if the female is receptive, he (gently) bites the back of her neck (to hold her) and mounts her. If she refuses he goes away—often he ejaculates by himself.
—I-626, Gail, 48 yrs., New York

Sometimes, when there are no females around, a guy does what a guy has to do:

December through March is the worst time for my male iguana. I found him a branch that seems to fit his "liking." I have seen him make love to this and seems quite fulfilled.   —I-737, Linda, 37 yrs., California

When my iguana went through his mating drive, he mounted my "Babar Elephant" (stuffed animal wearing green velvet clothing), bit the collar, and held on for more than 30 minutes. Also, the hemipenes were displayed with semen expelled.   —I-95, Pat, Missouri

There appears to be a window of opportunity or receptivity for the female to mate. "Captive iguanas are receptive for a period of about one week" (#23). Because this time of opportunity is different for each female iguana, only your female iguana knows but she can't tell you.

GESTATION

A little bit of information before we start this section on gestation: Humans get pregnant (refers to carrying a fetus and giving birth to live young). Reptiles become gravid (when the female carries eggs inside her body that will be deposited as eggs to hatch outside her body). Many people will say that their female iguana is "pregnant," but it would simplify communication if we all used the term "gravid" for iguanas with eggs.

As I have mentioned several times before, one of the biggest surprises to many people is that female iguanas can develop eggs without a male iguana being around, just like a chicken lays eggs without a rooster.

Sometimes it will be very apparent when a female is gravid (a "clutch mass" can make up as much as 40% of her total body mass [#29]), but other people have told me how their normal-looking iguana suddenly started dropping eggs all over the house.

To recap, here are some clues indicating that your female iguana might be gravid:
- At least 10" SVL
- Reduced consumption of food during the breeding season
- Belly looks larger, even perhaps while eating less food
- Acts a little crazy—frantic actions or facial expressions—or seems moody or withdrawn
- Wants to dig, get out, go everywhere in the house—restless

For those lucky enough to have a veterinarian with access to modern ultrasound equipment, you might be able to get visual proof of whether your iguana is gravid.

When I first found out in September that my female iguana had eggs, I was terribly excited. I jumped at the chance to be a part of my vet's ultrasound study on

the progression of eggs. I caught my iguana's eggs at a relatively early stage so she was ideal. Ultrasound is an excellent imaging medium for iguanas. She was put on her back on a very comfortable cushion, and the transducer was placed on her belly. You can easily see their heart pumping; you cannot see this in dogs and cats without a special machine. You can see their liver, bladder, spleen, etc. and best of all, eggs! You can't get a very accurate count but you can get a rough estimate and there is a definite progression of maturity. Ultrasound is completely harmless to the lizard and leaves no marks (you don't even have to shave them!). 						—I-795, Dawn, 24 yrs., Ohio

Toward the end of your iguana's gestation, it's important not to handle her except when necessary, as the eggs are large, soft, and can be broken inside her. That's usually a death sentence for the female.

She was huge and I think it was probably painful for her to be handled. The actual egg laying must have been an ordeal.
						—I-554, Anthony, 29 yrs., Texas

EGG LAYING (OVIPOSITION)

The female carries it [egg] for about a month before she digs a nest and lays the egg underground.
						—Gordon H. Rodda, iguana researcher (#27)

In the wild, female iguanas lay their eggs in burrows of sand or soil, often with long tunnels. If the soil is soft and sandy like the soil in La Mancha (see story on page 512), the tunnels could be quite long because of the easy digging. Burrows in hard-to-dig soil will not be as deep or as labyrinthine. Remember Dr. Dagmar Werner said that female iguanas are pretty lazy, so they will do the minimum to get by.

Nesting (or Egg-Laying) Box

During gestation, my female grew very large and started spending many hours digging at the substrate in her cage. I placed a large box of damp sand in the cage, in which she dug and re-filled many holes. She laid her eggs in the sand box. 						—I-282, Tom, 39 yrs., New York

Your gravid female needs an appropriate place to deposit her eggs. Because your iguana isn't in her natural environment, you **must** provide this place. It's not just a "nice idea"—it's an absolute requirement and may even save your gravid iguana's life (see "Egg Binding", page 549 of this chapter).

In Appendix H is a drawing of an ideal nesting (egg-laying) box with instructions for building and setting it up. The nesting box needs to be com-

SIDEBAR

Reptile Eggs: Changing the Face of the Earth Forever

"About 330 million years ago . . . there occurred an event of great significance in the history of vertebrate evolution: the development of the amniote egg. This is the special kind of egg laid by birds and reptiles which carries inside it, wrapped in a membrane, everything needed to nourish and preserve the embryo until it is hatched. . . . The particular importance of it . . . was that it made the animals which possessed it independent of the water—for the first time they could now lay and hatch their eggs on land. The reptiles, the first animals to develop the amniote egg, were thus the first who could live and multiply on the land, opening an entire new environment for their colonization."

—*The Illustrated Encyclopedia of the Animal Kingdom* (#47)

pletely set up and in place for at least two months prior to your iguana's egg laying. By putting the box out early, you allow time for your lizard to become familiar with the box and to feel safe and secure in it.

Almost all captive females (294 out of 318) presented with these nests preferred laying their eggs in the artificial nest rather than digging their own.
—Dagmar I. Werner, Central American iguana researcher (#20)

This nesting box is not just for the eggs laid by mated female iguanas. It also makes it easier for an unmated female iguana to lay her infertile eggs. Once your female iguana becomes sexually mature she could produce eggs once a year for a good percentage of her life, so the box will have years of future use. It's basically a sand-filled, square plywood box with a top, bottom, and a hole in the side for a tube (for entry and exit). It is simple and inexpensive to construct.

Although my iguana did lay her second clutch on the ground [egg box was not ready], I have several friends who have lost gravid iguanas, I believe because the iguanas could not find a suitable place to lay and became egg-bound. I always try to duplicate an animal's natural surrounding as best as I reasonably can. I believe this is what has given me the success I have had.
—I-780, Carl, Florida

I designed the egg-laying box in Appendix H based on the nesting concepts I saw at Dr. Werner's iguana farm in Costa Rica. The success of an artificial egg-laying chamber was apparent when Dr. Werner hatched more than 700 iguanas in her first year's attempt in 1984. Up to that point, nothing on this grand of a scale had ever been done in the world. She still uses her basic design, more than 10 years later, with great success.

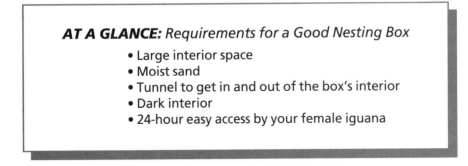

AT A GLANCE: _Requirements for a Good Nesting Box_
- Large interior space
- Moist sand
- Tunnel to get in and out of the box's interior
- Dark interior
- 24-hour easy access by your female iguana

What to Expect During Egg Laying

As with so much about iguana care, each individual female will have a slightly different experience with egg laying. This section presents a few general expectations and some scientific background, as well as stories from iguana owners who have been through the process with their female iguanas.

As an important side note, access to fresh water is always important to your lizard but this is <u>especially important</u> to a female when she is developing eggs. During gestation and after the eggs are laid, there is a chance she may become dehydrated. Besides the regular water you make available to her, you might try spraying water directly into her mouth from a clean misting bottle to encourage extra drinking at this time.

How Many Eggs to Expect

As you will see in the next group of quotations, there is a wide range in the number of eggs an iguana can lay.

A female [iguana] may lay between six and 70 eggs per clutch; average size is 41 eggs. . . . Clutch size is a function of body size. Larger females will lay earlier or they will lay larger clutches. . . . Clutch size is about 30 percent of the female's weight before laying.
—Dagmar I. Werner, iguana researcher in Costa Rica (#20)

My iguana laid 34+ eggs in my bathroom (breeding room) on January 29. She started at 10:30 p.m. (January 28) and laid approximately 6 eggs per hour until 4:00 a.m. (January 29). She was early. We did not expect her to lay until February. WRONG! She sat on my toilet tank and laid her eggs into a waiting towel. I had to take the eggs from her (off the towel and toilet tank) every half hour so they did not roll off onto the floor. It was truly an experience and far from a natural habitat. —I-775, Karen, 37 yrs., Arizona

My iguana [SVL: 17", TL: 3' 6", 7 yrs.] has laid eggs twice now. The first time she had a clutch of 34 eggs in a wooden box filled with sand. The second clutch was a year later and was composed of 43 eggs. Neither clutch was fertile and were discarded. Both egg-laying episodes occurred when my wife and I were out of town for the weekend. My iguana had the house to herself. I don't feel as if this was a coincidence. —I-554, Anthony, 29 yrs., Texas

She laid 11 of them over a two-and-a-half week period, which left her thin and exhausted, but she soon recovered and put on weight.
—conversation with pet owner at an international herpetological conference

I removed the eggs immediately after she was done laying them. I knew when she was done as she pulled away and covered them up. I lured her out of the cage by offering her some fresh collard greens. She came right out of the laying box and started eating it. I knew for sure that she started laying eggs at 10:10 p.m. last night because just a few minutes before that, I went in to get her bowl to feed her. She was done laying her eggs at 11:30 p.m. She laid 14 eggs in all. —I-735, Tammie, 31 yrs., Kansas

Figure 9.4 shows a few more examples of pet iguana egg-laying dates, numbers, and days between eggs being laid. This information is to help you get a feel for what happens with other iguanas so you will not be surprised when your female starts to lay eggs.

Egg Size

In a clutch of 41 eggs, the largest egg weighed 14.44 g [0.51 oz] and the smallest 13.22 g [0.46 oz], the mean weight being 13.78 g [0.49 oz]. The largest egg measured 43.0 mm [1.7"] long by 28.8 mm [1.1"] broad, and the smallest was 37.2 mm [1.5"] by 23.4 mm [0.9"]; the mean was 39.2 mm [1.5"] by 26.0 mm [1.0"].
—H. Mendelssohn, iguana researcher (#6)

My iguana's eggs were approximately 34 to 35.5 mm [1⅓"] long with a diameter of 24 to 24.6 mm [just under 1"] and a weight of 11.4 grams [0.4 ounce]. —I-714, Roger, 36 yrs., England

Egg Resorption

She reabsorbed her eggs. —I-775, Karen, 37 yrs., Arizona

Sometimes a female iguana will not lay her eggs but will reabsorb them (it's called egg resorption). Some of the many causes for this might be that the

Owner A

Date	Number of Eggs
20-Feb	1
25-Feb	13
4-Mar	1
10-Mar	1
11-Mar	3

Total of 19 in 21 days

Owner C

Date	Number of Eggs
1-Nov	1
2-6 Nov	10
7-Nov	22

Total of 33 in 7 days

Owner B

Day	Number of Eggs
1	5
2	0
3	1
4	6
5	0
6	2
7	4
8	2
9	4
10	1
11	1

Total of 26 in 11 days

Owner D

Date	Number of Eggs
Jan '89	41
1990	0
1991	0
Mar '92	50
Jan '93	63

Figure 9.4: The number of eggs and time from first to last egg laid varies from one iguana to the next, as indicated by these four separate owners (and the quotes in the text).

female isn't in good health, she's too "young," she got too stressed, or she can't find a proper place to lay her eggs. Resorption usually causes no negative effects to your lizard—but don't count on it happening. Always prepare an appropriate egg-laying site.

My female becomes visibly heavier about once a year, almost as if she may be carrying eggs. She will dig holes in the dirt in the flower pots and then lie in the holes, but I've never found any eggs. After about three weeks of appearing to be "pregnant," she will suddenly slim down again. I often wonder if she develops eggs and then her body reabsorbs them. Believe me, if there ever were any eggs, I would have found them! I look constantly! —I-467, Kris, 32 yrs., Florida

EGG INCUBATION

The mean clutch incubation time was 92.1 days.
—Tracy J. Miller, iguana researcher (#12)

Incubation of your female iguana's eggs is simplified with the incubator described in Appendix I. When you first find eggs in the nesting box, take them out and put them into the waiting incubator. It's important that when you place the eggs in the incubator, you maintain the exact orientation the eggs had when you found them (reptile eggs should not be turned).

Figure 9.5: Measuring eggs in Mexican jungle for iguana research project. Photo by: A. H. Iles

Place the eggs into the incubation medium so half of the egg is exposed with a little space left between them (1″ or so). The space between the eggs is important because if they are crammed together, they could elongate as they grow, causing malformed eggs. Sufficient space between the eggs also allows for proper circulation of the humid air in the incubator. The information necessary to properly set up and hatch iguana eggs is on the following pages and in Appendix I.

Fertile or Infertile Eggs?

Fertile

Before you can hatch iguana eggs, you need to find out if you have fertile or infertile eggs. If your female is older and was wild-caught or if you have a sexually mature male in with your female, you might have fertile eggs.

Sometimes fertile eggs have a little darkened spot that tends to be on the

---

AT A GLANCE: *How to Know if Eggs are Fertile*

Fertile eggs
• Large
• Chalky appearance
• Turgid, firm, resilient
• Oval shaped

Infertile eggs
• Smaller or excessively larger
• Pasty, yellowish looking
• May feel squishy, not firm
• Odd-shaped, deformed
• May get moldy or slimy

---

bottom portion of the egg (embryo "eye" spot—where the embryo is developing). You would see this only when you are moving the egg, say from the egg-laying box to the egg incubator. You may not be able to see it on all eggs; it depends on the thickness of the shell. Putting the egg near a low-watt light bulb (so it's not too hot) and looking through the egg ("candling") may be helpful in some cases.

Fertile eggs usually look much larger than infertile eggs. They are also firmer and chalky white in color. Iguana eggs are not hard and rigid like a chicken egg, but are flexible and have a leathery or rubbery texture. Be careful to handle the eggs only to move them, as excessive handling may reduce the natural antifungal properties found on the surface of the eggs.

All the eggs appear to be doing well at this time. One of the eggs was slightly sunken in at the time of laying, however it seems to be all right now; it has popped out a little today. —I-735, Tammie, 31 yrs., Kansas

Fertile eggs remain turgid and round. "Eggs with viable embryos generally increase in mass for approximately 60 days of development and then decline in mass as they approach the time of hatching" (#12). Near the end of the incubation period, fertile eggs start to indent or dimple.

Infertile

This year she laid 45 eggs. Six were obviously not viable. They were off color and pasty. Three were questionable and went bad within two weeks.
—I-780, Carl, Florida

If your female iguana was purchased as a hatchling or juvenile and has never been around any other iguanas, you can be assured that any eggs she lays will not be fertile.

Infertile eggs ("duds") are typically yellower, smaller, and perhaps more circular than the natural oval shape. One pet owner described the smaller eggs as "the size of large marbles." The eggs may also feel a little "squishy, like a marshmallow," or "slimy."

Infertile eggs have the tendency to grow mold or fungus on the outside of the shell. Fertile eggs [usually] resist the mold.
—I-772, Andy, 32 yrs., California

If the eggs are moldy they may contain a dead embryo or be infertile. Many kinds of mold or fungus can grow on an egg. Eggs that look moldy should be removed so they don't transfer mold or fungus to the other, good eggs.

The best way to tell whether an egg is fertile is to put it in an incubator and wait a few days. Infertile eggs can be regularly shaped, but if placed in an incubator for five to 15 days they completely lose their firmness and cave in, like a tire going flat.

Temperature and Humidity Requirements

Shells of iguana eggs are pliable and permeable to water.
—Dagmar I. Werner, iguana researcher (#20)

Temperature and humidity are the two key conditions an iguana egg needs to hatch. Too much or too little can either extend the hatching period or kill the developing iguanas. Much of the information in this section is from people who have successfully hatched iguanas in captivity. If you learn from their experiences, you can reduce most of the problems you might encounter in hatching your own iguana eggs.

Temperature

Thirty-four eggs were laid, and half were lost due to the wrong incubation temperature given to me. Once I got the right information, things went outstanding.
—I-326, Mark, 25 yrs., California

I used a heat mat to control the water temperature, but the mat was not accurate. Consequently, after 85 days the first hatchling appeared and the last one 13 days later.
—I-714, Roger, 36 yrs., England

Temperatures very near 30°C [86°F] are evidently required for the development of the eggs of the green iguana: A high mortality, rather than simply a retardation of development, occurs at temperatures only a few degrees above and below this level.
—"Thermal Requirements for Embryonic Development in the Tropical Lizard *Iguana iguana*" (#18)

When I was at the Belize Zoo in 1993 I got some first-hand information about their captive iguana breeding program. Tony Garel, who helped create this magnificent natural zoo, spent most of a day showing me around and explaining the different breeding techniques they used. The overall thrust of the experiments was to get the maximum growth and development of iguanas in captivity for later release back into the wild. He gave me a scientific paper

(#19) he co-authored that tested the effects of temperature and other factors on hatching.

Based on this and other studies, when you set up your incubator, keep it between 29°C and 31°C (84.2°F and 87.8°F). Any higher or lower, you could have deformed or dead hatchlings. Play it safe; aim for 30°C (86°F).

To get a feel for what egg temperatures are like for an iguana nest in the wild, look on page 568. These charts show actual nest temperatures and daily environmental conditions for two years of research. This was the research program I was invited down to help with in Mexico in 1992. Because of the weather condition called El Niño in 1992, the weather fluctuated dramatically (not shown on this one-month view chart), and the lizards hatched about three weeks later than normal. In your temperature-controlled egg incubator, such unpredictable fluctuations shouldn't happen.

I kept the water temperature at 86°F (30°C) and kept the vermiculite [incubation medium] slightly damp. Hatch was almost 50/50 males and females.
                                                            —I-780, Carl, Florida

Humidity

Something of very special interest: During the first month eggs may start losing their firmness. This could be an indicator that not enough water is mixed with the substrate in the incubator box. But most likely the egg is infertile. As the eggs age you may notice they shrink somewhat. Add water to the substrate and this should rehydrate the eggs.   —I-772, Andy, 32 yrs., California

[AUTHOR'S NOTE: With the incubator described in Appendix I, this dryness should not occur.]

Without a humid environment, iguana eggs won't hatch. In fact, if the medium used in the incubator dries out, hatching may not occur. Scientists have done research to measure the effects of dry and wet substrate media for incubating iguana eggs.

Eggs incubated on wet media weighed more late in incubation, and thus contained more water, than those exposed to dry media. The availability of water presumably affected the metabolism and growth of the embryos . . . and hatchlings from wet media contained more calcium and phosphorus than did [the iguanas] from dry environments.

Changes in mass of eggs over the course of incubation presumably reflect exchanges of water between eggs and their environment [an iguana's eggshell is permeable to water]. . . . Eggs could exchange liquid water across those parts of their eggshell contacting the substrate and water vapor across those surfaces exposed to air.
                    —"Influence of Moisture and Temperature on Eggs and
                        Embryos of Green Iguana (*Iguana iguana*)" (#19)

Nest Temperatures — 1991

	Time	Weather Conditions	Air Temp	Sand Temp	Halfway Temp	Nest Temp
May 29	5:07 PM	hot, partly cloudy	33°C	42°C	38°C	30°C
May 30	2:00 PM	hot, clear, E wind	33°C	47°C	34°C	30°C
May 31	1:35 PM	hot, clear	33°C	51°C	36°C	31°C
Jun 01	8:31 AM	hot, partly cloudy	29°C	32°C	35°C	30°C
Jun 01	1:21 PM	hot, partly cloudy	33°C	50°C	35°C	30°C
Jun 01	6:05 PM	hot, partly cloudy	31-32°C	44°C	37°C	30°C
Jun 02	5:31 PM	hot, partly cloudy	33°C	45°C	38°C	31°C
Jun 03	12:02 PM	hot, clear	34°C	52°C	36°C	31°C
Jun 03	5:49 PM	hot, partly cloudy	32°C	45°C	37°C	30°C
Jun 04	8:44 AM	hot, partly cloudy	30°C	31°C	34°C	30°C
Jun 04	12:07 PM	hot, clear	33°C	39°C	35°C	31°C
Jun 04	6:09 PM	hot, partly cloudy	32°C	36°C	35°C	31°C
Jun 05	12:24 PM	hot, clear	34°C	50°C	33°C	29°C
Jun 05	5:24 PM	hot, cloudy	32°C	38°C	34°C	30°C
Jun 06	6:28 AM	hot, cloudy	29°C	32°C	34°C	30°C
Jun 06	5:26 PM	hot, cloudy	32°C	37°C	34°C	30°C
Jun 07	6:22 AM	hot, clear	29°C	33°C	35°C	30°C
Jun 07	5:21 PM	hot, clear	33°C	43°C	34°C	31°C
Jun 08	2:28 PM	hot, clear	34°C	52°C	36°C	31°C
Jun 09	8:12 AM	hot, clear	29°C	33°C	34°C	30°C
Jun 12	11:28 AM	hot, cloudy	32°C	35°C	33°C	30°C

Nest Temperatures — 1992

	Time	Weather Conditions	Air Temp	Sand Temp	Halfway Temp	Nest Temp
Jun 04	8:00 AM	hot, partly cloudy	28°C	30°C	30°C	30-31°C
Jun 04	1:28 PM	hot, partly cloudy, W wind	33-34°C	55°C	34°C	32°C
Jun 04	5:27 PM	hot, cloudy	31-2°C	39°C	35°C	31°C
Jun 05	6:34 AM	hot, partly cloudy, NW wind	28°C	28°C	33°C	31°C
Jun 05	12:34 PM	hot, clear, W wind	34-5°C	58°C	37°C	33°C
Jun 09	5:13 PM	hot, partly cloudy	31°C	42°C	36°C	32°C
Jun 10	1:16 PM	hot, partly cloudy	33-34°C	52°C	34°C	31°C
Jun 10	4:30 PM	hot, partly cloudy	33°C	43°C	34°C	31°C
Jun 11	9:05 AM	hot, partly cloudy	30°C	33°C	32°C	32°C
Jun 11	12:16 PM	hot, clear	32°C	56°C	36°C	32°C
Jun 12	1:05 PM	hot, clear, W wind	34-35°C	60°C	35°C	32°C
Jun 12	3:05 PM	hot, clear, W wind	34°C	56°C	36°C	31°C
Jun 14	3:56 PM	hot, clear, W wind	35°C	59°C	38°C	32°C
Jun 14	4:56 PM	hot, clear, W wind	34°C	49°C	36°C	32°C
Jun 14	5:58 PM	hot, clear	32°C	39°C	35°C	31°C
Jun 19	11:20 AM	hot, partly cloudy	33°C	38°C	31°C	29-30°C
Jun 21	7:30 AM	hot, clear	30°C	29°C	31°C	30°C
Jun 21	9:34 AM	hot, clear	33°C	39°C	34°C	30°C
Jun 23	10:06 AM	hot, partly cloudy	33°C	38°C	34°C	30°C
Jun 25	9:06 AM	hot, partly cloudy	33°C	47°C	33°C	30°C
Jun 28	7:42 AM	hot, clear	31°C	30°C	33°C	30°C

Figure 9.6: These actual nest site temperatures in the wild give you an idea what is required for your iguana eggs to hatch in your egg incubator at home. Data supplied by Maria Socorro Lara López, La Mancha Research Station, Veracruz, Mexico

The incubator described in Appendix I not only has the eggs in a wet medium, but also has a pump in the tank that circulates water to create a humid environment with a constant temperature.

The Incubator

When I called around to find out what it would cost to purchase a commercially produced reptile incubator, the prices ranged from $300 to $500. Making your own incubator, described in Appendix I, saves you at least half the cost and it works as well as or better than some of the commercial models.

It's important to have the incubator completely set up and running at least two weeks prior to egg laying to allow time for the incubator's internal temperature to stabilize. If you have any doubt as to when your iguana will lay her eggs, set the incubator up earlier for safety.

One person said that the first year he had everything ready and when the eggs were laid they went right into the incubator. The next year he was busy with other things and then all of a sudden the eggs were laid. He ran around his apartment like a crazy man trying to find all of the equipment for the incubator. The third year, he said, everything was in place months ahead because he didn't want to be in frantic mode again. Take a warning from his experience.

HATCHING

I went to dinner with three friends the day my iguana laid her eggs. Weeks later, I came home from that same restaurant with the same three friends to find little iguanas hatching out of their eggs. I freaked out! I heard a noise as I took the lid off the incubator and saw one hatchling looking up at me from the corner. It was my first try, and I didn't expect anything to really happen.
—I-326, Mark, 25 yrs., California

[AUTHOR'S NOTE: See a photo of one of Mark's hatchlings in the color section of this book.]

When you think of iguanas hatching in captivity you probably first think of places like Latin America, where it's hot and humid. But Roger (I-714) of England had 30 eggs hatch: 20 males and eight females survived, one died, and one escaped and was never found.

Dr. Dagmar Werner estimates that in the wild, 95% of the hatchling iguanas die the first year from birds, snakes, coatimundis, and other predators. Raised properly in captivity, about 95% of your iguanas should survive.

Starting to Hatch

I found her first clutch started to hatch in 82 days and continued to hatch for five days.   —I-780, Carl, Florida

AT A GLANCE: Hatching Countdown

- Eggs hatch after about 70 to 90 days. Visually check on the eggs three times a week for the first 5-6 weeks, then every day for the next 4-5 weeks.
- Toward the end of incubation it's important to check the eggs a couple of times a day for indications of hatching readiness.
- Depending on the moisture content of the eggs, you may see swelling, dimpling, thinning, and even slight collapse of the egg close to hatching time.
- Let the hatchlings stay in their eggs if they don't come all the way out; don't force them out. "Most hatchling iguanas kept their heads out of their shells from six to 12 hours prior to their entire emergence" (#12). This time varies greatly among individual clutches.
- Once the yolk sac is absorbed by the hatchling, remove the lizard and place it in its new temporary home. Handle the hatchlings as little as possible because they are easily stressed, physically and mentally, at this time.

My first hatchling appeared 85 days after laying and the last one hatched 13 days later (98 days).   —I-714, Roger, 36 yrs., England

One person who has raised several clutches of eggs in his home told me: "The eggs take about 85 days from drop to pop." There is no set number of days it takes an iguana egg to hatch, and factors such as heat and humidity influence timing. But if you put your fertile iguana eggs into a correctly designed incubator, you should have hatchlings in about 90 days—sometimes sooner and sometimes later.

Below is part of a long, taped conversation I had with Tony Garel at the Belize Zoo about the iguana breeding project there. I extracted the information I thought would give you a clearer vision of the hatching process.

"You can sometimes see some movement in the egg," Tony said. "Then the next couple of days they hatch. Eggs of the same clutch hatch at about the same time unless there is a small egg in the group. You will also see a tiny depression in the egg before it hatches, and the egg will cave in because of rapid water absorption into the hatchling's body or because the hatchling punctures the egg. They use the longest claw on their hind foot to puncture the egg, to make a little slit, and you can see water ooze out of the egg a little bit . . . Each day there's a little less shape to the egg."

I checked two or three of the eggs in the "incubator room," but no action. I was tired and went to bed, turned out the light, but something mysterious was drawing me to check this one egg. I went to see and there she was—her little snout visible, working her way out. By morning she was fully out and walking in the incubator container. —I-274, Al, 38 yrs., Georgia

Immediately prior to hatching, [the eggs] lost their turgidity and became soft. More than 50% of the eggs exhibited dents in their shells at this time. Some also exhibited a loss of fluids that appeared as droplets over the shell surface.
—Tracy J. Miller, iguana researcher (#12)

Tony again: "Often the hatchlings have their yolk sacs attached to them after hatching in captivity. In the wild they would stay in their chamber [under-

Figure 9.7: Rare opportunity to see hatchling iguanas emerging from their underground egg nest. Photo: courtesy of Maria Socorro Lara López, La Mancha Research Station, Veracruz, Mexico

ground] and the sac is absorbed before they come out. Once they absorb their yolk sac at the zoo [at the breeding facility] we put the hatchlings out into our secure enclosure.

"A couple of days after hatching, no longer than a week, they don't eat anything. . . . They absorb the egg sac. Over time, the sac starts to desiccate, gets brittle, and falls off. All of our hatchlings had this egg sac." See the color photo section for a picture of Tony's iguanas eating real food.

Look at the chart on page 573 to get an idea of the size of some iguanas when they hatched in the wild. If you have hatchlings, you can compare yours to these wild ones.

Habitat and Food Requirements

Hatching a clutch of iguanas is a feeling like no other. It is the reward for a labor of love, rather than monetary pursuit, that makes it unique.
        —I-652, Amro, 22 yrs., California

My first clutch of hatchlings was a real highlight.   —I-780, Carl, Florida

To captive-raise iguanas you need the egg-laying box, incubation tank, and a fish-type aquarium to temporarily house the hatchlings until they get their future home. Food for hatchlings is the same as for juveniles except it must be chopped even finer or pulverized for easier eating and digestion.

Hatchling Cage (Temporary Home)

At the same time you are putting together the egg-laying box, you might as well assemble the cage for the hatchlings (if you think you have fertile eggs), or at least have all the parts in one location for easy access. The hatchlings' cage is just temporary housing, so it doesn't have to be elaborate like a normal habitat. Because the hatchlings can get stressed easily, locate this cage away from human activity and noise.

The size of the cage (aquarium) will depend on the number of eggs that hatch. If you have 50 viable eggs you should have two 50-gallon fish-type aquariums and divide the hatchlings between them. The lizards should be in these containers for no longer than three weeks. When they are eating and defecating on their own, you can sell or give the lizards away. Another option is to hold on to the lizards a little longer so they are bigger and stronger. For this you will need to build a nursery.

Nursery

The next step is to divide the lizards according to size by putting them into a nursery cage that has built-in dividers to separate the hatchlings into large, medium, and smaller or weaker iguanas. This will protect the smaller hatchlings from being threatened by their larger siblings and allow them all access to food and heat. The nursery can be a simple square or rectangular box with a

Born in 1991

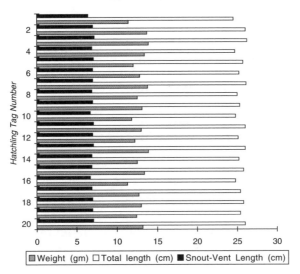

Born in 1992

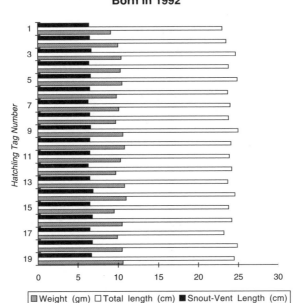

Figure 9.8: If you hatch iguana eggs at your place, compare their sizes with these measurements of iguanas that just hatched in the wild. Data supplied by Maria Socorro Lara López, La Mancha Research Station, Veracruz, Mexico

wooden bottom, glass front, plywood sides, hinged top with screening, and a draw catch latch (in front) so the hatchlings can't escape. A good size for this box would be about 4' x 3' x 3'.

I've included only a simple explanation for the design required to create these two hatchling containers. If you are attempting to breed and raise iguanas you should by now have a complete understanding of habitat size, heat, light, thermoregulating, and food requirements for these lizards. But here are a couple of additional points:

Like adult iguanas, hatchlings need a heat source at one end of their living space so they can thermoregulate. This heat source should be positioned so the lizard cannot get burned by it.

> The regulation of body temperature was examined in three of the 2-day-old hatchlings. Body temperatures were maintained between 30°C (86°F) and 40°C (104°F) most of the seven-hour observation period. The mean levels of body temperature for these animals were 34.6°C (94.3°F), 35.6°C (96.1°F), and 36.8°C (98.2°F), respectively.
> —"Thermal Requirements for Embryonic Development in the Tropical Lizard *Iguana iguana*" (#18)

Having limbs or branches under the heat source makes basking more natural and easy and allows the hatchlings to spread out without piling on top of each other to keep warm.

The substrate needs to be easily cleaned up or most people will not do it on a regular basis. Newspaper for the substrate is ideal considering the amount of defecation the lizards will generate. You also need to create a hiding place in the cage for any lizard that might be stressed out. And because the iguanas just came out of a very humid environment (the egg), you need to mist them several times a day.

Food

> In the first week after hatching, the hatchling must rely on stored energy and nutrients in the yolk sac before it begins to feed on its own.   —Conference on Nutrition of Captive Wild Animals (#13)

In the wild, iguanas hatch underground, where they stay for up to seven days to absorb their remaining yolk sac. This yolk sac looks like a yellow ball enclosed by a clear membrane, attached near where the iguana's navel would be (if it had one). Your captive-raised iguanas will live off their yolk sacs, like an attached lunch pail, for a while. Most hatchlings don't start eating real food until this egg sac is consumed.

Once the yolk sac has dried and fallen off, hatchlings can be encouraged to eat by putting a little mashed food directly on the sides of their face, but don't force them to eat it. It's just for them to taste and get used to. When you hand-

---

Eating Feces

It has been reported (source unknown) that wild newborn iguanas are often found in association with adults and have been observed eating adult feces, possibly to obtain bacteria/flora to aid digestion. [Bacteria are used for the breakdown of cellulose.] To test this theory, both years (1987 and 1988) the hatchlings were divided into two groups. Group one was fed the standard diet listed, while group two's diet was dusted twice with dried, ground adult feces. No difference in growth or development was noted and neither group appeared to have problems assimilating food.

—Scientific paper presented at International Herpetological Symposium (#11)

I have also heard and read about the wonders of hatchling iguanas eating feces, supposedly to inoculate their digestive and maybe immune systems with necessary microorganisms. Several years ago I saw a four-line comment, reportedly from Dr. Werner of Costa Rica, that said she believed that iguanas were eating the feces for protein.

Should adult feces be offered to hatchlings? The hatchlings noted above in the experiment seemed to do fine without the feces. But I wonder if a different result might have been obtained in his experiment using fresh (not dry) feces, which contain more live bacteria.

Feeding feces to hatchlings is a controversial topic. I don't know the real answer. One problem is getting feces that are not contaminated with parasites. One commercial iguana farmer who has been in the business a long time told me that they don't offer feces any more because of the potential for contaminating the hatchlings with parasites. They tried it in the beginning of their breeding operation, but discontinued it because they found it unnecessary and not worth the risk. More than 10 years later, they still don't inoculate with feces and have raised hundreds of thousands of healthy iguanas.

feed a hatchling this way, be careful not to hurt the little lizard's mouth, as it is very delicate.

Water should be available in a container and it is best to have it secured and off the cage floor about 1" to 2". Having it up high will prevent most of the lizards from accidentally defecating in it. If you have the water at the opposite end of the basking area, this also helps prevent the water from evaporating and the hatchlings from stepping in it. The water container should be cleaned any time you see feces in it. A cleaning mixture of bleach and water works best, but be sure to rinse the container several times with clear water to remove any bleach residue before filling it with fresh water. Also wash your hands thoroughly for you own protection.

New Homes

Don't lose sight of the most important goal in breeding iguanas: **GOOD HOMES FOR ALL OF YOUR HATCHLINGS. <u>You brought these little green guys into the world through your manipulation of life.</u>** As a god (very tiny "g") you must perform right action for the well-being of these creatures. Remember, with proper care they can easily live for 12 years. If they are not given a proper home and have to suffer for 12 years, this is on <u>your</u> conscience. If you figure you will hatch at least 20 iguanas, 20 x 12 years = 240 years of an enriched or suffering life! **IT'S YOUR RESPONSIBILITY. IF YOU CAN'T HANDLE IT—DON'T RAISE IGUANAS!!**

FUTURE OF BREEDING

In the future, I see exclusively farm- and captive-raised iguanas being sold, because of the pressure that people like yourself have put on the pet industry. This will surely be a great and harmonious shift from the way iguanas were taken in the past. The cost to raise iguanas on farms in Central and South America and even Mexico will be cheaper than paying someone to rip them out of the jungle.

There are also a few places in the U.S. that are raising *Iguana iguana* as a side line, along with more lucrative iguanas such as *Cyclura*. These places have to charge more for their hatchlings, but the animals will probably be in terrific condition because of the almost one-to-one care and the fact that the hatchlings don't have to fly thousands of miles to arrive at their destination. But because of the cheap price that *Iguana iguana* sells for, you won't see many places in the U.S. doing this on a mass scale, as in Latin American countries.

A possible negative result of getting hatchlings at such a cheap price ($10 to $60) could be a lack of real concern for their lives. In a "throw-away" society, if something is cheap and doesn't function correctly, too many people tend to just toss it and get another one. People have written to me and shared their concerns about this matter. I hope the price of iguanas remains high enough to reduce the possibility that iguanas will become disposable in some people's minds.

In coming years, I expect that farms and small breeders will set up some sort of quality-control system for their industry. Breeders that have excellent housing, food, and care for their iguanas will receive a special rating code or symbol (e.g., AAA bred) that will be displayed at the pet store or in their ads in herp magazines. Then the buying public will know that they are getting only the best iguanas.

I also predict that many breeders will emulate what some of the snake breeders have done and breed for certain physical traits, such as albino or two- and three-color animals. Maybe an iguana will be bred to have a very dark green color that doesn't change as they mature into adulthood. Maybe this iguana will have color banding of bright red or purple. Ah, give man a little science, too much time on his hands, and a desire to change a species (and make money), and there you have it.

Perhaps I am just old-fashioned, but for what it is worth I don't like this Frankenstein approach to life. I think that the people in this first wave of nature perversion will make some big bucks because it will be so unusual. I heard of some wholesale bidding on some (accidental) albino green iguanas that were farm-raised. The story goes that they were offered from $500 to $1,000 for each lizard, depending on who tells the story. But the iguanas died, supposedly because they were left outside like "normal" iguanas and couldn't take the sun (because they were albino).

I think one day Mother Nature is going to get really angry at all of the humans jerking her natural plan around, and then someone is going to get their butt kicked!

Conclusion

There is really no conclusion, because we still don't have all the answers for properly taking care of iguanas. But in the six short years I have been gathering information on these lizards, there has been a dramatic refinement of knowledge and better all-around care for iguanas.

Every year iguanas get more into the mainstream and are slowly losing their reputation as pets for weird people. But as the popularity of iguanas increases, and as our knowledge about them expands, my hope is that our wisdom also grows. As I said in the introduction, my intention with this book was actually to discourage people from getting iguanas as pets, unless they are fully aware of the responsibility and willing to make a real commitment to providing a great life for an iguana.

I know that the experiences I had with my iguana were powerful, profound, heartwarming, exciting, and fun. Za was a very special creature and his memory will live on through this book. It was because of Za's existence that this book was created.

If you decide to own an iguana as a pet, I hope the information presented in these pages will help your green friend enjoy a long, healthy, and happy life in your care.

Iguana Questionnaire Research

Thank you for letting me fill out one of your questionnaires. It has really been fun.
                                        —I-841, Bonnie, 23 yrs., Texas

I don't think you have missed anything in your questionnaire. It really made me think about my iguana a lot, and I even learned something by your questions.
                                        —I-940, Linda & Scott, 44 yrs., California

This questionnaire is extremely detailed and well thought out. I found it fascinating.
                                        —I-753, Kelly, 26 yrs., Pennsylvania

I can't think of anything you may have missed. You have asked a lot of in-depth questions. You have been more detailed and in-depth than I ever imagined. I have enjoyed participating in your project. I also hope some of the information given to you will be of some value.
                                        —I-773, Rick, 34 yrs., Nebraska

Thank you for caring about iguanas. I've tried to answer all your questions to the best of my ability. I wanted to cheat, but I didn't.
                                        —I-931, Wilson, 30 yrs., New Jersey

Iguana Owner Questionnaire

When I first decided to write an iguana book back in 1990, I had figured out most of the chapter topics and illustrations I wanted, based mostly on the experiences with my own iguana.

At the time, I knew very few people who had iguanas, and that was even when I lived in California. To find out if other iguana owners felt the same way I did about care requirements, I placed an ad in one of the reptile magazines, asking people to fill out a detailed questionnaire on iguana ownership. I got a good response and continued to put more ads in that and other reptile magazines for several years. I also handed out the questionnaire at herp meetings and reptile conferences until about 1995. Not only did I get some incredible quotations (used throughout the book), but I also got validation for what my pet-care book should cover.

The format of the questionnaire stayed about the same over the years, with three pages containing approximately 50 questions. The top part of the first page had a space for pet owners to fill in pertinent information about themselves (age, address, occupation, income, etc.) and about their iguanas (name, age, weight, length, country of origin, etc.). This top part was cut off and sent back to me along with their answers to the other 50 questions.

The main topics covered in the questionnaire were Food, Housing, Health, Up Close and Personal, and The Big Questions. Up Close and Personal included more in-depth questions about the pet owner's iguana, such as, "If you have more than one iguana, how do they get along with each other?" The Big Questions had to do with what the pet owners wanted to see in an iguana book.

Receiving more than 800 questionnaires gave me a very clear picture of the iguana community across the U.S., Canada, and parts of Europe. The answers ranged from a simple single page to a 28-page, double-spaced, typewritten response, as well as dozens of photographs and even a couple of videotapes. Much of this book is based on the comments and desires of these iguana owners.

As mentioned in the Foreword, every iguana owner's quotation in the book is coded for their privacy. I wanted to convey that the quote was from a real person but without identifying the individual. The solution was that everyone who sent for a questionnaire was assigned their own private code number.

In the text, you will see quotes followed by a capital "I", for iguana (owner), followed by the private code number. To let you know whether the person is a male or female, but to preserve anonymity, I included only their first name. I added the age and state or country the person is from to show the wide range of ages and locations for iguana owners. An example of the full code looks like this: I-626, Gail, 48 yrs., New York. To make the quotations stand out more clearly, they are italicized.

On the following charts are some interesting facts derived from the iguana questionnaires. In 1994 I stopped the "official" counting of questionnaires at I-800, but they kept coming in through 1995, so you might see code numbers up to I-940 in the book.

Veterinarian Questionnaire

A couple of years after beginning the iguana owner questionnaire research, I decided to add to my database of information by also contacting veterinarians. I got most of the veterinarians' names through recommendations from the people who answered my iguana owner questionnaire. The identities of veterinarians quoted in the book are protected by the same coding system that was used for the iguana owners, except with a "V" instead of an "I" before the code number (e.g., V-117, Dr. Dale, 38 yrs., Texas).

Figure A.1 (facing page): Included here are just a few results of my iguana questionnaire research from 1990 to 1994 (notice that I stopped tabulation of results at questionnaire number 800). I received questionnaire requests from nearly every U.S. state and from three other countries, and each year a high number of questionnaires was completed and returned. Slightly more women than men responded ("both" means that the questionnaire was completed by a couple or multiple family members). Although ages of respondents ranged from 8 to 71, most were in their 20s and 30s. Just a reminder: This was not a controlled scientific study, so don't draw too many hard conclusions from the information presented.

Requests By State/Country

State	Requests	State	Requests
AK	4	MT	2
AL	2	NC	9
AR	1	NE	6
AZ	13	NH	3
CA	215	NJ	24
CO	7	NM	5
CT	7	NV	4
DC	1	NY	60
DE	1	OH	28
FL	46	OR	48
GA	3	PA	41
HI	1	RI	2
IA	3	SC	1
ID	2	SD	1
IL	30	TN	7
IN	13	TX	26
KS	7	UT	9
KY	4	VA	20
LA	4	VT	1
MA	12	WA	23
MD	15	WI	13
ME	2	WV	3
MI	18	Canada	19
MN	11	England	4
MO	14	Germany	1
MS	4	TOTAL	800

Requested vs Returned Questionnaires

Year	Requested	Returned
1990	181	113
1991	179	108
1992	175	115
1993	163	84
1994	102	63
TOTAL	800*	481

*reached 800 questionnaire requests on 05/12/94

Respondents By Gender

Year	Male	Female	Both
1990	82	82	17
1991	82	89	8
1992	79	86	10
1993	75	78	11
1994	52	43	6

Respondents by Age (Returned Questionnaires Only)

Age	Number of Respondants	Age	Number of Respondants	Age	Number of Respondants
8	1	30	20	52	0
9	1	31	18	53	2
10	1	32	18	54	1
11	1	33	16	55	0
12	4	34	16	56	0
13	6	35	9	57	1
14	14	36	18	58	0
15	7	37	13	59	1
16	9	38	19	60	0
17	6	39	12	61	0
18	2	40	12	62	0
19	13	41	7	63	0
20	17	42	7	64	2
21	24	43	3	65	0
22	32	44	8	66	2
23	22	45	5	67	0
24	16	46	5	68	0
25	20	47	1	69	1
26	23	48	3	70	0
27	21	49	1	71	1
28	14	50	2		
29	18	51	0	Total	496*

*(304 unreported)

I sent out more than 150 questionnaires to veterinarians and got back fewer than 30, but the ones that arrived were very helpful. Not only did I get a number of good quotations, but I also received much useful information for Chapter 7, Medical Troubleshooting.

The veterinarian questionnaire contained about 30 questions, many of which were quite detailed. Perhaps that's what scared off many of the veterinarians from filling them out. As with the other questionnaire, this one had a top part to be cut off and sent back, with information about the veterinarian.

The three topics covered in the veterinarian questionnaire were:

- Personal information about the veterinarian (e.g., "What are your reasons for working with reptiles?")
- General medical questions relating to iguanas (e.g., "What are the four most frequent problems, in order, that cause clients to bring iguanas in for treatment?")
- General questions (e.g., "Do you recommend vitamin/mineral supplements, and if so what kind and how much?")

Invaluable Research

To my knowledge, my questionnaire research was the first time that anyone has surveyed large numbers of iguana owners and veterinarians to find out about captive iguanas in the "real world." The combination of the iguana questionnaire research and my other information sources on iguanas—conversations with leading researchers worldwide, scientific journals, interviews with people in all phases of the pet trade, trips to iguanas' native habitats, experience with my own pet iguana—helped give me a more realistic and in-depth understanding of the common green iguana.

APPENDIX B

Suggested Reading and Additional Information

The following resources for additional information on iguanas and iguana-related organizations and services is far from complete. My goal here is to provide a starting point for your further explorations of iguanas and their care.

WARNING! Because iguanas are so popular, many people are making videos and writing books about them. I have been sent a number of these materials by disgruntled iguana owners for my review. Some of them provide useful information, but many contain wrong information that could harm your iguana. As an example, one book recommended pea gravel as its first choice as a habitat substrate for iguanas. It appears that this author has never talked with a herp veterinarian, who would never recommend this dangerous substrate for an iguana.

Books

Reptile Medical Care:
Fredric L. Frye, DVM, MSc, CBiol, FIBiol
Biomedical and Surgical Aspects of Captive Reptile Husbandry, 2nd edition (2-volume set)
Krieger Publishing Co., Malabar, Florida, 1991

Douglas R. Mader, MS, DVM
Reptile Medicine and Surgery
W.B. Saunders Co., Philadelphia, 1996

For people who want to delve further into details of medical care for their iguana, these are two excellent books. They're not just about iguanas, but all kinds of reptiles. They are not designed for the casual reader, either in content or in price; these are *serious* veterinary books by two of the top herp veterinarians.

Iguana Science:
Gordon M. Burghardt and A. Stanley Rand
Iguanas of the World: Their Behavior, Ecology, and Conservation
Noyes Publications, Park Ridge, New Jersey, 1982

This quite simply is the book on iguanas from a scientific perspective. It covers all kinds of iguanas, not only *Iguana iguana*, and is pretty technical. It's a true classic.

Magazines

The Vivarium
Journal of the American Federation of Herpetoculturists
120 W. Grand, Suite 106
Escondido, CA 92025
(619) 747-4948

Reptiles
P.O. Box 58700
Boulder, CO 80322
(303) 666-8504

Reptile and Amphibian
RD #3 Box 3709-A
Pottsville, PA 17901
(717) 622-6050

These three magazines present scientific information and general articles about reptiles and amphibians, but are not written in the highly technical, often dry style of a scientific research paper. You don't have to have a college degree in science to pick up a lot of useful, up-to-date information on reptiles and amphibians from these magazines.

Major Herpetological and Scientific Societies

The advantage of being a member of a herp society is finding people like yourself who care about iguanas and many other reptiles and amphibians. They usually have monthly meetings, plus periodic special events and outings. Another benefit of herp societies is a monthly or quarterly newsletter or scientific bulletin. I belong to five of these organizations and only one is local here in Oregon. They all have something interesting to say through their newsletters, even if they don't always talk about iguanas.

If you want to find a herp society in your area, ask someone at a local pet store or your reptile veterinarian. If you don't get an answer, write to CHS (be sure to include a SASE with any correspondence) or call AFH.

CHS (Chicago Herpetological Society)
Membership Secretary
2001 N. Clark Street
Chicago, IL 60614

CHS is just one of hundreds of herp societies in the U.S., Canada, and the world. It is a local herp society based in Chicago, but it has worldwide membership and a high-class monthly publication. CHS is a non-profit organization, and its purposes are education, conservation, and advancement of herpetology. CHS is like your local herp society, except bigger and perhaps with more depth.

AFH (American Federation of Herpetoculturists)
120 W. Grand, Suite 106
Escondido, CA 92025
(619) 747-4948

AFH is a non-profit national organization whose purpose is to represent the interests of herpetoculturists through a variety of means. It disseminates essential information to individuals, societies, and institutions and documents herpetocultural accomplishments through its official publication, *The Vivarium* magazine. It also promotes responsible herpetoculture through education and legislative actions and aims to establish a general philosophy of herpetocultural education that could contribute to the conservation of biological diversity. AFH blends science about reptiles and amphibians into easy-to-understand and enjoyable articles presented in its magazine. It's definitely a worthwhile organization to join.

SSAR (Society for the Study of Amphibians and Reptiles)
Robert D. Aldridge
Department of Biology
St. Louis University
St. Louis, MO 63103

SSAR is the largest international herpetological society. It's a non-profit organization that was established to advance research, conservation, and education concerning amphibians and reptiles. SSAR puts out two publications quarterly: *Herpetological Review*, a news journal, and *Journal of Herpetology*, a scientific research journal. This organization is more for those interested in the scientific aspects of reptiles and amphibians.

IIS (International Iguana Society, Inc.)
P.O. Box 43061
Big Pine Key, FL 33043

IIS is a non-profit, international organization dedicated to the preservation of the diversity of iguanas through habitat preservation, active conservation, research, captive breeding, and the dissemination of information. This organization encompasses the entire family Iguanidae. Membership includes a subscription to *Iguana Times* magazine, which comes out about every four months. I have been a member from the beginning and recommend membership if you love all kinds of "iguanas."

On-line Services

HERP-NET (electronic bulletin board)
Mark Miller, Systems Administrator
P.O. Box 52261
Philadelphia, PA 19115
phone and fax: (215) 464-3561
modem access: (215) 464-3562 (works at 2400 baud; higher-speed connections are also available)

In addition, most of the major on-line services (e.g., America Online, Compuserve, Prodigy), the Internet, and the World Wide Web have various forums devoted to reptiles and places to discuss your green friend with fellow herpers. One warning: In cyberspace as in print, don't trust everything you read. Stick with reliable sources of information about iguana care.

Iguana Veterinarians

To find an iguana veterinarian in your area, talk to people in your local herp society or pet stores. Another option is to write or call:

Association of Reptile and Amphibian Veterinarians (ARAV)
phone: (610) 358-9530
write:
Wilbur Armand, Executive Director
6 North Pennel Road
Media, PA 19063

Iguana Rescue

The first Iguana Rescue Group was organized by some Florida residents who wanted better lives for iguanas that were discarded by their pet owners. In recent years, many more Iguana Rescue groups have begun and are now scattered across the U.S. If you want to start one up in your area or find out where one is located near you, write or call:

Deborah Neufeld
P.O. Box 423332   Or call:
Kissimmee, FL 34742-3332   Janet Truse
(407) 847-0725   (407) 957-5633

Iguana-Related Products

Because so many new iguana products come out constantly, it would be wrong to list only what's available now, thus limiting your selection. A new product "tomorrow" might also mean a better product than what is here "now." Also, this is an iguana care book, not a products catalog. To get current on what herp products are available, read the different herp magazines listed earlier.

Two exceptions to my "no recommendations" rule are the plastic netting sold mostly to aquaculturists (fish farmers) and the stainless steel reptile clippers that are the best for trimming iguanas' claws . . . so far.

Plastic Netting (for iguana habitat):
InterNet Inc.
2730 Nevada Ave. North
Minneapolis, MN 55427
1-800-328-8456

You will probably never see this product sold in any herp magazines. In fact, you are unlikely to see or hear about this product unless you are a professional aquaculturist. I recommend this product instead of wire screening for outdoor iguana habitats. It is also good for indoor habitats, for air vents or screened doors. You can get it by contacting the manufacturer directly. Please note: I still recommend wire hardware cloth for use around heat lights (for iguanas' protection); the plastic netting would melt.

Reptile Claw Clippers:
Four Paws Products, Ltd.
50 Wireless Blvd.
Hauppauge, NY 11788
1-800-835-0909

These clippers can be found in most pet stores, but if you have difficulty getting them, contact Four Paws directly.

Useful Conversion Tables

Dear Everyone on the Planet Except for U.S. Residents:

I realize that the metric system is the standard for measurements worldwide, and I apologize that this book gives mostly feet, inches, pounds, and degrees Fahrenheit, forcing some of you to go to the trouble of converting. But my publisher has estimated that more than 90% of the people purchasing this book will live in the U.S., so I have to write to my audience.

I considered putting metric conversions next to each length and weight listed in the book, but a prototype copy of this approach made the book look like a mess and distracted from the points being made.

To help you, I've included some convenient conversion tables to simplify any translations. Again, sorry for the inconvenience.

Thanks,
THE AUTHOR

Temperature Conversions*

Fahrenheit	Celsius
40	4
50	10
60	15
65	18
70	21
75	24
80	27
85	29
90	32
95	35
100	38
105	41
110	43
115	46
120	49

*Approximate. To convert Fahrenheit to Celsius, subtract 32, multiply by 5, and divide by 9. To convert Celsius to Fahrenheit, multiply by 9, divide by 5, and add 32. Water freezes at 32°F/0°C. Water boils at 212°F/100°C.

Length Conversions*		Weight Conversions**	
Inches/Feet	Centimeters	Ounces/Pounds	Grams/Kilograms
1/16″	1/4 cm	1 oz	30 g
1/8″	1/2 cm	2 oz	60 g
1/2″	1 1/2 cm	3 oz	85 g
3/4″	2 cm	4 oz	115 g
1″	2 1/2 cm	5 oz	140 g
1 1/2″	4 cm	6 oz	180 g
2″	5 cm	7 oz	200 g
3″	8 cm	8 oz	225 g
4″	10 cm	9 oz	250 g
5″	13 cm	10 oz	285 g
6″	15 cm	11 oz	300 g
7″	18 cm	12 oz	340 g
8″	20 cm	13 oz	370 g
9″	23 cm	14 oz	400 g
10″	25 cm	15 oz	425 g
11″	28 cm	1 lb	450 g
12″	30 cm	1 1/4 lb	565 g
13″	33 cm	1 1/2 lb	675 g
14″	35 cm	1 3/4 lb	800 g
15″	38 cm	2 lb	900 g
16″	41 cm	2 1/2 lb	1 1/4 kg
17″	43 cm	3 lb	1 1/3 kg
18″	46 cm	3 1/2 lb	1 1/2 kg
19″	48 cm	4 lb	1 3/4 kg
20″	51 cm	4 1/2 lb	2 kg
21″	53 cm	5 lb	2 1/4 kg
22″	56 cm	6 lb	2 3/4 kg
23″	58 cm	7 lb	3 1/4 kg
24″	61 cm	8 lb	3 3/4 kg
2 1/2′	76 cm	9 lb	4 kg
3′	107 cm	10 lb	4 1/2 kg
3 1/2′	122 cm		
4′	122 cm		
4 1/2′	137 cm		
5′	152 cm		
5 1/2′	168 cm		
6′	183 cm		

*Approximate. To convert inches to centimeters, multiply inches by 2.54. To convert feet to centimeters, multiply feet by 30.48. To convert centimeters to inches, multiply centimeters by 0.0937.

**Approximate. To convert ounces to grams, multiply ounces by 28.35. To convert pounds to kilograms, multiply pounds by 0.4536.

A Special Invitation

You are cordially invited to enjoy a special iguana pet-care update in the comfort of your home. Each year, I will mail a newsletter to everyone who writes to request it.

Learning and knowing about iguanas doesn't stop with this book, for you or for me. I will continue my travels to visit the lands where iguanas run free and where they are being raised in captivity. I'll gather the most timely information on iguanas and publish it annually in a newsletter. I believe that the more you know about your iguana, the better you'll be able to care for your green friend.

My yearly newsletter will feature several feature articles, updates on the latest research on iguanas, veterinarian Q&A, stories and tips from people who have iguanas as pets, photos, cartoons, and much more! The topics of the newsletter will vary, depending on what new information I discover, but might include new foods and products, nutrition research, health-care updates, or perhaps the latest news from iguana farms in Central and South America.

If you want this special once-a-year newsletter sent to you, write and ask to be put on the mailing list:
    Dunthorpe Press
    Attention: Iguana Newsletter
    P.O. Box 80286
    Portland, OR 97280

Enclose your name, mailing address, and whether you have an iguana as a pet. We will let you know by mail when the newsletter will come out, so if you move, please make sure we have your current address.

                    "Green Dreams,"
                    Iguana Jim

APPENDIX C
Iguana Pet Names

For all of you who need help in naming you lizard, here are some real iguana names taken from my iguana questionnaires. The most popular names were derivations of "iguana" ("Iggy," etc.) or names such as "Spike" that described some iguana-like physical characteristic. Surprisingly, mammal names—including "Spot," "Fido," and "Fluffy"—were also used. When it comes to iguana names, people are as colorful as their animals.

I've divided these names into categories solely for your entertainment. I admit that the decisions as to what names went into which category were sometimes arbitrary, so please don't get upset if you'd rather see "Peanut" in the food category or if you're appalled by some other grouping. Relax, it's just for fun!

Variations on "Iguana"

Big Ig	Hopmey d'Iguana	Igsy
Bwana	Icky	Iguana
Ed-Guana	Igfield	Iguana Don
Eeghana-guana	Iggums	Iguana Donna
Eguana	Iggy; Iggie	Iguie
Gibby	Iggy-Pop; Iggie Pop	Igwa
Guamy	Igmeister; Igmister	Little Ig
Guana	Ignatious	Oggi
Guans	Ignatz	Vwanna
Guano	Igor	Wanna
Guar	Igor Francis Greenleaff Iguana	Zig
Gwangi	Igster	Ziggy; Ziggie

Variations on "Lizard" or "Reptile" or "Dinosaur"

Dino	Izzy	Lizzy
Dragon	Kamoda	Puff
Isa Bean	Liz	Reptilous
Isa Liz[1]*	Lizard	T-Rex
Issy		

*Notes begin on p. 597.

Animal Names

Basset Hound	Lady	Pig Boy
Boomer	Lucky	Rhino
El Tigre	Old Scratch	Rover
Fido; Fydo	Pig; Pigg	Spot
Fluffy		

Plant Names

Basil	Daisy	Sweet Pea
Bonsai	Parsley	Tiger Lily
Buttercup	Petunia	Weed
Cypress	Sativa	Willow

Human Names: Female

Ada	Isabelle	Phoebe
Agatha	Isadora	Rhea
Ali	Jane; Jayne	Rita
Amanda	Julia	Ruby
Anna	Lana	Ruth
Cleo	Lu	Samantha
Collette	Lucy; Luci	Tina
Emmy	Marly	Victoria
Francine	Mary Jane	Wanda
Gini	Missy	Zelda
Gladys	Pauline	Zoë
Harriet	Peggy Sue	

Human Names: Male

Abraham	Fenwick	Malcolm
Al	Frazier	Max
Angus	Fred; Freddie	Milo
Anthony	Garth	Moe
Archie	Gary	Murry
Arthur; Art	George	Nigel
Barney	Grover	Norman
Ben	Gunther	Norton
Benjamin	Gus	Ozzie
Bernie	Guthrie	Pauly
Bud; Buddy	Hank	Pete
Bufford	Harry	Poindexter
Cecil	Henry	Quincy
Charlie	Herman	Ralph
Chester	Howie	Rex[2]
Clint	Ian	Riley
Cyrus	Ivan	Rocky

David
Denis
Dominik
Ed
Edgar
Eliot
Elmo
Emmett
Felix

Jack
Jackson
Jake
Jonathon
Kevin
Larry
Lars
Leo
Luigi

Sam
Sydney
Sylvester
Tom
Ty
Vernon
Waldo
Wally
Willie; Willy

Human Names: Male & Female Combos or Surnames

Barrett
Baxter
B.C.
B.J.
Boone
Darrell Van Horn

Higgins
Jamison
J.D.
Lister
Lyn, Bobbi, & Alex[3]
McGee

Ming
O'Malley
Phil/Phyllis
Quackenbush
Riley

Human Names: Hispanic

Cisco
Hector Sanchez
Jose
Juan
Juanita

Julio
Manuel
Pancho
Pedro

Pepe Mendez
Rico
Sergio
Tito

Famous People

Amos & Randy[4]
Archimedes
Birdman of Alcatraz[5]
Bogie
Bonnie & Clyde
Caesar
Calvin
Charles Darwin
Che
Cleopatra
Del Shannon

Dracula; Drac
Elvis
Genghis Khan
Geronimo
Ghandi[6]
Gucci
Hepburn & Tracy
Houdini[7]
Jack the Ripper
Michaelangelo
Napoleon

Picasso
Plato
Ringo
Robert Deniro
Sadam [8]
Sigmund
Stevie Ray
Talulah[9]
Tony Lama[10]
Twiggy

Terms of Endearment/Nicknames

Baby
Baby Brainless
Big Guy
Binkley
Booger
Bubba

Geezer
Itty Bitty
Junior
Little Fella
Little One
Mischief

The Queen Baby
Queenie
Rascal
Skimpy
Snaffoo
Snuggles

Butthead
Chichivo
Chickie-Ten
Chum-Chub
Coco
El Guapo & La Bonita
Foo Foo

Oodles
Oonie
Peanut
Pee Wee
Pekeyto
Precious
Princess

Sparky
Speck
Squeeze
Stinky
Sweetum
Tidbit
Weeney

Human Names: Fanciful

Egor
Glamis
LaMonte
Lothar

Ludwigga
Mercury Gabner
Nocona
Octavia

Rameth
Savannah
Suriana
Tiamat

Mythical, Biblical Names

Achilles
Athena
Bacchus
Beelzebub
Exodus
Goliath
Icarus

Lazarus
Medea
Minotaur
Ra & Isis
Sampson
Samson & Delilah

Satan
Solomon
Theseus
Thor
Wizard
Zeus

Human Names: Titles/Honors/Relations

Czar
Hero
Jewel of the Nile
Jr.

Lady Bean
Princess Buttercup
Princess Owasippie

St. Georgia
Uncle
Warrior

Book, Play, Movie, TV, Music Names

Al & Peggy[11]
Bert, Ernie & Oscar[12]
Brutus
Casper
Data
Don Juan
Drazil, Bilbo, Cinderella
Emma Peel[13]
Elvira
E.T.
Frankie & Johnnie
Franny & Zooey
Fred Flintstone
Godzilla

Goofy
Grimmi[14]
Grinch
Gulliver
Gumby
Ichabod
Kato
Kermit; Kermie
Larry, Moe & Curly
Lestat
Lurch
Merlin
Mogwai
Mr. Wizard

N'Toth[15]
Prufrock[16]
Pugsly
Rambo
Romeo
Sambo
Simba
Sinbad
Sir Galahad
Smaug[17]
Squiggy
Tarzan
Yoda

Behavior Names

911	Killer	Snoop
Blitz[18]	Lasher	Spaz
Bob[19]	Launchpad[23]	Splash
Bruiser	Leeper	Strider
Cheery	Mr. S[24]	Taz[27]
Damien[20]	Paralyzed[25]	Temere[28]
Dart[21]	Psycho	Topper[29]
Dizzy	Raider	Trouble
Flash	R.B.[26]	Vincent the Resilient
Flick	Shredder	W.B.[30]
Greedy	Shy	Weezie
Grunt	Sly	Wild Man Peyote
IFH[22]		

Physical Description Names

Digit	Large Marge	Rusty[33]
Emerald	Little Green Jeans	Simon Green
Fang	Little Green Pea	Smokey
Fatty	Little Green Sprout	Spike
Greenie	Malachite	Stripe
Greensleeves	Midori	Stubs; Stubbs[34]
Hardy	Mr. Green	Stubby
Iggy Long Green Finger	Negrite[32]	Stumpy[35]
Jade	Neon	Talon
Kelly	Poquito	Turq
Krinkle	Rasor	Verde
Lance[31]	Roksann, The Jade Dragon	Wrinkle

Geographic Locations: Town, Cities, Countries, etc.

Cairo [Egypt]	Paraguay [S. America]	Turlock [California]
Danzig [Germany]	Seneca [New York]	

"Things in the World" Names

Argyle	Dumpster	Ridge
Bog	Gizmo	Rooter
Crayola	Gyrm	Slick
Dirt	Onyx	X-Ray

Food Names

Kiwi	Pepsi & Coke	Sugar
Mango	Pickles	Tequila
Okra	Quiche	Tofu

Expressions

Bobalouie
Boluptuous
Iggy & Ziggy
IsHe[36]
Itchy & Scratchy

Major & Minor
Omega
Primero & Segundo
Ritz
Solo

Stormy
Tac-Toe
Trooper
Una
Yahoo

Miscellaneous "Z" Names

Za
Zammis
Zeek

Zeep
Zep
Zipp

Zogg
Zug Zug

Miscellaneous [or Names of Unknown Origin]

Boca
Chako
Checko
Chephern
Cire
Cousy
Cruise
Daines
Eguchan
Friskceils
Gallion
Galron & Toekey
Gilmer

Gingo
Gnarle
Hooch
Indi
Kingster
Mamu
Manilla
Mardak
Molo
Opus & Rufus
Quat-Loo
Queezer Berry
Rollo

Selley
Shabba
Smokey
Sneech
Snoop
Taneil
Teakie
Togon
Turk
Wallabert
Watashi
Yarkona

Notes

[1]owner wanted the name to start with an "I" and had gone to school with a person named Isa

[2]Rex became <u>Rexina</u> after "he" laid her first clutch of eggs

[3]all followed by human owner's surname

[4]a play on the real names of "Amos & Andy"

[5]because he escaped all the time at the beginning

[6]because he didn't eat for the first 4 days

[7]because he escaped all the time at the beginning

[8]for Sadam Hussein, because the iguana's so crazy

[9]for Talulah Bankhead, silent movie actress

[10]named after the boots

[11]as in Bundy, from the TV show *Married, with Children*

[12]characters from the TV show *Sesame Street*

[13]main female character in the TV spy series *The Avengers*

[14]named after the comic strip *Mother Goose & Grimm*

[15]female reptilian alien on the TV series *Babylon 5*

[16]from the T.S. Eliot poem "The Love Song of J. Alfred Prufrock"

[17]from *The Hobbitt*

[18]because he's extremely aggressive during mating season [also <u>Blitz, Jr.</u>]

[19]what an iguana's head does

[20]crazy iguana, paranoid, always defensive, dilated eyes, crazy look, looked wildly at his surroundings

[21]because every time the owner put the iguana down he ran away

[22]Iguana From Hell

[23]was mistreated by previous owner and would leap into the air whenever anyone came near him (in the beginning)

[24]at this time, "S" stands for "shithead"; he likes to bite and get aggressive

[25]had trouble with his back legs

[26]for Rotten Bitch

[27]after "Tasmanian Devil"—darts around the cage as if his tail were on fire

[28]Latin for "rash and inconsiderate"—but the owner loves him anyway

[29]because she climbs to the top of anything and everything

[30]full name is <u>Harvey Wall Banger</u>; when the owner first had him, whenever the owner tried to pick him up the iguana would dash across the aquarium until he hit a wall, then would turn around and do the same thing in the opposite direction

[31]because the owners' cat found the iguana in the back yard and had lanced it with her claw in an attempt to capture it (it's full name is <u>Sir Lancellot-Link</u>)

[32]Spanish for little black one; very sick and almost black when received

[33]very orange

[34]tail was broken when given to the current owners

[35]tail broke off when he was little

[36]as in "Is He gonna live or die?"

APPENDIX D

Construction of the Ultimate Iguana Habitat™

In the main text of the book, I discussed the principles for creating an excellent captive habitat for your green iguana. For those who want more details on actual construction, I've concentrated them in this appendix.

Over the years I have seen cages for adult iguanas that cost from $250 to more than $1,300, not including any of the habitat equipment. And most looked like they were designed for snakes or other reptiles that don't require large or tall spaces. The Ultimate Iguana Habitat is a great design and a good bargain if you decide to use it.

The construction guidelines for the Juvenile and Adult Habitat are basically the same, except the adult uses more materials and is larger in size. This appendix will give most of the details you'll need to construct one or both of these habitats.

BLUE PRINTS

I originally intended to insert or print a set of plans in this book so you could work directly from them to build the Ultimate Habitat. This idea turned out to be logistically impractical.

Instead, I offer the drawings and word descriptions in this appendix. In addition, on the following pages I will take the habitat apart by sections and describe how each is constructed. Although I have included what I hope are very detailed explanations of the construction, this book is not the forum for describing every single assembly detail.

As my publisher reminded me, this is a book about iguanas, not a manual for cage-building. Whether you do the building yourself, or get help from a more experienced builder, the descriptions of materials and construction—along with a little common sense, some understanding of how things go together, and a basic knowledge of how to use a few power tools—should provide the groundwork needed for a terrific habitat.

MATERIALS

The materials needed to build the structure of either the Juvenile or the Adult Ultimate Iguana Habitat will cost approximately $200 to $400, depending on which habitat you build, local materials costs, seasonal variations, and other factors. There will be

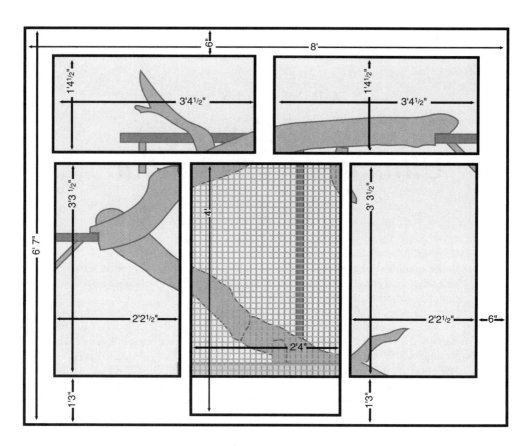

Figure D.1: Ultimate Iguana Habitat: Adult

additional costs for glass, timers, light bulbs, electronic equipment, and the materials to hook them up.

To make life simpler, it's easier to purchase the framing materials in 8' lengths. This is a common length at lumberyards and is easy to take home. The framing materials also include the door and interior support for the windows. The framing members you will be using are specially cut dimensions of 1½" x 2¼". They are cut from a standard 2x6 piece of wood. You will get two of these pieces from each board. All of this will be explained in the following pages in detail.

It's impossible for me to estimate the number of hours it will take to build your iguana's habitat. Some people work faster than I do, while others are much slower. If you decide to have your habitat built by a professional, the detailed descriptions in this appendix might provide enough of a guideline for doing a labor cost estimate.

The materials list is approximate, depending on how everything is measured, cut, and screwed.

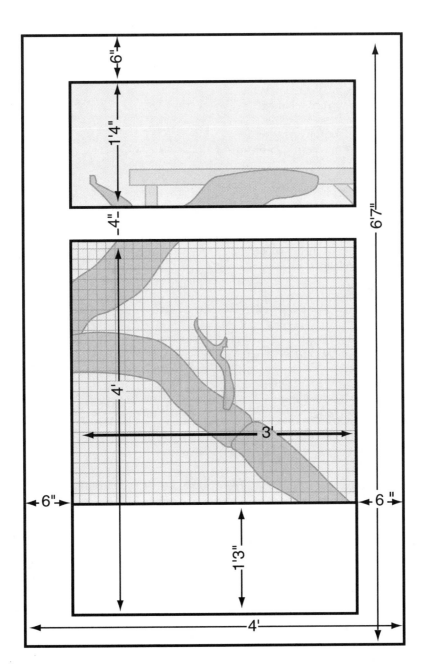

Figure D.2: Ultimate Iguana Habitat: Juvenile

Habitat Materials List (Approximate)	Juvenile	Adult
• Rough framing materials (2" x 6" x 8')	11 boards	13 boards
• Window frame (1x3)	9'	45'
• Trim		
— around glass, door, and vents		
($\frac{3}{4}$" x $\frac{1}{2}$" screen molding)	32'	75'
— to secure glass ($\frac{1}{4}$" round)	9'	52'
— wall corners, top and bottom		
($3\frac{1}{2}$" x $\frac{1}{2}$" primed MDS board)	36'	44'
• Plywood		
— Adult Habitat		
– ceiling (4' x 8' x $\frac{5}{8}$" CDX)	—	1 sheet
– floor (4' x 8' x $\frac{3}{4}$" CDX)	—	1 sheet
— Juvenile Habitat		
– ceiling and floor (4' x 8' x $\frac{3}{4}$" CDX)	1 sheet	—
• Masonite—exterior sheets (4' x 8' x $\frac{1}{8}$")	9 sheets	14 sheets
• Rigid foam insulation—walls (4' x 8' x 2")	$3\frac{1}{2}$ sheets	5 sheets
• Screws		
— to assemble the frame		
(Grabbers® $2\frac{1}{4}$" long)	30	30
— to secure glass to frame (#8 wood		
screws, $1\frac{1}{2}$" long)	3	12
— wall assembly (#10 wood screws,		
4" long)	40	48
• Flat washers ($\frac{1}{4}$" diameter hole)	40	48
• Nails—exterior sheets (18ga. $\frac{5}{8}$")	3 sm. boxes	6 sm. boxes
• Tile caulking—interior seal	3 tubes	5 tubes
• Paint	ask your paint salesperson	

Paint

> *We put eight coats of a waterproofing paint on the cage (we special ordered it from our local lumberyard/hardware store). It's totally non-toxic and odorless. You need to use twice as much as regular paint because it is very thin, but it's worth it.*
>
>   —conversation at a herp meeting

Whether you use the design described here or one of your own, you need to use the right paint on the inside and outside of your habitat. <u>Don't use any paint that may be toxic</u>. Tell the paint sales person that you want an environmentally friendly product to paint a room for a baby (human). Sometimes humans can understand protecting humans better than protecting reptiles.

Water-based paint is quick-drying and the paint brushes clean up with water. Oil-based paint is slower to dry and requires solvents such as thinner to clean the brushes, but some people feel it gives a better result than water-based paints. In either case, be sure to allow at least a few days for the paint to completely dry and for the smell to disappear. Remember, fumes are magnified inside an enclosed container.

CONSTRUCTING THE HABITAT, PIECE BY PIECE

Follow the instructions in the next pages to build the back wall, side walls, front wall, floor, ceiling, door, and windows for the Ultimate Iguana Habitat. Read all of this appendix at least once before starting to cut your first piece of lumber.

Walls

On page 605 you will see a detailed drawing (Figure D.3) of how all the habitat walls are constructed. They are lightweight, strong, and insulated with rigid foam insulation (R-value of about 13). All you have to do now is pick which size habitat you want to build.

The width of the side walls for the Juvenile and Adult Habitats can vary from 32" to 34". Except for specific cuts for windows and a door, the framing concept will be the same for both sizes.

The walls begin with a wooden frame consisting of the specially cut 1½" x 2¼" lumber. The lumber needs to be exactly 2¼" to accommodate the rigid foam insulation, which is 2" thick. The extra ¼" is necessary for a heat storage pocket—⅛" on each side of the insulation.

Non-Insulated Wall

Some parts of the country may not need an insulated cage like the one described. If your climate is always hot, you can use this same habitat concept but without the double-wall design.

Instead of using masonite (which won't work on single-wall construction) use either plywood or a product called melamine. Many of the finer-built kitchens use melamine for interior shelving and sometimes for the cabinet doors. It's a particle board construction (bits of wood chips compressed with glue) with a plastic-like laminate exterior. Any stain is easily cleaned up. For building the floor, you can use the same design as in the original Ultimate Habitat (minus the rigid foam insulation).

Another scenario might be that you have cold winters and hot summers. In this case, perhaps you could use the insulated cage design, but make a set of screens to replace the glass windows during hot weather. If all the glass area is converted to open screens, you'd have less chance of heat build-up inside the habitat. Or mix and match for your particular climate: Maybe the top glass is replaced with screen and the lower glass remains, or vice versa. Play with various options until you create the right conditions.

If you change from the original design, you become a pioneer. As a result, you have to solve your own problems that may come up. Good luck—pioneer!

Cuts

Most lumberyards will cut your boards to the exact thickness for little or no cost if done in the middle of the week, when business is usually slower. Ask them to cut some of their standard 2x6 framing material into two pieces 2¼" wide. Here's "builder's talk" for how these cuts are made: You will get two lengths of 2¼" out of the 2x6 (actual 5½") x 8' material (2¼" + 2¼" = 4½", plus ⅛" for each saw cut (¼") = 4¾" total, which means ¾" of material is waste).

IMPORTANT for the Adult Habitat only: The actual height of the habitat is determined by the height of the door (in your house). For example, if your house door opening is 6' 8", make the height of the habitat walls at least 1" less (6' 7") so the walls will fit through the door. The height of the Juvenile Habitat is not a problem because the walls can be turned on their sides (4') to come through the door.

Back Wall

Because the back wall has no openings for windows, doors, or vents, it is the most "basic" of the habitat walls. The following instructions work for both the Juvenile and Adult Habitats, except where indicted or obvious.

Frame

First, cut the framing members (1½" x 2¼") to the proper length and width of the wall. The frame should be glued and screwed together with screws called Grabbers (because they never let go!). Drill a pilot hole before driving the screws into the wood, to reduce the possibility of the wood splitting. IMPORTANT: **The 2¼" depth rests on the ground; this will be the depth or thickness of the wall.** This space (depth) will later be filled with the 2" insulation. If the 1½" side goes down on the ground by mistake, your insulation will stick above the wall edge about ½". You will have made a big mistake!

On the Adult Habitat (only), where the two sheets of masonite butt together, you will need an additional framing member to support these sheets.

Skin

The skin, or outer covering, of the habitat wall is made from 4' x 8' sheets of ⅛" masonite and requires pre-painting on both sides before it is attached to the frame. Many woodpressed products contain glues that can produce obnoxious odors. By pre-painting the masonite with two coats on each side, you help reduce or eliminate this potential problem. Using a paint roller makes this job go a million times faster.

SIDEBAR

What Lumber Numbers Really Mean

When a lumberyard sells you 2x6 framing material, it's really 1½" x 5½". Why the confusing terminology? Over a century of trying to make more profit, the dimensions of lumber have slowly been reduced from the original measurement of a true 2" x 6". This concept also applies to most of the other measured lumber (e.g., 2x4 is really 1½" x 3½").

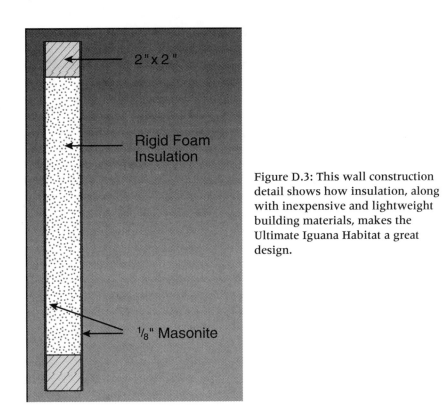

Figure D.3: This wall construction detail shows how insulation, along with inexpensive and lightweight building materials, makes the Ultimate Iguana Habitat a great design.

Because masonite is a hard substance, it needs to be pre-drilled about every 3"-4" and ¼"-½" from the edge.

Squaring

Once the frame is assembled, use a framing square (or the 3,4,5 squaring technique—Pythagorean's theorem) to make sure the wall is square. **IMPORTANT: Make sure the wall is square before nailing!** If all of your walls are a little out of square, even just a little, you'll have trouble assembling the habitat. Put the pre-cut and pre-drilled masonite section in place and nail it.

Insulation

Rigid foam insulation has foil on both sides and a kind of styrofoam center. Any pieces that are cut off from the original 4' x 8' sheet can be placed in smaller voids or pockets of the walls.

Once the masonite is secured, flip the wall over and cut the rigid foam insulation to fit inside the opening of the wall cavity. Put some glue on top of the frame, then the other sheet(s) of masonite, and nail it in place. What you have now is a masonite insulated sandwich that is strong and lightweight.

Side Walls

The side walls are constructed in the same way and in the same sequence as the back wall. The only difference is that these walls are shorter than the front and back walls, and they have vent holes.

The ceiling on both the Adult and Juvenile Habitats rests on top of the side walls. It's necessary that you <u>cut the side walls 3" shorter for the Adult and 3⅛" for the Juvenile Habitat (the thickness of the ceiling) than the front and back walls</u>. This way, when the top is put in position it will be flush with the front and back walls and will form a tight, interlocking connection.

You will be cutting out air vents on these side walls, but first look straight at the habitat (as if it were assembled). The vent on the left side is the lower vent. The bottom of the lower (left) vent is about 7½" off the room floor. The bottom of the upper (right) vent is 4' 6" from the floor (or just below the bottom of the upper glass window). Both vent openings are 14½" long, 3" wide, and centered in the middle of the wall.

Once you have the frame and the skin completed on both sides of the wall, it's time to cut out the vent holes. Because the Juvenile and Adult Habitats are essentially the same construction, the location of the vents is also the same.

First, lay out your measurements for the lower (left) vent on the masonite and cut the holes out with a circular or jig saw. Flip the wall over and make the same vent measurements again and cut them out. You now have a vent hole through the side of the habitat. Place lengths of the 1½" x 2¼" framing material around the inside edge of the vent hole to give it more support and backing for trim pieces that will be added later. Glue and nail these pieces in place.

Next, take some of the firm plastic netting (described on page 608, "'Non-Freedom' Door") and nail the ¾" screen molding on top of both sides of the wall to hold the netting in place. This also adds a decorative look to match the rest of the habitat trim coming up.

Do this same routine with the other side wall, except the vent location will be the higher one (right side).

Front Wall

The front wall, with its glass and the door, has the most measuring and cutting, but it's pretty straightforward. Again, look at the drawings to get a clearer picture of what you will be doing.

Assemble the front wall frame like the back wall. For the Adult Habitat, lay two sheets (4' x 8' each) of masonite, butted together side-by-side, on top of the frame, lined up with the edges of the frame, but do not nail the masonite yet. You will also need another framing member (Adult Habitat only) to support the two pieces of masonite where they butt together (except, of course, in the door opening). Mark the door and window openings from the drawing directly on the masonite. With a circular saw, delicately cut out the openings and any masonite that's too long.

Put the masonite back on top and nail it in place. Put framing members inside the openings like you did for the vents. These framing members go flush with the edge of the openings. Now nail them in place. These boards will be used later for backing to screw the window frames in place, for supporting the door, and for nailing on the trim.

Turn the wall over (you will need help with the Adult Habitat so nothing breaks) and cut insulation to fit the wall voids. With the insulation in place, put the two pieces of masonite (Adult Habitat) side by side. Nail the masonite and trim off any extra.

Now comes the delicate part of cutting the openings through the solid wall you just created. First, however, turn the wall over again (get help) so the cut-out wall is facing you. Hammer a nail through the masonite at each corner of the windows and door. Get some help again and turn the wall back over.

Where you see the nail holes, use a straight edge to connect these points. The outline should look like the windows and door that have already been cut out (on the other side). Cross your fingers and cut out the openings, then nail the perimeters of the opening to the framing material. The rest of the construction is a snap compared to what you just accomplished.

Floor

The size of the floor is the dimension of the inside of the habitat. The habitat floor is constructed like the walls, except that it needs ¾" plywood for strength to support your weight as you step in and out of the habitat. First make the frame, then cut and nail the plywood on the frame. Turn it over, and if you think you have extra insulation, you can put some in the voids. Then nail the masonite in place, and you now have a thermal barrier.

Your iguana's feces can soak into the open grain of the plywood, sometimes even when painted, so I recommend putting a plastic laminate covering on top of the plywood. (A well-known brand of plastic laminate is called Formica®. If you purchase a generic brand instead of the brand name, you can often save 30%. Many major paint or tile stores carry plastic laminate and can cut it to size for you.) This makes the floor impervious to urea, or just about anything else.

Another option is to use a full sheet of linoleum. Again, tell the salesperson that you want an environmentally safe product that's appropriate for a child's room. Small squares of linoleum are not recommended, as urea can get between the squares and eventually get into the plywood. You will need to use a special linoleum glue to secure this material in place.

The first cage had a solid linoleum floor. A breeze to clean and disinfect.
—I-808, Priscilla, 25 yrs., Iowa

Ceiling

Once again, the ceiling is like the wall construction except ⅝" plywood is used on one side of the frame instead of masonite (¾" will be used for the Juvenile Habitat).

The plywood side faces into the habitat and is what the 4' fluorescent light fixtures (full-spectrum lights) are screwed into. When purchasing the plywood, get the kind that has special glue able to withstand moisture (it's called CDX in most states). The plywood needs to be painted several times on both sides to seal the wood, as it will be exposed to high heat and humidity every day. Painting a light or white color will help to reflect the lighting better.

IMPORTANT: Be sure to put insulation in the ceiling, as this will help hold the heat in the habitat. Also, <u>before</u> you paint the plywood, make pencil lines where the fluorescent fixtures will be located. <u>Don't</u> paint these areas! I did, and the heat from the lights caused a disgusting odor. I had to go back later, remove the lights, and scrape the paint off to bare wood around the fixtures. What a pain!

Door

Now that the habitat is complete, it needs windows and doors to seal it up like a house. For my iguana's habitat, I had two kinds of doors; each had its own special purpose. You can either copy these ideas down to the letter or create your own door(s).

"Non-Freedom" Door

I called this first door a "non-freedom" door because my iguana could come out of his habitat only when I removed it. The frame was made out of ¾" thick wood stock, and the width was cut to the thickness of the habitat wall.

To help cool the habitat in the spring and summer, the back side of the door had a screen on it. Instead of wire mesh, which can cut an iguana's foot as it climbs, I used a plastic netting that is hard and smooth (used also for the side wall vents). I heard about this product when I was learning aquaculture many years ago.

I have resisted recommending specific products in this book, but no other alternative works as well as this plastic screen. The name of the product is "InterNet" and it's a strong plastic netting that's used by fish farmers. It is listed in Appendix B for your convenience because you will probably never see it advertised anywhere, not even in any of the herp publications.

I used the ¼" mesh size (product number XV-1170), which I stapled to the back of the door, then put the same ¾" wide window screen molding on top to give the door a finished look.

To keep the door from falling into the habitat, I again used the flat ¾" screen molding as a strip around the outside of the door. About ⅜" of the molding rested against the frame of the habitat, giving the door support. I used one eye hook latch on each side of the door frame to keep the door secured. If you have children you may want to beef up the security of the door.

To hold the heat in the habitat during winter, I put a piece of Plexiglas® (⅛") on the front, held in place with Velcro®. With 5-minute epoxy, I put one side of the Velcro around the door opening and the other piece on the Plexiglas. The Velcro made it easy to put on or take off the plastic. Because Oregon has some rapid weather changes, even in the spring I often attached the Plexiglas before I went to sleep at night as a precaution.

Freedom Door

This second door was created for my iguana when he was about 4 years old, and it was used <u>only</u> on warm days and when I was home. By then Za had proven that he could be trusted to come out of the habitat on his own and not get into trouble.

This door was similar to the "non-freedom" door except it was made out of ¼" stock and had ¹⁄₁₆" Plexiglas glued to the front and back of the door frame. This door was different because at the bottom it had an 11" x 27" opening for Za to move in and out of the habitat as he pleased (this was used only when I was home). I also painted the opening with some festive, bright, Mexican colors so he knew that this door was different from the other one—that he could get out.

At night when his lights went off he was always in his habitat, even if he had been out all day. As soon as he was inside I put his non-freedom door back on for security. It made me sleep better at night knowing the little "monster" couldn't get out. In the summer when I first woke up I would take the non-freedom door off and replace it with his freedom door. Allowing Za out was good for him and even better for me—I loved having him near me as much as possible every day.

Windows

The windows for the habitat are made from standard 1x3 (¾" x 2½") stock. Cut the material to the size of the window opening, then make a dado cut around the edge.

Nail and glue the pieces together. Place the glass into the dado groove, and put a strip of "quarter round" trim on top of the glass. When you nail the trim in place, don't angle the nails too sharply or you might hit and fracture the glass.

The finished, painted window frame slides into the window opening that has already been cut out. Don't put the window in place until the whole habitat is finally assembled (details coming up).

Around the outside of the window, use the same ¾" window screen molding used on the door, with ⅜" sticking into the opening. The window frame will enter from inside the habitat and will butt up against this wood. Using the same trim for the windows and door gives the habitat a uniform, finished, clean, professional look.

The best glass to use is cheap glass. Look back in Chapter 4, Housing, "Getting a Habitat Built," for ways of getting this glass. Glass ideally should be tempered, like the windshield of your car, so if you (or a child) happen to break the glass, it will shatter in small pieces. But tempered glass costs more and it is harder to get the exact size you need. My iguana's habitat had regular glass because it was cheaper and we don't have children or other animals in the house.

IMPORTANT: The Ultimate Habitat is designed to function with thermostats, cooling fans, backup heater, and full-spectrum lighting. To build this habitat and not use these items could cause major, perhaps even life-threatening, problems for your lizard. As an example, without the fans (set on a thermostat) in the summer, the habitat heat could get increasingly hotter until it becomes a killing box.

IMPORTANT: If the temperature of the room where your habitat is located happens to be 100°F, then the temperature in the habitat will surely be over 100°F. Even the best habitat fan system can't get the temperature inside the habitat much below the room temperature. Similarly, if you have a simple heater in the habitat and the room temperature is 50°F or so, it will be almost impossible to maintain 85°F in the habitat.

IMPORTANT: These precautions may sound obvious, but for some people maintaining a habitat is a new experience. The point is that many heaters and fans can correct only a specific range of heat or cold. If your habitat is in a room within the guidelines, everything seems to work fine. But outside these parameters nothing is for sure!

The original Ultimate Habitat is still working today, with more than six years of steady, reliable performance. The habitat operates in our living room (15' x 25') where temperatures never drop below 68 or 69°F or get above about 80°F. Under these conditions, the upper ledge area in the habitat stays at about 90°F, the next level down is about 85°F, and the bottom is about 80°F. Any temperatures above or below the tested baselines might cause problems for your habitat and lizard. Keep your room within the tested temperatures and you will have a very reliable habitat.

All of the equipment necessary to operate the Ultimate Habitat or any other type of habitat is explained in Chapter 4, Housing, "Habitat Equipment."

ASSEMBLY

Now that you have all the pieces, it's time to put them together.

Walls

The front and back walls screw into the side walls. But first you will need to make some pilot holes for the screws. The pilot holes should be just large enough so the screws slide easily through the first wall. You want the biting power of the screw to be in the second wall. The pilot hole for the second wall should be less than half the diameter of the screw you are using. This pilot hole will reduce the chances of the wood splitting, make screwing easier, and help the walls fit together tighter.

To hold the walls together, use #10 wood screws that are 4" long. Place six screws, equally spaced from each other, at each wall junction (total of 12 for the front and 12 for the back in the Adult Habitat). Use a flat metal washer for each screw to keep the screw head from pulling through the wall. Tighten down the screws until they are snug. I used an electric drill motor with a screw tip for faster assembly.

You will probably need some help holding the walls steady as you get ready to screw them together. Since I had no one to help me, I found it useful to use pipe clamps to hold the walls tight as I screwed them together.

First, place the floor of the habitat into position, then bring the long back and one side wall together. Make sure the corners are flush and square, then screw them together. Now bring the front and other side wall into place and do the same process again.

Next, screw the front and back walls to the floor section with six screws (and washers) per wall. Now is the time to put the habitat where you want it. After the ceiling, windows, and door are in place, <u>it may be too heavy or awkward to move</u> (Adult Habitat only). Put the ceiling in place and screw it into position with the same screw-and-washer routine as before.

With everything assembled, take a tube of tile caulking and put a bead of it around the whole inside of the habitat where the walls, floor, and ceiling meet. This will make the habitat air tight. Let the caulking set up overnight. You can come back later and paint it the same color as the inside of the habitat so it blends in better.

Trim

To add the finishing touch to the habitat, use MDS molding to create a "frame" around the front edge of the habitat (see the photo of my Adult Ultimate Iguana Habitat in the color section). MDS is a man-made wood product that is often less than half the price of regular wood. It's made out of compressed wood fibers and looks good painted. Don't glue these boards in place, as you will have to "pop" them off if you disassemble the habitat at a later date. Use small finish nails sparingly here. Pick widths that you feel are aesthetically balanced for your habitat. I used $2\frac{1}{2}$" x $\frac{1}{2}$" on the front and $3\frac{1}{2}$" x $\frac{1}{2}$" on the sides. Where two walls meet, join the MDS molding with a miter cut to make a perfect corner. These boards also cover up the area where the front and side walls meet.

Windows

Put the windows in the opening and secure them with a total of three screws for each window frame (use pilot holes to reduce the chance of splitting wood).

Ceiling

For the Adult Habitat, drill a hole in the habitat ceiling and run the power cord into the habitat, for the three 4' shop fixtures (for the full-spectrum lights). Next, connect the power cord to the individual light fixtures (IMPORTANT: make sure the power supply is disconnected first!), then screw the light fixtures (get the type that can be used around moisture) to the plywood ceiling. Note: The Juvenile Habitat has the same procedure, but it has only one or two 4' light fixtures, which will have to be angled to fit.

IMPORTANT: Put five or six ½" x 2½" x 2½" wood spacers (per fixture) between the plywood ceiling and the fixtures. If the fixtures are screwed directly to the ceiling the wood gets too hot. The spacers also allow heat from the fixtures to dissipate more easily.

Interior

Assemble the following parts and equipment. (The description of all of the special habitat equipment is in Chapter 4, Housing.)

Ledges (see Appendix F for more details)

- Screw the pre-assembled ledges to the inside wall of the habitat; see drawing on page 600.
- Use "toggle" screws as they can hold more weight and need no special backing.
- Adjust the height of the ledge depending on how large your lizard is. The lights should be about 6" to 8" from your iguana as it rests on the shelf. As the iguana gets bigger, you will need to lower the shelf away from the lights.

Ceramic Heater (with built-in thermostat)

- Drill a hole in the far left corner of the habitat ceiling (close to the front of the glass) so the power cord from the heater can be pushed up through the hole. This cord will eventually be plugged into your house outlet. Hint: To avoid drilling an excessively large hole in the ceiling to accommodate the width of the male plug end, cut the plug off and just run the wire through the small hole. Then put a new male plug end on the wire once it's outside the habitat.
- Screw the ceramic heater to the ceiling of the habitat (use a metal bracket if necessary). Face it toward the back of the habitat.
- To control heat loss, caulk around the hole where the cord came through the ceiling.

Fans

- Drill a hole through the right side wall for the power cords for the fans, and push the wires through the hole.
- Screw the fans under the right ledge in front of the air vent for better circulation, heat removal, and safety. Because it is under the ledge, there is less chance your iguana's tail will get hit by the fan blades. Also, orient the fan blades so they turn in the direction that will blow air into the habitat.
- Connect these wires to the thermostatically controlled environmental system you have purchased.

Self-Regulating Heat Source (Iguanamometer™)—Optional

The Iguanamometer is experimental and an option. Appendix E shows how to set up the actual device if you decide to use it.

- Drill a hole in the ceiling above the iguana's ledge in the far left corner. Shove the power cord, which brings power to the heat source, through this hole. Secure the ceramic holder for the heat bulb close to the ceiling.
- Install the heat bulb and wire cage (to protect your lizard from accidentally being burned).
- Put your Iguanamometer device in place according to the instructions in Appendix E.
- Connect the power supply cord to the heat bulb.

Multi-Plug Device (Power Strip)

- Screw this to the outside right-side wall, near the top. All plugs for the electrically operated devices will plug into this grounded strip.

Environmental Systems Control

- If you are using one of these systems, screw it into the same area as the multi-plug device.

Other Items

- Attach your limbs, ramps (if necessary), and artificial plants. You are now ready to turn on your habitat and will be able to relax for years to come, since everything is automatic. Let the habitat operate without your iguana in it for a couple of days to make sure the lights and heat work correctly.

DISASSEMBLY

In case you need to disassemble the Ultimate Habitat, simply follow the assembly process in reverse. The only special thing you will need to do is take a sharp knife and cut into all the corners inside the habitat where you put the caulking. Over time this soft putty turns semi-solid. You will also have to gently "pop" off the exterior corner trim. It's an artificial wood and can break or chip easily. If it does chip, put wood putty in the broken area, sand, repaint, and all is well again.

When I moved from California to Oregon, I disassembled my iguana's Adult Ultimate Habitat and the movers put the parts in the moving van. Nothing got broken during shipment, and everything worked when I put it together again. Life should always be so easy!

APPENDIX E

Iguanamometer™

The Iguanamometer™ is an ingenious self-regulating heating device for your iguana, which can be used inside or outside a habitat. As mentioned in Chapter 4, Housing, the Iguanamometer was designed by my friend Cris Shiebold, a talented engineer and president of the Shiebold Consulting Group.

For perspective, however, I should note that my iguana grew up big, strong, and healthy without the Iguanamometer. This device is an option for those people trying to achieve maximum effect of everything, and is by no means required apparatus for any iguana.

HOW IT WORKS

The Iguanamometer works like the automatic doors at some grocery stores, often called "electric eye." The big difference is that a heat source comes on instead of a door opening.

On one side of this device is a photo sensor (photo-electric switch), and on the opposite side is a low-wattage light that directs a light beam at the sensor (see page xx for a drawing of the Iguanamometer). When your iguana crosses the light beam (blocks the light), the heat source comes on. When the lizard leaves the space and the light beam reestablishes contact with the photo sensor, the heat source goes off. The reason your lizard leaves the area is that it is hot and wants to get away from the heat.

Training

You will have to physically put your iguana where the switch apparatus is located, perhaps many times, before it "understands" the process of using the Iguanamometer. For a more dramatic effect, try doing this in the morning before your iguana's lights come on, when its body is the coldest and it will feel the instant effects of the heat light. As mentioned in Chapter 4, Housing, Bruce A. Kingsbury wrote a paper proving that lizards <u>could</u> learn to self-regulate their heat with an external device. Be patient.

The Iguanamometer is a simple and efficient, yet advanced, thermoregulating device. But remember, it is cause and effect: If your iguana doesn't learn to use the device, it won't come on.

SETTING UP THE IGUANAMOMETER

Parts

The Iguanamometer can be constructed using simple parts that can be found at most large hardware stores. Refer to the drawing on page xx to picture how these parts work together.

Photo Sensor (Switch)

You need a photo sensor like the kind used to turn an outdoor light on automatically (one example is the Hemco part #758C, capacity 150 maximum watts). Get a sensor that is waterproof and that does not have a time delay. Many photo sensors have time delays built in to prevent false triggering of the switch. You want a sensor that turns the heat on as soon as the light beam is blocked. This way, the iguana makes the mental connection between its movements and the heat coming on. The photo sensor can be purchased at most hardware stores for about $9, and any brand with the right wattage, waterproofing, and without a time delay is fine.

All you have to do to the standard sensor is add a 1½" piece of plastic tubing over the end, which eliminates any background light from tripping the sensor. To secure your sensor in place, use whatever works for your particular situation, such as a hose clamp, or build it into the wall of the habitat. If used outside the habitat, be creative.

Low-Wattage Light Bulb

The sensor is very light-sensitive, so all you need is a simple 6-watt indicator or appliance bulb (e.g., General Electric part #656) to create a light beam. This bulb screws into a standard candelabra socket base and is placed directly across from the photo sensor. You can vary the distance from the light and the sensor, depending on how large your iguana is and your placement needs. (The set-up I used had a space of 8".) At a certain distance the light will be too far away from the sensor to make contact and will not work.

Some kind of hood or cover, such as a small capped tube of any heat-resistant material, needs to be put over the bulb to confine the light. Make sure this cover is large enough that it slides easily over the bulb without touching it (which might cause the cover to get too hot), but not so large that the light has too much space to bounce around in and loses its intensity.

Drill a hole into the side of the hood cover so the light beam can emerge. It can then be aimed directly toward the photo sensor. The hole should be at the same level as the photo sensor tubing, so the two can "look at each other." In my model, the "eyeball" hole was ¼".

Simply line up the light source ("eyeball") with the photo sensor and they are ready for action. Any object (e.g., your iguana) that breaks the light beam from the bulb to the sensor will switch the heat source on.

The Iguanamometer diagram on page 616 will help those who understand electrical devices; for everyone else, it will at least help you picture how it looks.

Heat Source

You can use any standard incandescent bulb (40 to 150 watts, or so) for the heat source—or ideally use the new kind of cone-shaped, ceramic infrared heating bulb

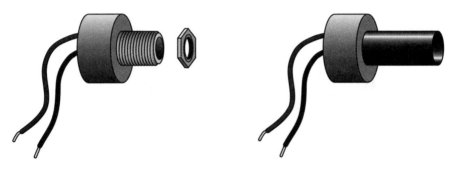

Figure E.1: Photo sensor switch: before and after deflector tubing is in place

designed especially for heating reptiles. The ceramic heating element screws into a light socket like an incandescent bulb, but it produces no light. It targets its long-wave infrared heat to penetrate deep into the lizard's body without generating a lot of excess heat in the habitat. This is important when used in enclosed habitat designs such as the Ultimate Iguana Habitat. You can find these heating bulbs at pet stores or through herp magazines.

Placement

In the Ultimate Habitat, the Iguanamometer would go at the left side of the iguana's top resting ledge area. Place the sensor on one side of the ledge, with the light source opposite it. The heat bulb (and its ceramic receptacle) can be placed in the far upper left corner of the habitat, where the iguana receives the heat but can't touch the bulb. The heat source also needs a protective wire mesh screen around it, so if the lizard accidentally comes in contact with the hot bulb it won't get burned.

For all habitat designs, place the sensor <u>away from normal activity</u> in the habitat, so the lizard has to make a conscious decision that it is going to the specific area to get warm.

It's important to locate the Iguanamometer so that the lizard can get easy access to it and has space to bask comfortably. And just as important, when the lizard wants to move out of the heat, there must be a limb, ramp, ledge, or something to make its exit easy, smooth, and safe. These things, plus the warmth of the lamp, will help the iguana <u>learn</u> the process more easily.

Reminder: Experimental!

The Iguanamometer is an experimental design at this time. With any new device or product, many things go right and a few things can go wrong. No problems have occurred to date with this device, and it functions according to the design, but it has not been in use for enough hours, or by a sufficiently large sample group, to take it off experimental status yet.

If you build an Iguanamometer, you will automatically become a researcher! One part of experimenting means "use at your own risk." Below are just a few possible problems that could arise. With luck, you can figure out and prevent any other future problem before it happens.

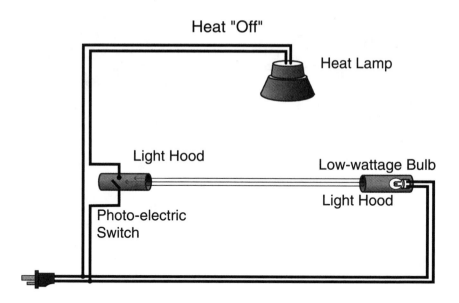

Heat "Off"

Heat Lamp

Light Hood

Low-wattage Bulb

Light Hood

Photo-electric
Switch

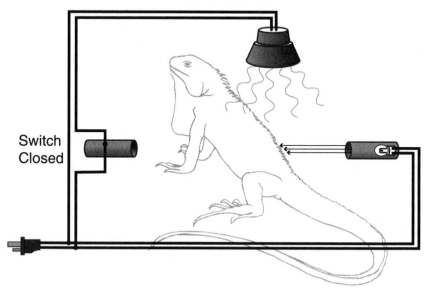

Heat "On"

Switch
Closed

Figure E.2: The Iguanamometer™ self-regulating heat control device

- Any loose material (e.g., stuffed sock) accidentally dragged into the light beam would make the light stay on, creating excessive heat. Keep loose items secured or as far away from the sensor as possible.
- If the light hood is not secured properly and is allowed to move, even a little, the "eyeball" hole may not look at the sensor and the heat light will never come on. The solution is to make sure the hood can't be knocked out of position.
- There might be some more, but that's all I can think of.

Write me and let me know how the Iguanamometer works for you.

APPENDIX F
Creating "Custom" Limbs and Ledges

If nature doesn't provide a limb of the exact length and shape to fit in your iguana's habitat, or if you decide to add ledges like those included in the Ultimate Iguana Habitat design, here are some hints for building customized climbing and resting areas for your iguana.

Creating "Custom" Limbs

You can create any limb configuration in your iguana's habitat simply by bolting or doweling different limb parts together (look at page 620 for a detail limb assembly drawing).

Permanent Limbs

If you want two separate limbs to be permanently joined together, drill a hole (maybe 1" to 3" deep, depending on the length of the limb) in the ends of both of them, put some 5-minute epoxy in the two limb holes, insert a wooden dowel, and push them together. When the resin hardens, you will have a single, strong "created" limb.

Limbs That Disassemble

I have one huge basking limb in my iguana's habitat, and the only way I could get it in there was in sections. If you want a limb that disassembles into parts, look at the "Temporary Attachment" portion of the limb drawing. (Note: The temporary attachment works only for side limbs, not end-to-end connections.) In this case, drill a hole partway into one limb and all the way through the other. Put the epoxy only in the partial hole.

Instead of a wooden dowel, use a steel support rod. The rod is called "all-thread" because its whole length is threaded to accept a nut. These rods are available in various diameters and lengths at most large hardware stores. The ones I used ranged from ¼" to ½" in diameter.

Cut the rod to the appropriate length, then shove one end of it into the hole that has epoxy and let it set up. Once the rod hardens in the hole, you can slide the other end into the limb drilled all the way through. Enough of the all-thread needs to stick out of the other limb to receive a flat metal washer and nut to strongly join the limbs together. To hide the metal nuts, epoxy (or use a hot glue gun) some plastic artificial plants on top of them.

With these attaching methods, you can create any limb angle or length you want. All you need are the limbs, wood dowels, all-thread, nuts, steel washers, electric drill motor and bits, hand saw, epoxy, and imagination. In the Ultimate Adult Habitat (interior) drawing in Chapter 4, Housing, you can get an idea of how several limbs joined together look.

Building the Ledges

Making ledges for your iguana to lie on is easy. When my iguana reached 5' and 13 pounds, his upper main ledge was 12" wide and 7' long. His sleeping and hiding ledge area (along the right wall of the habitat) was 8" wide and 2' long.

First, cut ⅝" to ¾" plywood to the desired width and length. Next, you need to cut a backing board for the ledge so you can attach the ledge to the wall of the habitat. This backing board is made of the same ⅝" to ¾" plywood and is about 3" wide and the length of the ledge. Put the ledge on top of the backing board's edge and glue and nail them together to form a 90° angle.

To make the ledge stronger, glue and nail a support brace under both ends of the ledge (see the Ultimate Adult Habitat [interior] drawing in Chapter 4, Housing). These support pieces will stiffen the ledge, so when your iguana rests on top it won't bend down. Another option is to put a solid triangular piece of plywood in the angle formed by the ledge and the backing board.

For extra safety and to make it easier for your lizard to move and turn around, glue and nail a 2" tall guard rail (made out of plywood) on the front edge of this ledge.

Securing the Ledges

The ledge unit is attached to the walls of the habitat with ¼" toggle bolts. If you are using the double-wall Ultimate Habitat design, the length of the toggles are 3¼". To secure the ledge to the wall, first pre-drill several ¼" diameter holes along the length of the backing board (if the ledge is 6' long, drill four to six holes). Next, hold the ledge where you want it on the habitat wall, make sure it's level, and mark the holes with a pencil.

Disassemble the toggles from the screw shaft. Put a metal washer on the screw shaft and shove this into the pre-drilled holes of the backing board, then put the toggle back on the screw shaft. Squeeze together one of the toggles (they fold back like a butterfly's wings) and this will be the diameter of the drill bit you will need next. Take this new-sized drill bit and drill holes through the interior wall (only) of the habitat (this assumes you're using double-wall construction like in the Ultimate Iguana Habitat) where you made your pencil marks. Now the butterflys can enter into the wall.

Push the backing board against the wall of the habitat and push the butterfly wings into each of the wall's holes. Once all butterflys are in the holes, slowly tighten down the screws until the toggles grab hold inside the habitat wall. You will have to pull the ledge away from the wall slightly to keep the toggles from spinning freely on the inside of the wall. Starting at your left, and working to your right, tighten each screw head the same amount until the board is tight against the habitat wall. If you don't tighten them equally, you won't be able to keep pressure on the other toggles and some of them will spin and won't tighten down.

(Note: If all of these directions sound too easy for you to understand, turn the book upside down, cover your right eye with your left hand, hold your left foot in your right

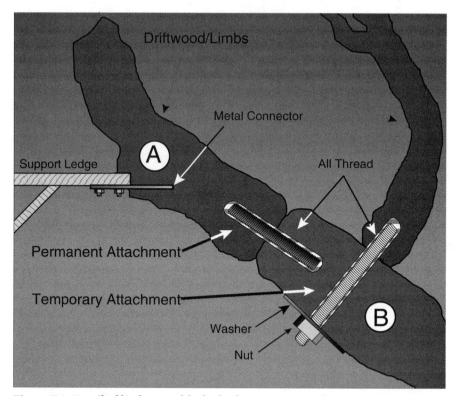

Figure F.1: Detail of limb assembly for both permanent and temporary "custom" limb attachments

hand, jump up and down in a counterclockwise circle while humming your favorite song—backwards—and now read!)

To keep your iguana from sliding off the slick plywood ledge surface, put a piece of indoor/outdoor carpeting (not astroturf) on top of the plywood. To secure the carpet to the ledge, use Velcro® strips glued in place with 5-minute epoxy. This way the carpet doesn't fall off the ledge as your iguana travels about in the habitat. When the carpet gets soiled, pull it up gently and the Velcro will let go; press the Velcro pieces together to put it back in place.

APPENDIX G:

Temporary Terrarium Set-Up (Hatchlings Only)

By design, a terrarium is an "open habitat," where the top is a wire mesh so the lizard can't escape—but heat does. This is in contrast to the Ultimate Iguana Habitat, which is "enclosed"; the top and all sides are solid and much of the heat generated inside stays there.

[In my iguana's cage,] there is ½" screen mesh on top to support the lights and provide ventilation. Unfortunately, the heat doesn't stay in the cage because of the mesh top.
—I-576, David, 24 yrs., New York

If you decide to use the temporary terrarium set-up, you will find a wide range of tank sizes. A good size to choose is 30" long, 12" wide, and 20" high, which sells for about $60. The pet store will also want to sell you a full-spectrum light, sticks for your iguana to climb on, heat lights, and a reptile heating pad that goes under the tank for warmth at night when the heat light is off. These are all important items, not just things the pet store is trying to sell to make money. The total bill could easily exceed $120, not including the iguana.

As I suggested in Chapter 4, Housing, "Terrarium," look in your local newspaper for a used terrarium and save perhaps half the original price.

The Set-Up

Placed on top of the terrarium's wire mesh is a full-spectrum fluorescent fixture; suspended above, but not on the wire, is a heat source for basking. As a side note, a full-spectrum light for this type of set-up (12" to 18") costs more than a 4' one used for the Ultimate Habitat.

The easiest thing to use on the bottom of the terrarium for a substrate to contain feces is newspaper. Even better is newspaper with two sections of paper towels masking taped to it. This arrangement is more absorbent and allows your iguana to wipe its vent more easily.

Next, you need to add some limbs for climbing and basking (thermoregulating). For comfortable basking by your hatchling, place one limb at an angle slightly off horizontal, running almost the full length of the cage. One end should be about 5" from the screened top of the terrarium, and the other end about 10" below the top. A second limb, extending from the floor of the terrarium and connecting to the basking limb, will act as a stairway or ladder. These climbing and resting branches not only provide optional height for thermoregulating, but also discourage your iguana from lying on the floor of the cage, which may be too cool and perhaps soiled with feces.

The iguana's water and food bowls should be heavy enough that they can't be accidentally knocked over (e.g., ceramic dog bowls). Put these bowls at the opposite end of the tank from the heat light, so the food doesn't dry out and the water won't evaporate. Also keep these bowls away from where your iguana normally defecates, if possible.

Iguanas need darkness at night, so attach a timer to the lights (like the kind used to turn an inside home light on and off at predetermined intervals while you are on vacation). To make sure the iguana has proper heat at night, purchase an under-terrarium tank heater from your pet store, and have the salesperson explain how these heaters work (they should not run the full length of the terrarium).

Young iguanas can get overloaded with the activities of a human household when first brought home, and one way to reduce this stress is to block the back side of the tank with paper. This way the lizard doesn't feel vulnerable from all directions at once. To create a more secluded place for your iguana for a while, wrap some additional paper on one end of the terrarium, perhaps where you iguana hides or sleeps, and extend it 7" to 10" high.

If your lizard still seems afraid (hides in the corner or under the substrate paper), build a private area. At the end of the terrarium away from the heat source and away from the spot where the lizard defecates, put a hide box (which is explained in detail in Chapter 4, Housing, "Hide Box"). This way the lizard has a place it can go to disappear from reality for a while. You can leave this hide box in place for a couple of weeks. If you find your lizard doesn't use it, take it out sooner.

Before you know it, your iguana will have outgrown this terrarium, and a larger habitat will be necessary. Look at the Ultimate Iguana Habitat in Chapter 4, Housing, or create your own design. In any case, get your lizard into a large habitat as soon as possible.

APPENDIX H

Egg-Laying (Nesting) Box

As mentioned several times in Chapter 9, Breeding, and Chapter 7, Medical Troubleshooting, sexually mature female iguanas can produce and lay eggs even if no male iguana is around. Without an appropriate nesting site, it is thought that captive female iguanas might hold on to their eggs instead of laying them. If this happens, serious medical problems can occur.

If you have a female iguana, a nesting box such as the one described here is a requirement. The box is simple to make, assembles and disassembles easily, and stores neatly in a small space so it can be reused every year.

Materials for the Nesting Box

The great thing about the materials used for the nesting box is that they are cheap and readily available at most lumberyards or home building supply stores. The measurements for all of the materials for the box are shown in the drawing on page xx.

Plywood

I find that plywood is the universal building solution because of its low cost and workability. Sometimes the price of 3/4" plywood is the same as 5/8"; if this is the case get the 3/4" because it is stronger. The standard sheet size is 4' by 8'. You need to get the type of plywood meant for outside use (i.e., that can take some water on it). There is a special glue used in this plywood that holds up well in wet weather, as opposed to regular plywood's glue, which falls apart when it comes in contact with water. In most states the designation for this exterior grade of plywood is called CDX.

For the nesting box shown on page 627, you'll need two pieces of 24" x 36" plywood (for the ends), two pieces of 24" x 48" (for the sides), and two pieces of approximately 36" x 48" (for the top and bottom). The actual measurements for the top and bottom will vary a little, depending on how you assemble the side pieces.

Backing

A backing block is necessary to hold the box together. For this project you will need 36 feet of a ¾" x ¾" solid wood material. Starting with the two ends of the box (24" x 36" sections), cut, glue, and nail the backing pieces flush with the outside edges of each end piece—like making a picture frame set on top of these plywood end pieces. Look closely at the drawing to see how they look. The side walls (24" x 48") will eventually screw into these end backing pieces.

On the side walls, also attach the ¾" wood stock pieces, but only along the top and bottom (i.e., the 48″ edges). This backing piece should be held back at each end ¾″ to accommodate the thickness of the "picture frame" end walls butting next to it. This backing will be used to secure the bottom and provide a stable base for the lid.

Coating

Even with exterior-grade plywood, you will still need to put a coating on the inside of the box to keep the moisture in the sand from soaking into the wood. Some options are marine-type varnishes, polyurethane, and even epoxy paints. Your best bet is to call a paint store and ask for a product that is safe around children. Safe for children is safe for green monsters—and environmentally friendly.

If you use these environmentally safe products you will usually have to apply at least two coats (layers). Be sure to build the box months ahead so the paint has time to dry to a hard finish. Even better, make the box in the summer and you won't have to worry whether it's dry or ready by egg-laying time.

For the best and longest-lasting box, also paint the outside. Sometimes putting a little extra time and effort in the beginning saves untold hours later. Be sure to coat the ends of the plywood several times; water is easily wicked into the wood through the ends, which causes the layers of the plywood to separate.

It's very important to paint all the individual pieces of the box <u>before</u> you assemble them. If you paint the box after it's assembled, you'll have real difficulties taking it apart for storage.

Pipe

For the iguana, the pipe that enters the nesting box replicates soil tunnels in the wild. Often females in the wild will fight over existing tunnels and nesting sites. When your female crawls into the pipe (tunnel), perhaps she will think that some other iguana has already been in there and done the hard work of digging for her. Once she is inside the box it's just like a big hole dug in natural soil. It's dark, moist, safe, and secure—all of the things a female iguana needs and wants to deposit her eggs.

Sometimes you have to show her the pipe entrance in the beginning by putting her in front of it; you may even have to coax her into the tunnel several times on different days. Keep showing her the tunnel entrance until she demonstrates her understanding by entering the tunnel on her own.

Start introducing her to the box at least two months before the time of egg laying. Normally eggs in the wild are laid from February to May. Play it safe; start early, because iguanas in captivity often invent their own egg-laying time schedules.

The entry pipe can be a length of ceramic, PVC (polyvinyl chloride), or concrete drain pipe. Another option is a paper tube used for storing rolls of carpeting (free at carpet dealers)—or use your own imagination.

PVC pipe is usually the easiest to obtain, but retail hardware stores rarely carry anything over 4″ in diameter. Depending on the size of your iguana, you will probably need at least 6″ in diameter. One solution is to call a commercial building supply store, which will have a wide variety of sizes to choose from. It may be a little difficult to get the pipe, but you only have to get it once in your lifetime. It's better to get a pipe that is too large in diameter than too small. Don't install a pipe that is so small that your iguana has to squeeze through it. <u>A narrow pipe could damage her delicate eggs.</u>

The length of the pipe is determined by how it is used. The best set-up is to have the nesting box next to the iguana's habitat, especially if the habitat is like the Ultimate Iguana Habitat design described in Chapter 4, Housing. If this is the case, cut a hole through your iguana's habitat wall, stick the pipe straight across, and you have the perfect solution. The pipe needs to be long enough to "feel" like a tunnel and needs to be secure so it won't wobble or move around. If it is not stable, the wobbling action will scare your female iguana from ever entering it.

It you use the PVC or any other material that is slick or smooth on the inside, you need to create a way for your iguana to get a grip as she climbs in and out of the pipe. The fastest solution is to epoxy (5-minute type purchased at a hardware store) small pieces of wood horizontally across the inside of the pipe, like a flat ladder.

The other option is to place the box near the habitat or somewhere in your house that is a little secluded and out of the flow of foot traffic. The angle of the pipe can be adjusted to your particular situation. Just remember that the box should be easy for your iguana to enter and exit—and accessible 24 hours a day!

Top Security

The top on the box will keep the area inside dark, just like a real burrow out in nature. Once the female iguana gets into the box she will thrash around as she digs, so it is also important to have a lid on the box to keep the sand from flying around the house.

The lid should open easily for you, but still remain very secure when in place. You don't want the lid to fall in on your iguana and scare her. If she gets spooked from a loose, chattering, or falling lid there is a good chance that she will never use the box again.

I suggest putting two or three hinges on the side of the box, as shown in the drawing on page 627. To keep the iguana from lifting the lid, add a draw catch in the center of the box, opposite the hinges (not shown). The draw catch holds the lid in place by pulling it down tightly with its compressing leverage action.

If you have children you may want to get the hasp type of draw catch that allows a small padlock to go through it. That way, no one but the person with the key can open the lid. Be sure to put the key in the same place every time so you don't forget its location.

Blocks (Feet)

Place blocks of wood under the bottom of the box on all four corners and one in the center, in case your moist sand becomes wet sand. These blocks will keep the box off the floor so you can see if water is dripping and correct the problem. The blocks can be as simple as pieces of scrap of wood that give you about 1½" of clearance between the floor and the bottom of the box.

Assembly of the Nesting Box

If you have a house that has lots of extra storage space, or an empty garage or barn, the fastest way to assemble the nesting box is with glue and nails. You end up with a large box that can't be taken apart and can be stored only as a "big box." The other solution is a box that can be taken apart and stored in easy-to-stack sections. That is how the box illustrated on page 627 is designed.

Place the entry pipe in front of the end wall and trace the outline of the pipe opening. Then take an electric saber saw and cut this circle out. Next, paint and seal the hole you just cut out.

Screws are the fastening device of choice because you can assemble and disassemble the box easily, unlike with nails, which are hard to remove. Use pan head, zinc-coated, number 10, 1¼″ long sheet-metal screws. These have more bite into the wood than the typical "wood" screws. Another option are the Grabber® drywall screws becoming popular at hardware stores. They are similar to sheet-metal screws in design but have a thread that really pulls and holds the wood together. It's my first choice, if available.

To assemble the box, start by screwing the two side walls into the two end walls. Before putting the screws in, make ¹⁄₁₆″ pilot holes with a drill bit. This helps prevent the screws from splitting the backing as the screws are driven in. Turn the box upside down and screw the bottom in place. If you are using the Grabber screws, you will need a metal washer for each screw, or else the screw head will pull right through the plywood.

The last step is attaching the top (hinges and draw catches) and inserting the pipe. If the hole was cut out properly, the pipe should fit snugly in the hole.

Substrate—Moist Sand

The best substrate for the box is sand. And the best sand to use is what they call "builders sand," which you can get at most lumberyards or building supply stores. Builders sand holds its form and sticks together better than other types of sand. It also holds more moisture, which is why brick layers use it. If you can't find this particular sand, other types will do.

Before you add the sand, check to see that the paint on the box is completely dry, because once the moist sand is added the paint will never dry. Take a moment to be sure that where you place the box is where you want it to stay. Once it is filled with moist sand it may be too heavy to move.

Fill the sand to a couple of inches below the bottom of the pipe (see drawing on page 627). The key is to have the sand lower than the entry pipe so your iguana won't be kicking and dragging sand easily into the pipe (which means all over the house). But you don't want the sand so low that your iguana has trouble getting back out of the pipe. Remember that she is loaded with eggs, and you don't want her to be forced into stressful body angles that could puncture an egg and eventually kill her as she crawls through the pipe.

Moisten the sand in a separate container, then put this sand in the nesting box. By mixing water and sand outside of the egg box, you retain control of the situation. If you mix water with the sand directly in the box, it's easy to add too much water to the mixture, and then it's nearly impossible to reduce this moisture mess. How wet is moist sand? You should be able to squeeze a handful into a ball that will hold together on its own.

If you think you have wet sand, you probably do. Off and on, however, you will need to add a little water to the sand in the box, to replace the water that evaporates each day. Add just a little water at a time, then mix and level the sand inside the box. Don't add too much water at one time and make a swamp out of the box, which also could breed bacteria, fungus, or mold.

Important

Make sure your iguana can get in and out of the box through the pipe. Open the lid a couple of times in the beginning when your iguana is in the box to make sure everything is working correctly and there is the right amount of sand (so she doesn't drag her body over the rough edge of the pipe getting out of the box).

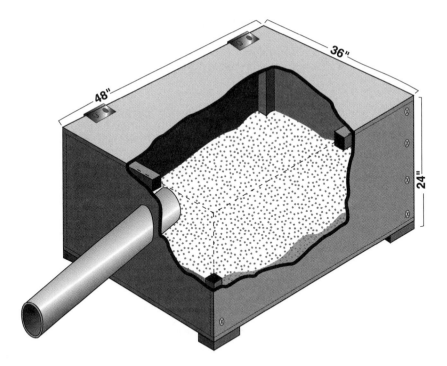

Figure H.1: Egg-Laying Box, with cutaway view of the interior and sand substrate

Put the box in the location you feel has the easiest access for your iguana. Remember that your iguana needs to be able to get into this box 24 hours a day. She can't be locked in her cage and have the box in another room of the house. This is an absolute!

When it gets close to egg-laying time, be sure to check the box every day for eggs (don't forget). The best time is when the iguana is not in the box. When the eggs are laid, they should be immediately taken out and placed into an incubation box, but the nesting box should remain in place for about a week more for transition time to let the female adjust to the eggs disappearing.

After the eggs were removed and the nests destroyed, females would generally again begin scraping material toward the nesting place and would continue to do so for two or three days.
—"Observations on a Captive Colony of *Iguana iguana*" (#6)

I have to tell you, I cried after we took her eggs out of the egg-laying box. She [SVL: 15", TL: 3' 3", 2 yrs.] kept looking for the eggs, going around and around the cage. Today she is still looking for her eggs. To me it's a sad time for her. Being a female I feel I can understand somewhat how she must feel. Even though I know we must do this for her eggs to survive, it's very sad.   —I-735, Tammie, 31 yrs., Kansas

When the egg-laying box is finished for the year, disassemble it, clean the plywood with a mixture of water and bleach, let it air dry, and stack the parts in a neat pile for next year's adventure. Also, get rid of the sand, which might have bacteria and mold growing in it. You will be putting new sand in the box each year.

Options

Many people over the years have sent me designs for egg-laying boxes. Most of them don't work, for various reasons. If you want to create your own box design, just use the basic principles I have stated earlier in this appendix and in Chapter 4, Housing, combined with your imagination and creativity.

As for optional containers, I was in a large home building supply store the other day and they had some big, tough plastic storage boxes for sale (32" long by 17" wide by 17½" high—perhaps you could even order a larger one). The top, which was very solid, came off in one piece with some quick-release latches. This container might work if you have a small female. All you would have to do is cut a hole for the pipe. There might be other options out there. Keep your eyes and ears open.

Egg Incubator

If you have fertile iguana eggs, the egg incubator described here will provide the appropriate environment for them to hatch.

The Incubator Set-Up

Below are the parts required for the incubator and a few brief comments for putting it together. The heater, thermostat, and water pump can be found at aquarium stores, fish supply warehouses, and through aquarium magazines. Look on page 631 for a detailed drawing of what the finished incubator looks like. This incubator can hold up to about 70 eggs.

Container

The best container is a 20-gallon (fish-type) aquarium (24" long, 16" high, 12" deep). Try to get a used one in the want ads of the newspaper or from a fellow herper to save some money. Be sure to disinfect the container with a bleach solution (one to two tablespoons of household bleach per cup of water), then rinse several times with clear water.

Lid

The incubator will lose most of its heat through its top, so a lid is essential. A styrofoam lid will help hold in both heat and humidity. You can purchase a thin sheet ($\frac{1}{4}$" to $\frac{1}{2}$") of styrofoam at stationery or art supply stores under the name "foam-core board," which usually has paper on both sides. If the incubator is in an exceptionally cold room you might need a thicker sheet of styrofoam ($\frac{3}{4}$" to $1\frac{1}{4}$"). You could double- or triple-layer the $\frac{1}{4}$" to $\frac{1}{2}$" pieces or look in the phone book under "styrofoam" for stores that sell thicker sizes.

You'll want the lid to be larger than the tank opening (maybe $\frac{1}{4}$" to $\frac{1}{2}$" overhang on all sides). Place the styrofoam on top of the incubation tank and trace the outline of the tank rim with a pencil (on the underneath side of the styrofoam). Remove the styrofoam and along this outline make a groove the width of the glass and about $\frac{1}{8}$" into the styrofoam. This groove allows the styrofoam lid to snap into place on top of the aquarium. You are not trying to get a hermetically sealed environment, just something to reduce heat and humidity loss.

Egg Boxes

You can use any type of container to put the eggs in, as long as it fits in the incubator and has a lid. One option is the plastic food storage containers ("tubs") that hold soft butter. Rubbermaid® and Tupperware® containers also come in a wide range of sizes. You can use several smaller containers or one big container.

Whatever the choice for container, make sure you sterilize it, and poke the containers with numerous ⅙″ to ⅛″ holes in the bottom and sides for gas exchange (because an iguana's eggshell is permeable to water). Then fill the boxes with incubation medium (see the next section).

> Eggs were placed on the vermiculite so that approximately half of their surface was in contact with the substrate and half was in contact with air trapped inside the covered containers. Consequently, eggs could exchange water with their environment in both liquid and vapor phases.
> —"Influence of Moisture and Temperature on Eggs and Embryos of Green Iguanas (*Iguana iguana*)" (#19)

The lids can stay on tight for the first 75 days, except when you remove them a couple of times a week to inspect for dud eggs. After that time, let the lid rest loosely on top of the container so when the eggs hatch, and if the lizards want to get out of the container, all they have to do is lift their heads up to push the lid aside. More likely, however, the hatchlings will remain in the container for a while until their yolk sac is absorbed.

Incubation Medium

People have used several types of incubation medium in the past, including sand, peat moss, vermiculite, perlite (these last two are the small, white plastic balls often found in potting soil), and combinations of all of these. I think it is best to go with what scientific researchers use:

> We opted to use vermiculite as an incubation medium, because vermiculite is clean, light in weight, and easy to use. The material is readily available from commercial sources, and it is graded for particle size before being packaged and shipped. Iguanas in a natural habitat clearly do not construct their nests in vermiculite. Nevertheless, eggs respond primarily to ambient temperature and water potential, thus the use of an artificial medium is unlikely to have affected results.
> —"Influence of Moisture and Temperature on Eggs and Embryos of Green Iguanas (*Iguana iguana*)" (#19)
> [AUTHOR'S NOTE: Grade #3 of vermiculite is the best if you can get it; courser grades tend not to compact.]

These same researchers liked vermiculite because "it was possible to control availability of water more precisely than with natural substrates." They used a water potential of −150 kPa—for all of us non-scientists, just mix equal parts of water and vermiculite. Make the mixture wet but not soggy. Mix this in a separate container, then scoop it into the egg boxes (the medium should fill the container halfway; see drawing on page 631).

Don't let the medium dry out! If you need to add more water to the medium, first pre-heat it to the temperature of the incubator. With the pump forcing water to circulate in the incubator, the medium should not dry out, though.

IMPORTANT: I have seen bags of so-called "sterile" vermiculite with bugs crawling

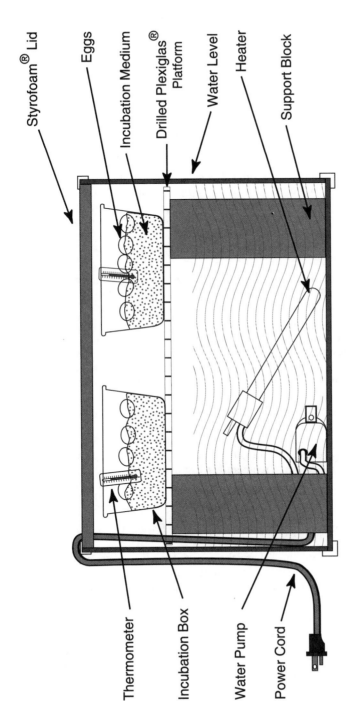

Styrofoam® Lid

Eggs

Incubation Medium

Drilled Plexiglas® Platform

Water Level

Heater

Support Block

Thermometer

Incubation Box

Water Pump

Power Cord

Figure I.1: Egg Incubator. Original concept courtesy of Amro Hamdoun

inside, so it is important to sterilize this material before putting it into the incubator. One way is to place it in a microwave oven for one minute at maximum heat. Be sure to let the vermiculite come to room temperature before placing eggs in it.

Water Pump

The type of pump needed in the incubator is called a "powerhead" pump. The powerhead pump circulates large volumes of water in a short period of time. The way it is set up in the incubator, it blows the water in the tank against the support blocks, thus distributing water and air to produce a humid environment throughout the tank. In the incubator described here, you want a pump that will circulate about 80 gallons of water per hour. These pumps are fairly inexpensive: about $15 at most aquarium stores.

To build a larger incubator, a good rule of thumb is to purchase a pump that turns the water over four times per hour (e.g., for a 20-gallon tank, get a pump that circulates 80 gallons per hour; for a 30-gallon tank, get a pump that circulates 120 gallons per hour). Use distilled water in the tank; regular tap water often has chlorine, fluoride, and sometimes heavy metals in it. Remember, an iguana's eggshell is permeable, so you want only pure water entering the egg.

Thermometer

Put one thermometer in each of the individual egg boxes so you get an accurate reading of each box's temperature.

Heater

Choose a brand recommended by your aquarium store salesperson. These heaters look like submersible test tubes, are about 12" long, and cost about $15 each. The most common ones are rated an average of 100 watts. If you can afford it, you may want to use two separate 50-watt heaters instead of one 100-watt variety. Two heaters mean that if one heater fails the whole system doesn't completely crash.

These heaters usually have a built-in thermostat, but don't rely solely on the factory calibration of the heater; always use thermometers placed in the egg boxes to see the true temperature. Factory calibrations may be off, but a thermometer rarely lies. If you are using a thermometer to verify the calibration, keep adjusting the heater in small increments until you get the desired temperature inside the egg boxes. This may take several hours, depending on how far off you are from the correct temperature.

Thermostat

A thermostat not only measures the temperature but also controls and adjusts it to the heat level you require.

The heater mentioned previously has a thermostat already built in, but many people recommend the use of an additional thermostat. This should be placed "in line" before the heater. This additional safety feature will provide a back-up in case the heater's thermostat fails and possibly overheats your iguana eggs. You don't want cooked eggs!

Get a pulse-proportioned thermostat, as seen in some herp magazine ads, or perhaps an electronic temperature controller with a remote probe. When you purchase the thermostat, tell the person selling it what you are doing with it and get all the necessary details to make it operate for your particular situation. A good thermostat is about $100 and worth it.

Platform

To make the platform for the egg boxes, take a ⅛" to ¼" thick sheet of clear acrylic plastic (the ¼" thickness has the best longevity) and drill ¹⁄₁₆" to ¹⁄₁₈" diameter holes about 1" apart. Look in the phone book under "plastic" for the nearest location and have them cut the platform to size, as acrylics require a special saw. If you have a drill motor and drill bits you could make the holes yourself and save money.

The acrylic should almost touch the sides of the tank (⅛" space all around). Once the iguana eggs hatch, this close tolerance will prevent the hatchlings from accidentally falling from the shelf into the tank water and drowning.

Supports

You will need something to support the acrylic platform that the egg boxes sit on. One suggestion is to use bricks or building (cinder) blocks, which you can purchase at most building supply stores. Scrub them thoroughly with a bleach and water solution, then rinse several times with clear water to remove any possible contaminants. Set them in the incubator tank gently, as glass and heavy objects don't mix.

APPENDIX J
References Cited

It was not my plan in the beginning to include a bibliography. I didn't want page after page of footnotes in the text of my book. It may look impressive, but who cares? All you really need are the <u>facts</u>. The original idea was to read and digest the hundreds of hard-to-swallow scientific journals I had collected over the years, then present the main ideas in a way that you could easily understand and relate to.

Having said that, I found numerous statements in these articles and books that are very powerful, and I have quoted them to help clarify or reinforce important points made in my book. These quoted references are listed by number (e.g., #9) in parentheses throughout the text. Don't be fooled by the select number of citations in this appendix; this is a meaty book. For every reference cited, I probably read half a dozen more that I didn't quote.

For all of you hard-core bibliographers who need a more comprehensive list of references, here's a simple suggestion. Make a list of the first, second, or third authors of the research papers referenced in this appendix, then go to your local library and look these names up in the periodical index. You can also look under the species name *Iguana iguana*.

If you live in a small town, the local library might not list any of these people. If you have a college or university nearby, try their library, or look on the Internet. Be aware, though, that even in large metropolitan cities with major universities, you may not be able to find the full complement of papers by these leading iguana researchers in either printed or electronic form. I was lucky that many of the authors sent their papers directly to me.

These citations are not in standard reference form (alphabetical order by the author's last name or sequentially as they appear in the book), for a good reason. The list grew (and got numbered) as I received and incorporated each new source into the text of the book.

1. Werner, Dagmar I., Esmeralda M. Baker, Elizabeth del C. Gonzalez, and Ines R. Sosa. "Kinship recognition and grouping in hatchling green iguanas." *Behavioral Ecology and Sociobiology*, Vol. 21, pp. 83-89, 1987.
2. Burger, Joanna and Michael Gochfeld. "The importance of the human face in risk perception by black iguanas, *Ctenosaura similis.*" *Journal of Herpetology*, Vol. 27, No. 4, pp. 426-430, 1993.
3. Gehrmann, William H. "Spectral characteristics of lamps commonly used in herpetoculture." *The Vivarium* (publication of the American Federation of Herpetoculturists), Vol. 5, No. 5, March/April 1994.

4. Greene, Harry W., Gordon M. Burghardt, Beverly A. Dugan, and A. Stanley Rand. "Predation and the defensive behavior of green iguanas (Reptilia, Lacertilia, Iguanidae)." *Journal of Herpetology*, Vol. 12, No. 2, pp. 169-176, 1978.

5. Ricklefs, Robert E. and John Cullen. "Embryonic growth of the green iguana, *Iguana iguana*." *Copeia*, 1973, No. 2, pp. 296-305.

6. Mendelssohn, H. "Observations on a captive colony of *Iguana iguana*." *SSAR Contributions to Herpetology Number 1: Reproductive Biology and Diseases of Captive Reptiles*, James B. Murphy and Joseph T. Collins, eds., 1980.

7. Phillips, John A. "*Iguana iguana*: a model species for studying the ontogeny of behavior/hormone interactions." *The Journal of Experimental Zoology Supplement*, Vol. 4, pp. 167-169, 1990.

8. van Marken Lichtenbelt, Wouter D. "Digestion in an ectothermic herbivore, the green iguana (*Iguana iguana*): effect of food composition and body temperature." *Physiological Zoology*, Vol. 65, No. 3, pp. 649-673, 1992.

9. Phillips, John A., Allison C. Alberts, and Nancy C. Pratt. "Differential resource use, growth, and the ontogeny of social relationships in the green iguana." *Physiology & Behavior*, Vol. 53, pp. 81-88, 1993.

10. Pratt, Nancy C., John A. Phillips, Allison C. Alberts, and Karen S. Bolda. "Functional versus physiological puberty: an analysis of sexual bimaturism in the green iguana, *Iguana iguana*." *Animal Behavior*, Vol. 47, pp. 1101-1114, 1994.

11. Cogan, Roger C. "The captive husbandry and breeding of the green iguana (*Iguana iguana*)." Proceedings of the 13th International Herpetological Symposium on Captive Propagation and Husbandry, Phoenix, Arizona, June 20-24, 1989. Michael J. Uricheck, ed.

12. Miller, Tracey J. "Artificial incubation of eggs of the green iguana (*Iguana iguana*)." *Zoo Biology*, Vol. 6, pp. 225-236, 1987.

13. Allen, Mary E., Olav T. Oftedal, David J. Baer, and Dagmar I. Werner. "Nutritional studies with the green iguana." Proceedings of the Eighth Dr. Scholl Conference on Nutrition of Captive Wild Animals, Lincoln Park Zoological Garden, Chicago, Illinois, December 8-9, 1989. Thomas P. Meehan, Steven D. Thompson, and Mary E. Allen, eds.

14. Phillips, John A. Center for Reproduction of Endangered Species, San Diego. Personal communication, 1992-1996.

15. Garel, Tony. Curator, Belize Zoo, Belize, Central America. Personal communication.

16. Burghardt, Gordon M. and A. Stanley Rand, eds. *Iguanas of the World: Their Behavior, Ecology, and Conservation*. Park Ridge, New Jersey: Noyes Publications, 1982.

17. Howard, C.J. "Notes on the maintenance and breeding of the common iguana (*Iguana iguana*) at Twycross Zoo." From *The British Herpetological Society: The Care and Breeding of Captive Reptiles*, 1980.

18. Licht, Paul and Walter R. Moberly. "Thermal requirements for embryonic development in the tropical lizard *Iguana iguana*." *Copeia*, 1965, No. 4, pp. 515-517.

19. Phillips, John A., Anthony Garel, Gary C. Packard, and Mary J. Packard. "Influence of moisture and temperature on eggs and embryos of green iguanas (*Iguana iguana*)." *Herpetologica*, Vol. 26, No. 2, pp. 238-245, 1990.

20. Werner, Dagmar I. "The rational use of green iguanas." In *Neotropical Wildlife Use and Conservation*, John G. Robinson and Kent H. Redford, eds. Chicago: The University of Chicago Press, 1991.

21. Packard, M.J., et al. *Copeia*, 1992, No. 3, pp. 851-858. As reported in "Herpetology

1993," *Bulletin of the Chicago Herpetological Society*, Vol. 28, No. 12, pp. 277-278, 1993.

22. Alberts, Allison C., Nancy C. Pratt, and John A. Phillips. "Seasonal productivity of lizard femoral glands: relationship to social dominance and androgen levels." *Physiology & Behavior*, Vol. 51, No. 4, pp. 729-733, 1992.

23. Rodda, Gordon. "The mating behavior of *Iguana iguana*." *Smithsonian Contributions to Zoology*, No. 534. Washington, D.C.: Smithsonian Institution Press, 1992.

24. Kingsbury, Bruce A. "Thermoregulatory set points of the eurythermic lizard *Elgaria multicarinata*." *Journal of Herpetology*, Vol. 27, No. 2, pp. 241-247, 1993.

25. Rand, A. Stanley, Beverly A. Dugan, Hebe Monteza, and Dalixa Vianda. "The diet of a generalized folivore: *Iguana iguana* in Panama." *Journal of Herpetology*, Vol. 24, No. 2, pp. 211-214, 1990.

26. McGinnis, Samuel M. and Charles W. Brown. "Thermal behavior of the green iguana, *Iguana iguana*." *Herpetologica*, Vol. 22, No. 3, pp. 189-199, 1966.

27. Rodda, Gordon H. "Sex and violence in South America: tactics for reproduction in the green iguana." Revised and edited transcript of a presentation made to the Tucson Herpetological Society, 21 November 1989.

28. Letters to the editor. *Iguana Times*, Vol. 1, No. 6, pp. 15-16, October 1992.

29. Rand, A. Stanley and Brian C. Bock. "Size variation, growth, and survivorship in nesting green iguanas (*Iguana iguana*) in Panama." *Amphibia-Reptilia*, Vol. 13, pp. 147-156, 1992.

30. Lara Lopez, Maria del Socorro. "Habitos alimentarios de la iguana verde (*Iguana iguana wiegmann*) in la region de La Mancha, Actopan, Veracruz." Thesis, Universidad Veracruzana, Facultad de Biologia, 1994.

31. Ball, James C. "A comparison of the UV-B irradiance of low-intensity, full-spectrum lamps with natural sunlight." *Bulletin of the Chicago Herpetological Society*, Vol. 30, No. 4, pp. 69-72, 1995.

32. Lazell, James D., Jr. "The lizard genus *Iguana* in the Lesser Antilles." *Bulletin of the Museum of Comparative Zoology*, Vol. 145, No. 1, 23 May 1973, Harvard University, Cambridge, Massachusetts.

33. McGee, Harold. *On Food and Cooking—The Science and Lore of the Kitchen*. New York: Collier Books, Macmillan Publishing, 1984.

34. "A reptilian pet peeve." *Health*, Vol. 9, p. 19, September 1995.

35. Alberts, Allison C., Lori A. Jackintell, and John A. Phillips. "Effects of chemical and visual exposure to adults on growth, hormones, and behavior of juvenile green iguanas." *Physiology & Behavior*, Vol. 55, No. 6, pp. 987-992, 1994.

36. Morganti, Thomas D. "Iguana strangled with human hair." From *The Bulletin of the Association of Reptile and Amphibian Veterinarians* Vol. 5, No. 3, 1995, as reprinted in *Get Behind BAARS* (newsletter of the Bay Area Amphibian and Reptile Society), Vol. XVIII, No. 11, November/December 1995.

37. Moyle, Matthew. "Vitamin D and UV radiation: guidelines for the herpetoculturist." Proceedings of the International Herpetological Symposium, Phoenix, Arizona, 1989.

38. Rossi, John. "Azalea, rhododendron sp. toxicity in a green iguana." *Bulletin of the Association of Reptile and Amphibian Veterinarians*, Vol. 5, No. 2, 1995, as reprinted in *Get Behind BAARS* (newsletter of the Bay Area Amphibian and Reptile Society), Vol. XVIII, No. 9, September 1995.

39. Alberts, Allison C. "Ultraviolet light and lizards: more than meets the eye." (Lizard Column), *The Vivarium* (Journal of the American Federation of Herpetoculturists), Vol. 5, No. 4, January/February 1994.

40. Garland, Cedric and Frank. *The Calcium Diet: Calcium Connection.* London: Penguin, 1990.
41. Sunshine-Genova, Amy. "Making scents of sex." *Men's Fitness,* April 1995.
42. Burghardt, Gordon M. and A. Stanley Rand. "Group size and growth rate in hatchling green iguanas *(Iguana iguana)." Behavioral Ecology and Sociobiology,* Vol. 18, pp. 101-104, 1985.
43. Personal research, unpublished.
44. Henderson, Robert W. "Aspects of the ecology of the juvenile common green iguana *(Iguana iguana)." Herpetologica,* Vol. 30, No. 4, pp. 327-332, December 1974.
45. Beltz, Ellin. "Herp news from around the world." *The Vivarium* (Journal of the American Federation of Herpetoculturists), Vol. 7, No. 4, p. 6, 1996.
46. Phillips, John A. "Does cadence of *Iguana iguana* displays facilitate individual recognition?" *Behavioral Ecology and Sociobiology,* Vol. 37, pp. 337-342, 1995.
47. Kastner, Jonathan and Marianna (eds. for Volume 9). *The Illustrated Encyclopedia of the Animal Kingdom,* Vol. 9. Milan, Italy: The Danbury Press, a division of Grolier Enterprises, Inc., 1970.
48. Rodda, Gordon H., personal communication, 1993-1996.
49. Walls, Gordon Lynn. *The Vertebrate Eye and its Adaptive Radiation.* New York: Hafner Publishing Co., 1963.
50. Bernard, Joni B. "Spectral irradiance of fluorescent lamps and their efficacy for promoting vitamin D synthesis in herbivorous reptiles." Doctoral dissertation, Michigan State University, East Lansing, Michigan, 1995.
51. Allen, Mary E., Olav T. Oftedal, and Ronald L. Horst. "Remarkable differences in the response to dietary vitamin D among species of reptiles and primates: is ultraviolet B light essential?" In: *Biological Effects of Light.* Berlin: Walter deGruyter & Co., in press, expected 1996. M.F. Holick and E.G. Jung, eds.

Acknowledgments

The scope of this book was vast, and doing it took a lot of help from many people and many sources. If you want to get a little insight into how this book came together, please read this section. To everyone listed here, and to the people described in "About the Illustrators and Photographers," I stand up and give you a round of applause and a grateful "Thanks!"

BACK IN THE BEGINNING

Over six years ago I contacted a person who knew a great deal about many animals; it was **Fredric L. Frye**, DVM. At one point in the conversation Dr. Frye said, "There is a demand for a pet-care book on iguanas, but take your time and do it right." Dr. Fred was the initial "kick in the pants" that kept me going for the first year. Over the years we have developed a good relationship. Thanks, Dr. Fred, for the first "jump-start."

Researching and writing this book had many ups and downs. Through these bouncy times it was the hundreds of **personal letters** from iguana owners that kept me going. "We really need a good iguana book." "Help save the iguanas." "Get people informed so I won't see such sad, sick iguanas in the pet stores and at people's houses."

And of course I could never have written this book without all of the hundreds and hundreds of **iguana pet owners and veterinarians** who filled out my detailed iguana questionnaire, or the people I talked with at herpetological conferences and pet stores. These people provided much background information, as well as the powerful quotations I used in the book to make specific statements sing.

RESEARCH CONTACTS

Digging through the scientific journals and other research sources to extract all the nitty-gritty information on iguanas took an enormous amount of time and effort. I was fortunate to receive assistance along the way from many of the top iguana researchers in the world.

Gordon M. Burghardt

is probably best known worldwide as the co-editor of the book *Iguanas of The World: Their Behavior, Ecology, and Conservation*, a collection of iguana scientific research papers. He is also the author of a number of important papers on iguanas. Locally, he's a Professor of Psychology and Zoology at the University of Tennessee at Knoxville, where his main field of study and research is with reptiles. Over the past four years, he has sent me hard-to-find scientific papers, the names of people to contact for further iguana research, valuable words of encouragement, and beautiful reptile postcards.

John A. Phillips

is the Deputy Director of CRES (Center for Reproduction of Endangered Species) in San Diego. He has a lot of quotes in my book because he has done so much to advance the research on iguanas over the years. His Curriculum Vitae overflows with honors, teaching stints, lectures, and page after page of research articles he's authored or co-authored. His research contributed to some important breakthroughs in iguana breeding and care. For more than five years he has helped me with specific iguana questions that have come up, as well as sent me a number of important iguana research papers. Twice I flew down to San Diego to see him and his iguana projects and to get his personal views on iguana-related subjects. For a man that has too many projects and too little time, he always had time to talk with me. That's pretty special.

Dagmar I. Werner

is affectionately called the "Iguana Mama" because she has helped raise so many iguanas (in her captive breeding program) to be released back into the wild. She is the President of Fundación Pro Iguana Verde in Costa Rica, Central America, which not only breeds iguanas in captivity, but also works with the local people to boost their economy while saving the rainforest (through the re-introduction of iguanas). She stands above all other iguana researchers for her non-stop devotion to iguanas and the environment. It was a true pleasure and "experience" to meet her and see her iguana farm in the jungles of Costa Rica some years back.

A. Stanley Rand

started the iguana research project in Panama with Dagmar Werner way back in 1983. About four years later it ended, and Werner went to Costa Rica while Rand remained in Panama doing other research for the Smithsonian Tropical Research Institute. He is the other co-editor of *Iguanas of the World* and is one of the "original" iguana researchers. When I was having trouble finding specific iguana research papers, he sent me a bundle through the mail that helped fill in more bits of the iguana puzzle.

Gordon H. Rodda

spent two years in the Llanos of Venezuela observing the breeding behavior of *Iguana iguana* for the Smithsonian (see reference #23). One well-known, bright iguana researcher told me that Gordon Rodda is one of the best observers of animals that he has ever seen. That's some praise. He has helped me refine the answers to some of my more challenging iguana questions over the last few years.

Maria Socorro Lara Lopez

was kind enough to share her egg research in the jungles of Mexico with me. She is an extremely dedicated, smart, and resourceful iguana investigator, who is now pursuing an advanced degree in biological research. Our paths will definitely cross again.

In addition, I would like to thank the Instituto de Ecologia in Xalapa, Mexico, especially **Alberto Gonzalez-Romero**, Director of the Department of Ecology and Animal

Behavior, for his friendly and professional help in getting me into La Mancha (a restricted research station). Thanks, too, for his continued interest in my research and this book.

On the other coast of Mexico, I also want to thank **Amos Palacios Ortiz** (MVZ), Director of the School of Veterinary Medicine and Zoology at the Universidad Autónoma "Benito Juárez" de Oaxaca. I was honored by his friendly, courteous, and personal attention when I met him there. He also made it possible for me to gain access to the research station at Playa Escobilla, a restricted area patrolled by military people with fully automatic weapons.

A bit further north on the Oaxacan coast, thanks to **Hector Cruz Reyes** for allowing me to work with him on his iguana project in Chacagua and for helping to get the boat and guides together for my personal research on the breeding iguanas in the area.

Lynn Wiegard is a pit bull when it comes to finding information. Once I gave her an assignment to find a particular scientific paper or subject, she didn't let go until she had completed her task. Over the years she has found information in her Canadian college town that wasn't available to me here in the States. She is brilliant, bright, and easy to work with, and her iguana is beautiful.

Amro Hamdoun, a graduate of the University of California at Davis, has had several successful hatchings of iguana eggs. He shared his knowledge of this process by showing me all the ins and outs of proper incubation and hatching. His design for an incubator is illustrated in Appendix I.

OUTSIDE EDITORS

Special thanks to **Cris Shiebold**, **Sue Stulz**, **Carol Sadler**, and **Peter and Marribel Iles** for patiently reading and editing each chapter in this book—and returning comments to me within the deadlines I imposed. I appreciate not only their patience but also their careful reading and comments. Every comment was useful, whether it made it into the final copy or not.

LAST BUT NOT LEAST

My heartfelt thanks to Amanda, "keeper of the gate" and never-ending supply of intelligence, energy, love, and enthusiasm for my project.

About the Illustrators and Photographers

ILLUSTRATORS

Illustrations of Iguanas

I had figured out most of the iguana line drawings I wanted for this book in the first year I started researching, but I needed to find the right person to do the job. There are many excellent illustrators I could have chosen, but I encountered one superior person: Kendal Morris.

Kendal Morris has had a lifelong interest in both reptiles and illustration. As a preschooler he caught lizards in his Tucson, Arizona back yard; later he kept virtual menageries of snakes, lizards, and other critters—from orphaned birds to long-horned beetles.

Kendal started drawing at an early age, too. One of his grade-school idols was naturalist and reptile illustrator Robert Stebbins. Kendal received his bachelor's degree in biology from MIT in 1983 and afterward studied science writing and natural science illustration at the University of California, Santa Cruz. He stayed on at UC Santa Cruz to teach science illustration until 1990. He now lives in Portland, Oregon, and is an illustrator, writer, and graphic designer for the U.S. Fish and Wildlife Service.

I gave Kendal my third-grade renderings of what I wanted drawn, and he put life and personality into that amorphic mess. Kendal said that illustrating **Green Iguana— The Ultimate Owner's Manual** was a lot of fun, allowing him to combine his long-standing interests in reptiles and illustration.

Graphics (Graphs, Charts, and Drawings)

I met **Morgan Odland** shortly after he had graduated from Reed College, a prestigious private school here in Portland. Morgan is a "Renaissance Man" about town: actor, director, researcher, and writer.

Morgan has a B.A. in English Literature from Reed College and also spent time in Paris, France, at the famous La Sorbonne University studying French, history, and architecture. He has traveled extensively, including a couple of trips to Central and South America, which made our work times together even more enjoyable. All of this is good background, but it was his talents with computer graphics that I tapped for this book.

For such a young guy (23 years), he grasped exactly what I wanted and needed to accomplish with the graphics for my book. The Mayan Canoe drawing in the introduction was the first thing I tested his skills on. He had to make this drawing from photos and bits of information I had gathered at Tikal, in Guatemala. After that "test run" I turned him loose on all of my graphics.

Every assignment I gave him came back better than I had expected. He took my rough designs and made them into sleek, clear, functional, and visually stimulating images. He also kept working with me over the years as more graphics were required as the book page count expanded, even while working at a "real" job at a local educational multimedia development company. He never once complained about having to fine-tune each drawing exactly perfect. Morgan Aaron Odland has a fine career ahead, in anything he wants!

PHOTOGRAPHERS

Cover

They say a picture is worth a thousand words, and I think this is true with the cover of my book. I wanted to show a personal relationship between an iguana and its owner—not an iguana just sitting on a tree limb by itself. This in essence is what my book is about.

Jon Deshler is an avant-garde commercial photographer here in Portland who is eclectic in his range of assignments and presentations. Like all fine photographers, he has an inner sense for details, which produces the desired results. In two separate sittings, Jon spent more than four hours shooting the front and back cover photos. I had a certain concept I thought I wanted for the front and back covers. Jon shot the concepts I wanted but also tried many other ideas he thought up.

The back cover photo was Jon's idea. He felt that with the close-up of the iguana on the front cover, people also needed to see what the iguana looked like "in total." I think he was right.

The final cover shot accomplished my original vision. The pet iguana (Za) is the main focus, but there is a connection with the pet owner (me). The way Za's hands are gently wrapped around my hand, his relaxed upper body, and his cute "grin" all express a relaxed, connected mood. It gives a feeling of a happy pet, which I hope all iguana owners will eventually achieve after reading this book. Jon fine-tuned our body positions to make this expression happen. It was truly a pleasure to be captured on film by such a well respected commercial photographer.

Inside the book

Special Shots of Iguanas in the Wild

Kevin Schafer is an internationally known nature photographer. He has had photographs in practically every worthwhile magazine, including *National Geographic, Smithsonian, Audubon,* and *Outside.* His photos also seem to be on every nature postcard of Belize, Central America. His work is everywhere because he captures nature in its essential beauty. He is also a strong environmentalist, and I think that is one of the reasons I got to have his photos in my book.

Kevin liked that my book does not encourage iguanas as pets and in fact discourages indiscriminate purchasing of these animals. To have such a world-renowned artist presenting his impressions of iguanas in my book is truly a blessing and a treat.

Iguana Habitat in the House

John McNally owns PhotoTek, Inc., a commercial photography company in Hillsboro, Oregon (near Portland). One Saturday morning, he loaded piles of equipment into his van and came to my house to shoot photos of the fully functioning Ultimate Iguana Habitat in my living room. I wanted to show how this large habitat can fit nicely into a room, even adding to the decor and overall look of the house. John set up the shot just right, overcoming all the challenges of space, lighting, and other details.

Hatchlings in the Jungle

Maria Socorro Lara Lopez (as you can read in Chapter 9, Breeding) invited me to participate in her research on iguanas' eggs in the jungles in Mexico. She is an astute researcher and cares deeply about the lives of iguanas, much like a pet owner—but from a scientific point of view. She never killed an iguana for her research or adversely interrupted the lizards' natural movements or life cycles, even during the egg research.

Because the iguana eggs didn't hatch while I was in Mexico, I left 10 rolls of film for Socorro to take photos of the hatchlings as they emerged from the sand. Without Socorro, I would never have gotten such great photos of iguanas hatching in the wild!

Iguana Skeleton

What a truly amazing find—getting photos of an iguana skeleton. This processes started in November 1993 and ended with the excellent photos by **David H. Lewis**, Clemson University, in March 1994. First, Deborah Neufeld of Florida (Iguana Rescue) told me about Dr. Richard Montanucci (Associate Professor in the Department of Biological Sciences, Clemson University), who told me about Dr. Stanlee Miller at Clemson, who was in charge of preparing a dead iguana to become a skeleton demonstration model.

When the skeleton was assembled, I asked David Lewis to shoot the iguana skeleton from about 15 different angles. One really cool angle was from underneath. David had to put the skeleton on glass and shoot from below.

The assemblage of the skeleton is impeccable, and so are the photos. I am proud to be the first one to show iguana owners what their green friends look like with no flesh on.

Iguana Sitting Up

It started with a simple photo that Laura Stinson sent me of her iguana sitting up for a treat. I had received several photos of iguanas sitting up, but not with such an outstanding, good-looking iguana as Iggy. Laura's husband, **Dave Stinson**, shot the photographs, and it took about six months to get to what you see in the book. It was my fault it took so long; I wanted Iggy to move a little higher, hands just so, etc. It meant a lot of shots, and time sending the photos back and forth between Canada and Portland. For a non-professional, Dave sure sent me some crisp, clear photos. Thanks to Laura and Dave, the book shows vivid proof that iguanas can be trained to sit up!

Hatchling Eating

I met **Tony Garel** at the Belize Zoo and Tropical Education Center when I was in Central America. It was a planned trip to pick his brain about the massive captive breeding program they had done with iguanas. When he was showing me all of his slides of the project, I saw this one special photo. It was part of his personal collection and he really didn't want to let it out of his sights. But he was kind enough to let me use it.

Thanks, Tony, for your breeding information and the loan of your great photo—and sorry it took forever to return the slide.

Oldest Iguana

Can you imagine the chance to meet the oldest pet iguana? I was lucky enough to see Iggy not once but three times before he died, at the ripe old age of 29. The owners, **Don and Maxine Burnham**, of California, were always generous with allowing me to see Iggy any time I was in the area.

Thermal Burn

I wanted a picture that would convey the importance of keeping the heat source (in this case a light bulb) away from an iguana. One of my iguana questionnaire respondents, **Ellen Broussard**, mentioned that her iguana had gotten burned very badly. The burn scar in the photo looks like someone spilled bleach on the side of her iguana Rex. And when her iguana died at 13 years old, the necropsy showed that the burn scar penetrated all the way to her iguana's ribs. In Ellen's defense, this accident happened back in the days when people just didn't have all of the answers. I hope Ellen's photo shows iguana owners the importance of properly protecting and supporting heat sources.

Iguana on Pillow

Charlene Nemec knows how to spoil her iguana, Rexina, with a pillow for her lizard to sleep on at night. Now that the iguana is spoiled, that pillow had better be in place each night before Rexina goes to sleep, or there will be trouble! Char did a great job of capturing Rexina's relaxed sleeping pose on film.

Hatchling on Hand

Mark Sanchez of California was completely surprised when his iguana eggs hatched—so surprised that he called me long distance in Oregon and shared the excitement over the phone. His wonderful photo of one of the iguanas that hatched, a tiny green lizard perched atop Mark's finger, is incredibly adorable. Sorry, Mark, that it took me three lifetimes to return the negative.

Index

Iguana from Venezuela in breeding season (notice the unusual rose-colored spines and face). Photo by: Kevin Schafer of Seattle, Washington

Full-body shot of Venezuela iguana. The photographer said when he got close to the iguana it was very aggressive and nasty—but it was breeding season. Photo by: Kevin Schafer of Seattle, Washington

Author in small canoe on lake Chacagua on the coast of Oaxaca, Mexico, doing research with local iguanas. Photo by: A. H. Iles

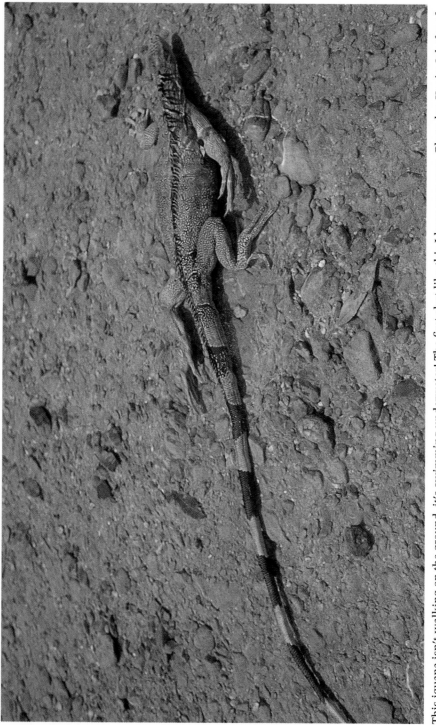

This iguana isn't walking on the ground, it's swimming underwater! The first shot like this I have ever seen. Photo by: Kevin Schafer of Seattle, Washington

Belize (Central America) hatchling iguana with plant juice on its face. Photo by: Kevin Schafer of Seattle, Washington

This four-phase photo shows an iguana hatching in the researcher's hand. Notice how calm and tame the emerging hatchling is. Photo: courtesy of Maria Socorro Lara López

This adult iguana is part of the breeding stock at Dagmar Werner's iguana farm in Costa Rica. The branded code on the side of the iguana is for genetic and breeding reference. Photo by: A. H. Iles

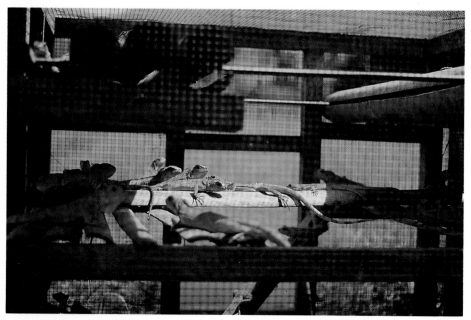

Beautiful, healthy hatchlings at Dagmar Werner's iguana farm. These iguanas will eventually be released into the jungle to help re-build the wild population. Photo by: A. H. Iles

Maria Socorro Lara López is holding a handful of iguanas that just hatched at her research area on the Gulf of Mexico, before setting them free. Photo: courtesy of Maria Socorro Lara López

This formal living room has all oak furniture, including the iguana habitat next to the couch. A beautiful, well-built iguana habitat can look great in any room of your house. Photo by: A. H. Iles

Close-up of the author's Adult Ultimate Iguana Habitat. The jungle effect was created with real wood limbs, plastic plants, and a hand-painted interior. Photo by: John McNally of Photo Tek Inc., Hillsboro, Oregon

Iguana habitats don't have to be ugly structures stuck in some back room. This habitat blends perfectly in the author's home in Portland, Oregon. Photo by: John McNally of Photo Tek Inc., Hillsboro, Oregon

Author's apartment living room when he lived in Los Gatos, California. In the window, on the large limb, is the author's iguana, Za, enjoying time out of his habitat with the "family." Photo by: James W. Hatfield III

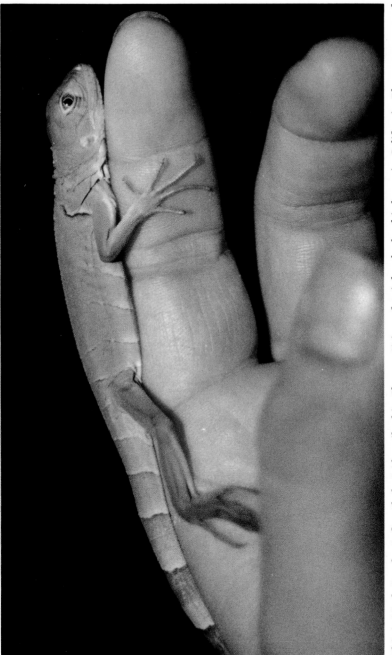

This is Mark Sanchez's first "baby" (described in Chapter 9) just after it hatched at his home in California. Photo: courtesy of Mark Sanchez

Iguana dressed up for a day's adventure. Photo: courtesy of Bryan Elwood

Captive-raised hatchlings having lunch at a breeding research station at the Belize Zoo. After the breeding program was completed, the lizards were released back into the jungle. Photo: courtesy of Tony Garel, Belize Zoo

This gorgeous wild-caught iguana in Hawaii will soon get a free airplane trip to the mainland. Hawaii doesn't want non-native species like iguanas throwing the islands' natural balance out of whack. Photo: courtesy of Duane Meier, Honolulu, Hawaii

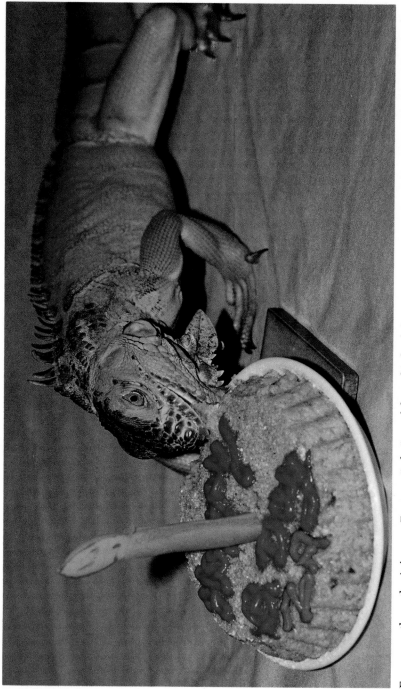

Every year the author's iguana, Za, got a "cake" to celebrate his birthday. The cake is made from vegetables ground up in a food processor. The candle is a carrot with a yellow crookneck squash "flame." Photo by: James W. Hatfield III